"This collection offers, at long last, the foundation of a g[...] transdisciplinary conversation about whiteness. The edito[...] range of work from a new generation of writers who bring insights to bear on a subject that has evaded sustained critique for too long. The book will infuriate those who are invested in maintaining the status quo; it will only encourage those who are determined to act together to change it."

**Vron Ware,** co-author of *Out of Whiteness: Color, Politics and Culture*

"This handbook provides a compelling, multi-level and wide-ranging investigation of the many ways in which white supremacy has ineluctably always been central to the notion of 'race' and racism in its various dehumanising and ever-destructive guises. Drawing on the insights of authors from a wide range of countries, contexts, and disciplines, this insightfully curated collection of chapters makes for captivating reading and adds significantly to extant scholarship on racism. This scholarly tour de force will undoubtedly become an important reference for scholars with an interest in the field whiteness and racism and the ever-changing articulations of racism."

**Norman Duncan,** Professor of Psychology; Critical Race Scholar; co-editor of *Race, Memory, and the Apartheid Archive: Towards a Transformative Psychosocial Praxis*

"What a wide-ranging and fiery examination of whiteness; its intersections, infusions and leaching logics across time, place and systems of colonial and racial domination. Apartheid, Hindu nationalism, indigenous genocide, oceanic colonialism and Goa, Meghan Markle, post-feminism, philosophical entrapment and Zionism are some of the topics through which authors complicate and decolonise critical whiteness studies. Drawing out theorising into activism, crucially the collection offers strategies towards a more equitable social world. A treasure trove for teachers, students and activists."

**Yasmin Gunaratnam,** Reader at Goldsmiths College, author of *Researching 'Race' and Ethnicity: Methods, Knowledge and Power* and *Death and the Migrant: Bodies, Borders and Care*

"It is hard to think of a more necessary critical renewal of whiteness studies than that presented in this detailed, challenging and incredibly insightful book. Authoritative and innovative, the editors and authors have done a great service to the topic and our understanding of it."

**Professor Nasar Meer,** University of Edinburgh, editor of *Whiteness and Nationalism*

"Our world is in turmoil. We live in the accumulated pain and emboldened geopolitical violence of 500 years of colonial history. This volume does not offer any balm for white wounds. Rather it is an insurgent call for racial justice. Bringing together a breadth of voices from across the Global North and South, the editors ask readers to critically reflect upon the connections and separations of the world through the varied formations of whiteness. This extraordinary volume is a provocation, a challenge, and a conversation, offering new constellations of possibilities to approach the field of critical whiteness studies; to interrogate whiteness within the calculated balances and sacrificial structures of the world; and to consider whiteness in relation, a method of working through the interpersonal. The chapters rumble with a thoughtful intensity that both activists and intellectuals require to carry forth visions of radical change, especially in these times when events in one part of the world cascades in another."

**Nalini Mohabir,** Concordia University, co-editor of *The Fire that Time: Transnational Black Radicalism and the Sir George Williams Occupation*

# ROUTLEDGE HANDBOOK OF CRITICAL STUDIES IN WHITENESS

This handbook offers a unique decolonial take on the field of Critical Whiteness Studies by re-historicising and re-spatialising the study of bodies and identities in the world system of coloniality.

Situating the critical study of whiteness as a core intellectual pillar in a broadly based project for racial and social justice, the volume understands whiteness as elaborated in global coloniality through epistemology, ideology and governmentality at the intersections with heteropatriarchy and capitalism. The diverse contributions present Black and other racially diverse scholarship as crucial to the field. The focus of inquiry is expanded beyond Northern Anglophone contexts to challenge centre/margin relations, examining whiteness in the Caribbean, South Africa and the African continent, Asia, the Middle East as well as in the United States and parts of Europe. Providing a transdisciplinary approach and addressing debates about knowledges, black and white subjectivities and newly defensive forms of whiteness, as seen in the rise of the Radical Right, the handbook deepens our understanding of power, place, and culture in coloniality.

This book will be an invaluable resource for researchers, advanced students, and scholars in the fields of Education, History, Sociology, Anthropology, Psychology, Political Sciences, Philosophy, Critical Race Theory, Feminist and Gender Studies, Postcolonial and Decolonial Studies, Security Studies, Migration Studies, Media Studies, Indigenous Studies, Cultural Studies, Critical Diversity Studies, and African, Latin American, Asian, American, British and European Studies.

**Shona Hunter** is Reader in the Centre for Race Education and Decoloniality (CRED), Leeds Beckett University, UK. Her publications include *Power, Politics and the Emotions: Impossible Governance* (2015) and various special editions and articles in *Social Politics: International Studies in Gender, State and Society, Critical Social Policy, Critical Arts: A Journal of South-North Cultural and Media Studies, Critical Race and Whiteness Studies Journal, Journal of Psychosocial Studies,* and *Policy Futures in Education.* She has held posts at the Universities of Birmingham, Lancaster, Leeds University in the United Kingdom and visiting positions at the Universities of Sydney, Australia; Mannheim, Germany; Cape Town, Rhodes; and Johannesburg, South Africa. Her scholarly interests are framed through an engagement with feminist anti-racist decolonial critique and include all aspects of welfare politics and governance, state practices, identities and the broader material-cultural-affective politics through which 'the' state(s) is enacted nationally and globally as a global colonial formation.

**Christi van der Westhuizen** is Associate Professor at the Centre for the Advancement of Non-Racialism and Democracy (CANRAD), Nelson Mandela University, South Africa. Her publications include the monographs *White Power & the Rise and Fall of the National Party* (2007) and *Sitting Pretty: White Afrikaans Women in Postapartheid South Africa* (2017), and articles in *African Studies, Critical Philosophy of Race* and *Matatu Journal for African Culture and Society.* She has held research fellowships with various universities, and previously worked as an Associate Professor of Sociology at the University of Pretoria. Her research focuses on identity, difference, ideology, and democracy in postcolonial contexts.

# Routledge Handbook of Critical Studies in Whiteness

*Edited by Shona Hunter and Christi van der Westhuizen*

Routledge
Taylor & Francis Group

LONDON AND NEW YORK

First published 2022
by Routledge
2 Park Square, Milton Park, Abingdon, Oxon OX14 4RN

and by Routledge
605 Third Avenue, New York, NY 10158

*Routledge is an imprint of the Taylor & Francis Group, an informa business*

*British Library Cataloguingn-ublication Data*
A catalogue record for this book is available from the British Library

*Library of Congress Cataloguing-in-Publication Data*
A catalog record has been requested for this book

ISBN: 978-0-367-40379-9 (hbk)
ISBN: 978-1-032-13934-0 (pbk)
ISBN: 978-0-429-35576-9 (ebk)

DOI: 10.4324/9780429355769

Typeset in Bembo
by MPS Limited, Dehradun

# Contents

Contents

# List of Figures

# Contributors

**Amanpreet Ahluwalia** is a writer, activist, and artist with 16 years of experience in social justice and community leadership development work. Aman brings her early involvement in theatre to her writing, focusing on the importance of bodily experience, powerful storytelling and emotional reflection work to honour what social change requires of us. Her recent work focuses on growing professional expertise, research, and practice by using lived experience of marginalisation as a force for ethical leadership and progressive social change. Aman is also the founder of *Birthing Ourselves*, a platform for growth and reflection for leaders focused on social justice from an intersectional perspective.

**Brittany Aronson** is an Associate Professor in Sociocultural Studies in Education at Miami University Ohio, USA. She teaches classes in sociocultural foundations, sociology of education, and multicultural education. In her scholarship, she focuses on preparing educators to work against oppressive systems as well as critical policy analyses of both popular and political discourse. Her research interests include critical teacher preparation, social justice education, critical race theory, critical whiteness studies, and educational policy. Dr. Aronson earned a PhD in Learning Environments and Educational Studies from the University of Tennessee in 2014.

**Neema Begum** is a Postdoctoral Research Associate at the University of Manchester Centre on the Dynamics of Ethnicity (CoDE), Britain. Her research is on the voting behaviour, political attitudes and representation of British Black and Asian people. Her PhD was on *British ethnic minority attitudes towards European integration and their voting behaviour in the Brexit referendum*.

**Colleen E. Boucher** is a Doctoral student at the University of Colorado Denver, USA, in the Critical Studies of Education programme. Research and publications have included the study of whiteness as it manifests in teaching practices, considering the many ways racism infiltrates curriculum and student–teacher interactions.

**Shefali Chandra** is interested in the sexual, affective, and racial relationship between India and the United States. Currently, Shefali is completing a book on the making of Indo-America as a spatial and cultural formation that is shaped by discourses of caste, race, and sexuality. *Penetrating America* explores the structural collaborations between sexuality, brahmanism, upper-caste power, whiteness, settler-colonial scripts, colour-blindness, racial capitalism, and heteronormativity. She also writes about the caste history of the English language project, and how whiteness nurtures upper-caste expansion. She is an Associate Professor in the Departments of Women, Gender and Sexuality Studies and History at Washington University in St. Louis, USA.

**William E. Cross Jr.** is a Professor Emeritus of Higher Education and Counselling Philosophy at the University of Denver, USA. His research and courses synthesise Africana Studies and Psychology, stressing the sub-fields of developmental, social and educational psychology. He is the author of *Shades of Black: Diversity in African American Identity* (1991), co-editor of *Meaning-Making, Internalized Racism, and African American Identity* (2016), and co-author of *Dimensions of Blackness: Racial Identity and Political Beliefs* (2018). He received the 2020 Gold Medal Award for Life Achievement in the Application of Psychology from the American Psychological Foundation. His forthcoming book is titled *Black Identity Viewed from a Barber's Chair*.

**Katerina Deliovsky** is an Associate Professor of Sociology at Brock University in Ontario, Canada. Her research and scholarly activities broadly encompass critical whiteness studies with an emphasis on white femininity and anti-racist feminism and methodology. A distinct but related area of scholarly inquiry is the critical sociology of mixed unions. A consistent theme animating her work is the development of an epistemologically deep and multi-dimensional theorisation of race, gender, power, and whiteness. Her current scholarship extends her critical whiteness focus to explore (white) women's sex/'romance' tourism and transnational relationships in, but not limited to, the Caribbean.

**Michelle Fine** is a Distinguished Professor of Critical Psychology, Women's Studies, Social Welfare, American Studies and Urban Education at the Graduate Center, City University of New York, USA. She is also Professor Extraordinarius in Psychology at the University of South Africa. As a scholar, expert witness in litigation, teacher and educational activist, her work centres on justice and dignity, privilege and oppression, and how solidarities emerge. She is the author, co-author/editor or co-editor of more than 20 books, including *Just Methods: Expanding the Methodological Imagination* (2017) and *Off White: Essays on Power, Privilege and Resistance* (with L. Weis, L. Powell and A. Burns, 2004).

**Phillip W. Gray** is an Assistant Professor of Political Science in the Liberal Arts Program at Texas A&M University at Qatar. He previously taught at the US Coast Guard Academy as well as at various universities in Hong Kong. Gray's main areas of research include the ideology and organisation of extremism, as well as Comparative Political Theory (CPT). His work has been published in various journals, including *History of Political Thought*; *Terrorism and Political Violence*; *Journal of Political Ideologies*; and *Politics, Religion, and Ideology*. His most recent book is *Vanguardism: Ideology and Organization in Totalitarian Politics* (2019).

**Katalin Halász** is a Leverhulme Early Career Research Fellow at Brunel University, Britain. She uses arts-based research methods to explore the lived experience of race and gender. She has staged a number of participatory and multimedia performances in the United Kingdom, Denmark, Germany, Brazil, and Bolivia, and has curated exhibitions in London. More on her artful sociological research can be found here: https://www.katalinhalasz.com/.

**Sarah Heinz** is a Professor of English and Anglophone Literatures at the University of Vienna, Austria. Her research and teaching focus on intersectional identificatory processes and the material and cultural practices through which these identifications are performed. She focuses on home spaces and practices and their representations in transnational contexts, and has published on representations of whiteness in Irish, Australian, Nigerian, and British literatures. Recent journal articles include 'Unsettling Australia: Disturbing White Settler Homemaking in Peter Carey's *True*

*History of the Kelly Gang*' (published in *Humanities, 2020*) and 'Revision as Relation: Adapting Parable in Chigozie Obioma's *The Fishermen*' (published in *Adaptation, 2020*).

**Tobias Hübinette** is an Associate Professor in Intercultural Education and Senior Lecturer in Intercultural Studies and in Swedish at the Department of Language, Literature and Intercultural Studies, Karlstad University, Sweden. He also teaches Comparative Literature and Gender Studies. His research is in the field of Swedish critical race and whiteness studies, which he is also actively trying to establish within Swedish academia. He has also been engaged with critical adoption studies. His books focus on Korean adoption and transnational adoptees, as well as on Swedish whiteness and Swedish racial formations and relations.

**Jamie Kherbaoui** is a critical community engagement practitioner working at Lesley University, USA, and an interdisciplinary scholar with research interests focused on the white saviour industrial complex. In 2019, she earned her M.Ed. in Community Engagement with a Concentration in Higher Education from Merrimack College, where she completed her Master's thesis qualitative research on how white individuals develop critical consciousness of white saviourism. In 2017, she received her B.A. in Sociology with a Concentration in Social Justice in Urban Education from Drake University.

**Mandisi Majavu** is a senior lecturer in the Department of Political and International Studies at Rhodes University, South Africa. His scholarship investigates the intricacies of racial formation across space and time, ranging from white racism and racial formation in South Africa to anti-black racism in Australia and New Zealand; from white missionaries and Christianity in 19th century South Africa to race and liberalism; and from gender and race in sports to the black diaspora. He focuses on the way in which these narratives intersect. Dr. Majavu is the author of the book *Uncommodified Blackness* (2017).

**Kendra Marston** is a Learning Advisor at Massey University, New Zealand. Her research predominantly focuses on gender, race, and class representation in popular media culture. She is the author of *Postfeminist Whiteness: Problematising Melancholic Burden in Contemporary Hollywood Cinema* (2018).

**Cheryl E. Matias** is a Professor and Director of Secondary Teacher Education at the University of Kentucky, USA. Her research focuses on race and ethnic studies in education, with a theoretical focus on critical race theory, critical whiteness studies, critical pedagogy, and feminism of colour. She uses a feminist of colour approach to deconstruct the emotionality of whiteness in urban teacher education. Her books are: *Feeling White: Whiteness, Emotionality, and Education* (2016) (Honorable Mention by the Society of Professors of Education); *Surviving Becky(s): Pedagogies for Deconstructing Whiteness and Gender* (2019) (nomination for the AESA book award); and *The Handbook of Critical Theoretical Research Methods in Education* (2021).

**Bernard Matolino** is an Associate Professor in Philosophy at the University of KwaZulu-Natal, South Africa. His latest book is titled *Afro-Communitarian Democracy* (2019).

**Ashley A. Mattheis** completed her PhD in the Department of Communication at the University of North Carolina at Chapel Hill, USA. Her work brings together cultural studies, media studies, and rhetorical criticism, through the lens of feminist theory to explore the material effects of cultural production and consumption online. Her areas of inquiry include the digital cultures of the 'Momosphere', the Alt-Right, the 'Manosphere', and #Tradwives, to understand how gendered logics promote racial discrimination and (re)produce dominant structures. Her dissertation, *Fierce Mamas: New Maternalism, Social Surveillance, and the Politics of Solidarity*, analyses how white women's strategic use of motherhood discourses works to reproduce structural whiteness.

**Aurelien Mondon** is a Senior Lecturer in politics at the University of Bath, in Britain. His research focuses predominantly on the impact of racism and populism on liberal democracies and the mainstreaming of far-right politics through elite discourse. His first book, *The Mainstreaming of the Extreme Right in France and Australia: A Populist Hegemony?*, was published in 2013 and he co-edited *After Charlie Hebdo: Terror, Racism and Free Speech* in 2017. His new book, co-written with Aaron Winter, is *Reactionary Democracy: How Racism and the Populist Far Right Became Mainstream* (2020).

**Amrita Pande**, author of *Wombs in Labor: Transnational Commercial Surrogacy in India* (2014), is Associate Professor in Sociology at University of Cape Town, South Africa. Her research focuses on the intersection of globalisation and the intimate. Her work has appeared in *Signs: Journal of Women in Culture and Society, Gender and Society* and many other journals. Her recent research explores the 'global fertility flows' of eggs, sperms, embryos and wombs, connecting the world in unexpected ways. She is an educator-performer, touring globally with a performance lecture series, *Made in India: Notes from a Baby Farm,* based on ethnographic work on cross-border gestational surrogacy.

**Ilan Pappé** is a Professor of History at the University of Exeter, Britain. He is the Director of the European Centre for Palestine Studies and a Senior Fellow at the Institute for Arab and Islamic Studies in the university. Prof. Pappé is the author of 20 books and numerous articles. His books include *The Ethnic Cleansing of Palestine* (2006) and *On Palestine* with Noam Chomsky (2015). His two recent books are *Ten Myths About Israel* (2017) and *The Biggest Prison on Earth: A History of the Israeli Occupation* (2017).

**Rory Pilossof** is a member of the International Studies Group at the University of the Free State, South Africa. His main research areas are land, labour, and belonging in southern Africa. His recent publications include *Labour and Economic Change in Southern Africa, c.1900-2000: Zimbabwe, Zambia and Malawi* (2021), with Andrew Cohen.

**Sherene H. Razack** is a Distinguished Professor and the Penny Kanner Endowed Chair in Women's Studies in the Department of Gender Studies, University of California, Los Angeles, USA. Her research and teaching focus on racial violence. She is the founder of the virtual research and teaching network *Racial Violence Hub* (RVHub.com). Her publications illustrate the thematic areas and anti-colonial, anti-racist feminist scholarship she pursues. Her recent books include *Nothing Has to Make Sense: Anti-Muslim Racism, White Supremacy and Law* (Forthcoming in 2022), and *Dying from Improvement: Inquests and Inquiries into Indigenous Deaths in Custody* (2015).

**Arun Saldanha** is a Professor in the Department of Geography, Environment, and Society at the University of Minnesota, USA. He is the author of *Psychedelic White: Goa Trance and the Viscosity of Race* (2007) and *Space After Deleuze* (2017), and co-edited *Geographies of Race and Food: Fields Bodies Markets* (2013/2014, with Rachel Slocum), *Deleuze and Race* (2013, with J. M. Adams), and *Sexual Difference Between Psychoanalysis and Vitalism* (2013). Arun's research interests include feminist theory, Marxism, psychoanalytical theory, and the Anthropocene. He is currently working on a hybrid project, *Prince from Minneapolis*, based on a symposium held in 2018.

**Mark Schmitt** is an Assistant Professor of British Cultural Studies at TU Dortmund University, Germany. His recent publications include *British White Trash: Figurations of Tainted Whiteness in the Novels of Irvine Welsh, Niall Griffiths and John King* (2018) and *The Intersections of Whiteness* (edited with Evangelia Kindinger, 2019).

**Lwando Scott** is a Next Generation Scholar at the Centre for Humanities Research (CHR), University of the Western Cape, South Africa. Lwando's research focus is on 'queering the postcolony' by engaging and challenging decolonisation, sexuality (queerness), gender, and culture. 'Queering the postcolony' is a continuation of Lwando's work in Queer African Studies. Lwando's Doctoral research was on same-sex marriage in South Africa, titled *'The more you stretch them, the more they grow': Same-sex marriage and the wrestle with heteronormativity*. Lwando was an Innovation in Science Pursuit for Inspired Research Fellow at Ghent University in 2016/17. He was awarded the Yale-Fox Fellowship at Yale University in 2013/14.

**Javeria Khadija Shah** is a sociologist in Visual and Social Cultures. Her work is interdisciplinary and aligns with visual arts, policy and education, in pursuit of social justice. Her research draws on person-centred methodologies that incorporate visual anthropology and narrative approaches to re-conceptualise societal positioning(s) of the individual. Dr. Shah is an academic at the Royal Central School of Speech and Drama, University of London, and a visiting lecturer at Leeds Beckett University, the University of Arts London, and the University of Winchester. In 2018, she set up the *Social Performance Network,* a research and practice-orientated platform on socialisation and its 'performance' in social world contexts.

**Theo Sonnekus** is a Research Associate in theDepartment of Visual Arts at Stellenbosch University. He has published widely on the representation of Afrikaner ethnic identity in post-apartheid visual culture and contemporary art, and on the intersection of whiteness and masculinity in queer urban spaces and the South African gay press. His current research centres on the race politics of a collection of monographs of homoerotic male nude photography produced and distributed in apartheid South Africa by the radical publisher *Alternative Books* (1981-1991).

**Yasuko Takezawa** is a Professor of Anthropology at the Institute for Research in Humanities of Kyoto University, Japan. Since 2001, she has been leading an international collaborative research project on race/ethnicity/migration, consecutively winning one of the largest grants from the Japanese government. She argues that race is not a modern Western construction, but has existed indigenously in the Middle Ages in Japan and Europe. Her English publications include 'Racialization and Discourses of 'Privileges' in the Middle Ages: Jews, 'Gypsies', and Kawaramono', in *Ethnic and Racial Studies* (2020) and *Race, Civilisation and Japanese Textbooks During the Meiji Period* in *Politika* (2021).

**Sitara Thobani** is an Assistant Professor at the Residential College in the Arts and Humanities, Michigan State University, USA. Her research focuses on formations of race, gender, sexuality, and religion in South Asian colonial and postcolonial visual cultures and representational practices. Sitara received her DPhil in Social and Cultural Anthropology from Oxford University, St. Antony's College. Her first book, *Indian Classical Dance and the Making of Postcolonial National*

*Identities: Dancing on Empire's Stage* (2017), demonstrates how this art form and attendant cultural performances serve as a site for the mutual constitution of Indian, diasporic and British national identities. She currently researches Hindu nationalism in transnational contexts.

**Samantha Vice** is a Distinguished Professor of Philosophy at the University of the Witwatersrand, South Africa. She works in ethics, aesthetics, and social philosophy, her latter work concentrating on white identity and racial privilege.

**Georgie Wemyss** is a Senior Lecturer and Co-Director of the Centre for Research on Migration, Refugees and Belonging at the University of East London, Britain. She was previously employed as a youth and community worker and in further education in London's East End. Her research and activism draw together anti-racist, feminist and anti-colonial scholarship with a particular focus on colonial seafaring histories, borders and citizenship. She is the author of *The Invisible Empire: White Discourse, Tolerance and Belonging* (2016) and co-author of *Bordering* (2019).

**Aaron Winter** is a Senior Lecturer in Criminology at the University of East London, Britain. His research is on the racism and the far right with a focus on identity, mainstreaming and violence. He is co-editor of *Discourses and Practices of Terrorism: Interrogating Terror* (2010), *Historical Perspectives on Organised Crime and Terrorism* (2018) and *Researching the Far Right: Theory, Method and Practice* (2020), and co-author, with Aurelien Mondon, of *Reactionary Democracy: How Racism and the Populist Far Right Became Mainstream* (2020).

# Acknowledgements

Bringing together a volume of the scope and scale of an International Handbook means that our recognition and thanks go to many people. To the contributors, first, who all in the context of extreme difficulty and uncertainty produced incisive, timely and well-crafted chapters with good humour, generosity and great commitment to a collective endeavour. It has truly been a pleasure to engage with them. We look forward to more.

Huge thanks go to Michelle Fine and William E. Cross Jr. who provided our Epilogue. Our admiration for Michelle and colleagues who produced *Off White* in its initial (1997) and later (2004) iterations is substantial. The approach we develop to connecting agencies, identities and systems as well as the commitment to asking new questions about materialities was influenced by the collective endeavours of both those volumes. In these, we were also able to see other projects on whiteness with deep political heart and commitment to resisting the dehumanisation it wreaks. In this regard, we are thankful to William E. Cross Jr's acceptance of the invitation to be involved in crafting the epilogue. To have a cultural psychologist and African American scholar so important to shaping the Black collective struggle to resist the white gaze on Blackness through ground-breaking deficit model busting ideas like 'Nigrescence', and then followed by volumes like *Shades of Black* (1991), is truly an honour. This volume should be read with all of these interventions as the precursors. In beautiful, contested conversation so many people globally contributing to the waft and weft of a collective writing against whiteness.

Our deep gratitude goes to South African artist Norman Catherine for his generosity in agreeing to the use of his work on the front cover. Given the aim of this handbook of bringing the Global South squarely into the global interrogation of whiteness, also using South Africa as a lens, it is apt to feature a foremost contemporary artist who is also renowned for his anti-apartheid work. We believe his evocative depiction of troubled and troubling racialised subjects captures the complexity of the intersecting orders of domination this handbook is grappling with. Our thanks also go to Janet Catherine.

At Routledge, thanks go to Emily Briggs, Commissioning Editor in Sociology, whose invitation spurred this project from conceptualisation. Her vision for a volume which was boundary breaking in terms of a mix of globality and multidimensional analysis bringing in the collective and collegiate emphasis on curation is what put our efforts in train. Thanks too, to Lakshita Joshi, Editorial Assistant, for administering, always to time and with efficiency and friendliness.

Thanks also to the two anonymous peer reviewers for their comments on the chapters by South African contributors.

Thanks to Sean Brown for formatting assistance in the last stages to manuscript submission, and to Dr. Olutobi Akingbade, postdoctoral research fellow at the Centre for the Advancement of Non-Racialism and Democracy (CANRAD), Nelson Mandela University, for editorial assistance.

For Shona, teaching in all its iterations is a lifeblood. Heartfelt thanks to my students in critical studies of whiteness over the years and especially on my current Critical Whiteness Studies module on the MA in Race Education and Decoloniality in the Carnegie School of Education at Leeds Beckett University. We dwell in the pain and loss of whiteness and produce joyful human resistance together through this dwelling. I really hope that this volume will honour their interest, tenacity and commitment to rehumanising themselves and the world through anti-racist activisms inside and outside their institutional locations. Thanks always to friends, family and compatriots many of whom are here either in soul or via the pen. I have had much happiness and fun learning from and working with my co-editor, comrade and friend Christi van der Westhuizen. Our criss-crossing experiences and sharing of interconnected respective South (hers) and North (mine) woes and joys challenge my understandings of my world in important ways. I will value that, continuing. I am proud of what we have achieved together.

Christi expresses wholehearted appreciation to Allan Zinn, director at the Centre for the Advancement of Non-Racialism and Democracy (CANRAD), Nelson Mandela University, for creating a nurturing environment in which research can flourish, and for the many conversations developing insight into South Africa's postcolonial conundrums. Warm thanks also to Prof André Keet, Deputy Vice-Chancellor for Engagement and Transformation, Nelson Mandela University, for countless incisive intellectual engagements and also opportunities to deepen critical thinking about race and anti-racist transformation. My gratitude also goes to Prof Norman Duncan, Vice-Principal: Academic at the University of Pretoria, for the opportunity to engage in anti-discrimination policy development and praxis in the Higher Education context, and for encouragement at crucial moments. For intellectual inspiration and collegial support along the highways and byways of academia, I thank Irma du Plessis, Andries Bezuidenhout, William Gumede, Karin van Marle, Danie Brand, Zohra Dawood, Allan Boesak, Elna Boesak, Zimitri Erasmus, Beata Mtyingizana, Denise Zinn, Mandisi Majavu, Andries van Aarde, Leslie van Rooi, Sonwabo Stuurman, Michelle Pressend, Matete Madiba, Malehoko Tshoaedi, Nisa Paleker, Derick de Jongh, Claire Kelly and David Moore. Taking the scalpel to whiteness to cut through its life-denying properties with my co-editor Shona Hunter has been a personally enriching and an intellectually expansive process for which I am grateful. It has been particularly inspiring to think together to bare global whiteness and dissect its North-South dynamics, inherent to whiteness' intractableness. Our shared commitment to the antiracist project provided the impetus to complete this project against the odds in the especially difficult time of a global pandemic. And lastly, as always, thank you to Melanie Judge, every step of the way.

# Preface

The interrogation of whiteness has long been pursued through the incisive critique of black thinkers such as W.E.B. Du Bois, Ida B. Wells, Frantz Fanon, James Baldwin, Steve Biko, and others. Decades after this work, intellectual scrutiny of the slippery object of whiteness has burgeoned into Critical Whiteness Studies (CWS), a distinct if loosely constituted area of academic and research inquiry. What was different in this relatively new field, was to name, home in and dissect whiteness as a distinct power formation within the structures of race, racism, and white supremacy that rose with and sustained colonialism, and today forms an essential part of coloniality. The impetus for expanding the focus from the racialised margins to whiteness as the centre of power in racial structures sprung from the recognition that whiteness was ill-defined, operated invisibly frequently and managed to retain traction over four centuries. Hierarchies have been organised with devastating results around whiteness, despite it being a phantasm of the Western mind construed from false attributions of human value on the basis of phenotype.

Toni Morrison's call to 'avert the critical gaze from the racial object to the subject' (1992: 90)[1] has been heeded from the first explorations in Critical Legal Studies (Lopez 1996) and Labour Studies (Allen 1994; Roediger 1991), to Education (Fine *et al.* 2004, 1997; Helms 1992) and Media Studies (Dyer 1997; hooks 1992), to Sociology (Feagin and Vera 1994; 2nd ed. with Batur 2000; Wellman 1993) and Feminist Studies (Frankenberg 1993; Ware 1992; Hall 1992). Since then, there has been a steady stream of special editions of key journals such as *Ethnic and Racial Studies* (2008), *Ethnicities* (2010) and *Social Politics* (2010), and the first special edition on whiteness in the African context (Van Zyl-Hermann and Boersema 2017).[2] Notable titles of books appearing since 2014 include Money and Van Zyl-Hermann (2020); Kindinger and Schmitt (2019), Eddo Lodge (2018), Van der Westhuizen (2017), Lundstrom and Teitelbaum (2017), Wekker (2016), Matias (2016), Weber (2016), Hunter (2015), Alcoff (2015), Willoughby-Herard (2015), and Sullivan (2014). These interdisciplinary contributions coalesce around critical interrogations of privilege; intersectionality; global and national racial regimes; the collusion of white respectability and good intentions in racist reproduction via institutionalised whiteness; white denial and ignorance; and the pervasiveness and codification of whiteness in everyday practices. The impetus behind this rapidly growing body of work is the recognition that whiteness forms the material, ideological, cultural, and affective centre of the unequal power structure of racism, which has proven to be not only remarkably adaptable to changing contexts but also resistant to dismantlement.

This preface outlines the structure of the volume, and also situates our approach as friendly critics in relation to the field that has contentiously come to be known as Critical Whiteness Studies. Disarticulating race implies the destabilisation of culture, embodiments and investments of white people. This is perhaps why so much of Critical Whiteness Studies addresses the issues of culture, identity and embodiment. Important as such analyses are, focusing on this outside of the machinery that produces whiteness risks merely repeating versions of the same racialising processes. This volume builds on newer, more explicitly integrated critiques that analyse whiteness as part of a broader racial formation, which is material, affective and discursive. Such work includes the South African-based Apartheid Archives project (Hook *et al.* 2013; Hook 2012; Straker 2004) and, from Britain, Sara Ahmed's *Queer Phenomenology* (2006) and *On Being Included* (2012). After the genesis of the project in the second quarter of 2018, as editors we set out with a critical and expansive approach to 'the field', seeking to extend the parameters of the critical study of whiteness. While not dispensing of the body, culture or identity, we sought to re-historicise and re-spatialise the understanding of bodies and identities as part of a global colonial world system which presently has whiteness at its heart. This is in response to criticisms about the ongoing parochialism of the field, which tends to be dominated by white scholars from the Global North, particularly from the United States and, more recently, from Britain and other Anglophile contexts. Asia, the Americas and the Caribbean, Africa, Australia, and New Zealand, as well as parts of Europe, have been underrepresented in the literature.

To upset the epistemological centre/margin relations of coloniality, Global North dominance is here challenged by including differently placed scholarship and a range of black authors. The volume features contributors reflecting on, and/or writing from, under-studied regions and countries: Africa (Matolino), Zimbabwe (Pilossof), South Africa (Vice, Sonnekus, Majavu), and other non-US settler states (Mattheis and Marston), India (Thobani, Chandra, Saldanha, and Pande), Israel (Pappé), Sweden (Hübinette), and Japan (Takezawa). Some make explicit South–South linkages and flows (Pande), or North–South connections (Thobani, Wemyss, Deliovsky, Hübinette and Heinz). While some contributors engage on Southern contexts whilst still located in the North (Chandra, Thobani, and Saldanha), others critique the Global North while located outside of it (Gray), alongside those located within (Razack, Begum, Mondon, Winter, Halász, Schmitt, Kherbaoui, Aronson, Boucher, and Matias). The terms of the debate in the volume extend to a broader set of questions around decolonial and Black politics (Shah, Ahluwalia, Matolino and Majavu); and spheres of human thinking and doing such as the Arts (Halász), Philosophy (Matolino); History (Majavu); Media (Heinz and Marston); and Religion (Razack). Therefore, the collection draws together, in one place, literatures from different national and disciplinary contexts, to create a conversation between established and emerging scholars towards producing an original take on the field's key questions.

As editors moving from transdisciplinary backgrounds, and being differently situated in the Global North and Global South, we believe the pursuit of anti-racism must be simultaneously intellectual and activist. Whiteness works as a knowledge formation imbricated with patriarchy, heteronormativity and capitalist relations. Racial justice remains out of reach if power is not brought in explicitly, with attention to white supremacy and the contributions of white people to its historical and current structures of domination. As we consider in more detail in our own chapter, grasping the nettle of whiteness becomes all the more urgent given the politics of the moment, as racial populisms of all hues rise with renewed impetus in the wake of the COVID-19 pandemic, both at global and national levels. Therefore, we aim to situate critical studies in whiteness as a core intellectual pillar in a broadly-based project towards racial and social justice, and the end of heteropatriarchy and coloniality.

Section I on 'Onto-epistemologies' troubles and extends the methodological basis for critical studies of whiteness. Arun Saldanha shifts the methodological parameters significantly, situating the onto-epistemic relation and expanding our methodological imaginary. He makes a historically and spatially expansive intervention at the beginnings of our contemporary global coloniality in Goa at the point mercantile capitalism was being established. But he shifts our sensibilities towards this by bringing us right into contact with the lived practices of the people making 'early whiteness' via a materialist ontology. Key themes of our contemporary global coloniality are there - religion, purity, sexuality - but in reworked form. The centrality of Northern European imperialism is disrupted through a beginning with the Portuguese. Sherene Razack takes us into the area of affect and its power to produce whiteness, and ensures the Islamophobic dimensions of culture, politics, and practice is understood and challenged. Katalin Halász focuses our attention on rethinking the body and affect together through gender and sexuality, and Mark Schmitt extends the notion of culture to better engage the body with attention to class by way of the idea of figuration.

Section II is on 'Conspiracies', and stands in dynamic tension with the first section. 'Onto-epistemologies' provides ways of thinking and doing in and out of race, while the 'Conspiracies' section interrogates those ways of thinking that aid and abet race, in the form of ideologies that reinforce or counteract whiteness. Problematising these conjunctions assist in explaining the longevity of race and racism across time and place. In the first chapter, Sitara Thobani finds unexpected transnational synergies between contemporary nationalist projects of India and the United States. Tracing the US's religio-racial taxonomy in its immigration laws and Supreme Court decisions, she shows how the Indian American diaspora's Hindu nationalist mobilisation enhances the politics of Trumpist whiteness. Ashley A. Mattheis takes up the transnational reactivation of white supremacism in the form of #Trad cultural narratives that mobilise traditional constructions of femininity and masculinity in service of utopic whiteness. This counter-position against feminism bridges liberal democratic and neo-fascist ideologies in contexts varying from Britain to its former colonies. Kendra Marston in her chapter also draws on online cultures to drill further into resurgent British white nationalism, using as lens the figure of Megan Markle as latest (unwanted) addition to the royal family. The #Megxit campaign against Markle is both a counter-reaction against postfeminism and a reassertion of Britishness as necessarily white. Mandisi Majavu then turns the dissection knife onto liberalism and socialism. Using the South African context as exemplar, he argues that these ideologies present themselves as colour-blind while being underpinned by whiteness as a normative value. The section ends with Ilan Pappé's chapter, which addresses a lacuna in scholarship on Zionism. While Post-Zionist and anti-Zionist scholarship probed Zionism as a Eurocentric settler colonial movement, it underestimated the racial and colour dimension in the formation of Israeli nationalist identity.

In Section III on 'Colonialities', we expand the range of colonialities usually considered in critical analysis of whiteness. Part of our concern is to consider the interrelationships and overlaps between Empires and the interdependent dynamics of nation building within this. Yasuko Takezawa's contribution brings a relational analysis to bear on the Japanese self-construction over time, breaking with the racialising dichotomies of coloniality to consider the complex power dynamics of the trilateral relationship between Japan, the West and Asia. Shefali Chandra's contribution moves us onto the symbolic relational constructions of American and Indian empires and the role of whiteness and caste within this. Rory Pilossof considers the shifting constructions of whiteness in Zimbabwe's postcolonising processes. Through this he raises questions around the particularities of colonisation on the African continent and the relationships and differences between African nations. In his chapter, Tobias Hübinette brings in an analysis of coloniality in a Nordic context. He challenges the notion of 'good' Sweden and makes a strong critique of the multiple and related colonialities still at play in Swedish adoption practices facilitating a colonially consumptive dynamic between North and South.

Section IV on 'Intersectionalities' brings the reader to the workings of whiteness at the level of identity: that is, the lived ways in which differences are intersectionally mobilised with or against other social categories to advance or rebut whiteness. In his discussion of contending settler masculinities in South Africa, Theo Sonnekus shows how whiteness and heteronormativity are co-constitutively bolstered through ethno-gender divisions in national identities. Staying with white heterosexuality but shifting the focus to femininities, Katerina Deliovsky casts a critical eye over sex/romance tourism literature. She finds that white heterosexual women reassert colonial tropes and reinforce racial hierarchies in the enactment of their newfound sexual 'autonomy' in Caribbean sex tourism locales. The theme of travelling tropes continues in Lwando Scott's analysis of media representations of 'the global gay' and white homonormativity, showing white gay men's reproduction of dominant power formations through the invisibilisation of black male sexuality. Turning to class, the section ends with a chapter by Neema Begum, Aurelien Mondon, and Aaron Winter on how #Brexit elite discourses seek to re-legitimise whiteness by interpellating the working class as white people 'left behind', detrimentally affecting immigrants and racialised minorities while undermining politics of solidarity across race and class lines.

Section V on 'Governmentalities' prompts a set of expanded questions on the spatial and temporal global orders which govern the intimacies of whiteness via ideas of the home, the body and in the broader public sphere through labour and institutional interactions. Amrita Pande looks at the way reproductive choice constitutes a desire for cosmopolitan and mixed whiteness. Georgie Wemyss develops a geographically and temporally expansive cross-empire analysis of the racialisation of British Indian seafarers. She shows powerfully and poignantly the ways in which these seafarers, the 'lascars' are always, wherever and whenever 'not quite white enough', to use Nayak's (2007) phraseology. Sarah Heinz's contribution explores the global constructions of the ideal home and related home making practices as white. In an interesting and powerful shift in the more usual global analysis of the White Saviour Industrial Complex, Jamie Kherbaoui and Brittany Aronson particularise the internal politics of the United States in a devastating critique of the contemporary and historical production of whiteness in this context. In the final contribution to this section, Javeria Shah returns us to one of the more studied contexts of British governmentality of whiteness, presenting us with a means to developing a multi-layered analysis of the global colonial using a 'whiteness ecology'.

In the sixth and last section, titled 'Provocations', the focus moves to points of friction within theorisations and lived experiences, as discussed in previous sections, to unpack dilemmas and debates that have made the critical study of whiteness especially lively in its short existence. Bernard Matolino opens the section with a confrontation of the discipline of African philosophy. He argues that a contemporary insistence that seeks to assert African philosophy by setting it up against whiteness as a vacuous ideology and epistemology traps African philosophy in circuitous protest thought. Can whiteness be suspended to free African thought? Continuing the exploration of epistemology but from the vantage point of lived experience, Amanpreet Ahluwalia problematises normative Critical Whiteness Studies and challenges scholars in the field to enable conversations that reflect the intricacies of both working and living towards racial justice. The next chapter serves as one answer to Ahluwalia's challenge: Samantha Vice resumes her scholarly inquiry into 'being white'. Vice argues that the subject racialised as white amid social conditions of injustice is presented with a paradox: her ethical confrontation with her white privilege runs up against the need to protect the self and personal projects and commitments. The section then segues to white reaction in the form of the relatively novel positionality of the Alt-Right and their practice of appropriation aimed at subverting recent social justice gains. Phillip W Gray analyses how the Alt-Right redeploy the Black Feminist concept of intersectionality to mobilise whiteness as resistance, bolstered with patriarchal masculinity and anti-neoliberal localism. The interrogation of new forms of aggressive whiteness continues in the section's concluding chapter. Colleen E. Boucher and Cheryl E. Matias argue that liberal colour-blindness has been superseded by whiteness as a form of 'evolutionary terror'. In reaction to the critical exposure of whiteness as centrepiece of the global architecture of racism, whiteness has emboldened itself to intensify its supremacist attack.

As can be seen from the discussion above, the volume brings materiality, signification, affect, and the body together. The intention is not to construct a new field. Neither does the volume seek to present a single perspective, theoretically, or methodologically. Very quickly into the project, as also for contributors Colleen E. Boucher and Cheryl E. Matias (see Chapter 28) the centrifugal nature of the notion of a 'field' of whiteness studies became too much of a re-racialising pull in terms of the representation of the scholarly endeavours collected in the Handbook and in our understanding as editors. Therefore, we have opted for the title *The Routledge International Handbook of Critical Studies in Whiteness* as it better captures the aim of understanding whiteness, rather than any intention to reflect, consider or constitute a field of scholarship. Mindful of Robin Wiegman's (2012) criticism of academic fields as fundamentally conservative, culturally exclusionary mechanisms – at least as they work in the context of the contemporary hyper-neoliberalising academic space – the Handbook is aimed at maintaining and emphasising the transdisciplinary nature of work on whiteness. We hope to start different conversations which cut into the race essentialisms that still haunt the predominantly social constructionist study of whiteness. Doubtless, the volume succeeds with some of the original intentions, but not with others. In emphasising the worldliness of whiteness, the volume may have sacrificed some of the livedness of the fine-grained empirical work that both editors have previously conducted. However, we regard this Handbook as an invitation to others to extend the decolonial analysis borne on whiteness here, especially around further empirical work on people in their bodies.

## Notes

1   Kovel's (1970) early work in Psychology should also be noted.
2   Journal articles include contributions written by the editors of this book: 'Reproducing and Resisting Whiteness in Organizations, Policies and Places' (Hunter *et al.* 2010) in *Social Politics: International Studies in Gender, State and* Society, and 'Race, Intersectionality and Affect in Postapartheid Productions of "the Afrikaans White Woman"' in *Critical Philosophy of Race* (Van der Westhuizen 2016). Abbas *et al.* (2013) published 'New Territories in Critical Whiteness Studies' in *Critical Race and Whiteness Studies,* and Samaluk and Pederson (2012) published 'Critical Whiteness Studies Methodologies' in *Graduate Journal for Social Sciences.* In 2019 the *American Behavioural Scientist* featured engagements with whiteness in 'Critical Race Theory and Sociology' (Christian *et al.* 2019) and Nasar Meer (2019) has brought together work on 'Whiteness and Nationalism' in *Identities: Global Studies in Culture and Power.* There has also been a steady range of high impact review articles produced ranging from Alastair Bonnett's 1996 essay in *Theory, Culture and Society* and in *Ethnic and Racial Studies,* through Anoop Nayak's (2007) contribution to *Sociology Compass,* to Steve Garner's reflections on shifts and upswellings in the field in *Ethnic and Racial Studies* and Chen's contribution to *Journal of Social Thought,* both in 2017. Others still focus on nation specific fields, like Inna Kerner's (2007) reflection on the German field and Lundstrom and Teitelbaum (2017) on the Nordic region. From a decolonial point of view and one that emphasises the sorts of critical connections with indigenous theorising we see as vital to the field, the contribution of the Australian Association of Critical Whiteness Studies and its many members and Chairs must be recognised. Especially the tireless work of Aileen Moreton-Robinson. We hope we honour that well in our own essay.

# References

Abbas, M., Burgin, S., Decker, J. and Hunter, S. 2013. New Territories in Critical Whiteness Studies, *Critical Race and Whiteness Studies Association Journal* 9(1) https://acrawsa.org.au/wp-content/uploads/2017/12/CRAWS-Vol-9-No-1-2013.pdf

Ahmed, S. 2010. *Queer Phenomenology: Orientations, Objects, Others*. London: Duke.

Ahmed, S. 2012. *On Being Included: Racism and Diversity in Institutional Life*. London: Duke.

Alcoff, L. M. 2015. *The Future of Whiteness*. Cambridge: Polity.

Allen, T. W. 1994. *The Invention of the White Race: The Origins of Racial Oppression in Anglo America*. London: Verso.

Bonnett A 1996. 'White Studies' The Problems and Projects of a New Research Agenda. Theory, Culture and Society. 13(2):145-155.

Chen, J. M., 2017 The Contentious Field of Whiteness Studies. *Journal for Social Thought* 2(1):15-27.

Christian, M. Seamster, L. and Ray, V. 2019. New Directions in Critical Race Theory and Sociology: Racism, White Supremacy, and Resistance'. *American Behavioural Scientist*. 63(13): 1731-1740.

Dyer, R. 1997. *White*. London: Routledge.

Eddo-Lodge, R. 2018. *Why I'm No Longer Talking to White People About Race*. London: Bloomsbury.

Feagin, J. R. and Hernán, V. 1995. *White Racism: The Basics*. London: Routledge.

Fine, M., Weis, L., Powell, L. C. and Wong, L. M., eds. 1997. *Off White: Readings on Race, Power, and Society*. London: Routledge.

Fine, M., Weis, L., Powell, L. C. and Burns, A., eds. 2004. 2nd ed. *Off White: Readings on Power, Privilege, and Resistance*. London: Routledge.

Frankenburg, R. 1993. *White Women, Race Matters: The Social Construction of Whiteness*. Minneapolis: University of Minneapolis Press.

Garner, S. 2017. 'Surfing the third wave of whiteness studies: reflections on Twine and Gallagher', *Ethnic and Racial Studies* 40(9): 1582-1597.

Hall, C. 1992. *White, Male and Middle Class: Explorations in Feminism and History*. Cambridge: Polity Press.

Helms, J. 1992. *A Race is a Nice Thing to Have: A Guide to Being a White Person or Understanding the White Persons in Your Life*. Kansas: Content Communications.

Hook, D. 2012. *A Critical Psychology of the Postcolonial: The Mind of Apartheid*. London: Routledge.

Hook, D., Stevens, G. and Duncan, N. 2013. *Race, Memory and the Apartheid Archive. Towards a Psychosocial Praxis*. Johannesburg: Wits University Press.

Hooks, B. 1992. Representation of Whiteness in the Black Imagination. In *Black Looks: Race and Representation*, ed. B. Hooks, pp. 165–178. Boston MA: South End Press.

Hunter, S. 2015a. *Power, Politics and the Emotions: Impossible Governance*. London: Routledge.

Hunter, S. 2015b. Being called to 'By the Rivers of Birminam': the relational choreography of white looking. *Critical Arts*, 29 (S1): 43–57.

Hunter, S., Swan E. and Grimes, D. (2010) Reproducing and resisting whiteness in organisations, policies and places, *Social Politics: International Studies in Gender, State and Society* 17(4): 407-422.

Kerner, I, 2007. 'Rassen', Körper, Identitäten: Kontingente Bezüge. In: Diehl, P, and Koch, G., eds *Inszenierungen der Politik. Der Körper als Medium*. München: Fink. 123-140.

Kindinger, E. and Schmitt, M., eds. 2019. *The Intersections of Whiteness*. London: Routledge.

Kovel, J., 1970. *White Racism: A Psychohistory*. New York: Pantheon Books.

Lopez, I. F. H. 1996. *White by Law: The Legal Construction of Race*. New York: New York University Press.

Lundstrom, C. and Teitelbaum, B. R. 2017. Nordic Whiteness: An Introduction. *Scandinavian Studies*, 89 (2).

Matias, C. E. 2016. *Feeling White: Whiteness, Emotionality, and Education*. Rotterdam: Sense Publishing.

Meer N. 2019. Whiteness and Nationalism. *Identities: Global Studies in Culture and Power*. 26(5)

Money, D. and Van Zyl-Hermann, D. 2020. *Rethinking White Societies in Southern Africa 1930s-1990s*. Oxon: Routledge.

Nayak A. 2007. Critical Whiteness Studies. *Sociology Compass*. 1(2):737-755

Morrison, T. 1992. *Playing in the Dark: Whiteness and the Literary Imagination*. Cambridge, MA/London: Harvard University Press.

Roediger, D. A. 1991. *The Wages of Whiteness: Race and the Making of the American Working Class*. London: Verso.

Samaluk, B. and Pederson, L. L. (eds) 2012. Critical Whiteness Studies: Methodologies. *Graduate Journal of Social Science*, 9(1) http://www.gjss.org/sites/default/files/issues/editorials/Journal-09-01--00-LundPedersen-Samaluk.pdf

Straker, G. 2011. Unsettling whiteness. *Psychoanalysis, Culture & Society*, 16 (1): 11–26.

Sullivan, S. 2014. *Good White People: The Problem with Middle-Class White Anti-Racism*. New York: State University of New York Press.

Van der Westhuizen, C. 2017. *Sitting Pretty: White Afrikaans Women in Postapartheid South Africa*. Scottsville: University of KwaZulu Natal Press.

Van der Westhuizen, C. 2016. Race, intersectionality, and affect in postapartheid productions of the "Afrikaans white woman". *Critical Philosophy of Race* 4 (2): 221-238.

Van Zyl-Hermann, D. and Boersema, J. 2017. Introduction: The politics of whiteness in Africa. *Africa*, 87 (4): 651–661.

Ware, V. 1992. *Beyond the Pale, White Women, Racism and History*. London: Verso.

Weber, B. 2016. Whiteness, WiG, and Talking about Race. *Women in German Yearbook*, 32: 189–202.

Wekker, G. 2016. *White Innocence: Paradoxes of Colonialism and Race*. Durham, NC: Duke University Press.

Wellman, D. T. 1993. *Portraits of White Racism*. Cambridge: Cambridge University Press.

Wiegman, R. 2012. *Object Lessons*. Durham, NC: Duke University Press.

Willoughby-Herard, T. 2015. *Waste of a White Skin: The Carnegie Corporation and the Racial Logic of White Vulnerability*. Oakland: University of California Press.

# Viral whiteness: Twenty-first century global colonialities

*Shona Hunter and Christi van der Westhuizen*

While the Coronavirus pandemic prompted some to stress its levelling effect as it felled even denialist presidents, cumulative mortality figures, and unequal vaccine access laid bare the cold and crude facts of the global order of coloniality. It works as a division of life in which race, class, gender, and geographical location still largely determine who is to live, and who is to die. African-Americans and racialised minorities elsewhere in the Global North suffered the most deaths, while poor communities in the Global South were especially hard hit. In most African states, infection numbers could give no indication of the actual extent of the virus' spread, due to low testing, and tracking capacity. Figures for excess mortality would be the only way to measure the real impact. Vaccine nationalism, bolstered by deadly capitalism, reared its head as states raced to be the first to scoop up millions of doses from pharmaceutical companies. Soon states in the Global North started with the process of vaccinating populations, the only sustainable way to save lives, while the majority of states in the Global South looked on. Global health care inequalities were proffered as a boon in a morbid echo of colonial medical abuses, as French doctors suggested that vaccine trials be conducted in Africa 'where there are no masks, no treatments, no resuscitation' (BBC 2020). Meanwhile, health protocols aimed at containing the virus provoked the drawing of political lines, with White Right supporters shunning the wearing of masks and social distancing, despite these being the only measures that could slow down the virus. The Yellow Peril was reconjured as Sinophobic politicians sought to capitalise on the virus's apparent origin in China. Spikes in racist hate crime followed.

Taking these observations together in the wake of the Coronavirus pandemic, liveability was afforded to some and not others, based on race, class, and gender hierarchies of humanisation and dehumanisation. The global crisis of health was exposed as borne from systemic, multilevel convergences of white supremacy, necro-capitalism and heteropatriarchy. Within this, whiteness on a global scale again designated an ordering of life, which redirected the crisis to its Others to bear the brunt: Those racialised and gendered, the poor, the older, the disabled, the medically sick, and others who are rendered vulnerable and disposable within a broader bio-politics of global colonial debility (Puar 2017).

In this opening essay, we situate the critical study of whiteness at this current global colonial juncture. We offer a decolonial analysis true to the praxis as well as the title by way of first showing how the deconstructionist impulse must translate into an onto-epistemic struggle

DOI: 10.4324/9780429355769-1

1

which recognises and refuses race as the way of organising and defining the human. This refusal is in concurrence with Mbembe's opposition to the mythologisation of whiteness that *all* racialised subjects can get lured into:

> Whiteness is at its best when it turns into a myth. It is the most corrosive and the most lethal when it makes us believe that it is everywhere; that everything originates from it and it has no outside.
>
> *(Mbembe 2015: 3)*

We proceed by developing a layered argument to show how whiteness works as a formation, a logic, and an assemblage through which global coloniality is enacted relationally in the interconnection between material, symbolic, and affective (Hunter 2015a, 2015b; Hunter et al. 2010). From this point of view, there is no such thing as white people, but there are people racialised as white, humans caught up in the racialising logics of global colonial forms of subjectification and who are constantly called to the many material, cultural and affective lures of whiteness. Whiteness falsely promises self-understanding and certainty in existence. But this self-understanding can only ever be achieved through the perpetuation of violence on the self and the other because of the mastery which is demanded through a commitment to the idea of race.

The Global North has maintained race thinking through the institutionalisation of whiteness as a (neo)liberal ideal to naturalise distinctions of life, creating disposable victims outside of whiteness and powerful oppressors inside. We reference the pandemic context to show how these distinctions work along the long-established colonial lines of innocence and guilt, and the way these lines are sustained in the contemporary moment through neoliberal processes of individualisation. These processes in turn work to frame diversity as a public good and whiteness as its guardian and arbiter. We then consider how this inside/outside whiteness dynamic translates into the study of whiteness itself, as well as into anti-racist politics and the contemporary public debate on whiteness. This binary dynamic is what this volume speaks back to. Critical studies in whiteness need to do better in pushing understanding beyond liberalism's terms because these terms are what create whiteness as a bureaucratic formation of coloniality. Neoliberalism's mix of necro-biopolitics depends on whiteness.

In this chapter, we trace key epistemologies from critical whiteness studies, shorthanded here as the 'invisibility–ignorance–innocence triad'. As the global war against racism gains momentum in the twenty-first century, these (neo)liberal mainstays of whiteness are augmented with explicit white supremacist re-instantiations, with Radical Right populisms rising to defend coloniality. South Africa serves here as an exemplar of global settler coloniality to consider how differentiations within whiteness work globally, connecting the Global South and Global North in complex ways (see also the chapter by Thobani in this volume). Rather than the oft-stated aim to visibilise and 'know' whiteness, we show how whiteness shifts between visibility and invisibility. Its self-proclamation to innocence is always under threat. The hyper-visibilisation of whiteness is key to how contemporary global colonial whiteness works through commodification: Through 'knowing' itself, declaring itself to be problematic and then 'cleaning up' itself to re-achieve innocence. But this relies on the same possessive, narcissistic mastery logic of coloniality, whereby the white subject knows and controls, mind over matter. We trace how hyper-visibilisation fits with the contemporary anti-racist focus on 'white fragility' as a form of white denial. Identifying 'white fragility' is purported to lead out of whiteness. For this to happen, it is suggested that the claim to white fragility be dislodged through deconstructive knowledge of the privilege and power that the white self asserts over the point of view and experience of the other. The counterargument made here, is that there is no way out of whiteness without deconstructing the binary terms of liberalism's lived dynamic.

This volume, as a whole, is curated to move beyond the deconstruction of colonial mastery internal to critical whiteness studies by bringing to bear a different way of thinking about whiteness as an onto-epistemic phenomenon. The goal is not to 'cleanse' white people and restore innocence to them, but to disestablish whiteness. Adapting Puar's concept of 'queer assemblage' to 'race-resistant assemblage' assists in this work, as it

> … moves away from excavation work, deprivileges a binary opposition … underscores contingency and complicity with dominant formations. This foregrounding of assemblage enables attention to ontology in tandem with epistemology, affect in conjunction with representational economies, within which bodies interpenetrate, swirl together, and transmit affects and effects to each other. (Puar 2007: 205)

The focus shifts therefore to understanding the materialisation of race. How does whiteness come to be as a process of historical violence which is repeated when race is lived in con-temporary, supposedly non-violent neoliberal forms? The bodies of race manifest practices of history; the present-day relationships between bodies convey history. Materialised through their connections to other things, ideas and affects, white bodies come to be through intersecting relations of domination and possession. This analysis throws into relief the complicated matter of denial and accountability, which is so contested in critical whiteness studies. Whiteness traumatises and retraumatises. In the present moment, this gains a new form in neoliberal demands to show the trauma. Whiteness now comes to rely on the dualism of white saviour/ traumatised victim, because what white subjects can 'save', they can contain and control. Pluralism and incompleteness are the basic threats to whiteness. Therefore, with this non-binary, or binary-resistant, analysis we propose rethinking whiteness in two related senses. First, as a deeply material matter which must be worked through. Second, as a matter of human practices which produce the deathly effects of whiteness.

## The politics of (white) crisis

Writing together apart in Britain and South Africa, as editors, due to a global pandemic and lockdowns, with a crisis of health curtailing our differently experienced everyday in both mundane and far-reaching ways, this unpredictable situation makes obvious again the nature of whiteness. Whiteness is a dynamic, shifting, but durable system of domination through, under, against and within which people live, work, and relate (Hunter 2015b; Van der Westhuizen 2007). Whiteness is fundamental to the reproduction of global coloniality, systematised through the intersection of racial capitalism and what is left of liberal humanism after its neoliberalisa-tion. It is a whiteness which feeds off and into the crisis discourse. Capitalism needs crisis. This current one must be read as another one of the many, ongoing 'flashpoints where capitalist crisis becomes racialised and where that racialisation seems to become a fix or an amplification in response' (Bhattacharyya 2018: 9). Grasping the nettle of whiteness becomes all the more urgent given the politics of the moment, as racial populisms of different hues surge at global and also national levels, seeking to augment or even supplant the neoliberal order. Therefore, unpredictable as it may be, this situation has a precedent in the context of the global racial order's reproduction and reinstation of whiteness, with echoes a century ago from the Spanish Flu pandemic followed by the rise of fascism. Interrogating the global racial order as magnified by whiteness is at the heart of the endeavour in this Handbook. This pursuit has an activist dimension, as part of an overall intellectual project of anti-racism, shared with Critical Race Theory and Black Feminist Theory. It builds on the work of black thinkers, concurring that there can be no racial justice without attention to white supremacy and the contributions of white people to its historical and current structures of domination.

Whilst this situation of a global pandemic was not what we imagined as editors setting out on this project in 2018, it brutally confirms the starting point for this volume which recognises that a 'racial attack on black people sits at the heart of global affairs and the emergence of social science; this attack has used analytics that disavow racial suffering and allegedly provide analytics for understanding its costs' (Willoughby-Herard 2015: 167).[1] Like Willoughby-Herard, we are concerned with processes of knowledge production as constituted by the 'axis of difference' central to the Western imaginary (Grosfoguel 2002): As first asserted by Edward Said (1978), the Western subject is contingent upon defining itself against an other, for example, its Oriental other or its African other (Baderoon 2014: 33). With the neo-conservative notion of the 'axis of evil', George W Bush's USA shifted the colonial global colour line further east with the figure of 'the Muslim terrorist': Abjected and therefore suitable for murder by drone attack, with civilian deaths mere 'collateral'; being under suspicion in any case, except when performing 'good Muslim' as per Western white requirements (Mamdani 2004). Inspired by historically and spatially expansionist approaches from black studies, decolonial, feminist, queer, post-structuralist, and postcolonial scholarship (Gilroy 2000; Hall 1996; Lewis 2017; Mbembe 2000, 2019; Moten and Harney 2013; Weheliye 2014; West 1993), we critically interrogate global whiteness (Willoughby-Herard 2015) produced through intersecting colonialities, transnational linkages, practices, philosophies whereby western subjectivity is produced through a hierarchy of human liveability. The valuation and hence validation of some lives over others, through a hierarchisation of grievability and precarisation (Butler 2004, 2009), is a global enactment of whiteness. This is most starkly demonstrated by the global inequality in the procurement of vaccines against the Coronavirus, with resources obtained as a result of colonialities of power determining who are to live, and who to die. Elaborated through modernity and Western European colonial 'worlding' (Wynter 1994) race is the defining idea through which categories of human value and levels of disposability are measured for the purposes of resource extraction and profit exploitation, and for justifying the subjugation and control of racialised people. As Morning (2011) has powerfully shown in the US context, this raciology continues to be naturalised through the transmission of essentialist notions of race across disciplines and at all levels of education. While, as Goldberg (2009) argues, the idea of race is not naturally violating, we regard the meanings and practices attached to whiteness in the context of coloniality as never innocent. These are always at work in the service of domination, and this domination materialises through their institutionalisation. Thus, whiteness from our point of view is a way into understanding the current global intersecting systems of precarisation, marginalisation, exclusion and abjection. Whiteness gives analytic purchase on this hydra-headed animal of power – on power formations that interlink and reinforce reciprocal dominations, marginalisations and oppressions. Analysing whiteness provides a way to speak back to these formations.

It is the relationship between contemporary racial ordering and the violent institutionalised racism at its heart which is exposed by pandemic conditions, through global interconnections, interdependencies and also marked discontinuities across the power geometries of South–North, East–West. True to form, in the Global North 'crisis tends to be declared and action called for when white middle-class people are affected' (El-Enany 2019: 51). The differential ramifications of the pandemic situation are not unique in their genocidal effects. There is longstanding and increasing evidence as to the contemporary institutionalised expression of colonially enacted genocide through the unequal ordering and distribution of health, social care and other forms of welfare (National Inquiry into Missing and Murdered Indigenous Women and Girls, 2019a, 2019b). This is built into colonisation and contemporary coloniality. Medicine – its development and institutionalisation – has been fundamental to the production and maintenance of colonisation and to the production of whiteness as an aspirational ideal (Anderson 2002; Bashford 2000; Doyal and Pennell, 1994; Hunter 2010; Stoler 2002; Doyal 1994). The destruction of indigenous health care, the creation of cordon sanitaire, quarantines and related internal forced migrations, the extractive movement of medical expertise from the Global South to North – these are some of the most evident examples. Epidemiologically and anthropologically derived evidence for the continuing uneven distribution of health between Global North and South is incontrovertible, with recent World Health Organisation (2020) data recording nearly 10,000 children dying *daily* from preventable causes in the Global South. There is growing mainstream recognition that this situation is an expression of institutionalised violence related to 'pathologies of power' (Farmer 2005). Indeed, the concentration on infectious disease prevention at the expense of public health activity in the Global South can be understood as part of this pathology, reproducing biomedical amelioration rather than addressing the systemic production of ill health.

Whilst the direct death tolls from COVID-19 appear to have bucked the usual uneven North-South patterning with the Global North thus far experiencing the highest death rates, the overall uneven distribution of global death due to the multiple and systemic impacts of COVID-19 looks likely to reflect the predictable pattern of inequality (Makau 2021; Schellekens and Sourrouille 2020). This is hardly surprising in the context of a Global Public Health System working 'as an apparatus of coloniality' whereby 'Public Health manages (as a profession) and maintains (as an academic discipline) global health inequity' (Richardson 2020a: 1). Also, unsurprising are the disproportionate racialised impacts of COVID-19 in the areas hardest hit in the Global North. In the context of the United States 'if they had died of COVID-19 at the same rate as White Americans, about 18,000 Black, 6,000 Latino, 600 Indigenous, and 70 Pacific Islander Americans would still be alive' (APM Research Lab 2020 cited in Richardson et al. 2021). Kherbaoui and Aronson in this volume link this to a 'White Saviour Industrial Complex': They argue, alongside community organisers and activists of colour, that it is 'disaster white supremacy that has built the foundation for the COVID-19 pandemic in the United States to be so much worse than in other countries' (Chapter 22 of this volume). This suggests an additional dimension to the 'pandemicity' identified by Eugene Richardson, whereby the 'linking of humanity through contagion' extends to the contagion of racism's impacts. The structural conditions of racialised minorities living across the Global North mean that these communities have born significantly the disproportionate impact of morbidity and mortality of COVID-19, as well as much of the burden of care. That caring burden itself is the result of extractive coloniality internal to nations, which has increased their risk and exposure. Evidence from across England and Scotland is reflected across Europe as well as the United States (Qureshi et al. 2020): Structural inequalities in housing, employment and income, pre-existing chronic health conditions, greater concentration in health professions and frontline care as well as the provision of other essential services, increased difficulty of social distancing, unequal access to health care, mistrust of state institutions (Laurencin and Walker 2020; Nazroo 2003; Nazroo and Bécares 2020). Then, there are the additional impacts of racism itself on the body and on health: Both in terms of premature violent death and increased incidence of post-traumatic stress disorder, depression, and broader mental health effects (Nazroo et al. 2020; Richardson 2020b; Wallace et al. 2016). This is a pandemic on a pandemic, racism being the other pandemic (Godlee 2020; Laurencin and Walker 2020).

## The neoliberal politics of white innocence

Human relationality – the truth of human interdependence, denied by some yet so continually obvious for others – is what is at stake. In this crisis situation, the material politics of perpetual neoliberal capitalist crisis intersects with the cultural politics of innocence. This politics of innocence is fundamental to the dialectical production of global whiteness and the human material and symbolic hierarchisation on which it depends. The disproportionate impact of the pandemic on black people is enabled by a neoliberal politics of white innocence, which shifts blame onto the hyper-individualised subject. According to Jackie Wang:

> The politics of innocence and the politics of safety and comfort are related in that both strategies reinforce passivity. Comfort and innocence produce each other when people base their demand for comfort on the innocence of their location or subject position. Perhaps it goes without saying there is no innately ethical subject position. ... When considering safety, we sometimes fail to ask critical questions about the co-constitutive relationship between safety and violence. We need to consider the extent to which racial violence is the unspoken and necessary underside of security, particularly white security. Safety requires the removal and containment of people deemed to be threats. White civil society has a psychic investment in the erasure and abjection of bodies onto which they project hostile feelings, allowing them peace of mind amidst the state of perpetual violence.
>
> *(Wang 2018: 286–287)*

Racialised patterns of imprisonment and other forms of social containment and expulsion, along with the assault on welfare and the urban poor so visible in the current moment, are not regarded as racist state violence because those on the receiving end are understood to be 'guilty', unworthy of support and therefore 'deserving' of their fate. Liberal discourses of fairness, deservedness and merit fuel racism and Islamophobia and justify the disposability of racialised others. The institutionalisation of this politics is elided through the discourse of white innocence.

Those figured through the projection of guilt are understood to be individually failing, responsible for and deserving of their own predicaments. Thus, blameworthiness is one aspect of the construction of racial others needed for systemic racial reproduction. Another aspect is the repetition of the figuration of *certain* racialised bodies and subjects as disproportionately failing and therefore as guilty. Intersections of gender, gender representation, sexuality, able-bodiedness, and politicised religious identity render some subjects more at risk in the white-dominated states of the Global North.[2] Increased vulnerability is interpreted as increased threat. Failure, whether supposedly due to vulnerability or malevolence or a toxic mix of both, is located *in* the individual. Under pandemic conditions, in a new twist on Social Darwinist biopolitics, neoliberalism's failing racialised subject bears the brunt of the historical in-dividualisation of illness as due to inherent weakness or malevolence (Sontag 1978) and the related metaphoric conflation of blackness with contagion (Swanson 1977). In the geopolitics of the twenty-first century, with the United States under pressure because of its dependence on Chinese capital, the supposed origin of SARS-CoV-2 in China is used opportunistically to expand these historical constructions in a xenophobic discourse. Neoliberal blameworthiness meets historical racialisation of disease.

While neoliberalism re-legitimises hyper-visibilisation of racialised subjects with a strategic 'celebratory' discourse of diversity, it invisibilises racism through the individualisation process. This individualising process divorces matters of race from the public domain and politics. Matters of race then become matters of ethics or morals, of personal offence or interpersonal expressions of race hate, or overt expressions of randomly targeted racism. Where these matters are legislated for, the framing is in terms of the state as the guardian of, and protector against moral aberration. South Africa's much debated Prevention and Combating of Hate Crimes and Hate Speech Bill currently before parliament could be read as an example of the function of hyper-individualisation to paper over the continuation of a highly extractive racial capitalism in the democratic era.

> When individual acts, driven by hateful 'sentiments' and 'beliefs', are presented as the primary motivators of violence, the social and historical conditions by which particular individuals and groups are rendered more, or less, vulnerable to violence, can be easily eclipsed. It is thus necessary to problematise the socially disconnecting hate crime discourse, in particular how it reduces prejudice to discrete and disconnected identity-based acts ...
>
> *(Judge 2018: 111)*

The constitutive violence necessary for the capital accumulation of coloniality and therefore fundamental to the development of nation states is denied through this individualising process. The advent of hyper or 'neo-neoliberalism' only extends this denial through individualisation:

> If neoliberalism concerns the intensification of privatised preference and experience, *neo-neoliberalism* is the hyper-extenuation of the neoliberal, its decoupling from any conscious modesty or humility, from any finitude. ... Neo-neoliberalism is the reach for the perfect replica and the perfectionism of the momentary, of making the everywhere and anywhere, any and every moment open to financialised investment, immediate and instantly mediated experience. It commits, where it commits to anything at all, to remaking and replication as the locally Same, as the particular instantiation of the unchanging Universal and therefore recognisable. Its trick it to be anywhere by going nowhere. A culture of pure replicability via a culture of cloning.
>
> *(Goldberg 2009: 363–364)*

This hyper-individualisation has the effect of bolstering the politics of whiteness as an epistemic-ontological process which enacts the forms of 'cultural cloning' (Essed 2005; Puwar 2004) able to contain the contradictions of race within a 'constrained mixture' (Goldberg 2009) of racialising articulations. Thus,

> *[n]e*oliberal whiteness comes to be [biopolitically] through its micromanagement of information, bodies; objects in general, via ever more complicated techniques for rendering the world of difference knowable in order to manage the threat to life (material, social and affective) that it presents. It works by the careful management and containment of difference, *bringing difference into sameness*, gathering allies as it does so. Therefore, an important consequence of the ability to define the world is the ability to bring difference inside to create inclusion. Normative (neo)liberal whiteness is extended through its silent *benevolent* outreach; through the very power to reach out and to offer inclusion to its excluded Others (women, older or queer subjects, for example); and thus through the power to make decisions about which groups come into its purview on the basis of which form of inclusionary/exclusionary bargains. Whiteness becomes civilisational and untouchable in its promotion of the general 'good'. Invitations to come into the human race operate as invitations into neoliberal whiteness.
>
> *(Hunter 2015a: 12)*

In this formulation, neoliberalism has the effect of flipping responsibility for violence and exclusion onto its victimised other, enabling whiteness to own the means by which morality and goodness are defined and responsibility and blame apportioned, located elsewhere with the guilty.

## Disturbed whiteness: Invisible/unknowing/innocent no more

Epistemology is central to white supremacy, as it is with the systemic forms of domination of heteropatriarchy and capitalism. The legitimation of some knowledges, experiences and voices at the expense of others serves to validate some subjects while disqualifying others from the status of 'fully human'. Critical whiteness studies' conceptual mainstays of invisibility, ignorance, and innocence, which speak to epistemologies of whiteness, need to be rethought in relation to the unique conditions of this historical moment. Peggy McIntosh's 1989 essay titled 'White Privilege: Unpacking the Invisible Knapsack' was one of the impactful early works that provided impetus to the fledgling field at that time, and framed subsequent thinking. While the idea of the invisibility of whiteness as a structural phenomenon has been productive, it becomes problematic when one brings in history, location, and politics. In short, whiteness has not been invisibilised everywhere, either today or in the past, and in those places where it was previously invisibilised, this is arguably no longer the case. At the intersections with gender, class, and ethnicity, 'degraded' or 'inferior' forms of whiteness have been very much visibilised – in co-constructive opposition to global 'whiteness incognito' or the 'Invisible Empire' – to justify violence, war, colonialism and apartheid, or to render internally othered or tainted whites available for disciplining and domestication into respectability and race purity regimes (Van der Westhuizen 2017; Wemyss 2009; Willoughby-Herard 2010; Wray 2006). Feminist studies of national colonial, and class formations expose particularly the investment in gender, sexual, and class corralling of female bodies as boundary of whiteness (McClintock 1995; Skeggs 1997; Stoler 1989). We regard a reassessment of what could be called 'the invisibility consensus' also as necessary in light of the work of black thinkers such as Fanon and Du Bois on hyper-visibilisation and invisibilisation, respectively. When invisibilised, whiteness seems to find its co-constitution in the hypervisibilisation of racial others, especially at the intersections with gender and ethnicity. Concurrently, the invisibilisation of whiteness stands in tension with the social invisibilisation of the understandings and experiences of people racialised as black. Indeed, it is vital to assert the vantage point from which whiteness is deemed to be operating invisibly: The white gaze is 'a racialised way of seeing that proceeds through the carefully cultivated refusal to see and acknowledge certain things and the suppression of other ways of seeing and experiencing the world' (Medina 2018: 248; see also Ahmed 2004). Whiteness involves a mind trick universalising itself as a pre-given norm to the extent that the foundational Western binarism of white/black is obscured. But subjects racialised by the operations of whiteness have no option but to see whiteness, its modes and effects, as in the work of Ralph Ellison (1952), Frantz Fanon (1963, 2006), and Steve Biko (1978). This necessary conspicuousness of whiteness is also true for subjects racialised as 'lesser' whites within intra-white hierarchies. Similar to masculinities, whiteness works in the plural to establish an order of whitenesses, arranged within boundaries that are continuously adapted in accordance with the vagaries of power, as seen historically with the shifting positions of Jewish, Irish, Italian, and Afrikaner whites (Brodkin 2002; Ignatiev 2009 [1995]; Painter 2010; Van der Westhuizen 2021).

Moving to innocence, the denial of violence implied in human disposability – upon which the notion of race rests – enables a politics of white virtue. This politics sustains white passivity in a range of ways, through its association with civility, nobility, goodness, forbearance, and/or feminine immaturity (Hunter 2010; McClintock 1995; Stoler, 2002; Van der Westhuizen

2016). All these articulations are linked to what has long been posited as one of the fundamentals of whiteness: Its wilful ignorance as a not-knowing accompanied by absolution of responsibility for racism and its effects (Dyer 1997; Ware 1992, 2015; Wekker 2016). The politics of white innocence is infused with an 'epistemology of ignorance' (Mills 1997), functioning as part of an active white defence of passivity in the face of implication in systemic racism. These machinations are oiled by (neo)liberal individualism, which obscures the systemic nature of racism by fixing racism onto individual white subjects as agentic racists. Thus, the politics of innocence and guilt fixes a global racialised hierarchy whereby white innocence feeds off black guilt justified through the supposed equation of blackness with violence, sexual permissiveness, criminality, indolence and a range of other (white defined) vices. This politics of innocence produces institutional stasis, a stuck-ness within a racialised human hierarchy, which is in reality actively produced. This stasis is dependent on ignorance about the unspoken marker in racialising practices, which is whiteness.

The mythology of perpetual crisis plays into the active reproduction of racial ignorance. In the Global North, a narrative is created around the extraordinary spectacle of abhorrent individually perpetrated racism whilst hiding the intersecting everyday relational cumulations, which enact a racially hierarchical order defined through whiteness. Visibilising certain racist enactments works to hide this systematic nature, associating them with certain forms of whiteness or certain expressions of white violence whilst maintaining the general definitional power of whiteness. This is part of the particularising power of whiteness identified by Robin Wiegman (1999) in her classic *Boundary2* essay whereby white liberalism obfuscates its violence through the positioning of racism 'out there'. Therefore, it has been important in anti-racist analysis to keep the everyday and the extraordinarily violent life-snuffing analytically connected. This creates a chance at disarticulating the 'fixed and material truth' of the racist white imaginary which is an imaginary in which *all bodies* are folded into the hierarchy of race in their everyday (Yancy 2017). In recent times, with the rise of Trumpism in the United States and Radical Right movements elsewhere, the spectacle of racist enactment has spawned a whiteness that is obvious, but we need to keep in mind the contextual conditions of systemic and institutionalised racism that have been invisibilised by such performance. What is the purpose of the performance and what are its effects?

The recent emergence of an obvious whiteness is here read as a reaction against the anti-racist and anti-colonial activisms of the past 400 years: These political, intellectual and artistic impetuses have forced whiteness into a political clearing. Most recently, this activism has been in the form of global #BlackLivesMatter civil society movements. Whiteness is left with no choice but to declare itself. At this historical juncture, where whiteness and its violences are being made apparent, the claim to innocence paradoxically requires the visibilisation of whiteness. It requires the active construction of whiteness within the racial imaginary – we might say, in the current moment, a *hypervisibilisation*. This hypervisibilisation appears to go against the grain of the earlier-described insights on whiteness, of invisibility, ignorance, and innocence. However, this apparent contradiction between hypervisibilisation in the context of invisibilisation/not-knowing serves as a reminder that whiteness works as a differentiated power geometry, with divergences and convergences across different contexts.

Currently, a political tide is on the rise in nation states in the Global North that seeks to violently reassert the national body politic as white. This is whiteness as an 'evolutionary terror', as Boucher and Matias describe this phenomenon in their chapter in this volume. Intensified by the pandemic, this politics is buoyed by a discourse not unlike tropes of illness (Sontag 1978) in its aim to purify the nation of all foreign objects, whether external or internal others. The past four centuries' rationalisations of race – with religion, biology, nationalism, culture – have all been mobilised in a cacophonic throng. Racialised others are deemed invaders infecting the white nation biologically and diverting it from its culturally ordained or scientifically verified course of natural superiority and domination. Others internal to whiteness (anti-racists, feminists, and queers) are deemed to be weakening the resplendent white nation from the inside: Biologically if they are women committing 'race suicide' by not keeping their bodies for white men only, and politically if they commit 'white treason' by siding with racial others. The politics of violent expulsion is also a politics of gathering those subjects true to whiteness, hence the rise of fascism with its object of the unity of a pure people, to be achieved by any and all means but especially violence. In Alt-Right versions of this politics, the racist colour-blind subterfuge of liberalism and the diversity-toting selective inclusivity of neoliberalism are overlaid with a politics cribbed from the struggles of the excluded, marginalised, and dehumanised. White people and particularly white men are centred as the new victims, in an opportunism claiming pain and victimhood in an attempt to displace the actually wronged. Intersectionality as the powerful theoretical and political tool that shifted feminist and anti-racist politics into a multi-pronged attack on interlinking dominations has been appropriated (see the chapters by Gray and Mattheis in this volume).

In the diversion from systemic racism to so-called 'identity politics', whiteness must reveal itself and state who its subject is, as constructed against its abjectified other. Peering closely at this whiteness, it is exposed in a form that repels even the suggestion of otherness, in contrast to both liberalism and neoliberalism's incorporation of selected others. This politics of abjection should be named for what it is: White supremacism, which must be brought back front and centre analytically as a vital section of the scaffolding of modern power that also comprises patriarchy, heteronormativity, and capitalism. After invading, dominating and extracting from indigenous peoples, legitimised by racialising, gendering and classing 'them' as inferior, and then opening Northern borders to augment demographically faltering local populations, whiteness in a *volte face* movement has increasingly in recent times sought to withdraw into its own otherless universe. To be exact, whiteness now seeks to withdraw into apartheid. As seen in the Nazi appropriation of colonial concentration camps, or in the contemporary relationship between the United States and Israel, the metropole learns from the colony, or at least, reproduces or emulates modes of expulsion and extermination first practised in colonial settings (see also Pappé in this volume). Apartheid returns as imaginary and practice, in Israel and elsewhere. To start with, apartheid was a colonial reboot of nineteenth-century forms of British colonial segregation. Further inspired by Jim Crow laws in the United States, it was cobbled together in South Africa in the mid-twentieth century at the very moment when the metropoles were withdrawing from their African colonies to shift into indirect colonialism, or coloniality. Here it comes again, global racism as Apartheid 2.0 for the twenty-first century. Reflecting on whiteness as a global power formation that is differentially operationalised according to contextual contingencies, it is useful to pay attention to its apartheid or colonial form to trace its current convolutions and possible futures (see also Money and Van Zyl-Hermann 2020).

## Apartheid 2.0

In understanding white people's variable wielding of invisibility, ignorance, and innocence, it is worth pausing at the country of apartheid, South Africa, as an unusual settler state. This volume contains several contributions that attend to South Africa as an exemplar illuminating structural, institutionalised, and identitarian dimensions of whiteness. While we note the caution against exceptionalising South Africa (Alexander 2003), it does serve as a microcosm of longevities in racial colonialities and also of anti-racist resistances and solidarities. Indeed, South Africa can be read as a harbinger of the many modes of deployment of race and racism, of the ways and means of whiteness and, crucially, of how to challenge racism and whiteness. As coloniality adjusted its grip globally to indirect or neo-colonialism from the mid-twentieth century onwards, South Africa at that very time deepened white domination and racial extraction with its brutal system of apartheid, a modernised and more minutely designed and enforced set of colonial technologies. Almost half a century later, amid the historical upheavals of the end of Communism, the fall of the Berlin Wall and the global hegemonisation of neoliberalism, South Africa again offered the unusual, as its white minority relinquished power in a transition to a constitutional democracy (Hyslop 2000):

> [M]any thought that South Africa's overthrow of institutionalised racism and its attempt to build a truly non-racial, modern and cosmopolitan society was the best gift Africa had ever given to the world. [It held the promise of] generat[ing] an alternative meaning of what our world might be, or to become a major centre in the global south.
>
> *(Mbembe 2006: np)*

Today, it is the only postcolonial African state that retains a sizeable white population. However, it is also unique among former British settler states in that white people form a demographic, political and, increasingly, cultural *minority*.

The varying functionality of invisibility to whiteness becomes apparent in the internal hierarchical differentiation of multiple whitenesses. The power contestations between two settler classes, which included the South African War of 1899–1902, partly explains the perennial re-entrenchment of whiteness through the intersectional wielding of other categories of differences – in this case, ethnicity and class. After the settling of a refreshment trading post at the Cape of Good Hope by the Dutch East India Company in 1652, increasing racialisation by the predominantly Dutch colonists was further exacerbated when the Cape colony shifted into the hands of Britain in 1806. British colonial authorities' violent geographical enforcement of racial segregation and movement control against the indigenous Khoi and Xhosa laid the groundwork for twentieth century colonial segregation and, between 1948 and 1994, apartheid. British imperialism sparked the counter-politics of African and Afrikaner nationalism at the fin-de-siècle before and after the war. Apartheid can be read as a culmination of the Afrikaner nationalist project to achieve an apparently contradictory move, by rising to unmarked whiteness while asserting ethnic particularity. However, when reading Britishness as an ethnicity transparent to itself but seeking to position all other ethnicities (Hall 1997), this emerges as a co-constitutive dynamic: British imperialists positioned Dutch or Boer whiteness as a degraded whiteness from especially the nineteenth century onwards. 'The Afrikaner' was a political counter-invention seeking to amplify European descent and, hence, the claim to whiteness for colonists to counter their sizeable slave ancestry due to significant miscegenation during the years of Dutch control. In a signature act of whiteness, both the moniker 'Afrikaner' and the language Afrikaans were appropriated from those designated to the newly constructed 'coloured' (mixed-race) identity on the basis of skin colour and phenotype. Contriving 'The Afrikaner' during the first half of the twentieth century was specifically to purge from the identity those racialised as 'coloured'. The racial expulsion was also a class project: Shifting from a large class of 'poor whites' to the embourgeoisement of the Afrikaner, in an aspirational relationship with white English-speaking South Africans (WESSAs). Here, gender and sexuality became crucial instruments of control. Installing female subjects to delimit this whiteness by reproducing the white nation or *volk* in body and morals is an essential plank in the scaffolding.

Internal sexual and gender others had to be subsumed or ejected. At first, the idea of apartheid in 1948 was ill-defined but eventually the Afrikaner nationalists sought to remake South Africa into the Afrikaner's own image, by projecting claimed racial and ethnic particularism onto others. While the intra-white ethnic division was reaffirmed at first, racial and ethnic divisions in the 'coloured' and the native/Bantu/black brackets, respectively, were multiplied many times over.

Apartheid's instatement of Afrikaners to whiteness was done, counter-intuitively, through the hyper-visibilisation of whiteness with apartheid geographies and spatialisation. Unmissably noticeable were ubiquitous sign boards directing the movement of bodies racialised as, at first, 'Europeans' and 'Non-Europeans' and, later, 'Whites' and 'Non-Whites', to demarcated sites. Spaces were hence racially reserved down to the microlevel, determining which doors could be entered, which seats sat on. Apartheid spatialisation was derived from Jim Crow laws and shared the mode of hyper-visibilisation, also in the form of white supremacist violence and spectacle. Jim Crow was part of white supremacist strategy against post-slavery Restoration in the United States (1865–1877), while apartheid was similarly (and partially) a reaction against the colonial liberalism of Jan Smuts' United Party government, which in the 1940s was considering some relaxation of segregation to allow for the creation of a category of colonial black insiders.

The spatial differentiations were class differentiations, to render whiteness equivalent to affluence and blackness to poverty, both ostensibly deserved. Apartheid was a biopolitics that intruded into minute bodily intimacies, with laws forbidding inter-racial and gay sex, and a necropolitics determining which bodies were disposable, especially in a racial capitalism de-pendant on black male bodies to perform deep-level mining. The creation of *Blank Suid-Afrika* was an everywhere representation of whiteness, to use Dyer's term (1997). But, different to Dyer's analysis of whiteness in the North, in this 'everywhere' whiteness, white subjects were not transparent to themselves – they understood themselves as white. Hence South African philosopher Samantha Vice's (2010: 326) contention: 'that one is white rather than black is always present to oneself and others'. The obvious macro and micro racialisations of apartheid created the presentness of whiteness to white and black people that Vice speaks of. In this sense, apartheid's hallowed object of *Blank Suid-Afrika* was aspirational, as is also revealed by the Afrikaans word 'blank', usually translated as 'white'. Similar to the English word 'blank', however, it suggests colourlessness, unmarkedness or transparency, rather than simply white. Afrikaners could not just assume whiteness. With bourgeois whiteness finally mostly achieved by the 1960s, the Afrikaner objective shifted in the 1970s to active rapprochement with WESSAs. As intra-white class interests dovetailed, the Afrikaner nationalist focus moved to ridding 'The Afrikaner' of its particularity and disappearing into globally hegemonic Anglo whiteness (Van der Westhuizen 2021). The transition to democracy and concomitant globa-lisation of Afrikaner capital in the 1990s, after years of anti-apartheid isolation and sanctions, accelerated this disappearing trick.

In further unpacking the white triad of invisibility–ignorance–innocence as wilful man-oeuvres, South Africa shows how highly visibilised production of racial spatialities went hand-in-hand with a knowing that racial inequality had to be enforced, with concomitant violence, as it was not a 'natural' state of affairs (see also Steyn 2001; Willoughby-Herard 2015). To state it simply, the makers of apartheid knew that white people were not naturally superior. J.G. Strijdom, who became the second apartheid prime minister, acknowledged in a letter in 1946 to D.F. Malan, the first apartheid prime minister, that urbanisation and education would allow black people to become 'civilised', which would make racist discrimination impossible and lead to equality. In 1954, the same Strijdom admitted that 'merit alone' was not enough to secure white domination and that racially exclusive franchise for white people was essential, whereafter the last people of colour who could vote were deprived of the right (Van der Westhuizen 2007: 57). Casting the timeline back to a century before, Boer and British settlers in the Cape Colony recognised the extreme injustice perpetrated against the Khoi and Xhosa peoples, with some admitting that colonial actions amounted to pillage and genocide (Mostert 1992). Whiteness in its settler mode was visibilised and intensely aware of its precariously constituted domination, partly because of its manifest injustice. But these facts have been subject to 'unremembering', Pumla Gqola's (2010: 8) phrase for 'a calculated act of exclusion and erasure'. Past racist violations of black people and people of colour's humanity are suppressed to normalise current white privilege and preclude corrective action – what Mills (2007: 31) calls 'the mystification of the past [that] underwrites a mystification of the present'. What can be called 'white unknowing' is an active turning away so as not to know the injustice on which white privilege is founded (Van der Westhuizen, forthcoming). But Afrikaner whiteness only shifted into the invisibility–ignorance–innocence triad as its subjects' affluence increased. In postapartheid South Africa, the lack of meaningful redistribution of wealth opened the door to 'a white opportunism of denial', which reactivates discourses of dehumanisation (Van der Westhuizen 2016). This mode fits with racial liberalism (Mills 2008), which refuses the past through 'cultivated amnesia, a set of constructed deafnesses and blindnesses' (p. 1391; also see Majavu in this volume) to proclaim innocence and hence invisibility, whether of whiteness or of the lived experiences of black people.

South Africa, as an exemplar of newly visibilised whiteness within global coloniality, shows how whiteness has historically alternated between strategies of hyper-visibilisation and invisibilisation of both white subjects and those positioned as racial others. As co-constituted power formation, the recent visibilisation of whiteness has been forced by newly impactful struggles against racism, in a sweeping confrontation especially in the Global North and in places such as South Africa. The invisibility–ignorance–innocence triad being historically contingent, it has been wielded by and large by what can be broadly called a liberalism-inflected whiteness. It is currently augmented with, if not supplanted by, rising global white supremacism, mirroring the replacement in government of 'softer' colonial liberalism in 1948 by apartheid's hardline racists. With the tearing away of Du Bois's veil through concerted anti-racist struggles, whiteness is confronted with its subsumed black other and knee-jerks into an attacking posture and mode. Racial liberalism's quietening violences are inadequate to the anti-racist groundswell, as can be seen in South Africa and in the Trumpist, neo-Nazi, and fascist reactionary upsurge in the Global North. White defiance has exploded in racist verbal and physical attacks ranging from social and mainstream media outbursts to killing sprees. The reversion is to the open and hostile drawing of a frontier with the assertion of white superiority.

White reaction emanates from whiteness' internally stratified others, another resonance traceable from the South African exemplar. Whiteness preys as much on internal differentiation as on external differentiation for its reproduction, underlining the importance of bringing in ethno-nationalism, class, gender, and sexuality. Differential class positions can provoke intensified efforts at reinforcing whiteness, especially when ethnically inflected. The intra-Afrikaner cross-class pact crumbled in the 1970s and was replaced by a cross-ethnic middleclass and elite pact with WESSAs, leading to the reform and official end of apartheid. This pushed a minority of 'losing whites', who were unable to achieve middleclass status, to reassert apartheid in original form. In the contemporary context of globalised neoliberal capitalism's necropolitical abjection of vast groups of people as disposable, including rendering 'the worker' increasingly superfluous, ethno-nationalism and class are again mobilised to buttress whiteness, as is discussed in the chapters by Thobani, Marston, Pappé and Begum, Mondon and Winter. Gender and sexuality are, similar to the orchestration of apartheid, again essential plains of control. More pressure is placed on female subjects to remain within the white fold, whether by reactivating biological destiny and the trope of woman/wife-as-mother, as seen in the chapter by Mattheis, or by unleashing negative affect against black women, as in Marston's chapter. Meanwhile, the (neo)liberal text continues running, as postfeminist white femininity and neoliberal 'global gayness' still accord some women sexual 'freedoms' and some queers respectability, as in the chapters by Deliovsky and Scott, respectively.

To conclude this section, whiteness has convulsed into a new permutation due to effective global anti-racist activisms. Alongside (neo)liberal whiteness with its invisibility–ignorance–innocence triad, a reactionary, more explicitly violent whiteness rears its head in the form of a globalised Apartheid 2.0: A self-emboldening that amounts to terror (see Boucher and Matias in this volume), drawing on histories of white racist extermination politics that underpins persistent global coloniality.

## Commodifying whiteness: Declaring denying and dematerialising whiteness

In the midst of the Global Pandemic came the global outpouring of grief and rage, the mass of protests and uprisings, thousands of newspaper column inches devoted to the need for anti-racist change and justice over the globe in response to the mass witnessing on social media of the death of George Floyd, a 46-year-old Black American man from Fayetteville North Carolina killed by a white police officer, suffocated in a choke hold for 9 minutes recorded and witnessed globally on social media. In the aftermath of Floyd's killing, the British writer and cultural commentator Otegha Uwagba finally felt moved to write her long planned personal essay on racism, 'Whites: On Race and Other Falsehoods', which despite her best intentions became an essay about white privilege (Uwagba 2020). The main thrust of her analysis of white privilege comes out of her lived experiences as a Black woman of the 'colossal burden' co-existing with white people, and how the outpouring of white emotion as part of the aftermath of this killing worked oppressively as part of the broader declarative mode of liberal and anti-racist whitenesses (Ahmed 2004). This burden is one that extends to the control exerted over her writing of the essay itself.

> [A]lthough I didn't want to write an essay where white people took centre stage ... that's exactly what I've done. It became clear to me that to write about navigating racism and not place white people at the centre of that narrative would be to elide the very thing I was trying to write about, because navigating racism really is a matter of navigating white people. Perhaps that conclusion seems obvious, but it took me a little while to get there, and to work through my competing desires about how to approach this essay. On re-flection, that push and pull – between what I wanted to do, and what racism necessarily requires of me – seems strangely apt, a facsimile of whiteness itself and the way it compels, overrides, distorts, and ultimately controls.
>
> *(Uwagba 2020: 4–5)*

What is implied by Uwagba, is the difficulty of resisting the serviceability of her work to whiteness and her black body to the anti-racist development of white people. The problem she articulates, demonstrates precisely the constitutive nature of whiteness as a consumptive, possessive *colonial dynamic* (Moreton-Robinson 2015) achieved through racism and its requirements. And which puts white and black people within a certain sort of relation, framed by whiteness. Much writing is resistant to but implicated in the fantasy of race whereby whiteness is operating as the 'master signifier' (Sashedri-Crooks, 2000) to establish the structure of meaning and chain of signification which organises human difference. And as Zimitri Erasmus

(2017) reminds us, none of us can be outside, above, or beyond race. Nevertheless, as she also notes together with Toni Morrison (1997), this does not mean that we should stop figuring out ways to struggle for race-specificity without the race prerogative. Living this tension is what it means to be a 'race critical anti-racist' (Lentin 2020): Neither repressed, nor beguiled by race.

Critical writing and communication about whiteness can never be understood from outside of the global coloniality which inaugurates this position of whiteness as mastery. From the point of view of attempting to write 'out' of the global coloniality of whiteness an important shift is to be made in understanding the epistemic and ontological power of whiteness as co-constitutive. This *co-constitutive* onto-epistemic power of whiteness has been underplayed in much of the earlier studies of whiteness. The focus tended to fall on privileging epistemic power over ontological power. This was done in an attempt to reject the biological and social essentialism so necessary in producing race and its master signifier white supremacy. Much of the work leading the significant recent developments in the empirically oriented critical analysis of whiteness situates itself from within a frame of critical race theorising. This includes the work of Sara Ahmed (2006, 2007, 2012), Yasmin Gunaratnam and Gail Lewis (Gunaratnam and Lewis 2001), Lewis 2000, Cheryl Matias (2016), Jasbir Puar (2007, 2017), Shirley Anne Tate (2014) and Arun Saldanha (2007) – to name a few of those influencing our approach. Given the challenges in communicating the experience of being racialised from outside of the terms set by whiteness, it is no accident that these works are developing a broader range of theoretical and methodological tools than is offered through critical whiteness studies' mainstay social constructionism. They are rooted instead in new understandings of affect and the body. One of the most notable contributions to the empirical corpus of the past 20 years is Nirmal Puwar's (2004) *Space Invaders* in which she elaborates the multiple impacts of racialised/gendered bodies *out of place* in the white somatic institutional norm which produces 'an encounter that causes disruption, necessitates negotiation and invites complicity' (p.1). Similar to Uwagba's intervention above, this varied body of work starts from the point of resisting the definitional power of whiteness. It asserts and reinforces Black agencies in a such a way that the micro-aggressive nature of race and racialising practice cannot be ignored. This is in contrast to the way that this can sometimes be when the starting point for an analysis is whiteness. It is a point demonstrated in different ways in chapters by Ahluwalia and Shah in this volume. The point is that Black bodies refuse and destabilise whiteness by their very presence. They produce an ontological disturbance which refuses the possessive dynamic of coloniality. They have to be engaged with or suppressed. Whilst it is arguably the work by Black people which has had at least as much if not the much bigger present and historical impact on the broader conversations on whiteness in the public sphere, the return is always to whiteness. This is precisely the dynamic so important to Reni Eddo-Lodge's *Why I'm no longer talking to White People about Race* (2017), which is one of the more important British-located texts inaugurating the recent rise in conversation on whiteness globally.

This brings us back to the point raised by Robin Wiegman (1999, 2012) about the problematic of particularity in any field, volume, collection or activity announcing itself through a debt to whiteness studies. This particularisation serves in the end to return itself to whiteness. This dynamic is exacerbated in the case of antiracist whiteness which is never an antithesis to white racial formation but only ever legible through it (Wiegman 2012: 196). The most commonly engaged social constructionist approach to highlighting, excavating and outlining white specificity shows that whiteness is not universal; it is contextual and produced relationally, interpersonally. It is something that white people do as a relational achievement, an enactment of power and across all spheres of life. However, the social constructionist approach does not necessarily show that whiteness, or indeed blackness as its foil, are not natural, nor are they reducible to white and black bodies. Much of the work in this area, generative as it has been, continues to fail to learn this *methodological* 'object lesson' (Wiegman 2012). It often stops short of an analysis that captures the full import of the fact that 'whiteness is the historical context in which modern Euro American culture is embedded' (Martinot 2010: 29) and therefore the one that *creates* the modernist idea of the self-contained liberal individual to support this. This means that it is whiteness *as an onto-epistemic relation,* a 'somatic norm' as Nirmal Puwar (2004) puts it, rather than an object in itself which belongs only to white people, which makes this inter-personal dialectical relation possible and intelligible in the first instance. This means dismantling the very notion of personhood as individual sovereignty which implies the conscious, knowing, and self-knowing, self-reflexive being which is of course the sort of being that could know and resist its own whiteness should that fancy or earnest goal take it. This is the quandary that much of whiteness studies finds itself in. As it seeks to deconstruct its object whiteness, it appears to destroy the means to resist it. As a social constructionist project the study of whiteness meets the impossibility of disestablishing whiteness without destroying itself. As such a project:

> Whiteness Studies was founded on an inescapable contradiction: its project to particularise whiteness was indebted to the very structure of the universal that particularisation sought to undo. This was the case because particularisation required an emphasis on the body and on reconstituting the linkage between embodiment and identity that universalism has so powerfully disavowed for the white subject. To particularise was to refuse the universal's disembodied effect. And yet the destination of the dominant theoretical trajectories in Whiteness Studies were never toward the white body but away from it in such a way that consciousness emerged as the methodological fix to the white body's universal authority – the very means to forge an antiracist white subject. One *saw* whiteness by *knowing* what whiteness had come to mean.
>
> *(Wiegman 2012: 160)*

Knowing the meaning of whiteness was, however, without knowing *how* it had come to be 'inside' the body.

This shift away from the body to sovereign consciousness reinstates the key problematic of race. This is because it continues to work from the basic position of privileging epistemology over ontology that supports the idea of race in its modern invention, where white people are subjects, black people are objects and indigenous peoples are absent. If we expand the imaginary of an analysis of whiteness to explore its globality as we must, learning from indigenous studies, we are able to better understand the importance of the fundamental rupture *of being* necessary to sustaining white supremacy *in general*; and then the importance of ignoring this globality of coloniality to sustaining this rupture in being. Summarising from Aileen Moreton-Robinson's devastating critique of the socio-discursive operation of patriarchal white sovereignty to settler coloniality (Moreton-Robinson 2015: 49–50; see also Majavu in this volume): 'Taking possession of Indigenous people's lands was a quintessential act of colonisation and was tied to the transition from Enlightenment to modernity, which precipitated the emergence of a new [white property owning] subject into history within Europe'. This is the process through which possessiveness became embedded in everyday discourse as 'a firm belief that the best in life was the expansion of self through property and property began and ended with possession of one's body' and the means by which it became fundamental to whiteness 'to be able to assert "this is mine" requires a subject to internalise the idea that one has property rights that are part of normative behaviour rules of interaction and social engagement'.

It is this dynamic of ownership established through violent dispossession which puts the subject and object in *violent* relation, whereby the black subject exists as a foil for whiteness. Furthermore, because *dispossession* cannot provide the requisite recognition of ownership required for the legitimation of white subjectivity, it also establishes the basic onto-pathology of whiteness. This is because, following Nicolacopoulos and Vassilacopoulos (2004: 41–42), 'modern Western subjectivity requires unmediated possession to ground itself securely, this sort of violence constitutes a fundamental disturbance of its ontological structure. Outwardly directed violence thus corresponds to an inwardly directed self-violation'. This is the lived mechanism through which global colonial whiteness is enacted materially, symbolically and affectively through the repressed violence of the possessive. This is a dynamic which is dependent on the idea of a whole subject which, once established, must be worked on to be maintained. This dynamic is at the root of the *violent* split in the relationality of being produced through colonisation, maintained through coloniality and increasingly through the public debate on the idea of institutional racism. It belies the fundamental split which is so significant in the reproduction of whiteness as a lived relation whereby the 'desire for whiteness' (Sashedri-Crooks 2000) operates as a protection against the fundamental anxiety related to the relationality of being. This is because exposing whiteness means challenging *white identification,* which in turn exposes the fundamental lack of wholeness in whiteness, due to the incomplete nature of human identity itself. Whiteness depends on the fantasy of wholeness, authority, and control of others as a way of controlling and understanding the self. Identification with whiteness is a way of guarding against the fundamental anxiety of being, of human vulnerability, of failure. Thus, the dismantling of race implies a fundamentally different way of thinking about identity and power which are fundamentally relational and *outside* of liberal narratives of the sovereign individual. This is a significant part of the explanation as to why whiteness maintains its power, because *all* of those subjects bound up in its chain of signification, whether 'white, black, yellow or brown' (Sashedri-Crooks 2000: 4–5; see also Thobani's chapter in this volume) have the promise of access to absolute wholeness. Disinvesting in the ideal of whiteness is a disinvestment in the possibility of the whole subject for everyone within the chain, not only for those racialised as white.

## The (neo)liberal rise of white fragility

From within the context of understanding the fundamentally repressive dynamic of coloniality at play in the enactment of whiteness, the rise of the notion of 'white fragility' popularised by the diversity consultant turned academic Robin DiAngelo (2018) makes sense as a 'better way' of thinking about white privilege. 'Better' in the sense that it appears to have the possibility of conceiving of the dynamic and relational nature of whiteness and the role of the possessiveness within this. The concept can certainly be powerful as a conceptual tool in highlighting and confronting a lack of white accountability for present and past racial injustices. It highlights the role of affect in these forms of social defence against the recognition of whiteness as a form of innocence. It is a powerful tool for rendering this in the context of interpersonal relationships and in the context of institutional life. The focus on 'white progressives' appears to respond to the contemporary manifestations of racism being experienced by people racialised as other to white (Ahmed 2012; Lewis 2000; Puwar 2004) in the context of their arrival into positions of leadership within the corridors of power. The concept speaks to 'everyday racism' (Essed 1991) concerns over repressive tolerance, blocked agency and progression within an ostensibly inclusive and supposedly benign liberal institutional context. White fragility is therefore a concept that appears to speak to the new antiracist terrain on which to fight racism and to be aware of and engaged with the agency of Black people in this, and in leading antiracist resistance.

However, developed in the US context, its direct transportability to different social realities is questionable, tied as it continues to be to the 'ground zero' history of America in the context of colonial expansion via slavery, as well as the difficulties produced through its thin concept of the (white) subject. Similar to earlier forms of racism awareness training (Katz 1978) it can work to re-essentialise identities, entrapping subjects into racial circuits of being, thinking and doing. A significant part of the problem is the reductive focus on 'how one aspect of white sensibility continues to hold racism in place: White fragility' (DiAngelo 2018: 2). Therefore, one of the reasons it is so popular is that it gets at the violence of the everyday experience of being racialised as other to white in liberal institutional spaces, and it gets that this experience relates to a denial of world view and to the related denial of the experience of racism as a fundamental part of that; and that this works even and *especially* where substantial inclusion appears to have been achieved. But the problems arising are similar to the training and work undertaken with reference to Peggy Macintosh's much earlier influential work on privilege. It has little of the necessary historical, philosophical or even psychological scaffolding necessary to understanding the psychic dynamic of ownership as socio-discursive phenomenon identified by Moreton-Robinson in her work. Furthermore, its rendering of white emotion as fragility also lends itself to the creation of a hierarchy of emotion, in which affect is rendered invalid if expressed by subjects racialised as white. White and Black subjects are understood to be in different affective universes. White subjects operate through 'emotions such as anger, fear, and guilt and beha-viours such as argumentation, silence, and withdrawal from the stress inducing situation' (DiAngelo 2018: 2). Affect is, alongside other modes, powerfully formative of subjectivity. The idea of 'white fragility' operating as a shorthand for whiteness raises the question whether white subjects may still 'be' at all, if all forms of affective enunciation are necessarily void when emanating from a white subject. The root of the problem is the subject-object binary that remains in play, if in a reversed manner.

Part of the criticism here is directed at what can be called a 'whiteness industry', akin to the 'diversity industry' (Ahmed and Swan 2006; Kandola and Fullerton, 1998; Swan 2010), which papers over complexities of subjectification as a socio-discursive historical process. This is a decomplexifying process which coincides with and is abetted by the postmodern narcissism of online life (Michel 2020). It facilitates 'handwringing whiteness', 'best whiteness' and 'essential whiteness', which all work to re-centre whiteness despite stated aims to do the opposite. 'Handwringing whiteness' refers to overly self-conscious, frequently autobiographical writing and other performances of 'awakenings' to whiteness. 'Best whiteness' refers to those white subjects who, through decontextualising hyper-individualisation and enactments of self-immolation, signal race traitorship for admission into opportunistic politics of advancement of select black others, a process that leaves systemically unequal power relations otherwise intact. 'Essential whiteness' is where the politics of subjects is read off skin pigmentation and phe-notype, with racialisation as white rendered a political and even ontological dead-end that obviates any possibility for ethical existence or inter-racial solidarities that pursue anti-racism. All of these show the extent of the destabilisation of whiteness, but also serve as strategies of co-option into, and re-entrenchment of, race thinking.

The concept of white fragility and others popularised in diversity training contexts, such as 'micro-aggressions' and 'unconscious bias', dilute the power and complexity such phrases may have had when they were first conceived (Ahmed and Swan 2006; Hunter 2015a; Swan 2010; Tate and Page 2018). This sort of superficial activity can impede moves to a more complicated struggle to become, such as the struggle that Erasmus (2017) identifies in her work in *Race*

*Otherwise*. Such a superficiality reinforces the process of speaking *about* whiteness rather than speaking *through* it (Hunter 2009, 2015a, 2015b). Speaking *about* whiteness manifests when people racialised as white are speaking in the declarative mode identified by Ahmed (2004), recognising their categorical positioning as a white person as though white privilege and the advantages accrued can be identified, objectified and understood in order to be disposed of (see also Shih 2014). Speaking *through* whiteness is the much more contested and messy activity where people racialised as white speak *through* relationships with others, from the context of those relationships, from within their bodies and intimacies together, through the living of their embodied histories (Hunter 2015b). A flattening of history is at play in concepts like white fragility which requires a related flattening out of affect and the expulsion of the body. There is little ability to see the complex intersections of whiteness: Not as a way to see the internal diversity with a view to establishing equivalences between experiences of oppression, but as a way of considering the connections and interplay which produce whiteness as supremacy (Bilge 2014; Levine-Rasky 2011; see also the Intersectionalities section contributions in this volume as well as the chapters by Ahluwalia, Gray, and Marston). There are, therefore, a number of problems with the way this translation of knowledge around white defence is occurring and the ways it is being translated into anti-racist practice.

## Conclusion: Rehumaning out of whiteness

What would it look like if subjects racialised as white were to be able to begin to speak, act, write, edit *through* whiteness rather than about it? Where 'speaking through' is not an endorsement, but an acceptance of the lived experience of the struggle to become more fully humanly connected to the world, and a rejection of the anti-relational divided self of global colonial whiteness. Writing well before the killing of George Floyd, George Yancy (2017) reflects on the process of 'white gazing' as 'a deeply historical accretion that normalises the making of Black bodies through a relationship to white power' (2017: 243; see also Fanon 2006). He is interested in the role of the gaze to produce the Black body as 'aesthetically deformed, morally disabled ... excessive, monstrous, disgusting, ... *distasteful*' (2017: 243). Yancy is interested in the transmogrification of Black bodies achieved through whiteness not because of what it tells about blackness, but for what this tells us about the ways in which white people are understandable from *within* a relational ontology. As Fanon wrote, and as Mbembe (2017: 44) elaborates, 'Blackness did not exist any more than Whiteness did', meaning that both categories refer to an absence, to a lack. In writing of Eric Garner's cries for breath during his killing, Yancy says:

> It is a call for help, crying out to others, a call that says 'Please hear me'. It implicates the white other. 'I can't breathe' challenges white perceptual practices, ones that have become sutured, held intact, seemingly impregnable. ... the white police officers at the scene have seemingly closed off the possibility of self-interrogation. Garner's cries for help were absorbed into an 'established white ontology'. To have heard his cries should have solicited (etymologically, to disturb) an urgent response from the police. [... But ... instead] Bearing upon their white bodies is effective white history, white systemic interpellative forces, white implicit alliances, white discursive regimes, white iterative processes of habituation, and white power and privilege. Baldwin argues that 'it is with great pain and terror' that one begins to realise that history has shaped, in this case, those white police officers, and those self-appointed white protectors of all things white and pure. It is with great pain and terror that they will come to see that they have inherited and continue to perpetuate their *white* frames of reference. Yet those ... white bodies avoided pain and terror. I would argue

that they remained sutured; sewn up and sealed, unable or unwilling to understand their relationship to white effective history; to understand the ways in which they have already been dispossessed by history, which already presupposes sociality and therefore vulnerability. More accurately, they fled from (covered over) their vulnerability; they refused to come to terms with the unsutured selves that they are: corporeal selves that are already exposed and beyond mastery.

*(Yancy 2017: 253–254)*

What is at stake here is what is at the root of the terror identified by Yancy and the difference between that terror and the fragility identified by DiAngelo. DiAngelo suggests that the loss of power is what is feared by white people, but without understanding the relationship of this loss of power to vulnerability. Yancy, on the other hand, is crystal clear about this link and the fact that the terror and pain provoked at the risk of losing power as a form of domination is about the exposure to the self as vulnerable, as fundamentally unfinished, as only ever in relation, as 'always already beyond ourselves, dispossessed by forces of interpellation, where the idea of automatic self and self-mastery is deeply problematic' (Yancy 2017: 256). The key to re-humaning through whiteness is coming to realise that the white subject was never the site of mastery in the first place. By attempting to practise livedness outside of this aspiration to mastery, a different orientation to the white body may be possible (Hunter, forthcoming 2021). This 'unsuturing' is not about returning whiteness and white subjects to comfort or innocence. Instead, the contrary: This 'unsuturing' relates to remaining open to threat and pain that potentially produces change. Because the recognition of subjective vulnerability implies the resistance to the idea of human self-determination. It places whiteness and whitened subjects in their fullest responsibility with themselves *and* others. This relationality also disrupts the idea of change as coming from within the white body. Social change is not in the gift of 'the white master' but achieved through a relationality where subjectivity is enacted by (at the very least) both in relation. It is this relationality which means that it is possible to resist whiteness. This does not mean that all white people are only ever defined through their implication in racism, but it does mean understanding that they have to work very hard not to be. This is why decolonising the mind is so important, where the meaning of this is not decolonising as a deep cleaning in another manoeuvre to control the body, but an understanding of the way of opening the mind (back) out to the body as the 'fractured locus' (Lugones 2010) for action. The starting point of such a move is coalitional because 'the fractured locus is in common, the histories of resistance at the colonial difference are where we need to dwell, learning about each other' (Lugones 2010: 753; see also Hook et al. 2013).

From this perspective it is no accident, nor any surprise that George Floyd's killing becomes a locus for the expression of white anger, anxiety and desire for solidarity or allyship with Black people. Importantly, this is *in the context of a global pandemic* that is daily exposing both the necropolitical nature of global colonial whiteness, as well as its hubris and complete failures to mastery. Police violence and individual death is conceivable from within a frame of coloniality because, as we argued earlier, a) crime can be understood as a site of violence, it is already the abject and b) the act of the killing itself is *ultra vires*, it is outside of the rules of liberal policing. This act is conceivable and therefore challengeable from within the liberal frame because there is blame to be apportioned, easily locatable within the perpetrating individual or individuals. These are the 'bad apples', bringing violence into 'our space', the root of 'our failure'. To understand this as aberrant is not difficult from within a liberal frame. The attachment of the violence to a racist dynamic supports the connection between racism, violence and irrationality. It is therefore challengeable from within a liberal frame whereby the efforts of white people still work to resist the violence of racism, resolve the pandemic and 'save the world'. It does not produce an ontological disturbance to whiteness as human mastery. This event and its re-cognition and the outpouring of emotionality around it *keeps whiteness in place*, not only at the felt level so immediately of concern to Uwagba (2020), but at the structural, systemic level. The black body works as a foil for whiteness to reproduce itself. As noted earlier, and as Alana Lentin (2020: 128) reinforces, '[c]olonisers reserve the right both to reduce Indigenous, Black, or migrant demands to performances of victimhood and to cast themselves as victimised in the face of these demands'. This is the ongoing repeated re-traumatisation necessary for the possessive dynamic to continue. The reversal of violence enables innocence. The outpouring of grief and emotion can be understood as the displacement of very real emotion onto the racialised other in the service of whiteness. George Floyd, yet another of the 'serviceable ghosts' (Cheng 2000) consumed in the bolstering of violent whiteness as a defence against the vulnerability of being human, sacrificed to the saviour dynamic of whiteness (see Kherbaoui and Aronson in this volume). The globality of analysis becomes all the more important here when trying to un-derstand the intimate subjectification of whiteness. This is precisely because sustaining this mythology of mastery has to happen on a world scale whereby the violence of coloniality is forever exportable, elsewhere, to other lands, other people, other times.

But this lesson about the fundamental relationship between whiteness and violence is a lesson which is more difficult to learn from the position of the Global North. Race is ex-perienced from within a context whereby racism as aberration is always already rendered other to the institutionalised quotidian day to day – losing a job, not getting a job, not being listened to, not being allowed to frame the terms of a meeting or conversation, experiencing other micro-aggressions, cultural mis-recognition and denial as 'non'-traumatic outside of the realm of 'real' life and death violence experienced by the real Other others, out there, over there temporally and geographically distant. Race, split off from itself, its history, the history of its embodiment. To be heard and to be seen, racism has to be deathly traumatising. Whiteness demands this sort of constant re-traumatisation of racialised others for its periodic catharsis. Within a hyper-possessive consumptive *neo*liberal context like the one we are living through now it is this feeding frenzy which provides its energy. This is what is at stake when whiteness is under threat: It feeds vampirically off the energy of Blackness and depletes the energy required to do hard anti-racist work (see Michel 2020). As Mbembe (2017) puts it,

[the] fantasy of Whiteness draws part of its self-assurance from structural violence and the ways in which it contributes on a planetary scale to the profoundly unequal redistribution of the resources of life and the privileges of citizenship. But that assurance comes also from technical and scientific prowess, creations of the mind, forms of political organisation that are (or at least seem to be) relatively disciplined, and, when necessary, from cruelty without measure, from what Césaire identified as a propensity for murder without reason.
*(2017: 46; see also the chapters by Matolino and Majavu in this volume)*

Before the current historical juncture, in which anti-racist struggles have forced the white supremacist underbelly of liberalism to the surface in retaliatory defence of whiteness, a white person in the Global North could go about their whole life almost never having any sort of obvious racially ontological disturbance. In the Global Southern context, as in South Africa, that is not possible. The embodiedness of the white subject is not deniable: Even if her quest is to combat racism and live an ethical life, she still cannot disinvest from whiteness. Instead, like what Samantha Vice (in this volume and in her previous work, 2010) is grappling with, she needs to learn to live through it as a human. This is where connecting the global dots is fundamental because the repression constitutive of whiteness is no longer possible. Whiteness here is related to whiteness there, as Aluwhalia (in this volume) shows at the subjective level. This is a lesson from the volume as a whole.

Ugandan scholar Mahmood Mamdani (2020) captures this in his interpretation of global coloniality, in which the Western nation-state is not a creation *apart* from colonialism but the *co-constituted* result of colonialism and the modern state. Ethnic cleansing is the primary mode through which both the modern state and the postcolonial state formed themselves, producing permanent majorities and permanent minorities by excluding 'those who would introduce pluralism' (p. 4). For Mamdani, democratic South Africa points a way out of this colonial division of 'settler/native'. This followed the realisation that racial identities are products of political processes and not eternal, as whiteness would have subjects believe. It enabled a vision that broke with apartheid to open the way to a new, politically forged community through a 'triple shift': The first shift was from seeking the end of apartheid, to offering an alternative to apartheid. The second was to replace anti-apartheid majoritarianism with non-racial democracy representing all South Africans. The third was to redefine the terms for governing South Africa to terms that denied apartheid's logic. Hence, the anti-apartheid movement 'internalised a novel political identity when it re-defined its target from white people to white power' (p. 346). Instead of substituting white rule with black rule, as South Africans could justly have done, a non-racial democracy was created. Following Erasmus (2017) and Satgar (2019), non-racialism is South Africa's unique contribution to the global war against racism. The principle, as entrenched in the country's democratic constitution (1996), has a century-long genealogy. Two strands must be distinguished, in order to avoid neoliberal 'post-race' colour-blindness (see Majavu's criticism in this volume). The liberal interpretation demands 'assimilation into dominant whiteness', while the anti-colonial or radical version 'defies colonial racial codification' and 'refuses to forget the ways in which race was used by colonists and what this meant for the struggles of and among the colonised' (Erasmus 2017: 37, 39). The latter has as its subject 'the anti-colonial non-racial subject' (p. 44). For Erasmus, radical non-racialism opens the possibility for 'political affinity as the foundation of political solidarity' (p. 42).

Reading Wynter, Erasmus argues for a human that is not 'always and inevitably racialised'. Even if racialisation will likely continue into the future, this fact should not 'absolve' us from working against race (pp. 44–45). Similarly, Mbembe (2017: 183) argues for 'a world freed from the burden of race, from resentment, and from the desire for vengeance that all racism calls into being'. This calls to mind the work of Gobodo-Madikizela (2004: 15), also with reference to South Africa, who asks: 'How can we transcend hate if the goal is to transform human relationships in a society with a past marked by violent conflict between groups? [...] Not closing the door to understanding may be one of the ways in which people can redefine their understanding of atrocities and see them as something that is, like evil in the self, always a possibility in any political system that has emerged from a violent past' (pp. 15–16). Her work speaks of the mobilisation of affect towards humaning ends, focusing on the productive possibilities of remorse and forgiveness.

Understanding begins with listening to one another's narratives (Gobodo-Madikizela 2014). But this should happen with the purposive inclusion of subaltern and marginalised voices – 'voicing' – which allows for the decolonising re-examination of racialised histories and opens the possibilities for alternative subjectivities, communal identities and futures (Stevens et al. 2010). Mbembe (2017) argues for restitution and reparation for those whose humanity was stolen through their subjection 'to processes of abstraction and objectification', to restore their intrinsic humanity. Similarly, Gobodo-Madikizela (2004: 125) insists that '[p]hilosophical questions can and should give way and be subsumed to human questions, for in the end we are a society of people and not of ideas, a fragile web of interdependent humans, not of stances'. She raises two points of significance. The first is that humans should be seized with ending the dehumanisation of others as something that can and has emerged in diverse human societies. The second is related to the first, in that ideas should not hold sway over human lives, which was and is the error of the Western paradigm (Mills 2007: 27; see also Matolino in this volume). Rehumaning here would speak to the concern that the actualisation of personhood depends on the restoration of both material and symbolic resources (Van der Westhuizen 2016) – the restitution of what Gobodo-Madikizela (2010) calls 'the necessities of life'.

Our approach in editing this Handbook builds out of this sort of point of view on rehumaning the subject of race. It is subtly, but significantly different from a social constructionist approach. We explore at multiple levels the global coloniality within which we are all positioned, re-spatialising and reorienting our discussions on how whiteness comes to be as part of a broader racial formation. This shift is what has informed our editing of this collection in bringing together authors who are pushing beyond representation, from various vantage points. What is holding the various contributions together is the interest in understanding the production of whiteness as lived, troubling the binaries of mind–body, structure–agency, rationality–emotion, past–present, truth–interpretation, and ontology–epistemology. This troubling enables a different set of questions about whiteness to those about how it can be known, to capture and control it. The more powerful questions come from people interested in disestablishing the substantial truth of whiteness as a means to becoming more fully human.

## Notes

1   From the expansionist vantage point of this volume, this crisis represents and exposes deep and extensive continuities of this global racial attack (Willoughby-Herard 2015), experienced and playing out differently through locally distinct intersections of power analysable in many flashpoints. This racial attack involves multiple racialisations in relation to the white centre, with the 'Muslim terrorist' and the Yellow Peril in reaction to Japan's and China's economic rise in the 1970s and 1990s, already noted, alongside the frontiers set against 'the African-American criminal' and the 'disposable African'. For example, the democratic-era Marikana massacre in South Africa of 34 black migrant worker miners by black police officers on the instruction of black office bearers in 2012 happens in the context of the co-option of a black political elite by a rapacious racial capitalism wrought during apartheid and colonialism, and which ensures that South Africa retains the ignominious status of most unequal country in the world. Israel's occupation of Gaza and the West Bank continues to be legitimised with colonial-racial discourses of dehumanisation of Palestinian people advancing the systematic seizure of Palestinian land, resources and homes, backed up by multiple assaults and killings in everyday interactions and activities like walking home, driving around town, going to the shops, to school or to work (Davis 2016; Spangenberg and Van der Westhuizen 2018). As Jasbir Puar (2017) elaborates on the Palestinian context, the right to maim exemplifies the most intensive practice of the biopolitics of debilitation, where maiming is a sanctioned tactic of settler colonial rule and an important source of value extraction from populations that would otherwise be disposable. In the United States, with its disproportionate levels of police killing and penal incarceration of African-American men, black social and physical death is primarily achieved through coded discourses of 'criminality' and mediated forms of state violence carried out by an impersonal carceral apparatus, consisting of a matrix of police, prisons, the legal system, prosecutors, parole boards, prison guards, probation officers, and so forth (Wang 2018: 266). So-called 'natural disasters' like the 2005 Hurricane Katrina in Louisiana expose the hierarchy of human life in the United States as starkly racially ordered through the inadequate and violent response to the hurricane's victims and the longer-term impacts of the flood destruction, as well as the neglect of flood protection and environmental erosion of wetlands by the oil industry which produced such disastrous impact of the winds and the rains. Similarly, the 2017 Grenfell Tower fire in London, England, where at least 72 people were killed, 70 injured and over 200 displaced and traumatised must be contextualised in terms of the intersection between neoliberalism and neo-coloniality. This intersection produced the neglect of the building and dangerously unsuitable external

cladding creating pre-disposability to burning, the racialisation of the collection of people living within it and the shambolic governmental response to the fire itself in terms of providing care and supporting those seeking justice for the survivors via the Public Inquiry (Bulley et al. 2019). Following El-Enany, we can conceive the 'epicentre of the fire to be located in European colonialism and transatlantic slavery' (2019: 51) – another example of collective colonially created precarity leading to the premature death, further impoverishment and displacement of racialised people. 'We are here because you were there' goes the rallying call popularised through the internationalist anti-colonial left struggles of Black communities in Europe in 1970s and 1980s (Kushnick 1993; Lewis 2017; Srilangarajah 2018). Srilangarajah (2018) identifies this call as the personal aphorism of the long-time Director of the British Institute for Race Relations and founding editor of the Journal *Race & Class,* Ambalavaner Sivanandan.

2    Examples of the figure of the 'black woman' include Sarah Reed suffering from mental ill health and dying in prison custody (in 2016); and Cynthia Jarret (in 1985) and Joy Gardner (in 1993) who were gendered 'deficient', 'ball-breaking' and 'aggressive' (Lewis 2017: 13), or of the criminalised 'young black man' like Trayvon Martin (died 2012, shot by vigilantes). Eric Garner (died 2014, suffocated during arrest) was caught at the intersections of threatening hypermasculinity, race and dis/ability (Aronson and Boveda 2017). Layleen Polanco died in 2020 without necessary medical care for epilepsy in solitary confinement, and Tony McDade was a victim of transphobic assault (shot dead by police as a murder suspect in 2020). Shemina Begum was recruited as a child by ISIS to travel to Syria and stripped of her citizenship as an adult on her attempt to return to Britain, while Talha Ahsan, a young British Asian poet with Asperger's syndrome, was denied citizenship, rendered without charge and extradited to the United States to be held in solitary confinement for three years.

# References

Ahmed, S. 2004. Declarations of Whiteness: The Non-Performativity of Anti-Racism. *Borderlands e-Journal,* 3 (2), viewed 10 December 2018, https://webarchive.nla.gov.au/awa/20050616083826/http://www.borderlandsejournal.adelaide.edu.au/vol3no2_2004/ahmed_declarations.htm

Ahmed, S. 2006. *Queer Phenomenology: Orientations, Objects, Others.* London: Duke.

Ahmed, S. 2007a. A Phenomenology of Whiteness. *Feminist Theory,* 8 (2):149–168.

Ahmed, S. 2007b. The Language of Diversity. *Ethnic and Racial Studies,* 30 (2):235–236.

Ahmed, S. 2012. *On Being Included: Racism and Diversity in Institutional Life.* London: Duke.

Ahmed, S. and Swan, E. 2006. Introduction. Doing Diversity. *Policy Futures in Education,* 4 (2): 96–100.

Alexander, N. 2003. *An Ordinary Country: Issues in Transition from Apartheid to Democracy in South Africa.* Berghahn Books.

AMP Research Lab Staff. 2020. The Color of Coronavirus: COVID-19 Deaths by Race and Ethnicity in the U. S. *AMP Research Lab,* 5 March, viewed 8 August 2020, https://www.apmresearchlab.org/covid/deaths-by-race.

Anderson, W. 2002. *The Cultivation of Whiteness: Science, Health and Racial Destiny in Australia.* Victoria: Melbourne University Press.

Aronson, B. A. and Boveda, M. (2017) The Intersection of White Supremacy and the Education Industrial Complex: An Analysis of #BlackLivesMatter and the Criminalization of People with Disabilities. *Journal of Education Controversy,* 12 (1): Article 6. https://cedar.wwu.edu/jec/vol12/iss1/

Baderoon, G. 2014. *Regarding Muslims. From Slavery to Post-Apartheid.* Johannesburg: Wits University Press.

Bashford, Alison (2000). 'Is White Australia possible?' Race, colonialism and tropical medicine. *Ethnic and Racial Studies,* 23, 248–271. 10.1080/014198700329042.

BBC, 2020. Coronavirus: France Racism Row Over Doctors' Africa Testing Comments, *BBC,* 3 April, viewed 28 January 2020, https://www.bbc.com/news/world-europe-52151722.

Biko, S. 1978. *I Write What I Like.* London: Bowerdean Press.

Bhattacharyya, G. 2018. *Rethinking.* London: Rowman & Littlefield International.

Bilge, S. 2014. Intersectionality Undone: Saving Intersectionality from Feminist Intersectionality Studies. *Du Bois Review: Social Science Research on Race,* 10 (2): 405–424.

Brodkin, K. 2002. *How Jews Became White Folks and What that Says about America.* New Jersey: Rutgers University Press.

Butler, J. 2004. *Precarious Life: The Powers of Mourning and Violence.* London: Verso.

Butler, J. 2009. *Frames of War: When is Life Grievable?* London: Verso.

Cheng, A. A. 2000. *The Melancholy of Race: Psychoanalysis, Assimilation, and Hidden Grief.* Oxford: Oxford University Press.

Davis, A. Y. 2016. *Freedom is a Constant Struggle: Ferguson, Palestine, and the Foundations of a Movement.* Chicago: Haymarket Books.

DiAngelo, R. 2018. *White Fragility: Why It's So Hard for White People to Talk About Racism.* Massachusetts: Beacon Press.

Doyal, L. and Pennell, I. 1994 [1979]. *The Political Economy of Health.* London: Pluto Press.

Dyer, R. 1997. *White.* London: Routledge.

Eddo-Lodge, R. 2017. *Why I'm No Longer Talking to White People about Race.* London: Bloomsbury.

El-Enany, N. 2019. Before Grenfell: British Immigration Law and the Production of Colonial Spaces. In *After Grenfell: Violence, Resistance and Response*, ed. D. Bulley, J. Edkins and N. El-Enany, pp. 50–61. London: Pluto Press.

Ellison, R. 1952. *Invisible Man.* New York: Modern Library.

Erasmus, Z. 2017. *Race Otherwise: Forging a New Humanism for South Africa.* Johannesburg: Wits University Press.

Essed, P. 1991. *Understanding Everyday Racism: An Interdisciplinary Theory.* London: Sage.

Essed, P. 2005 Gendered Preferences in Racialized Spaces: Cloning the Physician. In *Racialization: Studies in Theory and Practice*, ed. K. Murji and J. Solomos, pp. 227–247 Oxford: Oxford University Press.

Fanon, F. 1963. The Wretched of the Earth. New York: Grove Press.

Fanon, F. 2006. The Fact of Blackness. In *The Fanon Reader*, ed. A. Haddour, pp. 127–148. London: Pluto Press.

Farmer, P. E. 2005. *Pathologies of Power: Health, Human Rights, and the New War on the Poor.* 2nd edn. Berkeley: University of California Press.

Gilroy, P. 2000. *Between Camps: Nations, Cultures and the Allure of Race.* London: Allen Lane Penguin.

Gobodo-Madikizela, P. 2004. *A Human Being Died That Night.* Cape Town: David Philip.

Gobodo-Madikizela, P. 2010. A Call to Reparative Humanism. In *In the Balance. South Africans Debate Reconciliation*, ed. F. Du Toit and E. Doxtader, pp. 101–109. Auckland Park: Jacana.

Gobodo-Madikizela, P. 2014. *Dare We Hope? Facing our Past to Find a New Future.* Cape Town: Tafelberg.

Godlee, F. 2020. Racism: The Other Pandemic. *British Medical Journal*, 369: m2303. DOI:10.1136/bmj.2303.

Goldberg, D. T. 2009. *The Threat of Race: Reflections on Racial Neoliberalism.* Oxford: Blackwell.

Gqola, P. D. 2010. *What Is Slavery to Me? Postcolonial/Slave Memory in Post-apartheid South Africa.* Johannesburg: Wits University Press.

Grosfoguel, R. 2002. Colonial Difference, Geopolitics of Knowledge, and Global Coloniality in the Modern/Colonial Capitalist World-System. *Review (Fernand Braudel Center)*, 25 (3): 203–224.

Gunaratnam, Y. and Lewis, G. 2001. Racialising emotional labour and emotionalising racialised labour: Anger, fear and shame in social welfare. *Journal of Social Work Practice*, 15 (2):131–148.

Hall, S. 1996. New Ethnicities. In *Stuart Hall: Critical Dialogues in Cultural Studies*, ed. D. Morley and K.-H. Chen, pp. 441–449. London: Routledge.

Hall, S. 1997. The Local and the Global: Globalization and Ethnicity. In *Culture, Globalisation and the World-System*, ed. A. D. King, pp. 19–39. Minneapolis: University of Minnesota Press.

Hook, D., Stevens, G. and Duncan, N. 2013. *Race, Memory and the Apartheid Archive. Towards a Psychosocial Praxis.* Johannesburg: Wits University Press.

Hunter, S. 2009. Feminist Psychosocial Approaches to Relationality, Recognition and Denial. In *Theory and Scholarship in Equality and Diversity, Inclusion and Work: A Research Companion*, ed. M. F. Ozbilgin, pp. 179–192. London: Edward Elgar.

Hunter, S. 2010. What a White Shame: Race, Gender, and White Shame in the Relational Economy of Primary Health Care Organisations in England. *Social Politics: International Studies in Gender, State and Society*, 17 (4): 450–476.

Hunter, S. 2015a. *Power, Politics and the Emotions: Impossible Governance.* London: Routledge.

Hunter, S. 2015b. Being Called to 'By the Rivers of Birminam': The Relational Choreography of White Looking. *Critical Arts*, 29 (S1): 43–57.

Hunter, S. forthcoming 2021. Decolonizing Care: Relational Reckoning with the Violence of [White] Power. *Ethics and Social Welfare*, 15 (4).

Hunter, S., Swan E. and Grimes, D. (2010) Reproducing and Resisting Whiteness in Organisations, Policies and Places, *International Studies in Gender, State and Society*, 17 (4): 407–422.

Hyslop, J. 2000. Why Did Apartheid's Supporters Capitulate? 'Whiteness', Class and Consumption in Urban South Africa, 1985–1995. *Society in Transition*, 31 (1): 36–44.

Ignatiev, N. 2009. *How the Irish Became White*. New York/London: Routledge.

Judge, M. 2018. *Blackwashing Homophobia. Violence and the Politics of Sexuality, Gender and Race*. Oxon: Routledge.

Katz, J. H. 1978. *White Awareness: Handbook for Anti-Racism Training*. Norman: University of Oklahoma Press.

Kandola, R. and Fullerton, J. 1998. *Diversity in Action: Managing the Mosaic*, 2nd edn. London: Chartered Institute of Personnel and Development.

Kushnick, L. 1993. 'We're Here Because You Were There': Britain's Black Population. *Trotter Review*, 7 (2):17–19.

Laurencin, C. T. and Walker, J. M. 2020. A Pandemic on a Pandemic: Racism and COVID-19 in Blacks. *Cell Syst*, 11 (1): 9–10.

Lentin, A. 2020. *Why Race Still Matters*. Cambridge: Policy.

Levine-Rasky, C. 2011. Intersectionality Theory Applied to Whiteness and Middle-Classness. *Social Identities: Journal for the Study of Race, Nation and Culture*, 17 (2):239–253.

Lewis, G. 2000. *Race, Gender, Social Welfare: Encounters in a Postcolonial Society*. Cambridge: Polity Press.

Lewis, G. 2017. Questions of Presence. *Feminist Review*, 117: 1–19.

López, A. J. 2005. *Postcolonial Whiteness: A Critical Reader on Race and Empire*. Albany, New York: State University of New York Press.

Lugones, M. 2010. Toward a Decolonial Feminism. *Hypatia: A Journal of Feminist Philosophy*, 25 (4):742–759.

Makau, W. M. 2021. The Impact of COVID-19 on the Growing North-South Divide. *E-International Relations*, March 15, viewed 10 April 2021, https://www.e-ir.info/2021/03/15/the-impact-of-covid-19-on-the-growing-north-south-divide/.

Mamdani, M. 2004. *Good Muslim, Bad Muslim. America, the Cold War, and the Roots of Terror*. New York: Doubleday.

Mamdani, M. 2020. *Neither Native nor Settler. The Making and Unmaking of Permanent Minorities*. Cambridge: Harvard University Press.

Martinot, S. 2010. *The Machinery of Whiteness: Studies in the Structure of Racialization*. Ithaca: Temple University Press.

Matias, C. E. 2016. *Feeling White: Whiteness, Emotionality, and Education*. Rotterdam: Sense Publishing.

Mbembe, A. 2017. *Critique of Black Reason*. Johannesburg: Wits University Press.

Mbembe, A. 2019. *Necropolitics*. Durham, NC: Duke University Press.

Mbembe, A. 2015. Decolonizing Knowledge and the Question of the Archive, online lecture, viewed 17 March 2016, https://wiser.wits.ac.za/system/files/Achille%20Mbembe%20-%20Decolonizing%20Knowledge%20-and%20the%20Question%20of%20the%20Archive.pdf

Mbembe, A. 2006. 'South Africa's second coming: the Nongqawuse syndrome', 14 June, viewed 12 January 2021, <https://www.opendemocracy.net/en/southafrica_succession_3649jsp/.

McClintock, A. 1995. *Imperial Leather: Race: Gender and Sexuality in the Colonial Contest*. London: Routledge.

Medina, J. 2018. Epistemic Injustices and Epistemologies of Ignorance. In *Routledge Handbook of Philosophy of Race*, ed. P. Taylor, L. Alcoff and L. Anderson, pp. 247–260. New York/Oxon: Routledge.

Michel, N. 2020. Doing Good in Black Face: A Consuming Story. *Darkmatter Hub* (Beta) (15) Retrieved from <https://darkmatter-hub.pubpub.org/pub/0aclt8cj> 20.05.2021

Mills, C. W. 1997. *The Racial Contract*. Ithaca, New York: Cornell University Press.

Mills, C. W. 2007. White Ignorance. In *Race and Epistemologies of Ignorance*, ed. S. Sullivan and N. Tuana, pp. 11–38. Albany: State University of New York Press.

Mills, C. W. 2008. Racial Liberalism. *PMLA*, 123 (5): 1380–1397.

Moreton-Robinson, A., ed. 2004. *Whitening Race: Essays in Social and Cultural Criticism*. Canberra: Aboriginal Studies Press.

Moreton-Robinson, A. 2015. *The White Possessive: Property, Power, And Indigenous Sovereignty*. London: University of Minnesota Press.

Morning, A. 2011. *The Nature of Race: How Scientists Think and Teach about Human Difference*. London: University of California Press.

Morrison, T. 1992. *Playing in the Dark: Whiteness and the Literary Imagination*. Cambridge/London: Harvard University Press.

Mostert, N. 1992. *Frontiers. The Epic of South Africa's Creation and the Tragedy of the Xhosa People*. New York: Knopf.

Morrison, T. 1997. Home. In *The House that Race Race Built: Original Essays by Toni Morrison, Angela Y. Davis, Cornel West, and others on Black Americans and Politics in America Today*, ed. W. Lubiano. New York: Vintage.

Moton, F. and Harney, S. 2013. *The Undercommons: Fugitive Planning & Black Study*. New York: Minor Compositions.

National Inquiry into Missing and Murdered Indigenous Women and Girls, 2019a. Reclaiming Power and Place: The Final Report of the National Inquiry into Missing and Murdered Indigenous Women and Girls. viewed 12 April 2021, https://www.mmiwg-ffada.ca/final-report/

National Inquiry into Missing and Murdered Indigenous Women and Girls, 2019b. A Legal Analysis of Genocide Supplementary Report of the National Inquiry into Missing and Murdered Indigenous Women and Girls. viewed 12 April 2021, https://www.mmiwg-ffada.ca/wp-content/uploads/2019/06/Supplementary-Report_Genocide.pdf

Nazroo, J. Y. 2003. The Structuring of Ethnic Inequalities in Health: Economic Position, Racial Discrimination, and Racism. *Public Health Matters*, 93 (2): 277–284.

Nazroo, J. Y. and Bécares, L. 2020. 'Racism is the key to understanding ethnic inequalities in COVID-19 – despite what UK government says', *The Conversation*, October 27, viewed 12 April 2021, https://theconversation.com/racism-is-the-key-to-understanding-ethnic-inequalities-in-covid-19-despite-what-uk-government-says-1488.

Nazroo, J. Y., Bhui, K. S. and Rhodes, J. 2020. Where next for understanding race/ethnic inequalities in severe mental illness? Structural, interpersonal and institutional racism. *Sociology of Health and Illness*, 42 (2): 262–276.

Nicolacopoulos, T. and Vassilacopoulos, G. 2004. Racism, Foreigner Communities and the Onto-pathology of White Australian Subjectivity. In *Whitening Race: Essays in Social and Cultural Criticism*, ed. A. Moreton-Robinson, pp. 32–47.

Painter, N. I. 2010. *The History of White People*. New York: Norton.

Puar, J. K. 2007. *Terrorist Assemblages: Homonationalism in Queer Times*. Durham, NC: Duke University Press.

Puar, J. K. 2017. *The Right to Maim: Debility, Capacity, Disability*. Durham, NC: Duke University Press.

Puwar, N. 2004. *Space Invaders: Race, Gender and Bodies Out of Place*. Oxford: Berg.

Qureshi, K. *et al.* 2020. 'Submission of evidence on the disproportionate impact of COVID-19, and the UK government response, on ethnic minorities in the UK', *Global Public Health Unit at the University of Edinburgh*, 24 April, viewed 12 April 2021, https://ghpu.sps.ed.ac.uk/wp-content/uploads/2020/04/Qureshi-Kasstan-Meer-Hill_working-paper_COVID19-ethnic-minorities_240420.pdf.

Richardson, E. T. 2020a. *Epidemic Illusions: On the Coloniality of Global Public Health*. London: MIT Press.

Richardson, E. T. 2020b. Pandemicity, COVID-19 and the Limits of Public Health 'Science'. *BMJ Global Health*, 5: e002571. DOI:10.1136/BMJGH-2020-002571.

Richardson, E. T. *et al.* 2021. Reparations for Black American Descendants of Persons Enslaved in the U. S. and Their Potential Impact on SARS-CoV-2 Transmission. *Social Science & Medicine*, 276: 113741.

Said, E. 1978. *Orientalism*. New York: Pantheon Books.

Saldanha, A. 2007. *Psychedelic White: Goa Trance and the Viscocity of Race*. Minneapolis: University of Minnesota Press.

Sashedri-Crooks, K. 2000. *Desiring Whiteness: A Lacanian Analysis of Race*. London: Routledge.

Satgar, V. 2019. Seven Theses on Radical Non-Racialism, the Climate Crisis and Deep Just Transitions: From the National Question to the Eco-cide Question. In *Racism After Apartheid - Challenges for Marxism and Anti-Racism*, ed. Satgar V., pp. 194–216. DOI: 10.18772/22019033061.14.

Schellekens, P. and Sourrouille, D. 2020. 'The unreal dichotomy in COVID-19 mortality between high-income and developing countries', *Brookings Blog*, 5 May, viewed 10 April 2021, https://www.brookings.edu/blog/future-development/2020/05/05/the-unreal-dichotomy-in-covid-19-mortality-between-high-income-and-developing-countries/.

Shih, D. 2014. What Happened to White Privilege? Stanford University Arcade: Literature, the Humanities & the World. Viewed August, 30. 2018. http://professorshih.blogspot.com/2014/12/what-happened-to-white-privilege.html

Skeggs, B. 1997. *Formations of Class and Gender: Becoming Respectable*. London: SAGE.

Sontag, S. 1978. *Illness as Metaphor*. New York: Farrar, Straus & Giroux.

Spangenberg, I. J. J. and Van der Westhuizen, C. 2018. Kritiese besinnings oor die Israelse eiendomsaanspraak op Palestina/Critical Reflections on Israel's Claims on Palestine. *Litnet Akademies*, 15 (3). https://www.litnet.co.za/critical-reflections-on-israels-claim-to-land-in-palestine/. Viewed 21 February 2021.

Srilangarajah, V. 2018. 'We Are Here Because You Were With Us: Remembering A. Sivanandan (1923-2018)', *CEASEFIRE*, 4 February, viewed 15 June 2019, Ceasefiremagazine.co.uk/us-remembering-a-sivanandan-1923-2018.

Stevens, G., Duncan, N. and Sonn C. 2010. The Apartheid Archive: Memory, Voice and Narrative as Liberatory Praxis. *Psychology in Society*, 40: 8–28.

Steyn, M. 2001. *'Whiteness Just Isn't What It Used To Be': White Identity in a Changing South Africa*. Albany, New York: State University of New York Press.

Stoler A. L. 1989. Making Empire Respectable: The Politics of Race and Sexual Morality in 20th-Century Colonial Cultures. *American Ethnologist*, 16 (4): 634–660.

Stoler, A. L. 2002. *Carnal Knowledge and Imperial Power: Race and the Intimate in Colonial Rule*. London/Los Angeles: University of California Press.

Swan, E. 2010. Commodity Diversity: Smiling Faces as a Strategy of Containment. *Organization*, 17 (1):77–100.

Swanson, M. W. 1977. The Sanitation Syndrome: Bubonic Plague and Urban Native Policy in the Cape Colony, 1900–1909. *Journal of African History*, 18 (3): 387–410.

Tate, S. A. 2014. Racial Affective Economies, Disalienation and 'Race Made Ordinary'. *Ethnic and Racial Studies*, 37 (13): 2475–2490.

Tate, S. and Page, D. Whiteliness and Institutional Racism: Hiding Behind (Un)conscious Bias(2108) *Ethics and Education*, 13 (1):141–155.

Uwagba, O. 2020. *Whites: On Race and Other Falsehoods*. London: 4th Estate.

Van der Westhuizen, C. 2007. *White Power and the Rise and Fall of the National Party*. Cape Town: Zebra Press.

Van der Westhuizen, C. 2016. Race, Intersectionality, and Affect in Postapartheid Productions of the 'Afrikaans White Woman'. *Critical Philosophy of Race*, 4 (2): 221–238.

Van der Westhuizen, C. 2017. *Sitting Pretty: White Afrikaans Women in Postapartheid South Africa*. Scottsville: University of KwaZulu Natal Press.

Van der Westhuizen, C. 2021. *Reconstructed? White Afrikaans Women in Postapartheid South Africa*. London: Palgrave Macmillan.

Van der Westhuizen, C. Forthcoming. Apology as Pathway Out of White Unknowing. In *Making Sense of Sorry: Thinking Through Apology in Contemporary South Africa*, ed. M. Judge and D. Smythe.

Vice, S. 2010. How do I Live in this Strange Place? *Journal of Social Philosophy*, 41 (3): 323–342.

Wallace, S., Nazroo, J. and Bécares, L. 2016. Cumulative Effect of Racial Discrimination on the Mental Health of Ethnic Minorities in the United Kingdom. *American Journal of Public Health*, 106 (7): 1294–1300.

Wang, J. 2018. *Carceral Capitalism*. South Pasadena: Semiotext(e).

Ware, V. 1992. *Beyond the Pale, White Women, Racism and History*. London: Verso.

Weber, B. 2016. Whiteness, WiG, and Talking about Race. *Women in German Yearbook*, 32: 189–202.

Weheliye, A. G. 2014. *Habeus Viscus. Racializing Assemblages, Biopolitics, and Black Feminist Theories of the Human*. Durham, NC: Duke University Press.

Wekker, G. 2016. *White Innocence: Paradoxes of Colonialism and Race*. Durham, NC: Duke University Press.

Wemyss, G. 2009. *The Invisible Empire: White Discourse, Tolerance and Belonging*. Farnham: Ashgate.

West, C. 1993. The New Cultural Politics of Difference. In *The Cultural Studies Reader,* 2nd edn, ed. S. During, pp. 256–267.

Wiegman, R. 1999. Whiteness Studies and the Paradox of Particularity. *Boundary 2*, 26 (3):115–150.

Wiegman, R. 2012. *Object Lessons*. London: Duke.

Willoughby-Herard, T. 2010. 'I'll Give You Something to Cry About': The Intraracial Violence of Uplift Feminism in the Carnegie Poor White Study Volume, The Mother and Daughter of the Poor Family. *South African Review of Sociology*, 41 (1): 78–104.

Willoughby-Herard, T. 2015. *Waste of a White Skin: The Carnegie Corporation and the Racial Logic of White Vulnerability*. Oakland: University of California Press.

World Health Organisation. 2020. Children: Improving Survival and Well-Being, Viewed 30 April 2021 https://www.who.int/news-room/fact-sheets/detail/children-reducing-mortality

Wray, M. 2006. *Not Quite White: White Trash and the Boundaries of Whiteness*. Durham, NC: Duke University Press.

Wynter, S. 1994. No Humans Involved: An Open Letter to My Colleagues. *Forum N.H.I. Knowledge for the 21ˢᵗ Century*, 1 (1): 42–73.

Yancy, G. 2017. *Black Bodies: White Gazes: The Continuing Significance of Race in America*. Washington: Rowman Littlefield.

# Part I

# Onto-epistemologies: Theory against whiteness

This section provides the overall rationale and theoretical framing of the handbook *against* a white/black dichotomy and the various forms of racial realism (biological and cultural) through which this division works. It is a framework which works against racial realism's ontologising of race, whilst remaining aware of the real material damage produced through the epistemology of race. It brings together pieces which understand this contested interdependent relation between the ontology and epistemology, understanding the relational enactment of race as an onto-epistemic struggle. To establish this framing for the critical study of whiteness, this section includes a range of contributions which demonstrate two key and related points: *How* whiteness comes to be *through* human practices rather than existing *a priori*; and the ways intersecting dynamics of power are central to the mythology of racial realism on which this *a priori* assumption depends. As we argue in Chapter 1, when relationally understood, whiteness is never outsides of the epistemologies that produce it. Put differently, ways of knowing whiteness are fundamental to its production. This is an interdependent relation. Thus, the contributions frame our approach in opposition to binary modern social theory through which race is created as an object via the internalisation of white ideals and the externalisation of the idea of blackness. This is the means by which race becomes blackness and whiteness becomes humanness. This theoretical stance is anchored by contributions that focus on human practices, such as talk, looking, and emotional possession through ideological investments, material ownership, emotional fetishisations, and apparent disinvestments such as ignorance. This section follows directly from the calls we make in Chapter 1 to shift analysis in the direction of the relational onto-epistemic struggles through which whiteness is made, remade, resisted to move away from the idea of whiteness as located in white people, which continues to haunt most social constructionist approaches to whiteness. As such, the section sets up an anti-essentialist decolonial framing for analysing and understanding whiteness, which deconstructs the terms of coloniality and decentres white people from an analysis of whiteness. Each of the contributors offer different ways to achieve this decentring.

Arun Saldanha tackles the principal problematic of race and its relation to ocularity, the phenotypical proof of race supposedly in front of our eyes. His chapter presents a way to understand phenotype as a contested vehicle for racialisation. As he puts it succinctly, 'race is a cultural difference with biology as its material'. This observation is also suggestive of the

DOI: 10.4324/9780429355769-101

openness of race as a signifier. His analysis demonstrates how, in early-modern India's 'Golden Goa', race gets mixed up with phenotype through embodied style and leisure practices of East Indian 'Goan natives' and Portuguese capitalists, as these are recorded by a Dutchman Linschoten, reproducing whiteness for a European audience through his published musings on travel. Whiteness is assembled through this range of material practices and transported across the globe epistemologically, producing phenotype as raced. A racialised production came to be increasingly used for the purposes of domination to create distinctions between black, brown, and white, and within whiteness itself. 'For all the miscegenation and the cosmopolitan feasting, whiteness after Linschoten only became more obsessed with the purity it by definition could not capture,' as Saldanha concludes.

For Sherene Razack, the production of whiteness comes to be relationally through another aspect of culture: religion. Her analysis of whiteness is as a form of civilisational purity and entitlement that is systematised and consolidated through affect. In this contribution, anti-Muslim sentiment traverses the globe historically and spatially in the form of settler whiteness to create its modern enemy, the figure of the Muslim. Christian values translate into practices through the means of affect. Christian feeling is fostered through 'civilisational sagas', past and present, which connect Jews and Protestants in a global white settler project, as an organised white defence of national ownership, wealth, and as entitlement in the face of supposed socio-religious threats to property and life from Muslims.

Katalin Halász brings together these two aspects, the body and affect, to rethink the contested figure of white cis hetero womanhood and its situation in reproducing whiteness. Returning to the body in the present as historically produced, the intricacies of feeling are evoked through the intimate episode of a performance I LOVE BLACK MEN. Multidimensional materiality, significance and affect together produce the white woman. Halász shifts our attention more directly to the ways in which the onto-epistemic can illuminate moments of interruption in racist tropes, and to the body as battlefield, as agentic as well as reproducing racialisation. There is also a hint at the coalitional possibilities which might be brought into action through this understanding of bodily practices – in a potential reconfiguring of a chain of bodies 'off screen', in the sense of those who may be watching the performance, as well as those implied through the performance itself: 'black man' 'black women' and 'white man', the teacher. 'Performances of white femininities have an affective charge, induced by – but involving more than – visual discourse and racial regimes of representation.' In its engagement with performativities of the fleshy body, the contribution raises broader questions about artistic performance as disrupter of racial formation.

In the final contribution to this section, Mark Schmitt considers this potential for art and, in this case, literature specifically, as a means to play and produce the social. Following Toni Morrison's formulation, literature can be seen as the 'playground' for racial epistemologies which have impacts on the world. Revisiting the issue of racial purity by way of its failed 'tainted' whiteness, Schmitt is highlighting the importance of the contradictions in whiteness for its reproduction. The practices highlighted in the contributions by Saldanha, Razack, and Halász are necessary because of the contradictions in whiteness. As Hunter and Van der Westhuizen note in their opening chapter, this particularisation is what keeps whiteness in play. It is part of its hypervisibilisation, part of the contemporary play of white catharsis. The struggle between whitenesses in the struggle over the representation of fictional characters can be understood as one of the onto-epistemic struggles which, once comprehended as such, can demonstrate the inessential nature of whiteness and highlight the possibility for its challenge.

# Emerging whiteness in early-modern India: A Nietzschean reading of Jan Huygen van Linschoten

*Arun Saldanha*

## Emerging whiteness in early-modern India: a Nietzschean reading of Jan Huygen van Linschoten

The emergence of white identities during early modernity was indelibly marked by encounters between different bodies on the coasts of the Indian and Atlantic Oceans. This chapter uses the observations made by the late sixteenth-century traveller Jan Huygen van Linschoten during his stay in Goa to think through some conceptual issues pertaining to processes of racialisation in the Indian Ocean world. 'Golden' Goa, then the capital and most important economic node of the Portuguese *Estado da Índia*, exhibited both early forms of cosmopolitanism and the solidification of racial intolerance and prejudice. Proposing a 'physiological' approach derived from Nietzsche and Foucault, we can infer from Linschoten's account that racialisation was an incipient material process in which the variegations of human phenotype were central. However ambiguous in the light of cultural and genetic miscegenations and religious conversions, phenotype was from the beginnings of early modernity a central vehicle of social difference.

## The emergence of whiteness

Historical sociologists and historical geographers have contributed much to our understanding of how deep the racial dimension of the global present is (Bonnett 2000). Europeans started recognising themselves as white through a gradual hierarchical demarcation and coding of human phenotypical variation. As Michel Foucault (2003: 257) all too briefly noted in his lectures on biopolitics, the investment of European states in colonising populations went hand in hand with ethnic cleansing and racist typologies. In the wake of Foucault, Ann Laura Stoler (1995) kindled new research into the everyday and intimate nature of colonial regimes. Stoler demonstrates how an infatuation with the literary and the discursive blinds postcolonial theory to these more fleshy matters. A Foucauldian study of oceanic colonialism would ask in what ways the embodied encounters between sixteenth- and seventeenth-century Europeans on the one hand, and Africans, Asians, Australians, and Americans on the other, prefigured later regimes of white supremacy. My framework (Saldanha 2006, 2007) aims to affirm against most interpretations of Foucault that racialisation and the concomitant becoming-white of European bodies are not merely effects of racial 'discourses', but a material process that phenotypically variable bodies themselves are engaged in.

To obtain such a perspective on emergent materiality, we might retrieve the Nietzschean side of Foucault. Foucault's genealogical counter-method drew much of its critical force from Nietzsche's attack on the historiographical obsession with origins. Instead of attempting to represent the past as one continuous lineage running unproblematically from an origin to the present, Foucauldian genealogy is interested in what Nietzsche called *Herkunft*, which could be translated as 'descent',

> the ancient affiliation to a group, the bonds of blood, tradition or social class. The analysis of *Herkunft* often involves a consideration of race or social type. But the traits it attempts to identify are not the exclusive generic characteristics of an individual, a sentiment, or an idea, which permits us to identify them as 'Greek' or 'English'; rather, it seeks the subtle, singular, and subindividual marks that might possibly intersect in them in a network that is difficult to unravel.
>
> (Foucault 1977: 145)

Through Nietzsche, Foucault managed to privilege the messy contingencies of what he calls 'emergence'. What matters is the spatial arrangement and dissipation of bodies and things, not the personal agency and causalities identified in traditional historiographical writing.

This nonlinear sense of history is critical for a more complex understanding of race. The question 'How did Europeans become white when they were elsewhere, amongst visibly different populations?' has been answered extensively in the history of ideas. Nietzsche's suggestive turning towards an '[e]ffective history, on the other hand, shortens its vision to those things nearest to it – the body, the nervous system, nutrition, digestion, and energies; it unearths the periods of decadence and if it chances upon lofty epochs, it is with the suspicion – not vindictive but joyous – of finding a *barbarous and shameful confusion*' (Foucault 1977: 155, emphasis added). Nietzsche's new physiological approach to culture probes further than ideas or knowledge, into the concrete 'subindividual' power games, movements, affects, and 'confusions' of bodies – bodies of flesh, genes, sinews, neurochemistry, and sexual desire, greatly overflowing what writing and thought can make of them.

Ever since his brother-in-law and sister canonised him as the most erudite apologist of German and European supremacy, Nietzsche's relationship to the critical theorisation of whiteness has, of course, been extremely contentious. His more astute interlocutors like Gilles Deleuze in France and Walter Kaufman in the United States, nonetheless pointed out that the profoundly creative and irreverent force of his philosophy is not easily assimilable to any project of biopower. A collection called *Critical Affinities* made an important beginning in allowing Nietzsche to speak to some concerns in black studies (Scott and Franklin 2006). This chapter proposes, similarly, that the historical description of what Foucault's essay on Nietzsche calls *emergence* – here, the emergence of new uneven and ambiguous relationships between white and brown bodies under colonialism – is yet to learn much from Nietzsche. 'Emergence is thus the entry of forces; it is their eruption, the leap from the wings to the center stage, each in its youthful strength' (Foucault 1977: 149–150). Nietzsche's value for the study of colonialism and white supremacy can be drawn out from his critical investigations into corporeality and the circulation of energy, into the herd-like clinging to authoritarian leaders and stereotypical thinking and behaviours, and into the ever-present potential for decay and violence, all behind a façade of opulence and something Europeans called 'man'.

More than usually in the social sciences this will entail understanding racialisation as an embodied and otherwise *physical* phenomenon, 'constructed' not simply through language and mind but a whole host of ecological factors operating underneath or beyond the human realm. This means that the much-maligned biological dimensions of race – skin colour, body shape, immunity systems, genetic make-ups – are relevant to how bodies are historically positioned into racial hierarchies. This does *not* mean that racialisation – centered around the economic and cultural hegemony called 'whiteness' – follows automatically from phenotype. Physical differences are always overcoded and obscured by differences in the ways a body speaks, is dressed, comports itself, uses artifacts, worships, has sex, eats, walks. Moreover, the phenotypical body is itself altered by diet, exercise, medication, tanning, and so on. In short, race is a cultural difference with biology as its material. The upshot of this variability and contingency means that racial difference has never been a raster of distinct 'races'. Race is, like sexuality and class, an ongoing institutional process of social interactions and politicised meanings. However, through a modified 'physiological' approach, we can offer that this process inevitably encompasses blood relations, food, drugs, even the divine. This multilayered material nature of racialisation means that it is irreducible to any one of these components, while its outcomes are never given.

## Phenotypical encounter

The port and merchant city of Goa was during early modernity the proud capital of the Portuguese empire, the *Estado da Índia*. Conquered by Afonso de Albuquerque in 1510, Goa in the sixteenth century embodied a geographical concentration of cosmopolitan and economic experimentation on a par with Antwerp, Venice, Alexandria, Malacca, and Canton (Guangzhou). Dubbed 'Golden Goa' (*Goa dourada*) by travellers enthusiastic about its mercantile and ecclesiastical wealth, it was also the most intense node of missionary activity on the Indian Ocean rim. After many decades of corruption, disease, wars, and economic decline, it was abandoned as imperial capital in 1760. Of the old imperial city (which became Goa Velha or Old Goa), only the cathedral and a few ruined buildings remain. The territory of Goa was integrated into India in 1961.

As is well known, Portuguese colonialism was from the start highly ambivalent about the question of race. Officially, the Lusitanian empire claimed that it transcended racial differences under a shared Catholic faith and one language. In practice, the Portuguese continued everyday racism both subtly and legally in all of its colonies (Boxer 1963). Golden Goa is an apt place to start thinking about the emergence of a European 'will' to dominate the entire globe. Since medieval times, we can surmise that no mercantile or military intervention and societal crisis of Europeans was free from a particular coding of human phenotypes, starting with the Crusades and more ambiguously anti-Semitism. But it needs to be concretely ascertained how and why that coding operated, and from when we can talk about a racial *system*. I use 'phenotype' quite literally here, meaning the physical characteristics of a genetically related population of organisms as contingent expression of their genotype. As is clear in the case of anti-Semitism, inferring difference from phenotype is often not clear-cut. *Race* as a system of classification aims to group human bodies together into discrete and essential identities, but it necessarily fails to become fully coherent.

The Dutchman Jan Huygen van Linschoten worked as clerk for the Archbishop in Goa from 1583 to 1587, but his passion was geography. Reflecting a common feeling of the time, he was eager to learn of the world's diversity. His *Itinerario, Voyage ofte Schipvaert naar Oost ofte Portingaels Indien*, published in 1596 and immediately translated into other languages, is a key text in the history of European geography (Saldanha 2011).[1] Copiously illustrated and containing the latest maps and economic information, the *Itinerario* became a bestseller at a time Europe was becoming aware of the vast riches in Asia and the Americas could be directly imported. The book's descriptions of Goa's inhabitants should be understood not just as ideological distortions of reality, but as witnesses of how phenotypical differences were concretely negotiated through practice. This approach presumes a basically realist assumption that physical differences between populations exist independently of the mind and language, but that they are noticed, stereotyped, and elaborated only through social interactions. This does not mean that Linschoten's descriptions were 'objective', but that some striking elements of the actual situation in Goa can be inferred from his sensationalist descriptions. Within a planet entering a new phase of accelerations, Linschoten was living and writing from an important vantage point presaging centuries of white racism.

## Racial taxonomy

Let us first concentrate on Linschoten's remarks on the phenotypes he encountered. Goa harbored more than 60,000 residents by the early seventeenth century. The *Itinerario* constructs a detailed typology of the Goan populations, thereby demonstrating its role as node in flows of migrants and ideas across the Indian Ocean world: the Portuguese and the *mestiços*; Brahmins, and Hindus in general; Gujuratis; *Canares* and *Decanijns*, labourers and shop keepers from what is now called Karnataka; Arabs; Abyssinians; 'the Black People of Mosambique', slaves imported from the Southeast African coast; *Malabares* and *Nayros*, labourers and gentry from the Kerala coast; and Jews. Linschoten does not discuss many other nationalities known to have inhabited Goa, such as Armenians, Bengalis, Burmese, Chinese, Croatians, Danish, Dutch, English, Flemish, French, Germans, Italians, Japanese, Koreans, Malays, Ottomans, Persians, and Sinhalese. Most migrants were poor soldiers and sailors, but some were successful merchants, living in constant tension with the Portuguese rulers and clergy. Hence Linschoten's category 'white' was far from homogeneous.

Linschoten was already fully attuned to cataloguing differences of human phenotype, mentioning the skin colour of almost all the populations on his journeys outside Europe, even if black, brown, yellow, and white were more unstable categories than they would become. Of the Goan natives Linschoten noted, 'They are in a manner blacke, or of a dark browne colour' (1885 I: 261). Of the Gujurati Jains living in Goa, he writes:

> They are of a yellowe colour like the Bramenes and somewhat whiter, and there are women among them which are much whiter and clearer of complection than the Portingale women. They are formed and made both in face, limmes and all other things like men of Europe, colour only excepted.
>
> *(1885 I: 255)*

The contemporary hand colouring of the figures in some first edition copies of the *Itinerario*'s plates has Indian skin as light brown and slaves' as grey. The Portuguese and the Chinese all have bright pink cheeks. This sense of bodily difference, often mixing wonder with disgust, can already be found in Marco Polo or Ibn Battuta. By the late sixteenth century, however, it had become commonplace and had geopolitical implications.

Since early-modern geographical writing was done overwhelmingly by men unaccompanied by wives, it is not surprising much attention was given to local women, in particular their alleged addiction to sex. In fact, a persistent myth about Goa was that licentiousness was eroding its white identity. Linschoten realised very well that the *mestiços* undermined both the effort at racial segregation and his own typology of phenotypes:

> The Portingales in India, are many of them marryed with the naturall borne women of the countrie, and the children procéeding of them are called Mesticos, that is, half countrimen. These Mesticos are commonlie of yelowish colour, nothwithstanding there are manie women among them, that are faire and well formed. The children of the Portingales, both boyes and gyrls, which are borne in India, are called Castisos, and are in all things like unto the Portingales, onely somewhat differing in colour, for they draw towards a yealow colour: the children of those Castisos are yealow, and altogether like the Mesticos, and the children of Mesticos are of colour and fashion like the naturall borne Countrimen or Decaniins of the countrie, so that the posteritie of the Portingales, both men and women being in the third degrée, doe séeme to be naturall Indians, both in colour and fashion.
>
> *(Van Linschoten 1885 I: 183–184)*

The Nietzschean 'barbarous and shameful confusion' which Foucault illuminates is here exemplified. Since extremely few white women undertook the long and perilous journey to India, there was frequent marriage, concubinage, and rape between white soldiers and merchants on the one hand and brown and black women on the other. Albuquerque had in fact already promoted intermarriage as biopolitical settlement strategy. For the Dutch and the English, however, as for racist theorists in the centuries ahead, this genetic and cultural integration in the Portuguese colonies inevitably meant the loss of European vitality. It is an irony Nietzsche would end up inspiring Nazi ideologues to misread him to support their obsession about genetic purity.

Phenotypical difference is enhanced by all sorts of material inscriptions and adornments. The *caffares* (from the Arabic 'kafirs'), as the slaves from Mozambique and the East African coast were called pejoratively, Linschoten calls:

> Black as pitch, with curled and singed hayre both on their heads and beards, which is very little, their noses broad, flat and thicke at the end, great bigge lippes: some have holes, both above and under in their lippes, and some times besides their mouthes through their cheekes, wherin they thrust small bones, which they esteeme a bewtifying
>
> *(Van Linschoten 1885 I: 271)*

For Linschoten and his European readers, naked dark skin and piercings are grotesquely fascinating. However, racialisation is always a relational if asymmetrical process. The description above continues:

> there are some among them that have their faces and all their bodies over rased and seared with irons, and al figured like rased Sattin or Damaske, wherein they take great pride, thinking there are no fairer people then they in all the world, so that when they see any white people, that weare apparell on their bodies, they laugh and mocke at them, thinking us to be monsters and ugly people: and when they will make any develish forme and picture, then they invent one after the forme of a white man in his apparell, so that to

conclude, they thinke and verily perswade themselves, that they are the right colour of men, and that we have a false and counterfait colour.

*(Van Linschoten 1885 I: 183–184)*

As Linschoten repeatedly states that the *caffares* live 'like beastes', this momentary decentering of the European anthropological gaze and humanisation of the Africans could be written for comical effect. Note too the importance of clothing *on top of* phenotype. In any case, the passage illustrates the intensity of phenotypical encounter in which both whites and Africans, however unequal, might revel in its each other's absurdity.

White superiority did not come straight from theology or science. It was reproduced through reiterated embodied interactions between European and non-European bodies in which the former kept noticing those things he found compellingly *different* – whether disgusting or fascinating. François Pyrard de Laval, a French traveller, writes in his 1619 account of Goa:

You see there [at the market] very pretty and elegant girls and women from all countries of India, most of whom can play upon instruments, embroider, sew very finely, and do all kinds of work, such as the making of sweetmeats, preserves, etc. All these slaves are very cheap, the dearest not being worth more than 20 or 30 perdos, of 32½ sols each. Girls that are virgins are sold as such, and are examined by women, so that none dare use any trickery. [...] Some of these girls are very pretty, fair, and comely, others are olive-colored, brown and of all colors. But those to whom they are most attracted are the Caffre girls of Mozambique and other places in Africa, who are as wondrously black, with curly hair; they call these *Negra de Guinea*. It is a remarkable fact which I have observed among all the Indian peoples, as well males as females, that their bodies and perspiration have no smell, whereas the negroes of Africa, from both sides of the Cape of Good Hope, stink in such wise that when they are heated it is impossible to approach them: their savour is as bad as that of green leeks.

*(Pyrard de Laval 1888: II: 65–66)*

I quote this near-contemporary of Linschoten to point out that difference in the colonies was not only seen but also smelt, tasted, feared, touched, and laughed about. By repeatedly noting the sensory qualities of slaves, white people not only carried around demeaning stereotypes of black Africans in their heads but also learnt how to react to the presence of any black body as something not-quite-human, while affirming their own taken-for-granted humanity (Smith 2006). Social interactions are physiological and incite pathological exaggerations, they are not simply 'discursive practices'. And yet racism is never a necessary outcome of phenotypical and multisensory encounter.

## Fidalgos

As was just seen with Linschoten's description of slaves, the artifacts that bodies utilise are indispensable prostheses for racial distinctions. Goa's public spaces appear to have been rife with style consciousness. Linschoten's observations on the way the Portuguese in Goa underlined their whiteness through dress and comportment spurred the European imagination for centuries.

The Portingales are commonly served with great gravitie, without any difference betwéene the Gentleman and the common Citizen, townesman of soldier, and in their going, curtesies, and conversations, common in all thinges: when they go in the stréetes they steppe very softly and slowly forwards, with a great pride and vaineglorious maiestie, with a slave that carrieth a great hat or vaile over their heads, to keepe the sunne and raine from them.

*(Van Linschoten 1885 I: 193)*

White Goans quickly understood why the Nayro upper caste of Malabar chose to 'wear the nayls of their hands very long': to 'shew that they are Gentlemen, because the longnesse of the nayles doth let and hinder men from working or doing any labour' (Van Linschoten 1885 I: 282). Soon Portuguese aristocrats started growing their nails too. The fidalgo (literally 'son of a somebody') desire of the Portuguese to show off privilege, integral to the Portuguese aristocracy since the late Middle Ages though often more or less 'bought' in the colonies, was famous in Europe (Boxer 1948). The desire for distinction overcame the contempt that was otherwise held towards Indians, and fidalgos paradoxically 'went native' to exaggerate their status as colonists.

For fidalgos as well as priests, sailors, and soldiers, it was important to comport oneself as respectable subject. Greeting each other with what today would seem preposterous courtesy was central for a shared sense of being white.

When they méete in the stréetes a good space before they come together, they beginne with a great Besolas manos [hand-kiss], to stoope with their bodies, and to thrust their foot to salute each other, with their hattes in their hands, almost touching the ground.

*(Van Linschoten 1885 I: 194)*

This visible and collective monitoring by ritual greeting consolidated the identity of these men as Portuguese, as white, and as men. If disrespect was shown, harsh retaliation was an accepted way to reinstate the importance of honour:

when they séeke to bee revenged of any man that hath shewen them discurtesie, or for any other cause whatsoever it bee, they assemble ten or twelve of their friends, acquaintance or companions, and take him wheresoever they find him, and beat him long together, that they leave him for dead, or very neare dead, or els cause him to be stabbed by their slaves, which they hold for a great honor and point of honestie so to revenge themselves, whereof they dare boast and bragge openly in the stréetes.

*(Van Linschoten 1885 I: 194–195)*

Racial difference is thus played out *ecologically*, over and through the built environment. One of the most comfortable and largest hospitals of the world was then located in Goa. The Royal Hospital, however, admitted 'only Portingals, for no other sick person may lodge therein, I mean such as are called white men, for the other Indians have an Hospitall by themselves' (Van Linschoten 1885 I: 237). In fact, segregating the entire island of Goa from the mainland, all non-whites needed to be physically marked with ink to be identified at the city gates.

And the Indians, Decanijns, and other Moores and heathens, that are resident in Goa, and therein have their habitation, when they goe into the firme land to fetch their necessarie provisions, coming to those places which are called Passos [checkpoints], they must everye man have a marke, which is Printed on their naked armes, and so they passe over to the other side, and at their returne againe they must shew the same marke.

*(Van Linschoten 1885 I: 180)*

Linschoten's pictures of Portuguese colonial nobility became famous in Europe. He speaks of the music that accompanied the festivities of the Portuguese. Whiteness was achieved through an array of material and corporeal arrangements. Not just dress, parasols, and jewelry, but walls, greeting style, duels, and mode of transport (the Portuguese riding a horse or being carried around in a palanquin), even slaves and servants, were accessories to white bodies in the early-modern Indian Ocean world.

## On evil women

The intense role that sexuality played in the cohering of white masculinities in the writings of colonial regimes has been extensively theorised (McClintock 1995). Black and brown women were to white travellers prototypes of seductive and mysterious exuberance. Linschoten consolidated these perceptions like few other European authors of the late sixteenth century. Of Goa's white and *mestiço* women, in contrast, he reported mockingly: 'When they goe to church, or to visit any friend, they put on very costly apparrell, with bracelets of gold, and rings upon their armes, all beset with costly Jewels and pearles, and at their eares hang laces full of Jewels. Their clothes are of Damaske, Velvet, and cloth of gold, for silke is the worst thing they doe weare' (1885 I: 206). Within Goa's masculinist fidalgo culture white women were mostly invisible, jealously guarded by their husbands and locked up in their palanquins and houses. This was in telling contrast to how other women were treated. Most Portuguese *soldados* and sailors took Hindu women of lower castes as mistresses or wives, but these enjoyed little social standing. Many of the black women were used by their owners for sex work. As Linschoten told the Low Countries and England with a moral indignation that would soon prove hypocritical given the rest of Europe would soon expand the institution, slavery was completely entrenched in Goan society. The buying and selling of Africans was facilitated by a newly aggressive approach to trade and appropriation we now call capitalism. Wealthy households kept dozens, even hundreds of slaves, for domestic chores, production of handicrafts, and sex. Goa's clearest instance of early-modern racism is found in the sexual exploitation of African women slaves.

Linschoten's many misogynous statements on Indian women spurred a stubborn myth about the causes of the decadence of the Portuguese empire. All Golden Goa's vices, especially those connected to sex, were to be blamed on Indian women. Linschoten's description (1885 I: 250–251) of the practice, allegedly invented by Indian women, of drugging their husbands with the hallucinogenic plant datura (jimson weed) to be with their lovers, was repeated by many European travellers after him. Linschoten has a key place in the history of European stereotyping of sati, the ritual in which a Hindu widow throws herself into her husband's funeral pyre. Immediately outlawed by the Portuguese, the ritual had obsessed European scholars since Marco Polo. Linschoten's fanciful drawing of sati had etched the irrational exuberance of the ritual firmly into the European mind. Despite the obvious cruelty of the ritual, he is convinced even here the fault lies with Indian women:

The first cause and occasion why the women are burnt with their husbandes, was (as the Indians themselves do say), that in time past, the women (as they are very leacherous and inconstant both by nature, and complexion) did poyson many of their husbands, when they thought good (as they are likewise very expert therein): Thereby to have the better means to fulfill their lusts.

(Van Linschoten 1885 I: 278)

Of the Malabares, the labourers from Kerala, Linschoten first says reassuringly that 'Of face, body, and limmes they are altogether like men of Europe, without any difference, but onely in colour'. However, they were 'the most leacherous and unchast nation in all the Orient, so that there are verie few women children among them of seven or eight years olde, that have their maiden-heads' (Van Linschoten 1885 I: 207–208).

It is well-known European travel writing of the colonial era strongly sexualised black and brown women (McClintock 1995). But women of the Indian Ocean world – the mysterious Orient where spices came from – were perceived as especially immoral. 'For all the care & studie that ye women and wives of India have', Linschoten posited, 'is day and night to devise meanes to satisfie their pleasures, and to increase lust, by all the devises they can imagine, and to make their bodies the apter thereunto' (1885 II: 70). Even women-slaves 'leave their mistresses in the Churches, or slip into somme shoppe or corner, which they have redie at their fingers endes, where their lovers méet them, and there in hast they have a sport, which done they leave each other: and if she chance have a Portingal or a white man to her lover, she is so proud, that she thinketh no woman comparable unto her, and among themselves doe bragge thereof' (Van Linschoten 1885 I: 215–216). Sexual intercourse crossed and thereby consolidated racial boundaries.

In his misogyny, Linschoten was channeling Goa's general attitude amongst the white co-lonist class towards native women. A physiological genealogy of the emergence of racial dif-ference inspired by Nietzsche and Foucault understands these descriptions not just as extremely demeaning, but as skewed documents of actual desires and physical encounters: bodies divided by class, nation, and race were indeed having sex in the colonies. Linschoten's exaggerations reveal that elaborate affects pertaining to visibly distinguishable groups in Goa circulated amongst the white populace. His authority on the matter would be considered impeccable by men hungry for news of such tantalising matters. By repeating these stereotypes in talk and writing, further coherence of a transcontinental white identity was achieved. Nevertheless, already in the sixteenth century, whiteness – in this case, the cohesion of the Portuguese in the cultural and economic system of the Indian Ocean – was also felt to be a precarious structure, at mercy of the seductive lewdness of Indian women as well as the few white women becoming Indianised.

## Cosmopolitan pleasures

By entertaining certain feelings and prejudices, through architecture and a demeanor in public spaces, and with the use of artifacts such as expensive textiles and palanquins carried by African slaves, Goa's white population was materially distinguishing itself from the rest of the city. Yet, some practices complicated this labour of distinction. Culture that was shared across phenotypes mainly concerned the pleasures of sex, food, fashion, gambling, worship, bathing, drugs, and music. During the large *festas* in the *Estado da Índia*, chiefly organised by the church, the entire city participated. According to Charles Boxer (1948: 148), writing about the fidalgos in Macao, there were processions and games, parades with elephants and horses, and music played con-tinuously on loud trumpets and drums, while the fidalgos were dressed up in the most exquisite clothes. If Goa's festival and drug culture were studied 'from below', in their physiological effects, racial difference therefore indeed would appear messy and confused yet still obviously unequal.[2]

Some colonists have always seemed to have enjoyed going native, at least in some ways. In India, for example, the Portuguese quickly preferred eating rice with the hands and pouring water straight into the mouth like Indians still do (Van Linschoten 1885 I: 278). Most colonists eagerly changed food habits. Spices, of course, were the Indian Ocean's most wanted luxury item, used by all who could afford them. Boundaries between spice, intoxicant, medicine, aphrodisiac, magic potion, incense, and poison have never been clear-cut; the only thing that unites these is their rarity and desirability across heterogeneous populations (Turner 2004). Indeed, to Linschoten it was the use of spice for intoxication that exemplified the decadence of the Portuguese élite. One drug commonly used by both men and women to kill boredom was paan (betel nut).

> The Portingales women have the like custom of eating these Bettele leaves, so that if they were but one day without eating their Bettele, they perswade themselves they could not live: Yea, they set it in the night times by their Beddes heades, and when they cannot sleepe, they doe nothing els but chaw Bettele and spit it out againe. In the day time wheresoever they doe sit, goe, or stand, they are continually chawing thereof, like Oxen or Kine chawing their cud: for the whole exercise of many Portingales women, is onely all the day long to wash themselves, and then fal to the chawing of their Bettele.
>
> *(Van Linschoten 1885 II: 64)*

Attending to cosmopolitanism's pleasures and confusions should not blind us to the persisting economic and racial asymmetries. Only the Portuguese and wealthy *mestiços* had an excess of time to kill with paan. Only they could have slaves and native women working, playing music, and dancing for them inside their houses. In a passage worth quoting at length to elucidate this social stratification, Linschoten explains that while opium and bhang (marihuana leaves and flowers) were mixed with expensive spices and used as aphrodisiacs and sedatives amongst the wealthy, *mestiços*, and Muslim merchants, they were used by slaves, sex workers, soldiers, and the poor to simply cope with existence:

> Bangue is also a common meate in India, serving to the same effect that Amfion [opium] doth. [...] The Indians eate this seede or the leaves thereof being stamped, saying, that it maketh a good appetite, but useth most to provoke lust; as it is commonly used and sold in the shops, it is mingled with some poulder of the leaves and the seede together: They likewise put greene Arecca [areca nut] unto it, therewith to make a man drunke or in a manner out of his wits: Sometimes also they mixe it with Nutmegs and Mace, which doth also make a man drunke: Others (that is to saye, the rich and welthy persons) mix it with Cloves, Camphora, Ambar, Muske, and Opium, which (as the Moores likewise affirme) maketh a man pleasant, and forgetting himselfe, performing all kind of labour and toyle without once thinking of any paine: but onely laughing, playing, and sleeping quietly. The common women or whores use it when they meane to have a mans companie, thereby to be lively and merrie, and to set all care aside. It was first invented by Captaines and souldiers, when they had layne long in the field, continually waking and with great travell, which they desiring to rememedie and againe to comfort themselves, thereby to settle their braines doe use Bangue, in such manner as is foresaid. It causeth such as eate it, to reele and looke as if they were drunke, and halfe foolish, doing nothing but laugh and bee merrie, as long as it worketh in their bodies. It is verie much used by the Indians, and likewise by

some Portingales, but most by the slaves thereby to forget their labour: to conclude it is a certaine small comfort to a melancholy person.

*(Van Linschoten 1885 II: 115–116)*

It was Linschoten's astute observations on interracial sex, however – the most problematic of cosmopolitan pleasures – that resounded throughout a deeply Christian Europe. As Boxer (1963) argues, there was in the Portuguese empire simultaneously an ideology of racial equality, some promotion of intermarriage, and the maintenance of the medieval Lusitanian notion of *pureza de sangue* (purity of blood), which turned an archaic aristocratic concept into a new valorisation of whiteness. For most white men, purity was less an issue when it came to concubines or prostitutes. Unlike most later colonial regimes, there was considerable genetic exchange between amongst populations in Brazil and the Portuguese Indies. By cohabiting with white men, non-white women tried to augment their own status but thereby underlined the desirability of being white. Many natives and slaves were forcefully converted to Christianity, thereby to some extent 'whitening' themselves culturally, but again, underlining the superiority of the Catholic faith.

The pleasures of festival and interracial sex did little, in the end, to avert the ascendancy of modern racism. By the time the famous orientalist Sir Richard F. Burton visited Goa, miscegenation had long fallen out of practice and cultural boundaries between white and Indian were as strong as they were in British India. 'No better proof of how utterly the attempt to promote cordiality between the European and the Asiatic by a system of intermarriage and equality of rights that has failed in practice can be adduced', Burton wryly noted, 'than the utter contempt in which the former holds the latter at Goa' (1851: 86). From a relatively murky situation of self-obsessed pomp and rampant exploitation of slaves for sex, the colonial cities of the Iberian empires had by the middle of the nineteenth century become deeply entrenched in the biopolitical maintenance of racist hierarchy.

## Conclusion

The question in this chapter has been what white identities physically *consisted of* at a particular place and period in global history. Contemporary accounts such as Linschoten's suggest that even before anthropology and orientalism, phenotypical difference greatly mattered in everyday interactions and social stratifications, through both attraction (interracial sex, a traveler's curiosity) and feelings of superiority and disgust. Material culture, ways of moving and speaking and drinking, urban planning and policing supported the creation of a particular kind of Lusitanian whiteness.

The Portuguese version of colonisation was derided by northern Europeans. It was felt by the Dutch and the English – united through their Germanic languages, Protestantism, and eagerness to intercept the Portuguese import of spice – that the difference of climate and the passion of the tropics was irrevocably seeping into the European bodies of Goa, turning them rapidly into Indians. 'There die many men within the Towne, by meanes of their disordered living, together with the hoteness of the country', as Linschoten sums it up (1885 I: 185). He claims that tropical promiscuity meant a profusion of venereal disease, stomach ulcers, and drug overdoses. To Linschoten and his Dutch and English readers, as to Burton centuries later, the impurities of Portuguese whiteness in *Goa dourada* were not merely moral, but physiological, hereditary, and final.

It is essential that bringing a generalised physiology after Nietzsche into the genealogy of whiteness not be seen as opening the door to biological reductionism. Racialisation is a completely contingent process, and connections between phenotype and culture are only explicable after the fact. Practices like chewing paan and adultery were so widespread that they did not neatly map onto phenotypical variation. In a postcolonial world still dominated by white men and consumerist pleasures, it is clear that any ambivalences of whiteness in the colonies did not herald its demise. For all the miscegenation and the cosmopolitan feasting, whiteness after Linschoten only became more obsessed with the purity it by definition could not capture.

## Acknowledgements

This chapter is adapted from Saldanha, A. 2010. Whiteness in Golden Goa: Linschoten on phenotype. In *Indian Ocean Studies: Cultural, Social, and Political Perspectives*, ed. S. Moorthy and A. Jamal, pp. 339–359. London: Routledge.

## Notes

1   Jan Huygen van Linschoten, *Itinerario, Voyage ofte Schipvaert van Jan Huyghen van Linschoten naer Oost ofte Portugaels Indien* (Amsterdam: Cornelis Claesz, 1596). An English translation followed two years later. Quotes are from the annotated Hakluyt edition (Van Linschoten 1885).
2   See Saldanha (2007) for an ethnography of present-day music and drug culture in Goa which interestingly (but entirely contingently) repeats the emergence of white identities.

## References

Bonnett, A. 2000. *White Identities: Historical and International Perspectives*. Harlow: Prentice Hall.
Boxer, C. R. 1948. *Fidalgos of the Far East, 1550–1770: Fact and Fancy in the History of Macao*. The Hague: Martinus Nijhoff.
Boxer, C. R. 1963. *Race Relations in the Portuguese Empire, 1425–1825*. Oxford: Clarendon.
Burton, R. F. 1851. *Goa, and the Blue Mountains, or Six Months of Sick Leave*. London: Richard Bentley.
Foucault, M. 1977. 'Nietzsche, Genealogy, History'. In *Language, Counter-Memory, Practice: Selected Essays and Interviews*, ed. D. F. Bouchard. Ithaca: Cornell University Press.
Foucault, M. 2003 [1997]. *"Society Must Be Defended" Lectures at the Collège de France, 1975-76*, trans. D. Macey. New York: Picador.
McClintock, A. 1995. *Imperial Leather: Race, Gender and Sexuality in the Colonial Contest*. New York: Routledge.
Pyrard de Laval, F. 1888 [1619]. *The Voyage of François Pyrard de Laval to the East Indies, the Maldives, the Moluccas and Brazil*, 2 Vols., trans. and ed. A. Gray and H. C. P. Bell. London: Hakluyt Society.
Saldanha, A. 2006. Reontologising Race: The Machinic Geography of Phenotype. *Environment and Planning D: Society and Space*, 24 (1): 9–24.
Saldanha, A. 2007. *Psychedelic White: Goa Trance and the Viscosity of Race*. Minneapolis: University of Minnesota Press.
Saldanha, A. 2011. The Itineraries of Geography: Jan Huygen van Linschoten's *Itinerario* and Dutch Expeditions to the Indian Ocean, 1594–1602. *Annals of the Association of American Geographers*, 101 (1): 149–177.
Scott, J. and Franklin, A. T., eds. 2006. *Critical Affinities: Nietzsche and African American Thought*. New York: State University of New York Press.
Smith, M. M. 2006. *How Race Is Made: Slavery, Segregation, and the Senses*. Chapel Hill: University of North Caroline Press.
Stoler, A. L. 1995. *Race and the Education of Desire: Foucault's History of Sexuality and the Colonial Order of Things*. Durham, NC: Duke University Press.
Turner, J. 2004. *Spice: The History of a Temptation*. New York: Vintage.
Van Linschoten, J. H. 1885 [1598]. *The Voyage of John Huyghen van Linschoten to the East Indies*, 2 Vols., eds. A. C. Burnell and P. A. Tiele. London: Hakluyt Society.

# 3

# Whiteness, Christianity, and anti-Muslim racism[1]

*Sherene H. Razack*

Once we settle on the term, the questions begin: What is the psychosexual structure and historical character of whiteness that renders it so aggressive, so tortured, so interested in subjugation? Clearly something complex and elusive is at work in the phenomenon beyond prejudice (Allport 1958), no matter how sophisticated our typology of that complex event becomes.

*(William Pinar, The Gender of Racial Politics and Violence in America)*

Whiteness, defined variously by scholars as a social relation, an identity, an ideology and crucially, as property is an acquired competence, a constructed dominance over those who do not possess it. As Cheryl Harris (1993) brilliantly argues, *being* white ensures economic returns, a positional superiority that gives whiteness something in common with property: The right to exclude. Whites therefore have 'a possessive investment in whiteness', the historian George Lipsitz (2006) argues. To the extent that one can accumulate it, whiteness offers privilege. It is something that has to be protected and there is no better way to protect it than to ensure that the line is maintained between those entitled to it by virtue of their skin colour and other visible differences and those who must be kept out. To inhabit whiteness is to know oneself as entitled to the fruits of earth and to merit its bounty. It is to be committed to a system in which the earth's bounty is not shared with those undeserving of it. Whiteness is both an aspiration and a location in a social hierarchy, or even a set of locations (Frankenberg 1993). It is also a state of mind. It requires strong emotions about the entitlement of whites and the unfitness of others. As William Pinar (2001: 19) suggests, it is a tortured condition, riven through with anxiety and profoundly interested in subjugation.

One hundred years ago, the African-American sociologist W.E.B. Du Bois sought to describe this condition in 'The Souls of White Folk' (1999), an essay that is far less cited than his book *The Souls of Black Folk*. For Du Bois (1999), whiteness was an embodied condition characterised by 'a great mass of hatred', emotions principally directed at Black people who would lay claim to an equal humanity. Linking American whiteness to colonial aggrandisement the world over, Du Bois (1999: 23) put the connection between whiteness and property bluntly: 'It is the duty of Europe to divide up the darker world and administer it for Europe's good'. Whiteness is inevitably an emotional condition marked by aggrievement over lost

DOI: 10.4324/9780429355769-3

entitlement and racial hostility. It is a condition given over to racial fantasy. White 'orgy, cruelty, barbarism, and murder done to men and women of Negro descent' (Du Bois 1999: 19) were driven by everyday rages that take white people to 'the bottom of the world'.

> I have seen a man – an educated gentleman – grow livid with anger because a little, silent black woman was sitting by herself in a Pullman car. He was a white man. I've seen a great, grown man curse a little child who had wondered into the wrong waiting-room, searching for its mother: 'Here, you damned black ---'. He was white. In Central Park I have seen the upper lip of a quiet, peaceful man curl back in a tigerish snarl of rage because black folk rode by in a motor car. He was a white man.
>
> *(Du Bois 1999: 19)*

'I see these souls undressed and from the back and side', Du Bois (1999: 17) writes, considering what it is about whiteness that it should be so maniacally desired and so violently secured. His answer, 'that whiteness is the ownership of the earth forever and ever' (Du Bois 1999: 18) alerts us to the material and affective project of white supremacy, a racial project of accumulation created and sustained by 'tigerish snarls of rage' (Du Bois 1999: 19) directed at little Black girls and Black folk riding in a motor car.

Christianity gives content to whiteness, endowing colonialism and racial capitalism with a moral base and its cultural character (Bonnett 1998: 1038–1039). As Du Bois observed white entitlement to the land in the New World was defended as a God given right (Blum 2007). Beginning with his observation that in the settler colony whiteness is conflated with godliness, several scholars make the case that Christianity plays a prominent role in how white identity emerges in the United States. Edward Blum, a scholar of Du Bois, suggests that the role of religion in race-making may go unnoticed because religion is often understood as super-structural and not, as Du Bois saw, central to how subjects come to understand themselves as white (Blum et al. 2009: 3). 'Creating, defining, and defending whiteness', Blum (Blum et al. 2009: 5) shows, 'played a significant role in biblical debates over slavery'. Seeking divine sanction for slavery early on, whites relied on the bible to promote white power, unity and 'national whiteness' for a long time after the abolition of slavery. White people acted on their colonial impulses *as Christians*, imagining that their superiority mandated the occupation of Indigenous lands and domination of racialised others (Fessenden in Blum et al. 2009: 14). The conjoining of Christianity and white entitlement to the land gives American whiteness a distinct frontier aesthetic. With its emphasis on an aggressive gun toting masculinity, white settler whiteness combines with religious fervour, producing 'a conjunction of the sacred and vio-lence', that we see in militant religion the world over (Pieterse, 1993: 38). Anti-Muslim an-imus, a part of a basket of colonial fears easily develops into an affective politics where white Christians come to know themselves as a persecuted and vulnerable minority permanently under threat, denied their birthright as Anglo-Saxon and obliged to confront what is imagined to be a profoundly anti-Christian state that refuses to secure white Christian interests. In the school conflict I describe later, we see an example of how whites seek to gain power and to protect white entitlement through the idea of the Muslim as threat to white Christian life. Importantly, although the legal case that is discussed ultimately fails, the suit provides an op-portunity to enact a colonial fantasy of a conflict between white settlers and the foreign threat posed by Muslims. It provides the basis for a broader mobilisation of white politics and an anti-Muslim affect travels from the local to the national stage notwithstanding the setback at the local level.

## Historicising white Christian aggrievement

Emerging from the settler's conviction that whiteness and Christianity form the basis of entitlement to the land and its bounty, today's anti-Muslim groups are a part of a broader right-wing racial politics that include unqualified support for Israel, bans on abortions, gun rights, and immigration clampdowns. All such goals are in aid of the promotion and protection of what has been strategically referred to as 'Judeo-Christian values' and way of life. In practice, the politics of anti-Muslim groups entail a defence of a particular kind of whiteness, defined as the right to property, a right held against racialised others who are considered to be standing in the way of the prosperity of white Christians. White Christian aggrievement feeds on anti-Muslim racism as well as on anti-Black, anti-Mexican and anti-Indigenous racism, among others, accumulating grievances that find political expression. The Muslim comes to prominence in the white Christian imaginary whenever real live Muslims are seen to be threatening white life.

The founding of the state of Israel in 1948 thrust Muslims as the historical enemies of Christendom into another colonial fray (the first one being when Protestant settlers brought their old world Christian antipathies to America) and continues to have considerable impact on anti-Muslim feeling and the politics of the Christian Right in the United States. Imagined as the population standing in the way of a Jewish homeland in Palestine, a precondition for the eschatological scenario of the Rapture and the second coming of Christ. Christianity gives content to white power in this imaginary as the land (both America and Israel) is declared to belong to those who possess a God given right to it and who must defend it from those unworthy of sharing in its bounty. The events of 9/11 mark another watershed moment when anti-Islamic polemics surfaced with a vengeance from Christian evangelical sources, among other groups. Anti-Islamic polemics are often thought to originate in religious sentiment. Such is the claim made by Richard Cimino (2005) in his charting of American evangelical discourse on Islam. Defining evangelicals as distinguished by an emphasis on a personal relationship to Christ, the authority of the bible, and the importance of evangelising others, Cimino argues that it is Christian evangelical resistance to the new pluralism of American life that makes anti-Islamic discourses so attractive and useful. In essence, anti-Islamic discourses work to sharpen the differences between Christianity and Islam, helping to maintain the legitimacy of the former. Evangelical anti-Islamic feeling grows in the fertile soil of the sense of victimisation among evangelicals in the wake of the expansion of secular, liberal forces in American society. This explanation emphasises recent anti-Islamic feeling although it acknowledges its origins more than two decades earlier. Reviewing popular evangelical literature from 1991 to 2003, Cimino found anti-Islamic discourses to be central to all strands of the Christian evangelical movement. The texts of the Christian evangelical movement suggest, however, that aggrievement has a decidedly racial and patriarchal cast to it and that Israel looms large among anti-Islamic proponents.

If the racial project that is settler colonialism in North America has a Christian core, then evangelical values fuel the racial project in specific ways. The religious belief, for example, that social problems merely reflect individual problems enabled white evangelicals to attribute black inequality to personal failing and to resist any attempt at structural or systemic change (Cimino 2005: 11–12). As Michael Smith found in his late 1990s study, Christian evangelicals cling to the idea that the problem of race is the problem of a few wicked people. The protection of the biblical family that lies at the core of the evangelical belief system has always meant the white biblical family, as evangelical leaders such as Pete Peters openly averred. Ann Burlein, whose study of Peters and James Dobson shows the racial line that runs solidly through evangelical belief and politics, notes that the white biblical family is imagined as under siege from a host of 'unruly bodies' including sexual minorities, immigrants, and African Americans (Burlein 2002: 86). In the communities around Peters and Dobson, Burlein (2002) finds the biblical storylines of an embattled Anglo-Saxon and Anglo-Celtic peoples who consider themselves to be the 10 tribes of Israel and God's chosen people. Under siege by secular humanists and liberal multiculturalists, such Christians, although diverse in many ways, understand the bible-based family with its specific gender roles as key to the nation's (white) cultural heritage. Burlein shows that Peters was attempting to mainstream white supremacy through the bible, a biblicisation linking past and present and visible in the use of language such as harlots and infidels (Burlein 2002: 44). His brand of defence of Christianity required militias and gun rights. Dobson focused on the family as the bulwark against an urban and foreign takeover (Burlein 2002: 195). In the same vein, Sophie Bjork-James (2018) argues that in defence of a lost social order, the sexual politics of Christian evangelicals is white sexual politics, where whiteness is defined through opposing Queer and Trans rights. Anti-Muslim or anti-Islamic sentiment rides in on these old racetracks helping to shore up the white Christian family.

## Christian Zionism

Muslims have a starring role in white racial fantasies when the Christian evangelical movement turns to Israel and to the eschatological scenario of the Rapture. It can be difficult to understand the fervour of non-Jewish supporters of Israel, writes Martin Marty (2013) in his foreword to Robert O. Smith's *More Desired Than our Owne Salvation: The Roots of Christian Zionism*. In Marty's and Robert Smith's view, we can only understand this support if we consider today's Christian Zionists as the heirs of beliefs that emerged from sixteenth- and seventeenth-century English Protestantism. The historical line Smith (2013) traces from English Protestantism to contemporary Christian Evangelicals such as John Hagee, founder of Christians United for Israel (CUFI), and prominent Christian Evangelicals such as Jerry Falwell and Pat Robertson contains, as can be expected, a strong strain of antipathy to Islam and to Muslims. If the logic of the Christian evangelical line of political theology can be difficult to follow, it is instructive to consider its powerful affect. How Muslims matter to today's Christian evangelicals, and how these feelings sustain an undiluted support for the state of Israel is a story that begins much earlier that the events of 9/11. In his book, Robert Smith explains the theological basis that sustains Christian Zionism:

> Pouring Muslims, Catholics, and Jews into its apocalyptic mould and casting them in scripturally determine roles, the English Protestant tradition of Judeo-centric prophesy interpretation traced throughout this book exhorts the cultural heirs of English Puritanism to claim their status as instruments of God's redemption of the world.
>
> *(Smith 2013: 6)*

Importantly, the redemptive project holds a different place for Jews than it does for Catholics. Smith writes:

> the English Protestant tradition of Judeo-centric prophesy interpretation explored here constructed Jews as essentially occidental and, as eventual converts to Protestant faith and who would fight the enemies of Christendom, as standing on the correct side of the divide between civilisation and savagism.
>
> *(Smith 2013: 6)*

For Robert Smith (2013), American pro-Israel sentiment is mainly 'a religious impulse' that has meant that any support for the Palestinian position is construed as immoral, collapsed as it is with a general suspicion of Islam. 9/11 merely amplified such sentiments (Smith 2013: 9). Political discourse regarding the state of Israel turns on the cultural/moral and ideological affinity between Christians and Jews, an affinity I suggest is racially sustained as each group invests in the idea of manifest destiny. Theology, in other words, rides in on racial feeling and vice versa.

It is useful to reflect on the depth of the sentiments Robert Smith (2013) describes as cultural/moral and ideological, and which I maintain are deeply racial. Smith (2013) documents how the founding of the state of Israel was a deeply formative event for today's Christian evangelical leaders such as Hagee and Falwell. Support for Israel and suspicion of Islam were lessons absorbed at the kitchen table where Baptist parents impressed on their children the biblical origin of the founding of Israel. Christian publications that stressed God's will in creating the state of Israel were liberally sprinkled with a strong Orientalism and open suspicion of Islam. Christian feeling was often fostered through such civilisational sagas. Few Israeli leaders, Smith writes, could resist what might otherwise have been an uncomfortable alliance. A shared commitment to American and Israeli exceptionalism – each nation enacting a racial superiority over those whose lands it has seized – smooths over any lingering difficulties. Likewise, few American politicians can afford to dispute the declaration of Jerry Falwell that God will punish anyone who tries to take Israeli land. The strength of the theopolitical commitment to the Rapture and the racial frisson that comes with each drawing of a civilisational line give content to whiteness and legitimacy to settler projects the world over.

Robert Smith advises that we not consider merely quaint the Christian evangelical notion that political support for Israel is 'god's foreign policy' (Smith 2013: 16). What may seem quaint is in fact a solid political lobby and when Hagee issues claims that Catholics sponsored the Crusades, the Inquisition and the Holocaust and that the conflict in the Middle East is not over land but is over theology, he is able in Smith's words, to persuade significant sectors of Christians that God has 'racially excluded Palestinians from any claim on the land' (Smith 2013: 18). While not all Christian Zionists are evangelicals and not all evangelicals are Christian Zionists, scholars studying the correlation between religiosity and affinity to Israel note that what unites a diverse field of Christians on the issue of support for Israel is the perception that America is a unique moral community with a unique destiny (Smith 2013: 34). Manifest destiny, critical race scholars remind us, is a racially inspired and sustained project. As Smith discusses and as several polls show, it is a combination of whiteness and religious practice that likely produces unconditional support for Israel (Smith 2013: 36). Indeed, Black protestants can share the same religious orthodoxies as their white evangelical counterparts without strong support for American exceptionalism, their vilification of Muslims tempered by the history of slavery and the 'terrorists' in the big house (Smith 2013: 41–44). As scholars of non-white evangelicals show, anti-Islamic sentiment is deliberately fostered in the contemporary period but communities of colour such as the Koreans and Korean Americans Judy Han (2018) studies, in participating in Islamophobic workshops 'maybe following the trail of American footsteps but they are also calibrating their strategic proximity to the US empire' (Han 2018: 212).

If it is entirely possible that 'white evangelical support for the State of Israel is simpler and more basic than most theorists have assumed' (Smith 2013: 45), it is surely because racial feeling deeply animates responses to Palestinians. Christian Zionists are unabashed about their belief that it is Western civilisation that must be defended from the march of Islam. The historical Protestant perception of Catholics and Muslims (the Pope and the Turk) as enemies lends a solid base on which the contemporary civilisational divide is built and will not easily disappear from American life (Smith 2013: 47). Such sentiments framed 'the self-understanding of Anglo-American colonists' (Smith 2013: 126). Moors and Indians easily melded in the colonial mind. Similarly, American Republican politicians find it easy to equate the Jewish settler with the white settler, as Smith (2013: 178) documents. If there is any lesson to be drawn from the tracing of these historical lines, it is that the roots of anti-Muslim racism predate 9/11 and structure the emotional commitments and investments that underpin it. A solid racial line runs through its outwardly biblical base.

## Vengeance

In her study of the rise of Christian Zionism over the past two decades, Victoria Clark (2007) describes the violent Christian evangelical subject as a subject deeply invested in the idea of white Western superiority. Clark devotes a chapter in her book to 'taking Texan', the term from the late reverend Jerry Falwell who used it to refer to violent retaliation against anyone who attacks Christianity.

> Harking straight back to the Puritan ethos of Old testament eye-for-an-eye justice of us and them, good and evil, black and white, the language Falwell imagined talking to Hezbollah is rooted in the culture of descendants of the Puritan Scots who subdued the Irish for Cromwell and then departed for the Western extremity of the new World in the early nineteenth century. The idiom of hard men engaged in wresting the Wild West frontier of the future United States, first from its indigenous American-Indian inhabitants and then from Mexicans, Texan is pithy to the point of callous, in-your-face, and frequently humorous.
>
> (Clark 2007: 256)

Texan speakers use phrases such as 'God's foreign policy statement', 'Israeli of the heart', and make frequent references to the coming apocalypse. Quoting the biblical verse from Genesis 12:3 that those who support Israel will be blessed while those who do not will be cursed, those who talk Texan warn Israelis that they must never give up land that God has ordained for them. Defence of the land requires combatting the grand evil of Islamic 'fundamentalism' through pre-emptive strikes against Muslim communities (Clark 2007: 271). Clark (2007) maintains that for most Christian Zionists, belief in Armageddon, when Jesus returns to the earth and specifically to Jerusalem is not metaphoric. Christian Zionists deeply believe that they will survive the terrible destruction that is unleashed at the End Times and be whisked away to heaven. The rest of the world, Clark advises, urgently needs to understand the power of such beliefs and its impact on American foreign policy in the Middle East (Clark 2007: 5). Citing polls in 2006 that confirm that almost one half of all Americans believe that Israel was given to Jews by God and that 31% believe that this is so to facilitate the second coming, Clark suggests that such a heightened quotidian relationship to the Rapture has not occurred since the Crusades (Clark 2007: 5). The appeal of such beliefs surely lies in the work they do to install a superior Christian subject who is able to wrest both America and Israel from those who stand in the way of Christianity's triumph. The vengeful subject defending the world against Satanic enemies and usurpers is a subject drawn to the thunderous militaristic appeals of their pastors. Clark encountered such American Christian evangelical tourists on a tour of Jerusalem, subjects who were endlessly fascinated with the Israeli military and wanted the right to shoot one of their guns (Clark 2007: 185). Easily imagining themselves in a story of the Crusades or, equally, on the American frontier, what is unquestionably racial fantasy comes fully dressed as religious obligation. To be maintained, such powerful fantasies require a material base, one provided by racial capitalism at home and US imperial interests abroad. In the school conflict considered, we see Christian parents aggressively protecting white Christian life encouraged and sustained by organisations dedicated to the political goals of Zionism and conservative white Christianity, goals soaked in notions of white entitlement. Bringing together anti-Black, anti-immigrant, gun rights advocates, and conservative Christians, the school conflict illustrates how whiteness as property is made on the ground through the figure of the Muslim.

## Harnessing aggrievement in the classroom

The subject in whom whiteness, property, Christianity, and Zionism meet is a subject formed by a number of abject Others, among them the Muslim construed as "Islamic terrorist". A passionate defender of an America without Islam, the anti-Muslim Christian subject is featured in the school battle below often following a script circulated by Christian/Zionist organisations and individuals. Defending Christianity in an embodied, active way, outraged, and aggrieved white parents announce themselves as protecting their children from "Muslim terrorist" attempts to recruit Christian children. These scenes reveal the features of Christian anti-Muslim feeling and the close relationship such apparently religious feelings have to a deeply felt sense that white people must defend themselves from the foreigners bent on displacing them and remaking their world. They reveal as well the network of interests of Christian right, evangelical, and Zionist organisations who circulate narratives of these local conflicts nationally, depositing into the national psyche the feeling that white Christian America is threatened all round, and in its most vulnerable places by its historic Islamic foes.

In the fall of 2001, a teacher in Contra Costa County, Northern California in the small school district of Byron (1,500 students), using an apparently standard instructional guide in World History first developed in 1991 (Handy 1991), taught a unit on Islam to a seventh-grade class. The pedagogy of the unit emphasised simulation and students were encouraged to adopt roles as Muslims for three weeks to help them understand what Muslims believe. As a part of the role play it was suggested that students adopt Muslim names, recite Muslim prayers in class, memorise a passage from the Quran, and give up something for a day to understand fasting during the month of Ramadan. The students were also asked to formulate a critique of elements of Muslim culture. If the timing of the event shortly after 9/11, and the role play assignments and pedagogical approach were ill-advised, the exercise itself was modelled on a one-dimensional portrait of a medieval, conservative Islam (the manual emphasised 610-1100 A.D.) that emphasised Islam's archaic foreignness. An Orientalist framing of Islam became the basis for Christian resentment of an educational unit apparently meant to foster religious tolerance.

In 2001, the simulation exercise seemed guaranteed to attract the attention of Christian conservatives in the small rural school district. Students and parents sued the school district arguing that the activities in question crossed a line from education to endorsement of a religious practice and ultimately to religious indoctrination. The plaintiffs in the suit, Jonas and Tiffany Eklund and their two children particularly objected as Christians to the simulation exercise and to what they considered to be a too tolerant portrayal of Islam. They pointed out that only the unit on Islam required such role play. A federal district court in San Francisco found no constitutional violation in the school's practice, a decision that prompted online observers to name the judge in question as a 'Public Enemy', to condemn her support for abortions, and to suggest that she was an Al Qaeda supporter (Enemy Judge 2004). The US Court of Appeals for the 9th Circuit agreed with the lower court's decision and ultimately, the Eklunds lost their case in the Supreme Court where the decision to dismiss the suit emphasised the school district's argument that schools need to be able to address religion in the curriculum without fear of reprisal. The court concluded that the unit on Islam did not attempt to in-doctrinate (Eklund v. Byron Union School District 2005). That the Ecklunds failed in their suit does not alter the circulation of an anti-Muslim affect but instead sustains it. Law provides the stage on which the conflict is framed as one between normative white citizens and a foreign Muslim enemy. The participants perform a Christian colonial morality play even though the play's conclusion is that this time around, the enemy does not need to be engaged in battle. The script that is enacted provides the basis for a broader mobilisation of whiteness from the local to the national stage.

The Eklunds were not simply lone parents who disagreed with the teaching of Islam in the curriculum and who decided to challenge it in court. They were supported in their activities by the Thomas More Law Centre, an organisation that describes itself as a non-profit public in-terest law firm based in Ann Arbor, Michigan, whose mission is to: 'Preserve America's Judeo-Christian heritage; Defend the religious freedom of Christians; Restore time-honoured moral and family values; Protect the sanctity of human life; Promote a strong national defence and a free and sovereign United States of America' a mission it accomplishes 'through litigation, education, and related activities' (Thomas More Law Center 2019a). Firmly anchored in a politics of Christian, conservative values, the law firm has been involved in several lawsuits against school boards. The Eklund lawsuit was one in a concerted longer-term strategy re-volving around the teaching of Islam in schools, a strategy in which other conservative Christian groups such as ACT for America have actively participated for almost two decades (ACT for America 2020). For example, in 2011, ACT for America published 'Education or Indoctrination: The Treatment of Islam in 6th through 12th Grade American Textbooks' in which it took issue with the presentation of Islam as a religion of peace (ACT for America 2011). In 2019, the Thomas More Law Centre published what was billed as a special in-vestigative report that claimed to have uncovered evidence that 'Islamic propaganda was being forced on teachers in rural school boards' (Thomas More Law Center 2019b). This latter report, primarily directed at school boards who hired a Muslim consultant Huda Essa to lead a two-day seminar on Islam, maintains the same positions as in the earlier discussed Ecklund case, in-cluding arguments about the lack of attention to Christianity and Judaism, the suppression of Islam's propensity to wage war, and omission of its "terrorist" histories. Essa, the Law Centre charged, 'While quick to indict America as guilty of "cultural genocide"', was 'silent on the 1400 years of actual genocides, also known as jihads, in which Muslims wiped out Jewish tribes on the Arabian Peninsula, and slaughtered millions of Christians throughout the Middle East, North Africa and the European Continent' (Thomas More Law Center 2019b). As with a meme, the storyline of Muslims as historical aggressive marauders circulates widely, ensuring its repeatability intact.

The Thomas More Law Centre has devoted a considerable part of its relatively small budget (1.5 million) to cases involving banning Islam in schools. Its founder, Richard Thompson, a prominent Christian evangelical lawyer, is heavily involved in the anti-abortion movement and is a frequent media voice on Fox News among others (President and Chief Counsel 2019). The Eklund's suit also attracted the support of the Mountain States Legal Foundation, an organi-sation that filed a friend-of-the-court brief supporting their position (Trotter 2006). The Foundation lists its budget at 2.1 million and describes its mission as 'constitutional liberty, economic opportunity and the right to own and use property' (About Us 2020). Involved in several guns rights cases such as opposition to Boulder, Colorado's efforts to raise the minimum age for firearms possession to 21, as well as opposing environmental and Indigenous rights and the tearing down of Christian war memorials, the Mountain States Legal Foundation labels itself 'the spirit of the American West' committed to defending the frontier it imagines as one peopled by sheep farmers, ranchers, and miners who are under attack by governments opposed to white property interests. Indeed, the defence of America (and Israel) from marauding Muslims is often understood on the unabashedly colonial terms expressed by the Mountain States Legal Foundation. For its part, ACT for America, founded by Brigitte Gabriel, a notable Lebanese American anti-Muslim activist, identifies five issues of central importance to her organisation: Israel (and specifically efforts to change the definition of anti-Semitism to include criticism of Israel); Immigration reform (and specifically an end to sanctuary cities, the building of the Wall, and greater policing of migrants); anti-terrorism, defined as confronting the violence of radical Islam); military and law enforcement (and notably advocating for greater policing); and constitutional freedoms, a category in which can be found textbook reforms, and campaigns against honour killings and FGM, attributed to Islamic cultures.

Whether in legal briefs, blogs, special investigative reports, Fox News media appearances or columns in the *Jerusalem Post*, Christian evangelical groups and their supporters who share the political agendas mentioned earlier portray Islam as a terrorist group not a religion, and a people at war with Christianity. Decades long, the campaign began reaching new heights following the election of Donald Trump to the American presidency. In a letter to the Secretary of Education Betsy DeVos in 2017, the Christian Action Network – declared a hate group by the Southern Poverty Law Centre (Tyree and Metzgar 2017) – laid out its specific objections to the teaching about Islam in schools. The lesson plans indoctrinate children in the Islamic religion, the Network declared, and amount to 'a Sunday school class for Islam'. The curriculum also fails to devote sufficient time to Christianity, Judaism or Hinduism. The lesson plans must be removed, the organisation demanded, and the Secretary should issue a public announcement that anyone using these materials violated the Establishment Clause of the Constitution and should be prohibited from obtaining federal funding.

The Christian storyline discernible for the past 19 years is also circulated by *Middle East Forum*, the think tank founded by Daniel Pipes, one of the most prolific of Zionist individuals regularly publishing articles on the threat of radical Islam. Invoking the spectre of the "Islamic terrorist", Pipes (2002) wrote that the Eklund's lawsuit confirms that American children were being recruited for Islamic terrorism through schools. Suggesting that the students were forced to utter the words 'Allahu akbar' (God is Great) and duped into believing that the words are merely a common salutation in the Islamic world rather than a 'militant Islamic war-cry', Pipes (2002) even wondered whether John Walker Lindt, the soldier known as 'The American Taliban' might have been subjected to the same school curriculum as the Eklund children when Lindt was a child in California. As he (Pipes 2002) wrote in the *Jerusalem Post*, referencing The Thomas More Law Centre's and Richard Thompson's arguments in court, impressionable 12-year-olds, like the Eklund children, were at risk of being recruited to terrorism when they were exposed to material such as the simulation exercises. Interventions from Christian right organisations and Fox News repeat ad nauseam the logic that to teach about the Islamic world is to indulge in indoctrination, to engage in terrorism, and to denigrate Christianity and Judaism. As Christopher Bail found using plagiarism detection software, the same three-word phrases circulate throughout the media and are lifted verbatim from anti-Muslim organisations for legal projects such as anti-Sharia bills introduced in state legislatures (Bail 2019: 102–103).

## Conclusion

The white anti-Muslim subject varies locally but shares a Christian core. In America, that subject's Christian inflection is often, although not always, of the evangelical variety and maintains important links to Zionist Jews both in the United States and Israel. For this subject, whiteness, Christianity and the Muslim as archetypical enemy come together to provide a deep sense of purpose, selfhood, and national belonging. Such emotions feed anti-Muslim legal and political projects even as those projects themselves foster subjects who believe that in acting 'Islamophobically', as Ghassan Hage put it, they are protecting what makes their lives worth living (Hage 2017: 13). The anti-Muslim subject of the school conflicts is often someone who feels aggrievement and rage that home is being invaded and must be defended, emotions that circulate around the figure of the Muslim, although Muslims are seldom the only target. When these emotions are channelled into an organised defence of white entitlement through religion, they sustain a coalition of interests dedicated to the protection of a racial order. Law is the conduit through which anti-Muslim animus travels forging whiteness as it does so even when legal suits brought by white Christian parents fail. Deposited in the legal record and ready for transport to the national stage, the story of whiteness that is achieved through anti-Muslim racism gains ground each time it is performed, filling white Christians with the warmth of entitled belonging and righteous rage.

## Note

1   A version of this chapter will be appearing in *Nothing Has To make Sense: Upholding White Supremacy through Anti-Muslim racism*, Minn.: MN: University of Minnesota Press, forthcoming.

## References

ACT for America. 2011. *Education or indoctrination? The treatment of Islam in 6th through 12th grade American textbooks*, viewed 20 November 2020, http://d3n8a8pro7vhmx.cloudfront.net/themes/57365ca5cd0af55 ea6000001/attachments/original/1483921270/Education_or_Indoctrination_Executive_Summary.pdf?14 83921270.

ACT for America. 2020. Viewed 20 November 2020, https://www.actforamerica.org/.

Bail, C. 2019. *Terrified: How Anti-Muslim Fringe Organizations Became Mainstream*. Princeton: Princeton University Press.

Bjork-James, S. 2018. Training the Porous Body: Evangelicals and the Ex-Gay Movement. *American Anthropologist*, 120 (4): 647–658. DOI:10.1111/aman.13106.

Blum, E. J. 2007. *W.E.B. Du Bois, American Prophet*. Philadelphia: University of Pennsylvania Press.

Blum, E. J., Fessenden, T., Kurien, P. and Weisenfeld, J. 2009. Forum: American Religion and 'Whiteness'. *Religion and American Culture: A Journal of Interpretation*, 19 (1): 1–35. DOI:10.1525/rac.2 009.19.1.1.

Bonnett, A. 1998. Who Was White? The Disappearance of Non-European White Identities and the Formation of European Racial Whiteness. *Ethnic and Racial Studies*, 21 (6): 1029–1055. DOI:10.1080/ 01419879808565651.

Burlein, A. 2002. *Lift High the Cross: Where White Supremacy and the Christian Right Converge*. Durham, NC: Duke University Press.

Cimino, R. 2005. 'No God in Common': American Evangelical Discourse on Islam after 9/11. *Review of Religious Research*, 47 (2): 162–174. DOI:10.2307/3512048.

Clark, V. 2007. *Allies for Armageddon: The Rise of Christian Zionism*. New Haven: Yale University Press.

Du Bois, W. E. B. 1999 [1920]. *Darkwater: Voices from Within the Veil*. New York: Dover Publications.

Eklund v. Byron Union School District. 154 Fed. Appx. 648 (9th Circuit 2005), cert. denied, 549 U.S. 942. 2006. https://www.scribd.com/document/266923198/Eklund-v-Byron-Union-School-District.

Enemy Judge: No. 1 – Phyllis J. Hamilton. Free Republic, 2 June 2004, viewed 20 November 2020, http://www.freerepublic.com/focus/f-news/1146555/posts.

Frankenberg, R. 1993. *White Women, Race Matters: The Social Construction of Whiteness*. Minneapolis: University of Minnesota Press.

Hage, G. 2017. *Is Racism an Environmental Threat?* Cambridge: Polity Press.

Han, J. H. J. 2018. Shifting Geographies of Proximity: Korean-led Evangelical Christian Missions and the U.S. Empire. In *Ethnographies of U.S. Empire*, ed. C. McGranahan and J. F. Collins, pp. 194–213. Durham, NC: Duke University Press.

Handy, T. 1991. *Islam: A Simulation of Islamic History and Culture, 610-1100*. El Cajon: Interaction Publishers Inc.

Harris, C. I. 1993. Whiteness as Property. *Harvard Law Review*, 106 (8): 1707–1791. DOI:10.2307/1341787.

Lipsitz, G. 2006. *The Possessive Investment in Whiteness: How White People Profit from Identity Politics*. Philadelphia: Temple University Press.

Marty, M. E. 2013. Foreword. In *More Desired than Our Owne Salvation: The Roots of Christian Zionism*, ed. R. O. Smith, pp. xi–xiii. New York: Oxford University Press.

Mountain States Legal Foundation. 2020. 'About Us: The Spirit of the American West', viewed 20 November 2020, https://mslegal.org/about/.

Pieterse, J. N. 1993. Aesthetics of Power: Time and Body Politics. *Third Text*, 7 (22): 33–42. DOI:10.1080/09528829308576398.

Pinar, W. F. 2001. *The Gender of Racial Politics and Violence in America: Lynching, Prison Rape, and the Crisis of Masculinity*. New York: Peter Lang Publishing.

Pipes, D. 2002. 'Become a Muslim Warrior', *Jerusalem Post*, July 3, viewed 20 November 2020, https://infoweb.newsbank.com/apps/news/document-view?p=WORLDNEWS&docref=news/110B05BA2F16FA38.

President and Chief Counsel. 2019. *Thomas More Law Center*, viewed 20 November 2020, https://www.thomasmore.org/president-chief-counsel/.

Smith, R. O. 2013. *More Desired Than Our Owne Salvation: The Roots of Christian Zionism*. New York: Oxford University Press.

Thomas More Law Center. 2019a. *About the Thomas More Law Center*, viewed 20 November 2020, https://www.thomasmore.org/about-the-thomas-more-law-center-1/.

Thomas More Law Center. 2019b. 'Thomas More Law Center Uncovers Taxpayer-funded Islamic Propaganda Forced on Teachers – A SPECIAL INVESTIGATIVE REPORT', *Thomas More Law Center*, 22 August, viewed 20 November 2020, https://www.thomasmore.org/news/thomas-more-law-center-uncovers-taxpayer-funded-islamic-propaganda-forced-on-teachers-a-special-investigative-report/.

Trotter, A. 2006. 'Justices decline case about public school's Islamic-themed unit', *Education Week*, 10 October, viewed 20 November 2020, https://www.edweek.org/ew/articles/2006/10/11/07scotus.h26.html.

Tyree, E. and Metzgar, K. 2017. '"I think it's defamatory": Christian Action Network fighting back against hate group label', *ABC 13 News*, 23 August, viewed 20 November 2020, https://wset.com/news/local/i-think-its-defamatory-christian-action-network-fighting-back-against-hate-group-label.

# 4

# Affects in making white womanhood

*Katalin Halász*

I LOVE BLACK MEN I LOVE BLACK MEN I LOVE BLACK MEN I LOVE BLACK
MEN I LOVE BLACK MEN I LOVE BLACK MEN I LOVE BLACK MEN I LOVE
BLACK MEN I LOVE BLACK MEN I LOVE BLACK MEN I LOVE BLACK MEN I
LOVE MEN MEN I LOVE MEN I … [SIGH]

At the opening of *I LOVE BLACK MEN* (London 2011),[1] we see a black board on a stand
against a white wall. The board occupies the entire screen. Slowly, a white naked woman
approaches the board with a chalk in her hand and starts to write. We see the woman writing
but the words are not legible, they fade into the darkness of the board and the camera has not
moved closer. The only sound we hear is of the chalk on the board, which is slightly at odds
with her moving hand. It does not stop when she moves her hand and the chalk away from the
board, suggesting a continuity of the writing. Over the course of nearly two minutes out of the
total of four, we see the naked woman writing back-to-back on the board (Figure 4.1). Then
the camera angle changes and finally the words she has written become clear. 'I LOVE BLACK
MEN' in capital letters. She continues to write, her head and hands are now close to the
camera, but we cannot see her face as it is covered by her black hair (Figure 4.2). The performance is carried forward by the rhythm of the writing, which has covered the top half of the
board. She still has another half to go. By now the viewer could get a sense that her writing
would not change, she is repeating the same words over and over again. With the camera set at
the same place, we only see a segment of the board. She moves in the frame writing and when
she finishes at the end of the board, she moves across the camera to the beginning of the board
to start again. In the last row, the letters become a bit smudged, the words do not follow the
same order. She now writes MEN I LOVE MEN I (Figure 4.3). She then moves out of the
frame. The camera does not follow her; it is sternly fixed on the board for another 20 seconds.
The sound is of her moving around in the room perhaps, out of sight. Finally, we hear a loud,
exasperated sigh.

  The performance is of a simple act and is visually restricted. There are only two camera
angles. Set in black and white but slightly blurred and out of focus, the recording bears
comparison with the aesthetics of 1970s feminist performance/video art. The simplicity of the
writing and the sound of the chalk going on and on enables the viewer to drift off and return.

DOI: 10.4324/9780429355769-4

*Figure 4.1   I LOVE BLACK MEN.* 2011. Video still (black and white, sound).

The change of the camera angle in the middle of the piece helps to keep our attention on the naked woman and her performance, but we cannot decipher her thoughts or emotions, her face remains covered by her hair. The only and deeply corporeal reaction we get from her is a sigh.

We are made to endure the monotony of the white woman's labour, which can have contradictory effects. One can be bored and uninterested in her act. Or maybe curious or even enraged by yet another white woman demanding attention. In my reading, if one is open and engaged, the devastating effects of ideologies locked in bodies and their relationality can be brought close. As George Yancy writes: 'She performs her white body, ergo, I "become" the predatory Black' (2008: 23). The performance is hinged on and intends to subvert the power relation sustained by the essentialising sexual stereotype that dictates an elemental attraction between white women and Black men.[2]

In this chapter, I want to use the particular moment of the sigh as a vehicle to develop an argument about white female embodiment and its potentiality in fracturing whiteness. My initial point is that conceptualisations of heterosexual, cisgendered white womanhood in the North are too often reduced to the historical construction of the discursive figure of 'white woman'. While I place white womanhood firmly in histories of racism and structures of oppression, white domination and racial discourses, my critical focus is on the body and its affects. More specifically, on the interrelation of discourse and affect enacted in the body. From *I LOVE BLACK MEN*, I propose that the affective sensitivity of the situated white female body is at the core of the formation of white femininities. Through a key focus on the entanglements

*Figure 4.2   I LOVE BLACK MEN.* 2011. Video still (black and white, sound).

of discourse and affect, I investigate how discourse (in the form of a persistent stereotype of the hyper-sexualised Black male body), material and social relations and embodied practices (including the visual) are recruited together in the affective episode of the performance to produce white womanhood. I am drawing on recent theorisations of affect designated as '*relational dynamics* between evolving bodies in a setting' (Slaby and Mülhoff 2019: 27, emphasis in original). Moving away from inner feeling states and emotions, this definition emphasises changing bodily capacities or micro-powers in an affective relational encounter. Power in this Spinozian approach is intrinsically imbued with affect, the micro power that each individual holds is their *potentia*, their affective capacity to enter into relations of affecting and being affected. Further, as Jan Slaby and Rainer Mülhoff argue: 'Affective relations over time both establish and subsequently modulate – make, unmake, remake – individual capacities and dispositions. In other words, relational affect is a central factor in the process of subject formation' (2019: 27). Through *I LOVE BLACK MEN,* we can explore the ways in which affective relations are being formed around the discursive figure of the 'white woman', the interaction of multiple figurations that produces this situated and historical figure in the confines of the performance, and the white female body's potentia in making and unmaking this racial category.

My analysis takes place in an understanding of the body as a 'battlefield'. I am using Yancy's conceptualisation of Black and white bodies as never fixed and at rest, but constantly 'fought over' in moments of contemporary and past histories (2017: 36). While focussing foremost on Black bodies, Yancy argues that the white gaze projects fantasies, desires and meanings onto

*Figure 4.3   I LOVE BLACK MEN.* 2011. Video still (black and white, sound).

both, Black and white bodies. 'The larger white social imaginary' interpellates Black and white bodies in power but to different effects – blackness gets disempowered, and whiteness empowered (2017: 37). Through 'symbolic repetition and iteration that emits certain signs and presupposes certain norms' Black embodiment becomes fragmented and traumatised through distorted images projected on it (2017: 36). The same processes of symbolic iteration construct white bodies as 'the transcendental norm' (2017: 37). Importantly, these meanings and norms are assumptions of the body that can be defied, fractured, and disarticulated. For Yancy, the 'material force' of the body is interpreted through historical discourse. I developed and staged *I LOVE BLACK MEN* to push this argument further and show how the white female body responds affectively to racialising discourse and demonstrate that it is more than merely a matter to be interpreted. The battlefield that is the white female body in the performance holds the potential of its material force to intervene in dominant historical discourses. Thus, images, ideas, stereotypes are not simply inscribed onto the surface of the passively recipient white female body, they are fought over by its material life force, by its affective energies and intensities, its micro-powers.

I begin by situating the discursive figure of the 'white woman' in the temporal-spatial relations of North American slavery, colonialism, and anti-Black racism. In doing so, I am framing these temporal-spatial relations as my crucial points of departure in developing my argument on white female racial embodiment. This is a specific female embodiment: That of the heterosexual, abled bodied (importantly also in terms of procreation), cis white woman from the global North. While white femininities across the world are intersected by differently abled, queered, classed lived experiences and are generationally, religiously and ethnically diverse amongst other intersections, the North Western white heterosexual cis woman is crucial to establishing and maintaining contemporary global white supremacy and is thus extremely disposed to defensiveness. Dispelling the construction and protection of this particular discursive figure is a key driving force of the performance.

In the following section, I move on to consider how the performance recreates whiteness in the staged classroom and how affective relations are being formed in this space between absent present bodies under the white gaze. Finally, I turn to the white female body and its affective dimensions to argue that discourse and affect are mutually constitutive of white womanhood. I close by a purposefully anti-racist reading of the potentialities of white female bodies in re-making racial and gendered categories and thus disrupting whiteness. This is not to claim that white women can transcend whiteness or to produce a 'good' liberal anti-racist white position (Sullivan 2014) or to suggest anti-racism can or should be a source of white benevolence and pride (Ahmed 2004b; Hunter et al. 2010). Rather, my aim with the performance is to expand anti-racist scholarship with knowing whiteness through the body. As a white woman pro-fessionally active in anti-racist activism before pursuing academic and artistic research into whiteness, I have produced a series of art projects using bodies in performances to disrupt essentialising discourses of race and gender, which are at the root of racism. *I LOVE BLACK MEN* is one of these performances that attends to bodies and their inner, affective force holding the potential to dislodge race essentialism based on inscribing their surfaces with complementary meanings of white femininity and Black masculinity in the service of white supremacy. I do not claim uncritically that affect is emancipatory but intend to contribute to theorising whiteness through bodies understood not only as an effect of discourse.

## Inscribing white female bodies and the historical-discursive figure of 'white woman'

The historical context of the performance is North American slavery, colonialism and enduring post-slavery anti-Black racism. Within this context, the white female body in the performance appears on the scene as already produced historically – its surface has been a 'battlefield' of racialised discursive regimes inscribing meaning and effects. The white female body of the performer is 'totally imprinted by history and the processes of history's deconstruction of the body' (Foucault, 1977: 63). Michele Wallace writes that the slavery system forged a 'sacred white womanhood' on white women's status as property of white men, and her function to bear children for white men who would inherit his wealth and for this reason there could not be any doubt as to the father of the child (1978: 26). This status of the American 'Southern white woman' has changed, and by 1776, the 'legend of the Southern belle' was created, with a foremost decorative function (1978: 136). White women's bodies were constructed through an association with bodily limits, defined through their degrees of deviation from the white male body in the scientific thinking throughout the nineteenth century, a period when 'rather than *finding* evidence of racial difference, science was actually *constructing* or even inventing the very idea of race itself' (Ahmed 2002: 50, emphasis in original). It was the body, 'bodily difference and bodily hierarchy' that were the foundational idea behind the invention of race (Ahmed 2002: 50). In this ordering of bodies, white women's bodies were analogous to those of 'lower races', which according to Sara Ahmed 'allowed woman as a group to be racialized, and the "lower races" as a group to be feminised' (2002: 51). Although the body of 'white woman' was considered less evolved than that of the 'white man', due to her membership of the 'higher races' her bodily limits could (unlike the alleged bestiality and sexuality of the bodies of Black women) be transcended through the rules of 'virtue', 'chastity', and 'modesty' that protected and also hemmed her (Ahmed 2002). While in the eighteenth-century textual and visual technologies produced 'ideal' white womanhood as passive and dependent, by the nineteenth century the ideal of the white lady became 'respectable', to be proven by appearance and composed, controlled behaviour (Skeggs 1997).

These racialising discourses of the white female body are being brought alive in the performance with the use of a specific stereotype that interweaves femininity and masculinity with race and sexuality. *I LOVE BLACK MEN* operates with stereotyping as an act of social inscription, as writing on bodies. While acknowledging that there is no one true meaning, the piece employs stereotyping as a representational practice that fixes meaning (Hall 2013). As Stuart Hall states, in the 'racialised regime of representation', stereotyped means 'reduced to a few essentials, fixed in Nature by a few, simplified characteristics' (2013: 237). The stereotype that posits an elemental attraction of white women to Black men continuously reactivates the historically produced figure of the heterosexual, cis 'white woman' as vulnerable, sexually pure and restrained, a victim, in contrast to the fantasy of the predatory, excessive, exotic trope of 'black man' (Byrne 2006; Dyer 1997; Frankenberg 1993; Hall 1992; Harris 2000; McClintock 1995; Nava 2007; Ware 1992). As Wallace claims, 'what bothered America the most' was the alleged sexual attraction of the 'black man' and the 'white woman' (1978: 30). Protecting white women has been used as a reasoning to act on manic fears of white men over Black men's presumed overt sexuality and more importantly, on ending slavery, to continue to oppress people of colour economically, socially and politically through a continuation of violence in the form of lynching, mobs and most recently through mass incarceration (Davis 1981).

## The white gaze in the white classroom

I designed the space in which the performance took place to resemble a classroom: 'A site of effective (white) history' (Yancy 2017 : 9). Yancy writes about universities as 'part and parcel of white domination', as already given and familiar white spaces which white people perceive as non-racial (2017: 9). Whites inhabit and move in such places with the ease that stems from the lack of any self-awareness of their bodies, histories, and positions in power – with the ease of the oppressor. The performance recreates whiteness through a combination of various elements: The staging of the white educational space, the disciplining power of the white gaze, the objectification of Black subjectivity and the evocation of histories of racial violence that the stereotype has sustained over centuries. 'The historical power of the white gaze, a perspective that carries the weight of white racist history and everyday encounters of spoken and unspoken anti-Black racism' (Yancy 2017: 22) is enacted in the performance not only through the camera, but also by the invisible teacher who instructs the white woman to write on the blackboard. The woman, a sight without a voice, is under constant surveillance by the authoritative instructor who, it could be argued, is there to establish their power, not only by making her write but also through their freedom of being watched. Seeing, being seen and being not seen are visual perceptual practices of race that are interwoven with relational power positions: 'Visibility and invisibility are not simply states or conditions of being. Rather they characterise, express, reflect, or they are the effects of strategic relations' (Goldberg 1997: 82). Throughout the performance, there is only one body visible, that of 'white woman'. Although only she is to be seen, the defining presence of other members of what Ruth Frankenberg called the 'discursive family' is felt (1993: 81). Through a family of racial and gendered discursive tropes, the figure of the 'Black man' was constructed as sexually rapacious, from whom the 'white woman' victim must be saved by 'white man'. 'Black woman' in this constellation were deemed to be sexually promiscuous, not only to serve white men sexually but also to provide future labour force. These relational constructs give meaning to the figure of 'white woman' and affirm that however sexually exploited by 'white man' she might be, the 'ideal' and 're-spectable' 'white woman' is in the position of oppressor in relation to Black men and women. As bell hooks put it: 'To black women the issue is not whether white women are more or less racist than white men, but that they are racist' (1984: 124).

In the racial visual schema, seeing practices assert who is conferred with subjecthood and to whom it is denied (Byrne 2006). From the two 'family members' who the stereotype links together only 'white woman' is seen, 'black man' is not. From this point of view, the per-formance can be argued to reproduce oppressive relations and attests that the devaluation of Black subjects services whiteness by producing it as knowable and therefore as powerful (Hunter 2015). I would propose that 'white woman' too, is stripped of her own subjectivity. The white gaze is directed right at her. The woman's nakedness could suggest that she takes pleasure in her own body, but it could also be argued that as the performance evolves, her body is taken away from her, and turned into a sign of dis-possession, an object of sexual desire within the gaze. The oppressive ways of whiteness as reproduced in the staged white space of the classroom is brought to attention. 'White woman's image remains visible to the viewer, but her voice is not heard – only the sound of the chalk, the increasingly violent movement of her hand that makes the chalk shriek on the blackboard. She is not at ease any longer. She is made aware of her body, she becomes unsettled in the white space of the classroom – in her position in whiteness, which is that of the aggressor as well as the possessed object.

Written in the first person, the simple text of 'I LOVE BLACK MEN' is employed as a way to make her enact perceptions of her race, gender, and sexuality *inscribed* on her body – on the body of 'white woman'. Her whiteness and femininity, differences of race and gender, are reduced to the perception of visible differences of the white female body, the single most important means in producing beliefs and ideologies (Minh-ha 1989). The performance at-tempts to break the complementarity between 'white woman' and 'white man'. 'White woman' can be seen to be forced to patrol the definitional boundaries of the family, her race, and gendered heterosexuality that arguably draws her to 'black man'. In the discursive con-struct, 'white man' establishes and justifies his power over 'black man' by the need to safeguard vulnerable 'white woman' against a savage desire that 'white woman' is purportedly unable to regulate on her own. 'White woman' seems unable to take control of her subject position. She might be forever owned, disciplined, and controlled by 'white man', who must be reaffirmed as the saviour of her, the family, and humankind. She could be seen as having done something wrong or having not done something that she is expected or obliged to do. Like a schoolgirl, she must be disciplined by repeatedly writing-out lines of text on the chalkboard. Moreover, the act of repetitive writing reflects the repetitive nature of stereotyping practices and the performative process constitutive of identity. Repetition is the central act of the performance. 'The reiterative power of discourse' (Butler 1993: 2) that produces regulated models of being, which subjects are responsible for re-enacting and maintaining, is the backbone of the piece. The performance makes painfully clear the notion that whiteness is performative – that one has to act-out discursive conventions to become it. The repetitive writing is a visual articulation of the workings of disciplinary power and normative cultural ideas that render regulatory images of black and white bodies effective tools in processes of racialisation.

## Affects of the white female body

The corporeality of the racialised body occupies an uncomfortable position in the study of race and more so in studies of whiteness. The acknowledgement of the material and physical presence and the lived effects of racialisation stop at fears of reifying race as a biological reality and re-centring whiteness as the racial norm. Theorising whiteness as socially constructed, relational, and socially located (Brah 1996; Gunaratnam 2003; Lewis 2000) and placing racial bodies in historical context, processes of representation, and in specific sites, for example employment or racial violence partly resolves this dilemma (Knowles and Alexander 2005). These works focus on the externality of the racialised body and treat racialised bodies as objects/subjects of control constructed through power. Analysing processes of racialisation through white bodies is inherently different from doing so on Black bodies. Richard Dyer for example explains the 'ambiguous' position of white bodies in racialising processes by stating that, 'white people are something else that is realized in and yet is not reducible to the corporeal, or racial' (1997: 14). In his understanding, white people are made visible not through their bodies but by questions of power relations, and so white people are not reducible to their bodies in the same way as Black people have been by white supremacist thinking.

From *I LOVE BLACK MEN,* I want to propose a renewed focus on the complex interaction of the materiality of embodiment and the social construction of cultural ideas in the production of white womanhood. With the focus on the web of power relations in which white women play a profound role, the performance enables analysing the role of affect as a relation of power in making whiteness (Slaby and Mülhoff 2019). Rooted in social constructionism, critical whiteness studies denotes whiteness as an ongoing process of becoming, not a thing already out there: 'There are no white people as such only a (changing) set of idealized norms, practices, and investments that constitute a white racialized ideal' (Hunter et al. 2010: 410). Recent critical thinking on whiteness is concerned with the analysis of the social, symbolic, psychic and material processes, signs and strategies that combine to enact racialised power. Affect and emotion filters into critical whiteness studies (Ahmed 2007; Hunter 2010, 2014; Saldanha 2007; Shotwell 2011; Sullivan 2014), and there is a growing number of works that addresses affect in racialisation, othering and structural oppression (Blickstein 2019; Berg and Ramos-Zayas 2015; Chen 2012; Ngai 2005; Palmer 2017; Schuller 2018). This scholarship allows for a renewed engagement with the fleshy materiality of the racialised body that for long had been caught up in the cultural inscription model, in which cultural influence, ideology, and power shape the body through the mind (Blackman 2008).

My argument is that performances of white femininities have an affective charge, induced by – but involving more than – visual discourse and racial regimes of representation. There is a complex relationality at work between corporeal-affective and cultural inscription practices. This very conflict between the visual, external, culturally inscribed surface and the affective inner sense of the self is at the heart of the performance. Through a direct and clean black and white aesthetic, and employing repetition as a conceptual and artistic strategy, the performance enacts the ways in which 'cultural injunctions and subject positions might be literally written into the flesh of the body' (Blackman 2008: 72). The performance works with visual discourse on racial and gender differences, and with their visual markers that are culturally inscribed on the body, but it does not stop there. It further explores how the performance of any representational trope is deeply embedded in the sense of self and allows for the more profound, intersubjective, affective processes to coalesce with the image of stereotyped white femininities on the surface of the white female body. The naked body of 'white woman' is left bare, with no protection, and without the shield of respectability. Her body is marked as a site of racialisation.

I suggest, however, that there is more at play here than simply the intricate ways in which power shapes the body through discourse. The body is a process rather than a substance. Social and cultural practices and norms interact with the corporeal and physical in a dynamic relationality: The production of the racial body is performed as an affective process through multiple histories of stereotyping practices. The performance attempts to reproduce the silencing and ignoring of the 'dynamic nature of the body' (Shilling 1993: 104) inherent in social constructionism, whereby the body is passively written on, but fails. Affects surge to the surface, the white female body is trembling under the flow of affects. The body of 'white woman' is neither a simple 'inscriptive surface' (Grosz 1994: 23), nor pure biological matter. It is fleshy materiality that is lived and experienced by subjects positioned within cultural norms, power structures, and restraints. A complex relationality between discourse and affect could be detected here. Through the work of affects, the performance opens up the closure inherent in stereotyping. The way in which the performer is made to embody received ideas about Northern, heterosexual, cis 'white woman' indicates how stereotypes are perpetuated, and how they affect us at the very core of our personality, in our 'flesh'. Through the naked woman's repetitive writing on the blackboard, it becomes clear that the space of the staged classroom is a highly racialised and sexualised space, which then gradually blurs into a place where common-sense assumptions about the nature of identity and processes of identification are thrown into question through the very corporeal reactions of the white female body. Stereotypes are made to come apart and their assurances are gradually fading. Fantasies of sexual desire and the myth of the sexualised 'black man' that continue to haunt the collective imagination are re-viewed and unearthed through the body's engagement with this myth.

Acknowledging the work of affects allows us to conceptualise the white female body beyond the limiting focus of the external surface or appearance. Thinking through the interplay of political, social, cultural inscriptions and constructs with the materiality of bodies, attending to their felt orientations and lived relations to the world is made possible. This 'somatically felt body' (Blackman 2008: 30) is a 'battlefield': Through its openness to affect and to be affected it is continuously changing as a result of this dynamic relationality with the inside and outside. But affects surrounding 'white woman' are not arbitrary. Their nature and display are determined by the unfolding of the historical relations of the members of the 'discursive family', and by the power structures and systems of dominations of white supremacy and patriarchy. I suggest that the affective charge of white femininities does not belong to 'white woman' or to the performer performing 'white woman'. It belongs instead to the public sphere constituted along the discursive figures appearing in the performance – 'white woman', 'black man', and 'white man'. As Ahmed explains: 'Emotions are profoundly intersubjective. They happen in relation to others: Emotion is not simply something 'I' or 'we' have. Rather it is through emotions, or how we respond to objects and others, that surfaces and boundaries are made' (2004a: 10). At the end of the performance, nonetheless, the affective charge of white femininities seems to become internalised by the performer, herself a white woman. A complex act of embodied affective positioning is thus taking place: the transformation from a performer tasked to perform an act into a woman with her own histories, feelings, ideas, and subjectivity.

## MEN I LOVE MEN I .... [SIGH]

I see the performer struggling under the affective charge of white femininities. In the process of writing the text, 'I LOVE BLACK MEN' becomes smudged and broken until it reads 'MEN I LOVE MEN I' (Figure 4.4). The end of the performance could be read as the performer's intellectual and emotional struggle to comprehend the sentence and understand its implications,

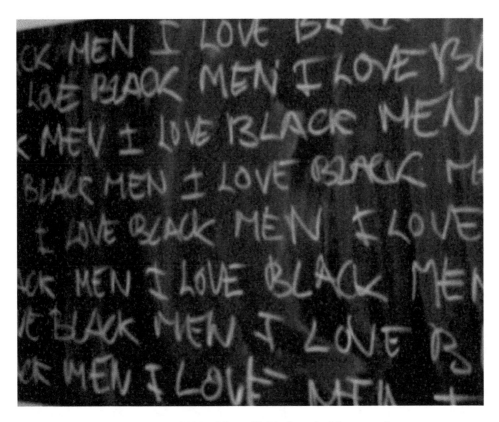

*Figure 4.4  I LOVE BLACK MEN.* 2011. Video still (black and white, sound).

to the point where racial and sexual differences are exhausted, forcing us to ask what they entail. What we hear is maybe a sigh of exasperation, exhaustion from the process by which the discourse becomes internalised and thrown back again into space. Through the sigh of affect, the body takes back her place in the discourse. The body of the performer is not 'a malleable entity that cannot speak back' (Blackman 2008: 16). Its living texture and materiality has ripped off the body the inscriptive cover of historical discourse. The white female body might have undergone a process of disorientation, an undoing, 'where the sensorial are shaken, unhinged' (Yancy 2017: 255). Understanding herself in the history of white supremacy, the performer could have reached 'a critical distancing from (or disruption of) various hegemonic norms', an opening of 'somatic and psychic closure' that she has inherited and perpetuated (Yancy 2017: 256). The last words of 'I LOVE MEN I' on the blackboard could be interpreted as a release from the fixing of boundaries, and as an invitation to include everything which previously did not belong. The eternal dance of Black men and white women has come to an end. Without the inscribed racial, gender, and sexual identification 'white woman' has been opened to love and receive love with humanity.

In my reading, the piece seeks to gradually dismantle the trope of the heterosexual white supremacist family, to refuse the racial and sexual contract of white womanhood. The attachment of emotions and the embracing of love and desire of Black males linked to white femininities seem to be pulled apart. In the process, the figure of 'white woman' is hollowed out, her body a container made vacant but willing to be filled: Affects of whiteness are left empty. And the commitment to the continuing heterosexual family project of whiteness seems to have been broken, the reproduction of itself and its most pivotal trope, 'white man'. In 1978, Wallace wrote: 'But all this is water under the bridge. At this point particularly, the sexual myths about white men, white woman, black men, and black women are just an accumulation of waste – wasted hope and wasted cockiness, born of insecurity and anxiety, which help to keep us all in our respective places' (1978: 13). In *I LOVE BLACK MEN*, I envisaged to leave this waste behind and form new, varied public bodies for white women, and the potential of performing anti-essentialist relations outside of colonial constrictions of cisgendered and heterosexualised white supremacist femininities.

## Notes

1  *I Love Black Men* was developed and staged as part of a visual sociology research on anti-racist white femininities. The performance was used solely for research purposes, to activate some of the concepts the research worked with: the relational construction of white womanhood through racial discourse, performativity, bodies, and performance as a sociological research method. Hence, there was no audience present; the performance took place in a studio in London with only the performer and me as the researcher present. Following *I Love Black Men,* the research has taken a new turn to focus more closely on the role of affect in racialisation and the production of white femininities. The consequent performances were staged in various art contexts in the United Kingdom, Brazil, Germany, and Denmark. For more information please see: <www.katalinhalasz.com>.
2  Many thanks to Shona Hunter for her suggestion on this point.

## References

Ahmed, S. 2002. Racialized Bodies. In *Real Bodies. A Sociological Introduction*, ed.M. Evans and E. Lee, pp. 46–63. Basingstoke and New York: Palgrave.

Ahmed, S. 2004a. *The Cultural Politics of Emotion*. New York: Routledge.

Ahmed, S. 2004b. Declarations of Whiteness: The Non-Performativity of Anti-Racism. *Borderlands e-journal*, 3 (2), viewed 10 July 2020, http://www.borderlands.net.au/vol3no2_2004/ahmed_declarations.htm.

Ahmed, S. 2007. A Phenomenology of Whiteness. *Feminist Theory*, 8 (2): 149–168.

Berg, U. and Ramos-Zayas, A. Y. 2015. Racializing Affect: A Theoretical Proposition. *Current Anthropology*, 56 (5): 654–677.

Blackman, L. 2008. *The Body: Key Concepts*. Oxford and New York: Berg.

Blickstein, T. 2019. Affects of Racialization. In *Affective Societies. Key Concepts*, ed. J. Slaby and C. von Scheve, pp. 152–166. London and New York: Routledge.

Brah, A. 1996. *Cartographies of Diaspora: Contesting Identities*. London and New York: Routledge.

Butler, J. 1993. *Bodies that Matter: On the Discursive Limits of Sex*. London and New York: Routledge.

Byrne, B. 2006. *White Lives. The Interplay of 'Race', Class and Gender in Everyday Life*. Oxon and New York: Routledge.

Chen, M. Y. 2012. *Animacies: Biopolitics, Racial Mattering, and Queer Affect*. Durham, NC: Duke University Press.

Davis, A. Y. 1981. *Women, Race and Class*. Visalia, CA: Vintage.

Dyer, R. 1997. *White*. London: Routledge.

Foucault, M. 1977. *Discipline and Punish*. London: Tavistock.

Frankenberg, R. 1993. *White Women, Race Matters: The Social Construction of Whiteness*. Minneapolis: University of Minnesota Press.

Goldberg, D. T. 1997. *Racial Subjects. Writing on Race in America*. London: Routledge.

Grosz, E. 1994. *Volatile Bodies: Towards a Corporeal Feminism*. Bloomington and Indianapolis: Indiana University Press.

Gunaratnam, Y. 2003. *Researching Race and Ethnicity: Methods, Knowledge, and Power*. London: SAGE.

Hall, C. 1992. *White, Male and Middle-Class. Explorations in Feminism and History*. Cambridge: Polity Press.

Hall, S. 2013. The Spectacle of the 'Other'. In *Representation*, 2nd edn, ed. S. Hall, J. Evans and S. Nixon, pp. 215–280. London: The Open University and SAGE.

Harris, H. 2000. Failing 'White Woman': Interrogating the Performance of Respectability. *Theatre Journal*, 52: 183–209.

hooks, B. 1984. *Ain't I a Woman?* Boston: South End Press.

Hunter, S. 2010. What a White Shame: Race, Gender, and White Shame in the Relational Economy of Primary Health Care Organisations in England. *Social Politics: International Studies in Gender, State and Society*, 17 (4): 450–476.

Hunter, S. 2015. *Power, Politics and the Emotions: Impossible Governance?* London: Routledge.

Hunter, S., Swan, E. and Grimes, D. 2010. Introduction: Reproducing and Resisting Whiteness in Organization, Policies, and Places. *Social Politics: International Studies in Gender, State and Society*, 17 (4): 407–422.

Knowles, C. and Alexander, C., eds. 2005. *Making Race Matter. Bodies, Space and Identity*. Basingstoke: Palgrave Macmillan.

Lewis, G. 2000. *'Race', Gender, Social Welfare: Encounters in a Postcolonial Society*. Cambridge, UK and Malden, MA: Polity Press.

McClintock, A. 1995. *Imperial Leather: Race, Gender, and Sexuality in the Colonial Contest*. New York: Routledge.

Minh-ha, T. T. 1989. Difference: A Special Third World Woman Issue. In *Feminism and Visual Culture Reader*, ed. A. Jones. Oxon and New York: Routledge.

Nava, M. 2007. *Visceral Cosmopolitanism: Gender, Culture and the Normalisation of Difference*. New York, NY: Berg.

Ngai, S. 2005. *Ugly Feelings*. Cambridge, MA: Harvard University Press.

Palmer, T. 2017. 'What Feels More Than Feeling?' Theorizing the Unthinkability of Black Affect. *Critical Ethnic Studies*, 3 (2): 31–56.

Saldanha, A. 2007. *Psychedelic White: Goa Trance and the Viscosity of Race*. London and Minneapolis: University of Minneapolis Press.

Schuller, K. 2018. *The Biopolitics of Feeling: Race, Sex, and Science in the Nineteenth Century*. Durham, NC: Duke University Press.

Shilling, C. 1993. *The Body and Social Theory*. London Thousand Oaks, CA and New Delhi: SAGE.

Shotwell, A. 2011. *Knowing Otherwise. Race, Gender and Implicit Understanding*. Pennsylvania: Penn State University Press.

Skeggs, B. 1997. *Formations of Class and Gender*. London: SAGE.

Slaby, J. and Mülhoff, R. 2019. Affect. In *Affective Societies. Key Concepts*, ed. J. Slaby and C. von Scheve, pp. 27–42. London and New York: Routledge.

Sullivan, S. 2014. *Good White People: The Problem with Middle-Class White Anti-Racism*. Albany: State University of New York Press.

Wallace, M. 1978. *Black Macho and the Myth of the Superwoman*. New York: The Dial Press.

Ware, V. 1992. *Beyond the Pale. White Women, Racism and History*. London and New York: Verso.

Yancy, G. 2008. *Black Bodies, White Gazes: The Continuing Significance of Race in America*. New York and London: Rowman and Littlefield.

Yancy, G. 2017. *Black Bodies, White Gazes: The Continuing Significance of Race in America*. New York and London: Rowman and Littlefield.

# 5

# What do cultural figurations know about global whiteness?

*Mark Schmitt*

Art is a human signifying practice that produces and constitutes knowledge. Literature, films, TV shows, music, paintings, and other art forms not only constitute and produce aesthetic knowledge, but also produce social and cultural knowledge. Cultural representations also intersect with other signifying practices and discourses in society and culture and are therefore instrumental in shaping the way we perceive our and other people's cultural identities. As Richard Hoggart (1971) has argued in a comparison of 'the literary and the sociological imagination',

> The literary imagination can give insights into the nature of society itself, insights which cannot be contained within a self-enclosed aesthetic world; insights which, it is often assumed, can affect a reader's own sensibility thereafter. [...]. [...] these works are at their best much more than reflectors or mirrors of their society, more than symptomatic evidence.
>
> *(1971: 260).*

What Hoggart says about literature can also be applied to other cultural representations which, in the broadest sense, narrate cultural and social identities. In this understanding of the inter-relation between representative art and society, '[l]iterary evidence does not simply illustrate that "X" is what a society believes, assumes, feels. It recreates what it seems like to be a human being or a society which believes, assumes or feels "X"' (1971: 270). Literary and other artistic representations thus fundamentally shape and interact with cultural epistemologies. Hoggart goes even further by proposing that through engaging with literature or other imaginative representations, we do not only learn about social facts, but can ideally engage with social and cultural knowledge in an active way: 'Many expressive phenomena are not only symptomatic of the consciousness of their age but themselves help to alter that consciousness' (1971: 271).

I take Hoggart's theorisation of literature as an 'inherently social practice' (Bailey et al. 2012: 19) and extend it to other representational, imaginative, and narrative practices. With regard to racial epistemologies, I argue that literature and film can be a 'playground' for racial epistemologies in that they have the potential to both solidify racial hierarchies of knowing as well as challenging these very hierarchies. Aesthetic and narrative figurations of whiteness and race can normalise white hegemony and privileged racial epistemologies, or they can experiment with them in a ludic way. This article will explore the potential of contemporary cultural texts

DOI: 10.4324/9780429355769-5

to produce and reflect racial knowledges. In the context of critical whiteness studies, the notion of unmarked (because unmentioned) whiteness in literary texts has been a prominent notion since Toni Morrison's seminal study *Playing in the Dark: Whiteness and the Literary Imagination* (1992). More recently, Reni Eddo-Lodge has made a similar point in her polemic *Why I'm No Longer Speaking to White People About Race* (2017).

Departing from these arguments, I will argue that rather than merely *re-presenting* racial identities, literary texts, films, popular music, and other cultural texts work towards producing *figurations* of raced, classed, gendered, etc. identities that are intricately linked to extratextual knowledge of and about these identities. I employ the concept of figuration as an epistemological frame, drawing from sociological theories (Hartigan Jr. 2005; Tyler 2008), literary theory (Korte and Zipp 2014), and my own analysis of figurations of tainted whiteness in British literature (Schmitt 2018a). This approach will bridge the gap between the disciplines of sociology and literary and cultural studies to comprehensively assess how figurations of whiteness (es) form a wide-ranging 'social imaginary' (Korte and Zipp 2014: 2, following Charles Taylor) that must not be merely regarded as (fictional) representations of a social reality, but actively shapes and interacts with it. Cultural figurations thus produce racial (and intersectional) and knowledge thereof. This chapter first summarises the main theses brought forth by Toni Morrison, Rebecca Aanerud, and Reni Eddo-Lodge concerning whiteness as an invisible norm in literary and filmic representations and will then connect the concept of figurations to the notion of whiteness and other racial identities as embodiment to come to terms with the question of how such default representational norms shape white epistemologies. This chapter illustrates this by specifically looking at two examples of different figurations of whiteness: James Bond as a figure of universal whiteness and fictional figurations of 'white trash' as hypervisible, non-normative, or 'tainted' forms of whiteness. This chapter argues that these two figurations of different whiteness represent the extreme ends of a spectrum of white identities. Both, however, embody similar knowledges of whiteness that help to constantly re-invent and perform whiteness. This chapter thus demonstrates that through the analysis of the social imaginary and its racial figurations, we can critically assess different racial epistemologies.

## Whiteness as invisible norm in literature

Toni Morrison (1992) and Rebecca Aanerud (1997) can be credited with having first explicitly dealt with the issue of representing whiteness as an invisible norm in Western literary texts. As Aanerud states, 'whiteness operates as an unmarked racial category' (1997: 37) in many literary texts. Literary representations thus become the symbolic backup of what Ruth Frankenberg (1993) has called whiteness' 'location of structural advantage' and 'set of practices that are usually unmarked and unnamed' (1993: 1). Toni Morrison, in a close reading of literary texts, has pointed out that whiteness is always an unspoken presence whereas non-white characters are often explicitly racially marked. In her reading of Ernest Hemingway's novel *To Have and Have Not* (1937), she remarks about a central character: 'Eddy is white, and we know he is because nobody says so' (1992: 72). This connects to Richard Dyer's (1997) analysis of the 'invisibility of whiteness as a racial position in white (which is to say dominant) discourse' (1997: 3). This invisibility equals the ubiquity of white characters which renders whiteness as a normative default identity and subject position in Western cultural representations. However, this ubiquity paradoxically comes about through an emptying of the racial signifiers of whiteness: 'Whites are everywhere in representation. Yet, precisely because of this and their placing as norm they seem not to be represented to themselves as whites' (Dyer 1997: 3). In other words: White people are everywhere in Western cultural representations, yet their omnipresence is rendered meaningless or unremarkable as racial fact – their bodies appear as normative signifiers which are not supposed to 'mean' a racialised identity, let alone a dominant one.

This is also echoed in British journalist Reni Eddo-Lodge's book *Why I'm No Longer Talking to White People About Race*. Her personal biographical reflection highlights the effect that the seemingly 'meaningless' omnipresence of white people in cultural representations had on her as a black woman growing up at the turn of the millennium and points to the epistemological repercussions of this type of representation. Eddo-Lodge remembers her experience of reading J.K. Rowling's *Harry Potter* novels (1997–2007) and other cultural texts as a black British girl in search for characters to identify with:

> After four-year-old me came to terms with the fact that I would never turn white, I found refuge in white fictional British and American characters that I could relate to. For so long, that fictional heroic character loved by so many has been assumed to be white, because whiteness has been assumed to be universal. It is in film, television and books that we see the most potent manifestations of white as the default assumption. A character simply cannot be black without a pre-warning for an assumed white audience. Black characters are considered to be unrelatable (with the exception of a handful of high-profile, crossover black Hollywood stars).
>
> *(2017: 134–135)*

Eddo-Lodge draws on recent debates about cases in which the notion of white universality in cultural productions became apparent. The 2014 discussion about black British actor Idris Elba as a potential successor of Daniel Craig in playing the next James Bond caused some controversy when a number of commentators including former Bond actor Roger Moore objected to the idea (cf. Eddo-Lodge 2017: 135). In a similar vein, the casting of black British actor John Boyega as a 'stormtrooper' in the recent entries in the *Star Wars* franchise (2015–2019) caused 'a new league of angry people [taking] to social media to call for a boycott of the film, calling it anti-white propaganda. This was because two of the film's heroes were black, and the film's villains were all white' (Eddo-Lodge 2017: 136). The interpretation of the casting of non-white actors as a conspicuous signifying gesture points to a rupture in representational white universality which signals that this universality is far from racially innocent. For the (white) fans of pop-cultural products and franchises, what is at stake in these cases is an emotional investment in the signifying regimes of whiteness in these cultural texts. Consequently, '[w]hen casting for film and TV *does* take the step to cast outside of whiteness, fans repeatedly reveal their ugly side, voicing their upset, disgust, and disappointment. Fear of black characters is fear of a black planet' (Eddo-Lodge 2017: 136). This is merely a selection of recent examples of the ongoing debate about diversity and representation of minority ethnic groups in cultural productions. Yet, the problem of hegemonic whiteness in representational art and its epistemological repercussions goes much deeper. In these examples, cultural representations, and especially those which are beloved as mass popular art, it becomes apparent that the arena of artistic representations of race and whiteness is something like a semiotic battleground on which white hegemony and its epistemology can be reinforced as well as challenged. The 'possessive investment in whiteness' (Lipsitz 2018) is articulated in the cultural arena, and, as Eddo-Lodge concludes, '[w]hite people are so used to seeing a reflection of themselves in all representations of humanity at all times, that they only notice it when it's taken away from them' (Eddo-Lodge 2017: 140).

To see what place is left for non-white subjects in this type of representational regime, Eddo-Lodge's argument can be connected to the theses of Stuart Hall's seminal essay on black art and representation, 'New Ethnicities' (1996). In the representational regimes of hegemonic white cultures, non-white identities are merely accorded the function of 'fetishisation, objectification, and negative figuration which are so much a feature of the representation of the black subject' (Hall 1996: 442). There are, however, also other 'negative figurations', which can, for instance, be found in the figurations of non-hegemonic, or 'tainted' whitenesses (Schmitt 2018a), which are far from invisible: They are hypervisible. Such figurations of hypervisible whiteness serve the normalisation and stabilisation of hegemonic whiteness because they mark the boundary between acceptable and less acceptable racial identities. Identifying such boundary figures is thus a necessary step for dismantling constructions of race and racial hierarchies.

## The figurations approach

The concept of figuration enables us to take into account various spheres and discourses which form the 'social imaginary' (Korte and Zipp 2014: 2) of which racial identities are an integral part. In this concept, no discourse or sphere is privileged over the other. The advantage of the figurations concept over the more conventional concept of representation is that it helps to analyse and theorise the performative aspect of how identities are figured across different spheres and discourses. In other words, a filmic or literary fictional character and their racial identity is not merely an illustration of this particular identity and what it means in the 'real' world, but it is actively shaping and interacting with the wider society. Thus, dominant ideas about certain individuals or communities can be naturalised, but also challenged. Fictional figurations of identities are as much part of the semiotic world of society as everything else. The concept thus helps to organically combine sociological and cultural studies research. I therefore draw on the sociological and anthropological use of figuration by researchers like Imogen Tyler and John Hartigan Jr. as well as on its use by literary scholars such as Korte and Zipp.

According to Korte and Zipp, 'literary texts mould images and imaginations of the world through their specific textual elements and structures' and consequently, a 'figurations approach will thus have to address levels of presentation that concern individual texts as well as their extratextual relations' (Korte and Zipp 2014: 12). This approach to the literary analysis of figurations can be compared to John Hartigan Jr.'s utilisation of the figurations approach for the sociological and anthropological analysis of social types that would usually be described as stereotypes, such as the American 'white trash' Hartigan Jr. focusses on in his research. Hartigan Jr. argues that the concept of figuration has several advantages over stereotypes:

> [F]igures call attention to the way people come to consider their identities in relation to potent images that circulate within a culture. Figuration is a drastic improvement over stereotype in that it captures the active way people subjected to certain debasing images are able to inhabit them in complex ways that involve critique and elaboration.
>
> *(Hartigan Jr. 2005: 16)*

The concept of figuration is thus more organic and versatile when it comes to describing the reciprocal effects of (fictional) representations in the wider society. As I have argued in my own analysis of the literary figurations of (British) white trash, Hartigan Jr.'s approach can be instrumental in bridging the gap between the analysis of sociological phenomena (i.e. the lived and experienced reality of raced identities) and the analysis of the representational and symbolic component of such phenomena in literary, film, or cultural studies (Schmitt 2018a: 51). The advantage of this type of analysis is that it offers ways to understand the interplay of the symbolic and the material. It thus enables the researcher engaging with the figurations approach to study the 'embodied knowledge' of racialised bodies (Levine-Rasky 2019: xii) – figures are on the one hand readable as symbolic representations of racial identities, and at the same time they are the very bodies that live and experience the reality of embodying this particular racial identity. As Castañeda argues, a 'figure [...] is the simultaneously material and semiotic effect of specific practices. Understood as figures, [...] particular categories of existence can also be considered in terms of their uses – what they "body forth" in turn' (Castañeda 2002: 3).

The analysis of figurations can help to deconstruct such epistemologies based on racial dichotomies. The analysis of the power of figures across discursive boundaries and across sociocultural spheres can help to establish new and alternative racial knowledges. Hartigan Jr. suggests that:

> [T]he point of producing racial knowledge is not to assemble it in order to characterize and define a particular group or order – such as whiteness or blackness – but rather to generate it as a basis for comprehending when, how, and if certain dynamics are racial, especially in situations where "race" is not ostensibly present.
>
> *(Hartigan 2005: 286)*

Cultural analysis which is dedicated to the study of artistic and cultural figurations of racial identities can be particularly productive in exploring racial epistemologies when it deals with texts that offer complex and sometimes subversive aesthetic re-negotiations of established epistemological frames. Examples of such challenging cultural texts can for instance be found in those figurations that offer narrative perspectives and focalisations that give voice to identities otherwise rendered marginalised, essentialised, or caricatured, if not plainly absent from the narrative.

In the following, I want to demonstrate how an analysis of figurations of white identities can elucidate the complex intersections of whiteness with other vectors of identity to produce embodied racial knowledges. I will look at two seemingly opposing figurations of whiteness: James Bond as a figuration of universal whiteness (and white masculinity) and figurations of white trash. Both are examples of a differentiation of whiteness that is part of a postracial imaginary of whiteness (cf. Wiegman 1999: 121). According to Robyn Wiegman, the discourse of postrace relies on images of 'liberal whiteness', which can manifest in a 'colour-blind moral sameness', whites as 'soldiers of civil rights' to be found in major US-American films such as *Mississippi Burning* (1988) and *A Time to Kill* (1996), or 'sentimental renderings of cross-racial relations', or 'celebrations of fundamental white male goodness' such as *Forrest Gump* (1994). At the same time, I argue, this 'liberal whiteness' relies on its polar opposite, which is to be found in hypervisible whiteness as it can be found in figurations of racist Southern whites which can also be found as contrast points in many of the cinematic examples listed earlier, such as *A Time to Kill*. I will show how such figurations are instrumental in 'strategic reinventions' of whiteness (Wiegman 1999: 124) and in the process of becoming white (cf. Wiegman 1999: 123).

## Embodied racial knowledge I: James Bond's universal whiteness

When in 2015, media rumors suggested that Idris Elba should be considered for the role of James Bond, a controversy ensued that pointed towards the racial blind spots of the character and its surrounding cultural franchise. The media was quick to consult sources who, by having been associated with the franchise in the past, constituted authorities on what shape the future of James Bond should take. Roger Moore, the actor who had portrayed Bond in a number of films from the 1970s to the 1980s, commented that 'although James has been played by a Scot, a Welshman and an Irishman, I think he should be "English-English"' (qtd. in *The Guardian* 30 Mar 2015). Ignoring the fact that even in Ian Fleming's source novels, Bond has been described as a man of Scottish heritage, Moore's idea of 'English-Englishness', i.e. an Anglo-centric idea of the character, might not explicitly refer to racial features, but by conspicuous omission, it becomes clear that, clearly, a black actor is not considered to be the ideal embodiment of this 'English–English' identity. Another authoritative voice of the franchise, the novelist Anthony Horowitz, was more explicit about the racial aspect. He acknowledged that Elba is a 'terrific actor', but that there would be 'other black actors who would do it better'. Horowitz stressed that 'it's not a colour issue', but that Elba is 'a bit too street' to play James Bond (qtd. in *Daily Mail* 29 Aug 2015). A few years later, actor Joanna Lumley said that the 'casting should be colour-blind', but that Elba did not fit the description of Bond in the novels (qtd. in *The Guardian* 09 May 2017). What all three commentators suggest is that there is a certain kind of cultural 'authenticity' that is at stake in the casting debate and that a particular figuration of James Bond should be preserved. What all comments have in common is that they want to stress that race (or 'colour') is not an issue, but that, clearly, Idris Elba is the 'wrong' kind of black actor to play the character.

In this discourse, whiteness – 'that great unspoken British value' (Hall 1999) – is once more left unsaid. Yet, whiteness looms large in the gaps. The fictional universe of James Bond is firmly situated in a post-imperial era of British history. Ian Fleming wrote his first Bond novels after the Second World War and addressed the great conflict of that time, the Cold War. Over the decades, the franchise has more or less transported this kind of spirit with various inflections. Eldridge Cleaver (1999) addressed the whiteness of James Bond in one of his essays in the 1968 collection *Soul on Ice*, 'The White Race and Its Heroes'. His interpretation of James Bond as one of the 'heroes' of the 'white race' seems to have been validated by the casting debate that took place almost half a century later: 'James Bond, offering the whites a triumphant image of themselves, is saying what many whites want desperately to hear reaffirmed: I am still the White Man, lord of the land, licensed to kill, and the world is still an empire at my feet. James Bond feeds on that secret little anxiety, the psychological white backlash, felt in some degree by most whites alive' (Cleaver 1999: 80). Building on Cleaver's argument, it can be argued that James Bond is the re-affirming figuration of a hyper-whiteness in a post-imperial age that amounts to a 'troubling intersectional cosmopolitanism' (Everett 2020: 197).

A look at one of the early Bond novels by Ian Fleming illustrates Cleaver's observations. In *Live and Let Die* (1954), the second novel in the original series, Bond is required to work with the FBI in the United States. Bond feels uneasy about having to operate in this cultural context because he feels that his embodiment of a British white masculinity will mark him as different and therefore visible in this context:

> Anonymity was the chief tool of his trade. Every thread of his real identity that went on record in any file diminished his value and, ultimately, was a threat to his life. Here in America, where they knew all about him, he felt like a negro whose shadow has been stolen by the witch-doctor. A vital part of himself was in pawn, in the hands of others.
>
> *(Fleming 2012: 2–3)*

Bond feels uneasy about having to work in the United States because he will lose his racial invisibility in an environment that has its own distinct racial and social hierarchies. His racist comparison 'he felt like a negro' signifies the loss of his racial invisibility – he now embodies a marked identity. That is, he loses the very quality associated with his superior male whiteness: The ability to move freely due to his unremarkable whiteness. Instead, he believes to get a glimpse of what it must be like to not be white and to be racially read as a marked body. A racist worldview pervades the whole novel, with Bond's superior M explaining to him his new assignment: To neutralise a black crime lord called 'Mr Big', who 'is probably the most powerful negro criminal in the world' (Fleming 2012: 21). Mr Big is described as 'not pure negro. Born in Haiti. Good dose of French blood. Trained in Moscow' (Fleming 2012: 22), and thus can be read as an embodiment of the fear of racial miscegenation while at the same time matching Bond's own mixed heritage: Fleming is eager to stress Bond's Swiss and Scottish parentage. However, for Bond, this 'mixing' is rendered as an advantage, a universal identity. When thrown into the cultural context of an American metropolis, however, his universality and invisibility is threatened and what Cleaver calls the 'psychological white backlash', that is, the reaction to the white fear of losing cultural hegemony by re-imagining oneself as maintaining dominance, is exposed.

Cleaver described the 1960s as a time when a politically aware white youth increasingly refused celebratory narratives of old white heroes and myths. An epistemological shift was taking place, with many young whites acknowledging complicity with cultural hegemony and demanding an interrogation of historical narratives of colonisation. However, the continued popularity of James Bond signals a backlash to this tendency. This can be seen emerging over the following decades, culminating in the 2015 casting debate. The Bond franchise has over the years performed what, following Robyn Wiegman, could be called 'strategic reinvention[s]' of whiteness (Wiegman 1999: 124). This can, for instance, be seen in the way the source material of the novel *Live and Let Die* was transformed two decades after the novel's publication in the film version (1973, dir. Guy Hamilton). Hamilton's film heavily draws on the iconography and aesthetics of American Blaxploitation films which were popular at the time of release (cf. Everett 2020: 199). The film stages Roger Moore's interpretation of Bond with the black Other in different guises, most prominently in a sequence which sees him entering the strange territory of Harlem, NY – a criminal space which is highly racialised and coded as exotic. Moore's 'considerably less intense and rather campy and flippant enactment of 007' (Everett 2020: 199), here works as an inflection of his hyperwhiteness: In the black environment of Harlem, he becomes hypervisible. It is notable that this film also entails the Bond character's first interracial sex scenes. As Anna Everett has concluded, these scenes are made palatable to contemporary audiences precisely due to Moore's campy embodiment of whiteness – in other words: An interracial encounter like this can only work within the codification as 'comic relief' (Everett 2020: 199). What becomes evident is a flexibilisation of Bond as a figuration of whiteness. Bond's whiteness is here defined through the encounter with black subjects which are rendered exotic and either threatening or sexualised. However, there is another encounter which can be interpreted as a stabilisation of Bond's whiteness in the film: The encounter with a Southern sheriff, played as a 'hillbilly' caricature by Clifton James, including exaggerated dialect, crude performances of masculinity, and tobacco chewing. This grotesque figuration of tainted and therefore hypervisible whiteness in a white space (the rural South) is yet again coded as comic relief and functions as a neutralisation of Bond's earlier hypervisiblity in Harlem. Bond's 'intersectional cosmopolitanism', which 'defines the limits of the Bondian universe' (Everett 2020: 204) is established vis-à-vis the Others that help to create his own differentiated whiteness: The black Other as well as the hyperwhite Other. Both Others are rather static, while they help to shape Bond's flexible figuration of whiteness. The early 1970s, which saw the release of *Live and Let Die* may not yet have been the supposedly postracial time of the 1990s and 2000, but the film's reinvention of Bond's whiteness certainly helped preparing the postracial 'popular imaginary' of whiteness (Wiegman 1999: 121).

However, the 2015 casting debate shows that Bond's whiteness itself is evaded and synonymously expressed in the demands for Bond to remain 'English'. As Anna Everett has pointed out, the reluctance of leading figures associated with the Bond franchise to accept the possibility of a black actor embodying Bond despite a 'transnational fandom advocacy for a black James Bond' (Everett 2020: 188) betrayed the issues at stake in the franchise's relationship with race and nationality. Vron Ware (2001) has described the link between Englishness and whiteness through their shared quality of semantic emptiness, or fleetingness: 'The content of Englishness, like whiteness itself, appears to be of a volatile nature, easily evaporating when put under pressure' (Ware 2001: 192). Thus, 'whiteness is synonymous with Englishness, forthcoming as a hidden, normative code that determines who is in or out on the basis of birth *and* complexion' (Ware 2001: 193). The 'volatile nature' of whiteness and Englishness poses an ontological and an epistemological challenge: How can we know something that seems to be so volatile, yet has such a profound effect on the lived realities and of people and on their perception and experience of the social world? The figurations approach can provide an answer to this question because it is precisely in the form of particular figures that whiteness is embodied even when it is not explicitly named. James Bond is such a figuration. To paraphrase Sara Ahmed (2007), Bond's whiteness cannot be 'faced' – it 'trails behind' his body 'as what is assumed to be given' (Ahmed 2007: 157). And one of the few moments that his whiteness can be realised (or 'faced') is precisely the moment when, to come back to Eddo-Lodge, this whiteness is about to be taken away or replaced by non-whiteness in the representational regime.

## Embodied racial knowledge II: white trash as hypervisible whiteness

The Southern sheriff in *Live and Let Die* points to a significant figuration of excessive whiteness which has gained some attention in what Wiegman has called the 'white trash school' of whiteness studies (Wiegman 1999: 122). Imogen Tyler has demonstrated how this figuration of abject working-class whiteness works in her analysis of the British 'chav', and more precisely, the 'chav mum' (2008). Tyler argues in support of the figurations approach as it 'refuses any binary distinction between the material and the semiotic, signs, and signifying practices are understood as having material effects that shape the appearance of and our experience of others. [...] we should understand mediation not only as representational (in a more structuralist sense) but as a constitutive and generative process. [...] it is through the repetition of a figure across different media that specific figures acquire accreted form and accrue affective value in ways that have significant social and political impact. [...] it is only when a range of different media forms and practices coalesce that these overdetermined figures materialize' (Tyler 2008: 18–19).

For the case of the 'chav mum', this means that a figurations approach accounts for both the fictional representation in, say, the form of the character Vicky Pollard in the sketch show *Little Britain*, and for the concrete social manifestation of such types who are subsequently decoded by the public as embodying this figure's characteristics. Vicky Pollard and the 'chav mum' in general are examples of the intersectional aspects of such figurations. They map out acceptable (ex negativo) and unacceptable performances and embodiments of femininity, sexuality, parenthood, whiteness, class, and (especially in the context of a show called *Little Britain*) nationality. These figurations of tainted whiteness are not exclusively to be found in the US-American white trash or British chavs, but can also be observed in the South-African 'zef' subculture, that is poor white liminal Afrikaans identities which have risen to pop-cultural prominence through musicians and performance artists Die Antwoord (cf. Marx and Milton 2011). The 'chav mum' as well as other figurations of abject working-class whiteness more general thus become what Matt Wray (2006) calls 'stigmatypes' (Wray 2006: 23) – figures which perform 'boundary work' in a culture by symbolically demarcating social and racial distinctions between groups of people. White trash is such a stigmatype because it demarcates the 'boundaries of whiteness' (Wray 2006: 23). These symbolic boundaries of who is and isn't counted as 'properly' white eventually have material effects on the lived reality of the people carrying this stigma. Stigmatyping figures produce a racial and social Other that in turn makes the Self of those who wish to distinguish themselves from the Other knowable. Thus, hierarchies of racial knowledge are established and maintained by stigmatyping figurations. In other words, we can only 'know' what it means to be white by defining it against identities which are perceived as non-white (or, in the case of white trash, not quite white).

This has also repercussions for the academic as well as for the cultural production of knowledge. As Imogen Tyler (2020) has shown in her work on stigma, the seemingly neutral knowledge production by (white) social scientists, for example has often caused the naturalisation of social and racial differences: 'These epistemologies work through producing and classifying human differences in ways which secure particular hierarchies of human value' (Tyler 2020: 114). Similar observations can be made for the cultural arena in which re-presentations and embodiments (i.e. figurations) of whiteness come to mean universal 'truths' while non-whiteness primarily figures as 'Otherness'. Stuart Hall (1999) has described this as 'a negative figuration, as reductive and simplistic' in his observations on the production of knowledge in cultural sites and institutions such as museums and art exhibitions.

The novels of Scottish writer Irvine Welsh, for example demonstrate the potential of negotiating figurations of hypervisible tainted whiteness. The main narrator of his novel *Trainspotting* (1993), Mark Renton, a drug-addicted unemployed young man from Edinburgh, describes himself, his upbringing in the town's Leith district and the entire nation of Scotland as 'a place ay dispossessed white trash in a country fill ay dispossessed white trash. Some say that the Irish are the trash ay Europe. That's shite. It's the Scots. The Irish hud the bottle tae win thir country back, or at least maist ay it' (Welsh 1993: 190). This interior monologue illustrates the novel's main literary and linguistic strategy of centering on the voice which would otherwise be marginalised in the canon of Anglophone literature, authentically rendering its regional and social dialect and thereby offering a satiric exploration of different manifestations of whiteness within Great Britain. In this case, the US-American stigmatype of white trash is appropriated for a self-deprecating auto-description which at the same time offers a historical scope by putting Scotland's tainted whiteness in the context of British imperialism and Anglo-Centric national hegemony. *Trainspotting*'s figuration of the Scottish working class as 'white trash' is in stark contrast to the grandiose figuration of omnipotent whiteness of James Bond who, in *Live and Let Die*, is juxtaposed with the caricature of tainted whiteness in the form of the 'hillbilly' sheriff. Renton's self-naming in *Trainspotting* playfully interrogates the hypervisibility of white trash as the product of Britain's history of colonisation and its class system. Following Jack Halberstam's reading of Renton's speech, his appropriation of a white trash identity as an outcome of Anglo-British imperialism, can be interpreted as a (deliberately) failed performance of whiteness (Halberstam 2011: 91). The narratologist Mieke Bal has argued that the choice of narrative focalisation constitutes a 'political act' (Bal 2009: 145). Consequently, by making Mark Renton, an example of a white trash figuration, the main focaliser rather than have him be focalised by another narrative agent, Welsh's novel deconstructs the privileged gaze of a hegemonic, invisible whiteness and offers a counter-narrative that destabilises notions of normative whiteness as a naturalised identity position.

In juxtaposition, the discussed figurations of whiteness demonstrate that, together, they map out a racial imaginary within which whiteness is differentiated within epistemological frames which are established precisely in the form of these cultural figurations. We 'know' James Bond's whiteness (and its intersections with gender, class, and national identity) through his confrontation with his Others. Societies structured in white hegemony also 'know' non-white identities through their juxtaposition with acceptable hegemonic whiteness or proximity to less acceptable whiteness. This became evident, for instance when British historian David Starkey commented on the young people partaking in the 2011 London Riots that 'the whites have become black'. According to Starkey's racist interpretation of the riots, the 'chavs' had 'become black' by identifying with 'black gangster culture' (cf. Schmitt 2018b). This has repercussions for the universalisation of certain forms of whiteness. The paradoxical effect of this universalisation of 'accepted' forms of white identity versus their 'unacceptable' Others is, however, that it shores up whiteness at the same time as it differentiates it in its multiplicity. Seemingly multidimensional racial identities are thus being flattened and limited in what is an acceptable performance of such an identity. However, the process of figuration is never entirely final, and offers potential entry points for re-claiming identities, as the example of *Trainspotting* demonstrates. Renton's failure of performing an acceptable white identity is embraced as an opportunity to interrogate forms of whiteness that are associated with nationalism, imperialism and middle-class norms of economic productivity. Thus, the cultural arena demonstrates the potential to offer non-normative racial epistemologies. Rather than fixed frames and representations, figurations can illuminate the processes of 'becoming white' (Wiegman 1999: 123).

## References

Aanerud, R. 1997. Fictions of Whiteness: Speaking the Names of Whiteness in U.S. Literature. In *Displacing Whiteness: Essay in Social and Cultural Criticism*, ed. R. Frankenberg, pp. 35–59. Durham: Duke University Press.

Ahmed, S. 2007. A Phenomenology of Whiteness. *Feminist Theory*, 8 (2): 149–168. DOI: 10.1177/1464 700107078139.

Bailey, M., Clarke, B. and Walton, J. K. 2012. *Understanding Richard Hoggart: A Pedagogy of Hope*. Chichester: Wiley-Blackwell.

Bal, M. 2009. *Narratology: Introduction to the Theory of Narrative*, 3rd edn. Toronto: University of Toronto Press.

Castañeda, C. 2002. *Figurations: Child, Bodies, Worlds*. Durham, NC: Duke University Press.

Child, B. 2015. 'Roger Moore denies racist comments about Idris Elba playing James Bond', *The Guardian Online*, 30 Mar 2015, viewed 31 July 2020, https://www.theguardian.com/film/2015/mar/30/roger-moore-denies-racist-comments-about-idris-elba-playing-james-bond.

Cleaver, E. 1999. *Soul on Ice*. Reprint. New York: Delta.

Dyer, R. 1997. *White*. London: Routledge.

Eddo-Lodge, R. 2017. *Why I'm No Longer Talking to White People About Race*. London: Bloomsbury.

Everett, A. 2020. Shaken, Not Stirred Britishness: James Bond, Race, and the Transnational Imaginary. In *The Cultural Life of James Bond: Spectres of 007*, ed. J. Verheul, pp. 187–206. Amsterdam: Amsterdam University Press.

Fleming, I. 2012. *Live and Let Die*. London: Vintage.

Frankenberg, R. 1993. *White Women, Race Matters: The Social Construction of Whiteness*. Minneapolis: University of Minnesota Press.

Halberstam, J. 2011. *The Queer Art of Failure*. Durham, NC: Duke University Press.

Hall, S. 1996. New Ethnicities. In *Stuart Hall: Critical Dialogues in Cultural Studies*, ed. D. Morley and K.-H. Chen, pp. 441–449. London: Routledge.

Hall, S. 1999. 'Whose heritage? un-settling "The Heritage", re-imagining the post-nation', *Reading the periphery.org*, n.d., viewed 31 July 2020, http://readingtheperiphery.org/hall2/.

Hartigan Jr., J. 2005. *Odd Tribes: Toward a Cultural Analysis of White People*. Durham, NC: Duke University Press.

Hoggart, R. 1971. *Speaking to Each Other II: About Literature*. London: Chatto and Windus.

Korte, B. and Zipp, G. 2014. *Poverty in Contemporary Literature: Themes and Figurations on the British Book Market*. Houndsmills/Basingstoke: Palgrave.

Levine-Rasky, C. 2019. Foreword. In *The Intersections of Whiteness*, ed. E. Kindinger and M. Schmitt, pp. 11–22. London: Routledge.

Lipsitz, G. 2018. *The Possessive Investment in Whiteness: How White People Profit from Identity Politics*. Philadelphia: Temple University Press.

Marx, H. and Milton, V. C. 2011. Bastardised Whiteness: 'Zef'-Culture, *Die Antwoord* and the Reconfiguration of Contemporary Afrikaans Identities. *Social Identities*, 17 (6): 723–745.

Moreton, C. 2015. '"This is something I have wanted to do all my life": James Bond is back with Pussy Galore for a steamy sequel to Goldfinger… Anthony Horowitz on his dazzling 007 debut Trigger Mortis', *Daily Mail Online*, 29 August, viewed 31 July 2020, https://www.dailymail.co.uk/home/event/article-3212827/James-Bond-new-book-Trigger-Mortis-written-Anthony-Horowitz-wanted-life.html.

Morrison, T. 1992. *Playing in the Dark: Whiteness and the Literary Imagination*. Cambridge, MA: Harvard University Press.

Schmitt, M. 2018a. *British White Trash: Figurations of Tainted Whiteness in the Novels of Irvine Welsh, Niall Griffiths and John King*. Bielefeld: Transcript.

Schmitt, M. 2018b. The Whites Have Become Black': Plan B's and George Amponsah's Representations of the 2011 English Riots and the Echoes of Stuart Hall's 'New Ethnicities. *Coils of the Serpent: Journal for the Study of Contemporary Power*, 3: 43–61.

The Guardian. 2017. 'Joanna Lumley: Idris Elba should not play James Bond as he doesn't fit description', *The Guardian Online*, 9 May, viewed 31 July 2020, https://www.theguardian.com/film/2017/may/09/idris-elba-james-bond-joanna-lumley-colour-blind-casting.

Tyler, I. 2008. Chav Mum Chav Scum. *Feminist Media Studies*, 8 (1) 17–34.

Tyler, I. 2013. *Revolting Subjects. Social Abjection and Resistance in Neoliberal Britain*. London: Zed.

Tyler, I. 2020. *Stigma. The Machinery of Inequality*. London: Zed.

Ware, V. 2001. Perfidious Albion: Whiteness and the International Imagination. In *The Making and Unmaking of Whiteness*, ed. B. B. Rasmussen et al., pp. 184–213. Durham, NC: Duke University Press.

Welsh, I. 1993. *Trainspotting*. London: Vintage.

Wiegman, R. 1999. Whiteness Studies and the Paradox of Particularity. *Boundary 2*, 26 (3) 115–150.

Wray, M. 2006. *Not Quite White: White Trash and the Boundaries of Whiteness*. Durham, NC: Duke University Press.

# Part II

# Conspiracies: Ideologies reinforcing whiteness

As whiteness draws on normative centres of power, such as patriarchal masculinity and heteronormativity, it also draws on kindred ideologies with correspondingly oppressive aims to reinforce itself. Drawing on epistemologies, ideologies work as political frames to produce systematised outcomes of differential identity-based access to life-giving resources. In other words, ideologies find succour in whiteness as knowledge construction and source of identity in their competitive quests to gain traction and attract adherents. Interrogating these conjunctions between ideologies and whiteness contributes to understanding the durability of racism and white supremacism as ideologies in themselves. In this section, the ideologies under scrutiny are nationalism, antifeminism, neo-fascism, postfeminism, liberalism, socialism, and Zionism. In the name of nationalism, with its exultation of an imagined community at the expense of constructed others, humans have instituted some of the most devastating systems of dehumanisation. The analyses on nationalism confirm how whiteness can be operationalised by subjects not racialised as white, and by subjects formerly regarded as of a 'degraded' whiteness. Exploring nationalist forms of identification further, the contributions also show how white reaction mobilises neo-fascism and nationalism in attempts to roll back the substantial gains of feminism. Even postfeminism's partial inclusion of acceptable racial, gendered, and sexual others transpires to be an affront to newly forceful and masculinist whiteness. In the opening chapter, Sitara Thobani invokes Fanonian analysis to argue that colonised people, in a psycho-affective attachment to whiteness, can reproduce the global logic of differentiating between racialised subjects in ways that reproduce white hegemony. Hence, in a twist of historical irony, Trumpist white nationalism in the United States finds an unexpected boon in resurgent Hindu nationalism in India. The Hindu diaspora's identification with the Trumpist white nation serves to legitimise ultranationalist claims to Hindu superiority in India. In the next contribution, Ashley A Mattheis examines how anti-feminism rears its head as part of the revival of fascism across Europe and in settler states ranging from the United States to Australia. Confirming the concurrence of (neo)liberal rationality with heteropatriarchal whiteness, antifeminism draws on systemic racist and patriarchal cultures in liberal democracies to appeal to women to return to a nostalgically framed utopic reproductive function that reinstalls whiteness as superior. Moving to postfeminism in contention with white supremacist nationalism, Kendra Marston in her chapter discusses the reactivation of the British royal family as the sign of the compulsory whiteness

DOI: 10.4324/9780429355769-102

of Britishness. Megan Markle as latest addition to the British royals serves as embodiment of postfeminist and neoliberal selective incorporation of racialised and gendered others, to which white supremacist nationalism reacts with racist and sexist discourses of expulsion. Liberalism's complicity with colonial and present-day racisms is explored in the next chapter. Mandisi Majavu finds that both liberalism and socialism in the South African context, despite professing 'non-racialism' and anti-capitalism, reasserted white people's authority over black people. He shows the historical imbrication of these ideologies with a racial paternalism which, in accordance with the themes of this handbook, normalises a positioning of white people as 'saviours' of black people while leaving whiteness undisturbed. At the confluence of colonialism and nationalism sits Zionism as a contradictory contemporary expression of European identification combined with ethnic and religious particularism. Ilan Pappé's chapter brings the critical study of whiteness to Zionism as the nationalism foundational to the state of Israel. Whiteness justified the secularisation of the Jewish identity – its shift from a religious to a national identity – and enabled the colonisation of a land occupied by racialised others, the Palestinians. As Zionism became hegemonic, the racialisation of native Palestinians, Arab Jews, and Africans was institutionalised.

# Trans/nationalist convergences: Hindu nationalism, Trump's America and the many shades of whiteness

*Sitara Thobani*

Shortly after securing the largest political majority in the history of independent India and thus winning his re-election in May 2019, Prime Minister Narendra Modi was greeted by some 50,000 Indian Americans at the 'Howdy Modi' Rally in Houston, Texas. This was not the first spectacle of diasporic zeal, dubbed 'Modi-mania', organised to honour the Hindu Nationalist Prime Minister; Modi had earlier appeared at New York's Madison Square Gardens in 2014, followed by similar events at Wembley Arena in London, England, and the Ricoh Coliseum in Toronto, Canada, to name a few. What made the Houston rally particularly noteworthy, however, was the presence of an equally nationalist and polarising president, Donald Trump of the United States. While Trump's history of holding sensationalist political spectacles, tailored mostly to white supremacist audiences and their sympathisers, is well known, what is less well known is that he too, every once in a while, catered to the Indian (national and diasporic) fans of his Indian counterpart.

Indeed, the largest rally Trump is believed to have ever addressed was at the Motera Cricket Stadium in Modi's home state of Gujarat (also the site of the infamous 2002 anti-Muslim pogroms), where 'Howdy Modi' was reciprocated with 'Namaste Trump' just five months after the two state leaders joined hands (quite literally) in Houston. While 110,000 people gathered in the cricket stadium to welcome Trump to Gujarat (with some diasporic rally-goers even traveling from the United States to do so), and another 100,000 lined the streets outside to greet the Presidential motorcade (Kumar 2020), anti-Muslim violence was erupting in the Indian capital following the introduction of the discriminatory National Registry and Citizenship Rights Act that together threatened the rights to citizenship (and by extension, the security and national belonging) of India's Muslim minority. More than just a PR stunt to promote US-India relations, Namaste Trump had the air of yet another American campaign rally for the President, featuring as it did criticism of mainstream (US) journalism, praise for Fox News, and even the soundtrack for Trump's stateside campaign (Kumar 2020). Thus oriented towards the political landscape in the United States, the rally in Gujarat also acted as an extension of Trump's attempts to court conservative Hindu support in the diaspora, the most notable example of which was the 'Humanity United Against Terror' (aka Hindus for Trump) 'charity' concert in

Edison, New Jersey, organised for the then Presidential Candidate by the Republican Hindu Coalition.

The relationship forged between the two distinct nationalist projects represented in Houston and symbiotically conjoined by segments of the diaspora – namely the Hindu nationalism of the Indian Prime Minister and the white nationalism of the US President – raises questions about the realignment of particular racial identities in a moment of escalation in ultraconservative and xenophobic politics globally. Tracing the work accomplished by a somewhat small but nevertheless powerful segment of the Indian diaspora can therefore reveal the productive nexus that exists between racialised subjects and the logic of whiteness, a relationship forged in the context of coloniality. Just as whiteness has shifted historically, so too has its alignments with other racialised subjectivities.

Addressing this history of racialisation and the violence that underpins it, Fanon (1986 [1952]) argued that race is organised through a hierarchical order produced in the crucible of colonialism. This order forced the colonised into fixed categories and asymmetrical relations that were normalised through the all-encompassing colonial project that fundamentally altered their languages, cultures, and histories (see also Fanon 2004 [1963]). Presenting itself as the natural order of things, this totalising taxonomoy gave rise to a psycho-affective affiliation with whiteness among colonised populations as the racialised subject internalised the logic of the very racial order into which they were fixed. Not only does this order promote racist attitudes towards Black and other colonised peoples on the lower rungs of the scale, but it also engenders a desire towards Europe – and white people and culture more generally – that continues to hold the colonised subject in its sway. Partaking in the 'same collective unconscious as the European', the colonised thus 'relives the same fantasies as a European' (Fanon 1986 [1952]: 191).

The construction of race (and through race, whiteness) is, in this analysis, both global and relational for the colonised subject, according to Fanon, 'does not compare himself with the white man qua father, leader, God; he compares himself with his fellow against the pattern of the white man' (Fanon 1986 [1952]: 215). It is with this point in mind that I historicise the different ways in which particular racialised subjects – segments of the Indian American community, in this case – have contributed to the construction of whiteness in the United States, and indeed continue to do so in the present. Crucially, as members of the diaspora, these actors weave together the history of colonialism in India with that of their resettlement in the United States. In other words, these subjects embody the very history of colonial racialisation and its extension into the transnational present. Focus on these subjects is therefore revealing of the ways in which contemporary race relations subtend the racial logic of coloniality in the contemporary context.

Whether through the bid to secure the rights of American citizenship in the early twentieth century discussed in the following section, or in the perpetuation of the scripted discourse of the model minority in the twenty-first century analysed in subsequent sections, these actors actively differentiate between various racialised subjectivities in ways that uphold the structures and perspectives of hegemonic whiteness. However, my focus on an ultraconservative segment of this diaspora – that is, on those members who openly profess their alignment with the supremacist politics of Hindu nationalism – further illustrates the complexities of the relationship between these racialised subjects and the whiteness to which they attempt to claim proximity. The global scope of the Hindu nationalist project, born in conversation with the colonial construction of race and now advanced in the transnational arena despite its territorial commitments in India, mediates the investments of these diasporic actors in the domestic politics of the United States. On the one hand, this orientation enables them to engage with US politics without threatening the racial order of the nation, to the benefit of white supremacy. On the other hand, as I also show here, this orientation further enables these diasporic actors to re-conceive whiteness through the claims they make to the physical space of the United States, thereby annexing this space to the global Hindutva landscape. Two distinct nationalist projects are perfected as a result in this convergence of interests.

## Race, religion, nationality: The many identities of the Hindu diaspora

Differentiated by religion, language, regional culture, caste, and class – not to mention patterns of multiple migration – the constitution of the Indian-American diaspora is indeed complex and deeply politicised (see Bhalla 2006, for example). Migrating from the post/colonial context of India, with its particular history of racial formation shaped by British rule, to the settler colonial context of the United States, where the history of slavery, the one-drop rule, and Jim Crow led to the construction of a racial binary calibrated to the opposition of white and Black,[1] and codified by law (Harris 1993), the racialised positioning of Indian-Americans has been far from fixed. Taking the colonies as the laboratory from which to study the supposed history and diversity of 'human evolution', Orientalist scholarship and pseudo-scientific studies of race established a precedent for the later designation of Indians as Caucasians (Bhatt 2001). According to these theories, Indo-European linguistic affinity was taken as evidence of a common ancestry Indians and Europeans supposedly shared, the embodiment of which was the imagined figure of the Aryan (Figueira 2002). Hence, a linguistic category was transformed into a racial one as European scholars projected onto the historical record their own colour-based ideas about race (Thapar 1993). However, the logical extension of this designation did not (unsurprisingly) lead to Indians being viewed as on par with Europeans; rather it was argued that, following ideas of social Darwinism, Indian 'Aryans' (as opposed to those who migrated to Europe) were a 'racial disgrace' and 'miserable bastards' due to their 'racial' miscegenation with other 'indigenous' peoples of the subcontinent (Koshy 1998: 297). Even when coupled with Europe through the hyphenated term Indo-European, the racial status of the Indian was tenuous at best.

Theories linking Indian civilisation to Aryan origins found rearticulation in the United States, indicating the powerful reach of colonial discourse beyond the colony and imperial metropole. Given that citizenship in the United States was extended only to those deemed 'white' (an arguably ambiguous but no less exclusionary category) or 'Black' (interpreted as 'aliens of African nativity and ... persons of African descent' [*United States vs. Bhagat Singh Thind* 1923]), migrants from the subcontinent, like those from elsewhere in Asia, had first to locate themselves within this racial binary before petitioning their bids for citizenship. The fact that South Asians, with one exception in 1970 (Koshy 1998: 286), did so by attempting to justify their inclusion into the category 'white' is often taken as evidence for their desire to distinguish themselves as racially superior. However, when read within their specific historical context, these bids for citizenship were clearly much more complex. Asian appellants seeking the rights of US citizenship had no choice, *by virtue of this very objective*, but to work within the legal framework and governing institutions that had already defined citizenship in racial terms (López 1996). Thus, rather than simply identify as white from the beginning (an identification that was foreclosed to them by the colonial-global construction of race), these subjects had to adopt the racial logic of the US legal system to make intelligible their claims. In doing so however, they nevertheless further reified the racial binary of the state through the very challenges they made to its exclusions.

The difficulties and contradictions of this racial logic are apparent in the oft cited 1923 case of Bhagat Singh Thind, a First World War veteran of the US Army who, after his initial success in becoming a naturalised citizen, was stripped of this status by the Supreme Court. Delivering the opinion of the court, Justice Sutherland displayed the legal acrobatics required to define race-based citizenship at a time when the very construction of race (and whiteness) as scientifically verifiable was under debate. Citing precedent established in the case of Ozawa vs. United States from the previous year, the Justice argued that 'the provision is not that any particular class of persons shall be excluded [from naturalisation], but it is, in effect, that only white people shall be included within the privilege of the statue' (*United States vs. Bhagat Singh Thind* 1923). The problem, as it appeared to the Court, was that the conventional (ahistorical) term 'Caucasian' was much too flexible, and not a neat synonym for whiteness as generally understood. 'It may be true that the blond Scandinavian and the brown Hindu have a common ancestor in the dim reaches of antiquity', explained the Justice referring to the theory of Aryan origins, 'but the average man knows perfectly well that there are unmistakable and profound differences between them today …' (*United States vs. Bhagat Singh Thind* 1923). Even the logic extending from the theory of shared Indo-European languages was called into question as it was argued that linguistic affinity was insufficient for racial fellowship. For, in the eyes of the Court, '[o]ur own history has witnessed the adoption of the English tongue by millions of negroes, whose descendants can never be classified racially with the descendants of white persons, notwithstanding both may speak a common root language' (ibid). Unlike language which could be cultivated, or place of origin which could be circumstantial, race was clearly imagined to be corporeal and hence unequivocal. With the differences between whiteness and blackness clearly demarcated, the racial positioning of the 'brown' subject was coming into sharper relief.

Reading this history of US immigration law and its placement of Asian subjects in American racial taxonomies, it becomes clear that the issue of the 'brown' Indian – like the Asian immigrant more generally (see Lowe 1996) – was more than just a question of determining whether they were assimilable (potential insiders) or alien (perpetual outsiders) to the nation. In a context in which citizenship was inextricably linked to white racial identity, the rights of the citizen in the abstract are more accurately viewed as instruments through which the asymmetrical racial boundaries of the nation are secured, as well as through which the nation itself finds its place in the global racial order. For, in upholding the whiteness of American citizenship, the courts were not only securing the internal racial borders of the state, but situating the United States within a global framework of whiteness. Denying inclusion to the racialised immigrant, the identity of the United States was confirmed to be white.

Equally significant, although somewhat overlooked in analyses of United States vs. Bhagat Singh Thind, is the extent to which the state operated on the parallel register of religion in addition to that of race in their reification of the Indian immigrant's identity. For, at the very centre of the case was the question of whether 'a *high-caste Hindu, of full Indian blood*, born at Amritsar, Punjab, India, [is] a white person within the meaning of § 2169, Revised Statutes' (*United States vs. Bhagat Singh Thind* 1923, emphasis added). Putting aside the fact that Thind was Sikh and not Hindu, this designation is striking for the way in which it racialises a religious identity which is then operationalised to function as a national category. In classifying turn-of-the-century migrants from India as 'Hindu', governmental agencies, along with the press and popular discourse more generally, drew on long-standing colonial ideas in which the figure of the Hindu/Hindoo (or more accurately, the Indian who was classified as 'Hindu/Hindoo') signified heathenistic idolatry and racial-cultural alterity (Koshy 1998: 302), as well as a sense of exotic intrigue and allure. Crucial to the discussion at hand and to which I now turn, such forms of interpellation, advanced through US legal precedent as well as in American popular culture more generally, served to legitimise (however inadvertently) the problematic equation of 'Indian' with 'Hindu' that lies at the heart of Hindu nationalist politics.

It is at this particular juncture that a discussion, albeit brief, of the development of a politicised 'Hindu' identity in the Indian context becomes significant. By Hindu I do not refer to the diversity of people who identify as followers of Hinduism, the amalgamation of myriad traditions, customs, and belief systems with its own history of development as a 'religion' (see King 1999). Instead my focus is on that specific identity produced through the work of certain nineteenth- and twentieth-century political activists and their adherents who sought to define the category Hindu in staunchly nationalistic terms. The earliest articulation of Hindu nationalist ideology in the late nineteenth and early twentieth centuries cannot be separated from the racial-colonial context in which it emerged, and drew heavily from European Orientalists. For these early ideologues, the alleged common origins of the Indo-Europeans were interpreted to suggest that Hindus were the first race and dispersed at one point to dominate the entire world (Jaffrelot 1998: 332). These ideas were refined by later activists, including V.D. Savarkar and M.S. Golwalkar, whose work gave form to the Hindu nationalism that underpins present day Hindutva politics; these later ideologues and their contemporary co-nationalists also professed admiration for European fascism (1998: 335–337), suggesting once more the global contours of their nationalist politics.

In short, Hindu nationalist ideology claims a privileged autochthonous status for Hindus in India, thereby equating the idea of an essentialist Hinduness (Hindutva) with a sense of national-cultural Indianness to the exclusion of religious minorities (specifically those whose religions cannot be appropriated as offshoots of Hinduism). Of these minorities, Muslims are characterised as posing the greatest existential threat to the Indian nation, historically and at present. Such an orientation complicates the idea of secularism, enshrined in the Indian Constitution, for the category Hindu is able to slip between religious and cultural registers, demarcating the limits of national inclusion and exclusion in both realms without being fixed in either. The various manifestations of the category Hindu in multiple registers also affords Hindutva ideals greater mobility, for despite its focus on defining the territory that is India in Hindu terms, this ideology continues to garner extensive support in the diaspora as well (see Bhatt and Mukta 2000; Burlet 2001; Zavos 2010).

These multiple and intertwined historical strands, from US immigration policies and citizenship law to the development of Hindu nationalist ideology, are encoded in contemporary invocations of a 'Hindu American' – as opposed to an Indian American – identity. Indeed, despite the shifts and contestations that have shaped the ways in which members of the Indian diaspora have – and have been – identified over the last century, the pointed use of the designation 'Hindu' among certain segments of this diaspora in the present nevertheless has the potential to calcify the nationalist vision of a Hindu nation from afar. In other words, the appellation Hindu American is noteworthy precisely because it now signifies an ideological affinity with, and political investment in, the Hindu nationalist project from outside the territorial context of the Indian nation while simultaneously positioning the diasporic subject in relation to the politics of US racial formations. As I now turn to discuss in the following sections, this designation is poised to advance Hindu supremacy while simultaneously upholding the global racial order that sustains the power of whiteness in the transnational present.

## Hindus for Trump and the business of whiteness

On the website of the Republican Hindu Coalition (RHC n.d.), the organisation claims that 'Hindu Americans in the United States come from many countries, principally India but also include Hindus from Nepal, Sri Lankan [sic], Caribbean, Indonesia, Bangladesh, New Zealand, Australia, Africa, and various parts of Europe. Additionally, Hindus include all faiths like Sikhs,

Jains, and Buddhists that were born in India'. Privileging India as both the principal homeland of Hindus, as well as the originary land of Hinduism and the other faiths it is (problematically) said to encompass, this claim enacts a key principle of Hindutva philosophy. However, the politics of the subcontinent is not the only site towards which the RHC orients itself, for this organisation also claims to have worked closely with the Trump Administration to represent Hindu American interests, and identifies as Honorary Co-Chairs figures such as Steve Bannon and Newt Gingrich. Moreover, the RHC actively campaigned for Trump during the Republican Primaries as well as the 2016 General Elections, despite the fact that the vast majority of Indian Americans tend to vote for the Democratic Party (Ramakrishnan et al. 2017). The RHC founder also reportedly pledged to raise $25 million to contribute to the infamous border wall (Kumar 2019), calls for which buoyed the Trump Campaign and remained a key policy item on the President's agenda throughout his tenure. In short, the RHC and its affiliate organisations (such as the American Hindu Coalition and Hindus for Trump) have taken an active role in advancing the white supremacy of this xenophobic Administration as much as they remain committed to furthering their Hindutva ideals in India and beyond (see Thobani, 2019).

In addition to representing the Indian nation as staunchly Hindu, the RHC also positions itself to represent 'Hindu Americans' as exemplary US citizens. For example, elsewhere on their website, the organisation boasts about the status of the 'Hindu Demographic' in the United States:

> [The] US has 4.2 million Hindu Americans with [sic] highest per capita income of any other group in the country. We have the highest education, highest proportion of managers, highest number of entrepreneurs (one out of ten), highest donations to charity and least dependence on government. Hindu Americans pay almost 50 billion dollars per year in total taxes.
>
> *(RHC n.d.)*

This statement is followed by various substantiating claims meant to present the Hindu American community as *the* model minority. Hindu Americans are described as sizable in number ('almost the same as [the] Jewish American population' (ibid)); the most highly educated ('67% have Bachelor's degree [sic] or more as compared to [sic] 28% nationally' (ibid)); the most respectably employed ('57.7% in professional or managerial jobs' (ibid)); and incredibly productive in their contributions to the US economy ('We are the nexus of small businesses that create more than 80% of all jobs in US [sic]' (ibid)).

Born of the anti-Black racism of the Moynihan Report[2] as well as the need to manage the shifting racial terrain in the wake of the civil rights movement of the 1960s, not to mention the need to atone for the history of anti-Asian racism and the Japanese-American internment in the United States, the model minority myth casts certain, particularly Asian origin, communities within the US racial hierarchy as exemplary due to their supposed 'good' attributes, including their presumed tight-knit family values, academic proclivity, and economic industriousness. However, as scholars have long pointed out (see Ball 2019), this mythology is problematic as it continues to mark Asian Americans as homogenous, shaped by cultural alterity (even if positively), and therefore as perpetual strangers to the US nation. This mythology further renders invisible the very real structural inequalities within and among Asian American communities, and maintains the status quo of the American racial hierarchy by pitting racialised communities against one another. Even more crucially perhaps, the mythology of the model minority serves as evidence of another myth, that of American exceptionalism, for the United States is presented as providing the conditions of possibility said to enable the successes these model immigrants and their descendants are able to achieve.

Given the ideological investment in the contemporary nationalist politics of Hindutva, politics that help consolidate the identities of a global Hindu community that actively ties itself to the Indian/Hindu homeland, the RHC and its cognates are perfectly situated to simultaneously advance this logic of US exceptionalism at a transnational level. Their ideological commitment to defining India in Hindu terms, and their narratives of Hindu supremacy in global terms, means that these diasporic nationalists have little investment in challenging the racism of the US state by asserting their rights to unequivocal national belonging as Americans. No longer caught in the struggle for citizenship due to the currency their economic privilege affords them in the globalised present, these diasporic subjects nevertheless serve a vital function in the demarcation of the boundaries of American whiteness as manifested via the Alt-Right and America First agendas that undergirded the Trump presidency. For their activities not only leave unquestioned the constitution of the US nation-state as internally cohesive and intrinsically white, they actually validate the specific politics of race woven into the very fabric of the United States, be it through their calls to secure the nation's borders against illegal immigrants or, as I also discuss further in the next section, their demarcation of the nation's presumed enemies. Take for example the following description, written by the RHC founder in the alt-right publication Breitbart:

> A deepened relationship between the US and India is already advancing the war against Islamic extremism by leaps and bounds. India is literally on the front line of the defence of freedom; it shares a 1,800-mile border with Pakistan, a nuclear weapons nation and one of the world's leading state sponsors of terrorism. (By contrast, the Texas-Mexico border is roughly 1,255 miles).
>
> *(Kumar 2017)*

The alleged affinity between Hindus and (white) Americans on which this rhetoric is predicated runs deeper than a set of shared interests or the identification of a common (in this case, Muslim) enemy; this affinity shapes the very constitution of the multiple political ideologies and national identities that are being deployed. Moving beyond the simple designation of 'Islamic extremism' as a threat supposedly shared by India and the United States, the statement stands out for its appeal to one of the most powerful tropes of the Trump campaign and presidency – the border. Coupled here with the border between Mexico and the United States, this reference to the *Indo-Pakistan border* presents it as a perfect corollary to US concerns regarding its own national boundaries, compounding US racial anxieties of 'illegal' immigration with the Islamophobic fear of 'extremist violence' in South Asia. The geographies of India and the United States are effectively made symbolically synonymous, metaphorically mapped onto one another via concerns to secure their (different) territorial boundaries. Not only does such seamless employment of Hindutva ideology and conservative white nationalism effectively legitimise the one through the other, it enables the Hindu nationalist to lay claim to the white nationalist space of the United States while simultaneously protecting the very whiteness of that space. The result is the perfection of Hindutva on the global stage through the very activities that legitimise the isolationist xenophobia associated with white nationalism in the United States. As I now turn to discuss, this perfection is also made possible by diasporic Hindu nationalists at the allegedly progressive end of the political spectrum.

## Hindus not for Trump and the model critique of the model minority

As the protests that erupted across the United States in the Summer of 2020 once again brought attention to the social, economic, and physical – not to mention fatal – violence that continues to be trained on the lives of Black Americans, various segments across the country – ranging from the corporate to the individual – rushed to profess solidarity with Black Lives Matter. Occurring during a global pandemic that revealed the fault lines of a society in which Black and Brown people are disproportionately impacted, these events propelled the issue of structural and systemic racism to the forefront of mainstream (acceptable) discourse. The protests and the racist violence they highlighted also led to an upswell of debates about racism in the United States and elsewhere within other communities of colour, most notably perhaps, among Indian Americans. Often public, these discussions were characterised by calls from and for members of these communities to interrogate their own forms of anti-Black racism, drawing on progressive concepts and the discourse of social justice.

As crucial a task as this call to challenge anti-Black racism is, the terms in which the debate was framed were nevertheless circumscribed by the global order of race I am tracing here. As such, these debates carried in their very articulation the potential to once again align with and uphold supremacist discourses in multiple registers. To elaborate this point, allow me to turn to the example of an article calling on 'Indian Hindu Americans to talk about Black Lives Matter' (Viswanathan 2020), published on *Medium*, an online platform that aims to bring together public thinkers, academics, and experts to foster critical dialogue. In it, the author – who identifies as a Democrat who would never cast a vote for Donald Trump – challenges her fellow Hindu Americans to forsake 'the broad assumption that anything associated with the *left* is necessarily anti-Hindu', claiming such a position will ultimately 'end up harming Hindus' (Viswanathan 2020). Instead, Hindu Americans should show solidarity with the Black Lives Matter movement, and put aside their concern 'that the very real threats facing India do not appear in these American protests or in the anti-racist paradigm of its protestors' (Viswanathan 2020). In this manner, the author advances the Hindu nationalist contention that Hindus face an existential threat in India, thereby revealing an ideological investment in Hindutva despite her identification with the political 'left'. This investment is made even clearer further in the article.

For example, the author draws on ideas of territory in ways that carry deep resonance with the Hindu nationalist relationship to land (*bhoomi*) in the Indian context. Situating the diasporic readers she addresses in a global Hindu nationalist landscape, she argues that:

> [W]hen you moved to the United States, this also became your Karma Bhoomi. The karma and history of this land impact you and your descendants. This is an important moment for us to ask ourselves individually and as a community what it means to be dharmic ['religiously' dutiful] for this land, which has a different karma, a different history.
>
> *(Viswanathan 2020, emphasis in original)*

Although allowing room for the history of genocidal violence on which the United States was founded, and to which the author refers in the article to a certain extent, the framing of US territory as the Hindu diasporic subject's *karma bhoomi* (land of one's karma, the force produced by one's actions) cannot help but recall the construction of India as *pitra bhoomi* (father land) and *punya bhoomi* (holy land) on which rest the foundations of Hindutva politics and its criteria of belonging (see Bakhle 2010: 154). The physicality of Indian territory – the *bhoomi* of the Hindus in the nationalist imaginary – is here exchanged in the abstract with the diaspora's relationship to its country of residence, thereby grounding Hindu nationalist ideals in the cartography of material life in the United States. Such a gesture enables the Hindu nationalist to lay claim to the physical space of the United States in ways that go above and beyond the boundaries of the American nation state, incorporating it into the global geography of Hindutva supremacy.

The appeal to Hindu nationalist ideals is not only made implicitly in the article, as in the above example, but in very explicit terms as well. Imploring her reader to not equate anti-Black racism and police brutality in the United States with contemporary state violence against Muslims in India, the author nonetheless draws on the presumed injury of Hindu history being 'misrepresented' in Indian and American textbooks in order to draw correlation with and elicit empathy for African-Americans, whose history has been 'similarly' obscured.[3] The contention that Hindus and Hinduism have been misrepresented in Indian history – be this history written by European colonialists or Indian secularists – is, of course, another issue of contention within contemporary Hindutva discourse and thus speaks volumes here. Building on this point, the author calls on Hindu Americans to educate themselves about systemic racism, albeit to pointedly Indian nationalistic ends:

> The more you learn about systemic racism, the more you can intelligently, dharmically, and powerfully unmask the false comparisons made by anti-Hindu forces about India. Instead of perpetuating the false correlation between India and the United States by saying 'if this was happening in India', call out how black American history is being unethically mined for anti-Hindu ends in India. Instead of downplaying African American history by reducing what is happening to one death or 'hurt sentiments', call out the egregious conflation that 'Muslims are the black people of India'. We are well positioned to point out the intellectual dishonesty in how some Indians are co-opting histories that aren't theirs. Consider this response:

> This is not **also** happening to Muslims in India. Do not conflate African American history with Muslim Indian history. To commandeer the Lives Matter [sic] hashtag is unethical and intellectually dishonest. It is **not** okay to steal the history of enslaved people and map it onto the history of settler colonists. Muslim ancestors **were** the settler colonizers. They were the enslavers. They were not stolen from their homeland by settler colonists and shipped across the ocean, only to be sold as property and forced to work on land that was stolen from indigenous people through genocide and broken treaties. Their descendents [sic] were not then subject to Jim Crow laws, segregation, mass incarceration, police brutality, prison labour, and the school-to-prison pipeline. Their contributions to society were not erased from textbooks, and their oppressors are not celebrated in statues and monuments in front of government buildings.
>
> *(Viswanathan 2020, emphasis in original)*

As this passage suggests, it is not so much the conflation of Black Lives Matter with the contemporary plight Hindus are presumed to endure in India that is of concern to the author; rather it is the parallel that activists have drawn between this movement, committed to dismantling the racial violence of the state, and the specific criticism levied at the Indian state for the Islamophobic violence it continues to perpetuate. In raising this point, I do not intend to imply that the Black Lives Matter Movement is synonymous with the struggle against state violence in India, although I maintain the necessity of a politics that recognises and emboldens the solidarities that can and have emerged between different movements against state repression worldwide. Rather, my intention is to track the work that the argument presented in this passage does in furthering Hindu nationalist narratives *through an engagement with the racial politics of the United States*. Despite the author's own calls to stand with Black Lives Matter (and, one would assume, the Black Americans who have built it), the movement and the people it represents are once again invisibilised, rendered secondary to the harm that has supposedly been done to Hindus in India. The global hierarchy of race is yet again left intact as the Black subject is once more obscured and the racialised Muslim subject vilified, even as the specific racism of the US state is opened up for (limited) critique.

Even more striking perhaps are the ways in which the discourse of Hindu supremacy is advanced to an even greater extent through the author's purportedly progressive stance. Using the language of settler colonialism, and gesturing towards the racist history of mass incarceration, police brutality and the school-to-prison pipeline in the United States, the author engages in a racial critique that is increasingly becoming more mainstream through the popularisation of social justice discourses. Such a position equips the 'progressive' Hindu nationalist to play the role of the 'exemplary Other' (Buck 2017: 2) who provides the foil that emphasises the danger posed by the 'threatening Other', symbolising what the latter 'should, but cannot be' (ibid). For here the Hindu nationalist demonstrates their comfort with, and *professed commitment to*, the language of social justice (unlike Muslims, as the argument goes), all the while obscuring the contemporary violence of the Indian state and maintaining the divisions of the global racial hierarchy.

## Conclusion

As conventional wisdom gives rise to laments about the increasing polarisation that was manifested in the 2016 US Presidential elections, and that came to characterise the subsequent political climate, striking are the points of intersection between distinct nationalist projects that are articulated to supposedly different ends of the political spectrum. As the analysis of the convergences between contemporary white nationalism and Hindutva in the Indian-Amerian diaspora presented here demonstrates, these intersections uphold the logic as well as the structures of whiteness, even when they result from the work of racialised actors. While the relationship between whiteness and racialised subjectivity may not be new, it is manifesting once more in the psycho-affective affiliation that Fanon recognised so clearly. Tracing its present-day iterations reveals the contemporary affinities that uphold the global racial order in the transnational present.

What the analysis presented here also demonstrates are the ways in which whiteness itself is reconceived and appropriated through the engagement of other ultra-nationalist projects. Produced in the same context of coloniality that contributed to the formation of whiteness, Hindu nationalism is here shown to also play a role in defining the present racial order. The global investments of diasporic Hindutva simultaneously leave be and lay claim to the whiteness of the US nation, thereby positioning its 'Hindu American' adherents to uphold the racial status quo. At the same time, this engagement garners greater legitimacy in the global arena for Hindutva amongst liberals and conservatives alike, thereby perfecting its politics in a transnational arena. Rather than detrimental to either project, that is, to white nationalism or Hindutva ideology, this relationship enhances the claims to supremacy of both, leaving intact the logic of whiteness.

## Notes

1 I capitalise the term 'Black' in line with anti-racist discourse, referring to the collective identity and sense of shared cultures and experiences that have resulted from the history of the global slave trade.

2 Sociologist Daniel Patrick Moynihan, serving as Assistant Secretary of Labour during the Johnson Administration, produced this report in 1965, which relied on racist tropes of single-mothered households and urban ghettos to explain the disproportionate levels of poverty amongst US Blacks, to the exclusion of analyses of structural inequalities.

3 For example, the author states: 'If you grew up in India, you might be aware of how Hindu history is misrepresented in Indian textbooks … You might also know how Hinduism is misrepresented in American textbooks and Indology departments … Now imagine how African-American history is misrepresented in Indian textbooks, if it is represented at all. And imagine how that under- or mis-representation has shaped your consciousness and awareness about the history of black oppression in this country'.

## References

Bakhle, J. 2010. Country First? Vinayak Damodar Savarkar (1883–1966) and the Writing of Essentials of Hindutva. *Public Culture*, 22 (1): 149–186.

Ball, D. 2019. America's 'Whiz Kids'? Ambivalence and the Model Minority Stereotype. *Sociological Spectrum*, 39 (2): 116–130.

Bhalla, V. 2006. The New Indians: Reconstructing Indian Identity in the United States. *American Behavioural Scientist*, 50 (1): 118–136.

Bhatt, C. 2001. *Hindu Nationalism: Origins, Ideologies and Modern Myths*. Oxford: Berg.

Bhatt, C. and Mukta, P. 2000. Hindutva in the West: Mapping the Antinomies of Diaspora Nationalism. *Ethnic and Racial Studies*, 23 (3): 407–441.

Buck, J. 2017. 'The world's best minority': Parsis and Hindutva's ethnic nationalism in India. *Ethnic and Racial Studies*, 40 (15): 2806–2822.

Burlet, S. 2001. Reawakenings? Hindu Nationalism Goes Global. In *Asian Nationalism in an Age of Globalisation*, ed. R. Starrs, pp. 1–18. London: Routledge.

Fanon, F. 1986 [1952]. *Black Skin, White Masks*. Charles Lam Markmann (Trans.). London: Pluto Press.

Fanon, F. 2004 [1963]. *The Wretched of the Earth*. Richard Philcox (Trans.). New York: Grove Press.

Figueira, D. 2002. *Aryans, Jews, Brahmins: Theorizing Authority through Myths of Identity*. Albany, NY: State University of New York Press.

Harris, C. 1993. Whiteness as Property. *Harvard Law Review*, 106 (8): 1707–1791.

Jaffrelot, C. 1998. The Idea of the Hindu Race in the Writings of Hindu Nationalist Ideologues in the 1920s and 1930s: A Concept Between Two Cultures. In *The Concept of Race in South Asia*, ed. P. Robb, pp. 327–354. London: School of Oriental and African Studies.

King, R. 1999. *Orientalism and Religion: Postcolonial Theory, India and 'The Mythic East'*. London: Routledge.

Koshy, S. 1998. Category Crisis: South Asian Americans and Questions of Race and Ethnicity. *Diaspora*, 7 (3): 285–320.

Kumar, A. 2020. 'India rolls out the MAGA carpet for Trump', *Politico*, 24 February, viewed 17 August 2020, https://www.politico.com/news/2020/02/24/donald-trump-india-spectacle-117112.

Kumar, R. 2019. 'The network of Hindu nationalists behind Modi's "Diaspora Diplomacy" in the U.S.', *The Intercept*, 25 September, viewed 17 August 2020, https://theintercept.com/2019/09/25/howdy-modi-trump-hindu-nationalism/.

Kumar, S. 2017. 'Trump's new alliance to end Islamic Terrorism', *Breitbart*, 21 February, viewed 17 August 2020, http://www.breitbart.com/national-security/2017/02/21/kumar-trumps-new-alliance-end-islamic-terrorism/.

López, I. H. 1996. *White by Law: The Legal Construction of Race*. New York: New York University Press.

Lowe, L. 1996. *Immigrant Acts: On Asian American Cultural Politics*. Durham, NC: Duke University Press.

Ramakrishnan, S. K., Lee, J., Lee, T. and Wong, J. 2017. *National Asian American Survey (NAAS) Post-Election Survey, [United States], 2016*. Inter-university Consortium for Political and Social Research [distributor], viewed 17 August 2020, https://naasurvey.com/wp-content/uploads/2017/05/NAAS16-post-election-report.pdf.

Republican Hindu Coalition. n.d. Viewed 17 August 2020, https://rhc-usa.org.

Thapar, R. 1993. *Interpreting Early India*. New Delhi: Oxford University Press.

Thobani, S. 2019. Alt-Right with the Hindu-Right: Long-Distance Nationalism and the Perfection of Hindutva. *Ethnic and Racial Studies*, 42 (5): 745–762.

United States v. Bhagat Singh Thind, 261 U.S. 204. 1923. Viewed 17 August 2020, https://supreme.justia.com/cases/federal/us/261/204/.

Viswanathan, I. 2020. 'Lost in Conflation: Calling in Indian Hindu Americans to talk about Black Lives Matter', *Medium: The Faculty*, 3 June 2020, viewed 17 August 2020, https://medium.com/the-faculty/lost-in-conflation-calling-in-indian-hindu-americans-to-talk-about-black-lives-matter-ff583a850acc.

Zavos, J. 2010. Situating Hindu nationalism in the UK: Vishwa Hindu Parishad and the development of British Hindu identity. *Commonwealth & Comparative Politics*, 48 (1): 2–22.

# 7

# #TradCulture: Reproducing whiteness and neo-fascism through gendered discourse online

*Ashley A. Mattheis*

Smiling white women in dresses, aprons, and high heels with their makeup done and hair coiffed extolling the virtues of marriage, homemaking, and family values. This is not an old television show, a black and white movie, or even a historical documentary, it is #Trad culture, the newest internet subcultural community to hit the news headlines. Although several articles point to problematic connections between #Trad culture and far-right online cultures, discussions of how extreme gender cultures online use narratives of tradition to forward specifically racialised, white ideals and values were left out of #Trad culture's mainstream media debut. #Trad cultures online, particularly 'Red Pill' related #TradWife forums on *Reddit*, are closely linked to the extreme gender cultures of the 'Manosphere', a loose group of male supremacist sites and forums (Ebner 2020). #Trad and Manosphere cultures share narratives of anti-feminism, a focus on 'traditional', binary gender roles, and promote a nostalgic view of a mythic past when people could be 'real' men and women without punishment. They also, crucially, share similar unmarked white epistemological framings where the universal constructions of 'man' and 'woman' are predicated on white norms, values, and experiences.

Importantly, the media focus on #Trad cultures as predominately within the United Kingdom and United States based misses the transnational scale of this culture. While the United Kingdom and United States may currently have larger populations of outspoken #Trad wife bloggers, the global scope of participants in social media communities on *Facebook*, *Twitter*, and *Instagram* come from across Europe, Australia, and Canada. As a recent Australian article interviewing multiple women identifying as #Tradwives suggests, the movement is growing in popularity and online presence (Judd 2020). Imagery from this broader group of online #Tradwives includes not only the 1950s housewife aesthetic, but also 'vintage' Victorian and homesteader aesthetics (Australia), traditional 'ethnic' dress (Montenegro and the Netherlands), and other markers of nostalgic (white) femininity tied to locally specific cultural histories.

#Trad discourses about gender foreground submissive femininity as a path to liberation that is also common in religious, particularly Evangelical Christian and traditionalist Catholic, milieus. This encompasses #Trad identified Christian influencers like *The Transformed Wife* and individual women posting on social media using #TradWife. It also includes offline groups seeking to forward traditional gender norms such as the 'True Woman' movement started in 2008 which now has 'ambassadors' in Brazil, Canada, Germany, Guatemala, Mexico, Puerto

DOI: 10.4324/9780429355769-7

Rico, South Africa, Switzerland, and 18 US States (Temples 2020). These 'True' women share aspects of #Trad life including a focus on stay-at-home mothering, submission to male headship, modest dress, along with sentiments of anti-feminism and homo/transphobia. This geographic scope indicates that #Trad ideologies are at least emergent if not becoming entrenched among participants who identify as white, culturally 'Western', and Christian.

This chapter takes up its critical exploration through an examination of how #Trad culture online acts as a gendered mechanism for reproducing whiteness and white social dominance. To do this, #Trad culture mobilises (white) femininity – a specific and historically significant intersection of dominant systems of race, gender, sexuality, class, and citizenship – to promote women's return to 'traditional' (white) gender roles as a solution to the problems of modernity. #Trad culture as a contemporary iteration of this specific constellation of race and gender relies explicitly on postfeminist notions of women's individual choice to return to femininity as a form of liberation. This, in turn, works to reanimate a white, middle-upper class, hetero-patriarchal and often explicitly Christian, social structure (Mattheis 2018). Importantly, this reproduction of whiteness occurs along a spectrum of presentations ranging from the quotidian to the extreme. These varied presentations embed (unmarked) white norms in mundane discussions of recipes, etiquette, and homemaking advice where white #Trad wife influencers dominate the blogs/vlogs.

Because #Trad culture relies on whiteness as an epistemological frame, it reproduces white identity even though some black and women of colour identify as #Trad wives. In this way, the worldview of #Trad culture idealises white norms and aspirations posing them as universal and biologically driven, gendered desires that have been obscured by feminism run amok. The implicit whiteness and explicit anti-feminism of the #Trad cultural worldview makes it a productive online community through which extreme-minded participants can launder overt white supremacy and neo-fascism by normalising extreme racial logics through gendered discourse. Thus, the ideological and discursive manoeuvres of #Trad culture are more than simple conjecture or articulations of individual experience, they have socio-political and material effects.

I argue that #Trad cultures' use of gendered ideals recuperates whiteness and promotes white social dominance from a conventional, if conservative, liberal democratic cultural stance.[1] As a contemporary practice of racial-gender-class power negotiation it is situated within a culture of 'reactionary democracy' (Mondon and Winter 2020) that enables while simultaneously disavowing the socio-political normalisation of (re)emergent forms of white supremacy and neo-fascism. Moreover, such recuperative practices stem from a long history of normative cultural racism (rather than from extremist subcultures) across the ideological 'West' including the United Kingdom and Europe as well as in former colonies especially in the United States, Canada, Australia, New Zealand, and South Africa. Throughout this history, particular configurations of gender and race have been articulated as a basis for both structural and individual modes of asserting white dominance and control. Mundane practices of recuperating white power such as micro-aggressive interactions,[2] as well as violent practices such as systematic police brutality and the ongoing extrajudicial murder of black people, each rely on gender as well as race to re-establish white social power.

To explore how #Trad culture reproduces whiteness, this chapter unfolds in two parts. First, I outline how #Trad culture constructs gender through white ideals of femininity and masculinity. I also contextualise #Trad culture's contemporary mobilisation of 'traditional' (white) femininity historically. Second, I map out how #Trad culture online acts as a bridge between normative, extreme white supremacist, and neo-fascist cultures. I show how gender is used systematically to uphold white power and social dominance as a structural component of normative culture as well as in white supremacist extremism and neo-fascism.

## Constructing #trad gender: mobilising 'traditional' white femininity in context

Women who participate in #Trad culture articulate their desire to return to 'traditional' gendered roles where men are 'strong' leaders and patriarchs, and they can be submissive helpmeets (Petitt 2020). In this capacity, #Trad women desire to be stay-at-home wives and mothers focused on primary roles as caregivers and domestic managers (Stewart 2020). #Trad women perform this gendered role through visible presentations of hyper-femininity and articulations of the benefits of submission to men as their 'head of household' (The Trad Wife Blog 2020). The scope of such participation ranges across multiple areas of preference including a 'back to the land' framework, a '1950s housewife' framework, and an overtly religious, Christian 'angel of the home' framework. Women publicly espousing these frames are also predominantly white and middle-upper class, although not exclusively.[3]

Gender in #Trad culture is idealised as biological, binary, heterosexual, and universal. Here, gender and biological sex are conflated, and heterosexual desire is framed through notions of biological and psychological sexual imperatives. This arrangement is then framed as universal: something all people share regardless of history, culture, or other social factors. In this way white, western heteronormative ideals of femininity and masculinity become fixed as trans-historical and trans-geographic 'facts'. Within this understanding of gender, women are characterised by femininity and men are characterised by masculinity as complementary sets of traits which lend themselves to the specific and different 'natural' roles of women and men. Ideal femininity is constructed as caring (emotional), soft, dependent, and characterised by a desire to please. And, ideal masculinity is constructed as rational (logical), strong, independent, and characterised as in-control. These idealisations are common to traditionalist, often conservative and religious, white western cultural constructions of gender (Whitehead and Perry 2019).

Caring, as a trait of idealised white femininity, is articulated through narratives of domesticity and portrayed visually through stylised imagery of 1950s (white) housewives. Linking care and domesticity in this ideal with the stated desire to be a submissive helpmeet, reifies notions of women's 'natural' roles as wife and mother. The capacity for care, as a (white) feminine trait, stems from women's 'emotional' natures which in backhanded fashion poses women as less logical and less suited to leadership. Rationality, alternately, is narrated as a basis for (white) male socio-political superiority and control through a framework of benevolent paternalism, where rational men have a duty to care for and protect their women and children.

Women's biological softness is posed as the basis for their carer–nurturer role and men's biological strength as the basis for their provider–protector role. Softness and strength are also seen as necessary predicates for developing successful heterosexual relationships in marriage. Dependence and independence as gendered traits reproduce white norms for gendered economic and labour relations. Here, feminine dependence on men is primarily a facet of economic security, and includes physical and emotional security produced by the provider aspect of masculinity. Thus, masculine independence, is predicated on the ability to provide effectively and protect women from the ills of society, a form of paternalist benevolence because of men's 'duty of care' for their dependents.

Women's 'desire to please' and men's ability to 'be in control' are the narrative framing which brings these feminine and masculine traits together in a unified matrix for performing gender. The feminine 'desire to please' as a narrative includes making family and friends happy, keeping a peaceful, beautiful home, and having a positive sexual relationship with their husband. The masculine ability to 'be in control' as a narrative includes developing the ability, judgment, and economic status to provide for and protect a family. Both are narrated as requiring sacrifices of the self. Feminine sacrifices are focused on subordinating one's needs for others, and masculine sacrifices are focused on performing labour for the well-being of the family.

In relation to gender roles, 'tradition' acts as a euphemism for whiteness thereby reproducing a nexus of white knowledge-power at the intersection of race and gender that reinforces and reconstructs white, hetero-patriarchal dominance as the basis of 'proper' socio-political, economic, and cultural order (Almeida 2015). Similarly, according to Christi Van der Westhuizen (2016), South African apartheid logics that were rooted in notions of white patriarchal dominance as 'order' are euphemised by white women postapartheid through narratives of 'proper' (white) morality. Such discursive framing is also a primary aspect of both white supremacist and fascist ideology which posits a return to traditional gendered roles and racial purity as the basis for the health and prosperity of the nation-state and society. In this way, narratives of 'tradition' are mobilised to support both systems: white supremacy and fascism.[4]

#TradWife culture revolves around a programme of elevating (white) motherhood. This is framed visually and discursively through nostalgic romanticism that obscures a long historical relationship between white mothers, the maintenance of white supremacy, and fascist nation-building. This history includes late eighteenth and early nineteenth-century governmental policies and programmes in the United States and Europe aimed at promoting white birth rates by 'educating' white women about 'companionate marriage'. It also includes eugenics programmes focused on eradicating blood-born impurities that placed a special emphasis on racial mixing (miscegenation) and people of colour as sources of hereditary malformation (Kline 2001).[5] And, it includes white mothers' direct participation in supporting white supremacy and white supremacist extremism throughout US history (hooks 1981; Jones-Rogers 2019; McRae 2018). Crucially, it ignores the flagrant use of maternalism within white supremacist and fascist ideologies that pose white women's most important role as the bearing and rearing of children in a 'traditional' (white) family setting (Durham 2007).

While it is true that participants in #Trad culture are not necessarily participants in extremist, white supremacist, or neo-fascist ideologies, supporters of these latter ideologies make incursions into #Trad culture precisely because they see it as useful. And, it is useful, as a productive site for the circulation of and radicalisation to extreme ideologies because it is *not* explicitly racist and extremist. Instead, it amplifies extant racialised and gendered discriminatory beliefs intrinsic to normative culture. Such beliefs are part and parcel of systemic racism and sexism entrenched in liberal democracies. As Mondon and Winter (2020: 53) argue, this is rooted in a fundamental contradiction within democratic liberalism because 'its central concern is the liberty of the individual', but 'the liberty of some individuals has always come at the expense of others, be they slaves, the poor, women, or foreigners'.

Thus, the normalisation of extreme ideologies predicated on racism and national purity depends upon being able to connect to currents of implicit racism in general culture. This is largely achieved by mobilising more socially acceptable misogynist, gendered discourses of tradition and heterosexist narratives promoting homo/transphobic ideas of 'natural' gender and sexuality as a corrective to feminist and queer notions of gender. Thus, notions of tradition as gendered provide a crucial site for the replication of whiteness-as-epistemology embedded in normative cultural expressions of racism, as well as the bolstering of whiteness-as-ideology which undergirds extreme, white supremacist and neo-fascist expressions of racism.

As black feminist scholars have long argued, gender is central to constructions of race and racialised tropes of gender are central to constructions of whiteness. Moreover, gender is a primary site through which whiteness is developed and maintained as a modality of structural power (Collins 2000; Crenshaw 1991; Higginbotham 1992; hooks 1981; Lorde, 2007). One of the earliest assertions of the link between gender and race comes from Sojourner Truth's (1851) speech at the Woman's Rights Convention in Akron, Ohio, where Truth outlines how whiteness is used to construct the category 'woman'[6]:

> That man over there says women need to be helped into carriages, and lifted over ditches, and to have the best place everywhere. Nobody ever helps me into carriages, or over mud-puddles, or gives me any best place! And arn't I a woman? Look at me! Look at my arm! I have ploughed, and planted, and gathered into barns, and no man could head me! And arn't I woman? I could work as much and eat as much as a man – when I could get it – and bear the lash as well! And arn't I a woman? I have borne thirteen children, and seen them most all sold off to slavery, and when I cried out with my mother's grief, none but Jesus heard me! And aren't I a woman?

Truth argues for her own classification as a woman because she does not meet the idealised standard of white femininity. The withholding of femininity from black women was an eco-nomic strategy of slavery in the United States. As Davis (1971: 205) notes, '[t]his was one of the supreme ironies of slavery: in order to approach its strategic goal – to extract the greatest possible surplus from the labour of the slaves – the black woman had to be released from the chains of the myth of femininity'. And, during the post slavery years in the United States, as Higginbotham (1992) notes, '[i]n contrast to the domestic ideal for white women of all classes, the larger society deemed it "unnatural", in fact and "evil", for black married women "to play the lady" while their husbands supported them'. In this way, 'traditional' notions of femininity are meant to exclude black women as Deliovsky (2008: 58, citing Elder 1998, Frankenberg 1993, and hooks 1992) asserts, '[f]emininity, then, far from being race-neutral, is always already raced as white'.

Traditional notions of white femininity are a modality through which white women have learned to assert power within white patriarchal culture. The lynching of Emmet Till in Money, Mississippi in 1955, is a stark example of how white women's claims of 'fear' generate excuses for white men to commit the murder of black men and boys with impunity. Still today, discourses of protecting the purity of white women remain foundational to the ongoing my-thology of the black male rapist used to pose black men as criminals and target them for discipline by the US state (Collins 2000; Wells-Barnett 1892). White women continue to assert this form of power today. Recently, in Central Park, New York, a white woman threatened to call the police when asked by a black male bird watcher to follow the park rules and leash her dog. In a video recording of the event, the white woman can be heard saying, 'I'm taking a picture and calling the cops … I'm going to tell them there's an African American man threatening my life' (Vera and Ly 2020). Explicitly weaponising her white femininity, the woman threatens to use the structural power of systemic police brutality in her effort to control the space and continue to do as she pleases. It makes clear that white women understand that their acquiescence to limitations on their gendered power can be offset through their whiteness which enables their access to specific forms of racialised social dominance. This power me-chanism is characterised by Van der Westhuizen (2016: 228–229) as '[i]ntersectional shifting in which the reduced status of the category "woman" is counterbalanced with the elevated status of whiteness and middle classness to gain ascendance'.

#Trad culture reanimates and circulates a contemporary version of the ideal white femininity that both Truth and Davis reference. It is an update of the historical configuration of normative middle-upper class, white femininity as fragile and pure, unsuited for public life and work outside the home and thus requiring the protection of white men through a system of benevolent paternalism. Under this system, the ideal social location for middle-upper class white women was domestic: marriage to a husband who could protect her and support her and their children.

As Merish (2000) argues, white women's civic identity – their liberal democratic subjectivity – developed through economic philosophies of early capitalism reliant on notions of free labour exchange. Thus, white women were positioned as free because they were able to choose to exchange their domestic (reproductive) labour through marriage. Moreover, as both Truth and Davis also argue, this positioning of white women as 'free' was only possible because it was framed in direct opposition to black women's status as slaves unable to freely choose to exchange their labour (Merish 2000). Underscoring this racialised construction of white women's freedom, black women were rendered the literal bearers and reproducers of un-freedom as racial purity laws assigned race to children based on the race of their mothers (Scales-Trent 2001). Such laws also made it necessary to protect white women's purity – to prevent them from having non-white children – who could destabilise the racial legal system. Thus, controlling white women's sexual behaviour became a principal aspect of the privileging white feminine performances (Higginbotham 1992).

Racial purity laws, which had existed since the colonial period, became more stringent and exacting as the slave trade slowed globally (Scales-Trent 2001). And while these laws prohibited miscegenation, this did not extend to punishing white men's rape of enslaved women. Because the progeny of such violence would also be enslaved, rape as a structural practice served multiple ends including increasing slave stocks and venerating white women's purity in relation to enslaved black women who were cast as 'Jezebels'.

Protecting white femininity was regularly used as a premise for bolstering white supremacy throughout the era of Jim Crow segregation in the United States. Here, the fragility of white femininity was posed against the threat of black masculinity, constructed as animalistic and hypersexual (Foster 2011). The common response to 'threats' against white femininity was lynching, which asserted white power through the application of unrestrained and unpunished violence including the murder of black men, women, and children by white men. Under Jim Crow, lynching was often a carnivalesque revelry in whiteness, performed at large social events that included hundreds, even thousands, of white viewers coming from distant areas to participate (Wells-Barnett 1892).

As slavery ended and segregation took hold, Malthusian and other 'blood' based scientific theories of social difference developed in the United States and Europe. These theories derived from racial science developed to support industrial slavery by 'objectively' proving the inferiority of black slaves and other people of colour (Schiebinger 1990). By the turn of the nineteenth century and through the First World War, controlling women's sexual reproduction became a focus of racial science. Promoting middle-upper class white women's fertility and limiting black and poor white women's fertility were embedded in social and institutional policies and practices which supported elite white interests under the cover of national improvement (Hobson and Margulies 2019; Kline 2001). During this period, the ideology of fascism began to develop and incorporate racial and gendered science. In the interwar years, the cross fertilisation between overt white supremacy and fascism led to a catastrophic outcome as Hitler and his Nazi regime would turn back to US racial purity laws and segregation practices to form their own systematic programme of genocide (Whitman 2017). Here again, white femininity – posed as non-Jewish, German whiteness – was a focus of Nazi anti-Semitism which was the German frame for racial supremacy.

Importantly, prominent expressions of fascism at the time – German and Italian – shared similar gendered concerns but expressed them in localised terms. Aryan femininity relied deeply on 'hereditary fitness' and maternity as women's duty to the state (Loroff 2011: 54) while Italian fascism relied on maternalism to forward conservative social values rather than a totalitarian state (De Grand, 1976). This pattern of broad gendered concerns expressed in localised terms remains active in neo-fascist and white supremacist expressions online. These expressions rely on a shared framework of women's maternal role but diverge in their specific expression in relation to national socio-political concerns and events (Mattheis 2018).

Contemporary, normative conceptions of 'traditional' (white) femininity also rely on this history but obscure that relation by universalising women's experience and romanticising 'traditional' gendered roles. #Trad cultural reliance on an aspirational model of 'traditional' femininity reanimates this historical relationality between gender and race. By repackaging domesticity, white femininity, and benevolent paternalism through 'feminist' languages of choice, liberation, and empowerment in nostalgic, postfeminist contexts, they romanticise 'traditional' (white) gendered experience and create cross-cultural legibility. In doing so, #Trad culture sanitises ideal white femininity from its historical role in producing forms of whiteness and white power specific to white supremacist and fascist ideologies.

## #Trad culture's relation to white supremacist and neo-fascist world views online

#Trad culture cannot be understood without contextualisation among white supremacist and neo-fascist ideologies that are (re)emergent across the globe. These developments are tied in many ways to the ubiquity of internet culture and the expansion of social media as regular aspects of daily life. Both racism and sexism have long run rampant on the internet (Marwick 2013) providing a cultural locus for white supremacist and neo-fascist narratives and ideologies to circulate widely. Popular discussions of women's role in online extremist participation often focuses on their capacity to soften extremist rhetoric, making these ideologies seem less dangerous and more palatable. However, developing research shows that women engaged with these ideologies take an active role in circulating them and that social media have increased their capacity to produce material and engage broad audiences (Mattheis 2018).

The replication of whiteness produced by #Trad culture online is entangled with extremist white supremacist and neo-fascist online cultures through shared narratives of anti-feminism and a nostalgic view of traditional gendered roles. This entanglement is especially apparent in extremist women's rhetoric and in engagements between #Trad wives and Alt-Right women in their online media programmes. This connection point is particularly productive because, as I have argued elsewhere, gendered and anti-feminist discourses produce highly effective and easily circulable online material (Mattheis 2019). Moreover, such material circulates across online cultures because misogyny and antifeminist humour and narratives are not stigmatised in the same ways as racist and xenophobic narratives.

It is #Trad culture's anti-feminism that most effectively enables its use as a bridge between mainstream, conservative, neo-fascist, male supremacist, and white supremacist extreme right-wing cultures across the globe. This is visible in the circulation of 'white identity' digital propaganda in the social media content on #Trad culture sites, as well as the language of 'red pilling' used in the *Reddit*-based #Trad culture (Ebner 2020).[7] In this way, the gendered logics of #Trad culture, including discourses of anti-feminism, maternalism, heterosexual marriage, anti-abortion, homophobia, and transphobia, link to gendered narratives across these other cultures. When paired with visuals of utopic whiteness, they provide direct avenues for engagement with extreme white supremacist and neo-fascist narratives about white women's reproductive role in preventing social collapse specifically the crises of Great Replacement and White Genocide. These narratives highlight the necessity of white men's control over white women's bodies, their sex and reproduction, as a primary focus of anti-feminist narratives touting the need for female submission to (white) male authority.

The theory of Great Replacement is a specific narration of the mythology of White Genocide. Both concepts are pillars in the ideology of contemporary white supremacist and racialised neo-fascist cultures which draw on earlier fascist fears about women's decadence as a mechanism for racial annihilation. They construct progressive leftism, or 'cultural Marxism', as a Jewish Conspiracy implemented by the 'Zionist Occupied Government' (ZOG), to exterminate the white race and white culture (Waltman and Mattheis 2016). A major component of this is the use of feminism as a tool to destroy the white race. In this narrative, the promotion of feminism by the ZOG is altering cultural norms through academic institutions and civil rights legislation in an effort to lull white people into complacency about the destruction of whiteness. Thus, feminism's 'liberation' of white women's sexuality and simultaneous promotion of multi-culturalism and LGBTQI+ sexuality are foundational to the decimation of white birth rates and the extermination of the white race and white culture. When this is paired with 'traditional' notions of white masculinity and femininity that espouse white men's mythical 'protector role' for white women, violence against the out-group, inclusive of racialised, LGBTQI+ or feminist 'Others', as well as 'social justice warriors', 'cultural Marxists' and anyone deemed leftist, becomes acceptable and is narrated by extremist women as a form of masculine care (Mattheis 2018).

While each online extremist culture expresses racialised, gender narratives through their own specific framing, they also engage with and share the others' materials when it is productive to further their goals. As such, contemporary figurations of gender and race in these online cultures share certain features. What is narrated in #Trad culture as social harm (posed by feminism and modern gender roles) becomes amplified in extremist online cultures as an existential threat of (white) societal collapse. What is presented in #Trad culture as a rejection of feminism, in extremist cultures online becomes militant, even violent, anti-feminism. And the mobilisation of whiteness as a gendered epistemology in #Trad culture becomes ontological, in extremist cultures, where race is the ultimate fact and reality of human being. Here, we can see how the historical uses of gender, particularly white femininity, to construct race become part of the contemporary moment as extremist narratives foreground the issue of protecting white women and girls from immigrant and refugee invaders as rapists; a clearly xenophobic adaptation of the trope of the black male rapist used to justify lynching and over-policing of black men in the United States (Mattheis 2018).

## Conclusion

#Trad culture online acts as a liminal space, a borderland, where white epistemologies are reconstituted, normalised, and circulated through narratives of gender framed by neoliberal and postfeminist notions of personal 'choice', individual responsibility, family, and 'free' thought (Christou 2020). Women's choice of 'tradition-as-liberation' then becomes registered as salvific through its juxtaposition with the failure of the state and decline of social order caused by an unnecessary and dangerous extension of feminism (Budgeon 2015; McRobbie 2009). #Trad cultural narratives leverage post-feminism through a particular strand of (white) nostalgia transposing the 'liberated' woman with the figure of the happy, perfectly put-together housewife as the ideal woman contented and fulfilled by keeping a perfect home and caring for her family. In this way, #Trad culture forwards a specifically white, feminised hope of return to a simpler time and golden past (Collins 2000; Deliovsky 2008; Truth 1851), a type of nostalgic vision and framing that is intrinsic to both white supremacist and neo-fascist ideology and narrative framing online (Mattheis 2018, 2019). Ultimately, whether #Trad culture does or does not fall under the rubric of narrowly defined white supremacist or neo-fascist ideology, it resonates with participants in those cultures as sharing an ideological position around gender and whiteness.

#Trad culture online showcases how gender, specifically notions of traditional (white) femininity, is used to reproduce whiteness while seeming 'not racist'. I have shown that #Trad culture's ability to reproduce whiteness through gender derives from gendered and racialised beliefs that are firmly rooted in normative white culture. Moreover, its position, drawn from normative culture, situates it within a long history of asserting white social dominance through gender and contemporary practices of reactionary democracy. Analysis of #Trad culture exposes how deeply entrenched whiteness remains as a racist structure of power and how it is interwoven with other normative structures of power (i.e. sexism, heterosexism, classism, and nativism) within the Gordian knot of 'difference' in liberal democratic societies. The normativity of white femininity within liberal democratic culture is what makes it an especially profitable site for the softening and normalisation of extreme ideologies. Thus, while #Trad culture defends its position as non-extremist, it is clearly intertwined with multiple extremist online cultures. To address this interconnection and cultural movements toward extreme political ideologies across the globe, acknowledging the normative reliance on racialised beliefs that shape notions of gender within #Trad culture is essential.

## Notes

1   I use terms other than 'mainstream' throughout to indicate the hegemonic nature of whiteness as embedded within conventional 'western' liberal democratic cultures.

2   D. W. Sue et al. (2007: 271) describe '[r]acial microaggressions' as 'brief and commonplace daily verbal, behavioural, or environmental indignities, whether intentional or unintentional, that communicate hostile, derogatory, or negative racial slights and insults toward people of colour'.

3   Understanding black women participants in #Trad culture or male participants in black masculinist cultures online is complex given the problematic portrayal of black 'matriarchal' dominance as destructive to black men and families – exemplified by the Moynihan report – rather than as a structural component of white racial, socio-political, and economic domination (Guy-Sheftall 1995). See also: <https://www.blackpast.org/african-american-history/moynihan-report-1965/#chapter3>.

4   Fascism is not always tied to whiteness, for example current aspects of Hindutva culture. However, in the ideological 'West', white patriarchy and fascism are integrated in distinct ways.

5   At this time in the United States (roughly the 1880s–1940s), status as a 'white' person was granted to Anglo, Northern, and Western Europeans but not granted to the Irish, Southern, and Eastern Europeans (Irving 2000). Thus, poverty as a marker of hereditary weakness was attached to multiple 'non-white' populations and used as a structural form of white economic control through gender.

6   The version included has been rendered by scholars in line with Truth's other speeches, as the historically 'known' version's vernacular is contested.

7   'Red Pilling' or taking the 'red pill' is a reference used in online misogynist and Far-Right cultures drawn from the film *The Matrix* to indicate their participants' awakening to 'reality' by coming out of the false consciousness of 'normal' society.

## References

Almeida, S. 2015. Race-Based Epistemologies: The Role of Race and Dominance in Knowledge Production. *Wagadu: A Journal of Transnational Women's and Gender Studies*, 13 (Summer): 79–105.

Budgeon, S. 2015. Individualized Femininity and Feminist Politics of Choice. *European Journal of Women's Studies*, 22 (3): 303–318.

Christou, M. 2020. #Tradwives: Sexism as a Gateway to White Supremacy. *Centre for Analysis of the Radical Right Blog*, viewed 1 April 2020, https://www.radicalrightanalysis.com/2020/03/23/.

Collins, P. H. 2000. *Black Feminist Thought: Knowledge, Consciousness, and the Politics of Empowerment*, 2nd edn. New York: Routledge.

Crenshaw, K. 1991. Mapping the Margins: Intersectionality, Identity Politics, and Violence Against Women of Color. *Stanford Law Review*, 43 (6): 1241–1299.

Davis, A.Y. 1971. Reflections on the Black Woman's Role in the Community of Slaves. In *Words of Fire: An Anthology of African-American Feminist Thought*, ed. B. Guy-Sheftall, pp. 200–218. New York: The New Press.

De Grand, A. 1976. Women under Italian Fascism. *The Historical Journal*, 19 (4): 947–968.

Deliovsky, K. 2008. Normative White Femininity: Race, Gender and the Politics of Beauty. *Atlantis*, 33 (1): 49–59.

Durham, M. 2007. *White Rage: The Extreme Right and American Politics*. New York: Routledge.

Ebner, J. 2020. *Going Dark: The Secret Social Lives of Extremists*. New York: Bloomsbury.

Foster, T. A. 2011. The Sexual Abuse of Black Men Under American Slavery. *Journal of the History of Sexuality*, 20 (3): 445–464.

Guy-Sheftall, B., ed. 1995. *Words of Fire: An Anthology of African-American Feminist Thought*. New York: The New Press.

Higginbotham, E. B. 1992. African-American Women's History and the Metalanguage of Race. *Signs*, 17 (2): 251–274.

Hobson, K. and Margulies, S. B. 2019. A Forgotten History of Eugenics: Reimagining Whiteness and Disability in the Case of Carrie Buck. In *Interrogating the Communicative Power of Whiteness*, ed. D. M. McIntosh, D. G. Moon and T. K. Nakayama, pp. 133–151. New York: Routledge.

hooks, b. 1981. *Ain't I a Woman: Black Women and Feminism*. Boston: South End Press.

Irving, K. 2000. *Immigrant Mothers: Narratives of Race and Maternity, 1890–1925*. Urbana: University of Illinois.

Jones-Rogers, S. E. 2019. *They Were Her Property: White Women as Slave Owners in the American South*. New Haven: Yale University Press.

Judd, B. 2020. 'Tradwives have been labelled "subservient", but these women reject suggestions they're oppressed', *ABC.net*, 23 February 2020, viewed 1 April 2020, https://www.abc.net.au/news/2020-02-24/tradwives-women-say-the-movement-is-empowering-not-oppressive/11960910.

Kline, W. 2001. *Building a Better Race: Gender, Sexuality, and Eugenics from the Turn of the Century to the Baby Boom*. Berkley: University of California Press.

Leidig, E. 2020. 'From incels to tradwives: Understanding the spectrum of gender and online extremism', *Impakter*, 21 May, viewed 21 May 2020, https://impakter.com/from-incels-to-tradwives-understanding-the-spectrum-of-gender-and-online-extremism/.

Lorde, A. 2007. *Sister Outsider*, 2nd edn. Berkley: Crossing Press.

Loroff, N. 2011. Gender and Sexuality in Nazi Germany. *Constellations*, 3 (1): 49–61.

Marwick, A. E. 2013. Online Identity. In *A Companion to New Media Dynamics*, ed. J. A. Hartley, J. Burgess and A. Bruns, pp. 355–364. Malden, MA: Blackwell. DOI: 10.1002/9781118321607.

Mattheis, A. A. 2018. Shieldmaidens of Whiteness: (Alt)Maternalism and Women Recruiting for the Far/Alt-Right. *Journal for Deradicalization*, 17: 128–161.

Mattheis, A. A. 2019. Disrupting the Digital Divide: Extremism's Integration of Offline/Online Practice. *Interventionen*, 14: 4–17.

McRae, E. G. 2018. *Mothers of Massive Resistance: White Women and the Politics of White Supremacy*. New York: Oxford University Press.

McRobbie, A. 2008. *The Aftermath of Feminism*. London: SAGE.

Merish, Lori. 2000. *Sentimental Maternalism: Gender Commodity Culture, and Nineteenth-Century American Literature*. Durham, NC: Duke University Press.

Mondon, A. and Winter, A. 2020. *Reactionary Democracy: How Racism and the Populist Far-Right Became Mainstream*. New York: Verso.

Petitt, A. K. 2020. *The Darling Academy*, viewed 15 January 2020, https://www.thedarlingacademy.com/.

Scales-Trent, J. 2001. Racial Purity Laws in the United States and Nazi Germany: The Targeting Process. *Human Rights Quarterly*, 23 (2): 260–307.

Schiebinger, L. 1990. The Anatomy of Difference: Race and Sex in Eighteenth-Century Science. *Eighteenth-Century Studies*, 23 (4): 387–405.

Stewart, A. 2020. 'Tradlife: The Restoration and Preservation of Traditional Family Values. Wife with a Purpose', viewed 15 January 2020, https://wifewithapurpose.com/.

Temples, A. June 2020 'Connect With an Ambassador, Revive Our Hearts', viewed 1, https://www.reviveourhearts.com/ambassadors/connect/.

The Trad Wife. 2020. 'The Trad Wife Blog', viewed 15 January 2020, https://thetradwife.wordpress.com/.

Truth, S. 1851. 'Arn't I a Woman', *BlackPast.org, An Online Reference Center for African American History*, viewed 1 June 2020, https://www.blackpast.org/african-american-history/speeches-african-american-history/1851-sojourner-truth-arnt-i-a-woman/.

Sue, D. W. *et al.* 2007. Racial Microaggressions in Everyday Life: Implications for Clinical Practice. *American Psychologist*, 62 (4): 271–286. DOI:10.1037/0003-066X.62.4.271.

Van der Westhuizen, C. 2016. Race, Intersectionality, and Affect in Postapartheid Productions of the 'Afrikaans White Woman'. *Critical Philosophy of Race*, 4 (2): 221–238.

Vera, A. and Ly, L. 2020. 'White woman who called police on a black man bird-watching in Central Park has been fired', *CNN.com, 26 May,* viewed 3 June 2020, https://www.cnn.com/2020/05/26/us/central-park-video-dog-video-african-american-trnd/index.html.

Waltman, M. S. and Mattheis, A. A. 2016. Understanding Hate Speech. *Oxford Research Encyclopedia of Communication*, 1–27. DOI:10.1093/acrefore/9780190228613.013.422.

Wells-Barnett, I. 1892. Lynch Law in America. In *Words of Fire: An Anthology of African-American Feminist Thought,* ed. B. Guy-Sheftall, pp. 70–76. New York: The New Press.

Whitehead, A. L. and Perry, S. L. 2019. Is a 'Christian America' a More Patriarchal America?: Religion, Politics, and Traditionalist Gender Ideology. *Canadian Review of Sociology*, 56 (2): 151–177.

Whitman, J. Q. 2017. *Hitler's American Model: The United States and the Making of Nazi Race Law.* Princeton: Princeton University Press.

# 8

# Hating Meghan Markle: Drawing the boundaries of British whiteness against postfeminist femininity

*Kendra Marston*

## Introduction

With an estimated global viewership of almost two billion, the royal wedding of Prince Harry to Meghan Markle in 2018 was heralded as a fairytale affair ushering in a more inclusive, modern era for the British monarchy due primarily to the Prince's unconventional choice of bride – a 36-year-old biracial American divorcée. Three years on, Markle has nevertheless proven a figure who reflects divisions in British society, with negative press coverage significantly contributing to the couple's 2020 decision to step back from royal life. A 2019 *Tatler* poll asking respondents if the Duchess of Sussex had been good for the monarchy had previously illustrated her divisive reception in concluding that 45% of those surveyed replied in the negative (Feigin 2019). Unflattering headlines have been splashed on a range of British tabloid covers from *The Sun* to *The Mirror,* but it is arguably in *The Daily Mail* where Markle has received the most notable and prolonged vilification. A high circulation tabloid known for inviting robust online commentary on 'Showbiz' articles, Markle has here been criticised for everything from narcissistic social climbing, familial neglect, over-spending on home renovations, and even concocting a fake pregnancy. It was *The Daily Mail,* and its *MailOnline* version too, that boasted an early headline about Markle being '(almost) straight outta Compton' and from 'a gang-scarred home' (Styles 2016).[1] Indeed, Markle's treatment is evidence of the continued harassment black women disproportionately face in the public sphere, and the psychological impacts of racism and sexism on black lives. As bell hooks (2014) argues, this has the capacity to wound irrespective of material privilege or, it would seem, the target's position in elitist and white-privileged systems.

Markle-targeting is striking in its emotive charge and constitutes a key site through which the role of negative affect in white nationalism and the co-generative relationship between neoliberal postfeminism and 'possessive investments in whiteness' (Lipsitz 1998) may be explored. Markle has been characterised in certain sectors of the British press and by a virulent online anti-fandom as a 'bad' object, whose presence corrupts a 'good' monarchy. Her construction as an illegitimate presence is here based not only on her race and class origins, but also her foreignness, feminism (Weidhase 2021), and association with a Hollywood industry defined by an awkward blend of unexamined capitalistic extravagance and social justice proselytising.

DOI: 10.4324/9780429355769-8

Staged fantasies of Markle's expulsion from the royal family and indeed from Britain – neatly encapsulated in the Twitter hashtag #Megxit – seek to preserve a fantasy of the British monarchy as an exclusive symbol of national heritage that is conservative, patriarchal, white and, importantly, legitimate. Here, Markle becomes a derided character in what Cornell Sandvoss calls 'a politics of against', which represents people through a dual concept of the elite and the undeserving, with the latter those who 'ought to be less privileged than themselves [the fans] but who are wrongfully rewarded by "the elite"' (2019: 135). *Daily Mail* top commenters (as judged by peer upvotes) predominantly interpret Markle's royal inclusion as a matter of wrongful reward, with most implicitly (or explicitly) upholding the idea that excessive wealth is acceptable but that there are those who deserve it and those who do not.

While Markle's celebrity image exemplifies markers of success defined by a postfeminist media culture in that it takes aspects of feminism into account (McRobbie 2009) while emphasising wealth, consumer-capitalism, and conventional beauty as markers of feminist success, this same image is interpreted by detractors as a desperate and failed effort on her part. The achievement of celebrity is, of course, more widely promoted in late capitalist postmodernity as a desirable culmination of a politics of liberal individualism and plays a normative role to advance the idealisations underpinning neoliberal postfeminism. However, the inclusion of women of colour and working-class women within this privileged world has long been fraught. While such women are not invisible in forms of media culture commonly identified by scholars as 'postfeminist', they have traditionally been marginalised and/or disparaged, for instance in reality media formats. The symbolic methods that postfeminist culture has deployed to privilege the white middle-class are thus invoked by white nationalists as a means of strengthening their claims of entitlement to the spoils of the economy in relation to those who they position as racial interlopers. This is a form of measuring, analysing and making the other accountable, which Ghassan Hage argues is instrumental to the white nationalist fantasy that they are 'masters of national space' (2000: 17).

*The Daily Mail* is the United Kingdom's third highest circulation paper and the second most visited English language site in the world, with a disproportionately female readership of upper working to lower middle-class status (Toolan 2016). Notable for its conservative and often sensationalist reporting on politics, the pro-Queen/anti-Meghan stance of most top commenters is perhaps unsurprising given the tabloid's incitement of readers 'to be full of envy, desire and resentment, yet not to challenge the position of the rich at the top of the social hierarchy' (Littler 2017: 133). While recognising that the ideological impetus of *MailOnline* articles creates the frame for the production of reader comments, this chapter places a greater emphasis on a thematic analysis of these comments to gauge popular preoccupations and enunciative patterns. Most celebrity Showbiz articles receive no more than a few hundred comments, yet articles and opinion pieces about the Duke and Duchess of Sussex routinely attract thousands, indicating an intensified enthusiasm for engaging in debate about the couple. To ensure greater observational reliability, only articles with more than 2,000 comments are included in this analysis. These range from the period of the 2018 royal wedding to Tom Bradby's 2019 ITV Africa documentary where the pair spoke of their despair at tabloid press mistreatment. Samples from the top 25 'most liked' comments are analysed. At the time of writing, popular *MailOnline* articles included Markle's appearances at Grand Slam tennis tournament Wimbledon in 2019 and at the British Fashion Awards, where she presented an award to Givenchy Artistic Director Clare Weight Keller; the couple's renovations of Frogmore Cottage in the British countryside; the Duchess's birth plans pending the arrival of son Archie and rumours of a feud with Kate Middleton, the Duchess of Cambridge.

## Markle as a postfeminist figure

Despite *MailOnline* commenters claims to the contrary, in many ways, Meghan Markle is an exemplary postfeminist figure. Postfeminism, both in early theorising and more recently, is described as a capitalistic sensibility in which female empowerment is largely reduced to the pursuit of financial success and active participation in consumer culture, rigorous self-monitoring, and the physical embodiment of beauty standards in adherence to a normative model of white, western, middle-class heterofemininity (Gill 2007, 2016; McRobbie 2009, 2015; Tasker and Negra 2007). At the time of Markle's rise to screen success, industry approaches to representational diversity were typically shallow and, in keeping with the neoliberal emphasis on individual responsibility for success or failure, rarely engaged with ongoing structural barriers to participation by people of colour (Projansky 2001). Black women who conformed to normative white heterofemininity were represented as living the American dream, just like the glamorous white women on screen. *Suits* (USA Network 2011–2019), the glossy legal drama that Markle starred in prior to marrying Prince Harry, perhaps exemplifies this type of show. Set in a prestigious Manhattan firm, *Suits* episodes revelled in tales of corporate treachery and ruthless ambition set in a world of sharp-edged aesthetic glamour. Markle played Rachel Zane, a talented paralegal with her sights set on becoming a lawyer at Pearson Hardman, a firm led by a black woman, Jessica Pearson (Gina Torres), whose powerful position demonstrates the feasibility of Zane's dreams. A convergence between postfeminist and post-racial obfuscation of the structural effects of whiteness is therefore facilitated by Markle as a symbol in media discourses.

However, postfeminist culture exists in some tension with the more conservative 'Princess' ideal, especially given Hollywood's recent partial sanctioning of feminist and anti-racist proclamations that nevertheless remain largely pro-capitalist in promoting forms of inclusion that pose little challenge to the prevailing economic order. Markle's alignment of her feminist identity with lifestyle branding, exemplified in her now defunct blog *The Tig,* is consistent with such an intertwining of activism and commerce. However, the royal family's quest to maintain their role in British constitutional life has long resided in a professed commitment to political neutrality and a degree of insularity from the political miasma into which celebrities are so fond of rhetorically wading. Such impartiality ostensibly befits the Queen's ceremonial role in presiding over a government that can veer to the left or right of the political spectrum yet also protects the monarch from burgeoning republican sentiment. Impartiality is therefore an ideal that elevates the monarch above her subjects' actions and follies as well as a vestige of innocence that shields the institution from accusations of past and present political wrongdoing. The Crown becomes a resilient symbol of timeless fairytale heritage, its Queens and Princesses, of which Kate Middleton is exemplary, symbolically upholding traditional ideals of white western femininity in their charitable benevolence, willingness to bear royal heirs, and diplomacy abroad (Shome 2001; Weidhase 2021). Meghan Markle, in contrast, is racially marked, which alludes to the injustices of Britain's colonial past, while her feminism speaks to gendered discontent in the political zeitgeist. Her presence thus fissures the illusion of transcendent timelessness and is an irritant to the monarchy as a 'racially exclusive form of divine sovereignty' (Randell-Moon 2017: 398) of the British nation, as well as its unofficial function as a comforting vehicle for white nostalgia.

In considering the affective dynamics of Markle anti-fandom, it is necessary to briefly return to debates on postfeminist media culture's supposed geographic and ethnic exclusions and the significance these might have to a growing interest in postfeminism's affective features. While scholars initially pointed to a white, middle-class bias in predominantly British and North

American media exemplifying postfeminist norms and accordingly focused their attentions on popular genres that confirmed this bias, the elisions of such an approach have since been identified (see Butler 2013; Dosekun 2015). In an influential piece particularly relevant for my argument, Jess Butler challenged the assumption that the scholarly focus on white women within postfeminist media studies could be attributed to an absence of diverse representation, citing numerous examples of women of colour enacting postfeminist identity, especially in the domains of music and reality television. Butler's point about the heightened visibility of women of colour on reality television is a pertinent one, for while Meghan Markle did *not* become famous as a result of reality television appearances, there have been repeated attempts in the anti-fandom to align her with this genre and its associations of inauthentic 'trash' culture. An association with reality television, a genre that Butler implies is less associated with the white middle-class, is therefore mobilised as a tool to destabilise the upward trajectory of a black woman who has found unequivocal success on postfeminist culture's terms. For in reality television, upward mobility is a *wish* to be granted by discerning judges and voters rather than a promise. In *MailOnline* commentary, anti-fans cast themselves as these discerning judges, and in associating Markle with a racialized form of television entertainment seek to render her an unviable form of royal femininity.

Reality show formats, in their various competitive guises, invite talent quest viewers to judge whether contestants are uniquely and 'authentically' talented or mere derivative copies of successful artists. They invite dating show viewers to assess if participants are involved in the competition for the 'right reasons', here translated as the pursuit of romance over fame and fortune. Spectatorial pleasure in such reality modes is in part derived from a heightened participatory element, with viewers playing a role in bestowing fame upon deserving contestants in a manner that may be experienced as more empowering than traditional fandom. Popular Markle criticism mimics reality show spectatorship in that her elevated celebrity status is treated by observers as highly precarious and conditional upon their approval that she is both a natural fit for her royal role and is motivated out of love and duty as opposed to money and power. Her perceived failure on the latter counts is framed as evidence of an alignment with a 'lower class' of celebrity linked implicitly to blackness, with Markle often compared to Kim Kardashian, an iconic albeit maligned reality star notorious for achieving a stratospheric level of fame disconnected from accomplishment.[2] The likening of Markle to Kardashian, a woman of colour considered by many as undeserving of fame, raises questions about the interrelationship between the public regulation of women of colour enacting postfeminism, the 'authenticity' (or lack thereof) of different kinds of celebrity, and how this judgement of authenticity may relate to peculiarly white interests, investments and fantasies, such as the investment in the British monarchy. One of Anne Rowbottom's (2020) interviewees in her study of dedicated royalists, for example, identifies the royal family as one of the last remaining symbols of a once great British nation. The participant explains that 'over the past 20–30 years we have lost our colonies, our industries and our British passports have been replaced by European ones, we have lost almost everything' (Rowbottom 2020: 37).

The levering of Markle into devalued categories of celebrity is driven by a vehement and collective affect, with reality television viewership notable for its striking association with 'hatewatching' (Gilbert 2019). Further consideration of celebrity hatewatching, powerful in its collective sociality, is necessary if scholarly analysis of postfeminism is to better understand its race and class dynamics and its relationship to investments in whiteness. As Sara Ahmed (2014) argues, emotionality is deeply embedded in structures of power and is boundary forming, with collective affect contributing to feelings of attachment and a sense of place. In this case, negative affect is projected at the racialized and abjected other as a means of safeguarding British identity as white. Correspondingly, Martha Nussbaum (2001) points out that one's emotional appraisal of external persons is closely related to one's perceived ability to flourish or to meet their own goals. In the case of Markle, there is a sense that her pathway to success was heavily calculated and thus 'unfair' in its flouting of the rules of the royal meet cute where a Prince traditionally recognises his future Princess for her innately royal (and gender appropriate) qualities. As Mara May commented on the article about fake pregnancy claims (Elson 2019), 'people don't like her cos she's a nasty little hypocritical trash. She uses people and is using harry. Who cares? Just don't put her on the papers every day' (1611 upvotes, 239 down). As capitalism rewards only a select few, the feeling that one has wrongfully missed out while another has been unfairly rewarded, or a sense that others are making misleading claims that will lead to unearned benefit, are not uncommon and likely shared by many. Therefore, investigations into how current iterations of postfeminism function within an interpersonal politics of resentment are necessary.

## The class–race–gender positioning of Markle

In *MailOnline* commentary, Markle is commonly referred to by the nicknames 'Meagain' and 'Sparkles' in reference to what anti-fans see as a narcissistic desire to claim a disproportionate share of the limelight and a reluctance to serve the public. The nickname 'Sparkles' mockingly references the glitz and glamour of Markle's Hollywood past but is invoked in a manner that distinguishes Markle as a striving minor celebrity who does not exhibit the required talent needed to reach the A-list on her own merits. On the article covering Markle's Wimbledon appearance (Morgan 2019), commenter Sesmarias writes 'she is utterly classless, a typical z list cheap actress', while Vye comments on her fashion awards appearance (Blott et al. 2018), 'she loves being fawned. Two-bit actress no one would have looked at if she had not become royal. What a tragedy for this country that she did' (16,597 upvotes, 1338 down). The charge that Markle did not only attain a high level of achievement as an actress again coincides with her alignment with 'low value' stardom, but also frames her public presentation as staged and mechanical – an amateur drama school performance to be scrutinised. This holds implications for how we understand the role of 'cruel optimism' (Berlant 2011) in the renegotiation of postfeminist media culture. If optimism is experienced as cruel when upward mobility fails to eventuate despite adherence to an individualistic and self-regulatory set of terms, then the public mockery of those who are seen to be 'wrongfully' enjoying these rewards can become a type of game. The players, knowledgeable of (and mostly committed to) the rules, can seek to 'correct' individual outcomes via a form of induced cruelty, presumably hoping to render the good life's rewards less palatable than they otherwise may have been.

The disparaging use of the nickname Sparkles is further significant given the centrality of sparkle and spectacle to fairytale makeover myth and postfeminist media culture alike, with Mary Celeste Kearney (2015) arguing that the appearance of glamorous luminosity is exclusive and often predicated on whiteness and class privilege. Kearney, drawing on Dyer (1997), points out that sparkle has a lineage in the representation of idealised female stars as heavenly and glowing, a look now purchasable through a glittering array of clothing and makeup, and which is symbolised though the imagery of many stars, including Princess Diana (Dyer 1997; Shome 2001; Weidhase 2021). Paradoxically, the framing of Markle's sparkle in inverted commas serves as a form of containment preventing full inclusion and resultant admiration, instead gesturing toward her apparent *desire* for an iconic marker of status that she holds no legitimate claim to. Such framing is aided by the implication that Markle's lower category of postfeminist celebrity, a judgement not inextricable from her race or class origins, reduces access to a more authentic kind of sparkle conferred through external recognition that one is unique, special or one-of-a-kind. Such sparkle best functions within a protected fantasy space where glamour and spectacle operate in a nostalgic, carefree and unapologetic manner, which is perhaps why it appears to befit and better circulate among dominant social groups. In a purely visible sense, monarchic sparkle is best observed at state banquets and awards ceremonies where royal women are granted full license to don tiaras and expensive custom gowns in the presence of esteemed guests. On visits to lower socio-economic British communities or indeed poorer Commonwealth countries, where there is greater potential for accusations of gross inequality and the monarchy's role within it to arise, sparkle must be tactfully dialled down to assist a symbolic bid to represent the human ordinary as opposed to divine extraordinary – an occasion for H&M and Zara rather than Givenchy. Important here is that strategic performances of anti-sparkle in the right circumstances allow it to thrive elsewhere, naturalising the right to sparkle for a 'deserving' elite that doubles as an aspirational fantasy for onlookers. The persistent and gleeful use of the nickname 'Sparkles' is additionally an inference that Markle's attempts to sparkle are not only poor but also mismanaged in that they occur irrespective of appropriateness, thus constituting a threat to the white nationalist fantasy.

Central to the discourse that Markle's sparkle is both overly earnest and poorly managed is an assessment that she is not only a poor imitator but also a calculated usurper of true 'originals', with comparator originals judged as deserving of their fame based on a superior level of talent or charisma. Reality television is of course preoccupied with separating the truly deserving from those who attempt to follow the rules but ultimately fail to convince, and as a result lose the game. Here, Markle is seen to not only fail the rules of the royal game but also to have never entirely succeeded on the terms of a competitive postfeminist culture either. Accusations of mimicry or co-optation are common methods of devaluation that protect practices, people or policies important to the assessor. At times, such judgements are somewhat tongue-in-cheek. The description of Megan Fox on forums such as *gamespot* or *Reddit as* a 'poor man's Angelina Jolie' (Squall18 2010; u/diamond9 2009), for example acknowledges Fox's close resemblance to a more established star, but also utilises a classed and gendered framework to allude to a kitschy cheapness in characterising Fox as an assembly line imitation of the true original. Such methods of devaluation seek to discredit the 'copy', or categorise enjoyment of the copy as a guilty pleasure, while working to preserve the original's merits and elite status. Likewise, reality TV competitions often ask us to spot the unique and authentic stars amid a sea of varyingly talented imitators. However, while mimicry of the celebrated is a performative element that reality television show spectators are encouraged to identify, 'Markle sparkle' is not merely judged as borrowed but as borrowed with sinister intent and as such she is characterised as the villain of the 'show'. Markle's royal performances are asserted to be *unnatural,* with evidence of a less aristocratic pedigree, a race and class identity that is decidedly out of step, to be collated and shared among the anti-fandom.

According to Weidhase (2021), certain quarters of the British Press have drawn comparisons between Markle and Princess Diana (in particular) in their shared love of fashion and dedication to humanitarian causes, which she argues constitutes a 'whitening' of Markle's image in that the pair are represented as sharing a transcendent glow. Yet, there is also an insidious counter narrative that asserts Markle does not innately have this glow but rather has a long history of carefully cultivating and performing the 'glow' of others in a plagiarism of authentic charisma. In Hollywood cinema, there has long been a fascination with stories of sinister female doubling that initially masquerade as tales of female fandom or friendship. Sianne Ngai (2005) points out that in films of envious and 'diseased selfhood' such as *All About Eve* (Mankiewicz 1950) and *Single White Female* (Schroeder 1992), the imitator does not attempt to achieve a union with her ego ideal, but rather seeks to transform the ideal into a pale imitation, a copy without an originating category, or as Ngai puts it, a 'bad example'. In anti-Markle lore, the Duchess is accused of plagiarising notable women from Eleanor Roosevelt to Maya Angelou and of copying Jennifer Lopez's wedding gown from *The Wedding Planner* (Shankman 2001). In Andrew Morton's (2018) biography *Meghan: A Hollywood Princess,* she is described by a 'childhood friend' as long intent on becoming 'Diana 2.0'. Prevalent on comment boards too are observations of Markle's apparent mimicry of Kate Middleton. Judging Markle's Wimbledon appearance (Brennan 2019), CSDNYC commented to 1104 upvotes and 70 down: 'Anyone else noticed she tried to recreate the photos of Catherine from a few days ago? The sunglasses, the sitting between 2 women, the standing shot ... Typical creepy narcissist behaviour'.

Discussing the title of *Single White Female,* Ngai argues that the raced adjective of the title constitutes an irritation in that no amount of consumerist or behavioural mimicry could ever result in the original and the copy becoming one. Racial difference constitutes a barrier to the narrative goal of indistinguishability, a barrier that is exploited here among Markle's detractors who accuse her of appropriating the (white) specialness of other royals. She *cannot* and *will not* succeed in the imaginary endeavour these royal watchers have created for her, for they have empowered themselves through their implication that they can always spot the difference. The positioning of Markle as imposter and imitator further serves to preserve nationalistic fantasies of what British, white royal femininity *should* be and is enabled by participatory forms of anti-fandom popular within a postfeminist media culture that fetishises competition (and especially competition among women) as spectacle. Interestingly, while Kate Middleton routinely restages famous photographs of Princess Diana, for example outside the hospital following the birth of Prince George wearing a similar polka-dotted dress to Diana's original when she first gave birth, in Bradby's Africa documentary it is only Prince Harry who is filmed retracing Diana's steps. As Harry is filmed alone meeting Angolan landmine victim Sandra Thijika 22 years after his mother was famously photographed doing so, it could be surmised that the producers knew that to draw too close a visual parallel between Princess Diana and Meghan Markle would be to invite a barrage of negative criticism.

## Markle as impurity invading the white British nation

Notable in the Markle anti-fandom is an espoused refusal to look on the Duchess as an object of desire, with many royal watchers instead collectively rejecting her as a role model to be adored or emulated in proclaiming her behaviour disgusting. While the British royal family receives income from public taxation, and Markle was independently wealthy prior to marrying Harry, there is a readiness in anti-Markle commentary to cast her as intent on reaping the rewards of a consumer society without doing any of the work. Commenters often describe her purchases and activities as an unwelcome drain on their finances and use metaphors of physical illness to voice their displeasure. As Ngai (2005: 335) explains, while desire and disgust may appear distinct and distant from one another, they are interrelated in the sense that the disgusting object 'makes an outrageous claim for desirability…imposing itself on the subject as something to be mingled with and perhaps even enjoyed'. Expressions of disgust with Markle are prevalent on *Daily Mail* comment boards, with many likening her presence to an unwelcome boundary infiltration that must be expelled. Commenting on Blott's 2018 article on Markle's appearance at the British Fashion Awards, for instance commenter Someone, Somewhere wrote:

> Enough. I'm sick of this woman. I'm sick of the million dollar wardrobe and the mother I'm going to have to pay for, I'm sick of the way she keeps cradling the bump I'm going to

have to pay for as if no other woman has ever gotten pregnant, sick of the fake, doe-eyed expression on her small mean face, sick of the rotten way she treats her dad, ex friends and pets and I'm sick of having her shoved off on me. She now gets more stories than the Kardashians and she's only MARRIED to the SIXTH in line to the throne.

*(4572 upvotes, 179 down)*

A feeling of financial victimhood is evidenced in the commenter's anger at Markle's extravagance and in their feeling of being forced to pay for Markle's dependents – in particular, it must be noted, her black mother. The commenter also resents Markle receiving public money as they have judged her to be absent the forgiving and charitable personality culturally associated with (white) Queens and Princesses who promote the nation and its leadership role internationally. Success as an ideal postfeminist subject, on the other hand, has long depended on putting the self first in keeping with a neoliberal individualistic ethos, a fact that commenters implicitly remind readers of when they post of Markle's selfishness. Despite Markle's attempts to conform to the royal model through her charitable work and patronages, her alternative characterisation as a 'gold digger', a 'hustler', and a 'welfare queen' associate her with race and gender stereotypes that accuse her of taking more from British society than she contributes. Ironically, such stereotypes are both produced by and indicative of neoliberal discourse, constituting a double bind for the postfeminist actor in relation to a defining myth of the British monarchy – that it is driven by public service and a communal good.

The term #Megxit is not therefore merely a cute word play on #Brexit, but rather is driven by a similar nationalistic sentiment in the form of micro-targeting that individualises key economic and social drivers within an interpersonal politics of resentment. As Weidhase (2021) notes, discourses of Markle manipulating Prince Harry contribute to her representation as 'unpatriotic' and correspond to fears of foreigners (i.e. the EU) limiting British sovereignty and agency. Plentiful are comments that Markle induces the urge to vomit, suggesting that the newest royal is an unwelcome national ingestion to be purged by the indignant citizen. In this manner, Markle's inclusion in the family is often likened to an unwelcome corporeal pathology – a blemish or parasite compromising the health of the body politic. Commenter Rhirhi, remarking on the Duchess's appearance at the British Fashion Awards, writes 'if Meagain cradles her bump once more I'm going to puke. Kate didn't do any of this kind of attention grabbing because she isn't a narcissist like Sparkles' (2513 upvotes, 68 down). It is relevant that this reaction is to Markle's pregnancy, as the child will not be white and thus constitutes an intrusion or parasite on the white, British nation. Markle's pregnancy also was the subject of a conspiracy theory, known on Twitter as #Moonbump, in which conspirators swapped thoughts on Markle's suspiciously fluctuating bump size and secretive post-birth plans. Moonbump served as the ultimate counter-fantasy of illegitimacy, in which Markle's perceived strategies could be exposed in an online game where an enlightened few could play at elevating themselves above the blindly obsequious.

## Conclusion

The British royal family is a powerful symbol of British nationhood and heritage as white, with the inclusion of Meghan Markle in this family seen by many to directly threaten such symbolism. Royal women embody the boundary that ensures the racial purity of the nation with the preservation of white nationalist fantasies requiring forms of boundary policing that disproportionately target female members of the 'firm'. Anti-fans have been able to harness Markle's association with postfeminist cultural discourses, which themselves 'conspire' to privilege whiteness, to police this boundary by emphasising her unfitness for royal life through a rejection of postfeminist identity. Yet, while Markle has been relentlessly taunted in online spaces like the *MailOnline* comments section, the Duchess herself claimed, in a heavily publicised interview with US talk show host Oprah Winfrey, that forms of racialized boundary policing also occurred within the institution. Speaking out about the family's failure to correct falsehoods about her in the British Press or to provide adequate care for her failing mental health, Markle shared that a senior royal expressed concern over how 'dark' her son Archie's skin would be. From this, we can infer that there was concern about how Archie's appearance may potentially alter the symbolism of the monarchy and its associated brand values. Therefore, the boundary policing that occurred throughout Meghan Markle's time as a working royal was a mutually reinforcing one, carried out by the British Press and public alike in service of an institution that is entirely cognisant of the version of 'Britain' they represent and its concomitant race, class, and gender politics. As such, the events of #Megxit can tell us much about the significance of white nostalgic symbolism for those seen to embody a reassuring ideal of nationhood as well as for those seeking to ease their anxiety in an increasingly polarised and inequitable world.

## Notes

1   Published pre-engagement, this article set a trend for Markle-related *Daily Mail* commentary in emphasising the (implicitly irreconcilable) distinction between Markle's allegedly 'troubled', 'tatty', and crime-ridden childhood neighbourhood and Prince Harry's 'palatial' upbringing. The author also outlines Markle's parents' history of money problems, foreshadowing later applications of the gold-digger stereotype.

2   In a *Daily Mail* article (Richardson 2019) on Meghan's awareness of being 'pitted' against Kate Middleton, for instance commenter Le-barn posted to an encouraging 1863 upvotes (and 50 down) that 'Kate is a young royal, Meghan is a reality TV contestant'. Meanwhile, the top (anonymous) comment reaching 5,729 upvotes to 395 down for a column about the 'sick trolls' claiming Markle to be faking her pregnancy (Elson 2019), read 'not sure about the bump, but everything else about the Duchess of Kardashian is absolutely false'. In the Fox documentary *Harry & Meghan: A Royal Crisis,* vocal critic Piers Morgan likened Markle to a 'mini royal Kim Kardashian', while Buckingham Palace was forced to issue a denial that the royal couple had hired the reality star's endorsement firm Sheeraz Inc. to build their brand on relocation to North America.

## References

Ahmed, S. 2014. *The Cultural Politics of Emotion*, 2nd ed. Edinburgh: Edinburgh University Press.

All About Eve. 1950. Film. Directed by J. L. Mankiewicz. USA: 20th Century Fox.

Berlant, L. 2011. *Cruel Optimism*. Durham, NC: Duke University Press.

Blott, U., Wheeler, O. and Linning, S. 2018. '"I'm celebrating Britain … my new home!" Duchess of Sussex STUNS onlookers in surprise appearance to honour wedding dress designer at Fashion Awards', *MailOnline*, 11 December, viewed 3 May 2020, https://www.dailymail.co.uk/femail/article-64 81215/Meghan-Markle-British-Fashion-Awards.html.

Brennan, S. 2019. 'Meghan channels tennis whites in a pleated skirt while Kate re-wears a green £2,150 D&G dress – as "duelling duchesses" quash feud rumours by sharing jokes as they watch Serena LOSE Wimbledon final', *MailOnline*, 13 July, viewed 3 May 2020, https://www.dailymail.co.uk/femail/ article-7243641/Kate-Meghan-end-feud-rumours-attend-Wimbledon.html-comments.

Butler, J. 2013. For White Girls Only? Postfeminism and the Politics of Inclusion. *Feminist Formations*, 25 (1): 35–58.

Dosekun, S. 2015. For Western Girls Only? Post-feminism as Transnational Culture. *Feminist Media Studies*, 15 (6): 960–975.

Dyer, R. 1997. *White*. London: Routledge.

Elson, J. 2019. 'Sick online trolls are claiming Meghan's baby bump is a FAKE prosthetic in bizarre conspiracy theory', *MailOnline*, 8 April, viewed 3 May 2020, https://www.dailymail.co.uk/news/article-6896153/Sick-online-trolls-claiming-Meghan-Markles-baby-bump-FAKE-prosthetic.html.

English, R. and Robinson, M. 2019. '"They could've moved next door!" Fury as it emerges Harry and Meghan spent 2.4 million of YOUR cash on Frogmore Cottage "to escape rift with Kate and William" – and final bill could hit 3m', *MailOnline*, 25 June, viewed 3 May 2020, https://www.dailymail.co.uk/news/article-7176813/How-Meghan-Harry-splashed-2–4m-taxpayers-cash-new-bathrooms-bedrooms-kitchen.html.

Feigin, S. 2019. 'Meghan Markle Tatler Survey: Nearly Half of Brits don't think Duchess of Sussex has been good for Royal Family', Evening Standard, 25 October, viewed 18 August 2021, https://www.standard.co.uk/insider/royals/meghan-markle-tatler-survey-nearly-half-of-brits-don-t-think-duchess-of-sussex-has-been-good-for-royal-family-a4271076.html

Gilbert, A. 2019. Hatewatch with Me: Anti-Fandom as Social Performance. In *Anti-Fandom: Dislike and Hate in the Digital Age*, ed. M. Click, pp. 62–80. New York: New York University Press.

Gill, R. 2007. Postfeminist Media Culture: Elements of a Sensibility. *European Journal of Cultural Studies*, 10 (2): 147–166.

Gill, R. 2016. Post-postfeminism? New Feminist Visibilities in Postfeminist Times. *Feminist Media Studies*, 16 (4): 610–630.

Hage, G. 2000. *White Nation: Fantasies of White Supremacy in a Multicultural Society*. New York: Routledge.

Harry and Meghan: An African Journey. 2019. Documentary. Directed by N. Lippiett. UK: ITV.

Harry and Meghan: The Royals in Crisis. 2020. Documentary. USA: Fox.

Hooks, B. 2014. *Sisters of the Yam: Black Women and Self-Recovery*, 2nd edn. New York: Routledge.

Kearney, M. C. 2015. Sparkle: Luminosity and Post-girl Power Media. *Continuum: Journal of Media & Cultural Studies*, 29 (2): 263–273.

Lipsitz, G. 1998. *The Possessive Investment in Whiteness: How White People Profit from Identity Politics*. Philadelphia: Temple University Press.

Littler, J. 2017. *Against Meritocracy: Culture, Power, and Myths of Mobility*. London: Routledge.

McRobbie, A. 2009. *The Aftermath of Feminism: Gender, Culture and Social Change*. London: SAGE Publications.

McRobbie, A. 2015. Notes on the Perfect: Competitive Femininity in Neoliberal Times. *Australian Feminist Studies*, 30 (83): 3–20.

Morgan, C. 2019. 'Meghan is joined by two old friends at Wimbledon as she makes surprise appearance to cheer pal Serena Williams to victory (so they could be Archie's secret godparents?)', *MailOnline*, 5 July, viewed 3 May 2020, https://www.dailymail.co.uk/femail/article-7214133/Duchess-Sussex-makes-surprise-appearance-Wimbledon-cheer-pal-Serena.html-comments.

Morton, A. 2018. *Meghan: A Hollywood Princess*. New York: Grand Central Publishing.

Ngai, S. 2005. *Ugly Feelings*. Cambridge: Harvard University Press.

Nussbaum, M. C. 2001. *Upheavals of Thought: The Intelligence of Emotions*. Cambridge: Cambridge University Press.

Projansky, S. 2001. *Watching Rape: Film and Television in Postfeminist Culture*. New York: New York University Press.

Randell-Moon, H. 2017. Thieves Like Us: The British Monarchy, Celebrity, and Settler Colonialism. *Celebrity Studies*, 8 (3): 393–408.

Richardson, H. 2019. 'Meghan Markle is "aware" she is being "pitted against" future queen Kate Middleton and finds the situation "challenging", a source tells People magazine', *MailOnline*, 25 November, viewed 3 May 2020, https://www.dailymail.co.uk/femail/article-7722387/Meghan-Markle-aware-pitted-against-future-queen-Kate-Middleton-source-claims.html-reader-comments>.

Rowbottom, A. 2020. Subject Positions and 'Real Royalists:' Monarchy and Vernacular Civil Religion in Great Britain. In *British Subjects: An Anthropology of Britain*, ed. N. Rapport, pp. 31–47. Oxon: Routledge.

Sandvoss, C. 2019. The Politics of Against: Political Participation, Anti-fandom, and Populism. In *Anti-Fandom: Dislike and Hate in the Digital Age*, ed. M. Click, pp. 125–147. New York: New York University Press.

Shome, R. 2001. White Femininity and the Discourse of the Nation: Re/membering Princess Diana. *Feminist Media Studies*, 1 (3): 323–342.

Single White Female. 1992. Film. Directed by B. Schroeder. USA: Columbia Pictures.

Squall18. 2010. 'Do you agree with this saying: Megan Fox is the poor man's Angelina Jolie', *Gamespot*, viewed 17 May 2020, https://www.gamespot.com/forums/offtopic-discussion-314159273/do-you-agree-with-this-saying-quot-megan-fox-is-th-27331281/.

Styles, R. 2016. 'EXCLUSIVE: Harry's girl is (almost) straight outta Compton: Gang-scarred home of her mother revealed – so will he be dropping by for tea?', *Daily Mail*, 2 November, viewed 17 May 2020, https://www.dailymail.co.uk/news/article-3896180/Prince-Harry-s-girlfriend-actress-Meghan-Markles.html.

Suits. 2011-2019. USA Network. TV, Netflix.

Tasker, Y. and Negra, D., eds. 2007. *Interrogating Postfeminism: Gender and the Politics of Popular Culture.* Durham, NC: Duke University Press.

Toolan, M. 2016. Peter Black, Christopher Stevens, Class and Inequality in the Daily Mail. *Discourse & Society*, 27 (6): 642–660.

u/diamond9. 2009. 'Megan Fox: The poor man's version of Angelina Jolie', *Reddit*, viewed 17 May 2020, https://www.reddit.com/r/offbeat/comments/8ufgs/megan_fox_the_poor_mans_version_of_angelina_jolie/.

Weidhase, N. 2021. The Feminist Politics of Meghan Markle: Brexit, Femininity and the Nation in Crisis. *European Journal of Cultural Studies* [Online]. https://doi.org/10.1177%2F1367549420980010

The Wedding Planner. 2001. Film. Directed by A. Shankman. USA. Sony Pictures.

# 9

# Colour-blind ideologies: The whiteness of liberalism and socialism

*Mandisi Majavu*

## Introduction

This chapter aims to historicise the evolution of colour-blind ideologies in South Africa from the nineteenth-century Cape Colony to twentieth-century apartheid South Africa. En route, this chapter demonstrates ways in which colour-blind ideologies were used by Whites to portray themselves as possessing an 'objective authority' and 'expert knowledge' to solving the so-called 'Native question' (Bateman 2008). Thus, Blacks who challenged this White narrative were demonised as being divisive and 'anti-White'.

Biko (2004: 21) argues that White leftists and White liberals have always pretended to know 'what was good for the blacks and told them so'. Biko (2004: 21) demonstrates that this has historically manifested itself 'in the "non-racial" set-up', which has often been achieved in 'a one-way course, with whites doing all the talking and the blacks the listening'. Biko (2004: 26) identifies Whiteness as the fundamental basis on which White-Black relations and social interaction occurred in the late twentieth century, a social situation in which Whites assumed the role of 'a perpetual teacher and the black a perpetual pupil'. Thus, Biko (2004: 26) argued against 'the intellectual arrogance' of White thinkers who believed that their intellectual leadership was *sine qua non* in the intellectual production of Black liberation politics.

Inspired by Steve Biko, this chapter contradicts the official narrative that positions colour-blind ideologies as the hotbed of politics against White racism in South Africa. Part one of the chapter traces the ideological roots of colour-blind ideologies to the nineteenth-century worldview of White missionaries in the Cape Colony. It illustrates ways in which White missionaries' colour-blind views on race shaped and influenced what is often referred to as Cape liberalism. The second part of the chapter demonstrates the ways in which Cape liberalism was resuscitated in the early twentieth century by White liberal institutions such as the Joint Councils of Europeans and Natives – to cultivate political solidarity and collaboration among racial groups in a way that did not disrupt White control of South Africa. To that end, the twentieth-century liberals centred the concept of 'non-racialism' in their liberal conversation about race and racism. The third part of the chapter proves that by the mid-twentieth-century Whites had weaponised non-racialism; they claimed that a race analysis was a 'false consciousness', and asserted that apartheid was a 'class struggle' that affected every working class person, and that both poor Whites and Blacks were equally marginalised and oppressed by the apartheid system (Rodriguez and Freeman 2016). The chapter concludes by pointing out that in post-apartheid South Africa, colour-blind ideologies have not resulted in the erosion of White racism (Song 2018).

## Racial liberalism in the Cape Colony

In the nineteenth century, White missionaries' views on race were culturally shaped by a racialising monogenism discourse. The monogenism perspective is premised on the view that 'blacks represented a "degenerate" form of the white race', and thus the return of the Black race to a White type is possible through various social options – such as converting to Christianity, acquiring Western education, imitating Whites, or through 'perpetual crossbreeding' between Whites and Blacks (Daut 2012). Monogenism regards all human beings as descendants of Adam, and therefore grants Black people a place in humanity, albeit as humans who had 'degenerated' but could 'improve' again to achieve civilisation in a relatively short time (Curtin 1964). Samuel Johnson's (1765) dictionary captures the eighteenth-century definition of degeneracy as 'departing from virtue of our ancestors', 'a falling from a more excellent state to one of less worth', and 'forsaking what is good'. According to Raymond Williams (1983), the word 'civilization' was preceded in the English language by the word 'civilize'. In the seventeenth and eighteenth centuries, the word 'civility' was used to describe an 'ordered society' (Williams 1983: 48). John Ash's (1775) dictionary gives the eighteenth-century definition of civilisation as 'the state of being civilised' and 'the acts of civilising'; he defines civilise and civilising as 'to reclaim from savageness' and 'to instruct in the arts of civil life'. Similar to Johnson's definition, Ash's (1775) dictionary defines savage and savageness as 'ferocity', 'wildness', and 'a man untaught'. According to Williams (1983: 48–49), Ash's definition of the word 'civilisation' is premised on the 'general spirit of the Enlightenment', and to that end communicates 'an achieved condition of refinement and order', as well as a 'progressive human self-development'. By the nineteenth century, the definition of the earlier-mentioned words had become part of the public epistemology (Williams 1983).

To make sense of White racism of nineteenth-century White missionaries in the Cape Colony, this chapter locates and frames the worldview of these missionaries within a wider historical context. Although the White missionaries advocated for the political freedoms of Black people, they did so in such a way that confirmed the racialising discourse about Black people. Theirs was a racialising discourse because, first and foremost, it reinforced racial colour categories that were rooted in monogenism moral and social frameworks (Hoquet 2014). White missionaries in the Cape Colony merged a monogenism intellectual framework with liberal intuitions and sentiments to produce a locally flavoured racial liberalism, which has historically been referred to as Cape liberalism. It is racial liberalism in the sense that it promoted the idea that the 'white man's burden' was, among other thing, to establish a 'civilised society' for 'savages' who were residents of a Hobbesian state of nature, which was characterised in terms of wilderness, violence, and wasteland (Mills 1997).

The racial liberalism promulgated by White missionaries and other White liberals in the Cape Colony included a commitment to the abolition of slavery, a class-based limited franchise for people of colour – while foregrounding a British cultural and moral supremacy – and 'an implied authority on the part of the colonizer/missionary' (Bateman 2008: 73). This strand of racial liberalism was saturated with 'imperial discourse' that advocated for a 'benign' colonial project that went hand-in-hand with a racialising reclamation project to uplift, civilise, and reclaim Africans 'from their delight of licentious barbarism unto the love of goodness and civility' (Bateman 2008; Spenser 1763: 18). It is against this background that British critics of British colonialism in the Cape Colony, like Saxe Bannister (1830), advocated for a colonial project that was based on a 'humane policy' and justice. Bannister (1830: vi) wrote:

> If we, the civilized, could not, physically exist in the same land with the barbarian and the savage without destroying them, it would be a paramount duty to discourage the extension of colonies; but history, early and recent, where the civilized have been just, shows all men to be capable of improvement; and the same experience also shows, that doing justice is the grand means to ensure the amelioration and the mutual safety of the most dissimilar races.

This discursive combination of White racism and egalitarianism norms was not particularly unique to the Cape Colony. Rather, it was a profoundly influential ideology among White missionaries of the nineteenth century. Cape liberalism was part of a global movement that took place in the nineteenth century (Rich 1980). Britain's Victorian liberalism laid the discursive foundation for Cape liberalism (Wilburn 2013). South African liberals regarded the Victorian model of liberalism as 'the yardstick by which to judge much of their own actions and achievements' (Rich 1980: 13). The Victorian model of liberalism has been described as ideologically sympathetic to the British Empire. Thus, Jennifer Pitts (2005: 11) argues that liberal thinkers in Britain in the early decades of the nineteenth century were convinced that Europe's civilisation gave the Europeans the authority to 'suspend, in their relations with non-European societies, the moral and political standards they believed applied among themselves' (Pitts 2005: 11). According to Cooper (2002: 17), 'by the nineteenth century, Britons considered themselves to be a distinct, special, and superior race, set apart by a shared superior Western civilization'.

In a nutshell, both White missionaries and the colonial government in the nineteenth-century Cape Colony subscribed to a colonising discourse, which was based on the Victorian model of liberalism. Cape liberalism was responsible for the Ordinance 50 of 1829, which removed 'the Cape Coloureds from their status of indentured servants and establishing formal legal equality' (Rich 1980: 16). Furthermore, due to Victorian liberalism, slavery was abolished by the British Parliament 'throughout the British Empire, including the Cape Colony of southern Africa, in 1834' (Watson 2012: 1). When the colonial government in the Cape Colony was granted representative institutions by the British government in 1853, Cape liberalism introduced a colour-blind voter franchise (Trapido 1964). However, to qualify for the franchise, one had to reside at a property valued at £25 (Trapido 1964). Moreover, as soon as the number of potential African voters increased and therefore threatened to overwhelm White voters, the government of the Cape Colony raised the property value qualification to £75 (Wilburn 2013). Additionally, a literacy test was introduced as another criterion to qualify for suffrage (Wilburn 2013). Francis Wilson (2011: 5) explains that there were very few educated Africans with property qualifications in the late nineteenth century, and even they had no power 'in an overwhelmingly racist society'.

This chapter argues that overall the liberal freedoms introduced throughout the Cape Colony in the nineteenth century were 'tightly circumscribed, in some respects even illusory' (Watson 2012: 1). Socially, Whites were regarded and behaved like colonial overlords of Blacks. Social and racial relations were deeply shaped by a racial liberalism that reinforced a racialising hierarchy with those considered to be 'White', Christian, and 'civilised' at the top of the hierarchy, while those identified as 'Other', 'Hottentots', 'Caffres', African, 'heathen', and 'savage' were at the bottom of that hierarchy (Cleall 2012). Whites in the Cape Colony utilised a monogenistic inflected vocabulary to describe and to talk about the 'natives'. For instance,

Reverend Thornley Smith (1848b: 991) described the population in the Cape Colony as 'not merely inhabited by emigrants', but containing a mixed population, for example: 'There are not only found in them the refined European, but also the rude and barbarous Kaffir, the swarthy Negro, and the idolatrous Hindoo'. Among other things, the ideological function of this monogenistic racialising discourse was to confirm the racist discourse that White missionaries and White settlers knew 'something objectively just by looking at a person's skin colour; that all the "negroes" were slaves, for example' (Daut 2015: 20).

Moreover, one of the defining features of Cape liberalism was the notion that colonies were 'indispensable to every seafaring and commercial nation' like Great Britain (Smith 1848a: 881). Writing in The Wesleyan-Methodist magazine in the mid-nineteenth century, Reverend Thornley Smith (1848a: 882) further observed that:

> It is doubtless in the order of a superintending Providence, and accordant with the spirit of the original command, 'Increase and multiply, and replenish the earth, and subdue it,' that man should go forth, and occupy those countries which are lying waste, or are but thinly peopled, but which, if cultivated, would yield a rich supply of all the necessaries of life.

Hence, British colonisation in South Africa could not 'be condemned as a whole' (Smith 1848a: 882).

> Evils have been associated with it; but these evils are not necessary parts of the system; and as the principles of justice and humanity spread, they will be separated from it, and be numbered only among 'the things which were.

Slave abolitionists and Christian missionaries in the late eighteenth century and early nineteenth century subscribed to racial liberalism and used it to advocate for colonialism of 'backward lands'; not for 'sordid greed', but for the purpose of spreading European civilisation (Kiernan 2015). Missionaries saw the imperial project as consisting of spreading European civilisation, peace and 'good governance to the unenlightened' (Magubane 1997: 19). The idea of 'Europe's "mission" dawned early, but it was taken seriously in the nineteenth century' (Kiernan 2015: 24). Christian missionaries saw themselves as playing a vital role in Europe's imperialistic projects. As far as missionaries were concerned, their role required them to exercise authority over indigenous people on the one hand, while acting as a restraint to aggressive colonial forces on the other (Lester 2009). On the ground in the colonies, missionaries imposed their version of Christian, humanitarian imperialism, which clashed with the objectives of the secular settler societies (Lester 2009). Sir Thomas Fowell Buxton, an English Member of Parliament and an abolitionist, helped to disseminate the missionaries' humanitarian narrative throughout the British Empire (Lester 2009). Secular settler societies in Australia, New Zealand, and the Cape Colony viewed the missionaries' narrative as threatening their access to the British government and public opinion in Britain, because it portrayed secular settler societies as immoral for overseeing violent colonial projects in places like the Cape Colony (Lester 2009). Missionaries and missionary societies like the London Missionary Society exercised their greatest influence in the Cape Colony between 1806 and 1840 (Magubane 1997).

By the end of the 1800s, however – partly due to the 100-year Frontier Wars that the Dutch and British fought against Blacks throughout the nineteenth century in the Cape Colony, and partly due to the South African mineral revolution of the late nineteenth century and the demand for cheap labour it created – the missionary narrative about Blacks undergoing an improvement process was replaced by an anti-Black racist discourse that portrayed Blacks as 'lazy', 'thieves', 'war-like', and 'irreclaimable savages' (Crais 1992: 249; Maylam 2001). Furthermore, the rise of scientific racism in the late nineteenth century, which spread throughout South Africa, was employed by secular Whites to displace racial liberalism as an official narrative of the industrialising South Africa.

The Anglo-Boer War, which took place from 1899 to 1902, ushered in a new century with an organised and much more collective White supremacist project in South Africa. The conflict between Whites (British and Afrikaans) was partly for the control of the South African diamond and gold mines (Bolt 1984). Unlike the mainstream South African historiography that often foregrounds the conflict and struggle between the Afrikaners and British imperialism as a driving historical force of South African history, this chapter rather puts a discursive emphasis on the shared adherence to White supremacy by these White groups (Willoughby-Herard 2015; Wright 1980). The difference between the Boers and the British colonists is that the Boers were never invested in a reclamation project, nor were they interested in 'improving' the so-called 'Caffres'. As far as the Boers were concerned, the role of Blacks and other people of colour was to slave away for Whites, either as servants or labourers. The industrialisation of the South African economy in the post Anglo-Boer War period, with scientific racism fully operational in the background, finally created conditions which were amiable to the Boer racism.

White unity through the establishment of the Union of South Africa in 1910 was achieved at the expense of Blacks 'and all the necessary pre-conditions were established for the creation of apartheid' (Lake and Reynolds 2008: 210). According to Lake and Reynolds (2008: 211), Alfred Milner, the key imperial official in South Africa from 1897 to 1905, wrote a letter in 1897 to his friend Herbert Asquith, a British liberal politician, saying that to bring about the unity between the English and Afrikaners, 'You have only to sacrifice the nigger "absolutely" … There is the whole crux of the South African position'.

## The afterlife of racialism: A deranged narrative

After the racist Union of South Africa was established, a nebulous and vague 'White speak' of racialism became a deranged narrative that cast a long shadow over the twentieth-century thinking space. The eight-year peace and reconciliation process between the two White groups was often characterised by mistrust and in-group favouritism which both groups understood as 'racialism'. Both the English and the Afrikaners often accused each other of 'racialism'. Liberals of all hues saw themselves as being engaged in a bitter struggle against 'racialism'. One of the ideological functions of racialism in the twentieth century is that social groups could use it to describe whatever antipathetic feelings a group showed for another group – and this could be done without ever mentioning White racism. Instead, the 'White speak' of racialism emboldened White liberals and White communists in the twentieth century to monitor racialism among Blacks. Good politics meant, among other things, to be opposed to racialism. It did not matter that White liberals and White communists lived lives of White privilege at the expense of Blacks. What mattered was that one had to be 'non-racial'. What non-racialism did for both the White liberals and White communists is that it freed them up to play their social roles of being colonial overlords, while treating their liberal and Marxist ideologies as some kind of daytime political projects. White liberals could live their White lives characterised by racist White norms in a separate White part of town, without experiencing any psychological discomfort engendered by the blurring of moral values in their lived experiences. This is the parallel colonial universe within which South African Whites were situated and in which they operated throughout most of the twentieth century.

Once White liberals tapped into this deranged narrative of racialism, they ran wild with it, and swiftly centred the concept of 'non-racialism' in their 'race relations' conversations. White liberals such as David Rheinallt Jones and Charles Loram were the chief architects behind this twentieth-century liberal project. They belonged to 'a circle of like-minded English-speaking white liberals who were concerned with race relations and solving "the Native Question"' (Davis, 2003). Other prominent White liberals who resurrected White liberalism in the twentieth century include Edgar Brookes, 'Lovedale principal James Henderson, [and] the Quaker philanthropist Howard Pim' (Davis and Brundage, 2003). They were committed to fighting racialism, but 'when it came to race relations, their political ideology was one of segregation' (Davis and Brundage, 2003). Manning Marable (1976: 309) describes them as being 'politically liberal yet racist in perspective'. It was these White liberals who helped spread the idea of fighting racialism, which by this time political activists and liberals of all hues simply referred to as non-racialism. They achieved this goal by creating colonising institutions called the Joint Councils of Europeans and Natives to cultivate and improve 'race relations' between Whites and Blacks in a way that did not disrupt White control of South Africa (Haines 1991).

The widely held view among historians is that the ideological form that these Councils took was largely shaped by the influence of James Aggrey and Thomas Jesse Jones of the Phelps-Stokes Education Commission, which toured South Africa during the early 1920s (Haines 1991). The Phelps-Stokes Education Fund was an American liberal project which was founded in 1911 to 'improve' the racially oppressive situation of African Americans, as well as to civilise and uplift Africans on the continent through education (Yellin 2002). Marable (1976: 305) identifies Anson Phelps-Stokes, the President of the philanthropic Phelps-Stokes Fund and the Secretary of Yale University at the time, as someone who 'shared many of the same organisational affiliations, social prejudices and petite bourgeois sensibilities of his counterparts in the British empire – Howard Pim, Rheinallt Jones, John Harris, Travers Buxton, and Loram'.

Although the Phelps-Stokes Fund Directors, Anson Phelps-Stokes and Thomas Jesse Jones, paid lip-service to the liberal universalistic belief of the value of all humans, they were dedicated and energised by the idea of cultural superiority of people of European descent (Yellin 2002). In its 'white search for black order', the Phelps-Stokes Fund supervised and regulated all the Fund's efforts for equality in America and in Africa (Yellin 2002: 320). The Phelps-Stokes Fund was part of the American Commission on Interracial Cooperation, set up to improve interracial cooperation and understanding between White Americans and African Americans (Cole 1943). Much of its work was carried out through other organisations, including the Phelps-Stokes Fund (Cole 1943). Phelps-Stokes Fund Director Jones 'carried the story of the Commission to South Africa, with the result that able leaders there inaugurated a similar movement with excellent results' (Cole 1943: 458).

From the early 1920s, Charles Loram became the South African representative of the Phelps-Stokes Fund, a role for which he received a regular allowance (Haines 1991). Loram is regarded as a liberal 'pioneer of race relations' and 'the famous expert on Native education' in South Africa (Heyman 1972: 41). Through Loram, the Phelps-Stokes Fund financially supported the Joint Councils throughout the 1920s. From the beginning of 1928, they were also funded by the Carnegie Corporation (Haines 1991). By the 1930s, Joint Councils had been formed in most of the major urban centres in South Africa (Haines 1991).

The Joint Councils shaped the political ideology of the South African left. Libertarian Socialists, such as Eddie Roux and Clare Goodlatte, and Fabian Socialists such as W.M. Macmillan, Mabel Palmer, and Don Molteno, found an ideological home in the Joint Council movement (Haines 1991), which contributed to the political education of the South African political leaders of the early twentieth century, including D.D.T. Jabavu, Dr. A.B. Xuma, Selby

Msimang, Z.K. Matthews, John Dube, Oliver Tambo, and Bram Fischer (Badenhorst 1992; Haines 1991). The Joint Council also served as a place to meet new people and network with like-minded people. For instance, Bram Fischer developed a friendship with Xuma through them (Haines 1991). People like 'John Dube … R. V. Selope-Thema, Selby Msimang, A. B. Xuma, were all leading members of both the Joint Councils and the ANC', and moreover, 'the history of the ANC during this period was inextricably linked to the Joint Council movement' (Badenhorst 1992: 138).

## Radical Whites weaponise non-racialism

In the 1920s, the White socialist camp viewed the racist White working class in Johannesburg, which saw itself as White labour and on that basis advocated for and argued for anti-Black racism, as a true revolutionary vanguard (Drew 1991). According to Drew (1991: 162), until 1924, most White communists 'thought that a white working class vanguard would lead the socialist movement'. The political worldview of early twentieth-century White socialists 'arose from the tradition of British labour and Eastern European exiles' who cared more about Russian and European political problems than the existential conditions of Black people in South Africa (Drew 1991: 188). 'Certainly in the early 1930s, communist and Trotskyist politics in South Africa still tended to reflect Russian and European struggles as opposed to being integrally part of, and emanating from, the South African struggle' (Drew 1991: 188).

Be that as it may, White socialists paid lip service to the political need to build a colour-blind working class movement (Drew 1991). As far as the Communist Party of South Africa was concerned, 'the proletarian united front … was colour-blind' (Drew 1991: 286). Although White labour fought against the idea of Black freedom well into the 1930s, 'the Party continued working in all-white popular fronts, trying unsuccessfully to attract white labour' (Drew 1991: 290). Because South African White labour was highly committed to anti-Black racist norms and racist intuitions, White socialists were entangled in this web of White racism. Consequently, some White radicals cut their political teeth in White racist unions and in White nationalist organisations. White 'anarchists' or 'syndicalists' like W.H. 'Bill' Andrews and S.P. Bunting are examples of this. Both Andrews and Bunting began their political careers as committed White nationalists and members of the South African Labour Party (SALP), which represented White workers in the 1910 South African racist elections. The SALP's White supremacist politics included, among other things, the rejection of

> the separation of coloureds from whites and supported their advancement and membership of the SALP providing that they did not undermine 'white standards' … Coloureds were defined as 'persons other than whites, including Cape Malays, but excluding natives or Asiatics'.
>
> *(Ticktin 1973: 443)*

Long before Andrews was the chairman of the SALP, he sat on the committee of the White Labour Association (Ticktin 1973). Bunting was not only a member of the SALP, but he was also a member of the 'White Expansion Society', whose aim was to promote the rapid expansion of a permanent White population in South Africa to create a White ethnostate (Drew 2003). According to Drew (2003), there is 'no precise evidence' of when Bunting began to focus on Black labour, but some writers date the change of Bunting's politics to 1915. White historians tend to downplay the racist past of these so-called 'syndicalists' or 'anarchists'. For instance, according to Simons and Simons (1969: 89), although 'Andrews and other socialists of the time may not have been racists, they certainly excluded the African from their vision of the ideal commonwealth'. This is the same Andrews who, when he was the chief spokesperson and national organiser of the White engineers' union, wrote to the Mining Commission advocating for anti-Black racist employment policies because Blacks, 'if unchecked would rise to the top and endanger the state itself by reason of their numbers, vitality and low standards' (Simons and Simons 1969: 88).

According to Badenhorst (1992), prior to the 1940s, the ANC was constrained by the influence of Christianity and liberal White organisations such as the Joint Councils. Badenhorst (1992: 138) argues that a characteristic of this period was the White liberal ideology 'of co-operation and dialogue', which was acted out through a 'spate of European-Bantu Conferences between 1923 and 1936'. However, the intensification of White racism, which culminated with the establishment of a White supremacist state in 1948 – apartheid – convinced some Black activists that as a political animal, non-racialism was a dog of White racism, which would never bark at its master (Sherlock Holmes cited Doyle 2001; Harris 2020). Non-racialism showed itself not only to be a false narrative, but also a shameless public performance of White paternalism. Badenhorst (1992: 140) explains that the ANC started to radicalise after 1939, 'a process that continued through the 1940s, and intensified after the 1946 miner's strike'. The 'growing disenchantment with white liberals and missionaries' became intense during the 1940s (Badenhorst 1992: 140).

In this context, Black radicals considered 'the idea of a black united front to fight white racism' (Drew 1991: 138). Thus, Black radicals within the African National Congress (ANC) resolved to form the ANC Youth League (ANCYL) in 1944 (Drew 1991). The new Black radicals in the ANC 'were less likely to accept white liberal appeals of equality through passive cooperation' (Badenhorst 1992: 188). Thus, the ANC Youth League began by injecting a strongly racial conception of African nationalism that stood counter to 'Western civilisation' (Badenhorst 1992: 189). The ANCYL's political ideology was influenced by two strands of thought – Garveyism, and what Drew (1991: 354) approvingly terms 'a moderate, Africanist stream'. These two political traditions within the ANC disagreed on the political role that was to be played by White activists and White socialists within the ANC. The Garveyists within the ANC believed in the Garveyism political philosophy of Africans determining their own po-litical destination, and to that end a development of an 'Africa for the Africans' political movement (Drew 1991). The Garveyists were purged from the ANCYL in the late 1950s, which led to the formation of the Pan Africanist Congress (PAC) in 1959 (Drew 1991).

This is the time around which White activists and White socialists weaponised non-racialism in the service of a White saviour narrative that portrayed Blacks as being highly susceptible to what White activists diagnosed as a racialised false consciousness. White activists were con-vinced that Black radicals suffered from some kind of political disorder, which made them highly resistant to White influence and therefore dysfunctional. The White saviour socialist script was analogous to the White missionaries' reclamation project in the way it spoke in racialised, patronising, and condescending terms about Black radicals (Bateman 2008). Both White narratives are characterised by 'an exaggerated sense of white import coupled with a severely low estimation of the ability of people of colour to sort out their own troubles' (Hughey 2014: 41). This White discourse positioned Whites as people who always knew what political ideologies and worldviews were best for 'Natives'. Furthermore, this White narrative empowered Whites with powers to police and surveil Blacks with the aim to root out political disorders, such as racialised false consciousness often expressed through a Black Nationalist language. To that end, White activists wielded non-racialism like a weapon, intent on using it at a moment's notice to beat back what they perceived as a threat to 'class alliance' of the colour-blind working class movement they wanted to build.

According to Everatt (2012: 7), in the 1950s, some Whites 'used their own non-racialism to accuse the ANC of being racist' for not allowing Whites to join the movement. To fight against White racism in the 1950s, the ANC worked with the South African Indian Congress (SAIC) under the aegis of the Congress Alliance, a political structure that, among other things, facilitated political solidarity between Indians and Blacks (Everatt 2009). White activists weaponised non-racialism to demand that they be included in this political structure. Everatt (2009: 97) recalls that 'the major problem facing the "Europeans" was whether they fitted into the struggle? And if they did, where?'. In addition to not being able to join the ANC, White activists in the 1950s were alienated by the anti-White sentiments that were increasingly being expressed by a militant nationalistic faction within the ANC (Everatt 2009).

The ANC and the SAIC advocated for White liberals, Marxists and communists to form '"a parallel white organisation" which would join the Congress Alliance' (Everatt 2009: 98). Such an organisation launched nationally in 1953 as the South African Congress of Democrats (SACOD) (Everatt 2009). SACOD provided a political home for White liberals, Marxists, and communists within the Congress Alliance (Everatt 2009). However, some White liberals, Marxists, and communists were opposed to the idea of a parallel White organisation. For example, Danie du Plessis – former Communist Party of South Africa (CPSA) Johannesburg District Chairperson – opposed the formation of SACOD and 'called for a single, non-racial congress' (Everatt 2009: 121). Additionally, 'a considerable number of rank and file CPSA members refused to join the white congress' (Everatt 2009: 122). Du Plessis and his supporters called for a single, non-racial congress opened 'to all South Africans who are prepared to fight for its programme and aims and under one leadership elected by all' (Everatt 2009: 121). Many Whites in SACOD were 'deeply uncomfortable' with their position in the Alliance, and as far as they were concerned, 'the struggle for equal right for all races was obscuring the "real" struggle, which was class-based and aimed at substantive equality for all' (Everatt 2009: 5).

To achieve their political goals, these White activists deployed non-racialism to argue for colour-blindness, while simultaneously demonising Black radicals who foregrounded White racism in their political orientation (Hughey 2014). White activists argued that a race analysis was false consciousness and had no role in progressive organisations, and thus Black radicals who argued for the inclusion of the race question in the political agenda were 'easily portrayed as racial ideologues who are oversensitive or dishonestly playing the race card for sympathy' (Hughey 2014: 116). Aside from the ability of Whites to effectively fight Black radicals, the history of White missionaries, White liberals, White socialists, and White activists in South Africa shows their 'inexplicable talent for transforming' the mindset of Blacks so that they came to accept their values and worldview (Hughey 2014: 39). It is against this discursive backdrop that Everatt (2009: 3) asserts that,

> there were too few anti-apartheid whites to make any numeric impact; but they did have a powerful influence on the nature of the struggle, including ideology as well as the strategies and tactics used – and were visible testament to the non-racialism that all espoused, albeit in different ways and taking different forms.

Indeed, these 'few anti-apartheid Whites' have had a powerful influence in the struggle against White supremacy in South Africa. It is partly for this reason that non-racialism features in the Freedom Charter (a political statement that informed the core principles of the anti-apartheid struggle), as well as in the 1996 post-apartheid South African Constitution. Furthermore, in post-apartheid South Africa, non-racialism is deployed to undermine and question claims of White racism. Mangcu (2015: xviii) argues that 'the concept of non-racialism has come to take on a different meaning in post-apartheid South Africa, used more now to defend than to fight racial inequality'. In post-apartheid South Africa, non-racialism's repudiation of race categories has not resulted in the erosion of White racism, or even racial thinking for that matter (Song 2018). To use Sara Ahmed's insight (2009: 47), the post-apartheid commitment to non-racialism has effectively been translated into a prohibition on the use of the words 'race' and 'racism', because the herd mentality is of the view that to 'speak of racism is to introduce bad feeling'. The corollary is that non-racialism's repudiation of race analysis makes it impossible to bear adequate witness to the full meaning of the anti-Black racism manifestation in post-apartheid South Africa (Heng 2018). Non-racialism's avoidance of 'race' not only undermines our ability to challenge Whiteness in post-apartheid South Africa, but it also hinders our ability to recognise the specificity of many types of racist experiences in post-apartheid South Africa (Song 2018). What further complicates the situation is that non-racialism is not just an obscure academic theory that has nothing to do with how people experience race in post-apartheid South Africa. Rather, non-racialism is a constitutional right in post-apartheid South Africa (Suttner 2012). According to Suttner (2012), non-racialism is also not simply a clause of the South African Constitution, but a fundamental value of the post-apartheid South African society that is linked to notions of unity, freedom, and nationalism.

Erasmus (2017), Satgar (2019), and Soudien (2019) claim that 'radical non-racialism' is not about colour-blindness. However, the historical trajectory of the concept explored in the preceding sections suggests that non-racialism was introduced to the political elite of colour in South Africa in the late nineteenth century and disseminated throughout South Africa in the early twentieth century, by White liberals from Anglo Saxon countries like Britain and the United States of America. In the White liberal imagination, non-racialism was a discursive short-hand for colour-blindness. Furthermore, the White liberals behind the Joint Councils deployed non-racialism as an organising tool to cultivate political solidarity and collaboration among racial groups in South Africa. For these White liberals, non-racialism was neither an intellectual tool to unpack racialised social relations, nor was it a project to disrupt widespread racist norms, values, and belief in the White culture. These White liberals viewed race analysis as a counter-productive project.

## Conclusion

In the final analysis, my contention is that not only have the progressive projects of White missionaries, Cape liberals, and White socialists downplayed and in certain instances outrightly denied White racism, they have historically refused to acknowledge that Whiteness is a normative value that underwrites them. Whiteness has served as a normative value for these projects in the sense that they have historically been framed, consciously or not, within the White saviour narrative. In this narrative, Whites have historically played the role of 'a messianic white character' who redeems 'dysfunctional Others' from barbarism and false consciousness (Hughey 2014: 8). Moreover, the 'dysfunctional Others' in this White narrative have historically been portrayed as only redeemable if 'they consent to assimilation' and the full acceptance of the world view of their benevolent White 'benefactors of class, capital, and compassion' (Hughey 2014: 8).

Another important finding of this chapter is that all colour-blind ideologies, whether they claim to be liberal-based non-racialism or Marxism, become a way to avoid talking about racial justice (Goldberg 2002). Hence, non-racialism has historically been used by Whites in South

Africa to keep the intellectual door shut to theories, concepts, and analyses that can name and hold accountable White racism and anti-Black racism (Heng 2018). Claiming to disavow racial categories and 'race thinking', nineteenth-century liberal colour-blind ideologies and the twentieth-century concept of non-racialism have historically promised to lead many Black political figures to a racial Kumbaya while leading them down the garden path. What non-racialism does not advertise, but has historically achieved with breath-taking effectiveness, is that it shields Whites from being implicated in a parasitic White supremacist system that historically benefitted Whites educationally, economically and politically, at the expense of Blacks.

# References

Ahmed, S. 2009. Embodying Diversity: Problems and Paradoxes for Black Feminists. *Race, Ethnicity and Education*, 12 (1): 41–52.

Ash, J. 1775. *The New and Complete Dictionary of the English Language*. London: Printed for Edward Dilly Charles Dilly and R. Baldwin.

Badenhorst, C. M. 1992. 'Mines, Missionaries and the Municipality: Organised African Sport and Recreation in Johannesburg c1920–1950', PhD thesis, Kingston, Ontario: Queen's University

Bannister, S. 1830. *Humane Policy: Or, Justice to the Aborigines of New Settlements Essential to a Due Expenditure of British Money, and to the Best Interests of the Settlers. With Suggestions how to Civilize the Natives by an Improved Administration of Existing Means*. London: Thomas and George Underwood, Fleet Street.

Bateman, F. 2008. Defining the Heathen in Ireland and Africa: Two Similar Discourses a Century Apart. *Social Sciences and Missions*, 21 (1): 73–96.

Biko, S. 2004. *I Write What I Like*. Johannesburg: Picador Africa.

Blind, K. 1896. Problems of the Transvaal. *The North American Review*, 162 (473): 457–472.

Bolt, C. 1984. Race and the Victorians. In *British Imperialism in the Nineteenth Century*, ed. C. C. Eldridge, pp. 126–147. London: Macmillan.

Clark, G. B. 1881. *British Policy Towards the Boers: An Historical Sketch*, 4th edn. London: William Ridgway, Nineteenth Century Collections Online.

Cleall, E. 2012. *Missionary Discourses of Difference Negotiating Otherness in the British Empire, 1840–1900*. Hampshire, New York: Palgrave Macmillan.

Cole, W. E. 1943. The Role of the Commission on Interracial Cooperation in War and Peace. *Social Forces*, 21 (4): 456–463.

Cooper, J. 2002. 'Invasion in Writing: London Missionary Society Missionaries, the Civilizing Mission, and the Written Word in Early Nineteenth-Century Southern Africa', MA thesis, Kingston, Ontario: Queen's University.

Crais, C. C. 1992. *White Supremacy and Black Resistance in Pre-Industrial South Africa: The Making of the Colonial Order in the Eastern Cape, 1770–1865*. Cambridge and New York: Cambridge University Press.

Curtin, P. D. 1964. *The image of Africa: British Ideas and Action, 1780–1850*. London: MacMillan.

Daut, M. L. 2012. The 'Alpha and Omega' of Haitian Literature: Baron de Vastey and the U.S. Audience of Haitian Political Writing. *Comparative Literature*, 64 (1): 49–72.

Daut, M. L. 2015. *Tropics of Haiti: Race and the Literary History of the Haitian Revolution in the Atlantic World, 1789–1865*. Liverpool: Liverpool University Press.

Davis, R. H. 2003. Up from Slavery for South Africans: C.T. Loram's Abridged Edition of Booker T. Washington's Classic Autobiography. In *Booker T. Washington and Black Progress: Up from Slavery 100 Years Later*, ed. F. W. Brundage. University Press of Florida.

Doyle, A. C. 2001. *Memoirs of Sherlock Holmes*. London: The Electric Book Company.

Drew, A. 1991. 'Social Mobilization and Racial Capitalism in South Africa, 1928–1960', PhD thesis, Los Angeles: University of California

Drew, A. (2003). Will the Real Sidney Bunting Please Stand Up? Constructing and Contesting the Identity of a South African Communist. The English Historical Review, 118 (479), 1208–1241. 10.1093/ehr/118.479.1208.

Dubow, S. 2006. *A Commonwealth of Knowledge: Science, Sensibility, and White South Africa, 1820–2000*. Oxford and New York: Oxford University Press.

Erasmus, Z 2017, Rearranging the Furniture of History: Non-Racialism as Anticolonial Praxis. *Critical Philosophy of Race*, 5 (2): 198–222.

Everatt, D. 2009. *The Origins of Non-Racialism: White Opposition to Apartheid in the 1950s*. Johannesburg: Wits University Press.

Everatt, D. 2012. Non-Racialism in South Africa: Status and Prospects. *Politikon*, 39 (1): 5–28.

Gladstone, W. E. 1910. 'Lord Gladstone on Racialism', *Rhodesia Herald*, 23 September, Nineteenth Century Collections Online.

Goldberg, D. T. 2002. *The Racial State*. Massachusetts: Blackwell Publishers.

Haines, R. J. 1991. 'The Politics of Philanthropy and Race Relations: Joint Councils of South Africa c.1920–1955', PhD thesis, School of Oriental and African Studies, University of London.

Harris, S. 2020. 'A conversation with Caitlin Flanagan', *Sam Harris*, podcast, 13 May, viewed 15 May 2020, https://samharris.org/podcasts/203-may-13-2020/.

Heng, G. 2018. *The Invention of Race in the European Middle Ages*. Cambridge: Cambridge University Press.

Heyman, R. D. 1972. C. T. Loram: A South African Liberal in Race Relations. *The International Journal of African Historical Studies*, 5 (1): 41–50.

Hoquet, T. 2014. The Genealogy of Race in the Eighteenth Century: Biologization of Race and Racialization of the Human: Bernier, Buffon, Linnaeus. In *The Invention of Race: Scientific and Popular Representations*, ed. N. Bancel, T. David and D. Thomas, pp. 41–71. New York, NY and Abingdon, Oxon: Routledge.

Hughey, M. 2014. *The White Savior Film: Content, Critics and Consumption*. Temple University Press: Philadelphia.

Jacottet, E. 1904. The Ethiopian Church and the Missionary Conference of Johannesburg: An Open Letter from the Rev. E. Jacottet, of the Paris Evangelical Missionary Society, to the Assistant Secretary of the Special Conference of the African Methodist Episcopal Church held at Pretoria in August, 1904. *The Christian Express*, December, 34 (411).

Johnson, S. 1765. *A Dictionary of the English Language: In which The Words are deduced from their Originals, and Illustrated in their Different Significations by Examples from the best Writers, vol. 1, 3rd edn*. London: Longmans, Green, Eighteenth Century Collections Online.

Kiernan, V. 2015. *The Lords of Human Kind: European Attitudes to Other Cultures in the Imperial Age*. London: Zed Books.

Lake, M. and Reynolds, H. 2008. *Drawing the Global Colour Line: White Men's Countries and the International Challenge of Racial Equality*. Cambridge: Cambridge University Press.

Lester, A. 2009. Humanitarians and White Settlers in the Nineteenth Century. In *Mission and Empire*, ed. N. Etherington. Oxford: Oxford University Press.

Magubane, Z. 1997. 'From Noble Savage to Native Problem: Images of South Africans in British Colonial Discourse, 1806–1910', PhD thesis, Harvard University, Cambridge, Massachusetts.

Mangcu, X. 2015. Preface. In *The Colour of Our Future: Does Race Matter in Post-Apartheid South Africa?*, ed. X. Mangcu. Johannesburg: Wits University Press.

Marable, M. 1976. 'African Nationalist: The Life of John Langalibalele Dube', PhD thesis, Maryland: University of Maryland

Maylam, P. 2001. *South Africa's Racial Past: The History and Historiography of Racism, Segregation, and Apartheid*. Aldershot: Ashgate.

Mills, C. W. 1997. *The Racial Contract*. Cornell University Press: New York.

Nauright, J. 1996. Colonial Manhood and Imperial Race Virility: British Responses to Post-Boer War Colonial Rugby Tours. In *Making men: Rugby and Masculine Identity*, ed. J. Nauright and T. J. L. Chandler, pp. 121–139. London: Routledge.

Pitts, J. 2005. *A Turn to Empire: The Rise of Imperial Liberalism in Britain and France*. Princeton and Oxford: Princeton University Press.

Rich, P. 1980. 'The Dilemmas of South African Liberalism: White Liberals, Racial Ideology and the Politics of Social Control in the Period of South African Industrialisation, 1887 to 1943', PhD thesis, University of Warwick, United Kingdom.

Rodriguez, J. and Freeman, K. J. 2016. 'Your Focus on Race is Narrow and Exclusive': The Derailment of Anti-racist Work Through Discourses of Intersectionality and Diversity. *Whiteness and Education*, 1 (1): 69–82.

Satgar, V. 2019. Seven Theses on Radical Non-racialism, the Climate Crisis and Deep Just Transitions: From the National Question to the Eco-cide Question. In *Racism After Apartheid: Challenges for Marxism and Anti-Racism*, ed. V. Satgar, pp. 194–216. Johannesburg: Wits University Press.

Sauer, H. 1910. 'Speech by Mr Sauer, His Views on Racialism: More Anti-Dutch Feeling than Anti-English, The Future of South Africa', *Diamond Fields Advertiser*, 16 February, Nineteenth Century Collections Online.

Seely, J. 1908. 'Racialism Dead', *Rhodesia Herald*, 13 November, Nineteenth Century Collections Online.

Simons, H. J. and Simons, R. E. 1969. *Class and Colour in South Africa 1850–1950*. Harmondsworth: Penguin.

Smith, T. 1848a. 'Sketches of South Africa', *The Wesleyan-Methodist magazine*, 4 August, Nineteenth Century Collections Online.

Smith, T. 1848b. 'Sketches of South Africa', *The Wesleyan-Methodist Magazine*, 4 September, Nineteenth Century Collections Online.

Song, M. 2018. Why We Still Need to Talk About Race. *Ethnic and Racial Studies*, 41 (6): 1131–1145.

Soudien, C. 2019. *Cape radicals: Intellectual and political thought of the New Era Fellowship, 1930s–1960s*. Johannesburg: Wits University Press.

Spenser, E. 1763. *A View of the State of Ireland as it was in the Reign of Queen Elizabeth*. Dublin: Laurence Flin, in Castle-Street, and Ann Watts, in Skinner-Row, Eighteenth Century Collections Online.

Suttner, R. 2012. Understanding Non-racialism as an Emancipatory Concept in South Africa. *Theoria: A Journal of Social and Political Theory*, 59 (130): 22–41.

Templin, J. A. 1968. God and the Covenant in the South African Wilderness. *Church History*, 37 (3): 281–297.

Templin, J. A. 1999. The Ideology of a Chosen People: Afrikaner Nationalism and the Ossewa Trek, 1938. *Nations and Nationalism*, 5 (3): 397–417.

The Christian Express. 1911. 'Nation Union from Mlomo oa Bantho the New Native Paper Published at Johannesburg We Take the Following', *The Christian Express*, XLI (493).

Ticktin, D. 1973. '*The Origins of the South African Labour Party 1888-1910*', PhD thesis, Cape Town: University of Cape Town.

Trapido, S. 1964. The Origins of the Cape Franchise Qualifications of 1853. *Journal of African History*, 5 (1): 37–54.

Watson, R. L. 2012. *Slave Emancipation and Racial Attitudes in Nineteenth-Century South Africa*. New York: Cambridge University Press.

Wilburn, K. 2013. 'Friend of the Native?': James Sivewright and the Cape Liberal Tradition. *South African Historical Journal*, 65 (2): 271–292.

Williams, R. 1983. *Keywords: A Vocabulary of Culture and Society*. London: Fontana.

Willoughby-Herard, T. 2015. *Waste of a White Skin: The Carnegie Corporation and the Racial Logic of White Vulnerability*. Oakland: University of California Press.

Wilson, F. 2011. Historical Roots of Inequality in South Africa. *Economic History of Developing Regions*, 26 (1): 1–15.

Wright, H. M. 1980. The Burden of the Present and Its Critics. *Social Dynamics*, 6 (1): 36–48.

Yellin, E. S. 2002. The (White) Search for (Black) Order: The Phelps-Stokes Fund's First Twenty Years, 1911–1931. *Historian*, 65 (2): 319–352.

# 10

# Zionism as a movement of whiteness: Race and colour in the Zionist project

*Ilan Pappé*

## Introduction

Whiteness is not usually referred to as an object of interest for scholars who work on Israel, Zionism and Palestine. In fact, race as a concept hardly appears even in the most critical Israeli or Palestine studies, apart from few works such as a recent book by Ronit Lentin (2009). Israel, as one scholar rightly noted, considers itself colour-blind; but it is not. The absence of race as an analytical or descriptive tool in Israeli scholarship explains the marginality of whiteness as a concept. However, once the Ethiopian Jews arrived in Israel, whiteness as a research topic became more common among critical observers, who applied it not only to the case of Africans (Jews and non-Jews), but also to the Mizrahi Jews[1] who came originally from Arab and Islamic countries back in the 1950s.

## Post-Zionist scholarship

From the late 1970s onwards, a group of knowledge producers in Israel challenged the hegemonic Zionist narrative of the past and offered an alternative interpretation of the present realities in the Jewish state. This challenge is described in many sources as 'the Post-Zionist Movement'. It began in the late 1970s, with a small group of academics who claimed that Israeli policies towards the Jews who came from Arab and Islamic countries, and against the local Palestinian minority, were discriminatory in nature and pushed these communities into the geographical and social margins of the local society.

The next development was the emergence of the 'new history': A group of professional historians who accepted major chapters in the Palestinian narrative of the 1948 Nakba (catastrophe) and in particular blamed Israel for the massive expulsion of the Palestinians and the destruction of their homes and livelihood. This was followed by what one can call the post-Zionist decade of the 1990s: A burst of academic works, cultural productions and political activism revisiting critically the whole Zionist and Israeli history, from the very early formative years of Zionism to the more recent past.

The outbreak of the second Intifada (October 2000) and shift in Israeli politics to the right, brought an end to this wave of soul searching in the Israeli academia and the general critique on

DOI: 10.4324/9780429355769-10

Zionism from within petered out, and almost disappeared entirely. The local society it seems opted for an even harsher version of Zionism; an extreme brand of religious nationalism fused with the settler colonial vision of a de-Arabized Palestine.

However, there was one exception: The research and cultural works on the Mizrahi Jewish experience in Israel continued. The more critical view on Mizrahi Jews, which refers to them as Arab Jews, was maintained in this century due to the fact that the blame for their abysmal treatment was cast solely on the Labour party (the left in Israel) and its establishment, which were in power until 1977. It was replaced in that year by a right-wing coalition, led by the Likud party, and which still dominates Israeli politics today. This collation exploited the Mizrachi discontent and plight as an electoral asset in successive election campaigns and is committed at least on paper to allow this critique to be expanded. The first part of this chapter follows the gradual integration of the concept of whiteness into the analysis of the condition of Mizrahi Jews in Israel.

The second part describes a different, but complimentary, interest in whiteness in Israeli academia and activist circles (as yet it is not a topic of general discussion). This is the issue of whiteness as it appears in racist policies toward Africans (Jewish and non-Jewish) in Israel.

The final part of the chapter links the two case studies and shows that the discrimination against Mizrahi Jews, Ethiopian Jews and life seekers from Africa, gave more impetus for the need to include whiteness in the discussion of discrimination within the Jewish state.

Racism in Zionism is interconnected to positions in its early days towards non-Zionist Judaism and its ongoing attitudes towards the Palestinians. As a recent research by Etan Bloom has shown, leading Zionist ideologues such as Arthur Rupin, depicted the diaspora Jews, who refused to become Zionists, as inferior blacks: A 'Jew' in early Zionist discourse was a black Jew who was an anathema to the new white Jew, the Hebrew person (Blum 2011).

The more important feature of Zionism was and is its institutional and societal racism towards the Palestinians, wherever they are, be it under direct or indirect, Israeli control. The dehumanisation of the indigenous people of Palestine, which is the ultimate form of racism, enabled the Zionist movement to employ every possible means at its disposal to remove Palestinians from their homeland. Whether considered 'red' or 'black', the definition of people by their colour as a justification for their genocide or removal is characteristic of settler movements such as Zionism and the white settlers of North America and South Africa. Thus, the analysis in the following pages towards blackness/whiteness within the Jewish society in Israel is inseparable from the settler colonial dehumanisation which is at the heart of the Zionist attitudes towards, and perceptions of, the Palestinian people.

## The Arab Jews

The Jews who came from Arab and Muslim countries suffered from various degrees of discrimination from the European Jewish establishment. As Susan Abulhawa (2017) writes 'these Jews were not embraced as brethren by European Zionists'; the European Jewish (Ashkenazi) leadership shared in the beginning of the Zionist project Ze'ev Jabotinsky's view that:

> We Jews have nothing in common with what is called the Orient, thank God. To the extent that our uneducated masses [Arab Jews] have ancient spiritual traditions and laws that call the Orient, they must be weaned away from them, and this is in fact what we are doing in every decent school, what life itself is doing with great success. We are going in Palestine, first for our national convenience, [second] to sweep out thoroughly all traces of the Oriental soul.
>
> *(Quoted in Abulhawa 2017)*

When the first Arab Jews arrived in large numbers, in the early 1950s, such racist attitudes were common among the political and professional leadership that oversaw the process of absorption of the Arab Jews. Some scholars claim that they were also brought as cheap labour, substituting the Palestinians working force the Jewish state needed to build its infrastructure. However, it seems that the government pushed these immigrants to non-skilled work out of ignorance and racism. Their occupational situation indicated their location on the socio-cultural pyramid of the Jewish society in Israel.

On arrival, as Ella Shohat (2006: 143) observed in her memoirs, the Arab Jews experienced discrimination on every level, with a gradual improvement towards the end of the twentieth century. But even today, there is correlation between the social stratification of the Jewish society and one's ethnic origins. Ashkenazi veteran men enjoy the highest socioeconomic ranking (when you examine house values, family income and level of education) (Cohen et al., 2019). Moreover, their representation in the upper echelons of politics, academia, business, and the media were much higher than their proportion of the population (Lissak 1999). This is a dynamic situation, and the gaps are closing but they are still there (Shenhav 2006).

While the early research focused on the origins of the discrimination and its nature, the more critical scholarship shifted its interest to the questions of identity and socio-cultural references. This shift produced a new terminology. First, there was a recognition of the Mizrahi as an ideological position, not just an ethnic identity. Chetrit (2005) called people who identified with the Mizrahi plight the 'neo-Mizrahim' which included also Jews who did not come from Arab countries. However, quite soon after he too adopted that new and more radical reference Arab Jews.

A small group of Mizrahi scholars, mainly anthropologists and sociologists, regarded the term 'Arab Jew' as a more appropriate category for the Mizrahi Jew. By adopting this term, these activists and scholars stressed the ethnic Arab identity of these Jews. This reification challenges the Zionist claim that the Arab Jews were a distinct national, and not only religious group, within the Arab world. Ella Shohat (2017) also refutes the claim that these Jewish communities' dialects were an indication of a separate national identity, and she shows that they were local and regional dialects shared by others. Shohat in one of her earlier work (1988) argued that the use of the term Mizrahim is in some sense a Zionist achievement as it created a single unitary identity separated from the Islamic world. Framing these communities as such runs against the national ethos and therefore is not common among Israeli researchers. Zionist historiography could not accept a hyphenated Arab-Jewish identity and embarked on a programme to remove the 'Arabness' and the 'Orient' off the Jews from the Arab world after they arrived in Israel. To ensure homogeneity, the powers that be focused on religious commonality and a romanticised past. This homogeneity was assured by sustaining the binary logic wherein Jews and Arabs were posed as cultural and political antagonisms. Yehuda Shenhav (2006: 140) called it the attempt to de-Arabize the Arab Jews.

## The Arab Jews as black Jews or the Ashkenazi Jews as white Jews

Probably one of the first scholars to refer to whiteness in this context was Smadar Lavie (1991), who saw the Israeli project of bringing over one million Jews and non-Jews form the ex-Soviet Union in the 1990s as an attempt to whiten the Israeli Jewish society. This observation triggered a wider interest in whiteness in the study of the Israeli society. The issue of whiteness was not at first part of the post-Zionist critique that focused on the Arab Jews. It was more an issue of ethnicity and culture and less a question of race. However, some developments in the study of whiteness alerted critical scholars in Israel working on the Arab Jews and made the notion relevant to their inquiries. They even found a Hebrew word, 'Lavnut', for this term. It seems that *Lavnut* associated whiteness less with classical racism and more as a reference to a cultural identity which until the 1990s in Israel was regarded as a social position or reification. When these scholars familiarised themselves with the concept of whiteness, they considered the possibility that *Lavnut* was a racial (though not racialised) social category characterized by a privileged position in society – very much in line of the works of scholars such as Frankenberg (1997: 1–35), Lewis (2004), and Roediger (2007).

The first theme that was explored was the link between whiteness and the Zionist project of creating a new Jew. It began with Raz (2004) who examined whiteness in the early Zionist propaganda films. Raz showed how these movies were used to whiten Eastern European Jews, almost turning them into Aryan figures and in the process conveying the image of a new white Jew that was reborn in Palestine.

What Raz and others found was that the human engineers of the Zionist project were determined to dissociate the Jews of Europe from their 'blackness'. Anti-Semites referred to Jews as non-white persons in nineteenth-century and early twentieth-century Europe. For many in the continent, European Jews were the blacks of Europe or the 'white negroes' (Gileman, 1991). Even German Jews were cognizant of that fact and saw it as a feature that would hinder any attempt to assimilate in their society. As Moses Hess wrote: 'The black curly hair will not turn into yellow by baptism' (quoted in Raz 2004: 126–127), or as Daniel Boyarin (Raz 2004: 126–127) puts it 'the best denotation…for the "race" of the European Jew seems to be off-white'. Thus, an important part of the Zionist project in Palestine was to reincarnate the Jew as a white person.

The next stage was to find out how whiteness and Euro-centric or Western-Centric (Ashkenazi in the local jargon) identity and culture dominated the Israeli Jewish society ever since its inception and until today. The research here was influenced by the study of whiteness in the United States. Whiteness became associated with upper middle-class symbols and culture. It was an ethnic identity representing an elevated social status which involved mostly leisure-time activity and one which was not stigmatised, and did not interfere with the economic, social, and other imperatives of everyday life.

All these attributes and characterisations cast a new and clear definition of *Ashkenaziyut* (Western Jewishness or Eurocentric Jewishness) in Israel. It seems that the American whiteness has much in common with whiteness in Israel: Both categories are associated with European ancestry and both are identified with power structures. They are also flexible identities as observed by Mary Waters (1990) with regard to the United States where Americans of European ancestry can often choose the background they wish to identify with, making their ethnicity voluntary and optional. These similarities between American whites and the Ashkenazim suggest that the study of Ashkenazi Jews offers a valuable opportunity to examine the construction of whiteness in an Israeli context.

Based on such conceptual frameworks, these scholars exposed the Ashkenazim, as the dominant white group in the local society (Chinski 2002; Sasson-Levy 2013; Yadgar 2011). Thus for instance, Orna Sasson-Levy (2013), inspired by the work of Richard Dyer (1997), defined whiteness in Israel as a signifier for the rest of the society or as the 'unmarked marker' (unmarked insofar as it is identified with a 'neutral' universalism while serving as a criterion against which all other groups are marked and racialised). No less relevant, in her view, was Rosaldo's argument (1989) that the social invisibility of whiteness is characteristic of those who hold full citizenship and institutional power in the nation state. Thus, the place of power remains hidden and needs to be deconstructed. And finally, she analysed whiteness in Israel as becoming the 'tyranny of the transparent', referring to a famous reference by Homi Bhabha (1998: 23).

## Becoming white in Israel

In their search to understand if you can become white, if you are an Arab Jew, these scholars also followed with interest the transformation of the Jews in the United States into whites. It took time for the Jews to be regarded as whites, due to early hurdles in in social mobility (Brodkin 1998; Levine-Rasky 2020) but they are now part of whiteness in America (even if here and there new anti-Semites like to cast doubt about it).

From this perspective, you could also become white when whiteness was not directly associated with colour. Arab Jews could be 'Ashkenazified', a pejorative term with an implied sense of blame—for engaging in deception and for becoming estranged from one's 'authentic' self. Hence, though, some Arab Jews can, and sometimes do, join the category of Ashkenaziness; namely joining an exclusive group, which confers privilege and power on its members.

In a way as Frantz Fanon (1967: 8) noted black persons know they are black only in relationship with a white person or when they want to become white. Only rarely was the recognition of white dominance and the difficulty of joining related to the situation of the Palestinians in Israel. But when it is done it became clear how relevant it is. As can be seen by the work of Sharon Rotbad (2015) when she compared 'the White City' of Tel-Aviv (an adjective granted to it by UNESCO because of its Bauhaus heritage) to the black (Arab) city of Jaffa. The visible colour of the buildings hid a much deeper narrative of past colonisation and present racism.

Very few people were aware in Israel of the discussion on whiteness; it was confined to niche academic journals or publications and was conducted in a language not always accessible, or attractive, to everyone. The language became less academic and the phenomenon of whiteness more visible with the arrival of the Ethiopian Jews.

## The Ethiopian Jews

In two operations, operation Moses (1984) and operation Solomon (1991), the *Beta Israel*, the Jewish community in Ethiopia, immigrated to Israel. The push factors were famine and an ongoing civil war; the pull factors were an association with Judaism that was a few thousand years old. They are about 130,000 (2018 numbers) living in Israel, around 30% were already born in Israel.

In a curious way, the issue of colour was an argument for and against their immigration before the final decision to bring them over was made by the government. Their 'blackness' was quoted as a reason not to bring them by some among the policy makers, while others thought that their 'blackness' will depict Israel as a progressive state and society. Whatever the motives after they had arrived, their real confrontation with racism has just begun.

Their initial predicament was the decision to locate them next to the poor towns, where mostly north African Jews lived. From the onset, the immigrants' rural background was ignored. They came from strong close-knit communities and they were offered housing and locations that immediately turned into slums adjacent to urban centres. Overall, the Israeli Jewish society proved to be a white racist society when it came to accepting 'black Jews'. In hindsight, researchers found out that even programmes put in place to combat racism against Ethiopian Jews were themselves plagued by racism.

Even the early stages of absorption that began in transition camps in Ethiopia, or on arrival, were marred by overt racism. The people were delayed on the way out since Israeli Rabbis doubted their Jewishness under the Israeli Law of Return. All in all, scholars observed that, *a priori*, the authorities deemed the Ethiopian Jews to be particularly problematic as a kind of a group 'with special needs'. They were considered to lack parenting skills and therefore their children were separated, without parents' consent, and sent to boarding schools. One scholar called this approach cultural racism (Ben-Eliezer, 2004). In fact, what is common to the absorption process of the Arab Jews and that of the Ethiopian Jews is what Deuardo Bonilla-Silva (1997) termed 'institutional racism'. This also accounts for the absence of Ethiopian university graduates from the media, academia, architecture, and other more prestigious professions. The other side of the coin is their overemployment in unskilled jobs, even if they possessed academic degrees.

The early difficulties of absorption were replaced by tough existence on the social and economic margins of the local society. They became the poorest group in Israeli society and their main predicament has been the inaccessibility of the labour market. Such high level of unemployment within an environment of poverty, deteriorates the younger generation to criminal activity and increase tensions inside the family household. Despite the fact that only a small group is attracted to crime, its existence sustains a racist attitude and treatment by the Israeli policy and other law enforcement agencies. This means that Ethiopian Jews, very much like African-Americans and the black community in Britain, were likely to be stopped, searched, and indicted in the criminal system. As mentioned, the community forms only 2% of the population but 18% of the under aged prison population are Ethiopians (the kind of disparities you encounter in places such as the United States and the United Kingdom).

This is accompanied by numerous acts of police brutality, reminiscent of similar assaults in the United States against African-Americans. The first infamous case was in April 2015 when Israeli policemen assaulted, unprovoked, a young Ethiopian soldier. The police claimed he was the attacker, but a video released later proved his claims.

Occasionally, cases of racist abuses made their way into the Israeli media after the arrival of the Ethiopian Jews. One famous such case was in 2009 where school children of Ethiopian ancestry were denied admission into three semi-private religious schools in the town of Petach Tikva. At least in this case, the government reacted quite swiftly and forced the school to accept the children.

Worse was the blood donation scandal. Hospitals in Israel dumped in the garbage blood donations given by Ethiopian Jews. Israeli health authorities claimed it was a reasonable move as there was a higher likelihood of HIV in Africans. Maybe even more severe was the Depo-Provera scandal. Israeli hospitals in 2010 began prescribing contraceptive drugs like Depo-Provera to the community. This was seen as a deliberate sterilisation policy. Human rights organisations that followed the case claimed that this was not the only contraceptive offered to the Ethiopian women. The figures were staggering, despite the government's claim that their actions were based on a voluntary participation in a family planning programme. It seemed that 60% of women receiving this contraceptive are Ethiopian Jews, while Ethiopians made up only 1% of population. As on scholar observed 'the gap here is just impossible to reconcile in any logical manner that would somehow resist the claims of racism'.[2] Later even more damning evidence, included by a hidden camera, proved beyond doubt the racist nature of this policy. Although the government denied such a policy, the programme stopped.

More invisible layers of racism were noted later on in the treatment of Ethiopian Jews in hospitals and mental health clinics etc. The pattern was always the same, a media exposure of an act of racial discrimination, a government apology and no systemic change in sight. One such case with the segregation imposed on parents in kindergartens and elementary schools in several towns in Israel: Ethiopian toddlers and children were forced to study in segregated classes.[3]

The attention to such incidents became more widespread when the first Ethiopian Jews made it to the parliament, the Knesset. Public awareness also grew due to a series of very charged demonstrations that followed cases of particular police brutality or incidents of rampant racism incidents affecting all walks of life in Israel; and there were quite a few of them in this century.

As often happened in situation of racism, the authorities highlighted the individual stories of success and there are quite a few of Ethiopian Jews achieving success in sport, diplomacy, culture, and politics. These exceptions, however, did not prove the rule.

As happens in such cases, an unhealthy process of internalisation of whiteness can be detected in the younger generation. Research on Ethiopian high school children found out that many of them were craving for a white normality or whiteness in general (Mula 2018). Indeed, very much as in the case of the Arab Jews, white normality meant to be accepted as a proper Israeli Jew; namely as close as possible to being a European Jew.

This was noted and challenged when a handful of Ethiopians entered the academic circles and published their own works on the topic. They employed critical race theory, pointing to the relevance of recognising race as a sociological category which is relevant to the Israeli society.

Frantz Fanon became particularly an important compass in explaining the complexity of the relationship with whiteness for a black person, 'The white man is sealed in his whiteness. The black man in his blackness', wrote Fanon (1967: 12) and thus provided the foundation for the critic on the search for whiteness. But this is a difficult path to follow. The phenomenon of cultural racism which rationalises inequality by casting the blame on the minorities themselves (for failing to adapt to the White way of life) is also affecting these communities, in particular the Ethiopian Jews and deserves further research (Shenhav, 2006). What is need most it to apply the settler colonial paradigm, and within it the ethnic cleansing policies, to the case of the Ethiopian Jews. The similarities are there but a bold and expanded analysis of such nature is still needed.

On the other side of the coin, it seems that the African American struggle inspires a new generation to explore racism in society and the ways to push forward the struggle for equality and justice.

## The black Hebrews

They call themselves 'the Black Hebrew Israelites'. These are African Americans who believe they are descendants of the ancient Israelites of the old testament. They are generally not accepted as Jews by the Jewish establishment in Israel, so in many ways the self-reference as Hebrew Israelites or Black Hebrews, was adopted because of this rejection.

They arrived in Israel in 1969, on the basis of the Israeli Law of Return, that granted automatic citizenship to any Jew who immigrates to Israel. Their case was discussed by the government for quite a while and finally in 1973, it ruled that the group did not qualify for automatic citizenship. As a result, the Black Hebrews were denied work permits and state benefits. The group responded by accusing the Israeli government of racist discrimination.

The involvement of American legislators in their affairs revised somewhat the policy toward this group. A compromise was reached which allowed members of the group to work and have access to housing and social services. Their situation improved when in 2003 they were given permanent residence.

## Refugees and life seekers from Africa

In 2010, the movement of immigrants from Africa to Israel began to be noted as a substantial phenomenon. For the next three years, about 55,000 life and work seekers arrived in Israel. In 2013, Israel built a wall on its border with Egypt to stop immigration and expelled quite a few of the immigrants and by 2018, there were about 30,000 such refugees in Israel.[4]

Human rights organisations in Israel regard most of the refugees who came from Africa as legitimate asylum seekers, while the government preferred to look at them as labour seekers and not refugees. The official position does not tally with the reality on the ground. The people who arrived mainly from Eritrea, the Sudan and Somalia, should be protected under the 1951 UN convention on the status of refugees; of which Israel is a signatory. In the United States, Eritrean, and Sudanese refugees, who arrived at the same period were treated as refugees. It seems that the government policy is motivated by a wish to satisfy racist undercurrents, in particular, among right wing voters or more disturbingly, this serves as another manifestation of the impossibility of having a state that is both Jewish and democratic.

This is a relatively small number of black people whom official Israel finds hard to accept. The Supreme Court in Israel until now was the main bulwark against their deportation. The government tried to deport them either to their home countries, but this was strongly condemned by the UN so the government tried to convince third countries, such as Rwanda in Africa to accept the deportees, a plan that so far has failed.

Only a handful of refugees were fortunate enough not to be imprisoned or awaiting deportation. They were able to request a temporary permit to stay, which needed to be reviewed every three of four months. The majority were not able to pursue this avenue. They stay illegally in the poor neighbourhoods of Tel-Aviv and in the southern city of Eilat. Their Jewish neighbours, who are themselves marginalised and deprived, display racist attitudes towards them, instigated by right wing parties such as the Likud.

The residents' main claim is that the refugees are responsible for an increase in the crime rates in their neighbourhoods; a claim that is allegedly substantiated by the police. In their frequent demonstrations, they demand the deportation of the Africans; but there are also demonstrations of support for the refugees organised by local human rights organisations. In a special ruling on a related case, one of the Supreme Court judges in Israel noted that in fact the level of crime committed by the refugees is much lower than in the society in general (Arbel 2013).

The situation of these African refugees deteriorated after 2018, when the Israeli Knesset passed a law that ruled that those who refuse to leave would be jailed. Many of them were jailed already in the regular jail system. When this practice was condemned as unconstitutional by the Supreme Court, the government built an open detention centre, named *Holot* (sands in Hebrew) in the Negev desert. However, the Supreme court intervened again and ruled that the conditions in *Holot* are 'unbearable violation of the refugees' basic rights'. The centre was closed and the legal status of these refugees is still hanging in the air.

A further blow to their existence occurred when a de facto 20% salary cut had been imposed on them (through taxing their employers) by the Israeli government driving them into deeper poverty. It was clearly part of an attempt to drive them out.

There are not many scholarly works on this community and there are even fewer that relate to them within the study of whiteness. But, they are the ultimate victims of whiteness in Israel. This is clear when one examines the rhetoric of Israeli politicians in positions of power. One of Israel's two chief rabbis, Rabi Yitzhak Yosef, called black people, in general but referred to the Africans in Israel in particular as 'monkeys' in his televised weekly sermons. No one in Israel reacted. A leading politician told the press: 'The Sudanese are a cancer in our body'. Another politician suggested enclaving them in a special city in the desert.

The economic correspondent of Haaretz claimed that their presence would not allow Israel to close the gap between the rich and the poor. The white racism is manifested in other more tragic ways as happened when an immigrant from Eritrea was beaten to death by a mob, accusing him of an act of terrorism he had no connection to (namely he was seen as a black Arab and not as a Jew). All of this shows that in the case of African refugees, raw anti-black racism is rampant is all walks of life and quite widespread.

## Conclusion

A recent American visitor to Israel wrote: 'No one informed me that there is considerable racism/ discrimination here for people of colour ... I expect this in the deep South of my country (US) but not in the holy land'.[5]

Indeed, many do not associate racism of colour with Israel. But it seems that what is common to the attitudes towards the Ethiopian Jews, the Black Hebrews and the life seekers from Africa is that the majority of Israeli Jews are either indifferent or ignorant about these minorities' experience of racism and discrimination.

If we use Robert Boyd's (2003) conceptualisation of colour as signifier, we can say that whiteness in Israel is a signifier in the society that impacts social position, economic conditions, and cultural attitudes. It is a similar signifier of Europeanness, or the alleged Europeanness of the Ashkenazi Jews. As Hagar Salamon (2003) put it, you cannot become an Ashkenazi because of your colour. *Hishtakenzut* (becoming an Ashkenazi) does not help if your colour is not white. There is thus no route to integration even if you are a black Jew. Only when the Jewishness of the state would be replaced by a state identity based on equality and democracy, at least the institutional racism towards black people might disappear.

The discussion on whiteness in the context of Zionism and Israel is much more than just exposing racist attitudes towards anyone who is not white. It is an important entry point for understanding the transformation Judaism underwent as a faith and a collective identity through its Zionisation process. The settler colonial nature of Zionism meant that Judaism ceased to be a global monotheistic religion and instead it became an ideology that orientated a certain group of Europeans, who were persecuted because of their religion and who chose to become a national group, towards the colonisation of someone else's homeland. Whiteness therefore justified first the secularisation of the Jewish identity and then the colonisation of 'black' Palestine, so to speak. Thus, racialisation – as a crucial factor of the settler colonial project of nation building – determined the attitude and policy towards the indigenous population.

At later stage, once Zionism became the hegemonic ideology of the Jewish state the racialisation of the other, be it native Palestinians, Arab Jews, or Africans, was institutionalised. Racialisation is still the principal forger of the collective Jewish identity in the state of Israel. For many years, it was regarded as colour blind racialisation, but the truth is that Whiteness is a crucial part of this racialisation and its disastrous impact of so many people who live in historical Palestine or used to live there.

## References

Abulhawa, S. 2017. 'Invention of the Mizrahim', *Al-Jazeera Online*, 20 September, viewed 15 March 2019, https://www.aljazeera.com/indepth/opinion/invention-mizrahim-170920103701750.html.
Arbel, E. 2013. Adam v. The Knesset. *Supreme Court of Israel*, 16 September.

Ben-Eliezer, U. 2004. Becoming a Black Jew: Cultural Racism and Anti-Racism in Contemporary Israel. *Social Identities*, 10 (2): 245–266.

Bhabha, H. 1998. The White Stuff (Political Aspects of Whiteness). *Arts Forum International*, 36: 21–23.

Blum, E. 2011. *Arthur Rupin and the Production of Pre-Israeli Culture*. Leiden: Brill.

Bonilla-Silva, E. 1997. Rethinking Racism: Toward a Structural Interpretation. *American Sociological Review*, 62 (3): 465–480.

Boyd, R. 2003. Were Black Entrepreneurs Displaced From the Retail Trade by White Immigrant Merchants? A Study of Northern Cities in the Early Twentieth Century. *Journal of Socio-Economics*, 32 (2003): 447–455.

Brodkin, K. 1998. *How Jews Became White Folks and What That Says About Race in America*. New Brunswick: Rutgers University Press.

Chetrit, S. S. 2005. The Neo-Mizrahim: The Mizrahi Radical Discourse and the Democratic Rainbow Coalition. In *Mizrahi Voices: Toward a New Discourse on Israeli Society and Culture*, ed. G. Abutbul et. al., pp. 131–152. Tel-Aviv: Masada [Hebrew].

Chinski, S. 2002. 'Eyes Wide Shut': On Acquired Balkan Syndrome in the Israeli Arts. *Theory and Criticism*, 20 (Spring): 57–86.

Cohen Y. *et al.* 2019. Mizrahi-Ashkenazi Educational Gaps in the Third Generation. *Research on Social Stratification and Mobility*, 59: 25–33.

Dyer, R. 1997. *White: Essays on Race and Culture*. London and New York: Routledge.

Fanon, F. 1967. *Black Skin, White Masks*. New York: Grove Press.

Frankenberg, R. 1997. Local Whiteness, Localizing Whiteness. In *Displacing Whiteness: Essays in Social and Cultural Criticism,* ed. R. Frankenberg, pp. 1–35. Durham, NC: Duke University Press.

Gileman, S. L. 1991. *The Jew's Body*. London and New York: Routledge.

Ginzburg, K. *et al.* 2013. Perceived Racism, Emotional Responses, Behavioral Reponses and Internalized Racism among Ethiopian Adolescent Girls in Israel. In *Proceeding of the 14th Facet Theory Conference: Searching for Structure in Complex Social, Cultural and Psychological Phenomena*, 501–518.

Lavie, S. 1991. 'Arrival of the new cultured tenants', *The Times Literary Supplement*, London, 14 June: no. 4602.

Lentin R. 2009. *Traces of Racial Exception: Racializing Israeli Settler Colonialism*. London: Bloomsbury.

Levine-Rasky, C. 2020. 'Jewish Whiteness and its Others'. *The Journal of Modern Jewish Studies*, 19 (3): 362–381.

Lewis, A. E. 2004. 'What Group?' Studying Whites and Whiteness in the Era of 'Color-Blindness'. *Sociological Theory*, 22 (4): 623–646.

Lissak, M. 1999. *The Great Aliya of the 1950s: The Failure of the Melting Pot*. Jerusalem: Bialik Publishing [Hebrew].

Mula, S. 2018. 'I am totally Normal'. Judaism, Israelism and Whiteness as Identity Anchors in the way Ethiopian Pupils Cope with Racism. In *Israel. Gilui Da'at: An Interdisciplinary Journal for Education, Society and Culture*, 14: 13–42 [Hebrew].

Raz, Y. 2004. Marked: The Construction of Ashkenazi Whiteness in Zionist Cinema. In *Eastern Appearances/Mother Tongue: A Present that Stirs the Thickets of Its Arab Past*, ed. Y. Nizri, pp. 132–152. Tel Aviv: Bavel Publication [Hebrew].

Roediger, D. R. 2007. *The Wages of Whiteness: Race and the Making of the American Working Class*. London: Verso.

Rosaldo, R. 1993. Culture and Truth: The Remaking of Social Analysis. Boston, MA: Beacon Press.

Rotbad, S. 2015. *White City, Black City: Architecture and War in Tel Aviv and Jaffa*. Cambridge: MIT Press.

Salamon, H. 2003. Blackness in Transition: Decoding Racial Constructs Through Stories of Ethiopian Jews. *Journal of Folklore Research*, 40 (1): 3–32.

Sasson-Levy, O. 2013. A Different Kind of Whiteness: Marking and Unmarking of Social Boundaries in the Construction of Social Ethnicity. *Sociological Forum*, 28 (1) (March).

Shenhav, Y. 2006. *The Arab Jews: A Postcolonial Reading of Nationalism, Religion and Ethnicity*. Stanford: Stanford University Press.

Shohat, E. 2006. *Taboo Memories, Diasporic Views*. Durham, NC: Duke University Press.

Shohat E. 2017. The Invention of Judeo-Arabic. *Interventions, International Journal of Postcolonial Studies*, 19 (2): 153–200.

Waters, M. C. 1990. *Ethnic Options: Choosing Identities in America*. Berkeley: University of California Press.

Yadgar, Y. 2011. Jewish Secularism and Ethno-National Identity in Israel: The Traditionist Critique. *Journal of Contemporary Religion*, 26 (3): 467–481.

# Part III

# Colonialities: Permutations of whiteness over time

The contributions in this section show how the shifts and continuities of whiteness over time relate to the establishment of global coloniality. Attention is paid to the multiplicities of whiteness as part of an overall hierarchical racial ordering, which works to systemically exclude people racialised as outside of whiteness (as black, brown, yellow, red, minority ethnic, and so on) from material and cultural resources. The locations move outside of the whiteness studies mainstay of Global North Western European Coloniality, centering the little considered colonialities of Japan, India, Zimbabwe, and Sweden. The section therefore pushes against a singular analysis of Global Northern dominance in understanding colonialism by refusing the more usual Western European starting points. It nevertheless recognises that these expressions of coloniality are enacted in relationship to an overall globality of whiteness whereby Global North Western European coloniality must be engaged with as an economic and cultural power. The contributions show how whiteness works to produce bargains and coalitions between differently categorised whitened subjects as a way of establishing and maintaining resource power and territorial ownership fundamental to nationalist ambitions. It also considers how these ambitions are achieved across Global South and North and within South and North in an inter-connected web of imperial dominations held together through mythologies of not quite whiteness as well 'outsiderness'. Yasuko Takezawa considers how in Japan the construction of the 'Asian Race' over time works as a historical response to not being included in Western European whiteness, whereby Japan becomes the 'saviour' for neighbouring countries of Asia, legitimising dominations internal to Asia. Everyday shifts in whiteness, who is classed as 'in' and who is classed as 'out' and how these divisions are established and form the inter-related histories of coloniality, are also considered. Inter-connected mythologies around whiteness produce collaborations and clashes between groups, framing ideas of good white subjects and bad white subjects, wherein white, male middle class heteropatriarchal ideals recognisable from within that Global North Western European nineteenth century coloniality constitute the pinnacle. Thus, differentiated European colonialisms work collectively to establish whiteness as a multifaceted symbolic ideal which justifies territorial domination, even in relationships of warring conquest, such as the English and Boers in South Africa. This too impacts neighbouring contexts. For example, as considered by Rory Pilossof, whiteness in Zimbabwe is created and downplayed against its nearest neighbour South Africa, as a way of

DOI: 10.4324/9780429355769-103

distinguishing itself from the troubled politics of its neighbour and establishing Rhodesian identity as successfully independent from Britishness. Nations like Japan look East and West to establish superiority within coloniality. The rise of whiteness is considered as fundamental to US Imperial expansions as well as to the bolstering of Indian nation building in distinction to US Imperialisms. Following Shefali Chandra's argument, whiteness is the 'lever' in our current global coloniality. The intersecting practices of religion, philanthropy and education and their transitional roles in supporting colonial control for economic expansion are considered, as well as how forgettings of intra-European colonial conquest enable whiteness to remain invisible in some places, such as Nordic contexts. Contemporary transnationalisms such as in the case of those working through Swedish adoption practices, considered by Tobias Hübinette, are exposed for their ongoing extractive dynamic; adoption as body snatching. But this colonial dynamic constitutes a key part in the construction of an exceptional Swedish white anti-racist goodness, reminiscent of historical representations of colonial violence as innocent benevolence.

Thus overall, the situation is of complexity whereby whiteness shifts and changes. The section exposes the agencies of contexts outside of the Global North Western to maintain whiteness within a broader global colonial formation, sustained, and resisted through various inter-connected dynamics of power and resistance. The section also poses challenges to selective narratives around colonisation which serve to reinforce fixed positions of (black) colonised and (white) coloniser.

# 11

# How (not) to become white

*Shefali Chandra*

## How (not) to become white

Writing from Lahore in current day Pakistan, a young British Indian writer, Kanhaiya Lal Gauba (1899–1981), sought to inform his fellow English-educated Indian colonial subjects of the racial and sexual desires of white American women. Previously, 'abnormally passionate women' would mistress 'Red Indians or Great Danes', he wrote. But today, that predilection has been replaced by a preference for 'Negro Butlers'. The year was 1929; the inter-war period was studded with the global awareness of a rising American power, and the possibility of a world-wide decolonisation from European rule, in tandem. Two years before, the American journalist Katherine Mayo had published *Mother India* (1927) to global acclaim and outrage; the book presented a scurrilous depiction of Hindu sexuality and the inability of Indians to govern themselves.[1] Gauba responded to Mayo in 1929; his book was entitled *Uncle Sham: A Strange Tale of a Civilization Run Amok.* By invoking images of inter-species and inter-racial sex, Gauba caricatured, proliferated and produced whiteness. He disseminated a particular kind of whiteness, characterised by female sexual excess and by distinctions between Continental and American racial regimes. More subtly, as I show, he incited the upper-caste obsession with endogamy. It is my argument that in engaging with America and American power, Gauba manufactured whiteness to instantiate the reach of caste over and beyond the emerging Indian nation. By caricaturing whiteness, some Indians like Gauba quietly re-centred another racial project: That of caste. They both embraced whiteness as well as denied it, but they did so in the service of upper-caste power. The commitment to caste ensured that they would (not) become white. By revealing the symbiotic relationship between caste and whiteness, my chapter probes the mutuality and inter-dependence of racial regimes under twentieth-century global capitalism.

## Whiteness as a lever

Critical ethnic studies' scholars recognise that South Asian Indians align with whiteness (Koshy 2001; Mazumdar 1989). Each twist in the tale of American domestic history has enabled Indians to forge fresh and beneficial ties with whiteness. From the historic *United States vs. Bhagat Singh*

DOI: 10.4324/9780429355769-11

*Thind* case of 1923, the era of Cold War cosmopolitanism and the Immigration Act of 1965 to the ceaseless appetite of neoliberal multiculturalism and Silicon Valley industries for technically trained software engineers following the Immigration Act of 1990, we learn that subcontinental Indians have presented as white, or as racially ambiguous, and in that way have benefitted from the racial disparities of the United States and the insatiable needs of global capitalism, in tandem. While broadly accurate, the scholarship tends to portray the Indian contract with whiteness as inevitable and also, as similar to that crafted by all Asian groups. That story suits a cursory anti-racist conviction in whiteness as the dominant, overarching force. The assumption that Indians have and always will adjust themselves to the superior power of whiteness actually absolves upper-caste Indians from a long history of racism.

Taking up the challenge posed by the editors of this collective project, and in particular the notion of the relationality of whiteness, I proffer a deeper analysis in this chapter. As I show, Indians have not merely accepted whiteness and attempted to shape themselves to its dictates. Rather, embedded in the more obvious history of alignment, lies a critique of and power over whiteness. In their engagement with a rising American power, Indians actively shaped whiteness to suit the exigencies of a new imperial terrain. Positioning themselves between a waning empire and a rising one, some Indians manufactured whiteness so as to distance themselves from it, and thereby garnered tremendous amounts of power. Indians used whiteness as a lever to suppress the interrogation of caste, to render themselves racially in-nocent, and thereby to catapult themselves into a world dominated by US power.

## 'European ladies really exceed all bounds'

Through the eighteenth and especially the nineteenth century, British colonial ethnographers worked to codify caste, to fix and limit its boundaries and its internal sub-categories (Cohn 1996). Employing the services of Indian priests in this endeavour, these state-employed scholars consolidated the broad features of the caste system. Alongside that assiduous process of enu-meration, caste groups emerged anew, disappeared, and negotiated their relative positions vis-à-vis the colonial state as well as other castes. Caste continued its dynamic march, sometimes oblivious to and at other moments assisted by, the colonial effort to collate and categorise society through the empirical detailing of professional, culinary, sartorial, linguistic, and marital markers. The period of colonial rule consolidated the hegemony of upper-caste practice and power in determining the attributes of caste as a system. And sexuality, always a marker of caste identity, now became a primary indicator of boundaries between caste groups (Chakravarti 2019). Marriage became decisive to gender and caste status. Sex outside marriage was libelled as prostitution and native elites worked to establish that prostitution was outside Hinduism itself (Gupta 2001; Mitra 2020). Prostitution increasingly marked that which was not a caste Hindu practice; it was the denigrated other, beneath and unclean. Simultaneously upper-caste women celebrated their commitment to those rituals that established nubile or marital status. Today an animated debate structures much of the scholarship on caste: Was caste a colonial invention or did it predate the colonial encounter (Bairy 2010)? Indeed, much ink has been spilled. But as I find in my research, that question misses a far more pressing aspect of the constantly mutating history of caste power. Rather than ponder the longevity and reach of the colonial bureaucratic administrative regime, I propose instead that the Indian upper-caste project shaped ideas of colonialism and as I show here, empire. A focus on sexuality is essential to this insight: Throughout the Indian engagement with British colonialism and American empire, upper-caste men crafted a critique of white female sexuality. I argue that they did so to render upper-caste regimes as hegemonic.

The theme of white female sexuality emerged as an explosive subject in upper-caste writing, it then reverberated through the engagement with American power. An early portrayal of the sexually excessive white woman appeared in response to the inauguration of an Indian girls' school in western India. An inflammatory newspaper article, deceptively entitled 'Strishikshan' (women's education), appeared in the Marathi language newspaper *Poona Vaibhav* in 1884. The article first described Indian female prostitutes: They do not 'allow any difference or distinction to exist between males and females'. With that, it veered towards a detailed comparison with white female sexuality. 'Same is the state of our educated European rulers', complained the writer of this piece. The article depicted European women in their baths, titillating their Indian servants while in the nude. It then specified each feature of the sexual relationships between European women and men. Moreover, the 'relation which exists in the case of a European pair is exactly the same as that is seen between a prostitute and her master in this country'. Mimicking the detached objective voice of colonial ethnography, the writer produced a detailed description of 'the dance of these people, which is called a ball ... would really put our prostitutes to shame ... a mode of recreation among western people ... played by all people, young and old, poor and rich'. Regardless of class or gender, European behaviour was shameful even by the standards of native prostitutes; Europeans did not differentiate cultural practice by gender or social status. The invocation of shame was productive, it produced gender, policed sexuality, and thereby ranked caste. Resonating with the arguments made by shame theorists, here too the sentiment was marshalled to instantiate hegemonic and exclusionary projects; shame links to whiteness across diverse colonial formations.[2] All Europeans were beneath prostitutes, unclean and hence, outside of caste. Strishikshan continued in the descriptive mode, detailing the consumption of caste-taboo and sensual items such as 'fruit, wines, and flesh' at these occasions, and the customary dress that 'keeps the ladies' hands and chest entirely uncovered ... the gentleman's dress ... also ... keeps the chest entirely uncovered ... any lady and any gentleman may dance together ... it is a rule, as it were, that the chests of both must unite at each stroke [of the dance]'. Later, according to the writer, after the dance the couple retires to private adjacent rooms for 'rest, and spend there a considerable time in agreeable conversation'.

The most mundane activities such as bathing and commonplace social interactions, were described in piercing detail to make the case that European women were more unchaste – therefore impure – than native prostitutes. Worse, even the institution of marriage did not insulate Europeans from their perusal of sexual pleasure, and for that reason, as the writer concluded in his article, while Indian prostitutes could have some shame, the Europeans knew none. 'We say', it concluded, 'that prostitutes of this country can have some modesty, but that European ladies really exceed all bounds'. The repeated invocation of shame exposes the project to fix and regulate gender. The correlation of 'bounds' with the sexual conduct of native prostitutes and white women hints at the desire for markers such as those respected within caste society. European women were being assessed through the very caste optic that favoured educated Hindu male power. Food, marriage, hygiene, and sex configured the terms of that assessment. In the comparison between native prostitutes and European female sexuality, the author implicitly produced the chastity and marital orientation of the Hindu female as the norm. Without ever mentioning caste Hindu sexuality, the writer of this piece projected upper-caste sexuality as hegemonic and as superior. Furthermore, European women were inferior even to Indian prostitutes: They could not be incorporated into caste. Rather, they were the necessary outsiders; their practices and desires marked the boundary of caste. The writer literally cast prostitution and European sexuality as the foil against which to elevate the chastity of the upper-caste Hindu woman.[3] Fortifying the binary between prostitution and marriage, the silent referent in the piece was the upper-caste norm: The chaste Hindu wife's life-long devotion to the marriage contract, concomitantly her subjection to the punitive rituals of enforced widowhood, child marriage, and endogamy. Caste had always hinged on the silent production of relative value between sex and virtue; in this case, European women were being brought into the analysis to further elevate Brahmanical practice and authority.

## 'A civilization run amok'

The similarities between the Marathi article from 1884 and Gauba's 1929 *Uncle Sham,* with its observations on American female sexuality, are striking. Born in 1899 in Lahore, Pakistan, Kanhaiya Lal Gauba was the son of the wealthy and iconoclastic industrialist, banker and first Hindu Minister of colonial Punjab, Lala Hariskrishna Lal Gauba. His 1974 memoirs recount the extreme wealth to which he was accustomed from an early age, the European tutors, the multilingual and poly-religious upbringing. His tutors named him Walter, and it was as 'Wal' that he went about his life both in India as well as in Britain. 'Wal' records how his wealth, and his light-skin colour protected him from hostilities aimed at Indian students at Cambridge over the inter-war years. The racial-economic nexus, in other words, bolstered him from the very start. A keen debater at Cambridge, successful barrister and a famous convert to Islam, Gauba's personal biography makes evident his prominence amongst the Anglicized bi-cultural brokers of the inter-war years.

*Uncle Sham* sold almost as many copies as Mayo's book and he profited professionally as well as monetarily from the success of his rebuttal. He composed the book in three swift months, based on sources sent to him by friends, sources ranging from the Chicago Commission on Race Relations to *True Story Magazine.*[4] The politics of citation are of vital importance. With the exception of the inter-racial Chicago Commission, Gauba reproduces 'the world around certain bodies', predominantly white, male, and American.[5] Even in critiquing whiteness, he overlooks yet reproduces and further disseminates the disproportionate grip that white men had on shaping the parameters of culture, race, and virtue. Beneath his visible contempt for American women, lay an identification and affinity with white power. Despite that, no publisher wanted to carry the book, and the first edition was self-published, at the Times Press that he owned. It sold 5000 copies overnight, claims Gauba, and from then on, stayed in print for at least 20 years (a 31st edition was issued in 1944). More than 20,000 paperback copies were sold in a week over a single, subsequent re-print the very first year. It was reviewed around the world, translated into several languages and even pirated in Japanese and French. The book was initially banned in the United States, but that was almost immediately rescinded.[6] Claude Kendall put out three re-prints within a year at $3 a copy, but with one passage permanently deleted from the original: 'The preference for Negroes by white women of America'.[7]

The readership for *Uncle Sham* stretched across continents. It seems however that Gauba first planned the book in conversation with other English educated, upper-caste Indians. The use of English as the language of communication, and Gauba's smooth facility with British and American, rhetorical and cultural references, exposes the coalition of transnational and caste privileges.[8] The very title of the book, *Uncle Sham: A Strange Tale of a Civilization Run Amok* bristles with references to an elite Anglophone world. 'Uncle Sham' draws on the British colonial, Malay-derived term deployed at that time to characterise unruly, or irrational, colonised subjects, 'to run amok' (Yule and Burnell 1903). As Gauba recalls, he first broached the idea for the book in his own Lahore-based English language newspaper, *The Sunday Times,* where he penned a weekly column. It was here that he suggested that the fitting response to Katherine Mayo need not entail a scrupulous correction of Mayo's 'facts', as had already circulated in the countless titles produced by Indians following the publication of her book.

Rather, the response should flip the script and focus instead on the sexual debauchery of the United States. Gauba's readers were moved by his advice and wrote in, encouraging him to be the one to pen exactly such a 'hot and smoking reply'. Gauba proceeded to overlook the small fact of never having visited the United States (as against Mayo's three-month long sojourn in India) and launched 'one of the world's best sellers' (Gauba 1974: 82, 87).

Gauba's rebuttal of Mayo resolutely centres US Empire. The cruelty of the Spanish-American war, subjugation of the Philippines, the massacres in Haiti, the take-over of Nicaragua, the Virgin Islands, Honduras, Guatemala, and the support for Japanese sub-regional imperial interests – every form taken by the US global grab is elicited and censured in this work. Greed, cruelty, and unbridled sexuality cohere 'Americanism'. The morally bankrupt 'average American[s]' of this civilisation are white, being 'the descendants of the Pilgrim Father [who] disgusted with the bigotry of the Mother Country, went across the seas and set up their institutions of freedom ... [t]heir sons became the great moral giants of history, the super-dentists, the par excellence manufacturers of Flit'[9] (p. 17). The disappearance of Indigenous people in his description, as of settler violence, rebounds to centre white people even as his wider assertions appear critical of white power.[10] Eventually as he shows, 'the institutions created by the early founders of the American Constitution became prostituted to business organisations, such as oil, steel, and rail-road, the Ku Klux Klan, the priesthood and the professional grafter' (p. 26). The partnering of capitalism with racism, and his depiction of that relation as resembling prostitution: These were the co-ordinates of Americanism and white supremacy. Intriguingly overlooking the work of his contemporary, W.E.B. DuBois (1868–1963), Gauba suggests that capitalism is inherently, and necessarily racist. But, it is important to retain an awareness here of Gauba's audience. White supremacy and its organised violences are presented to shock an *Indian* audience, English-reading and upper-caste. Prostitution is invoked, repeatedly, to translate and to provide semantic coherence. The question to ask therefore is how it was possible for Gauba, and his audience, to suspend an awareness of caste atrocities while collectively condemning the United States? To probe further, how did the depiction of American Empire and racism permit Indians to deflect attention away from the existence of caste violence?

When he has been studied at all, Gauba has been portrayed as characteristic of an established pattern of anticolonial intellectual production. It is commonplace to situate works such as his amidst the transnational circulation of imagery, strategy, and language that shaped the vocabulary of nationalists and anti-race activists in India and America, respectively. In discussing the inter-war years, the historian Gerald Horne (2008) has argued that a 'major rhetorical device used by South Asians before 1947 was to rebut negative assessments of India ... by pointing to glaring flaws in the budding superpower that was the United States – notably its treatment of African Americans' (Horne 2008: 71). Horne even mentions Gauba (although mischaracterises him as a woman) as he elicits the links between Indians bringing down the British Empire and African-Americans dismantling the 'Empire of Jim Crow': Both groups centred the American treatment of African-Americans. The process by which colonised Indians and African-Americans reached out to one another, built analogies between caste and race, and disseminated each cause to their respective national audiences has also been celebrated in the recent years by South Asianists like Vijay Prashad, Nico Slate, and Gyan Pandey. Such assessments portray Indians as anti-race and anti-imperial agents, who extended themselves across the globe to shape international solidarities in their quest to end the British Empire. But this conception has been perilously inattentive to sexuality, even as it might, at times, consider the role of gender. The image of Indians polarised against Empire, of the common political interests shared by 'the darker nations' and subjugated peoples of the world, obscures the generative role of sexuality and thereby ends up simplifying history along the binary of white/non-white. Simultaneously and therefore, it nimbly side-steps the history of upper-caste power.

## 'Lovemaking and necking a national pastime' (Gauba 1929 Horne 2008: 80)

Sex is unequivocally at the core of Americanism in Gauba's vision, and it is the white woman who is the architect of American sexuality: 'The Eve of to-day bears a close resemblance to Adam. She is masculine in her strength, she goes to the barber and uses a Gillette, she has no use for howling brats, she attends office and receives a cheque on pay day, which buys her smokes and pays for her nocturnal pleasures' (p. 63). Echoing the concerns voiced in *StriShikshan*, Gauba incites the fear of gender blurring. The sexual drive of American women starts early, a 14-year old boy enjoys hunting and shooting, but his 12-year old sister would be involved in a very different kind of sport. Sexuality is firmly conjoined with race:

> [I]n certain races puberty and precocity come at an early age, but it appears that in hybrid communities, where races have intermingled, the sex urge opens at an early age and in an emphasized form. The race mixtures that constitute the American nation perhaps account for the very early sex stimulus in American children.
>
> *(Gauba 1929 Horne 2008: 65)*

His pronouncements on miscegenation stoked the upper-caste investment in endogamy. Gauba's agenda is to establish the inferiority, via alteration, of the white race. Specifically, this is the American white race for the 'average English girl enters life at eighteen, fresh as the new rose; the average American girl of the same age is according to all authorities the prostitute's successful rival' (p. 70). In other words, he crafts American exceptionalism via its endemic sexual excess.

America has made a mockery of marriage, Gauba claims, this by way of the technologies of birth control, the new economic freedom desired by women, the craving for a life beyond discipline and responsibilities, and the uses of blackmail. Matrimony is a business, and in the case of the white American, marriage incorporates prostitution: 'The professional prostitute is usually in the trade about six years. Apparently both trial marriage and the regular trade start and end much about the same time. Then the altar, two years of respectability and appearance, then alimony and divorce or adultery by consent' (p. 95). The four fruits of the American matrimonial tree are, in his view, 'separation, divorce, venereal disease and sterility' (p. 103). Strikingly, it is white women who are the drivers of this horrible state of affairs, women who 'would shrink from killing even the mouse that nibbles at their foot, yet do not hesitate deliberately to kill their own offspring' (p. 110). A nation of female murderers, invested more in their appearance, their pleasures and freedom from responsibility, has spurred an avoidance of 'maternity', so much so that the entire race, lacks the 'innate love for children'. This proves the 'defect in character, some perversion, some degeneracy' (p. 111).

The innocence of the white man is an intriguing outcome of Gauba's relentless castigating of white female sexuality. The rampant cases of sexually transmitted diseases, that claims some 90% of the United States' population 'infects not only the guilty, but also the innocent, so that one half of American young men … every other man' is infected in this manner. As a result, 'one half of the population, for one reason or another, is not propagating the species' (p. 113). Sexual diseases are transmitted because of female moral degeneracy. Another aspect of this moral failing is the 'secret polygamy' endemic to the United States. Other parts of the world have rightly legalised polygamy: 'In many races it is deemed to be an effective bulwark of the foundation of society' (p. 113). But in America, the 'abnormal sex urge arising out of race complex ... explains the divorce figures, the extraordinary extent of venereal disease, and the early impotency of many American husbands and the traffic in Negro waiters' (p. 115). Gauba's reference to a *race complex* crafts an inter-locking assemblage, sutured by the vectors of race, interracial progeny, prostitution, deceit, polygamy, and sexually transmitted disease. The American assemblage stands in implicit contrast to the ideals of purity, chastity, and sexual abnegation cherished by upper-caste norms. Americans are abnormal, the 'satisfaction of sex hunger by resort to Negroes should be regarded as abnormal, the normal sex instinct of race preservation would be the mating between members of the same race' (p. 116). The vast number of interracial liaisons and their growing frequency are 'regarded in many quarters as one of the greatest menaces with which our white civilization is faced' (p. 116). The collective pronoun here is sarcastic, for his goal throughout the book is to eviscerate whiteness by staging distance from it.

Gauba was writing at the height of Jim Crow laws, a time when America was drenched with the violent policing of (the threat of) inter-racial sex. Shuddering at the possibility of sexual relations between races, Gauba evokes the passions of all those opposed to marriage outside a socially recognised group; he does so in speaking to an upper-caste audience. It is instructive here to invoke the primary place of endogamy in undergirding the caste system as theorised by Gauba's contemporary, Dr. Bhimrao Ramji Ambedkar (1891–1956). '*Endogamy is the only characteristic that is peculiar to caste*' the young Dalit scholar stressed in his doctoral defence at Columbia University in 1917, it was the upper-castes that were invested in its maintenance, and they did so through the regulation of female sexuality.[11] Endogamy guarantees the perpetual replication of the system. Sex and the rituals of sexual regulation (sati, child marriage and enforced widowhood) are essential to upper-caste hegemony and caste is always a system of relationality, 'caste in the singular number is an unreality. Castes exist only in the plural number'. Undeniably the foremost theorist of caste, Dr. Ambedkar went on to reveal how caste maintains its hold through a pyramidic logic of graded inequalities, with an 'ascending scale of reverence and a descending scale of contempt' (Ambedkar 1947: 26). There is an important difference between inequality and graded inequality, and it is the latter which is the differentiating feature of the sexual-caste complex. Graded inequality ensures that there is always a group beneath even an unprivileged caste, such that 'each class being [somewhat] privileged, every class is interested in maintaining the system' (Ambedkar 1935: 101–102).

To connect back to Gauba, I argue that he manufactures and transmits contempt via sexuality, thus exposing his own, caste-informed, standpoint. The white female desire for African-American men differentiates 'our standards' from Caucasian ones, he then proceeds to map this distinction on the separate realms of intellect and appearance.

> To the average individual, intercourse with the Negro is abhorrent. From records of universities and teaching societies it appears that intellectually the Negro is perhaps a little below the average of our standards, but from all Caucasian standards of appearance his hideous black skin, heavy limbs, coarse matted hair, and heavy protruding lips are in every respect the antithesis of what is regarded as beautiful.
>
> *(Gauba 1929 Ambedkar Ambedkar 1935: 116)*

I have struggled with reproducing these lines but have ultimately elected to do so to foreground upper-caste ideas of Blackness, the inverse symbiosis of caste with race. Gauba separates intellect from physique, stressing 'intellect' when discussing 'our' and 'Caucasian' standards but excessive, and hideous, corporeality in the case of the 'Negro'; the latter coded male. The caste-specific distinction between intellect and labour instantiates the white/Black binary. Again, Gauba reproduces hegemonic subject positions by circulating stereotype as 'knowledge'. Crucially, he extends the pyramidic structure of reverence and contempt identified by Ambedkar upon American society. To borrow from Jennifer Morgan here, I propose too that Gauba activates a 'negative symbolic' system.[12] The revolting sexuality of the white woman is substantiated by inciting anti-Blackness. White women are the semantic glue, 'they' cohere anti-Blackness upon upper-caste codes of endogamy and thereby perform negative symbolic work. It is in this way that Gauba reinforces the split between caste and race: The contempt that Indians might feel for Black males is not respected by white women. The wide prevalence of inter-racial desire, sex and progeny establishes that all Americans are beneath (upper-caste) Indians. A caste-specific code allows him to both reject whiteness as well as to materialise it, and in this way, to (not) become white.

With this citational practice, whereby whiteness is produced through sex to scrutinise its claims to civilisational dominance, Gauba returns to the phenomenon of prostitution, 'practically unknown among savage races and despite current opinion to the contrary, appears to have developed as an institution of civilization' (p. 124). He invokes, without references, cases from Uganda, Australia (prior to the advent of the white settler), and 'the Takue' of East Africa to establish the absence of prostitution amongst them. Such 'savage races' avenge acts of prostitution with terrible retribution, he claims, albeit without any annotations. Prostitution was barely known among such 'primitive races and tribes ... till civilization arrived with its culture and its license' (p. 124). Isabel Hofmeyer has powerfully stated that 'Africa has long been conscripted as an invisible boundary of Indian nationalism, the "uncivilized foil" to Indic civilization, the bottom tier in a hierarchy of civilizations'. The invocation of tribe and race as non-Indian, and specifically, Black and African serves Gauba in rendering a hierarchy of race, colour, and civilisation. Caste hovers silently and yet centrally over this analysis, by way of prostitution, Gauba renders American inter-racial sex as distinct and 'beneath' African tribal customs.

The American form of prostitution is not only restricted to the hiring of 'the female body for the gratification of male lust' but also includes 'the hiring of the male body for the satisfaction of feminine passion'. Who, he thunders, 'are these women who take no hire' (p. 125)? The answer cannot be belaboured enough. Gauba references *Prostitution in the United States* and jumbles the numbers and the descriptions to provide a vivid picture of a nation engaged recklessly and uproariously in sexual commerce. Here, he casually switches his style to that of a participant observer,

> [t]ravelling in the United States, cases came to my own observation of hotels which were nothing more or less than glorified brothels, where, for a small gratification, introduction to women in the hotel could be obtained, and where the Negro establishment supplemented their income by obliging women patrons.
>
> (Gauba 1929 Ambedkar Ambedkar 1935: 128)

Once again, he renders America white by its sexual practices, the 'Negro establishment' is named and marked so that the implicit allusion is to white women as the universal category. None of the passages or authorities that he cites actually corroborate his theory on male prostitution or of 'Negro and Mongolian attendants popular with female custom'. However, it would take a careful reading to distinguish between the facts that he constructs, and the ones that he cites.[13] American sexual excess is irrefutable, for unlike in the 'East' there is no such case of the 'hereditary prostitute' in America (p. 130).

Savarna (upper-caste) apologists of the caste system often propounded the unique cultural benefits of a system that freed its adherents from the burden of learning or choosing a profession.[14] In reality, it would often be the most vulnerable who would be expected to inherit professions, as we have many cases from the same period of upper-caste men such as Gandhi and Gauba who smoothly rejected their inheritances. It was convenient and economically useful for these men to believe that caste provided a pre-ordained path, that it harmonised social relations. Indian prostitution might be terrible and unclean, but elites could claim that caste contained its spread. In America, the absence of a hereditary prostitute caste, amidst the rampant cases of venereal disease, inter-racial sex, under-age sexual activities: All these established that the prostitute-conjugal binary so essential to the Hindu caste system carried no salience in the United States. The Empire had seriously run amok. And it was the dog-fucking, face-shaving, racially lustful white woman who had driven the country to this stage in history.

## Conclusion

In the final analysis, the white woman, object of Indian revulsion and contempt, would not be incorporated into the graded hierarchies of caste. She remains outside caste, but necessarily so. Rejecting the voluminous debate on whether Empire created caste, I maintain instead that it was the Indian caste project that needed Empire. This was an Empire of sex and race, of white power and anti-Blackness, of prostitution, shame, the failure of marriage, gender blurring, and venereal disease. Colonial regimes built extreme forms of authority by scrutinising 'native' sexuality, and some Indians easily understood the value to be gained from observing, commenting on, and thereby fixing sexuality. Despite the seeming imbalance in global power, writing about sexuality accrued authority. It enabled colonised men to speak in the name of India and thereby, to assess 'America'. They sexualised whiteness and rendered it emblematic of 'America', in the process, split caste from race and thus positioned themselves as racially innocent (Chandra 2020). Whiteness was a lever, it catapulted the upper-caste man to the position of global critic. Aligning whiteness with sex, the anti-imperial critic enshrined upper-caste cultures. Caste was obscured and absolved of the very charge that was levied against white racial supremacy.

It might be comforting, to some, to situate the nineteenth-century Marathi language essay, and Gauba's global blockbuster, in the context of resistance: Colonised subjects returned the gaze, they parodied the British obsession with sexuality and thereby lampooned the moral presumptions of an Empire built on racial difference. However, by locating the constituent elements of sexuality in the long, and culturally coded history of caste, I have drawn attention instead to the continuous replication of the marriage/ prostitution binary, the use of the English language, the dissemination of sexual caricature as knowledge, the contempt for labouring bodies. The critique of Empire enables the splitting off of caste from race, casteism from racism; 'Blackness' congeals as a barrier against the identification of Indian racism. Here, in other words is the production of Indian innocence via 'race'. It is a cunning move by which the signifier race, and especially the signifier 'negro' deflects an upper-caste recognition of its own racism. The fantasy of a rampaging prostitution, the hegemony of Empire, the investment in caste and particularly in endogamous marriage, the derision of female desire, and the fabrication of Blackness all congeal to populate the primer on how (not) to become white.

## Notes

1 Mayo's book was a global success; Mrinalini Sinha describes it as 'an international cause celebre'; it sold 395,678 copies worldwide in under 30 years of being in print (Sinha 2006: 1).

2 Eve Sedgwick stresses that shame becomes 'the place where the question of identity arises most originally and most relationally' (2003: 37).

3 Elsewhere, I have shown how the controversy over this case actually augmented the authority of upper-caste men (Chandra 2011).

4 Gauba, *Uncle Sham*, 7. He lists his sources as the *Literary Digest* and *Current History*, H. L. Menkin's *Americana*, Dr. Edith Hooker's *Laws of Sex*, Woolston's *Prostitution in the United States*, various Macfadden publications and Judge Lindsey's *The Revolt of Modern Youth* and *Companionate Marriage*. Gauba mines Mr. Stephen Graham's *New York Nights*, Viscount Bryce's *Modern Democracy* and *American Commonwealth*.

5 Sara Ahmed describes citation as 'a rather successful reproductive technology, a way of reproducing the world around certain bodies' ('Making Feminist Points' Blog post entry in *Feministkilljoys*, 11 September 2013, viewed 1 June 2020, <https://feministkilljoys.com/2013/09/11/making-feminist-points/>.

6 The book was reviewed extensively, and immediately *Foreign Affairs* noted Gauba's achievement in drawing a 'lurid, grotesque, and extremely uncomplimentary picture of our civilization'. William Langer, Uncle Sham *Foreign Affairs,* October 1929.

7 Gauba, *Friends and Foes*, 86.

8 I have demonstrated how Indian English is produced by the intimate and social politics of caste (Chandra 2012).

9 Flit was an American invented insecticide, first manufactured in 1923 by the Standard Oil Company (later renamed ExxonMobil). Flit contained a significant amount of DDT and was also inflammable. It stayed in common use industrially as well as domestically in many developing nations until the 1990s.

10 In a powerful and arresting analysis, Shaista Patel (2016) unpacks a contemporary move that resonates with Gauba's: The way that upper-caste sexual cultures thrive through the re-narration of Indigeneity. .

11 B.R. Ambedkar, 'Castes in India. Their Mechanism, Genesis and Development' in *Indian Antiquity,* May 1917, XLVI: 3–22. The text is republished several times; I refer to the online edition, viewed 1 June 2020, http://www.columbia.edu/itc/mealac/pritchett/00ambedkar/txt_ambedkar_castes.html. Emphasis in original.

12 Morgan shows how early modern European descriptions of African women entailed 'identifying Others through the monstrous physiognomy of the sexual behaviour of women'; these were mobilised to condone the pillage of Africa and theft of American lands, pp. 169–170.

13 In another instance, he casually cites passages from a *Report of Social Service Committee*, Toronto 1915, to buttress his claims.

14 Gandhi's references to the utility of the inheritance of labour are scattered through his writings. See for instance, *Young India,* 27 October 1927, p. 357; *Young India,* 4 June 1931, p. 129 and *Collected Works of Mahatma Gandhi*, 'An Example to Copy', 29 July 1933.

## References

Ahmed, S. 2013. 'Making Feminist Points', *Feministkilljoys*, September 11, viewed 1 June 2020, https://feministkilljoys.com/2013/09/11/making-feminist-points/.

Ambedkar, B. R. 1917. Castes in India. Their Mechanism, Genesis and Development. *Indian Antiquary*, May, XLVI: 3–22, viewed 1 June 2020, http://www.columbia.edu/itc/mealac/pritchett/00ambedkar/txt_ambedkar_castes.html.

Ambedkar, B. R. 1935. Untouchables or the Children of India's Ghetto. In *Writings and Speeches, Vol. 5*, ed. B. Ambedkar, 1989. Bombay: Government of Maharashtra.

Ambedkar, B. R. 1947. Who were the Shudras? How they came to be the Fourth Varna in Indo-Aryan Society? In *Writings and Speeches, Vol. 7*, ed. Babasaheb Ambedkar Dr, 1990. Bombay: Government of Maharashtra.

Bairy, R. 2010. *Being Brahmin, Being Modern*. New Delhi: Routledge.

Chakravarti, U. 2018. *Gendering Caste: Through a Feminist Lens*. New Delhi: SAGE Publications.

Chandra, S. 2011. Whiteness on the Margins of Native Patriarchy: Race, Caste, Sexuality and the Agenda of Transnational Studies. *Feminist Studies*, 37 (1): 127–153.

Chandra, S. 2012. *The Sexual Life of English: Languages of Caste and Desire in Colonial India*. Durham, NC: Duke University Press.

Chandra, S. 2020. Decolonizing the Orgasm: Caste, Whiteness and Knowledge Production at the 'End of Empire'. *South Asia: Journal of South Asian Studies*, 43 (6): 1179–1195.

Cohn, B. S. 1996. *Colonialism and Its Forms of Knowledge: The British in India*. Princeton NJ: Princeton University Press.

Gauba, K. L. 1929. *Uncle Sham: A Strange Tale of a Civilization Run Amok*. Lahore: Times Press.

Gauba, K. L. 1974. *Friends and Foes*. New Delhi: Indian Book Company.

Gupta, C. 2001. *Sexuality, Community, Obscenity: Women, Muslims and the Hindu Public in Colonial India*. New Delhi: Palgrave Macmillan.

Hofmeyer, I. 2016. Foreword. In *Africa in the Indian Imagination: Race and the Politics of Postcolonial Citation*, ed. A. Burton. Durham, NC: Duke University Press.

Horne, G. 2008. *The End of Empires: African Americans and India*. Philadelphia: Temple University Press.

Koshy, S. 2001. Morphing Race into Ethnicity: Asian Americans and Critical Transformations of Whiteness. *Boundary 2*, 28 (1): 153–194.

Langer, W. L. 1929. Some Recent Books on International Relations: Uncle Sham. *Foreign Affairs*, 8 (1): 156–168.

Mayo, K. 1927. *Mother India*. London: Harcourt Brace and Co.

Mazumdar, S. 1989. Racist Responses to Racism: The Aryan Myth and South Asians in the United States. *South Asia Bulletin*, 9 (1): 47–55.

Mitra, D. 2020. *Indian Sex Life: Sexuality and the Colonial Origins of Modern Social Thought*. Princeton NJ: Princeton University Press.

Morgan, J. L. 1997. 'Some Could Suckle over Their Shoulder': Male Travelers, Female Bodies, and the Gendering of Racial Ideology, 1500–1770. *The William and Mary Quarterly*, 54 (1): 167–192.

n.a. 1884. Strishikshan. *Poona Vaibhav* [The Glory of Poona]: 24 August: 1–2.

Pandey, G. 2013. *A History of Prejudice: Race, Caste and Difference in India and the United States*. New York: Cambridge University Press.

Patel, S. 2016. Complicating the Tale of 'Two Indians': Mapping 'South Asian' Complicity in White Settler Colonialism Along the Axis of Caste and Anti-Blackness. *Theory & Event*, 19 (4). muse.jhu.edu/article/633278

Prashad, V. 2001. *Everybody was Kung Fu Fighting: AfroAsian Connections and the Myth of Cultural Purity*. Boston: Beacon Press.

Prashad, V. 2007. *The Darker Nations: A People's History of the Third World*. New York City, NY: New Press.

Sedgwick, E. 2003. *Touching, Feeling: Affect, Pedagogy, Performativity*. Durham, NC: Duke University Press.

Sinha, M. 2006. *Specters of Mother India: The Global Restructuring of an Empire*. Durham, NC: Duke University Press.

Slate, N. 2012. *Colored Cosmopolitanism: The Shared Struggle for Freedom in the United States and India*. Cambridge, MA: Harvard University Press.

Yule, H. and Burnell, A. C. 1903. *Hobson-Jobson: A Glossary of Colloquial Anglo-Indian Words and Phrases, and of Kindred Terms, Etymological, Historical, Geographical and Discursive. The Anglo-Indian Dictionary*, 2nd edn. London: J. Murray.

# 12

# 'Good Sweden': Transracial adoption and the construction of Swedish whiteness and white antiracism

*Tobias Hübinette*

## Sweden and the Nordic countries as the world's most transracially adopting region and country

This article provides a critical historicized analysis of the Nordic countries as being the world's leading transracially adopting region with Sweden as the principal case study. The purpose is to account for and examine how the development of transracial adoption and the construction of a particular form of Swedish whiteness and white antiracism took place *in tandem* in Sweden ever since this Nordic and Scandinavian country pioneered the global practice of transnational adoption itself together with the United States in the 1950s and 1960s. In other words, the Swedes have not only adopted more foreign-born and non-white children per head than any other Western country – Sweden also contributed to institutionalize the practice of transnational adoption itself side by side with the United States during its first decade in the 1950s. Sweden and the United States thereby turned transnational adoption into a permanent global forced child migration and a naturalised reproduction technique in the West by transforming it from a temporary rescue operation for war children and mixed-race children in 1950s' South Korea to an institutionalized and commercialized reproduction method for Westerners run by an adoption industry which Kimberly McKee (2016) calls the transnational adoption industrial complex.

The Nordic countries encompassing the sovereign states of Sweden, Denmark, Finland, Norway, and Iceland as well as the Finnish autonomous territory Åland and the Danish autonomous territories Greenland and the Faroe Islands are oftentimes left out within postcolonial studies even if the two leading nations of the Nordic region Sweden and Denmark once ruled over several overseas colonies in the Americas, Africa, and Asia and they were also both involved in the transatlantic slave trade. Furthermore, Denmark is still clinging to the Inuits' Greenland or Kalaallit Nunaat while Sweden, Norway, and Finland still rule over the Samis' Samiland or Sápmi. It is only lately that this negligence has been challenged by academicians, authors, artists, and activists alike and among historians a couple of collections of academic

DOI: 10.4324/9780429355769-12

articles has recently come out as a corrective to this postcolonial amnesia (Naum and Nordin 2013; Weiss 2016).

The Nordic region, and specifically the three Scandinavian kingdoms of Sweden, Denmark, and Norway, has also for a long time been seen as the homeland for the most pure, superior, and valuable version of whiteness and branch of the white race, that is Nordic whiteness or the so-called 'Nordic race', according to Western racial thinking as it developed from the nineteenth century and onwards. This idea of the white Scandinavians as being the whitest of all whites on earth was during the twentieth century both a cherished self-image among the Scandinavians themselves as well as the image of the Scandinavians in the outside world and in particular of the white Swedes (Broberg and Roll-Hansen 2005; Duedahl 2017; Kjellman 2013; Kyllingstad 2014). Up until the end of the past century, the Nordic countries were also arguably much more white and racially homogenous than the rest of the Western world as the inhabitants of the Nordic countries emigrated to the United States and to other overseas settler states and very few immigrants found their way to this peripheral part of Europe. It was therefore only after WW2 that immigration slowly but steadily started to change the demographic make-up also of Northern Europe.

Due to this combination of the discourse of the Nordic race and the demographic fact that non-white and non-Western immigration came late to the Nordic region, Scandinavia with Sweden as the prime example has become a powerful symbol for today's pan-Western Far Right as on the hand being the homeland of the 'super whites' and on the other hand being lethally threatened by non-white 'mass immigration' and by an imagined 'globalist' establishment wanting to destroy the 'white elite' of the Western world (Norocel et al. 2020). In other words, the Northern Europe and the Nordic region is on the one hand seen as the bastion and homeland of the whitest of all whites in the world while on the other hand this part of the West is more threatened than any other Western region by non-white immigrants and minorities as this part of Europe cannot by all means 'fall' and 'perish' as it harbours something like the heart of whiteness itself.

At least since the 1960s and 1970s, in particular Sweden and to a lesser extent Norway has also been regarded as being the most good, the most humanitarian and the most ethical white Western nation of the world because of among others its history of being by far the world's biggest development aid donor, of its generous refugee policy which until recently was arguably the most generous in the whole West, of its radical and firm antiapartheid, antisegregationist, anticolonial, and antiimperialist line toward the rest of the West including harsh criticism of French, British, and American racism and of its active economic, cultural, political, and even military support for the so-called Third World, the former colonies in Latin America and the Caribbean, Africa, the Middle East, Asia and Oceania and the Global South (Hübinette and Lundström 2014; Pitcher 2014: 54–72). The general image of the Nordic region and especially of Sweden as being something like the paradise on earth for all kinds of progressive polices, antiracist attitudes, and social justice initiatives with the world's most advanced welfare system is connected to transnational and transracial adoption. This image is intimately related to the fact that Sweden, Denmark, Finland, Norway, and Iceland have altogether and since the end of the 1950s adopted around 100,000 foreign-born children out of whom the vast majority derive from Latin America, Africa, and Asia (Howell 2006; Högbacka and Ruohio 2020; Hübinette 2007; Lindgren 2010; Myong and Andersen 2015; Yngvesson 2010).

This makes the Nordic region the most transnationally adopting region in the world proportionally and per head given that not more than 27 million people are scattered around this geographically vast region of Northern Europe. As the absolute majority of these 100,000 foreign-born adoptees have been adopted by white Scandinavian singles or couples and as the majority of the adopted children derive from the postcolonial world, most transnational adoptions to and in the Nordic countries are also transracial. Among the Nordic countries, Sweden has adopted the most non-white children from the Global South and with its 60,000 foreign-born adoptees, the country is espousing the highest number of transnational adoptions per head in the whole world and possibly in world history.

## The hegemonic narrative of transracial adoption

The hegemonic narrative both within and outside of the Nordic countries when it comes to explaining and understanding that the Nordic region is the world's leading transnationally and transracially adopting region says that the Nordic countries are among the most affluent in the world while most adopted children derive from poor and war stricken former colonies outside of the West. In other words, the world record transnational and transracial adoption numbers are usually explained by Nordic benevolence and generosity, and by Nordic international engagement and humanitarianism. The same dominant narrative on transnational adoption nowadays also adds that the Nordic countries are both the most gender equal and the most socio-economically class-equal region in the world as well as the world's safe haven for LGBTQ people and for people with disabilities and for practically all other minorities, and therefore more or less everyone is able to adopt in the Nordic countries including same-sex couples, singles, and upper middle-aged persons contrary to most other Western countries where there are more or less strong restrictions on who can adopt or not.

Additionally, it is arguably only in Sweden among all Western nations where the transnational adoption of non-white children has become so intimately linked to the construction of a good and ethical whiteness and of white antiracism. To be able to unpack and understand this intimate relationship between transnational and transracial adoption, Swedish whiteness and white antiracism it is necessary to go back to a public debate that took place in 1960s' Sweden concerning the adoption of non-white children from abroad and which in hindsight can be conceptualised as the foundational moment when this specific form of white antiracism was formulated and became an intrinsic and integrated part of Swedishness itself as well as of the image of Sweden in the outside world. In other words, the birth of Sweden as the biggest adopting country in the world was also the birth of 'good' and antiracist Sweden.

## The development of transracial adoption in Sweden

Sweden in the 1940s, 1950s, and 1960s, and even in the 1970s, was probably one of the most racially homogenous Western countries after decades of a racially motivated strict anti-immigration regime which was explicitly directed towards Roma people between 1914 and 1954, and in 1931 for example, a government authority recommended that 'coloured races under no circumstances, Negroes not even as temporary visitors, should be allowed entrance in the country except for certain rare exceptions' (Ericsson 2016: 153). This strongly negative and hostile attitude at that time towards practically everyone that could not pass as a white Swede and a white Scandinavian was also acted out against the small national minorities of Sweden and especially during the inter-war years including the Roma, the Travellers, the Jews, the Finnish speakers and the Samis, and as late as 1960 not even 3,000 inhabitants of Sweden derived from Africa, Asia, or Latin America taken together (Statistiska centralbyrån 2019).

However, already from the end of the 1950s, the first adopted children from other countries arrived in a then predominantly white Sweden and in the beginning they were mostly from South Korea, where transnational adoption itself as we know of it today was born as an institutionalised practice in the aftermath of the Korean War (Hübinette 2003). Both Sweden and the other two Scandinavian countries took part in the war on South Korea's side with field hospitals and as Sweden, Norway, and Denmark decided to stay in the war-torn country and together established what was then South Korea's most advanced medical hospital in its capital Seoul, especially Sweden came to pioneer and lay the ground for the global practice of transnational adoption itself together with the United States. It is therefore no coincidence that the world's biggest adoption agency, Holt, is American while the second biggest Western adoption agency, Adoption Centre, is Swedish as the two countries were the two main Western receivers of Korean children from an early stage and soon also of children of colour from numerous other countries in the Global South.

In 1971, at the first international conference on transnational adoption which took place in Milan, Italy, a participating representative from the Swedish Agency Adoption Centre boasted to *New York Times* that 'other countries show us their trust by sending brown, black and yellow children to pinkish parents' as Sweden had already then become the biggest adopting country in the world per head (Hoffmann 1971). Interestingly enough, during the same year the white American expat journalist Ruth Link wrote about how the previously predominantly white country slowly but steadily started to change demographically on a racial level due to the massive influx of adopted children of colour that characterized 1970s' Sweden:

> It was while shopping for gloves one day at Åhléns department store – where I noticed two Swedish parents with their little Korean daughter, after just having seen two others with their African daughter in the purse department – that I realized new colour was being added to Sweden's tall, fair, often blond and almost bland homogeneity. Like a strip of chocolate in the Swedish vanilla, the new tots were melting into the picture.
>
> *(Link 1971: 50)*

In 1970, the number of inhabitants deriving from Africa, Asia, and Latin America had also increased to 13,459 people representing 0.17% of the then total Swedish population and a good number of them were adopted children, and in 1980 as many as one out of three of all immigrants of colour in Sweden or about 17,000 people were adoptees from the Global South meaning that transnational and transracial adoption constituted a substantial part of non-white and non-Western immigration itself to Sweden for several decades in a row (Statistiska centralbyrån 2019).

## The construction of a good and ethical Swedish whiteness

While the US involvement in and engagement with the early years of transnational adoption was intimately linked to what Christina Klein (2003) has coined Cold War Orientalism and which Arissa Oh (2005) has named Christian Americanism, that is a sentimental structure of feeling and a then powerful ideology combining American post-war empire building rhetoric of saving and protecting the weak and the needy from the 'barbarism' of 'world Communism' with Christian missionary zeal, the Swedish one has a somewhat different origin as Sweden stayed neutral during both Second World War and the Cold War. In the 1960s and partly also in 1970s' Sweden, a public debate raged in the Swedish media and among Swedish experts, professionals and politicians concerning if Sweden would institutionalize the practice of transnational adoption or not. In the debate, the old Swedish establishment of medical doctors, child care experts and scholars stood in opposition to radical Left-leaning journalists, cultural figures and activists who belonged to the so-called 1968 movement (Hübinette 2020).

While the old establishment continued to defend a certain kind of classical Swedish racial thinking from the mid-war years which argued that the white Swedes belonged to the Nordic race and would therefore not benefit from the adoption of children of colour from the former colonies as the children would most certainly marry and reproduce with white Swedes as adults and thus give rise to so-called race mixing, which was seen as something negative in itself as the white Swedes were considered to be purer and more valuable than any other white nation, the winning camp started to craft and formulate a new vision of Sweden as the most fitting white nation in the world to receive non-white children for adoption. This ideological manoeuvre became the starting point and foundational moment for the construction of a good and ethical Swedish whiteness and of a particular white antiracism which today has come to permeate the thinking of practically all white Swedes regardless of political views. At that time, however, in the 1960s and 1970s, it was considered to be both utopian and avant-garde and in all respects extremely radical.

The pro-transracial and transnational adoption camp of 1960s' Sweden can in hindsight be said to have identified with what Raka Shome (2011) calls global motherhood and which Antoinette M. Burton (1994) has named the white woman's burden in her study of early British Feminists and their relationship to the British Empire. The famous Swedish Feminist Eva Moberg, who was a public celebrity in Sweden in the 1960s and 1970s, argued for example in 1964:

> Today, it is impossible to find a country that could be better suited than Sweden for an adoption on a larger scale of children from developing countries... Prosperity, social security, low nativity, political neutrality, no colonial burden, good reputation among the developing countries, racial prejudices on retreat ...
>
> *(Moberg 1964: 57)*[1]

Moberg and the other enthusiastic proponents for transnational adoption portrayed Sweden as almost being the potential white mother and white protector of the so-called Third World and in practice of all non-white people on earth including also the African-Americans and as being in opposition to all other Western countries which were seen and portrayed as aggressive and masculine imperialists and racists waging colonial wars such as the United States and France and/or oppressing their racial minorities such as the United States and the United Kingdom. As a result of the lobbying of the pro-transracial and transnational adoption camp, a government investigation was commissioned in 1964, which eventually led to the institutionalization of transnational adoption in and to Sweden from the end of the 1960s and through this almost overnight transformation of Sweden as previously being totally obsessed by preserving its perceived racial purity and white superiority to embracing the mass adoption of non-white children from Latin America, the Caribbean, Africa, Asia, the Middle East and Oceania, Sweden, purged its own colonial past both in front of itself and in front of the rest of the world including both the Global North and the Global South. Catrin Lundström and myself have argued in our theoretical model of understanding the modern history of hegemonic whiteness in Sweden and of Swedish racial formations, that this shift was crucial and decisive. The transformation from race conscious and race obsessed Sweden to antiracist Sweden or rather antiracial and colour-blind Sweden according to David Theo Goldberg's definition of anti-racialism (Goldberg 2009: 10), was in all respects avant-gardistic also on a Pan-Western level:

> Before that, Sweden had played an absolutely vital role in the construction of the white race and of race thinking itself, both as the projection ground par excellence for what can

be called whiteness deluxe, and as a world-leading knowledge production centre for scientific racism. This time, Sweden again played an equally if not even more crucial role during and after the dramatic years of decolonization and the civil rights movements in the 1960s and 1970s, by creating a new kind of antiracist whiteness for the future at a time when the final and violent end of Europe's global empires had resulted in both a fundamental crisis regarding the centuries-old belief in white supremacy, and even in a crisis for whiteness itself. We argue that Sweden therefore contributed to preserving whiteness in the new postcolonial order, and in a new society characterised by increased diversity due to postcolonial migration, as still being fit to continue to rule the planet, in spite of the fact that the colonies were now politically independent.

(Hübinette and Lundström 2014: 430)

Within the Swedish national context, the non-white adoptees were above all bestowed with the task to turn the white Swedish masses into antiracists and to realize the vision of a colour-blind Sweden. In 1963, Anna Wieslander, who was symptomatically also an educator at the world's largest development aid government authority Sida or the Swedish International Development Cooperation Agency, wrote for example that 'intimate and long-lasting contact creates human understanding that means the end of prejudices' when she argued that the children from China, Latin America, the Arab countries and sub-Saharan Africa must be brought to Sweden in great numbers to be adopted by white Swedes as a way to eradicate the racial prejudices in Sweden, and she ended her op-ed piece by hoping that in a future Sweden 'it is my belief that only when there is a little Negro child in every school or an Arab in every workplace does the propaganda already begun in schools and the media have its full effect' (Wieslander 1963).

Furthermore, already in the 1960s and 1970s and throughout the following decades and still today, adoptees of colour have also been heavily used in Swedish visual public culture to communicate diversity, multiculturalism, and antiracism on for example information brochure covers and posters, in outdoor adverts and television commercials and in novels, plays, songs, and films while their non-white bodies are at the same time exoticised to an extent which borders on fantasies of eating the other according to Richey Wyver's analysis of the commodification of adoptees' bodies in adoptive parents' memoirs and in Swedish companies' commercials (Wyver 2018, 2019). The leaving behind of race obsessed Sweden was in other words made possible by exploiting the non-white bodies of the transnational adoptees, who thereby played a pivotal role in the birth and construction of a good and ethical Swedish whiteness and of a white antiracism for the future.

## Decolonising 'good Sweden'

In contemporary Sweden, the exceptional idea of 'good Sweden' and the self-image among white Swedes as being the practically only ethical whites of the world has remained intact since the turning point in the 1960s and 1970s when it comes to transnational adoption and transracial adoptees. Johanna Gondouin (2012, 2016), who has studied how adoptive families are represented in Swedish media, argues that 'transnational adoption thus became a manifestation of modernity, the expression of a nonprejudiced, national attitude' (Gondouin 2016: 103). While it is today more or less commonplace in other adopting Western countries to at least accept the voicing of a postcolonial critique of transnational adoption in the public and in the political sphere, and both within and outside of the academia, this is still not the case in today's Sweden. Barbara Yngvesson (2012) has argued that Sweden is a special and unique case among the receiving Western countries as transnational adoption came to play such a central role when it came to demarcating the borders of the national body and of Swedishness itself:

> The founders of international adoption in late 1960s Sweden argued that Sweden was 'a well prepared soil for the idea of inter-country adoption to grow', because of its egalitarian ethos, the absence of racism, the fact that Sweden had 'no colonial history ...'.
>
> *(Yngvesson 2012: 332)*

By writing itself out of post-colonial and post-imperial Europe and by even abolishing the word race as being the first state to do so through a unison parliamentary decision already in the beginning of the 2000s, Sweden entered the new millennium as a white innocent nation, to speak with Gloria Wekker (2016), and to an extent which by far exceeds Wekker's own Netherlands as Sweden is arguably seen as the most innocent white nation in the world and both among Western and non-Western countries. Even though a strong Far Right backlash has hit Sweden as well after the so-called refugee crisis year of 2015 when Sweden took in the most refugees per head in the Western world amounting to over 160,000 people, transnational adoption and adoptees of colour are still firmly located within the Swedish national body as still playing a fundamental role in upholding and reproducing the self-image of a good Swedish whiteness and white antiracism.

It is therefore no surprise that the Far Right (National Socialist in origin) party the Sweden Democrats, which became the third biggest party in the 2018 election with 17.5%, have explicitly stated in the party programme from 2011 that the adoptees of colour belong to Sweden and to Swedishness. Furthermore, this party has even made use of adoptees of colour in its visual propaganda material such as in propaganda films that have been screened on national television during parliamentary election campaigns (Wyver 2020). Such an open display of adoptees in the political propaganda of a Far Right Western party can only take place in Sweden where transnational adoption has become such an integrated and embedded part of the white nation and of the national psyche and where transracial adoptees are playing such a fundamental role to reproduce the image of good and ethical Sweden in the world and of antiracism as being the national ethos of all white Swedes. In other words, a Far Right party with Nazi origins openly, unashamedly, and perversely embracing adoptees of colour and according them a central position within the national imaginary can only exist in Sweden. This is because of the role of the adoptees as the beloved mascots of the white Swedish nation whose presence serves the function of continuously saving and cleansing Sweden from a colonial past and from racial prejudices and even 'helping' a former Nazi party to cleanse itself of its past.

In the 1960s and 1970s, the adoptees of colour were needed to rebrand and recreate Sweden from a race obsessed and 'super white' nation to an antiracist and progressive country at a time of decolonization and civil rights movements and today they are still needed to fuel the upholding of 'good Sweden' and even to 'prove' that the Sweden Democrats are not racists and that even this Far Right party adheres to white Swedish antiracism. In this way, the adoptees are not just the children of their Swedish adoptive parents – they are on a symbolic level the children of Sweden itself as transnational and transracial adoption to Sweden has not just been a reproduction technique for individuals as the practice also has a use value in itself to the white nation which in the Swedish case translates into 'good Sweden' similar to how Ghassan Hage (1998) argues that white multiculturalists find a use value in immigrants in Australia. However, while Hage talks about the cultural Otherness of Australian immigrants, the Swedish case is solely about the racial Otherness of the adoptees as they are in all other respects culturally Swedish. This centring of race in the form of the adoptees' non-white bodies an otherwise colour-blind country thus becomes a reminder of Sweden's race obsessed and not so distant past. As Richey Wyver reminds:

> The adoptee body represents a fantasy of regaining a complete control over the national space, where nonwhite bodies can be positioned and fully trusted to behave on the White Swede's terms.
>
> *(Wyver 2020: 913)*

Finally, in the future, to be able to decolonize 'good Sweden', to deconstruct white Swedish innocence and benevolence and to challenge the transnational adoption industrial complex it is necessary for Sweden to start to accept that the mass adoption of children of colour from the postcolonial world has come with a huge and irreparable price, and both in the countries of origin and for the adoptees themselves. In the recent years, more and more adoption corruption scandals have been revealed and it is nowadays well known that for example the majority of Sweden's thousands of adoptees from Chile and possibly also from the other Latin American countries were made 'adoptable' by being kidnapped, trafficked, and sold to the Swedes. In fact, in March 2021 the then current Swedish Social Democratic and Green Party government finally acknowledged this fact through its Minister of Social Affairs who in a parliamentary debate promised to initiate an official investigation into the dark side of Sweden's 'glorious' transnational and transracial adoption history, which has resulted in numerous first mothers and birth families in Latin America, Africa, and Asia being practically robbed of their children. Increasingly, more and more adult adoptees of colour have also started to speak out about the heavy psychic cost and affective labour including staggering suicide rates and a general record high mortality rates that comes with being forced to uphold good white Sweden and white Swedish antiracism on their very shoulders as this impossible task have not protected them from being exposed to everyday racism, racial discrimination, and racially motivated hate crimes.

## Note

1   This and all other translations from Swedish to English are mine.

## References

Brännström, L. 2016. 'Ras' i efterkrigstidens Sverige. Ett bidrag till en mothistoria ['Race' in post-war Sweden. A contribution to a counter-history]. In *Historiens hemvist. 2. Etik, politik och historikerns ansvar [The home of history. 2. Ethics, politics and the responsibility of the historian]*, ed. P. Lorenzoni and U. Manns, pp. 27–55. Göteborg: Makadam.

Broberg, G. and Roll-Hansen, N., eds. 2005. *Eugenics and the Welfare State: Sterilization Policy in Denmark, Sweden, Norway, and Finland.* East Lansing, MI: Michigan State University Press.

Burton, A. M. 1994. *Burdens of History. British Feminists, Indian Women, and Imperial Culture, 1865–1915.* Chapel Hill, NC: University of North Carolina Press.

Duedahl, P. 2017. *Fra overmenneske til UNESCO-menneske. Racebegrebet i Danmark 1890–1965 [From Super Humans to UNESCO Humans. The Concept of Race in Denmark 1890–1965].* Odense: Syddansk Universitetsforlag.

Ericsson, M. 2016. *Historisk forskning om rasism och främlingsfientlighet i Sverige. En analyserande kunskapsöversikt [Historical Research on Racism and Xenophobia in Sweden. An Analysing Knowledge Review].* Stockholm: Forum för levande historia.

Goldberg, D. T. 2009. *The Threat of Race: Reflections on Racial Neoliberalism.* Hoboken, NJ: Wiley-Blackwell.

Gondouin, J. 2012. Adoption, Surrogacy and Swedish Exceptionalism. *Australian Critical Race and Whiteness Studies ejournal*, 8 (2). Viewed 21 February 2020, https://acrawsa.org.au/wp-content/uploads/2017/12/CRAWS-Vol-8-No-2012.pdf.

Gondouin, J. 2016. Feminist Global Motherhood: Representations of Single-Mother Adoption in Swedish Media. In *Critical Kinship Studies*, ed. C. Kroløkke, L. Myong, S. Adrian and T. Tjørnhøj-Thomsen, pp. 101–116. Landham, MD: Rowman and Littlefield.

Hage, G. 1998. *White Nation: Fantasies of White Supremacy in a Multicultural Society*. Annandale: Pluto Press.

Hoffmann, P. 1971. Adoptive Parents, at Milan Conference, Tell of Fighting National Barriers and Ask World Standards. *New York Times*. 19 September, 27.

Högbacka, R. and Ruohio, H. 2020. Black and White Strangers: Adoption and Ethnic Hierarchies in Finland. In *Adoption and Multiculturalism. Europe, the Americas, and the Pacific*, ed. J. H. Wills, T. Hübinette and I. Willing, pp. 177–198. Ann Arbor, MI: University of Michigan Press.

Howell, S. 2006. *The Kinning of Foreigners. Transnational Adoption in a Global Perspective*. Oxford: Berghahn.

Hübinette, T. 2003. The Adopted Koreans of Sweden and the Korean Adoption Issue. *Review of Korean Studies*, 6 (1): 251–266.

Hübinette, T. 2007. Sverige unikt som adoptionsland [Sweden – a unique adoption country]. *Välfärd*, 7 (2): 3–5.

Hübinette, T. 2020. Transnational Adoption and the Emergence of Sweden's Progressive Reproduction Policy. A Contribution to the Biopolitical History of Sweden. In *Adoption and Multiculturalism. Europe, the Americas, and the Pacific*, ed. J. H. Wills, T. Hübinette and I. Willing, pp. 223–238. Ann Arbor, MI: University of Michigan Press.

Hübinette, T. and Lundström, C. 2014. Three Phases of Hegemonic Whiteness. Understanding Racial Temporalities in Sweden. *Social Identities. Journal for the Study of Race, Nation and Culture*, 20 (6): 423–437. DOI: 10.1080/13504630.2015.1004827.

Kjellman, U. 2013. A Whiter Shade of Pale. Visuality and Race in the Work of the Swedish State Institute for Race Biology. *Scandinavian Journal of History*, 38 (2): 180–201. DOI: 10.1080/03468755.2013.769458.

Klein, C. 2003. *Cold War Orientalism: Asia in the Middlebrow Imagination, 1945–1961*. Berkeley, CA: University of California Press.

Kyllingstad, J. R. 2014. *Measuring the Master Race: Physical Anthropology in Norway, 1890–1945*. Cambridge: Open Book Publishers.

Lindgren, C. 2010. *Internationell adoption i Sverige. Politik och praktik från sextiotal till nittiotal [International Adoption in Sweden. Policy and Practice from the 1960s to the 1990s]*. Stockholm: Myndigheten för internationella adoptionsfrågor.

Link, R. 1971. The New Swedes. Chocolate Children Are Melting into the Swedish Vanilla. *Sweden Now*, 5 (11): 50, 51–55.

McKee, K. D. 2016. Monetary Flows and the Movements of Children: The Transnational Adoption Industrial Complex. *Journal of Korean Studies*, 21 (1): 137–178. DOI: 10.1353/jks.2016.0007.

Moberg, E. 1964. Vill ni rädda ett barn [Do you want to save a child]. *Idun-Veckojournalen*. September 11, 24–25, 57.

Myong, L. and Andersen, N. T. 2015. From Immigration Stop to Intimizations of Migration: Cross-Reading the Histories of Domestic(ated) Labor Migration and Transnational Adoption in Denmark 1973-2015. *Retfærd: Nordisk Juridisk Tidsskrift*, 38 (3): 62–79.

Naum, M. and Nordin, J. M., eds. 2013. *Scandinavian Colonialism and the Rise of Modernity: Small Time Agents in a Global Arena*. New York, NY: Springer.

Norocel, C., Saresma, T., Lähdesmäki, T. and Ruotsalainen, M. 2020. Discursive Constructions of White Nordic Masculinities in Rightwing Populist Media. *Men and Masculinities*, 23 (3–4): 425–446. DOI: 10.1177/1097184X18780459.

Oh, A. 2005. A New Kind of Missionary Work: Christians, Christian Americanists, and the Adoption of Korean GI Babies, 1955-1961. *Women's Studies Quarterly*, 33 (3–4): 161–188.

Pitcher, B. 2014. *Consuming Race*. New York, NY: Routledge.

Selman, P. 2002. Intercountry Adoption in the New Millennium: The'Quiet Migration' Revisited. *Population Research and Policy Review*, 21 (3): 205–222. DOI: 10.1023/A:1019583625626.

Shome, R. 2011. 'Global Motherhood': The Transnational Intimacies of White Femininity. *Critical Studies in Media Communication*, 28 (5): 388–406. DOI: 10.1080/15295036.2011.589861.

Statistiska centralbyrån. 2019. 'Folkmängd efter födelseland 1900-2018 [Population number according to birth country 1900–2018]', viewed 25 March 2020, https://www.scb.se/contentassets/2b133080e4 8d4f5ba012947e5dc6b79e/be0101-folkmangd-fodelselander-1900-2018.xlsx.

Weiss, H., ed. 2016. *Ports of Globalisation, Places of Creolisation: Nordic Possessions in the Atlantic World During the Era of the Slave Trade*. Boston, MA: Brill.

Wekker, G. 2016. *White Innocence: Paradoxes of Colonialism and Race*. Durham, NC: Duke University Press.

Wieslander, A. 1963. De har ljusare framtid här [They have a better future here]. *Stockholms-Tidningen*, 3 April, 3.

Wyver, R. 2018. Mimicry, Mockery and Menace in Swedish International Adoption Narratives. *Borderlands e-Journal*, 17 (2), viewed 25 February 2018, http://www.borderlands.net.au/vol17no2_2018/wyver_mimicry.pdf.

Wyver, R. 2019. Eating the (M)Other. Exploring Swedish Adoption Consumption Fantasies. *Genealogy*, 3 (3), viewed 25 February 2020, https://www.mdpi.com/2313-5778/3/3/47. DOI: 10.3390/genealogy3030047.

Wyver, R. 2020. From Flat-Packed Furniture to Fascism: Exploring the Role of the Transracial Adoptee in Fantasies of Swedish Goodness. *Interventions. International Journal of Postcolonial Studies*, 22 (7): 897–915. DOI: 10.1080/1369801X.2020.1718534.

Yngvesson, B. 2010. *Belonging in an Adopted World. Race, Identity and Transnational Adoption*. Chicago, IL: Chicago University Press.

Yngvesson, B. 2012. Transnational Adoption and European Immigration Politics: Producing the National Body in Sweden. *Indiana Journal of Global Legal Studies*, 19 (1): 327–345.

# 13

# Japan's modernisation and self-construction between white and yellow

*Yasuko Takezawa*

This essay focusses on changes in geography textbooks and education policies as a lens through which to examine how a modernising Imperial Japan interpreted racial classifications and geographical divisions constructed in the West, then distorted that knowledge while coupling it to Japan's position in the world, thereby making and remaking the 'European Race' and the 'Asian Race' in the process. It will also discuss how the pursuit of 'whiteness' and its ultimate failure triggered initially by American exclusion of Japanese immigrants at the beginning of the twentieth century came to have a determining impact not just on Japanese immigrants but on the aims and self-definition of leaders at home in Japan.

By employing the notion of 'epistemic violence', the term coined by Gayatri Chakravorty Spivak, Ruth Frankenberg, in her book, *White Women, Race Matters*, problematises 'the production of modes of knowing that enabled and rationalised colonial domination from the standpoint of the West, and produced ways of conceiving 'Other' societies and cultures whose legacies endure into the present' (Frankenberg 1993: 16). As Frankenberg points out, the production of knowledge related to a racial hierarchy with the European Race at its pinnacle entails 'epistemic violence' toward 'the rest' of the world. The imposition of racial meaning in its contemporary sense and a related conceptualisation of whiteness where there was not any before is a fundamental violence and building block of coloniality.[1] This essay will examine the related process by which the Japanese government in alliance with their political and intellectual leaders, amid the construction of the modern Japanese nation-state and the expansion of its empire, tried to make its own subjects internalise distorted and fabricated images of self and other through textbooks which exerted a powerful influence over epistemological formation. Through my presentation of the historical evidence, I show how this is related in complicated ways to the construction of whiteness.

This chapter comprises three sections that link and build with each other to put forward the argument set forward earlier. The first section considers the mutual impressions that outward appearances made on the Japanese and the Europeans who had come to Japan for missionary work and later trade during their encounters from the sixteenth and seventeenth centuries. It clarifies the disparity between this period and the modern period under the influence of imported Western race theory. Japanese textbooks are the focus of the second section, in particular the textbooks that served as a means to explicate the development of Japanese interpretations of

DOI: 10.4324/9780429355769-13

racial hierarchy after the Meiji Restoration in 1868. The third section examines the US political and social environment related to the series of exclusions of Japanese immigrants in the United States, which became the catalyst for the early twentieth century Japan's belief that it would never be able to 'join Europe' because of its 'Yellow Race'.

## Before Europeans became 'white' and Japanese became 'yellow'

Most Japanese, even today, have internalised the discourses on Europeans as the 'White Race' as a 'biological category', although in daily conversations, Japanese skin colour is described as '*shiroi* (white/light)' or '*kuroi* (black/dark)', as it has been so since pre-moden times. However, visual and non-visual materials depicting the encounter between Europeans and pre-modern Japan demonstrate a perception of skin colour that differs from modern racial classifications.

Many European missionaries who came to Japan in the sixteenth and the early seventeenth centuries had depicted Japanese skin colour as 'white' in their reports back to their homelands, as demonstrated in the following accounts by García de Escalante Alvarado, purportedly the first missionary who mentions the appearance of the Japanese: 'The inhabitants of these islands are good-looking, white, and bearded ... The women have mostly very white complexions and are very beautiful' (Demel and Kowner 2013: 46).[2]

On the end of the Japanese perceptions, close observations of *Nanban Byōbu* [illustrated folding screens depicting the arrival of Europeans] produced in the sixteenth and seventeenth centuries (reproduced in Sakamoto 2008) reveal that skin colour of the Europeans was un-marked in the eyes of the premodern Japanese artists.[3] Instead, it was relative differences such as height, nose size, and facial hair that attracted their attention (Wagatsuma 1967). Similar characterisations of Europeans are found in the writings by Japanese scholars of Dutch learning during the seventeenth and the early eighteenth centuries.

Alternatively, the 'whitest' people portrayed in the screens are the Japanese women indoors, who are painted lighter than the European men. The nobles, the samurai, and wealthy merchant men are depicted with lighter skin, whereas Japanese men who performed work outdoors have a darker hue. In other words, the skin hue variation among the Japanese served as an indicator of status differences in premodern Japan.

## The reception of Western race theory

Fearing the increasing influence of Christianity, in 1612-1613 the Tokugawa shogunate issued an edict banning Christianity across the nation. In the 1630s, a series of isolationist laws cut off all contact with foreign countries, with only a handful of exceptions: The shogunate maintained formal diplomatic and trade relations with Korea and the Ryūkyū Islands, and maintained trade relationships with Holland and Qing-dynasty China.

The first known writing to discuss racial classifications of European origin can be traced back to *Shinkiron* [A Private Proposal], written by Watanabe Kazan,[4] a scholar of Dutch learning, in 1838. The book presented four races for human division: 'Tartar', 'Ethiopian', 'Mongolian', and 'Caucasian'. In *Gaikoku jijōsho* [On Matters Foreign] (1839), he discusses 'the races east of the high northern sea',[5] in which he includes Japanese as well as Chinese. The term 'jinshu' that Kazan employs is now the established translation for the English word 'race' in the sense of racial classification, but it is worth noting its use at such an early date.

Watanabe Kazan also writes, 'I have heard the English have found an island close to Japan and landed there' (Watanabe 1971 [1839]: 31), referring to English ships appearing in Japanese waters, repeatedly making illegal landfall and clashing with local fishermen. In 1806 and 1807, the Russians attacked the shogunal army's northern bases on the islands of Sakhalin (Jp. Karafuto) and Iturup (Jp. Etorofu). He expresses his deep anxiety, sensing Europe's expanding colonialism in Asia and its looming shadow over Japan: '(W)ithin Asia, only the three countries of China, Persia, and our country have avoided the "defilement of Westerners"' (Watanabe 1971 [1839]: 49).

An argument arises among some intellectuals who learned about 'Europe' and 'Asia' through Dutch learning against Japanese use of the West's arbitrarily defined term 'Asia'. For example, Aizawa Seishisai, in his 1833 work *Tekiihen* (The Unswerving Path of Righteousness) argues: 'To include our land of the gods in this blanket term is a grave insult to all that is virtuous. Accordingly, let us not use it to describe ourselves' (Yamamuro 2001: 2).

The spatial perception that accompanied such designations and geographical divisions involved more than just the drawing of lines on a map, however; in the context of the moment, it re-presented a tug of war between the powers, a question of survival of the fittest. Japan witnessed the Opium War (1840–1842) between England and the Qing dynasty, the Arrow War (1856–1860) which pitted an Anglo-French alliance against the Qing, and the resulting cession of Hong Kong.

In 1853, under orders from President Millard Fillmore, US Navy Commodore Matthew Perry arrived in Japanese waters at the head of four massive black battleships, and pressured the Tokugawa shogunate into opening Japan's borders. The following year Japan and the United States signed the US–Japan Convention of Peace and Amity (commonly called the Treaty of Kanagawa), which brought more than 200 years of isolationist policy to a close. Thereafter, travel and study in the United States and Europe by Japanese increased dramatically, enabling *bakumatsu* (the end of the Edo period) intellectuals to acquire greater knowledge of the outside world and its theories of race.

In 1868, having wrested power back from the shogunate, the Meiji Emperor began what came to be known as the Meiji Restoration, a series of reforms centred around policies of industrialisation, enriching the nation and strengthening the military, and so-called 'civilisation and enlightenment'. As Western international law came to be applied to non-Western countries such as Japan and China, and East Asia was compelled to accept unequal treaty terms like extraterritorial consular courts and fixed low import–export duties, the Meiji government adopted a national strategy of strengthening the nation and hastening its 'civilisation and enlightenment' to catch up to the West and create a relationship on an equal footing (Yamamuro 2001: 41). One measure into which the Japanese government poured a great deal of energy was the nationwide propagation of elementary education.

In the year of Meiji 5 (1872), the newly established Ministry of Education began to establish at least a single elementary school in every school district across the country with the goal of universal education. They would have to wait 30 years for the establishment of compulsory education, however. Translations or adaptations of texts imported from Europe and America were used for the majority of the textbooks studied during the first decade of the Meiji period.

The Ministry of Education initially designated three books as foreign geography textbooks, among them *Sekai kunizukushi* (1869), a one-million copy best-seller of the time, and *Yochishiryaku* (1871), which printed 150,000 copies by 1875 (and continued to print new editions). *Sekai kunizukushi* was created by Fukuzawa Yukichi, one of the most influential intellectuals during the early Meiji period. In his introduction, Fukuzawa stresses that the book is a translation of excerpts assembled from various European and American books. Accordingly, the book divides humans into four categories: 'Chaos' (*konton*); 'barbarian' (*ban'ya*); 'as yet uncivilised (*mikai*) or half-civilised (*hankai*)'; and 'civilised' (*bunmeikaika*). It describes the 'most inferior people', 'chaos', giving the 'Natives' (*dojin*) of Australia and of inner Africa as its examples. The 'barbarians' included the Tartars in northern China, and 'natives' of Arabia and northern Africa. The book lists China, Turkey, and Persia as examples of nations 'as yet un-civilised (*mikai*) or half-civilised (*hankai*)'. Finally, the 'civilised' (*bunmeikaika*) were described as those who value manners, and actively engage in academic work, the arts, and farming. The United States, England, France, Germany, and the Netherlands are presented as exemplars (Fukuzawa 1869: 14–17). *Sekai kunizukushi* also included a discussion of China's defeat in the Opium (Anglo-Chinese) War, a war which resulted in indemnity payments and the transfer of Hong Kong to Britain.

*Yochishiryaku* was written by a Ministry of Education bureaucrat, Uchida Masao, who had studied in the Netherlands and later travelled around the world during the last several years of the Edo period. In the 'Introduction' to *Yochishiryaku,* Uchida credits the work of J. Goldsmith (whose real name is Richard Philips) as one of the main texts he drew from (Goldsmith 1868). Ostensibly adapting from Goldsmith's original book, *Yochishiryaku* also provides a discussion of the five races and the stages of civilisation. It lists China, Siberia, and Turkey as 'half-civilised' countries, and European countries and the United States as 'civilised' countries (Uchida 1871).

Through these and other related books, used as textbooks and read widely by intellectuals during the early Meiji period, the Japanese discovered that countries such as China, Turkey, and Persia, which boasted the most prosperous histories in Asia, were still seen as 'half-civilised' by the West. Kikuji Nakamura points out as the characteristics of early-Meiji geography textbook:

> The pre-Restoration reverence for China vanished completely, to be replaced by a powerful interest in the West and consequently a prejudiced and contemptuous view of Asia, and of China in particular.
>
> *(Nakamura 1984: 65)*

The Meiji 20s (1888–1897) rapidly advances the Westernization of Japan's educational and political systems as well as its military and economic power. The Constitution of the Empire of Japan was proclaimed in Meiji 22 (1889), Article 1 of which stipulated that 'The Empire of Japan shall be reigned over and governed by a line of Emperors unbroken for ages eternal'. This emphasis on a single unbroken lineage was clearly a means of legitimising the emperor's rule.

In the 'Fundamental Principles' (Meiji 24/1891), the moral training curriculum emphasised 'working to foster respect for the Emperor and a spirit of patriotism, and laying out the essentials of one's duty to the nation' (Ministry of Education 1891). This emphasis on the importance of fostering a patriotic spirit is reflected in one of the world geography textbooks: 'Rather than studying the various countries of the world, [our students] should learn the ways in which our empire is superior to them, and by studying its features, learn how beautiful its natural and geographical features are, and how gentle its climate is' (Noguchi 1896: 2–3). It demonstrates how the study of world geography shifts its emphasis from gaining knowledge of foreign countries to recognising the 'superiority' and 'beauty' of Japan by this time.

During this decade, the First Sino-Japanese War (Meiji 27/1894 to Meiji 28/1895) broke out over ambition to exert influence and authority over Joseon Korea. Wang Ping argues that Japan's victory in the First Sino-Japanese War was a defining moment in which Japan started to nurture a sense of superiority, not just vis-à-vis China but throughout Asia. He maintains:

> [After the First Sino-Japanese War,] it was a simple matter for Japan to replace the model of '*Civilization = the West* vs. *barbarian = the East*', with '*Japan = civilization = the West* vs. *China = barbarian = the East*'.
>
> *(Wang 2004: 264)*

The Ministry of Education revised the law governing elementary schools again in Meiji 33 (1900), ordaining compulsory education at public elementary schools free of charge, leading to attendance rates topping 90%.[6] The geography curriculum 'should in summary promote a thorough understanding of the general state of our nation, and contribute to the fostering of a spirit of patriotism' (Ministry of Education 1900: 9).

As Japan's internal and external dominance and colonisation intensified, the country was paying increasing attention to its surrounding peoples and minorities, while openly admitting that they all belong to the yellow race. This is reflected in the descriptions of the 'Han Race' and the 'Taiwanese Race' which began to appear in textbooks. *Middle School Geography of Our Nation* (1901) states:

> While the inhabitants of our nation all belong to the yellow race [*jinshu*], they can be divided into the following five racial groups [shuzoku] according to their language, customs, disposition, and appearance: The Yamato Race [shu], the Ryūkyū Race [shu], the Ainu Race [shu], the Han Race [shu], and the Taiwanese Race [shu]. This text reveals a contempt for the Ainu and the people of Taiwan: 'While daring by nature, they are an ignorant and uncivilised race [shuzoku], and are rather to be pitied'. As for the 'Han Race', 'They reside in Taiwan, largely having come over from the Fujian and Guangdong regions during the Ming dynasty'. Regarding the 'Taiwanese aborigines', it says, 'Their customs and practices are little different from those of the Chinese, and the wild tribespeople are largely savage and bloodthirsty'.
>
> *(Satō 1901: 26, 28)*

Japan gained exclusive command and colonial control of the Korean Empire beginning in 1910 through the peace treaty that ended the Russo-Japanese War. Thereafter, Japan continued the expansion of its colonial rule through military invasion in the surrounding nations of Asia. Section 1 of the first volume of the state-sponsored textbook *Upper-Level Elementary Geography Volume Two* (1912) sings the praises of the Empire of Japan – 'Blessed with an Emperor of unbroken lineage at its head, and abounding with a spirit of loyalty to one's lord and love for one's country' – after which it lists the eight great powers of the world: the United Kingdom, the United States, Germany, France, Russia, Austro-Hungary, Italy, and finally 'this nation' (Ministry of Education 1912: 48).

Around this time, mentions and descriptions of the races residing in the neighbouring countries under Japanese colonial rule begin to appear in textbooks. Although other Asian ethnic groups are mentioned, the Japanese (Yamato) people are consistently touted as superior.

The revised 1929 edition of *Standard Elementary Geography* includes full descriptions of 'China, Siberia, India, and Southeast Asia' alongside those of Europe and America, in an attempt to educate students about the countries with which Japan had deep ties vis-à-vis resources and trade (Ministry of Education 1929).

According to Japanese intellectual historian Shin'ichi Yamamuro, a 'discourse of East-West harmony' aimed at both the West and the East appeared in Japan after the Russo-Japanese War, and some began to tout the idea that Japan had a mission to enlighten the rest of East Asia in its capacity as the leader of Asian civilisation. In the 1920s, as the looming confrontation over China and the anti-Japanese movement (described later) in America materialised, and war with the United States started to seem inevitable, the discourse of an East–West showdown with Japan representing the East gathered steam (Yamamuro 2001: 50–53).

The notion that Japan had a mission to bring civilisation to the rest of Asia was a colonialist mentality which had much in common with the 'Manifest Destiny' that was used to legitimise US colonisation and territorial expansion in the nineteenth century. In the case of Japan, however, an imperialisation movement to turn the peoples of Taiwan and Korea, formerly in the control of other countries, into subjects of Imperial Japan followed, and the 1937 invasion of China helped ramp up the ideological legitimisation of incursions into Asia under the guise of Japan as a saviour liberating Asia from the control of white Westerners.

The paternalistic attitude of Japan as the saviour of Asia comes through most powerfully in the following passage from *Elementary School Geography*, compiled by the Ministry of Education in 1943 at the height of the Asia-Pacific War, three years after the establishment of the Greater East Asia Co-Prosperity Sphere.

> Not understanding Japan's sincere intentions, some portion of the Chinese who have yet to see the light are borrowing the power of America and Britain to resist Japan. We must and will open their eyes without delay, and proceed with the establishment of Greater East Asia. Nay, this establishment has already begun. Under Japan's guidance, the occupied territories are improving steadily, transport is developing rapidly, and the exchange of goods is flourishing (Ministry of Education 1943: 82).

On the surface, "Japan's sincere intentions" meant the liberation of their Asian brothers and sisters from the racism and aggression of America, Britain, and their allies; but in truth Japan's intention was for their own expansion of power and colonial rule in Asia, and their struggle with America for control over the resources of the Pacific. The geographical label "Greater East Asia" was more useful to Japan than colour terms such as "white race" and "yellow race" in its calling for the unity of the co-prosperity sphere. Nonetheless Japan took the very same racial hierarchy which had humiliated them, switching out the criterion of skin color for their own interpretation of "civilization," whilst positioning themselves at the apex in place of Caucasians, and then they applied these results to the various national/ethnic groups of Asia. In doing so, they hoped to spread the discourse that Japanese rule was protecting Asia from the great powers of the West. In other words, whilst Japan was on the one hand setting up the whiteness of countries like England and America as a threat and as an enemy of Asia, on the other hand it was attempting to transfer the racial and colonial control that accompanied whiteness within that framework onto themselves.

## A decisive break with the ideology of 'leave Asia and join the West'

The number of Japanese intellectuals traveling and studying abroad began to increase around the latter half of the 1880s, many of whom personally experienced racial slurs and became self-conscious for the first time about their own skin colour (Majima 2012). While some among the elite who emigrated to the United States turned a contemptuous eye on the behaviour and appearance of the Chinese labourers making the long journey aboard the same vessels, the same contemptuous eye was turned on Japanese immigrant labourers, coming from farming villages in rural areas of Japan (Azuma 2005; Takezawa 2016).

Following Japan's victory over Russia in 1905, the 'Yellow Peril' that appeared in Europe in the late nineteenth century fed into an increasingly vociferous orchestrated call for the expulsion of Japanese immigrants on the West Coast, the same call that succeeded in the enactment of the Chinese Exclusion Act of 1882. Lothrop Stoddard's 1920 book, *The Rising Tide of Color Against White World-Supremacy,* by emphasising the dangers posed by Japan's victory in the Russo-Japanese war, the first time in 400 years of history that 'coloured race' had defeated the white race, stirred up fears of an Asian threat to the white race (Stoddard 1920). Accordingly, by the 1920s the characterisation of Chinese and Japanese as a 'yellow' and perilous race had become fully accepted by the West (Keevak 2011). Non-Anglo-Saxon European immigrants, in particular, the working class Irish immigrants, actively led calls for the expulsion of the Japanese as well as the Chinese as 'unassimilable' and the 'Yellow Peril', an act which was inextricably linked to their own process of acquiring whiteness (Ignatiev 1995; Roediger 2002).

The United States Naturalization Act of 1790 restricted the right of naturalisation to those considered to be 'a free white person'. However, since Asians were not considered within their assumptions at that time, whether 'white person' referred to European descendants or those with pale skin hue had been ambiguous. Thus, the 1910 census lists the 420 Japanese and 1,368 Chinese as naturalised citizens, who had ostensibly fulfilled the prerequisite of being 'a white person' (Bureau of the Census 1914).

The exclusion of Japanese in America under the law from citizenship (and hence whiteness), occurred in the 1922 *Takao Ozawa vs. United States* case. In the *Ozawa* decision the Supreme Court ruled that Japanese are not Caucasian, but Mongoloid, therefore not eligible for naturalisation.[7] The fact that Ozawa was a light-skinned, pious Protestant who spoke fluent English and attended University of California, Berkeley, before moving to Hawai'i only reinforces the political and social nature of the construction of Japaneseness and 'yellowness' in American soceity. After Ozawa's ruling, Japanese nationals were excluded from the right to naturalisation until the Immigration and Naturalization Act of 1952.

The US Congress passed the Immigration Act of 1924, which included an article completely banning Japanese immigration to the United States. Now the prohibition of Japanese immigrants, which Japanese leaders were well aware was motivated by racism against the Japanese, was no more a regional issue on the West Coast, but the official decision of the United States as a country, resulting in a high rise of anti-American sentiment, as well as the emergence of discussions framing the international relations as the white race versus coloured races (Hirobe 2017: 94–95).

On top of the series of exclusionary acts against Japanese immigrants in the United States, such as the California Alien Land Law of 1913, the race-based justifications in the 1922 Supreme Court decision, plus the complete prohibition of immigration from Japan under the Immigration Act of 1924 – the rejection of the Japanese Racial Equality Proposal at the 1919 Paris Peace Conference, the proposal derived from the smouldering discontent about American treatment of their country fellows but it was rejected by the United States and by its allies – is known among historians as having been so humiliating to the Imperial Japanese Government and Japan's intellectual class that it shook the very basis of Japanese identity as they attempted to join the ranks of the West as a 'civilised nation'. Emperor Hirohito, whose war responsibility was never seriously challenged either by postwar Japan nor the US, mentioned after the Second World War, in particular these two shocking incidents to Japan in reference to the causes of the war: 'When we look for the causes of the Greater East Asia War', he said, 'they lie in the past, in the peace treaty after World War I' (Peter Wetzler 1998: 10, quoted in Horn 2004: 36); Hanihara Masanao, the Japanese Ambassador to the United States, wrote in his correspondence with Secretary of State Hughes, that the 1924 Japanese Exclusion Act 'would naturally wound the national susceptibilities of the Japanese people'(Majima 2013: 400).

Imperial Japan, however, applied to neighbouring countries in Asia the European and American racial hierarchy that had so humiliated and infuriated them. Artfully, the inventors of the Japanese-led hierarchy switched out the criterion of skin colour for their own interpretation of 'civilisation', positioning themselves at the apex in the place of Caucasians, and applying the method to the various peoples of Asia. In doing so, they hoped to spread the idea that Japanese rule was protecting Asia from the dangerous powers of the Allies. In other words, while positioning the whiteness of the British Empire, the United States, and other allies as a threat and as an enemy of coloured peoples in Asia, they simultaneously attempted to transfer the racial and colonial control that accompanied the framework of whiteness to themselves.

What further complicated the situation was the multiple layered structure of racisms and supremacisms, in other words, not just Japan's supremacism over other Asian peoples, but the Allies' preceding white supremacism over non-white nations and coloured peoples, plus the strong resentment of white supremacism by some Asian nations and African American soldiers at the initial onset stage of the war. John Dower asserts that Japan's late entry onto the world stage as a major colonial power 'challenged not just the Western presence but the entire mystique of white supremacism', which has been assumed for long decades of expansion by other colonial powers from Europe then much later America (Dower 1986: 5–6). A wider transnational scope of analysis is presented in *Race War* in which the author Gerald Horn gives detailed descriptions of the resentment of white supremacy, particularly of the British Empire and America. Even pro-Japan feelings, Horn argues, among many, if not all, in India, the Philippines, Burma, and other Asian countries as well as African Americans all suffering from white supremacy. Some nationalists in Burma felt that Tokyo 'represented a resurgent Asia against European domination' (quoted from Robert H. Taylor 1984: 8, in Horn 2004: 202). Japan's struggle and war against the Allies appeared to them the first challenge in modern times against white supremacy, which they soon found to be an illusion as under the heated trials and tribulation of war, Japan engaged in a succession of war crimes against Asian nations and peoples.

With Japan's defeat in the Second World War, the postwar occupation, and the process of reconstruction, government policy, and public sentiment towards America made a sharp U-turn. For the generation that had experienced the occupation in particular, American material culture and lifestyles became the model to strive for, idealised in a certain sense just as it had been beforehand in the early Meiji period. Kazuomi Sakai argues that Japanese self-directed criticisms, embodied in common expressions such as, 'Compared to Japan, [America is] ... 'stem from an idealisation of Western culture, proving that contemporary Japanese people and society are still controlled by structures born of what Sakai calls 'dominant whiteness' (Sakai 2005).

## Conclusion

This chapter has examined historical changes in Imperial Japan and its elites' discourses surrounding Japaneseness, constructed in relation to the West and to the rest of Asia, from a premodern Japan that was not colour-conscious in its encounter with Europeans through to the reception of race theory at around the time of the Meiji Restoration, then onto the rise of nationalism in the mid-Meiji period and the subsequent imperial expansion and colonialism that continued until Second World War.

According to materials originating from the seventeenth and early eighteenth centuries, the Europeans outward otherness was marked by the size of their noses, the shape of their eyes, or the colour of their hair, and skin colour as an index of 'difference' was virtually a non-factor. With the introduction of Western race theory to Japan, however, the indices of self/other awareness changed drastically. It was in learning of the term 'Asia' and the geographical designation it represented, arbitrarily created by the Western other, and of the classification of the 'Asian' or 'Mongoloid' race, that late-Edo intellectuals began to become aware of the imbalances in their relationship with the West. Nevertheless, with the influx of Western knowledge, technology, and lifestyle during the early Meiji period, Western learning in general came to acquire a special authority – including theories of race, which reflected the 'epistemic violence' of whiteness that accompanied Western expansion.

Japan had no traditional notion of skin colour through which to understand the difference between themselves and the Europeans, and lacked the experience of physical colonisation and forced obedience and repression at the hands of the West that other Asian nations had undergone, so in its sudden rush to modernisation, the country inarguably underestimated the power that white discourses surrounding skin colour and 'racial difference' would exert in all arenas. Meiji politicians and intellectuals conflated modernisation with Westernization, mistakenly assuming that through the civilising process they could join the ranks of the West, and pushed towards 'Leave Asia and Join the West'.

Beginning around the time of the First Sino-Japanese War in the mid-Meiji period, the focus in school education also shifted from simply following in the footsteps of the West to nourishing a spirit of patriotism and loyalty to the emperor. After the advent of free compulsory education and Japan's victory in the Russo-Japanese War, the curriculum shifted to further emphasise nurturing students' patriotic spirit.

On the other hand, through the series of what Japan perceived as humiliations the country endured from the 1900s through the early 1920s, beginning with the exclusion of Japanese immigrants in the United States, the Japanese were for the first time confronted with the realisation that no amount of civilisation would procure them whiteness and a place at the same table as the West. Japan pivoted toward the establishment of the Greater East Asia Co-Prosperity Sphere. During the Asia-Pacific War, and state-sponsored textbooks emphasised Japan's role as a saviour for the neighbouring countries of Asia, protecting them from Western infraction, which served to legitimise Japan's own invasions, plundering of resources, and other forms of violence. Intellectuals held diverse views on Asia, but their voices were drowned out amid the chaos of an imperial government run amok.

The Japaneseness that Imperial Japan sought was constructed in the trilateral relationship between Japan, the West as a signifier of absolute global hegemony, and Asia, whose colonisation at the hands of the West was attributed to their 'lagging civilisation'. Unlike the Western experience, which tends to be understood in terms of the dichotomies between white and non-white, the coloniser and the colonised, Imperial Japan constructed the Japanese identity through its negotiations, clashes, and self-righteous sense of solidarity and identification with the two 'others' of Asia and the West. While the racial hierarchies constructed in the West and the geopolitical dynamics of Asia formed an interwoven structure, the interpretation and realisation of whiteness has fluctuated in the space and the time between illusion and reality.

It is beyond the scope of this chapter to examine Japanese experiences in other regions of the world, or Japan's complex relationship with the West (and America in particular) and the other countries of Asia from the period of the US occupation to the present. Nonetheless, the legacy of the struggle surrounding whiteness and racial hierarchy that began in the Meiji period continues to influence the view of 'others' both inside and outside of Japanese society even to this day. The case examined in this chapter has wider implications in understanding how the epistemic violence entailed in whiteness, while continuing to reproduce the racial hierarchy and post-colonialism by the 'West' on the global level, can be negotiated, twisted, and used by rulers in their pursuit of power, colonialism, and resources within the 'Rest' [of the West].

## Notes

1   This does not mean the non-existence of what I call racialisation in premodern Japanese society. The *Kawaramono*, who were engaged in animal slaughtering and leathercrafting, a minoritised group most of whom later came to be called *Burakumin* as they still are today, had been severely discriminated against with the mythical belief that they were of different 'species'/'race' originated in the East Asia Continent (Takezawa 2020).
2   For detailed discussions of initial perceptions by Europeans of the Japanese, see Kowner (2014: 67–100).

3   Portuguese and Spanish people were called '*Nanban-jin'*, a term adopted from the Chinese taxonomy of the time, 'nan' meaning south because the European ships came from the south of Japan, 'ban' barbarians.

4   In this essay, the name order of Japanese historical figures takes the Japanese style according to which a surname comes first then a given name, whereas the remaining Japanese names follow the English style. Watanabe Kazan is usually called by his given name (Kazan), unlike writers and others from the Meiji period onwards, who are known by their surnames.

5   Judging from the Chinese characters used in his writing, it probably refers to Lake Baikal in Siberia.

6   'Meiji Education', National Archives, http://www.archives.go.jp/exhibition/digital/meiji/contents3_04/.

7   Takao Ozawa vs. United States, 260 *U.S. Reports* 178 (1922).

# References

Azuma, E. 2005. *Between Two Empires: Race, History, and Transnationalism in Japanese America*. Oxford: Oxford University Press.

Bureau of the Census. 1914. *Chinese and Japanese in the U.S. 1910*. Dept. of Commerce.

Demel, W. and Kowner, R. 2013. Early Modern European Divisions of Mankind and East Asians, 1500-1750. In *Race and Racism in Modern East Asia: Western and Eastern Constructions*, ed. R. Kowner and W. Demel, pp. 41–57. Leiden: Brill.

Dower, J. 1986. *War Without Mercy: Race and Power in the Pacific War*. New York: W. W. Norton & Company.

Frankenberg, R. 1993. *White Women, Race Matters: The Social Construction of Whiteness*. Minneapolis: University of Minnesota Press.

Fukuzawa, Y. 1869. *'Sekai kunizukushi' [All the Countries of the World, for children written in verse]*. Tokyo: Keio gijuku-zōhan. Digital Collection of Keio University Libraries, viewed 25 January 2021, https://dcollections.lib.keio.ac.jp/en/fukuzawa.

Goldsmith, J. 1868. *A Grammar of Geography for the Use of Schools, with the Maps and Illustrations*. London: William Tegg.

Hirobe, I. 2017. *Jinshu Sensō toiu Gūwa [An Allegory of the Race War]*. Nagoya: Nagoya University Press.

Horn, G. 2004. *Race War: White Supremacy and the Japanese Attack on the British Empire*. New York: New York University Press.

Ignatiev, N. 1995. *How the Irish Became White*. New York: Routledge.

Keevak, M. 2011. *Becoming Yellow: A Short History of Racial Thinking*. Princeton: Princeton University Press.

Kowner, R. 2014. *From White to Yellow: The Japanese in European Racial Thought, 1300-1935*. Montreal: McGill-Queen's University Press.

Majima, A. 2012. Skin Color Melancholy in Modern Japan: Male Elites' Racial Experiences Abroad, 1880s–1950s. In *Race and Racism in Modern East Asia: Western and Eastern Constructions*, ed. R. Kowner and W. Demel, pp. 391–410. Leiden: Brill.

Ministry of Education. 1872. 'Shōggakō Kyōsoku Gaihyō: Meiji 5 nen 11gatsu 10ka Ministry of Education futatsu bangai' [Chart of Regulations for Elementary Education: Addendum to the Ministry of Education Notification of November 10, 1872], viewed 25 January 2021, http://www.mext.go.jp/b_menu/hakusho/html/others/detail/1318006.htm.

Ministry of Education. 1891. Fundamental Principles of Education. Tokyo: Ministry of Education.

Ministry of Education. 1900. 'Shōgakkōrei, Shōgakkōrei-shikō-kisoku, Shōgakkōrei-kaisei-no-yōshi oyobi sono shikōjō chūijikō Yoryō' [Elementary Education Edict/Elementary Education Edict Implementation Regulations/Summary of Amendments to the Elementary Education Edict and Guidelines for Implementation]. Tokyo: Ministry of Education, viewed 25 January 2021, https://dl.ndl.go.jp/info:ndljp/pid/992598/16.

Ministry of Education. 1912. *'Kōtō Shōgaku chiri Kan-ni' [Higher Elementary School Geography, Vol. 2]*. Tokyo: Nihonshoseki.

Ministry of Education. 1929. *'Jinjō Shōgaku chiri-sho' [Standard Elementary Geography]*. Tokyo: Tokyo shoseki.

Ministry of Education. 1943. *'Shōtōka chiri' [Elementary School Geography]*. Tokyo: Nihonshoseki.

Nakamura K. 1984. *Kyōkasho monogatari: Kokka to kyōkasho to minshū*. (A Story on Textbooks: Nation, Textbook and People). Tokyo: Horupu shuppan.

Noguchi, Y. 1896. *Chūgaku bankokuchishi jōkan [Middle School World Geography, volume 1]*. Tokyo: Seibidō.

Roediger, D. 2002. *Colored White: Transcending the Racial Past*. Berkeley: University of California Press.

Sakai, K. 2005. 'Dominanto na hakujinsei' wo koete: Kindai Nihon no futatsu no kao [Beyond the 'Dominant Whiteness': Double Faces of Modern Japan]. In *Hakujinsei towa nanika [White is whiteness?]*, ed. T. Fujikawa, pp. 147–156. Tokyo: Tōsui shobō.

Sakamoto, M., ed. 2008. *Nanban byōbu shūsei [The Nanban Byobu Collection]*. Tokyo: Chūōkōron bijutsu shuppan.

Satō, D. 1901. *Chūgaku honpō chiri kyōkasho (Middle School Textbook of Japanese Geography)*. Tokyo: Rokumeikan.

Stoddard, L. 1920. *The Rising Tide of Color Against White World-Supremacy*. New York: Scribner.

Takezawa, Y. 2016. Shifting Grounds in Japanese American Studies, In *Trans-Pacific Japanese American Studies: Conversations on Race and Racializations*, ed. Y. Takezawa and G. Y. Okihiro, pp. 13–35. Honolulu: University of Hawai'i Press.

Takezawa, Y. 2020. Racialization and Discourses of 'Privileges' in the Middle Ages: Jews, 'Gypsies', and Kawaramono. Ethnic and Racial Studies, 43 (16): 193–210.

Takezawa, Y. 2021. Race, Civilization and the Japanese: Textbooks During the Meiji Period. *Politika*. https://www.politika.io/en/article/race-civilisation-and-the-japanese-textbooks-during-the-meiji-period

Uchida, M. 1871. *Yochishiryaku (Condensed Geography)*. Tokyo: Daigakunankō.

U.S. Reports. 1922. Takao Ozawa v. *United States*, 260.

Wagatsuma, H. 1967. The Social Perception of Skin Color in Japan. *Daedalus*, 96 (2): 407–443.

Wang, P. 2004. Nihonjin no Chūgokukan no rekishiteki hensen ni tsuite [On the Historical Changes of the Japanese 'China Perception']. *Hiroshima Daigaku Management Kenkyū*, 4: 261–269. DOI:10.15027/18007.

Watanabe, K. 1971 [1838]. Shinkiron [A Private Proposal]. In *Nihon shisō taikei 55 [Japanese Thought System 55]*, compiled with notes by S. Satō et al., pp. 66–72. Tokyo, Iwanami shoten.

Watanabe, K. 1971 [1839]. Gaikoku jijōsho [On Matters Foreign]. In Nihon shisō taikei 55, ed. S. Satō et al., pp. 18–42. Tokyo, Iwanami shoten.

Yamamuro, S. 2001. *Shisō kadai toshiteno Ajia [Asia as a Subject of Intellectual Thought]*. Tokyo: Iwanami shoten.

# 14

# The evolution of whiteness in Zimbabwe: Any white will do?

*Rory Pilossof*

## Introduction

Whiteness studies in southern Africa have flourished in the last decade. This is partly due to a growth in the literature on whiteness itself, which has moved out of the American academy, and expanded to find a footing in research and critical discourse across the Anglo-speaking world. As scholars and researchers continue to confront patterns of privilege and racial disparity, whiteness has proved a useful analytical tool to do so. It is also, however, due to circumstances and events in the two main settler colonies in the region, Zimbabwe and South Africa. In South Africa, the Rhodes Must Fall movement and the Decolonise the curriculum campaign have shown how central race is to the experiences of many young South Africans (Van Zyl-Hermann and Boersema 2017). In addition, white, and particularly Afrikaner, fears of targeting by the state have led to increased proclamations of victimhood and ethnic cleansing in South Africa. To this end, 'farm murders' have been weaponised to prove white landowners have been attacked and victimised. In Zimbabwe, the state, facing a host of social, economic, and political crises at the turn of the millennium, embarked on a chaotic, violent, and highly charged land reform programme, ostensibly to redress the colonial and racial imbalances of the past. This fast-track land reform programme (FTLRP) directly targeted the country's white farmers, blaming them for the slow pace of land reform and lack of development in Zimbabwe. Since 2000, the number of white commercial farmers fell from 4,500 to less than a couple of hundred in 2020.

The eviction of white farmers and land-owners, concomitant with other political, social, and economic crises, resulted in a spurt of academic research on whites and white farmers, creating a significant body of literature on 'whiteness' and its iteration in a post-colonial setting (Fisher 2010; Hughes 2010). Much of this work was anthropological, with a focus on contemporary issues of whiteness. A key critique of this work is that it largely framed 'whites' as a homogenous group and offered little differentiation in the experience and outlook of this group (Hammar 2012; Pilossof 2014; Pilossof and Boersema 2017; Wylie 2012). In addition, the longer history of Zimbabwe as a settler colony and the formulation, construction and genealogies of thinking that created various forms of whiteness in Zimbabwe/Rhodesia have been largely ignored. This chapter seeks to complicate the term whiteness and its application in

DOI: 10.4324/9780429355769-14

Zimbabwe. A key aim of the chapter is to illustrate the significant drivers in the construction of specific forms of whiteness in Zimbabwe/Rhodesia, and how these have evolved over time. It will also compare some of the events and processes in Zimbabwe to other settler localities, especially South Africa, to show both how whiteness in Zimbabwe has differed or played out in similar ways to other locations. Finally, this chapter concludes with a discussion on the place of whiteness in the post-colonial setting, and the ambiguities of its application and use.[1]

A number of historians of southern Africa have sought to investigate the tensions and anxieties of the colonial project (and its beneficiaries) with the care, exactness, and sympathy that has been devoted to those who have were the subjects of colonial rule (Law 2012; Pilossof 2012; Roos 2005). A central tenant to this new scholarship has been examining the 'the staying power of white power, privilege, and supremacy' (Van Zyl-Hermann and Boersema 2017: 651). Much research has looked at how white populations in southern Africa have responded to the shift from colonial/settler rule to majority rule, yet 'historical, racialized inequalities persist on the continent, and new social arrangements and institutions, as well as the global reach of capitalism, seem to reproduce racial disparities on the ground' (Van Zyl-Hermann and Boersema 2017: 652).

Part of the motivation for this work is that whites in southern Africa have been particularly vocal in narrating their own experiences in the region. Often these narratives are burdened with problematic readings of the past, various forms of racism and victim politics (Pilossof 2012). As I have pointed out elsewhere:

> The ... deliberate targeting of white farmers and landowners [in Zimbabwe] created an international groundswell of sympathy and concern for the country's small but still significantly influential white population. Endowed with the skills (and skin colour) to access and participate in the West's fascination with white experience and suffering in Africa, these 'white Africans' were able to exploit and promote their plight as it happened.
>
> *(Pilossof 2009: 623–624)*

There is a significant literature on the formation of the settler state in Rhodesia, political and racial attitudes of the white population, and the political rebellion led by Ian Smith in 1965, where Rhodesia declared itself independent under white minority rule. International interest in Zimbabwe, and the ability of whites there to tell and promote their own versions of events, have meant that there is an established literature on the country and its colonial past. The academic scholarship on Zimbabwe's settler history, has highlighted that whites and white society have a rich and complicated history in Zimbabwe/Rhodesia, despite its relatively small size. The white population of Zimbabwe/Rhodesia was always small. Colonial occupation started only in 1890. By 1911, there were only 11,000 white residents. This grew to 35,000 in the 1920s, as more migrants from the region and the metropole sought to capitalise on opportunities in Southern Rhodesia. This white population rose to just over 80,000 by end of Second World War. After Second World War, driven by post-war resettlement schemes and expansion of commercial farming opportunities, more white settlers came to Southern Rhodesia. By the time of the Unilateral Declaration of Independence (UDI) by the Ian Smith regime in 1965, the white population was 220,000, which then peaked at 275,000 in 1975. From independence in 1980, the white population shrunk as many whites many refused to live in 'black Africa', and the political and economic crises of the 1990s and 2000s, resulted in more whites leaving. Today, the white population is estimated to be less than 30,000 (Hartnack 2015). For comparison, the African population of Zimbabwe was in the region of 1.5 million in

1936. This rose to over 3.7 million in 1965. By 1992, the total population of Zimbabwe was 12.5 million and this rose to an estimated 13 million in 2012 (Phimister and Pilossof 2017: 221).

## Coloniality and the settler occupation of Zimbabwe

The arrival of white settlers in the form of the 'pioneer column' on the Zimbabwean plateau in September 1890 marked the beginning of the colonial conquest. Initially, the settlers who came to this part of Africa were primarily interested in finding a 'Second Rand', gold deposits comparable to those found in South Africa on the Witwatersrand in the 1880s. Cecil John Rhodes' British South Africa Company (BSAC), which had the charter to control this region, did not immediately seek to dominate the African populations that resided there. While smaller Shona polities were gradually absorbed, the Ndebele were left undisturbed until the latter part of 1893 when their kingdom was violently overthrown. Although huge tracts of the best land in both Matabeleland and Mashonaland were alienated on paper to white settlers, most Africans stayed where they were, some of them retaining the capacity to resist any further incursions. However, in 1896, Ndebele and Shona uprisings were quelled, and by 1898, both groups had been subjugated (Phimister and Pilossof 2017: 216–217). This opened up the space for a slowly expanding settler presence, initially in gold mining, and latterly, as mining failed to live up to the hopes of the BSAC, directed towards commercial agriculture. The early white settlers were a mix of British and South African (and mostly men) looking to the frontier for adventure and fortune (Hartnack 2015: 287). Land became a keystone of white settlement and measures were put in place to cement white land holding.

As the colony became more established, however, the small white population began to grow and various agricultural, manufacturing, and industrial activities took root (Pilossof and Rivett 2019: 248; Rubert 1998). Shortly after the Second World War, the Federation of Rhodesia and Nyasaland was established. Federation was officially formed on 1 September 1953, and it would only last just over ten years, as it dissolved on 31 December 1963. Initially, the Federation performed well economically, but it soon encountered difficulties and opposition spread across the three territories. For Cohen (2017), Federation was a bold experiment in political change during the end of empire and constituted one of the most intricate episodes in decolonisation. Later, I will discuss in more detail the 'liberal' aspects of Federation and the potential for racial partnership at the time. After Federation, the ruling Rhodesian Front (RF) pushed for do-minion status.[2] This was not forthcoming from the colonial powers, and instead of allowing majority rule, the settler state took the radical step of declaring a Unilateral Declaration of Independence (UDI) in 1965 to protect and preserved white rule. This move resulted in pariah status for the small colony and lead directly into a protracted liberation war which lasted until 1980, when majority rule was finally secured.[3] This process of uncoupling from the empire was vastly different to many of Rhodesia/Zimbabwe's neighbours. As will be expanded on later, the belief that the white settlers in Rhodesia could maintain control of the state, both reinforced constructions of whiteness, but also had to contest with a range of social and political realities that undermined white domination of the state.

After the liberation war and independence, many white Rhodesians left Zimbabwe. In addition, most whites who remained retired from public and political activity (Sylvester 1986). There was a conscious decision to become 'apolitical', and focus on remaining in Zimbabwe. This apoliticism, which I have also called 'affirmative parochialism' elsewhere (Pilossof 2012), echoes with what Van der Westhuizen (2017) has termed 'inward migration'. Since race was such a clear marker, white people in Zimbabwe used it as a means to justify staying out of politics, as this was now a 'black' arena. They often claimed limited agency thus withdrew from public life. This 'apoliticism' shifted at various times in the post-colonial setting, but boiled down to a process whereby white elites essentially refused to speak out against the ruling government to keep hold of positions of wealth and privilege. This process has played out in a slightly different way in South Africa, where the Afrikaner population has at the same time retreated from public view, but there have also been some sections of the Afrikaner community that have been very vocal about their perceived victimhood after the end of apartheid in 1994. Loud and prominent voices within the Afrikaner community had led these discourses, such as the ex-trade union Afriforum (Van Zyl-Hermann 2014). English-speaking white South Africans have been less prominent in this way, however. In Zimbabwe, there was no unified with voice to speak for whites after 1980, and apoliticism was the predominant form of engagement from the 1980s onwards.

Robert Mugabe, the new leader of Zimbabwe, took the conscious decision to promote racial reconciliation and asked the country's white population to remain in the country and assist with its growth and development. During the 1980s, Zimbabwe was seen as a post-colonial success story and one where racial tensions had been overcome. However, as the state became more corrupt and authoritarian in the 1990s, white support for opposition movements became apparent by the turn of the millennium. Nowhere was this more evident than when white farmers, in a rare moment of political action, were seen to be hosting an opposition rally and donating large sums of money to the main opposition party, the Movement for Democratic Change in 2000 (Selby 2006: 254). Mugabe and the ruling Zimbabwe African National Union – Patriotic Front (ZANU-PF) were reported to be outraged by this change of tack, and commercial farmers became direct targets of the state. From 2000 onwards, the urban and rural white population fell dramatically in Zimbabwe as many emigrated the country.

This very brief overview of white occupation in Southern Rhodesia/Zimbabwe touches on a few key points that address issues of coloniality in Zimbabwe. The ones I want to address here are (1) land and identity, (2) unity and differences, and (3) and politics and forms of liberalism.

## Land and identity

The white population was never more than 5% of the total population of Zimbabwe. Of that white population, white farmers were only a small fraction, between 5% and 10%. Yet, throughout the country's history, the prototype white Zimbabwean or Rhodesian has been a white farmer or land owner. The events of the fast-track land reform programme and the eviction of white farmers enhanced this representation, but even after 2000, most whites were urban residents. Throughout the twentieth century, this was the case. There have been attempts to correct this portrayal. Caute (1983: 88–89) observed, 'Most white Rhodesians were not pioneering farmers hacking down the bush and bringing the barren, arid veld to life. They were townsmen before they left Britain or South Africa and townsmen they remained after their arrival in Rhodesia'. The urban white population always outnumbered the rural white population, yet land ownership and control are key components of white identity and framing. Godwin and Hancock (1996) also noted this in their detailed look at white reactions to the end of colonial or settler rule in Rhodesia. White farmers are only a small part of that community, although they have been connected in a variety of ways to its other white populations in the country, be it through politics, social interaction, and commercial necessity (Pilossof and Boersema 2017). Yet control and management of the land and the 'bush' has been central to the colonial occupation of Zimbabwe, and the ideological construct of Rhodesia in the settler population. It is no mistake that those on the forefront of land and land control, white farmers, have become such prominent markers of 'white society', both in the colonial and post-colonial period.

In addition to control of the land, nature as a place of refuge and recreation have been important aspects of white experience in Rhodesia/Zimbabwe. A central thesis in Hughes's *Whiteness in Zimbabwe* (2010) was that connection to the landscape is/was important to white belonging in Zimbabwe. For Hughes, the co-production of white identity and environmental stewardship is fundamental to understanding much of the white experience in Zimbabwe. Forms of coloniality created structures that allowed whites to control land, make it feel like the land was empty and unoccupied, and thus allowing whites to have it and use it. These manifestations of coloniality and whiteness have been long studied in Zimbabwe. Chennells (1982) shows how settlers have placed themselves into rural landscapes and the colonial practices that allowed them to do so. By seeing the land as empty, it offered space for ownership, control, and recreation. The settler myth of empty land can also be found in Australia and South Africa (Marks 1980; Moreton-Robinson 2015). There are similarities across these three settings, converging on the colonial aim of justifying white land occupation and alienation, whilst also undermining indigenous forms of ownership, political organisation, and rights to belonging. In Zimbabwe, the empty land motif has developed alongside white ideas of recreation and conservation. Duffy (2000) has shown the important links between race, development and conservation in Zimbabwe, while McGregor (1995) has shown how colonial conservation legislation created modes of acceptable development. In other writing, Hughes (2006: 827) commented that within Zimbabwe, there was always an 'ambiguity in the entire enterprise of conservation: Between an ideal of the wild and the merely pretty'. For urbanites, getting out into 'the bush' and having forms of recreation that revolve around national parks, water bodies, and game viewing have been very popular. More research needs to be done on white urban forms of connection with nature and how this relates to forms of belonging. In addition, the complicated histories of human displacement (in favour of nature and wildlife very often) that surround national parks and popular recreation places needs more recognition. Lake Kariba is a great example of this (Colson 1971; Hughes 2006; Tischler 2013).

## Unity and cohesion

Before 1965, Rhodesia had wanted to ensure the right sort of immigrant came to the country, being ideally someone from Britain. This belief in the right immigrant created tensions. Kenrick (2019: 44) has observed, 'the consistent predominance of British and English-speaking South Africans within the Rhodesian population perhaps accounted for the continuation of ethnic discrimination towards other groups of European immigrants such as Jews, Greeks, Afrikaners, and Portuguese'. There were many ethnic tensions between different white communities in Southern Rhodesia, and these minorities faced a great deal of discrimination (Kosmin 1981). Before 1965, there were hierarchies within white society, with an imagined 'British' identity at the pinnacle. While 'British', or 'English' ethnicity or identity is as constructed as any other, as Hall (1997) has shown, Britishness became a valuable trait for white immigrants in Rhodesia. However, after 1965, this policy changed. Due to sanctions and its pariah status post-UDI, the Rhodesian state shifted tactics and sought to attract white immigrants from wider sources. After aspiring to create a settler state in the metropole's image, the ramifications of UDI meant a new approach was needed. Instead of being selective, the state adopted a stance where basically any white would do. This was a deliberate strategy, as Brownell (2008) has noted. After UDI, Rhodesia was 'apparently prepared to accept any number of Afrikaners and Mediterranean immigrants'.

Mlambo (2002) and Brownell (2008, 2011) have outlined how white migration into and out of Rhodesia was a constant issue for the authorities. Migrants were transient, and there was a very high turnover. Consistent outflows of whites took on more significance after 1955. From 1955 to 1979, a total of 255,692 immigrants arrived in Rhodesia, but over the same period, 246,047 emigrants left (Brownell 2008: 595). This rate of turnover is especially noteworthy considering that the total white population, during this same period averaged only 228,583. Because of the high turnover of population, the state:

> [P]assed a resolution that white immigration should be as 'unselective as possible' and that more jobs should be reserved for whites in Rhodesia, which was an obvious effort to increase white numbers solely for political purposes. More importantly, the fear that blacks would overwhelm the non-racial electoral franchise of the 1961 Constitution was the driving force behind the introduction of the 1969 Constitution. These electoral anxieties, spurred by the new racial demographic information, were exploited and articulated through RF propaganda for the 1969 Constitution, which capped Africans' political potential by removing parity with whites to a distant future and delinking it from population.
>
> *(Brownell 2008: 609)*

The transient nature of the settler population created pressures within white society. After the Second World War, white Rhodesian settlers were keenly aware of the need to speak with one voice, in particular when it came to the colonial metropole in London. 'Whatever objections an individual might have toward the commonly declared interests of the settler population', wrote Kennedy, 'it was essential that they not be allowed to jeopardize the outward display of white solidarity' (1987: 181). White Rhodesians deemed unity vital for presenting a front to the British in negotiations about the status of the colony. As independence was claimed across the African continent, the white settler community hoped to retain political power in an independent Rhodesia.

During the period of political rebellion, the state continued trying to promote unity – and display harmony – in the white community, and to have members of that community act as one in their defiance in the face of local and international pressures (Godwin and Hancock 1996: 15). The white community wanted to demonstrate that it could run the country independently of Britain, and could work with local African populations to allow a slow and gradual evolution of political integration that would eventually see majority rule come to Rhodesia. However, this could only happen, many white Zimbabweans argued, after a long and sustained period of white control (White 2015). Many Rhodesians believed that they could follow the South African example and have an autonomous white-run state, or at least be conferred with dominion status like that seen in Canada and Australia (White 2015).

Godwin and Hancock have observed that there is/was no underlying or overarching unity among the white community in Zimbabwe. Solidarity within it has sometimes been illusory and has also waxed and waned over the course of a century. Various political factors have increasingly created wedges to separate farmers from these town-dwellers, and at times have brought them closer together. Ultimately, however, it shows that this solidarity has been a political game, a front for desired ends. This complicates the narrative on whiteness, and several authors, such as Kennedy, Godwin and Hancock and Selby have shown by noting certain fissures in white society and how they have ebbed and flowed over time.

The transience of white Rhodesians again marks another difference to white populations in South Africa. South Africa, and Afrikaners in particular, have not had as high rates of emigration or population turnover. Longer histories of settler belonging in South Africa have meant that these populations are more established, and can claim a longer 'belonging'. This has seen whites in South Africa, at times, be much more confrontational to the post-colonial state. The forms of whiteness there are not as passive and apolitical, but often much more vocal and ready to directly address public political concern (see above on apoliticism). Rhodesian and Zimbabwean whites more often than not chose to flee rather than fight.

## Liberalism

In the 1950s and 1960s, Rhodesia became a popular option for those seeking a place in the Empire. Mlambo has noted that the 'post- Second World War immigrants from Europe ... tended to be more liberal in their attitudes towards the Africans' (Mlambo 2009: 113). This liberalism, however, has to be qualified. As Law (2012: 24) has noted, 'Those who belonged to the ranks of Rhodesia's liberals still believed in gradual change and only favoured the co-option of "educated" Africans into the existing system'. That said, others have labelled the Federation as high point of multiracial partnership, and any genuine attempts at forging lasting and evolving multiracial interaction ended in the 1960s and rise of RF (Blake 1966: 284–345; Law 2012: 151). However, the liberals were a diverse group with a range of ideas about race, gender, politics, and class (Hancock 1984: 7). As one of the most notable liberals of the time, Diana Mitchell, has stated, 'liberalism was the only word we could've applied to ourselves ... liberalism for me was always a misnomer but it was always a shortcut to saying that we didn't despise blacks' (Law 2012: 176).

The literature on the politics of whites (liberal or otherwise) during the second half of the century is large in Zimbabwe. Law (2012) has examined liberalism in detail, as has Hancock (1984). The more right wing politics have also been scrutinised (Pilossof and Rivett 2019) and the moves towards UDI and the fallout in the white community (White 2015). In regards to whiteness, Law's work stands out. She engages in depth with the conceptual framework of whiteness and endeavours to come to a workable and useful application of the concept. Her work focuses on the changing roles and futures of women in Rhodesia from the 1950s to the 1980s. A key concern of hers, adopting a phrase from Cooper, is how various 'redefinitions of political space' resulted in women mobilising 'to claim new futures' (Cooper 2002: 2; Law 2012: 214). Law analyses how education and class were important factors in the formulation of political attitudes of women and how they sought to engage in public and private spaces. As Law (2012: 45–46) is aware, liberalism 'was predicated on a highly paternalistic understanding of race relations in as much as the white liberals wanted to co-opt "moderate" and educated Africans into the existing order'. This order was clearly defined by the understandings of whiteness of the time. Importantly, Law clearly illustrates both the changing role of women in Rhodesian politics during this contested and turbulent period and the fluid nature of gender relations in this settler society. Law has rightly noted that too much work in Southern Africa has conflated the terms 'whiteness' and 'identity', and insists that the two need to be separated to give whiteness any significance. Furthermore, much of the whiteness writing from Southern Africa often 'lapses into myopia with scholars indulging and exploring their own sense of white identity' (Law 2012: 45). Law also recognises that while writing on the topic is dominated by sociologists and anthropologists, 'it is a literature that nonetheless raises valuable theoretical questions that assist the historicisation of a white Rhodesian identity'. Her own work shows the changing attitudes towards work, home life and political involvement in Rhodesia, and how these interacted with whiteness issues of the time. The separation of whiteness and identity is important because whiteness in not about 'whites' per se. It is about power, privilege and race and understanding how these become embedded in various forms of hierarchy in society. Various forms of privilege, and how other groups or elites might mimic patterns power or status, is key to exploring whiteness, and this should be distinct to idea of being white.

Law makes an important contribution to evolution of white identity in Rhodesia. Her predecessors include Kennedy (1987), Shutt and King (2005), Phimister (1988), Caute (1983), Chennells (2004), and Godwin and Hancock (1996). However, I would argue that what is still needed is a better understanding of the various 'white' minorities (Italians, Greeks and Afrikaners, for example) in Zimbabwe and Rhodesia. This could provide insights that would historicise the development of ethnic differences and identities, and in doing so aid understandings of white experiences in Zimbabwe.[4] Clearly, a limited understanding of whiteness during the colonial or settler period undermines much of the current focus of whiteness precisely because of the lack of historical depth and the failure to understand the trajectories of whiteness, and how these have evolved and changed over time. However, as has been illustrated earlier, much of the research on what 'Rhodesian identity' was has been carried out by a generation of scholars that pre-date whiteness. As Arnesen (2001: 6) has commented, the construction of race, a key tenant of whiteness studies, has long been a central concern of social and cultural historians. Indeed, he goes as far as to say 'whether or not whiteness scholars want to admit it, it is safe to say that, among most academics in the humanities, save for the rare crank, we are all social constructionists now'. The instance that whiteness studies is 'discovering' something new and unresearched is often overemphasised and obscures much of the existing literature on white identity, the construction of social strata and the history of white superiority in Southern Africa, and as a result, a great deal of important work is often left out of the whiteness canon. This chapter has illustrated much of the important work on identity and white privilege in Zimbabwe that came before the term whiteness was coined. While the term whiteness originated in American academia, the topic and issues of whiteness have long been pursued by historians and social scientists working in and on southern Africa, as well as numerous locations outside the United States. Such work can help deepen understandings of whiteness and its relevance to contemporary debate, and, thus, needs to be remembered in the discussions.

Liberalism, conservation, and ethnic unity are three key themes in the study of whiteness in Zimbabwe and southern Africa. The history of these practices provide valuable insights to whiteness scholars. This work is provided by many current researchers, and by scholars who predate the term whiteness. These early works are critical for developing deeper understanding of current contestations over whiteness in southern Africa, and other settler states. Whiteness in southern Africa is further complicated because unlike many parts of the Western world, whites are so prominent, due to historic patterns of levels of privilege and power. This makes the study of whiteness in post-colonial Africa problematic, because whiteness is often looking for hidden processes of continuing privilege or superiority. However, what this chapter has tried to do is show that 'white' and 'whiteness' is not a consistent theme in Zimbabwe's past and that there are important undercurrents that deserve considered investigation. This continues in the postcolonial period, where caricatures of what 'white' and what 'privilege' are need to be better understood and nuanced to appreciate white presence in the region better, as well as the long-term impacts of different forms of coloniality.

## Conclusion

This chapter has outlined the rise in whiteness studies in Zimbabwe and the key literature in this scholarship. It has also tried to show some of the contextual reasons as to why whiteness studies have become so popular in southern Africa after 2000. It has also highlighted ways in which it is possible to complicate and disambiguate the term whiteness and its application in Zimbabwe. In doing so, it has shown some of the significant drivers in the construction of specific forms of whiteness in Zimbabwe, and how these have evolved over time. Importantly there is a large scholarship that either predates or does not use the term whiteness, yet addresses many of the key concerns of whiteness – race, identity, power, and privilege. These contributions need to be acknowledged and the findings brought into the whiteness debates to deepen and enrich current discussions.

Finally, whiteness has always been marked in Africa, due to the politics of settler colonies and minority rule and privilege in the region. As a result, whiteness is highly visible in Zimbabwe and southern Africa. The literature on whiteness in Africa shows how the visibility of whiteness matters for its politics. As pointed out earlier, white Zimbabweans have been vocal and active in narrating their own experiences. This has given much material for scholars of whiteness to look into and research. However, as Hughes has pointed out, there are dangers about writing on those who can write back. His book was widely criticised by white Zimbabwean scholars. He noted of the reviews of his book, 'In different ways, their comments … underscore the perils in documenting highly literate people who "write back". More tellingly, they expose the enduring uncertainty of tolerance and integration in Harare and beyond' (Hughes 2015: 305). The case of Zimbabwe illustrates how the politics of whiteness and representation are intimately connected. This chapter has also tried to briefly highlight potential similarities and differences in whiteness and coloniality in Zimbabwe and the South Africa, the two biggest settler colonies in southern Africa. Hopefully, this can help open more avenues for discussion about whiteness and colonial histories in Africa and further afield.

## Notes

1  While there is no definitive time frame for this chapter, the insights into the post-colonial setting are relevant in the 2010s and 2020s.
2  Dominion status was used as a term to refer to self-governing colonies in the British Empire, such as Australia, Canada, and New Zealand. These territories had more legislative independence that other colonies and had large, white, settler populations.
3  Rhodesia was a unique settler colony because of UDI. Through this process, the white settlers broke away from the British colonial control to instill their own leadership and maintain white control of the state. While the new settler government proclaimed vague promises of a gradual movement to majority or black rule, it was clear this was a token gesture to appease international opinion. Britain had insisted there would be no independence in Rhodesia/Zimbabwe independence without majority rule and universal suffrage.
4  There is very little work on these white minorities in contemporary Zimbabwe either, and many of these smaller white communities have reduced radically in size since the 1990s.

## References

Arnesen, E. 2001. Whiteness and the Historians' Imagination. *International Labor and Working-Class History*, 60: 3–32.

Blake, R 1966. *A History of Rhodesia*. London: Metheun.

Brownell, J. 2008. The Hole in Rhodesia's Bucket: White Emigration and the End of Settler Rule. *Journal of Southern African Studies*, 34 (3): 591–610.

Brownell, J. 2011. *The Collapse of Rhodesia: Population Demographics and The Politics of Race*. London: I. B. Tauris.

Caute, D. 1983. *Under The Skin: The Death of White Rhodesia*. London: Allen Lane.

Chennells, A. 1982. 'Settler Myths and the Southern Rhodesian Novel', PhD thesis, Harare: University of Zimbabwe.

Chennells, A. 2004. The Mimic Women: Early Women Novelists and White Southern African Nationalisms. *Historia*, 49 (1): 71–88.

Cohen, A. 2017. *The Politics and Economics of Decolonization in Africa: The Failed Experiment of the Central African Federation.* London: I. B. Tauris.

Colson, E. 1971. *The Social Consequences of Resettlement: The Impact of the Kariba Resettlement Upon the Gwembe Tonga.* Manchester: Manchester University Press.

Cooper, F. 2002. *Africa Since 1940: The Past of the Present.* Cambridge: Cambridge University Press.

Duffy, R. 2000. *Killing for Conservation: Wildlife Policy in Zimbabwe.* London: James Currey.

Fisher, J. 2010. *Pioneers, Settlers, Aliens, Exiles: The Decolonisation of White Identity in Zimbabwe.* Canberra: ANUE Press.

Godwin, P. and Hancock, I. 1996. *'Rhodesians Never Die': The Impact of War and Political Change on White Rhodesia, c. 1970–1980.* Oxford: Oxford University Press.

Hall, S. 1997. The Local and the Global: Globalization and Ethnicity. In *Culture, Globalization, and the World-System,* ed. A. D. King, pp. 19–39. Minneapolis, MN: University of Minnesota Press.

Hammar, A. 2012. Whiteness in Zimbabwe: Race, Landscape and the Problem of Belonging. *Journal of Peasant Studies,* 39 (1): 216–221.

Hancock, I. 1984. *White Liberals, Moderates and Radicals in Rhodesia, 1953–1980.* New York: St. Martin.

Hartnack, A. 2015. Whiteness and Shades of Grey: Erasure, Amnesia and the Ethnography of Zimbabwe's Whites. *Journal of Contemporary African Studies,* 33 (2): 285–299.

Hughes, D. M. 2006. Whites and Water: How Euro-Africans Made Nature at Kariba Dam. *Journal of Southern African Studies,* 32 (4): 823–838.

Hughes, D. M. 2010. *Whiteness in Zimbabwe: Race, Landscape, and the Problem of Belonging.* New York: Palgrave Macmillan.

Hughes, D. M. 2015. To Lump or to Split: Perils of Portraying Zimbabwe's Whites. *Journal of Contemporary African Studies,* 33 (2): 300–304.

Kennedy, D. 1987. *Islands of White: Settler Society and Culture in Kenya and Southern Rhodesia, 1890–1939.* Durham, NC: Duke University Press.

Kenrick, D. W. 2019. *Decolonisation, Identity and Nation in Rhodesia, 1964–1979.* London: Palgrave Macmillan.

Kosmin, B. A. 1981. *Majuta: A History of the Jewish Community of Zimbabwe.* Gweru: Mambo Press.

Laurie, C. 2016. *The Land Reform Deception: Political Opportunism in Zimbabwe's Land Seizure Era.* New York: Oxford University Press.

Law, K. 2012. *Gendering the Settler State: White Women, Race, Liberalism and Empire in Rhodesia, 1950–1980.* Abington: Routledge.

Marks, S. 1980. 'The Myth of Empty Land', *History Matters,* viewed 2 December 2020, https://historymatters.co.za/content/south-africa-myth-empty-land-shula-marks-1-january-1980-south-africa.

McGregor, J. 1995. Conservation, Control and Ecological Change: The Politics and Ecology of Colonial Conservation in Shurugwi, Zimbabwe. *Environment and History,* 1 (3): 257–279.

Mlambo, A. S. 2002. *White Immigration into Rhodesia: From Occupation to Federation.* Harare: University of Zimbabwe Press.

Mlambo, A. S. 2009. From the Second World War to UDI, 1940–1965. In *Becoming Zimbabwe: A History from the Pre-colonial Period to 2008,* ed. B. Raftopoulos and A. S. Mlambo, pp. 75–114. Harare: Weaver Press.

Moreton-Robinson, A. 2015. *The White Possessive: Property, Power, and Indigenous Sovereignty.* Minnesota: University of Minnesota Press.

Phimister, I. 1988. *An Economic and Social History of Zimbabwe 1890-1948: Capital Accumulation and Class Struggle.* London: Longman.

Phimister, I. and Pilossof, R. 2017. Wage labor in historical perspective: A study of the de-proletarianization of the African working class in Zimbabwe, 1960–2010. *Labor History,* 58 (2): 215–227.

Pilossof, R. 2009. The Unbearable Whiteness of Being: Land, Race and Belonging in the Memoirs of White Zimbabweans. *South African Historical Journal,* 61 (3): 621–638.

Pilossof, R. 2012. *The Unbearable Whiteness of Being: Farmers' Voices from Zimbabwe.* Cape Town: University of Cape Town Press.

Pilossof, R. 2014. Reinventing Significance: Reflections on Recent Whiteness Studies in Zimbabwe. *Africa Spectrum,* 49 (3): 135–148.

Pilossof, R. and Boersema, J. 2017. Not All Whites are Farmers: Privilege, the Politics of Representation, and the Urban–rural Divide in Zimbabwe. *Africa,* 87 (4): 702–719.

Pilossof, R. and Rivett, G. 2019. Imagining Change, Imaginary Futures: 'Conditions of Possibility' in Pre-Independence Southern Rhodesia, 1959–1963. *Social Science History*, 43: 243–267.

Roos, N. 2005. *Ordinary Springboks: White Servicemen and Social Justice in South Africa, 1939–1961*. Aldershot: Ashgate.

Rubert, S. 1998. *A Most Promising Weed: A History of Tobacco Farming and Labor in Colonial Zimbabwe, 1890–1945*. Athens, OH: University of Ohio Press.

Selby, A. 2006. 'Commercial Farmers and the State: Interest Group Politics and Land Reform in Zimbabwe', PhD thesis, Oxford: University of Oxford.

Shutt, A. and King, T. 2005. Imperial Rhodesians: The 1953 Rhodes Centenary Exhibition in Southern Rhodesia. *Journal of Southern African Studies*, 31: 357–379.

Sylvester, C. 1986. Zimbabwe's 1985 Elections: A Search for National Mythology. *The Journal of Modern African Studies*, 24 (2): 229–255.

Tischler, J. 2013. *Light and Power for a Multiracial Nation: The Kariba Dam Scheme in the Central African Federation*. Basingstoke: Palgrave Macmillan.

Van der Westhuizen, C. 2017. Afrikaners in Post-apartheid South Africa: Inward Migration and Enclave Nationalism. *HTS Theological Studies*, 72 (4).

Van Zyl-Hermann, D. 2014. Baas or Klaas? Afrikaner Working-Class Responses to Transformation in South Africa, ca. 1977–2002. *International Labor and Working-Class History*, 86: 142–158.

Van Zyl-Hermann, D. and Boersema, J. 2017. Introduction: The Politics of Whiteness in Africa. *Africa*, 87 (4): 651–661.

White, L. 2015. *Unpopular Sovereignty: Rhodesian Independence and African Decolonization*. Chicago: University of Chicago Press.

Wylie, D. 2012. Not Quite a Refutation: A Response to David Mcdermott Hughes's *Whiteness in Zimbabwe*. *Safundi*, 13 (1–2): 181–194.

# Part IV

# Intersectionalities: Differences (de)stabilising whiteness

Whiteness is not monolithic. Indeed, as per the anti-essentialist stance from which this handbook moves, it would be more accurate to speak of whitenesses in the plural. This approach aims to underscore and differentiate among the plethora of positions of whiteness, and to account for the power effects of whiteness criss-crossing gender, sexual, class, and other differences, in all their complexity. This section drills down to bring the reader to the workings of whiteness at the level of identity: The lived ways in which differences are intersectionally mobilised with or against other social categories to advance or rebut whiteness. Multiple strands of differentiation are unpicked, exploring how subjects may at any given moment simultaneously occupy normative and non-normative positionalities. The power otherwise associated with whiteness as normative centre can be reduced if a subject is also identifiable by marginalised, objectified, excluded, or abjected differences. Therefore, the operations of power in the bolstering of some identities in relation to others can be exposed, such as white middleclass women in relation to economically insecure black men. Notably, in what has been called 'intersectional shifting' (see Chapter 7), others internal to whiteness wield their whiteness to compensate for the power deficit incurred due to an intersecting stigmatised positionality, such as femininity in the case of women and gay men. The analyses also show that ethnicity and class can be deployed to paradoxical effect, both to claim whiteness and (re)secure economic entitlements. Theo Sonnekus illustrates in the opening chapter how masculinity at the intersections with ethnicity and class works to accrue the benefits of whiteness, as seen in the competition for dominance between Afrikaner and white English-speaking masculinities in South Africa. In the next chapter, Katerina Deliovsky critically discusses the literature on sex tourism. She analyses how heterosexual white women's newfound sexual autonomy in former colonial contexts such as the Caribbean reify tropes that reinforce unequal racial power structures. As a counterpart to Deliovsky's chapter on white women's conflicting race–gender positionality in relation to patriarchy, Lwando Scott investigates gay white men, who also hold a contradictory position, in this case in relation to heteronormativity. The pursuit through neoliberal consumption of 'the global gay' as necessarily white and middleclass involves an equalisation of male beauty with whiteness and a fetishisation of black male sexuality. In the final chapter in this section, the focus shifts to the opportunistic use of class by British political

DOI: 10.4324/9780429355769-104

elites. Neema Begum, Aurelien Mondon, and Aaron Winter argue that the projection of voters who supported Brexit and Trump in Britain and the United States, respectively, as 'the white working class' shifts the responsibility for socio-economic inequalities from elites and onto immigrants and racialised minorities.

# 15

# 'Africa is not for sissies'[1]: The race for dominance between white masculinities in South Africa

*Theo Sonnekus*

## Introduction

This chapter offers a concise history of the conflicting claims to dominant white masculinity in South Africa in the colonial era and during apartheid. I therefore propose a selective trajectory of white machismo in strife vis-á-vis historical events or contexts variously marked by trauma, subjugation, and humiliation, as well as associated attempts at rehabilitation. The main protagonists of this narrative are the British, who gained control of the Cape of Good Hope in the early nineteenth century, and the Afrikaners, descended mainly from the Dutch, whose colonising mission to South Africa commenced nearly two centuries earlier. While the trope of the pioneer (of being 'first') emerges as a major point of contention in this history of competition between two settler whitenesses, it figures amongst a variety of discourses deployed by opposing British and Afrikaner forces in the race for the seat of power during the nineteenth and twentieth centuries. This exploration first builds on the robust notion that sheer whiteness is never secured once and for all, but variously struggled for, gained, lost, and reclaimed. Second, I attend to whiteness as contingent on (and modified by) accompanying aspects of identity with which it intersects – in this case, ethnicity and gender.

The development of Afrikaner ethnic identity presents the singular case of a historically rural, impoverished, and subaltern white minority that expended a considerable amount of energy to obtain material and symbolic gains through the vehicle of an imagined coherent *volk* (nation) that could challenge and ultimately supplant their wealthier and more powerful British counterparts. Such power imbalances ultimately invite perspectives on whiteness as a fiercely circumscribed construct that maintains strict boundaries between the invited and uninvited, or marked and unmarked. Projects for economic upliftment and claims to cultural sophistication, which figure prominently in the history of Afrikaner nationalism, are therefore discussed as strategies for obtaining middle-class respectability – the raw material of whiteness. In the case of the Afrikaners, for example their ethnicity historically figured in British social discourse as an indelible sign of difference that restricted bonafide entry into the fold of whiteness. As I will illustrate, the Afrikaners were therefore considered 'not quite' white. Yet, this chapter also anticipates that the ideological and political gambits deployed by the Afrikaners to conflate ethnic and national identity resulted in a near reversal of markedness, by which the legitimate

DOI: 10.4324/9780429355769-15

belonging or 'indigeneity' of white English-speaking South Africans (WESSAs) were called into question.

I explore the implications of gender identity in the construction of whiteness via the concept of hegemonic masculinity, which describes the manner in which a single, apparently homogenous, group of men assumes authority over another.[2] Hegemonic masculinity and whiteness are therefore conceptually similar, because both constructs operate by means of expulsion: They constantly survey the boundaries that separate, and hierarchically organise, subjects in terms of their adherence to an imaginary ideal. Such strategies are often inextricable from violence, which manifests at material and symbolic levels. The devastation of the Afrikaners, or Boers, and subsequent emasculation of Afrikaner men by British forces during the South African (Anglo-Boer) War (1899–1902), is exemplary in this regard. Yet, hegemonic masculinity is not monolithic or necessarily accepted via acquiescence. Instead, as explored in this chapter, the history of this conflict teems with discourses of disdain for British masculinity and the simultaneous veneration of Afrikaner masculinity. Maintaining hegemonic masculinity also depends on the capacity of the group for whom it holds significance to deploy political, economic, and cultural influence. The locus of hegemonic masculinity (like that of whiteness) therefore shifts according to changing power relations. Thus, the institutionalisation of Afrikanerdom in the twentieth century effectively relegated WESSA men to an inferior position in selected social milieux. In this regard, I focus specifically on the history of compulsory military conscription in South Africa (1968–1993) to explore the various ethnocentric, racist, homophobic, and misogynistic discourses deployed to fortify apartheid-era Afrikaner masculinity.

## Fighting for whiteness on the frontier

This history begins with a slight. Definitions of the term 'Afrikaner' fluctuated significantly during the early years of colonisation before resolving in 'white Afrikaans-speaking South African' under the auspices of Afrikaner nationalism. The term initially referred to people of colour in the Cape Colony but developed to define a linguistic community of black, brown, and white people who spoke Afrikaans, a creole language derived mainly from Dutch (Giliomee 2009). A later inflection, namely 'Afrikanen', was however promoted as a signifier for white citizenship, thus wresting ownership from indigenous peoples to unify the two main settler populations at the Cape (Giliomee 2001). The British, however, had no intention of adopting this designation, ultimately spurning what could be considered an invitation to parity. Such an act of closing ranks seems typical, given the generally disparaging view of Afrikaner ethnic identity in English social discourse during colonialism and in the early twentieth century.

In the imperial imaginary, the Afrikaners were marked as belonging to an entirely different, and degenerated, class of settler, based on their perceived backwardness or primitivity: Their largely agrarian societies and pidgin language (Afrikaans), for example placed them hierarchically closer to indigenous peoples and further removed from whiteness in this particular schema of social Darwinism. Such perceptions also indicated that the 'lack of apparent European-style evolution' amongst the Afrikaners threatened to undermine white supremacy and impede the imperial project of white expansion into Africa (Van der Westhuizen 2017: 27). A significant development in the study of whiteness has been to resist thinking of 'being white' as *essentially* embodied or corporeal, and therefore uniform, since white identities are subject to major differentiations at conceptual or discursive levels (Steyn and Conway 2010). In the history discussed here, the beneficiaries of the conceits of the British Empire thus emerged as the holders of the economic and cultural capital needed to manufacture knowledge of whiteness in a narcissistic fashion, that is, as corresponding to a particular brand of respectable, bourgeois

Englishness. Yet, they rarely needed to articulate such an ethno-racial position, given that 'British identity was seen as the most outstanding example of the "universal" identity ... that colonial "others" (as well as other Europeans) needed to aspire to' (Johnson 2002: 171).

To be legitimately white, therefore, is to be sovereign. This logic is explicit in the histories of white people assuming custodianship of the colonised and their territories. Once the British seized control of the Cape, however, the Afrikaners were largely excluded from influential decisions about the status and futures of indigenous peoples: While their relative access to white privilege secured, for instance the right to own land, they nonetheless figured as the subjects (rather than agents) of European imperialism. The tense negotiations for power amongst Afrikaner and British constituencies at the Cape reached an impasse exactly because slavery was abolished throughout the vast colonies of the British Empire in the early nineteenth century. Perceptions of political bullying and the devastating material effects on Afrikaner farms that depended on slave labour are therefore often cited as the main reasons for a significant number of Afrikaners defecting from the Cape to establish independent Boer republics in the interior of South Africa.

At this stage, it is useful to note that the terms 'Boer' (farmer) and 'Afrikaner' have historically been used interchangeably (Barris 2014), thus attending to the pastoral origins of Afrikaner identity, elevating it to near mythic status. The *plaas* (farm) is also the site of the emergence of an enduring archetype of Afrikaner masculinity: The upright patriarch and progenitor of whiteness, whose divinely ordained authority bore down on immediate domestic relationships, the natural landscape and its attendant fauna and flora, as well as slaves and other colonised peoples (Du Pisani 2004). As a microcosm of masculine autonomy, the *plaas* therefore figured as a self-contained space onto which a fantasy of utter possession and control could be projected – a spell broken by the imperial decree of abolition. Perceptions of emasculation, and being denied the prerogative of white rule, therefore occasioned highly charged anti-English sentiments amongst selected Afrikaner constituencies.

I propose that the pronounced affective dimension of this schism resulted from troubling (and ultimately collapsing) the synergy of white privilege and patriarchal control, depreciating each in turn. The Afrikaners who travelled north seeking self-governance, via the Great Trek (1835–1845), thus attached to themselves an alternative designation, *voortrekkers* (pioneers), which manifested distinct expressions of masculinity to call British dominance into question. The precarity of life on the frontier encouraged the rehabilitation of Afrikaner masculinity, because the experiences of dislocation and adversity placed Afrikaner men at the centre of a mythological narrative steeped in displays of physical and mental toughness, perseverance, and valour. A prominent example in this regard is The Battle of Blood River (1838), during which the *voortrekkers* defeated the Zulu despite being considerably outnumbered; an event propagated by Afrikaner ideologues as incontrovertible evidence of the *volk*'s divine right to African soil. Such discourses of bravado at once positioned Afrikaner men as the victims of British imperialism, and self-made agents of a newfound independence from it.

The South African War, and militarisation of Afrikaner and British men in general, offers a particularly productive site from which to explore the animosities, and associated habits of derision, that shaped negotiations between settler masculinity and whiteness at the end of the nineteenth century. Military conscription amongst Afrikaner men was largely organised along the lines of the commando system, comprising networks of guerrilla militia deployed to defend and survey the frontier, and eventually the Boer republics of the Orange Free State and the Transvaal[3] (Giliomee 2009). Boer commandos promoted an ethos of egalitarianism belied by a deeply paternalistic hierarchy in which older men disciplined and assumed custodianship of Boer youths in an informal, familial fashion (Swart 1998). The lack of institutional uniforms, training, and disciplinary codes amongst Boer forces, however, figured in the imperial imaginary as further evidence of the Afrikaners' rudimentary state – in other words, their disconnection from European gentility and its white reflection.

The vigorous, unkempt beards of Boer leaders were particularly contentious in this regard, because they signified authority and maturity in Afrikaner gender politics (Swart 1998), but appeared 'uncouth' compared to the dapper dress and fine grooming of British military personnel. These men occupied a venerated position in imperial discourses on progress, civilisation, and the onus of interrupting the degeneration of lesser peoples. Such demonstrative and highly organised modes of masculinity thus supported ideologies which sought to naturalise the superior sensibilities of British white men vis-à-vis derisive comparisons with racial 'others'. Representations of 'naked, bestial-faced African troops [pictured alongside] beautifully uniformed British soldiers' were, for example strategically reproduced in the Victorian press to propagate the notion of the Empire's resplendent modernity (Anderson 2008: 13). However, Anglophile whiteness as humanity par excellence emerged not only from the binary opposition of white and non-white, but also from the particularisation of whiteness itself – Lord Kitchener's caricature of the Boers as 'uncivilized white savages with a thin white veneer' is especially telling in this regard (Kitchener, cited in Steyn 2001: 26). Thus, in the milieu of the South African War, the perceived crudeness of Afrikaner forces apparently betrayed their cultural, moral, and cerebral shortcomings, confirmed by their eventual defeat. However, it does not follow that the Afrikaners necessarily acquiesced to their expulsion from the ranks of dominant settler masculinity.[4] While they lacked the material means to challenge British hegemony, their discursive arsenal burgeoned.

In the period after the war, narratives of the brutalisation of the *volk*, reiterating the incineration of vast areas of the Boer republics and internment of Boer women and children, for example proliferated to demonise the British and simultaneously paint Afrikaner patriarchs as righteously struggling to secure a home for posterity. In their settler imaginary, the Afrikaners had paid for the land in blood from the moment their ancestors set foot on the continent, and to the extent of achieving 'an embeddedness in Africa' (Rodéhn 2016: 74). Thus, by extinguishing the European origins of the Afrikaners, the discourses of nascent Afrikaner nationalism asserted an indigenised whiteness inaccessible to British imperialists, who, by that designation alone, retained political, cultural, and affective connections with the metropole. By way of this logic, which placed actual indigenous peoples under erasure, the British had arrived in South Africa belatedly, taking illegitimate ownership of a 'motherland' already claimed two centuries earlier. At a colloquial level, notions of the Afrikaners' inimitable kinship with the land found expression in ethnic slurs, notably manifest in the context of the military, intended to mark British subjects as hopelessly foreign, and ultimately unfit to rule South Africa. The term *rooinek* (red neck), meant to ridicule the sunburnt skin of British soldiers, is emblematic in this regard, as it implies a certain deficit in terms of ideal frontier masculinity – a European pedigree (even a 'delicate' state of whiteness) forever estranged from, and ill-equipped for, the climate and topographies of Africa.

The formation of the Union of South Africa in 1910 was a significant ideological move towards entrenching preferential political and social treatment for white South Africans, while the tentative coalition between Boer and Brit enabled the construction of a common black menace in need of surveillance and control (Giliomee 2009). Yet, the constant oscillation between gaining and losing ground, which continued to frustrate the Afrikaners' attempts at autonomy, deferred any simple resolution to the scramble for dominant whiteness at the beginning of the twentieth century. It is pertinent in this regard that the years of union were also marked by widespread and severe Afrikaner poverty, mainly inherited from the economic blows of the South African War and compounded by late Afrikaner urbanisation (Davies 2009).

Efforts at assuaging the 'poor white problem' persisted well into the mid-twentieth century, with Afrikaner ideologues fearing that class divisions amongst the Afrikaner people threatened to erode the nationalist ideal of a homogenous *volk*, unified in their ethnic pride, white respectability, and political aspirations. Furthermore, the stigma of degeneration historically attached to Afrikaner identity, and still expressed in English social discourse at the time, meant that impoverished Afrikaners were especially vulnerable to perceptions of having regressed to 'blackness': While fears of miscegenation prompted stricter control over Afrikaner women, recently urbanised, working-class Afrikaner men faced with limited options for employment, for example deigned to take on 'kaffir work' (Willoughby-Herard 2007) – the types of unskilled manual labour derisively associated with the black majority. Those who secured employment in cities were also compelled 'to speak a foreign language – English – like a conquered race' (Swart 1998: 741), again finding their interests subordinated to those of the 'old enemy'.

A tangible sense of disenfranchisement thus emerged amongst the Afrikaner poor, 'who assumed they were entitled to the material and social privileges of whiteness, but could not afford a "white" urban lifestyle' (Roos 2016: 123). Such grievances bring the intersection of whiteness and economic, social, and cultural capital, as well as internalised beliefs about their interdependence, into stark relief. Afrikaner masculinity, as well as the paternalistic structure of the Afrikaner family, was similarly compromised by economic hardship. While some Afrikaner men suffered the 'indignity' of parity with black labourers, others reluctantly surrendered the role of bread-winner to unmarried female family members, many of whom tended to relocate to urban areas significantly earlier than their fathers and brothers (Bozzoli 1983), whose male labour was, in some instances, deployed to salvage Afrikaner farms.

Concerted efforts at extending welfare services and other forms of state-sanctioned economic protection to selected Afrikaner communities in the mid-1920s (Roos 2016), however, significantly shifted the class status of some Afrikaner families, subsequently rebalancing patriarchal authority: During the inter-war years, and for a significant period thereafter, numerous Afrikaner women were being extracted from public welfare and political work and the job market to resume their domestic roles (and invisible labour) as wives and mothers (Van der Westhuizen 2017). Thus, by imitating the 'basic unit of Victorian bourgeois society' (Van der Westhuizen 2017: 108) – which presented female 'leisure' as the by-product of male industriousness and success – prosperous Afrikaners could begin to challenge the enduring perceptions of their exclusion from notions of middle-class respectability, and, by association, legitimate whiteness. Though Afrikaner poverty was never completely eradicated, a new confidence emerged amongst aspirational Afrikaner constituencies who perhaps anticipated that the growing influence of Afrikaner nationalism would eventually overturn the subaltern status of the *volk* in a momentous fashion.

## The making of *moffies* and men in apartheid South Africa

Following the electoral victory of the National Party (NP) in 1948, a powerful ethnic politics could indeed finally be mobilised: With a cabinet comprised mostly of English-speakers considered troublingly royalist and partial to the advancement of WESSA communities (Giliomee 2009), the defeat of the ruling United Party signalled that the Afrikaners had finally succeeded at becoming the dominant white group in South Africa. To establish their hegemony, the NP implemented various social, economic, and political apparatuses (subsumed under apartheid) in the post-1948 period to secure the privilege and power of the *volk*.[5] In a radical attempt at ideological streamlining, memories of the trauma and humiliation inflicted on the Afrikaners by the British during the South African War figured as apologia for the apartheid regime in certain iterations of nationalist fervour – apparently, 'in 1948 [the Afrikaners] had regained what they had lost in 1902' (Grundlingh 2004: 370). To enforce such notions of reparation, the nationalist movement materialised its triumph via signifiers ranging from the national flag and anthem, to memorial sites, visual art, civic buildings, and street names commemorating nationalist personages and the historical struggles of the *volk*. Thus, for most of the twentieth century, the Afrikaners were immersed in a public sphere that ubiquitously exulted their sovereignty.

At its peak, Afrikaner power extended across various proto-nationalist platforms, such as the press, public broadcaster, culture industry, and education system, to institutionalise (and negotiate an esteemed position for) Afrikaans and its related forms of cultural expression (Botma 2008). Such processes of institutionalisation strategically suppressed the creole origins of Afrikaans by relegating brown and black variants of the language to the sphere of the colloquial, thereby claiming that standardised (or literary) Afrikaans was unambiguously 'the language of white people' (Van der Waal 2008: 62). The post-1948 period also bears witness to the gradual displacement of WESSA men from high-ranking positions in the civil service and 'in the first twenty years of NP rule, the number of [Afrikaner bureaucrats] doubled' (Giliomee 2009: 493). With the power of the state and tremendous growth in Afrikaner-dominated industries, especially agriculture, behind them, the Afrikaner middle-class therefore expanded rapidly, reaching unprecedented numbers (O'Meara, 1983). Many Afrikaners, but especially the elite, could now comfortably assert self-concepts based on notions of progress, modernity, and cultural sophistication, thereby powerfully negating their historical exclusion from the upper echelons of (British) white propriety.

While compelling evidence exists of the political involvement of Afrikaner women in shaping the nationalist movement (Van der Westhuizen 2017), Afrikaner men routinely emerge in historical narratives as the primary agents of the reformation of the *volk*. The Afrikaner *Broederbond* (League of Brothers), a secret society founded in 1918, for example played an instrumental role in establishing Afrikaner power before and during apartheid. The *Broederbond*, by that very designation, restricted its membership to male, conservative Afrikaners, and attracted prominent politicians, academics, entrepreneurs, and church leaders. As a collective, they sought to secure the political, economic, moral, and cultural well-being of Afrikaners via an unwavering loyalty to the NP, the establishment of co-operative financial institutions that could alleviate Afrikaner poverty, and a cultural wing, the *Federasie van Afrikaanse Kultuurvereniginge* (Federation of Afrikaans Cultural Associations), which ensured the continued public use and legitimacy of Afrikaans (Freschi 2009).

The Afrikaner elite could in effect construct a sense of hegemonic masculinity premised on nationalist sentiments and a puritan, heteronormative form of Christianity, which engendered a profound distrust of 'outsiders', whether in terms of their liberal politics, 'deviant' sexualities, or racial and ethnic identities. Apartheid-era hegemonic Afrikaner masculinity could therefore be considered a microcosm of the state's widespread fixation on restricting contact with (or exposure to) cultural and political influences considered *volksvreemd* (foreign to the nation): State-sponsored media incessantly warned against the danger of 'non-Afrikaans movies, books, and music', while international travel and notions of cosmopolitanism figured in the apartheid imaginary as damaging to the moral character of the *volk* (Marlin-Curiel 2001: 155).

By the 1960s and 1970s, however, such myopic views became the basis for increasing dissension amongst aspirational Afrikaners in particular, who viewed the paternalistic attitudes of the regime as anathema to their capital interests and appetite for 'modernising' stimuli. At this stage, Afrikaner capital elites also 'began to side with their [WESSA] counterparts "across the

ethnic divide", preoccupied with the imperatives of liberalisation very much against the nationalist tradition' (Davies 2012: 396). Any historical understanding of the declining support for
Afrikaner nationalism should therefore make a case for an initial 'unravelling from within'
(Blaser 2012: 3), as *verligte* (enlightened) Afrikaners gradually defined themselves in opposition
to *verkrampte* (conservative) Afrikaners, who valued traditions not as a constructs to be sur-
mounted, but as sanctified essences of ethnic identity. Additionally, as African anti-colonial
movements in neighbouring countries, including Namibia (then South West Africa – SWA),
Angola, and Zimbabwe (then Rhodesia), threatened to spill over into South Africa and
strengthen internal black pro-democracy forces, the white population grew increasingly
paranoid that the state had failed to establish a compelling sense of national security. To assuage
such fears, the government implemented compulsory military conscription for all white men of
school-leaving age in 1968 (initially for a period of nine months and then two years from 1977
until 1993) to defend the South African border during the SWA-Angolan Bush War
(1966–1990) (Edlmann 2012).

The explicit racialisation of the call-up (all white men) is of major significance to this exploration in terms of the complex intersection of whiteness and masculinity in the history of
apartheid. First, with conscription in full effect, the definition of hegemonic masculinity had
come to depend on extant racial and gendered hierarchies extolled within the South African
Defence Force (SADF), where 'white militarised men were regarded as the "highest" form of
life', followed by women and black men, for whom there was very little, if any, reverence
(Edlmann 2012: 260). Second, with the apparent threat of decolonising forces at their doorstep,
the NP could no longer afford to stigmatise and divide white South African men (the guardians
of the nation-state) at the level of their ethnic identities (Conway 2008). Thus, the potential
benefits of white unity, in theory at least, significantly outweighed the ideals of an inward-
looking and essentially cohesive Afrikaner identity, which, as I have mentioned, had already
started disintegrating. Yet, it does not follow that intra-white competition had been eliminated
from the SADF, or that the legacy of animosity between Afrikaner and WESSA men had
completely receded from collective memory and everyday discourse.

Military slang in the context of the SADF is a pertinent case in this regard. The terms 'hairy
back' and 'rock spider' were, for instance regularly deployed by hostile WESSA conscripts to
denigrate their Afrikaans-speaking counterparts via historically charged notions of the
Afrikaners' assumed crudeness and stupidity. Yet, as an entity of the state, the SADF was
dominated by Afrikaans in terms of formal training, as well as shared (relatively unbiased)
colloquialisms for which there were apparently no English equivalents (Gibson 2010). Such
modes of linguistic authority meant that Afrikaner conscripts, especially those who harboured
anti-English sentiments, were at an advantage in terms of the ease with which they could
neutralise Afrikaner-centred slurs with dismissive, nearly institutionalised, attacks of their own.
In view of this, *soutpiel* (salty prick) holds the distinction of being effectively endemic to the
history of the SADF and is especially revealing in terms of the continuing fixation on the threat
of 'male others' within the purview of hegemonic Afrikaner masculinity. *Soutpiel* is intended to
conjure a mocking image of having one foot in South Africa and another in Britain, with one's
genitalia dangling in the ocean, thus representing a dubious, at best conflicted, commitment to
the nation-state. Like *rooinek*, which marked the white male English body as a site of un-
belonging in the militarised spaces of the nineteenth century, *soutpiel* reaffirmed that 'within
state institutions, and especially the armed forces, Afrikaners were the real insiders' (Baines
2014: 509).

Conceptions of apartheid-era masculinity were also overdetermined by various misogynistic
and homophobic discourses which sought to discipline white men who outright rejected, or

failed to excel at, military training: They were thus 'portrayed as sexually "deviant" and associated with effeminacy, weakness, cowardice, and of being incapable of achieving "true" manhood' (Conway 2004: 208). The homophobic slur *moffie* (faggot), which permeated SADF communities, thus operated as a catch-all term to shame any deviation – and not only *actual* homosexuality – from the state's prescriptions of hypermasculinity (Van der Wal 2019). In other words, conscientious objectors to the call-up and 'border war', as well as white men who absconded from military conscription, were subject to being marked as 'faggots'. Yet, it is telling that one of the main detractors of the SADF, the End Conscription Campaign (ECC), was largely (although not exclusively) comprised of WESSA men since its inception in 1983 (Conway 2008).

The insider–outsider binary which underscored hegemonic masculinity during this time, and operated at a level of white ethnic differentiation, was therefore further entrenched by consistent attempts on the part of the state to vehemently deny the existence of Afrikaner homosexuality. In such discourses, homosexuality typically figured as a 'foreign' influence, completely alien to Afrikaner identity. In the 1960s, as the threat of homosexuality increasingly troubled the apartheid imaginary, police reports of 'indecent' practices in South African cities, for instance alleged that such proclivities were most pronounced amongst white English-speaking men (Jones 2008). The fear that male homosexuals could elude the state's gaze via participation in practices traditionally associated with heteronormativity, especially sports, was similarly inflected by ethnic stigma. Soccer, fencing, and squash, the sports that were associated with WESSA men during this time, were apparently prone to such deceits, while rugby – wrested from WESSA hands to become a salient marker of Afrikaner masculine identity in the post-1948 period[6] – was considered an impossible option for *moffies* (Jones 2008).

Thus, the figure of the *soutpiel* had also become pathologised as the potential 'carrier' of moral corruption, supported by controversy surrounding the decriminalisation of homosexuality in England (and Wales) in 1967, a year shy of the introduction of compulsory military conscription and the Immorality Amendment Bill, which sought to outlaw homosexuality in South Africa. Nationalist ideology and attendant state apparatuses such as the SADF thus ultimately manufactured a compelling scapegoat onto which a litany of imagined masculine failures, whether in terms of heterosexual virility or loyalty to the state, could be projected to valorise Afrikaner masculinity. Yet, by the time of the transition to democracy in 1994, and the implementation of constitutional rights regardless of race, gender, or sexual orientation, the gradual decline of Afrikaner nationalism had culminated in its total collapse, irretrievably severing Afrikaner masculinity from state power and, therefore, any institutionalised claims to hegemony.[7]

## Conclusion

Read against the main theoretical tenets of contemporary Critical Whiteness Studies, this history attends to how 'meanings of white race reach into concepts of labour, gender, and class' (Painter 2010: xi), thereby demanding intersectional approaches premised on the pluralities of whiteness, and resulting intra-white conflicts. This chapter proposed that the categorisation of white masculinities in South African during colonialism and apartheid operated at a multi-directional level, characterised by denigrations and admonishments hurled from one ethnic in-group to another. In this history, Afrikaner men first challenged imperial perceptions of their inaptitude for the expansion and guardianship of white sovereignty by asserting a masculine identity centred on the mythologised figure of the *voortrekker*. Further to this, early iterations of

Afrikaner national identity (emergent during and after the South African War) sought to un-dermine British hegemony by manufacturing a powerful connection between Africa and the Afrikaner people, thereby creating value-laden divisions between hardy/indigenous (Afrikaner) and delicate/foreign (British) whitenesses. Bolstered by the state, and with numerous material and symbolic advantages at their disposal, such discourses continued to circulate in the post-1948 period to elevate Afrikaner men to a hegemonic position premised on heteronormative, militarised, and nationalist modes of masculinity. WESSA men, by contrast, were painted as liberal, lily-livered, and effete, thus unable to protect white rule from black encroachment – a sheer reversal of the discourses of infirmity that Afrikaner men were subject to a century earlier. Finally, the capacity of Afrikaner men to extol their virtues in relation to WESSA men along these lines also extended to the period of South Africa's transition to democracy: In this context, the former NP leader F.W. de Klerk's popular phrase, 'Africa is not for sissies', intimates that brokering peace with people of colour and defusing the threat of civil war was a feat that only 'real' (that is, Afrikaner) men could have accomplished.

## Notes

1   A colloquially popular phrase attributed to F. W. de Klerk, the last state president from the period of white rule in South Africa (Dubin 2006).

2   As constructs of exclusivity, hegemonic masculinity and whiteness enforce boundaries that are at once inward- and outward-looking. At a macro-level, women and black men are the primary targets for the projection of difference in discourses on white masculinity. However, this chapter focuses almost exclusively on the dynamics of internal hegemony: The struggle for power and legitimacy *between* white men (Connell and Messerschmidt 2005). I therefore cannot fully account for the historical development and complexities of South African femininities, or the tenacity of indigenous (black) masculinities, which continued to exist along the lines of specific gender regimes that could be considered hegemonic on their own terms (Morrell, Jewkes and Lindegger 2012).

3   The main catalyst for the war was the discovery of gold and other rare minerals in the interior of South Africa, where the Boer republics had been established. Hence, the risk of the Afrikaners 'gaining access to economic activities which would generate fiscal resources and allow them to challenge British power' partly motivated the Empire's military campaign (Trapido and Phimister 2008: 51).

4   The war also destabilised power relations between Boer men and women, who (in the absence of male family members) had 'spawned female household heads [and] female farmers', thereby challenging the previously secure notion of the paterfamilias (Bradford 2000: 211). Thus, in the period directly fol-lowing the war, Afrikaner men first reasserted their dominance in relation to Afrikaner women.

5   When the NP came to power in 1948, the Afrikaners made up 57% of the white population in South Africa and outnumbered potential WESSA voters by 135,000 (Giliomee 2009). At the same historical juncture, 'Africans' (that is, black people) – who were effectively excluded from participation in the electoral process – comprised 68% of the total population (Giliomee 2009). The victory of the NP was therefore perceived not only as a hard-fought triumph over British imperialism in terms of national governance, but also as a salve for the 'menace' presented by the black majority.

6   While rugby was widely embraced by Afrikaner men, they had very little power in terms of the politics and administration of the sport prior to 1948 (Allen 2003). After the NP came to power, however, the *Broederbond* 'took steps to put its own people in positions of authority in the rugby establishment', thus usurping a sport with a distinctly British heritage to challenge the 'imperialist hegemony that had introduced [it] in the first place' (Allen 2003: 53).

7   The notion that the disintegration of Afrikaner nationalism has precipitated a 'crisis' of masculinity for a major constituency of Afrikaner men is often cited in contemporary research, including perspectives on the discourses deployed to rehabilitate Afrikaner patriarchy in the post-apartheid period. See, for example Sonnekus (2013) and Van der Westhuizen (2017: 149–175).

# References

Allen, D. 2003. Beating Them at Their Own Game: Rugby, the Anglo-Boer War and Afrikaner Nationalism, 1899–1948. *The International Journal of the History of Sport*, 20 (3): 37–57.

Anderson, C. E. 2008. Red Coats and Black Shields: Race and Masculinity in British Representations of the Anglo-Zulu War. *Critical Survey*, 20 (3): 6–28.

Baines, G. 2014. Masculinities, Militarisation and the End Conscription Campaign: War Resistance in Apartheid South Africa. *Journal of Contemporary African Studies*, 32 (4): 508–510.

Barris, K. 2014. The Afrikaner Grotesque: Mediating Between Colonial Self and Colonised Other in Three Post-Apartheid African Novels. *English in Africa*, 41 (1): 91–107.

Blaser, T. 2012. 'I Don't Know What I Am': The End of Afrikaner Nationalism in Post-apartheid South Africa. *Transformation: Critical Perspectives on Southern Africa*, 80 (1): 1–21.

Botma, G. J. 2008. Paying the Field: The Cultural Economy of Afrikaans at Naspers. *Ecquid Novi: African Journalism Studies*, 29 (1): 42–63.

Bozzoli, B. 1983. Marxism, Feminism and South African Studies. *Journal of Southern African Studies*, 9 (2): 139–171.

Bradford, H. 2000. Regendering Afrikanerdom: The 1899–1902 Anglo-Boer War. In *Gendered Nations: Nationalisms and Gender Order in the Long Nineteenth Century*, ed. I. Blom, K. Hagemann and C. Hall, pp. 207–225. Oxford: Berg.

Connell, R. W. and Messerschmidt, J. W. 2005. Hegemonic Masculinity: Rethinking the Concept. *Gender & Society*, 19 (6): 829–859.

Conway, D. 2004. 'All these Long-Haired Fairies Should be Forced to do Their Military Training. maybe they will Become Men'. The End Conscription Campaign, Sexuality, Citizenship and Military Conscription in Apartheid South Africa. *South African Journal on Human Rights*, 20 (2): 207–229.

Conway, D. 2008. The Masculine State in Crisis: State Response to War Resistance in Apartheid South Africa. *Men and Masculinities*, 10 (4): 422–439.

Davies, R. 2009. *Afrikaners in the New South Africa: Identity Politics in a Globalised Economy*. London: Tauris.

Davies, R. 2012. Afrikaner Capital Elites, Neo-Liberalism and Economic Transformation in Post-Apartheid South Africa. *African Studies*, 71 (3): 391–407.

Du Pisani, K. 2004. 'Ek Hou van 'n Man wat Sy Man kan Staan': Puriteinse Manlikheidsbeelde in die Afrikaanse Kultuur tot 1935. *South African Journal of Cultural History*, 18 (1): 80–93.

Du Pisani, K. 2012. Shifting Sexual Morality? Changing Views on Homosexuality in Afrikaner Society During the 1960s. *Historia*, 57 (2): 182–221.

Dubin, S. C. 2006. *Transforming Museums: Mounting Queen Victoria in a Democratic South Africa*. New York: Palgrave Macmillan.

Edlmann, T. 2012. Division in the (Inner) Ranks: The Psychosocial Legacies of the Border Wars. *South African Historical Journal*, 64 (2): 256–272.

Freschi, F. 2009. The Business of Belonging: *Volkskapitalisme*, Modernity and the Imaginary of National Belonging in the Decorative Programmes of Selected Commercial Buildings in Cape Town, South Africa, 1930-1940. *South African Historical Journal*, 61 (3): 521–549.

Gibson, D. 2010. Constructions of Masculinity, Mental Toughness and the Inexpressibility of Distress Among a Selected Group of South African Veterans of The 'Bush War' In Namibia. *Journal of Psychology in Africa*, 20 (4): 613–621.

Giliomee, H. 2001. Voëlvlug van 'n Afrikanergeskiedenis van 350 jaar. *Historia*, 46 (1): 5–24.

Giliomee, H. 2009. *The Afrikaners: Biography of a People*. Cape Town: Tafelberg.

Grundlingh, A. 2004. Reframing Remembrance: The Politics of the Centenary Commemoration of the South African War of 1899–1902. *Journal of Southern African Studies*, 30 (2): 359–375.

Johnson, C. 2002. The Dilemmas of Ethnic Privilege: A Comparison of Constructions of 'British', 'English' and 'Anglo-Celtic' Identity in Contemporary British and Australian Political Discourse. *Ethnicities*, 2 (2): 163–188.

Jones, T. F. 2008. Averting White Male (Ab)normality: Psychiatric Representations and Treatment of 'Homosexuality' in 1960s South Africa. *Journal of Southern African Studies*, 34 (2): 397–410.

Marlin-Curiel, S. 2001. Rave New World: Trance-Mission, Trance-Nationalism, And Trance-scendence in the 'New' South Africa. *The Drama Review*, 45 (3): 149–168.

Morrell, R., ed. 2001. *Changing Men in Southern Africa*. Pietermaritzburg: University of Natal Press.

Morrell, R., Jewkes, R. and Lindegger, G. 2012. Hegemonic Masculinity/Masculinities in South Africa: Culture, Power, and Gender Politics. *Men and Masculinities*, 15 (1): 11–30.

O'Meara, D. 1983. *Volkskapitalisme: Class, Capital and Ideology in The Development of Afrikaner Nationalism, 1934-1948.* Cambridge: Cambridge University Press.

Painter, N. I. 2010. *The History of White People.* New York: W.W. Norton.

Reid, G. and Walker, L., eds. 2005. *Men Behaving Differently: South African Men since 1994.* Cape Town: Double Storey.

Rodéhn, C. 2016. (Re)doing Men in Museum Exhibitions? Masculinities and the Democratization of Heritage in South Africa. In *Critical Perspectives on Masculinities and Relationalities: In Relation to What?*, ed. A. Häyrén and H. Wahlström Henriksson, pp. 67–96. Switzerland: Springer.

Roos, N. 2016. South African History and Subaltern Historiography: Ideas for a Radical History of White Folk. *International Review of Social History*, 61 (1): 117–150.

Sonnekus, T. 2013. 'We're not faggots!': Masculinity, Homosexuality and the Representation of Afrikaner Men Who have Sex with Men in the Film *Skoonheid* and Online. *South African Review of Sociology*, 44 (1): 22–39.

Steyn, M. 2001. '*Whiteness Just Isn't What It Used To Be': White Identity in a Changing South Africa.* Albany, NY: State University of New York Press.

Steyn, M. and Conway, D. 2010. Introduction: Intersecting whiteness, interdisciplinary Debates. *Ethnicities*, 10 (3): 283–291.

Swart, S. 1998. 'A Boer and His Gun and His Wife are Three Things Always Together': Republican Masculinity and the 1914 Rebellion. *Journal of Southern African Studies*, 24 (4): 737–751.

Trapido, S. and Phimister, I. 2008. Imperialism, Settler Identities and Colonial Capitalism: The Hundred Year Origins of the 1899 South African War. *Historia*, 53 (1): 45–75.

Van der Waal, K. 2008. Essentialism in a South African Discussion of Language and Culture. In *Power, Politics and Identity in South African media: selected seminar papers*, ed. A. Hadland, E. Louw, S. Sesanti and H. Wasserman, pp. 52–72. Cape Town: HSRC.

Van der Wal, E. 2019. Masculinities at War: The South African Border War and the Textual Representation of the 'Moffie'. *Journal of Literary Studies*, 35 (2): 62–84.

Van der Westhuizen, C. 2017. *Sitting Pretty: White Afrikaans Women in Postapartheid South Africa.* Pietermartizburg: UKZN Press.

Willoughby-Herard, T. 2007. South Africa's Poor Whites and Whiteness Studies: Afrikaner Ethnicity, Scientific Racism, and White Misery. *New Political Science*, 29 (4): 479–500.

# 16

# White femininity, black masculinity, and imperial sex/romance tourism: Resisting 'whitestream' feminism's single story

*Katerina Deliovsky*

## Introduction

In her popular TED Talk 'The Danger of a Single Story', Chimamanda Ngozi Adichie (2009) contends that stories matter. Many stories matter. She points out that some stories are used to dispossess, to malign and to break the dignity of people. But stories can also be used to em-power, to humanise and to repair human dignity. Stories do not exist in a vacuum, Adichie argues, and as such, it is impossible to talk about stories without talking about power – how they are told, who tells them, when they're told, how many stories are told; they are all dependent on power. Moreover, she argues, power is the ability not just to tell a story of a people, but to make it the definitive 'single story' of those peoples.

While Adichie speaks of stories in the context of fictional literature, her argument is not limited to that genre. Sociology, too, tells stories, as do all other academic disciplines. The cognitive terrain and the sociopolitical contexts of their stories exist within habitats of power. In this context, this essay is a meta-story of the 'single story' – specifically, of the history, categories of analysis and geographies of power that Feminism tells about the issue of sex/romance tourism. But being a story about stories, this essay considers the possibility of counter-stories and what they might say about the power of epistemology.

The particular counter-story this chapter tells is situated in critical narratives of whiteness and the 'peculiarities' of white femininity (Deliovsky 2010). Until some important interventions, such as Ruth Frankenberg's The *Social Construction of Whiteness: White Women Race Matters* (1993), the racialised and privileged location of white femininity was not given due attention by most white feminists (see also Spelman 1988; Stoler 1989; Ware 1992). It had been a 'presence-absence' (Sandoval 2000) animating monistic feminist theoretical articulations of womanhood. This presence–absence precipitated a call from 'subaltern' (Spivak 1988) feminists that white feminists delve into and map out the various particularities of whiteness and the privileging of white women within structures and relations of racialised gender power – locally, nationally, and globally (hooks 1984; Lugones and Spelman 1995; Moraga and Anzaldúa 1981).

DOI: 10.4324/9780429355769-16

A review of feminist literature, however, suggests these critical interventions have not fundamentally altered the single story that hegemonic white middle class feminism tells (Clark Mane 2012). It remains, indeed, the case that haunting the monistic conception of 'woman' is the presence–absence of white femininity. Theoretically and methodologically, then, this counter-story insists on the interrogation and explication of complex positionalities of power, privilege, and subordination within Feminism and its related fields. The aim here, in the words of Clare Hemmings (2011), is to tell 'stories differently'[1] (2011: 2) and to move towards feminism's 'promise' as an emancipatory politic. This movement necessitates resisting the hegemonic dominance of white feminist thought and recognising that feminism, as bell hooks states, 'is a theory in the making' – a work in progress – whereby feminists 'must necessarily criticise, question, re-examine, and explore new possibilities' (2011: 11).

Towards these goals, in the first section of this essay, I briefly recall some of the counter-stories produced by 'subaltern' feminists to delineate where the stories still need to go. The second section applies the lessons of the critical assessment to contemporary research on white women's sex/romance tourism in the Caribbean with local black men. These sex/romance tourist relations occur within 'white imperial tourism' (Alexander 1997) – the commodified tourist space for the consumption of sexualised and eroticised black bodies. This essay parses what I believe are representative samples of this sex/romance tourism literature into two broad approaches: (1) Gender/feminism approach and (2) political economy approach.[2] Specifying the strengths and limitations of those approaches, this essay mobilises counter-hegemonic 'story-telling' by sketching an alternative approach grounded in a Fanonist inspired antiracist and critical race feminism.

## Recalling feminist stories of the past: An abbreviated epistemic history

In the period known as the 'culture wars', the countering of 'second wave' whitestream feminism's single story was seriously taken up over the 1980s and 1990s in the Global North and South. Calling attention to problematic conceptualisations of equal oppression among all women and in some cases among men, critical interventions were launched by black American feminist scholars (hooks 1984), Chicana feminist scholars (i.e. Moraga and Anzaldúa 1981), postcolonial transnational feminists (i.e. Mohanty 2013), and a small coterie of white American feminists (i.e. Spelman 1988).[3]

It was argued that what has passed as 'mainstream' feminism in the Global North should have been more appropriately named 'whitestream feminism' (Grande 2003). That is, a 'feminist discourse that [was] not only dominated by white women but also principally structured on the basis of white, middle-class experience; a discourse that serve[d] their ethno-political interests and capital investments' (Grande 2003: 330). This dissembling obscured the lived reality and struggles of black, indigenous, lesbian and bi-sexual, poor/working class and women of colour in both the Global North and South. In resistance, counter-hegemonic stories took account of capitalism, colonialism, imperialism, and racism to trouble totalising discourses of gender and patriarchy. Asserting that concepts of 'woman' and patriarchy were universalising, abstract and synthetic categories, counter-hegemonic stories claimed that whitestream feminism: (a) Could not capture the complexity of racialised gender power and; (b) created a false parallelism of oppression between women *and* a false parallelism of domination between men.

Despite the epistemological and methodological interventions, they have not moved 'from margin to centre' (hooks 1984) to give way to more complex epistemologies of gender, race, and power within whitestream feminism (Grande 2003). Chandra Mohanty (2013), in fact, contends that by '"doing … whiteness as usual", … hegemonic feminist knowledge production traffics antiracist feminist scholarship across borders, domesticating women-of-colour epistemology in ways that either erase or assimilate it into a Eurocentric feminist globality' (2013: 981). As such, the conceptual logic of universal male privilege and female subordination remains intact, operating at a latent level, granting both 'innocence' (Wekker 2016) and 'positional superiority' (Said 1979) to the power of white femininity and thus to white feminism. Furthermore, within this conceptual logic, essentialisations of masculinity are grafted onto 'patriarchy' (often concealed through the mantras of class, gender, and race), positioning it as universally oppressive and dominating. This positioning includes subaltern masculinities, despite white patriarchy's denigration and brutalisation of men of colour (Curry 2017).

In the following Section 2, I trouble this persistent decontextualisation of patriarchy and gender towards reframing understandings of racialised gender power in the research on white women's sex/romance tourism in the Caribbean with local black men. This reframing is particularly important in the context of white women's sex tourism because it disturbs the assumed privileged gender position of (black) men (particularly in intersectional accounts) to seriously (re)consider how, 'being gendered [and racialized] men could ... be [a] source of oppression' (Mutua 2013: 347) rather than a source of privilege.

## Sex/romance tourism: Gender/feminism, political economy, and sketches of an alternative approach

As early as Frantz Fanon's classic anticolonial tract, *The Wretched of the Earth* (1968), scholars have registered interest in sex tourism. Focus on women as sex tourists is thin, though it is bourgeoning. My interest is with the social-sexual behaviour of white tourist women with local black men. A survey of the literature from the vantage point of feminist theory and methodology, presents two primary approaches: (1) Gender/feminism and (2) the political economy (Deliovsky 2021). This behaviour has been variously called 'cross border sexual and intimate relations' (Frohlick 2013), 'romance tourism' (Pruitt and LaFont 1995) and 'sex tourism' (Sanchez Taylor 2006). The differing labels indicate key ideological distinctions relevant for the single versus counter-hegemonic stories of feminist theory. In both instances, however, what is being described are interpersonal, sexual–economic relationships between tourists and locals/migrants that follow from contemporary and historical patterns of inequity rooted in colonialism, imperialism, and slavery (Sanchez Taylor 2011). This chapter endeavours to situate both approaches and their respective labels in relation to the single story of whitestream feminism.

## Sex/romance tourism and the gender/feminist approach

Among the first scholars to focus their research exclusively on this phenomenon of white women's sex/romance tourism in the Caribbean with black men is Deborah Pruitt and Suzanne LaFont in 'For Love and Money: Romance Tourism in Jamaica' (1995). To distinguish heterosexual male sex tourism from other tourist sexual encounters in the Caribbean, they name this phenomenon 'romance tourism'. They argue that contrary to male sex tourism, the encounters between primarily (European and American) white women and Jamaican men are potentially transformative of gender relations. Pruitt and LaFont (1995) maintain

> [w]hereas sex tourism serves to perpetuate gender roles and reinforce power relations of male dominance and female subordination, romance tourism in Jamaica provides an arena for change ... Each of them are engaged in manipulating and expanding their gender repertoires.
> *(1995: 423)*

As such, it is argued 'gender is constitutive of the relationship, not ancillary to it' (p. 423). And it is travel/tourism, Pruitt and LaFont argue, that creates the social space whereby these 'romantic' relationships are able 'to transform traditional gender roles across cultural boundaries, creating power relationships distinctive from those existing in either native society' (p. 436). In this context, Pruitt and LaFont argue white women are accorded 'new opportunities ... to liberate themselves from patriarchal authority [read: white male patriarchal authority] relations and redefine "woman"' (p. 437).

Redefining 'woman' rests on the socio-economic disparity between the tourist women and the local men because, according to Pruit and LaFont, it affords the women the exploration of a 'more dominant role in the tourism relationship' (p. 427). As such, Pruitt and LaFont conclude that power in romance tourism is fluid between the genders: 'Rather than the purview of men, dominance is rooted in various attributes such as economic power, physical strength, and personality characteristics that may reside with the man or the woman' (p. 437). To buttress their conclusion, they argue that given this fluidity,

> dominance and power are not static, but are shifting and situational, constantly negotiated and contested. As the partners in these relationships play off traditional social and gender repertoires, as well as the immediate circumstances of finance and cultural capital, the power in the relationships fluctuate between them.
>
> *(1995: 437)*

With some thematic overlap with Pruitt and LaFont's analysis, an addition to the literature on sex/romance tourism is Susan Frohlick's monograph *Sexuality, women, and tourism: Cross border desires through contemporary travel* (2013). Her anthropological account, by her own declaration, attempts to paint a more nuanced picture of these 'heterosexual crossborder relations' (Frohlick 2013: 179). And she does so to challenge what she believes is a predominant political economy framework that situates sex tourism

> as a unidimensional exertion of power where, in their pursuit of racialized exotica and erotic experiences, heterosexual Western women (often stereotyped as older, unattractive and desperate women) are seen to wield ... extraordinary economic power over disenfranchised non-Western men.
>
> *(2013: 180)*

For Frohlick, her feminist ethnography in Costa Rica (Puerto Viejo specifically) challenges this so-called 'unidimensional framework of power' that constructs the white tourist women as 'despicable' and tries to offer a more complicated account by asking the question 'Who's using who[m]?' Frohlick's answer is '... a mix of exploitation and instrumentality on *both* sides ...' (p. 180, italics mine) is the framework she puts forward.

Frohlick contends that the asymmetries of political economy place white tourist women in positions of relative power over local black Costa Rican men because their financial resources 'and also crucially, their mobility – related to their passports and citizenship in [Global North] countries ... grant them the access to go almost anywhere in the world they can afford to go' (p. 180). She maintains gender discourses, however, enable local men masculinised power regardless of socio-economic standing that enable them to 'control the town's public and semi-public spaces of leisure and informal economies and engage in performances of hyper-masculinity' (p. 179). This 'hyper-masculinity' grants the men, according to Frohlick, 'physical and symbolic power *over* heterosexual (and bisexual) tourist women for whom being desired by men is highly seductive and valued' (p. 179, italics added). In this context, she maintains 'international travel engenders eroticism through exoticism' but, it is 'locality and actual corporeal gendered beings that shape the outcomes of sexual exchange' (p. 172).

No doubt, Frohlick and Pruitt and LaFont both labour to bring complexity to a social phenomenon that has been given little in-depth scholarly attention. In the final analysis, however, and contrary to their 'good' intentions, they do a disservice to understanding how racialised gender systems and identities are inextricably intertwined, given colonialist and white supremacist contexts of transnational dominance.

Frohlick's assertions of 'mutual exploitation' and Pruitt and LaFont's notions of 'mutually imbricating cycles of exploitation' suggest an equivalent partnership of sorts through the checks and balances of their respective class, gender, race locations. They assume the 'hypermasculinity' of the local men counters the economic power and mobility of the tourist women and consequently, they are positioned on a relatively equivalent terrain of power. Such over determinations of the micro-dimensional aspects of these relations elide the ways the white women's embodiment within colonial, imperial, and racist contexts mobilise the political and economic power of the Global North *and* the racialised gender power accessible to the women in these transnational locations. If we, indeed, follow Frohlick's line of reasoning regarding the 'physical and symbolic power' of the local men, and Pruitt and LaFont's argument of gender/power fluidity in romance tourism we are left with an uncomfortable conclusion. And that is that the gender/feminist approach to women and sex/romance tourism is an instrumental methodology which appropriates for white women the best of all worlds. On one hand, they are powerless as victims of a white heteropatriarchy that constrains and restricts their autonomy at home and, therefore, they are granted innocence in the practicing of power. On the other hand, they get to exercise racialised gender power and transcend 'heteropatriarchy' vis-à-vis cross-border travel and sex/romance with poor 'black' men in the Caribbean who have physical and symbolic power over them. The evasions and elisions of white women's racialised gender power and consequently black men's racialised gender dis-empowerment – reflecting a pervasive lacuna in 'whitestream' feminist understandings of race, gender, and power – allow for these seemingly contradictory conclusions. As such, the black male sex/romance worker becomes the straw horse for white women's sexual and personal liberation in these 'white imperial' (Alexander 1997) locations.

Such gender-focused, race-absent (with a splash of class) analyses are troubling for the reasons highlighted, and because they diminish and/or erase the actual vulnerabilities and traumas experienced by black men who are sex/romance tourist workers. These erasures are made possible because racialised gender evasions and elisions provide the analytical space for tropes of black masculinity to easily slip into the theoretical void and function as what Tommy Curry (2017) calls *genre* (rather than gender) – 'a cog in a conceptual scheme that reduces Black male life to the examples, or proof, of a predetermined abstraction' (p. 203). The reduction of poor and working class black men to a *genre* enables moralistic denunciations of them such as unsavoury, licentious, and manipulating. As a result, capturing the full humanity of black men as complex material beings made in and by history and vulnerable to sexual exploitation in these sex/romance tourist contexts (and beyond) is rendered a conceptual and, therefore, a material impossibility.

From a Fanonist perspective black men are overdetermined as a 'sociogenic' a priori in the white cultural imaginary, from which not even researchers are immune. In the end, by claiming both parties engage in mutual exploitation or that power, like a fluid, fluctuates between them enables gender/feminist researchers to disavow the significance of race (and class) while over-determining gender (as this social category is essentialised as female only) in their framings of power and subjectivity.

## Political economy approach

Highlighting some of the conceptual and theoretical problems associated with existing analyses, Sanchez Taylor (2001, 2006) points out that the distinction between romance tourism and sex tourism is often split along gendered lines. Women's encounters are more likely to be categorised as 'romance tourism', whereas men's encounters are often referred to as 'sex tourism'. Her ethnographic research suggests sexual–economic exchanges between tourist women and local men in Jamaica and the Dominican Republic, map onto and are 'predicated on the same global economic and social inequalities [of structural adjustment managed by the World Bank, the International Monetary Fund and the World Trade Organization] that underpin the phenomenon of male sex tourism' (Sanchez Taylor 2006: 44). And as such, any distinction on the structuring dynamics that informs both processes is problematic. Furthermore, male and female sex tourists may exhibit similar 'sex tourist' behaviour yet are conceptualised differently.

It is in this context that Sanchez Taylor (2006) launches a criticism of the 'overlooked' similarities between men and women tourists from the 'overdeveloped' Global North. She argues these overlooked similarities shared 'between male and female sex tourism reflects and reproduces weaknesses in existing theoretical and common-sense understandings of gendered power, sexual exploitation, prostitution and sex tourism' (2006: 42). Much of this failing rests on the fact that 'North American and European feminist' (p. 45) discussions on sex work is informed by a Radical Feminist approach. This view largely ignores male sex work and focuses on female sex workers as 'victim[s] of male sexual violence ... or whether they are engaging in "free choice" prostitution wherein female prostitutes are autonomous agents choosing to sell their sexual labour' (p. 45). Male sex work, according to Sanchez Taylor, has been overlooked because victimisation in this tradition is a 'gendered' concept (Lamb 1999) that is essentialised as the descriptive property of 'woman'. Women are constructed as victims and men as their victimisers. Given the refusal of an alternate possibility, it is consequently difficult to conceptualise the ways men might be sexually exploited by women (Curry 2017). She explains that Radical Feminist theory, for example posits sexuality as a fundamental location of male power and it is in the heterosexual sex act that 'women submit to men, and men affirm their masculinity and patriarchal power by penetrating the female body' (p. 47).

This theorisation of gender power as male domination fixes female and male relations in as master/slave framework and treats them as undifferentiated social groups. Consequently, Sanchez Taylor argues, it obscures the importance of age, class and race 'for an individual's social power and life chances' (Sanchez Taylor 2006: 47). This point is crucial because much of the research on sex tourism generally begins from the premise 'that it represents a form of prostitute use and can, therefore, be primarily explained in terms of patriarchal power relations' (p. 45). In this framework, women cannot actually be sex tourists (and men cannot be prostitutes), hence, the term 'romance tourism'. These essentialist conceptualisations of gender, sexuality, and patriarchy 'preclude the possibility that a woman can sexually exploit a man' (p. 44), and conceals the ways women are sexual agents, especially if racialised power dynamics are obscured or ignored (see also Sanchez Taylor 2001).

As a result of such taken-for-granted configurations, we have limited insight into how gender within these sex tourist relationships is multi-varied and complex and that 'in some circumstances, women can pursue a social ideal of heterosexuality without automatically placing themselves in a subordinate position' (Sanchez Taylor 2006: 52). Importantly, Sanchez

Taylor emphasises, 'if [White] women are not necessarily subordinated by the heterosexual sex act, then it becomes possible to recognise that they too can, in certain circumstances, sexually exploit [black] men' (p. 52). This recognition necessitates an epistemic project that rejects claims of 'mutual exploitation' and the 'theoretical privileging of [male] gender power over questions of racism and racialized power' (Sanchez Taylor 2001: 258).

## An alternative approach: Anchoring sex/romance tourist relationships in a diverse analytics and politics of agency/power

The necessity of the epistemic project to which Sanchez Taylor alerts us requires an alternative approach. This approach must seriously engage with Sanchez Taylor's anticolonial insights by anchoring the 'thick descriptions' of the gender/feminist approach in the political economy of sex/romance tourism. Additionally, and more importantly for me, it requires a Fanonist in-spired antiracist and critical race feminism's analytics and politics of agency/power. The objective is to open up new possibilities for epistemological and methodological (re) framings that do not evade or obscure complex racialised gender power dimensions through essentialising analytic categories.

Anne McClintock's 'articulated categories' (1995) is one possibility. Describing the conceptual framework that informed her examination of power and Western Imperialism, she explains '...race, gender and class are not distinct realms of experience, existing in splendid isolation from each other; nor can they be simply yoked together retrospectively like armatures of Lego' (McClintock 1995: 5). They are articulated categories, McClintock argues, and are not 'reducible to, or identical with, each other; instead, they exist in intimate, reciprocal and contradictory relations' (p. 5). These categories, for example placed colonial white women 'ambiguously' in the imperial process. While marital, property, and land laws and 'the in-tractable violence of male decree bound [Colonial women] in gendered patterns of disadvantage and frustration' (p. 6), McClintock explains, the women nonetheless experienced 'the rationed privileges of race' that located them 'in positions of decided – if *borrowed* – power', (p. 6, italics mine) over both colonised women and men. As such, and central to the alternative approach, white women were/are not unfortunate 'onlookers of empire' (p. 6), but 'complicit both as colonizers and colonized, privileged and restricted, acted upon and acting' (p. 6; see also Kitossa 2002; Ware 1992) – all in relation to a degraded colonised other. It is through this under-standing of articulated categories that we can counter the single story and examine white women's sex tourism with black men as a site for the reproduction of relations of dominance and through which the historicity of empire articulates itself as – 'white imperial tourism' (Alexander 1997) – to produce racialised gender power.

Focused on the context of 'white imperial tourism', the conceptual logic of articulated ca-tegories enables the possibility to avoid the essentialist and stultifying categories of whitestream feminism and the commodification and exoticisation of black men as a *genre*. These connections are realised through a Fanonist inspired antiracist and critical race feminism examination of ex-isting sex/romance tourist narratives. Before doing so, it bears repeating here that white women's striving for autonomy and sovereignty in these sex/romance tourism contexts occurs within and is made possible by the very structuration of contemporary 'white imperial tourism'. It has created the place, space, and conditions for white women to pursue 'personal growth and/or en-vironmentalism and mid-life transformations' on and through the locations, cultures, and bodies of black local men (and women). As such, these sex/romance tourist relations can never be intimate and erotic spaces of 'mutual exploitation', or of romance, companionship, and personal transformation outside of the inequities of 'white imperial tourism'.

Be that as it may, 'practices of knowing and not-knowing' (Wekker 2016) ignore, obscure or minimise how sex/romance tourism in the Global South is located within profound asymmetries of power, which position both white men *and* women as 'imperial tourists' (Alexander 1997: 68). These asymmetries provide the 'imperial tourist' as the 'invisible subject of colonial law' (1997: 68), with a population in her/his service; thus, enabling a high degree of personal and sexual command over themselves and colonised others (see also Davidson and Sanchez Taylor 2005). Yet, recognition of the processes and structures instrumental to 'white imperial tourism' is denied through the theoretical evasions/elisions of gendered racialised power that construct colonised black men as 'with gender power' and complicit and/or active in their own sexual/racial exploitation and white women as 'without gender power' and innocent and/or ignorant of the process.

The emphasis on the inseparable role of white imperial tourism and the racialised gendered dimensions that shapes the men's and women's sexual/erotic exchange is not simply theoretic conjecture – it is actually revealed in the narratives of female sex/romance tourist themselves. Such representative narratives can be found in Frohlick's ethnography. In one narrative, for example Frohlick (2013) recounts her research participant's (Carolyn), description of her two sexual encounters 'with a "really beautiful rasta" and "a pretty rasta"':

> They are really amazing in bed. Not in a giving way at all. Not like they're going to perform oral sex for an hour to you. No. They're in really good shape most of them. A lot of them surf so they're strong through the middle. Powerful, passionate, crazy sex. Crazy wild *jungle sex* [emphasis added].
>
> *(Frohlick 2013: 144)*

In prodding Carolyn to expand on the notion of 'jungle sex', Frohlick asks 'How different are they as lovers from Canadian guys?' (read: Most likely 'white guys' since these were her first sexual encounters with black men) (p. 144). Carolyn responds that,

> A lot of women don't like to admit it, but I think they like to be manhandled, not have to be in charge, not have to initiate things. It's macho … The two that I had sex with, they're just powerful. More *animalistic*. None of this 'Are you okay?' None of them are ever going to give you a massage. None of them are ever going to give you oral sex. It's just *powerful* [emphasis added].
>
> *(2013: 144)*

Indeed, perceiving the sex with black men as 'not giving' and the men being perceived as 'macho', 'powerful', and 'more animalistic' than (white) Canadian men, resulted in 'crazy wild jungle sex' that was intensely pleasurable for Carolyn. We can certainly extrapolate from this narrative that sex with the black man as a *genre* amplified Carolyn's erotic excitement, but this is only one possibility for what made her experience of the sex so 'powerful and animalistic'.

Pointing to a possibility is Gargi Bhattacharyya's (2002) Fanonist inspired analysis on power disparities and erotic racism. She argues that 'without the sense that the object of desire is lesser, dangerous, and forbidden – alluringly other and beyond any everyday social contact – there is no exoticist dynamic' (Bhattacharyya 2002: 106). In this context, Carolyn's designation of the sex as more powerful and animalistic is precisely because the black man is imagined not as a fully formed human being, but as an animal (See Fanon 1986 [1952]). Bhattacharyya explains that '…there is something about being socially disadvantaged, or even degraded, that makes for exoticisation'

(2002: 104). The power inequity between the exoticist (white women) and the exoticised (black men) 'heightens the sexual hit' (p. 102). Bhattacharyya states,

> When we examine the cultural products of exoticism, each instance comes from a very tangible set of political relations ... In exoticism the desired object is your slave, your enemy, your absolute other – the desire may fixate on the anticipation of danger of the pleasure of dominating the weak or the adventure of an alien and forbidden experience, but each scenario demands that the object has less agency and access to mainstream power than the one who desires.
>
> *(2002: 107)*

Bhattacharyya extrapolation of the one who desires versus the one who is desired, clearly challenges notions of exploitation as 'mutual' or conceptions of power as 'fluid' and 'shifting'.

The narratives of the sex/romance tourists themselves are, again, particularly illuminating of the inequities of 'exoticism' in 'white imperial tourism'. Examining another narrative taken from Frohlick's (2013) ethnography, she recounts how unabashedly her participant, Annabelle, seemed in expressing her desire to have sexual relations with any local man that appealed to her – '"I want this one and this one!" she exclaimed, referring to the "hot" bodies of local men who were in her eyes, "gorgeous", "hard" and "beautiful" [and "exotic"]'. Racial overtones are evident in her narratives of 'cross border' sex, Frohlick reports, 'including stereotypes about 'black guys' as naturally skilled dancers and athletes' (2013: 128). As Annabelle and 'her friends go out on their nightly jaunts to the town's hot spots to seek out the sexiest local "hotties"' Frohlick explains 'the local men are objectified as hers for the picking' (p. 128).

It is within the context of 'white imperial tourism' that white women can invert the traditional white heteropatriarchal gender script and objectify these men as theirs 'for the picking'. White women's positional superiority, their whiteness – their racial and to some degree class assignment relative to the men's – grants them the social/racial mobility to engage in these sex/romance tourist encounters. But more importantly in some ways, the construction of the women as without power and innocent (and victimised by rapacious black men) disguises the extent and quality of their participation in white domination. Kate Davy (1995) explains that, paradoxically, white women can never 'fully embody the unembodied dimension of white masculinity, for to 'embody' is still [their] definition and destiny' (p. 197). And while they can never fully embody white masculinity, sex/romance tourism in the Global South positions these women, even white working-class women, to enact power conferred by their whiteness. These sex tourist relationships rely on 'explicit and comprehensible power disparity' to fulfil its erotically charged potential, but white women's role 'as the subject who desires' gets muddied by arguments of mutual exploitation. And this is made possible precisely because it is the disenfranchised hypersexual Black man as a *genre* who is the 'object of her desire'.

## Conclusion

I want to close this essay by reiterating this point – the epistemic and discursive race-neutral account of gender and patriarchy identified in the gender/feminist approach on sex/romance tourism reflects a pervasive lacuna in 'whitestream' feminism's theorisations of race, gender, and power. This omission is and can be addressed by the mobilisation of the counter stories of white feminist hegemony – an alternative approach – representing the transition from deconstruction to reconstruction and an open engagement with the histories of colonialism, imperialism, and racism.

Fanon (1986 [1952]) contends, referring to the deeply embedded and pervasive 'single story' about the black *man* as solely determined by his precocious genitalia (which is the mark of his unalterable negation demanded by white 'civilisation'), there are '… legends, stories, and above all historicity' (p. 112). Historicity in these sex/romance tourist contexts, refers to an a priori 'field of racial and sexual visibility' (Butler 1993: 17; Fanon 1986 [1952]) forged in colonial violence that profoundly affects all aspects of these relationships. Serious consideration needs to be given to the disjuncture between analytical categories established by disciplines for how they synchronise with historical patterns of colonialism, imperialism, and racism. In this case, the single story of feminism frames and imposes meaning on how white tourist women and black local men themselves experience the sex/romance tourist relationship in ways consistent with how media discourses and popular culture conceptualise and interpret them through a range of prisms. In the final analysis, this phenomenon makes it all the more important for countering the single story of gender versus genre established by whitestream feminism. What I conclude here is that researchers/scholars (white, feminist, and otherwise) must be attentive to the hearing of this historicity as the backdrop and source of the drama, not just in the context of sex/romance tourism, and in how their research is implicated in the epistemic violence of a single story.

## Notes

1 I appreciate Clare Hemmings (2011) work on the political grammar of feminist storytelling in *Why Stories Matter: The political grammar of feminist theory*. But I take issue with her assertion that 'feminist theory … occupies a position of reflexive non-innocence' (p. 2) that can potentially 'break open' the global power relations that feminist theory is entangled in. This claim is, itself, a story about feminism that needs a counter-story.
2 There is a larger body of scholarship that explores women's sex/romance tourism as part of a broader examination of sex work as a whole, including men's sex tourism. There is also research that examines women's sex/romance tourism with Asian, Southeast Asian, and African men. I do not analyse these scholarships.
3 These accounts do not focus on the theory of patriarchy specifically, but on challenging the monistic accounting of gender.

## References

Adichie, C. N. 2009. 'The danger of a single story' [online]. *TEDGlobal 2009*, viewed 24 June 2020, https://www.ted.com/talks/chimamanda_ngozi_adichie_the_danger_of_a_single_story.

Alexander, M. J. 1997. Erotic Autonomy as a Politics of Decolonization: An Anatomy of Feminist and State Practice in the Bahamas Tourist Economy. In *Feminist Genealogies, Colonial Legacies, Democratic Futures*, ed. M. J. Alexander and C. T. Mohanty, pp. 63–100. New York: Routledge.

Bhattacharyya, G. 2002. The Exotic. In *Sexuality and Society: An Introduction,* ed. G. Bhattacharyya, pp. 102–197. London: Routledge.

Butler, J. 1993. Endangered/Endangering: Schematic racism and white paranoia. In *Reading Rodney King, Reading Urban Uprising*, ed. R. Gooding-Williams, pp. 15–22. London: Routledge.

Clark Mane, R. L. 2012. Transmuting Grammars of Whiteness in Third-Wave Feminism: Interrogating Postrace Histories, Postmodern Abstraction, and the Proliferation of Difference in Third-Wave Texts. *Signs*, 38 (1): 71–98.

Crenshaw, K. 1989. Demarginalizing the Intersection of Race and Sex: A Black Feminist Critique of Antidiscrimination Doctrine, Feminist Theory, and Antiracist Politics. *University of Chicago Legal Forum*, 1 (8): 139–167.

Curry, T. J. 2017. *The Man-Not: Race, Class, Genre, and The Dilemmas of Black Manhood*. Philadelphia: Temple University Press.

Davidson, J. O. C. and Sanchez Taylor, J. 2005. Travel and Taboo: Heterosexual Sex Tourism to the Caribbean. In *Regulating Sex: The Politics of Intimacy and Identity,* ed. E. Bernstein and L. Schaffner, pp. 83–99. New York: Routledge.

Davy, K. 1995. Outing Whiteness: A Feminist/Lesbian Project. *Theatre Journal,* 47 (2): 189–205.

Deliovsky, K. 2010. *White Femininity: Race, Gender and Power.* Halifax: Fernwood Publishing.

Deliovsky, K. 2021. White Femininity, Black Masculinity, Sex/Romance Tourism, and the Politics of Feminist Theory: Theorizing Desire and Erotic Racism. In *Appealing Because He is Appalling : Black Masculinities, Colonialism, and Erotic Racism,* ed. T. Kitossa, pp. 105-139. Edmonton, Alberta, Canada: University of Alberta Press.

Fanon, F. 1968. *The Wretched of the Earth.* New York: Grove Press.

Fanon, F. 1986 [1952]. *Black Skin, White Masks.* Charles Lam Markmann (Trans.). London: Pluto Press.

Frankenberg, R. 1993. *The Social Construction of Whiteness: White Women, Race Matters.* Minneapolis: University of Minnesota Press.

Frohlick, S. 2013. *Sexuality, Women, and Tourism: Cross-Border Desires Through Contemporary Travel.* New York: Routledge.

Grande, S. 2003. Whitestream and the Colonialist Project: A Review of Contemporary Feminist Pedagogy and Praxis. *Educational Theory,* 53 (3): 329–346.

Hemmings, C. 2011. *Why Stories Matter: The Political Grammar of Feminist Theory.* Durham, NC: Duke University Press.

hooks, b. 1984. *Feminist Theory: From Margin to Center.* Boston: Sound End Press.

Kitossa, T. 2002. Criticism, Reconstruction and African-Centred Feminist Historiography. In *Back to the Drawing Board: African Canadian Feminisms,* ed. N. Wane, K. Deliovsky and E. Lawson, pp. 85–128. Toronto: Sumach Press.

Lamb, S. 1999. *New Versions of Victims: Feminist Struggle with the Concept.* London: New York University Press.

Lugones, M. and Spelman. E. 1995. Have We Got a Theory for You! Feminist Theory, Cultural Imperialism and the Demand for the 'the Woman's Voice'. In *Feminism and Philosophy: Essential Readings in Theory, Reinterpretation and Application,* ed. N. Tuana and R. Tong, pp. 494–507. Boulder: Westview Press.

McClintock, A. 1995. *Imperial Leather: Race, Gender and Sexuality in the Colonial Contest.* New York: Routledge.

Mohanty, C. T. 2013. Transnationalist Feminist Crossings: On Neoliberalism and Radical Critique. *Signs: Journal of Women in Culture and Society,* 38 (4): 967–991.

Moraga, C. and Anzaldúa, G. E. 1981. *This Bridge Called My Back: Writings by Radical Women of Color.* Watertown, MA: Persephone Press.

Mutua, A. D. 2013. Multidimensionality Is to Masculinities What Intersectionality Is to Feminism. *Nevada Law Journal,* 13: 341–983.

Pruitt, D. and LaFont, S. 1995. For Love and Money: Romance Tourism in Jamaica. *Annals of Tourism Research,* 22 (2): 422–440.

Said, E. 1979. *Orientalism.* New York: Vintage Books.

Sanchez Taylor, J. 2001. Dollars are a Girl's Best Friend? Female Tourists' Sexual Behaviour in the Caribbean. *Sociology,* 35 (3): 749–764.

Sanchez Taylor, J. 2006. Female Sex Tourism: A Contradiction in Terms? *Feminist Review,* 83: 42–59.

Sanchez Taylor, J. 2011. Sex Tourism and Inequalities. In *Tourism and Inequality. Problems and Prospects,* ed. S. Cole and N. Morgan, pp. 49–66. Wallingford, Oxfordshire, UK: CABI.

Sandoval, C. 2000. *Methodology of the Oppressed.* University of Minnesota Press.

Spelman, E. 1988. *Inessential Woman: Problems of Exclusion in Feminist Thought.* Boston: Beacon Press.

Spivak, G. C. 1988. Can the Subaltern Speak? In *Marxism and the Interpretation of Culture,* ed. C. Nelson and L. Grossberg, pp. 271–313. Basingstoke: Macmillan.

Stoler, A. 1989. Making Empire Respectable: The Politics of Racial and Sexual Morality in Twentieth-century Colonial Cultures. *American Ethnologist,* 16 (4): 634–660.

Ware, V. 1992. *Beyond the Pale. White Women, Racism and History.* New York: Verso.

Wekker, G. 2016. *White Innocence: Paradoxes of Colonialism and Race.* Durham: Duke.

# 17

# Paradoxes of racism: Whiteness in *Gay Pages* magazine

*Lwando Scott*

Never again, and yet again and again, even now, never more so before our very eyes. Seeing but not; seeing but not believing; believing but immediately not my problem, our problem; seeing and believing but frozen from action, too distracted or busy or unconcerned to do anything about it; acting but not in concert, not concertedly.

*(Goldberg 2009: 156)*

## Introduction

The earlier mentioned passage is from Goldberg articulating the 'paradoxes of racism' in 2009, and his articulation remains relevant as it eloquently captures racism's continuation in 2021. It is in the context of the continuation of racism, 'yet again and again', that I return to the analysis of *Gay Pages* (2020) magazine. It is a return, because in 2007 I wrote my honours thesis on the representation of black gay men, or rather the lack thereof, in *Gay Pages* magazine (Scott 2007). At the time, the magazine was 13-years old, and had never had a black person on the cover.[1] I, a black queer postgraduate student at the time, still fashioning my own queer identity, I was looking for black queer representation everywhere, and it was hard to find; ironically, especially hard to find in *Gay Pages* magazine. In 2019, I had my first 'return' to *Gay Pages*, while attending the *Queer African Visualities* conference at Northwest University. Two white gay men, representatives from *Gay Pages*, spoke about an upcoming cover of *Gay Pages*, the first cover that would feature a black man (see Figure 18.1). However, there was still a catch; the cover would feature the black man with his white partner. The *Gay Pages* representatives were pitching this inter-racial cover with the first black face as 'progress' at *Gay Pages*. I, along with others at the conference, objected to the idea that *Gay Pages* was making 'progress', instead argued that the magazine continues to synonymise whiteness with gayness, and consequently anti-black. In this regard, South African scholars Sonnekus and van Eeden (2009: 92) have pointed out that 'whereas black men appear infrequently in queer publications like Gay Pages, images of white men grace nearly every advertising image, cover and feature article'. Therefore, to label having an inter-racial cover 24 years into the magazine's existence in a country with majority black population as 'progress' is reaching. Given the history of the overrepresentation

DOI: 10.4324/9780429355769-17

of whiteness in *Gay Pages* magazine covers, the question then becomes, what is the function of this sole inter-racial cover? What does this inter-racial cover do, given the historical omission of blackness on the cover?

My honours thesis titled *How 'Race' is Implicated in the Construction of Gay Identities in South Africa's Gay Media: An Inspection of Gay Pages Magazine* was researched and written in 2007 (Scott, 2007). Through content and discourse analysis, I critiqued the lack of black representation in *Gay Pages*, and how this omission of blackness continuously constructs Africanness and gayness as mutually exclusive. Since then, other South African scholars have also engaged the whiteness, and subsequent lack of blackness, in *Gay Pages*. The work of Sonnekus and van Eeden (2009) and Carolin (2019) are great examples, where they have interrogated the intersections of race, sexuality, and other cultural meanings of *Gay Pages*. Similarly to my thesis' conclusions, Sonnekus and van Eeden (2009) and Carolin (2019) critique the lack of representation of black men and the casting of whiteness as the only representation of gayness thereby creating white gay hegemony. Ironically, *Gay Pages* is outdone by magazines geared towards the heterosexual market that have come a long way with racial representation (Sonnekus and van Eeden 2009). In this then, it becomes important to critically think about the intersections of race and sexuality in post-apartheid South Africa. Heeding the arguments of Nast (2002) about queer patriarchs and queer racism, it becomes necessary for us to question the overrepresentation of whiteness, and the negation of blackness in the presenting of gayness in *Gay Pages*.

The social conditions, including the politics of sexuality, in post-colonial and post-apartheid South Africa necessitate an understanding of the ramifications of colonialism and apartheid, systems that perpetuated white supremacy. South Africa was colonized by the Netherlands in 1652 and Great Britain in 1795, where the indigenous people who resided in these parts of the world were disposed of their land and livestock (Mellet 2020; Oliver and Oliver 2017). The land dispossession of indigenous people was through a series of wars throughout the eighteenth century (Laband 2020; Ngcukaitobi 2018). These wars led to dispossession that was followed by the Anglo-Boer War, where two independent Boer states and Great Britain battled over land (Nasson 2011). The white settler invasions, the wars, and the dispossession of land for indigenous people altered the history of what we now know as South Africa. Post the Anglo-Boer War South Africa was unified in 1910 in a new country called the Union of South Africa, but the unification was only for white settlers and discriminated against indigenous populations. Pivotally, in 1948 the National Party continued and intensified racial discrimination and segregation with even harsher discrimination towards indigenous people in a racial legal system called apartheid (Clark and Worger 2016; Gordon 2017). In racialized apartheid South Africa, 'Slegs Blankes' (Whites Only) philosophy and signage governed and segregated people in all spheres of life including the social, political, economic, and geographical areas. The apartheid system formally ended in the early 1990s with the release of political prisoners who had been arrested for defying apartheid laws, and the first democratic elections took place in 1994, where Nelson Mandela became president. In 2021, we are living in democratic South Africa, but the legacies of colonialism and apartheid discrimination, segregation, and economic disparities continue, albeit with modifications. Similarly to other postcolonial contexts, in a Fanonian sense, South Africa suffers from postcolonial problems captured in Fanon's (1963) seminal *Wretched of the Earth*. This then means that the politics of sexuality are not, and cannot be divorced from serious engagement with colonial and apartheid legacies as those legacies remain in the everyday navigation of social life. Therefore, white gay men's identities are implicated in the continued constructions of whiteness in post-apartheid South Africa.

In democratic South Africa, while the South African Constitution is lauded as the most liberal in the world, and the first to include protection against discrimination for sexual orientation, queer people's lived realities are heavily shaped by apartheid inscribed racial identities. Throughout the post-apartheid era, the gay and lesbian movement, through the constitutional protection, fought for and gained civil rights, culminating, as it were, in the legalisation of same-sex marriage (Judge et al. 2008; Massoud, 2003). However, access to these civil rights is mitigated by race and class, meaning that white queers, who because of colonial and apartheid legacies, are more likely to be middle class, are shielded from discrimination by virtue of their whiteness and access to economic resources. Whereas black queers, who because of colonial and apartheid legacies, are more likely to be the working poor, and are subjected to harsh discriminations and violence, and are not shielded by economic resources (Mkhize et al. 2010). What becomes apparent in democratic South Africa is the mechanisms in which whiteness is deployed, in this instance by *Gay Pages*, and by white queers in general, to solicit white solidarity in the aims to soften difference. The aim here is the integration of white men who have sex with men into existing power structures (Carolin 2019), an important theme in the sexuality politics in post-apartheid South Africa as exhibited by the successful fight for inclusion, which can also be read as assimilation, into heteronormativity, via same-sex marriage (Scott 2019a).

Introduced through colonialism and strengthened through apartheid legislation, white supremacist values and ideals continue to plague post-apartheid South Africa. South African scholars writing on race – Steyn (2001), Erasmus and De Wet (2003), Steyn and Foster (2008), and Van der Westhuizen (2017) – all demonstrate the continuities of resistant whiteness in post-apartheid South Africa. According to Mills (2003) white supremacy is a 'global social system' (p. 36) that 'clearly comes into existence through European expansion and the imposition of European rule through settlement and colonialism' (p. 38). It is a system where European history, culture, and society dominates and denigrates non-European peoples socially, politically, and economically, often through violent means. What underpins white supremacy is the supposed 'superiority' of European descended people and the supposed 'inferiority' of non-Europeans. *Gay Pages*, South Africa's longest running gay publication, introduced in 1994, ironically at the dawn of democracy, is a concentration of white supremacy. The magazine is a demonstration of the refusal of whiteness to give up power and privilege, a refusal really, to exist *with* blackness. Here then, Canadian scholar Rinaldo Walcott's (2021) articulations about black freedom become relevant, that we are living in the time of the long emancipation, characterised by legal reform, likes of which are found in post-apartheid South Africa, but we are yet to arrive at freedom, which would entail substantive radical change where black people are no longer regarded as sub-human.

Through an intersectional analysis, this chapter interrogates the white supremacist characterisation of gayness in *Gay Pages*. In this chapter, I am reflecting on *Gay Pages*, and advancing three inter-related points. First, *Gay Pages* peddles white supremacist notions, and through its centring of white cis-normative male bodies actively contributes to the suppression and erasure of black queers. Second, the dominant white representations in *Gay Pages* tell us much about the continued racist assumptions about beauty, and desirable bodies in the gay subculture in post-apartheid South Africa. The racism of *Gay Pages* is linked to racial fetishisation where blackness is characterised as unique, hence a singular black cover in *Gay Pages* history, and how this functions as the denial and misrepresentation of black sexuality. Third, in conclusion, I am arguing for radical queer politics that foreground the intersection of identities and social positions as shaped by colonial and apartheid history. I am arguing for an expansive sexuality politics that takes intersectionality seriously both as a theory of understanding queer South

African lives, and as appreciating the different lived realities experienced by those queers. The kind of politics, the kind of engagement, and the kind of LGBTI community that is being set up by the white supremacist representations in *Gay Pages* are detrimental to building solid LGBTI communities grounded in freedom, built on radical change. Furthermore, while I write about 'black gay men' here as a collective, I am mindful that black gay men are not monolithic; that they themselves as a group are diverse, but they share, as diverse as they are, the systemic disadvantage of non-representation in *Gay Pages*.

## *Gay Pages* magazine

*Gay Pages* magazine, like other magazines, is a cultural institutional and plays a role in reflecting and representing communities. *Gay Pages* was created and is currently edited by Rubin van Niekerk, to represent and cater to the gay community. *Gay Pages* was one of the few gay publications available in South Africa at the dawn of democracy. *Gay Pages* was first published in 1994, the same year South Africa held its first democratic elections and Nelson Mandela became president. *Gay Pages* describes itself as the largest gay publication in South Africa, published by Association Business Network PTY (Ltd) in Johannesburg. The magazine positions itself as the premier gay magazine in South Africa, published every season, therefore four publications a year. *Gay Pages* is a glossy magazine that features high end products and premium brands with a clear target market of middle-to-upper-class gay men. The magazine has a continuous stream of advertising hotels, expensive cars, travel destinations, and gay cultural events like Pride. While the magazine has more than a fair share of men in tiny designer speedos and underwear, it has a respectability aesthetic that shies away from 'too' much sex. The respectability aesthetic of *Gay Pages* is constituted by a white male cisgender performance that is all too aware to not be too sissy-like, and is hinged on normative middle-class heterosexual norms that are positioned as antithesis to blackness [see Joshi, (2012) on respectable queerness].

## The focus on the cover

In this chapter, while the focus is on the magazine and its politics of representation in general, the analysis was sparked by and narrows in on the inter-racial cover of the Autumn 2019 issue of *Gay Pages*. The image on the Gay Pages Autumn 2019 cover is of a white man and a black man. It is a head and shoulders shot, and both men are shirtless, young looking, and well groomed. The white man is standing behind the black man in an embrace, where the white man's head rests on the black man's back. The black man is taller than the white man, and almost tilts his head backwards in the embrace. They are both looking to their side with serious non-smiling faces. There is even a bit of a frown in their foreheads. The black man has metallic glittery dust on his neck, and the white man has pink dust on his. The image looks like a studio image with a background almost resembling the skin colour of the black man, almost fading into the background, while still visible. The black man has a shaved head, and the white man has a full head of black hair.[2]

As described in the introduction, when I first learned about the inter-racial cover, it was introduced as 'progress' for *Gay Pages*. The inter-racial cover left me with many questions; it was peculiar given the history of no black person on the cover for 24 years of the magazine's existence. The cover image is also of an inter-racial couple; therefore, the magazine cover still has a white face to accompany the black face. Why is this the case? This remains the only issue of *Gay Pages* with a black person on the cover, and I can't help but wonder what this means for future covers. The singular inter-racial cover seats uncomfortably in the history of white covers, and the white covers since the inter-racial cover. It is the discomfort brought about by this singular inter-racial cover, a discomfort that was evident when some of us expressed concern over the billing of the cover as 'progress' for *Gay Pages*, that I want to interrogate in this chapter using intersectionality. Considering the history of *Gay Pages*, the history of colonialism, and that of apartheid, what exactly is the function of this cover?

## Racism and intersectionality

In theorising about the disruption of Johannesburg Pride in 2012 by a group of feminist black lesbians called *One in Nine*, I argue for the importance of intersectionality as a tool of understanding the fissures in the sexuality movement in South Africa (Scott 2017). Similarly writing about the pride disruption, South African scholar and activist Judge (2018: 100) argued that 'the Pride protest was a performative destabilisation of norms that regulate who is eligible for recognition and signalled a refusal of the deniability of particularised queer subjectivities'. The message was clear, in advancing queer politics in South Africa it is necessary to address anti-black racism in politics of sexuality. Scholars and activists working in the field of sexuality have to examine the multiple ways that race and ethnicity intersect with sexuality in different contexts and what that means for political mobilisation (Gamson and Moon 2004). The particularity of the intersection of sexuality and race becomes visible in the racist politics of *Gay Pages* and its covers, and warrants critique that zeros in on race representation in sexuality. The critique of white supremacy advanced here is built on the knowledge that race is socially constructed (Sussman 2014) and thus has no biological basis, but racism's effects are real. The recognition of race as a social construct does not automatically undo the structural violence created through anti-black social and economic structures that privileged whiteness in apartheid and in many ways continue to privilege whites in post-apartheid (Carolin 2019). In all its unrealness, through history, race matters because the social life, in other words the power that race has gained over the centuries has meant that people make use of race to make sense of their lives and those around them, even as it shifts and its meanings contingent on politics of the day (Erasmus 2017). The meanings made, contested, and renegotiated allude to an ongoing process, one that is uneven and seldom linear, and in many ways a process that post-apartheid South Africa is steeped in. It is in this context of contestation and renegotiation of the meanings of race, particularly within sexuality, that I am problematising *Gay Pages* and its continued white supremacist representations. In the wake of the fall of apartheid, post-apartheid South Africa endeavours to create a society built on democratic principles that foreground non-racialism, and it is in this spirit of non-racialism that I find the white supremacy of *Gay Pages* destructive and reductive in the building of a new South Africa.

Writing about intersectionality, I find myself always gravitating towards Kath Weston's (2011: 15) opening line in *Me, Myself and I*, where she writes 'gender is about race is about class is about sexuality is about age is about nationality is about an entire range of social relations'. While speaking from outside the South African context, I go back to this articulation because it enables a way to use intersectionality, to think with intersectionality through South African sexuality politics. The power of intersectionality lies in its ability to hold many points of entry, and articulate how they impact on each other as their crisscross and particularise individual experiences. In the South African context, often, racial identity is thought of and spoken as if it is the master identity, but people's realities point us to a multiplicity of identities that are often drowned by the dominant discourses. It is becoming more important for the post-apartheid context to take seriously how race, gender, class, sexuality, and a variety of other social identities and positions largely determine the liveability of a South African life.

The theory of intersectionality was introduced by American feminist scholar Kimberlé Crenshaw (1991), arguing about the invisibility of black women's struggle in both the white dominated feminist movement and the male dominated antiracism movement. Intersectionality was built on the scaffolding that was established by black feminists who foregrounded the particularity of black women's struggle in a simultaneously racialized and gendered world. The book titled *All the Women Are White, All the Blacks Are Men, But Some of Us Are Brave* edited by Hull et al. (1982) perfectly captures the foundations of intersectionality as theorised by black feminists. The collection is regarded as a landmark anthology in women's studies, and cemented a crossroad in understanding the simultaneous implication of different identities and positions. Even prior to the edited text, intersectionality was captured in a statement issued by black feminists of the Combahee River Collective (1977) when they stated that 'we also often find it difficult to separate race from class from sex oppression because in our lives they are most often experienced simultaneously'. The appreciation of multi-identity oppression and its complexity is vital for understanding the problematics that are presented by *Gay Pages* and its history of white supremacy.

The multi-axis framework of intersectionality is useful in making sense of oppression because it enables us to see how race, as a historical construct, is implicated in the struggle for sexual freedom in post-apartheid South Africa. In advocating for multi-axis framing, Crenshaw (1989: 14) argues that 'single-axis framework erases Black women in the conceptualisation, identification, and remediation of race and sex discrimination by limiting inquiry to the experiences of otherwise-privileged members of the group'. Similarly, then, when we speak about sexuality and race in South Africa referencing *Gay Pages*, there has to be an appreciation of how race and sexuality intersect and affect people's lives. In this particular chapter, the focus is on the effects of the intersection of sexuality and race, and how the omission of blackness in *Gay Pages* demonstrates how white supremacy is entrenched in LGBTI communities in post-apartheid South Africa. When we are able to appreciate the complex ways in which race and sexuality intersect, we are able to see that white gay men's identity as a sexual minority does not erase their racial privilege; indeed, white gay men rely on racial privilege to enable liveable lives for themselves at the expense of black gay men.

## The continued construction of homosexuality as white

In writing about the Afrikaans women's magazine *Sarie*, Van der Westhuizen (2017: 67) describes the magazine as 'a technology of heteronormativity'. I would amend this slightly and describe *Gay Pages* as a technology of homonormativity. Duggan (2002: 179) articulates homonormativity as 'a politics that does not contest dominant heteronormative assumptions and institutions, but upholds and sustains them'. In this then, *Gay Pages* is invested in preserving and showcasing a particular kind of white middle-class gay subjectivity. In other words, *Gay Pages* takes sexuality and masks it with already familiar hegemonies of race, class, and gender. Indeed, 'the racialization of gayness as marker of whiteness further reinforces how sexuality and race are mutually implicated in the hierarchised representation of queer subjectivities' (Judge 2018: 96). When black gay men are not part of the gay world, this neglect or erasure or forced non-participation in that gay world is partly a legacy of colonialism and apartheid. In post-apartheid South Africa, hegemonic whiteness within sexuality, that is to say white gay men, continue past injustices, and getting away with it because they are also victims of homophobia. Indeed, '*Gay Pages* routinely constructs a normative position of the male queer subject as white' (Sonnekus and van Eeden 2009: 95). It is in this matrix of homophobia's victims but racially oppressive that we find white gay men utilising and reproducing white privilege. Queer racism has been gaining scholarly attention in texts such as the edited book by South African scholars Camminga and Matebeni (2019), Mkhize et al. (2010), and Tucker (2009). With all this examination, what becomes apparent is the multiple ways in which white supremacy asserts itself in post-apartheid South Africa, and how white LGBTI people are invested in racist systems of oppression—like segregation, class assertion, and other exclusions—because they benefit from them. It is under these conditions that it becomes imperative for us to spotlight white LGBTI people and how they assert and benefit from white supremacy at the detriment of black sexual minorities.

What is at play here with *Gay Pages* is what Steyn (2001: 36) termed apartheid logic, built on 'the rigorous systems of laws that was designed to guard white supremacy'. *Gay Pages* and the white men who run it are oblivious to inter-related forms of inequality when you factor in race and class into sexuality. The continued neglect of black bodies and black voices in *Gay Pages* demonstrates the power systems involved in the continued racialization of South Africa in post-apartheid. In *Gay Pages*, if the covers are anything to go by, being gay has been singular for the past 24 years in South Africa; that is to say, white, male, cisgender, and middle class. The continuous reiteration of white bodies on the cover of *Gay Pages* sends a powerful message of affirming white gay identity while simultaneously negating black queer existence. The negation of black queers is linked to what Mbembe (2001: 1) termed the 'negative interpretation', where Africans, in this case queer Africans, are seen through stubborn Eurocentric pathologies. The history of racial apartheid, and the continued negation of black queers in post-apartheid cannot be undone or be rectified by a singular random inter-racial *Gay Pages* cover pitched as 'progress'.

The monolithic representation and reproduction of gayness in *Gay Pages* misses much about the vibrancy and expansiveness of cultures of men with same-sex desires in post-apartheid South Africa. In writing about the period just after South Africa's first democratic elections, South African writer Gevisser (2000: 131) observed that 'perhaps not surprisingly, too, the life in Pretoria is very white. Walk through Steamers, the throbbing gay bar that spills over three floors, on a Saturday night, and you'll be hard pressed to see a black face in the crowd of thousands. Pretoria has large black townships; why, then, are there no black people at steamers?' The picture painted by Gevisser (2000) of racial segregation in post-1994 South Africa in the mid-1990s remains as demonstrated by Tucker (2009) and Soldaat (2019). The politics of black exclusion in Pride marches in Johannesburg (Scott 2017) and Cape Town (Scott 2019b) have led to the creation of alternative Pride marches and the carving out of space by and for black people within LGBTI communities (Soldaat 2019).

It goes without saying that *Gay Pages* is a 'gay lifestyle' magazine, meaning that it is an aspirational magazine designed to construct and represent the 'gay lifestyle'. The representation is that of white gay men only. In this, *Gay Pages* 'legitimises a certain kind of life as the 'good gay life' through repudiating another kind of gay life' (Judge 2018: 97), black gay life. The term lifestyle is complicated because it is linked to the commodification of the gay identity (Pellegrini 2002), a commodification process aided by magazines like *Gay Pages*. In his study of the Pink Map of the city of Cape Town, South African queer academic Rink (2013: 83) argues that 'shifts in consumption patterns, and the nature of the citizen-consumer can be seen through changes in listings that are present in the *Map*. What was once a map that appealed to readers through shared notions of sexual citizenship has become one where the common pursuit of consumption is the overarching focus'. Democratic South Africa with its progressive sexuality legislation has created an environment where LGBTI people can be visible and can participate in South African life openly. A participation that is also heavily shaped by consumption. The prioritisation of queer consumption has consequences in the South African landscape considering the income inequality that is largely shaped by race, where because of apartheid legacies whites are largely middle-class whereas black people largely make up the working poor. In this context then, those who are able to participate in queer consumption, white gays, are assimilated in post-apartheid citizenship, whereas those who can not, black queers, are excluded.

In the mainstream 'gay scene' in South African cities, and in *Gay Pages* magazine there is an ongoing desire to replicate and reproduce Northern queer sensibilities and aesthetics even though they are incongruent with the local landscape. Indeed, 'a particular group of white queer men in Cape Town (and elsewhere in South Africa) are striving to emulate a no doubt essentialistic class of queer identity that itself is derived from images in part derived from overseas' (Tucker 2009: 149). Necessarily then, through queer geographies or sexual geographies, we must understand that space matters (Visser 2016). Therefore, attention must be given to the local ways in which space and identity are articulated, because the Global North hegemonic construction of gayness that is taken up by publications like *Gay Pages* is problematic in the local context. As Altman (2001) has argued, much is lost in the eagerness for universalism of sexuality articulated through western discourses and culture. In this then, 'the notion of urban gay life as community and the gay village as an expression thereof requires rethinking' (Visser 2016: 59), particularly when we consider the history of colonialism and then apartheid in South Africa and how the legacies of these racist systems, as they pertain to space, are still entrenched. If we take *Gay Pages* as a space, then Browne and Brown's (2016: 1) articulations that 'there is nothing innate or natural to either space/place/environment or sex and sexualities, … geographies have shown how sex and sexualities are created in, through and by space, place and environment' are of importance. As the largest gay publication in South Africa, *Gay Pages* magazine occupies a powerful space in the public culture. The symbolic representation on the cover of *Gay Pages* cannot be underestimated when we consider the continued struggle for sexuality freedoms in post-apartheid South Africa (Judge 2018), particularly for black queer people. Considering symbolic representation of the magazine, considering the work it does on display on the magazine stand, considering the colonialism and apartheid legacies, considering the continued struggle for sexual freedom for black queers, *Gay Pages* is implicated in the violence against black queers. The space occupied by *Gay Pages* is a political space, and the continued white cover is an investment in white supremacy. Furthermore, considering *Gay Pages* as a space, and considering apartheid laws that segregated South Africans by race, *Gay Pages* occupies a space where their magazine cover policy remains 'Slegs Blankes' (Whites Only).

It is important to remember that *Gay Pages* chooses the particular racist construction and articulation of gayness where blackness is ignored, and by doing so contributes to the violent alienation of black queers in this country and feeds into 'homosexuality is unAfrican' discourses. In a country, indeed a continent, where queer activist fight against the notion that homosexuality is a western import, *Gay Pages* reinforces this narrative by constructing gayness as synonymous with whiteness. The consequences of the conflation of gayness with whiteness is visible in the ways that homophobic violence is experienced disproportionately by black LGBTI people compared to white LGBTI people in South Africa (Judge 2018; Mkhize et al. 2010). Furthermore, the continuous lack of representation in *Gay Pages* perpetuates negative self-perception of black queers, because the lack of representation constructs black queers as non-existent. The question then becomes, what becomes of gay desire in a white supremacist gay world? What becomes of the ways in which black gay men come to understand themselves and their desires? And also, what becomes of white desires?

## Race and desire

African psychologist Ratele (2004: 145) argues that 'Desire in racist cultures is misrecognised, that is to say 'perverted', and this can be seen in how race relations transmogrify into sexual relations'. The singular black cover in the history of *Gay Pages* is an inter-racial cover of a white and a black man. The black man was not alone but accompanied by whiteness. In this instance, whiteness provides a buffer for the blackness, it whitewashes the blackness. The cover is seemingly acceptable because it contains whiteness, therefore the blackness is tamed, kept from looming large and not centred on *Gay Pages*. This inter-racial cover is similar to 'some of my best friends are black', a retort often used by white people accused of being racist. This cover is linked to a long history of a singular black person being seen as the exception from the 'rest' and therefore can be in the company of white people. *Gay Pages* is quick to pat themselves on the back and sell this singular inter-racial cover as 'progress', but this cover is a ruse, it is smoke and mirrors. Therefore, it must be clear that the singular inter-racial cover in the history of *Gay Pages* does not represent 'progress' or solidarity, rather it is designed to placate, and is not seriously looking to transform the magazine. Furthermore, considering the history of *Gay Pages*, it will take more than an inter-racial cover to address the white supremacist ethos of the magazine.

*Gay Pages* is a magazine that sells aspiration and designates what is desirable. As demonstrated by Rink (2013), queer consumption goes not only beyond the selling and consuming of merchandise but is also implicated in the selling and consumption of bodies. The cover of a magazine is designed to entice, to draw you in, and to give an idea of what is inside. Following this, *Gay Pages* says much about what is desirable, and consequently what is not desirable. The white supremacist idea of black bodies being undesirable is made only more complicated by the fetishisation of black bodies for the white gaze. This is partly exemplified by the singular inter-racial couple cover in the history of the magazine's existence. The warped forms of fetishisation is captured in Gordon's (1997: 128) articulation that 'in an anti-black world, a black penis, whatever its size, represents a threat'. Gordon's articulations are linked to Ratele's misrecognised and perverted desire. In the case of *Gay Pages*, the omission of the black body, and the black penis speaks to a long history of the 'swart gevaar' (black danger) from apartheid, where there was a perceived security threat from black people. The 'swart gevaar' also functions as metaphor for the supposed looming danger of blackness in the white imagination since the advent of colonization. This is bigger than just South Africa in that the 'threat' that Gordon is referring to is the one that enables the gunning down of unarmed African-American men in broad daylight while being filmed and sparking a world-wide Black Lives Matter movement, and white policeman still getting away with murder. It is also this 'threat' that means the white gaze can project its desires for the Other in degrading ways, as exemplified in the exploitation and violent treatment of Sarah Bartman (Abrahams 1996).

Arnfred (2004: 20) wrote that 'sexual pleasure and desire have rarely been objects of study for scholars studying Africa'. Indeed, the scholarship on African sexual pleasure and desire has historically been limited to negative depictions from the imaginations of Europeans. For Ratele (2004: 142), 'kinky politics follows the fetish of, and refetishises, race. There can be no racism without this constant re-fetishisation. Indeed, one could say, racism is kinky politics as it always involves a sexual warping of identity politics'. By kinky politics, Ratele is talking about racialized perversions at the intersections of race and sex for heterosexual South Africans. The representations of African sexual pleasure are slowly changing, as exemplified by the articulations of pleasure and desire in the works of South African queer artist Zanele Muholi (Corley 2016, in an interview with Corley) and the academic work of Matebeni (2013). The negation of African people's pleasures and desires through the negation of black gay men or their re-presentation as a unique fetish is a denial of black sexuality. Here, I am making the argument that the non-representation of black gay men is tantamount to misrepresentation. It is a negation that perpetuates white supremacist notions about beauty and who can be seen as desirable.

The question then becomes, how do we address the legacies of colonialism and apartheid in the ways that racialized people in South Africa could fully *see* each other. One possible solution to the problem of race fetishisation was proposed by Ratele (2004: 144), who argued that:

> Young men and women should be encouraged to have good, 'normal', sexual intercourse at the earliest opportunity with another person of another race or ethnic group before they reach a certain age. [...] Most crucial, though, good interracial sex could have deep significance for reconstructing our national politics.

I appreciate Ratele's take on developing healthy sex education and encouraging honest discussions with young people about their bodies and developing sexuality. However, people like South African race theorist Erasmus (2010) have argued that contact theory is too timid for race and racism and have argued rather for creative political imaginaries that will aid antiracism work. While seemingly opposite, I see both Ratele's radical inter-racial sex and Erasmus's push for a more political engagement as strategies that are rooted in antiracism. They seek more creative ways to undo racism and the kind of sexual stereotypes and fetishisation built on white supremacy. These are creative solutions that *Gay Pages* is in desperate need of, where they can interrogate the long-established racism within their articulation of gayness. The problematic I am raising here is not a question of begging to be 'let in' by whiteness, but a principled call for radical queer politics that endeavours to create freedom for liveable black queer lives, while also recognising the compromised humanness of white gay South Africans. My intervention here is interested in creating a queer futurity that takes seriously the intersections of race and sexuality, and what these intersections mean for queer lives.

## Conclusion: Radical queer politics

The narrative of the 'master' race purported by whiteness continues to plague post-apartheid South Africa (Steyn 2001; Van der Westhuizen 2017), and publications like *Gay Pages* are invested in reproducing this narrative. *Gay Pages* is not unique in this regard, as demonstrated by Van der Westhuizen (2017); other publications, like *Sarie*, remain invested in the grand narratives of whiteness and its supposed superiority. Perhaps, it would have been naive to expect whiteness in post-apartheid South Africa to go down without a fight. At this juncture, it would serve us well to remember the depths of structural racism in South Africa after 1948, a kind of racism that Derrida (1985: 291) called 'the ultimate racism in the world' in a piece aptly titled *Racism's Last Word*. If we consider the insidiousness of white supremacy, and how people are still grappling with it the world over, then we must take heed of Erasmus's (2017) call for creative political imaginaries.

Through the writer Toni Morrison, Erasmus (2017: xxiii) argues, 'in the ongoing process of our liberation we must create openings in the racial house. We must refuse to live by its rules of dominance and its significations'. Taking on the challenge of refusal, in this chapter I am arguing against the racism perpetuated by *Gay Pages*. My refusal of the racism perpetuated by *Gay Pages*, and those who support the magazine without questioning its philosophy, is inspired by the simple yet radical words of Jacque Rancière (1999: 19) about 'the equality of anyone and everyone'.

The whitewashing of same-sex desire in *Gay Pages* works against the principles and the advancement of constitutional democracy in post-apartheid South Africa. *Gay Pages* and those involved in its production should take heed of Crenshaw (1991) and others advocating for intersectional politics if true sexual freedom is to be achieved; because we cannot kid ourselves—there is no queer freedom without black queer freedom or indeed human freedom. My refusal of *Gay Pages*, and what the magazine represents, is grounded in a commitment to radical queer politics that take seriously intersectionality. By radical queer politics I mean that there has to be a recognition of history, and how history shapes the lives we live today. That the intersection of race, class, and a myriad other identities and social positions are important in post-apartheid sexuality politics. Here, while I am writing about representation in a predominantly gay male magazine, but the politics I am advancing have implications for queer people beyond *Gay Pages* and gay male representations. As demonstrated by the disruption of Johannesburg Pride by the black lesbian feminist group *One in Nine* (Scott 2017), a radical queer politics is not only needed, but is necessary for our survival. The post-apartheid sexuality landscape has to advance politics that will benefit all of us, and not just some of us. A sexuality politics that recognises all of us has to take intersectionality and the particularity of our social positions because of our axis of difference seriously. To paraphrase Flavia Dzodan (2011), the post-apartheid sexual revolution will have to be intersectional, or it will be bullshit.

## Acknowledgement

I would like to thank Melissa Steyn and iNCUDISA for encouragement and intellectual guidance with my initial thoughts and ideas about Gay Pages magazine during my Honours studies. I also acknowledge the Centre for Humanities Research of the University of the Western Cape for the Next Generation Scholar position that facilitated the writing of this paper.

## Notes

1  After this article went to print, Gay Pages has since had their first solo black cover for the Autumn/ Winter 2021 edition.
2  I wanted to reproduce the image of the Autumn 2019 front cover of *Gay Pages* for this chapter, but my request for copyright permission from the publishers was ignored. I settled with a description of the image. The image can be found on their website, https://gaypagessa.com/editions/.

## References

Abrahams, Y. 1996. Disempowered to Consent: Sara Bartman and Khoisan Slavery in the Nineteenth-Century Cape Colony and Britain. *South African Historical Journal*, 35 (1): 89–144. DOI.10.1080/02582479608671248.

Altman, D. 2001. *Global Sex*. Chicago: University of Chicago Press.

Arnfred, S. 2004. Re-thinking Sexualities in Africa: Introduction. In *Re-thinking Sexualities in Africa*, ed. S. Arnfred, pp. 7–34. Sweden: Almqvist & Wiksell Tryckeri AB, viewed 1 June 2020, https://www.diva-portal.org/smash/get/diva2:240493/FULLTEXT03.pdf.

Brown, G. and Browne, K. 2016. An Introduction to the Geographies of Sex and Sexualities. In *The Routledge Research Companion to Geographies of Sex and Sexualities*, pp. 1–10. London: Routledge. DOI: 10.4324/9781315613000.ch7.

Camminga, B. and Matebeni, Z. 2019. *Beyond The Mountain: Queer Life in 'Africa's Gay Capital'*. Pretoria: Unisa Press.

Carolin, A. 2019. South African *Gay Pages* and the Politics of Whiteness. *Social Dynamics*, 45 (2): 234–249. DOI: 10.1080/02533952.2019.1619273.

Clark, N. L. and Worger, W. H. 2016. *South Africa: The Rise and Fall of Apartheid*. London: Routledge.

Corley, I. 2016. An Interview with Zanele Muholi. *Wasafiri*, 31 (1): 22–29. DOI:10.1080/02690055. 2016.1112570.

Crenshaw, K. 1989. Demarginalizing the Intersection of Race and Sex: A Black Feminist Critique of Antidiscrimination Doctrine, Feminist Theory and Antiracist Politics. *University of Chicago Legal Forum*, 1 (8): 139–167. https://chicagounbound.uchicago.edu/cgi/viewcontent.cgi?article=1052&context=uclf.

Crenshaw, K. 1991. Mapping the Margins: Intersectionality, Identity Politics, and Violence Against Women of Colour. *Stanford Law Review*, 43 (6): 1241–1299.

Derrida, J. 1985. Racism's Last Word. *Critical Inquiry*, 12 (1): 290–299.

Duggan, L. 2002. The New Homonormativity: The Sexual Politics of Neoliberalism. In *Materializing Democracy: Toward a Revitalized Cultural Politics*, ed. R. Castronovo and D. Nelson, pp. 175–194. Durham, NC: Duke University Press.

Dzodan, F. 2011. 'My feminism will be intersectional or it will be bullshit!', *Tiger Beatdown*, 10 October, viewed 14 January 2021, http://tigerbeatdown.com/2011/10/10/my-feminism-will-be-intersectional-or-it-will-be-bullshit/.

Erasmus, Z. 2010. Contact Theory: Too Timid for 'Race' and Racism. *Journal of Social Issues*, 66: 387–400. DOI:10.1111/j.1540-4560.2010.01651.x.

Erasmus, Z. 2017. *Race Otherwise: Forging a New Humanism for South Africa*. Johannesburg: Wits University Press.

Erasmus, Z. and De Wet, J. 2003. *Not Naming 'Race': Some Medical Students' Experiences and Perceptions of 'Race' and Racism at the Health Sciences Faculty of the University of Cape Town*. Cape Town: Institute for Intercultural and Diversity Studies in Southern Africa.

Fairclough, M. 1995. *Media Discourse*. London: Arnold.

Fanon, F. 1963. *The Wretched of the Earth*. New York City: Grove Press.

Gamson, J. and Moon, D. 2004. The Sociology of Sexualities: Queer and Beyond. *Annual Review of Sociology*, 30: 47–64.

Gay Pages. 2020. https://gaypagessa.com, viewed 1 September 2020.

Gevisser, M. 2000. Mandela's Stepchildren: Homosexual Identity in Post-apartheid South Africa. In *Remapping Sexualities*, ed. P. Drucker, pp. 111–136. London: Millivres Ltd.

Goldberg, D. T. 2009. *The Threat of Race: Reflections on Racial Neoliberalism*. Hoboken, NJ: Wiley-Blackwell.

Gordon, D. M. 2017. *Apartheid in South Africa*. New York City: Bedford/St Martin's.

Gordon, L. 1997. Race, Sex, and Matrices of Desire in an Antiblack World: An Essay in Phenomenology and Social Role. In *Race/Sex: Their Sameness, Difference and Interplay*, ed. N. Zack, pp. 117–132. New York: Routledge.

Hull, A. G. T., Bell-Scott, P. and Smith, B. 1982. *All The Women Are White, All the Blacks Are Men, But Some of Us Are Brave: Black Women's Studies*. New York: Feminist Press at City University of New York.

Joshi, Y. 2012. Respectable Queerness. *Columbia Human Rights Law Review*, 43 (1): 1–45.

Judge, M. 2018. *Blackwashing Homophobia: Violence and the Politics of Sexuality, Gender and Race*. London: Routledge.

Judge, M., Manion, A. and de Waal, S. 2008. *To Have and to Hold: The Making of Same-Sex Marriage in South Africa*. Cape Town: Jacana Media.

Laband, J. 2020. *The Land Wars: The Dispossession of the Khoisan and AmaXhosa in the Cape Colony*. South Africa: Penguin Random House.

Massoud, M. F. 2003. The evolution of gay rights in South Africa. *Peace Review*, 15 (3): 301–307. DOI: 10.1080/1040265032000130896.

Matebeni, Z. 2013. Intimacy, Queerness, Race. *Cultural Studies*, 27 (3): 404–417. DOI:10.1080/09502386. 2013.769151.

Mbembe, A. J. 2001. *On the Postcolony*. Berkeley, CA: University of California Press.

Mellet, P. T. 2020. *The Lie of 1652: A Decolonised History of Land*. Cape Town: Tafelberg.

Mills, C. W. 2003. White Supremacy as Sociopolitical System: A Philosophical Perspective . In *White Out: The Continuing Significance of Racism*, ed.A. W. Doane and E. Bonilla-Silva, pp. 35–48. New York: Routledge.

Mkhize, N., Bennett J. Reddy, V. and Moletsane, R. 2010. *The Country We Want to Live in: Hate Crimes and Homophobia in The Lives of Black Lesbian South Africans*. Cape Town: Paul & Co Pub Consortium.

Nasson, B. 2011. *The Boer War: The Struggle for South Africa*. United Kingdom: The History Press.

Nast, H. 2002. Queer Patriarchies, Queer Racisms, International. *Antipode*, 34 (5): 874–909.

Ngcukaitobi, T. 2018 . *The Land is Ours: South Africa's First Black Lawyers and the Birth of Constitutionalism* . South Africa: Penguin Random House.

Oliver, E. and Oliver, W. H. 2017. The Colonisation of South Africa: A unique case. *HTS Teologiese Studies/Theological Studies*, 73 (3). DOI:10.4102/hts.v73i3.4498.

Pellegrini, A. 2002. Consuming Lifestyle: Commodity Capitalism and Transformation in Gay Identity. In *Queer Globalizations: Citizenship and the Afterlife of Colonialism,* ed. A. Cruz-Malavé and M. F. Manalansan IV, pp. 134–145. New York: New York University Press.

Rancière, J. 1999. *Disagreement: Politics and Philosophy.* Minneapolis: University of University Press.

Ratele, K. 2004. Kinky Politics. In *Re-thinking Sexualities in Africa*, ed. S. Arnfred, pp. 139–156. Sweden: Almqvist & Wiksell Tryckeri AB, viewed 1 June 2020, https://www.diva-portal.org/smash/get/diva2 :240493/FULLTEXT03.pdf.

Rink, B. 2013. Que(e)rying Cape Town: Touring Africa's Gay Capital with the Pink Map. In *Tourism in the Global South: Heritages, Identities and Development,* ed. J. Sarmento and E. Brito-Henriques, pp. 65–90. Lisbon: University of Lisbon.

Scott, L. 2007. 'How "Race" is implicated in the Construction of Gay Identities in South Africa's Gay Media: An inspection of Gay Pages Magazine', Honors thesis, University of Cape Town.

Scott, L. 2017. Disrupting Johannesburg Pride: Gender, Race, and Class in the LGBTI Movement in South Africa. *Agenda*, 31 (1): 42–49. DOI:10.1080/10130950.2017.1351101.

Scott, L. 2019a. '"The more you stretch them, the more they grow": Same-sex marriage and the wrestle with heteronormativity', PhD/Doctoral thesis, University of Cape Town. http://hdl.handle.net/11427/30912.

Scott, J. 2019b. Disruption and Withdrawal: Responses to 21st Century Prides from the South. In *Beyond the Mountain: Queer Life in 'Africa's Gay Capital'*, ed. B. Camminga and Z. Matebeni, pp. 168–182. Pretoria: Unisa Press.

Soldaat, F. 2019. Black Lesbian Politics and Organising Spaces. In *Beyond the Mountain: Queer Life in 'Africa's Gay Capital'*, ed. B. Camminga and Z. Matebeni, pp. 137–144. Pretoria: Unisa Press.

Sonnekus T. and van Eeden, J. 2009. Visual Representation, Editorial Power, and the Dual 'Othering' of Black Men in the South African Gay Press: The Case of *Gay Pages*. *South African Journal for Communication Theory and Research*, 35 (1): 81–100. DOI:10.1080/02500160902906661.

Steyn, M. 2001. *'Whiteness Just Isn't What It Used to Be': White Identity in a Changing South Africa.* Albany, New York: State University of New York Press.

Steyn, M. and Foster, D. 2008. Repertoires for Talking White: Resistant Whiteness in Post-apartheid South Africa. *Ethnic and Racial Studies*, 31 (1): 25–51. DOI:10.1080/01419870701538851.

Sussman, R. 2014. *The Myth of Race: The Troubling Persistence of an Unscientific Idea.* Cambridge, MA: Harvard University Press.

Taylor, Y. 2011. Complexities and Complications: Intersections of Class and Sexuality. In *Theorising Intersectionality and Sexuality*, ed. Y. Taylor, S. Hines and M. E. Casey, pp. 37–55. United Kingdom: Palgrave MacMillan.

The Combahee River Collective. 1977. 'The Combahee River Collective Statement', viewed 16 September 2020, https://americanstudies.yale.edu/sites/default/files/files/Keyword%20Coalition_ Readings.pdf.

Tucker, A. 2009. *Queer Visibilities: Space, Identity and Interaction in Cape Town.* United Kingdom: Wiley-Blackwell.

Van der Westhuizen, C. 2017. *Sitting Pretty: White Afrikaans Women in Post-apartheid South Africa.* KwaZulu Natal: University of KwaZulu-Natal Press.

Visser, G. 2016. Sexualities and Urban Life. In *The Routledge Research Companion to Geographies of Sex and Sexualities,* ed. G. Brown and K. Browne, pp. 55–62. London: Routledge.

Walcott, R. 2021. *The Long Emancipation: Moving Towards Black Freedom.* Durham, NC: Duke University Press.

Weston, K. 2011. Me, Myself, and I. In *Theorising Intersectionality and Sexuality*, ed. Y. Taylor, S. Hines and M. E. Casey, pp. 15–36. United Kingdom: Palgrave MacMillan.

# 18

# Between the 'left behind' and 'the people': Racism, populism and the construction of the 'white working class' in the context of Brexit

*Neema Begum, Aurelien Mondon, and Aaron Winter*

## Introduction

Britain's exit from the European Union, popularly known as 'Brexit', has commonly been represented as a democratic revolt of the so-called 'left behind', defined as both 'white working class' and 'the people'. It has been argued that this 'revolt' had been brewing since the turn of the century, serving as vindication of this very thesis. The election of Donald Trump five months later seemed to confirm the trend – the 'white working class' had awakened to reclaim its democratic standing and make its voice heard. This narrative was well rehearsed. Perhaps most symbolically, Nigel Farage (2016), one of the main protagonists of the Brexit saga, wrote in an opinion piece in *The Telegraph* a month before the US Presidential election:

> The similarities between the different sides in this election are very like our own recent battle. As the rich get richer and big companies dominate the global economy, voters all across the West are being left behind. The blue-collar workers in the valleys of South Wales angry with Chinese steel dumping voted Brexit in their droves. In the American rust belt, traditional manufacturing industries have declined, and it is to these people that Trump speaks very effectively …

Similar takes became commonplace and reiterated not only by the very actors benefiting from these electoral successes and this ideological realignment, but increasingly by their opponents.

Building on a wealth of literature which has demonstrated that such readings are not only inaccurate, but also politically dangerous and divisive, this chapter aims first to challenge the idea that Brexit was indeed a (white) working-class revolt, and then explore the impact of and underlying ideology behind the construction and perpetuation of such narratives. Our focus will be on racialization and the construction of the working class and 'the people' as white. First, we turn our attention to what was represented in the campaign, coverage, and subsequent analysis and what was not. We then deconstruct what the 'white working class' narrative is predicated on and its political and ideological function, paying particular attention to the

DOI: 10.4324/9780429355769-18

representation of white male victimisation and grievance claims. Finally, we explore what is really at stake in this reactionary backlash and its misguided depiction.

Our argument is that the focus on the white working class has not only racialized and divided the most diverse section of our society, but also displaced racism, white supremacy, and Brexit itself onto the working class. In the process, it not only served to exculpate the middle and upper classes and rendered their racism and white supremacy relatively invisible, but also allowed elites to serve and protect their own economic and political interests, while appearing to be looking out for the so-called 'legitimate' concerns of the 'left behind'.

## Brexit as a white working-class revolt

The 'left behind' became an increasingly common concept used in relation to growing support for the far right and hard Eurosceptic United Kingdom Independence Party (UKIP), which saw the party make significant inroads in the 2014 EU Elections. According to Ford and Goodwin (2017), they are older, less-skilled and less-educated white working-class men who have lost out in the process of rapid social and economic changes such as deindustrialisation, globalisation and mass immigration. Economically 'left behind', they were also presented as culturally left behind by multiculturalism and liberal social values and argued to have driven support for Brexit. However, contrary to claims that Brexit and Trump's election were working class revolts, what we witnessed was largely a legitimisation of racism, realignment of the right and resurgence of the far right. Narratives placing so-called 'left-behind' as core to these 'populist' waves served a clear purpose in the discourse of right-wing politicians eager to get a semblance of popular support behind their otherwise elitist and exclusionary platforms. The working class, whose mythologisation had been constructed over centuries of struggles, hagiography, and demonization, proved a particularly potent ally for the far right to claim, at a time when it was easy to show that it had been abandoned by the centre left.

Interestingly, this narrative was not simply used by politicians for clear short-term electioneering goals, it was also espoused by many prominent commentators in the media and academia, on both sides of the political spectrum. It was not a surprise to see the right-wing press and commentators exploit the idea: *The Daily Express* talked about a 'working class revolution' (Gutteridge 2016) and *Spiked!*, a right-wing libertarian website, claimed 'The Brexit vote was a revolt against the establishment' (*Spiked!* 2016). However, it was perhaps more unexpected to see the more left-leaning media follow suit. In what represents a fairly typical hot take on Brexit and Trump, Caroline Crampton (2016) wrote in *The New Statesman* about 'what the working class revolt is really about'. While her analysis was indeed correct that it was race and not economic anxiety that had driven some of the vote for Brexit and Trump, she nonetheless succumbed to the idea that it was indeed something pushed predominantly by the 'white working class'. John Harris (2016), writing for *The Guardian*, in the aftermath of the referendum, claimed that 'Britain is in the midst of a working-class revolt'. The divide in British society was clear and simple: 'From ardent leavers in Merthyr Tydfil and undecided people on the English-Welsh borders to university students in Manchester who were 95% for remain, my Guardian colleague John Domokos and I have sampled just about every shade of opinion'. On one side, the white working class of the South Wales Valleys and other depressed industrial areas, on the other, the affluent and educated, predominantly London-based cosmopolitans. Even if Harris admitted that 'to be sure, there are many nuances and complications among leave voters', these nuances were really not worth blurring such a poignant picture:

[M]ake no mistake: in an almost comical reflection of the sacred lefty belief that any worthwhile political movement will necessarily be built around the workers, the foundation of the Brexit coalition is what used to be called the proletariat, large swathes of which are as united as in any lefty fantasy, even if some of their loudest complaints are triggering no end of anxiety among bien-pensant types, and causing Labour a great deal of apprehension.

This was music to the ear of *Guardian* readers: solace is to be found in the centre-left middle class rather than the poor, uneducated, or oppressed. These trends and narratives have endured and been further fuelled by 'the fall of the red wall' in the 2019 General Election, when traditionally Labour seats in the North turned to the Conservative party, despite evidence that this was not driven by a shift in working class vote to the right (Dorling 2020).

This elite narrative placing the blame squarely on the shoulders of the (white) working class was predicated on the populist hype, which by then had gripped much of public discourse across the west (Glynos and Mondon 2016). That this was pushed both by those who thought it was a positive development and those who worried about it as a threat to establishment politics, fed into the racist, nativist, but also anti-elite narrative pushed by the far right, despite being led by and benefiting part of the establishment. For Farage, a former stock broker, Brexit was a victory for 'ordinary people, for good people, for decent people' (Peck 2016), one which confirmed that concerns over immigration, as well as Islam, came first and economic grievances second (Hall and Maddox 2016). Often, the Leave. EU campaign tapped into far right strategies, most notably with its use of a Nazi-esque image of refugees crossing from Croatia to Slovenia in 2015, with a banner reading 'Breaking Point: the EU has failed us all' (Stewart and Mason 2016).[1] It was therefore not surprising to see the far-right rally behind Farage (Lyons 2016). While the Conservative-led Vote Leave was the official campaign for Brexit, the UKIP-led Leave. EU received much coverage as Nigel Farage had been instrumental in leading the agenda on the issue since the 2014 European election.

A number of academic analyses also participated in either reproducing, constructing or informing the narrative. Arguments about the white working class 'left-behind' became common to explain the resurgence of far right parties as it was argued right-wing populists were able to attract former left-wing voters alienated by the convergence of the mainstream left and right and their focus on the middle class and ethnic minorities (Norris and Inglehart 2019). For Ford and Goodwin (2017), support for Brexit was to be found within the working-class 'left-behind' who fear a loss of order and identity in 'a more diverse and rapidly changing Britain', championed by a homogenised and mythologised, 'multicultural', socially liberal elite.

Despite such widespread and mostly homogenous coverage, claims that Brexit was a working-class revolt are untenable. According to Danny Dorling (2016), 'of all those who voted for Leave 59% were middle class (A, B, and C1), and 41% were working class (C2, D, and E)'. Such claims are further dampened when looking at the geography of the vote, with 52% of people who voted Leave living in the southern half of England. For Derek Sayer (2017: 96), the discrepancies between the result in Scotland and Northern Ireland who voted overwhelmingly for remain (62% and 55.8%, respectively) and Wales and England who favoured Brexit (52.5% and 53.4%) reinforce the need for a more nuanced approach as 'there is no consistent correlation with income levels across the regions that might help explain these disparities in class terms'. Were it simply a question of class qua income for example, Scotland and Northern Ireland, whose gross disposable household income (GDHI) is lower than the UK's average, would have been fertile ground for Brexit. Based on similar data, Wales, whose GDHI is lower than all the English regions, returned a stronger remain vote (albeit with a Brexit majority). While the analysis of the vote already provides us with a number of caveats to counter the hegemonic narrative placing the blame firmly on irrational working-class voters for the Brexit decision, the inclusion of abstention as a variable allows us to weaken such generalising claims further (Mondon and Winter 2018, 2020).

## Brexit and the 'left-behind': what was the white working class Brexit narrative predicated on?

Key to the narrative pitting Brexit as a popular revolt relies on an ideological definition of 'the people' as an unrepresented population with a grievance and claim to the nation, its past and future, against elites and interlopers. In this case, the ideological definition of the working class is as essentially white and indigenous: 'While the populist character of the campaigns and their portrayal in the mainstream media pitted a constructed "people" made up of workers against an out-of-touch or contemptuous elite who fails to represent them, its nativist/racist/xenophobic basis pitted whites against "classless" immigrants, refugees and representatives of multi-culturalism and diversity who threaten jobs, resources, and nation' (Mondon and Winter 2018). According to Steph Lawler (2012), looking at media representations of white working-class people in a pre-Brexit period, but in the context of debates about English national identity and multiculturalism, 'whiteness that has come to be used as a signifier of white working-class existence'. On the other hand, diversity is often equated with affluence: Leave-voting areas are characterised as white, working class or 'left behind' while 'multicultural' cities populated with degree-educated, middle-class professionals are presented as being part of the liberal cosmo-politan elite (Hobolt 2016). In this way, ethnic minorities serve as a backdrop to the lives of white, liberal middle-class professionals. Working-class ethnic minorities are often erased, de-spite common, and even exacerbated experiences of poverty and precarity with the 'white working class' (compounded by racial inequality), or they are seen as sharing in the wealth and cultural resources of the white middle classes in cosmopolitan, Remain-supporting towns and cities. The conflation of diversity with affluence and that ethnic minorities (and immigrants) may be part of this 'liberal cosmopolitan elite' underpin claims of white victimhood, projected onto the white working-class, that ethnic minorities or immigrants are overtaking or even oppressing them. Their whiteness which should, in their eyes, grant privilege, is instead thought of as a liability. For Virdee and McGeever (2018: 1811),

> This racializing nationalism has borne a particularly defensive character since the 2008 crisis. It is defined not by imperial prowess or superiority, but by a deep sense of loss of prestige; a retreat from the damaging impact of a globalised world that is no longer re-cognisable, no longer British.

This operates through what has been described by Miri Song (2014) as a culture of racial equivalence: this 'post-race' narrative does not negate race or racism, but allows for the discursive placement of whiteness in a position where it has lost its historical power (globally and domestically) and appears thus in decline, vulnerable and subject to victimisation by others. This construction was expressed and mobilised in the context of Brexit and again in response to the toppling of slave trader Edward Colston's statue in Bristol during protests that followed the police killing of George Floyd in 2020. Protests against monuments to the legacy of the British Empire and role in slavery, such as that of Cecil Rhodes at Oxford University, were taken to be an attempt to erase British history and former greatness, as well as being 'anti-white'. Despite the elite status of these individuals and some of the institutions their statues watch over, the narrative and the identification, if not conflation, of

Britishness and whiteness with the working class, particularly in a globalised, post-industrial and post-colonial era, negates its white privilege and renders it the 'people'.

In this context, it has become increasingly accepted in elite circles, that the political divide in British society is no longer between the left and right, with the former being the representative of workers and the latter of the elite. Instead, constructions of the Brexit narratives pushed the idea that the new battle lines were between a cosmopolitan middle class 'soft left' and a more grounded, ethnocentric 'left-behind', eager to return the nation to its heyday. This tapped into David Goodhart's conception of the 'Somewheres' and the 'Anywheres' (2017):

> The old distinctions of class and economic interest have not disappeared but are increasingly over-laid by a larger and looser one – between the people who see the world from Anywhere and the people who see it from Somewhere.
>
> *(2017: 3)*

The Anywheres are the urban elite, while the Somewheres 'have usually 'ascribed' identities – Scottish farmer, working class Geordie, Cornish housewife – based on group belonging and particular place, which is why they find rapid change unsettling' (p. 3). Within the Somewheres, the 'left-behind' white working class was particularly hit: these 'older white working class men with little education have lost economically with the decline of well-paid jobs for people without qualifications and culturally, too, with the disappearance of a distinct working-class culture and the marginalisation of their views in the public conversation'. While it is well documented that neoliberal globalisation has benefitted a small elite at the expense of most, Goodhart's 'frame' focuses on identity, conveniently whitewashing the fact that those at the sharp end of inequalities are predominantly ethnic and migrant communities, but that they also share far more in common with the so-called 'white working class', than with 'Home Counties market town *Daily Mail* readers' he associates them with (Goodhart 2017: 4). As Joe Kennedy (2018: 83) points out in his powerful critique of those he terms 'authentocrats':

> That poor people live in cities, that many provincial working-class people are left-wing (and, vitally, not white) and that more than a few people in supposedly left-behind constituencies are materially well-off is neither here nor there to them.

In Goodhart's simplistic account, Londoners do not feel a particular attachment to their city or even their particular area of London, nor do other city dwellers; there are no (multiracial) working-class poor there suffering from unequal access to education, housing, and other public services. You would also be forgiven to think that the views of ethnic minorities are less marginalised than that of the white population. Finally, absent from this picture are the large swathes of wealthy England that voted to leave, for both 'cultural' and economic reasons, putting those so-called Somewheres most at risk. In this, Goodhart's approach epitomizes the contemporary reactionary moment: his extremely simplistic account conflates wilfully elitist neoliberal politics with their internationalist left-wing opponents, in order to defend the interests and appease the anxiety of the ageing privileged middle and upper classes in the United Kingdom. As Gurminder Bhambra (2017: 226) notes, 'what is being described is a relative loss of privilege rather than any real account of serious and systemic economic decline that is uniquely affecting white citizens'.

As is typical amongst far right legitimisers (Mondon and Winter 2020), Goodhart treads a fine line between the extreme and the mainstream, denouncing the most egregious acts of racism and discrimination, but justifying the more latent aspect of our reactionary moment as if they were democratic demands, all the while ignoring the existence and reach of systemic racism. His supposedly non-racist credentials are strengthened by his claims that some ethnic minorities are Somewheres and have voted for Brexit – which of course ignores the fact that their reasons to vote for Brexit were very different (Begum 2020). While around two-thirds of ethnic minorities voted to Remain in the EU, for many this was largely a vote against Leave which they associated with a rise in support for white nationalism and racism. Of the ethnic minorities who supported Brexit, this included criticism of the EU over the Refugee Crisis and freedom of movement for privileging (Eastern) European immigration over the Commonwealth, where many of their families originate (Begum 2020).

Goodhart's focus on 'cultures', their equal worth whether native or immigrant and the necessity to protect all and thus keep them separate, is not original either. It is in fact reminiscent of the *Nouvelle Droite*'s approach taken in the 1970s and 1980s as parts of the extreme right attempted to recalibrate their racist ideology to suit the post-racial hegemony, moving away from blatant biological racism based on the superiority of the white race, towards more cultural forms based on the necessity to protect all cultures and thus prevent mixing (see Bar-On 2013; Mondon 2013).[2] It is no surprise that Goodhart's work has been praised in *Eléments,* the main *Nouvelle Droite* publication 'for European Civilization'. The *Nouvelle Droite*'s approach was based on the reading of Antonio Gramsci, and in particular a belief that to achieve political power, one first needs cultural power. This approach can be witnessed in Goodhart's writing: the seemingly quaint and inoffensive veneer of the Anywheres and Somewheres cracks in the conclusion in particular where the author provides some leads towards 'better societies' which are often reminiscent of far right proposals. Goodhart advocates for a clearer and more punitive division of the population between those who really belong and those who do not, but also between those deserving of the help of a national welfare state and the 'scroungers'. Here, our analysis shows that there is more Thatcherism and neoliberalism, and continuities of these under New Labour,[3] in the British new right in the twenty-first century than old-school working-class labour.

While Goodhart was somewhat of a trailblazer in the United Kingdom on these issues, a number of prominent academics have pushed similar arguments in recent years, with more or less nuance or ideological ambitions. As others, he has also embraced a euphemisation strategy, calling parties and politics previously widely described as radical or extreme right, or racist, simply populist. This shift towards less stigmatising and unclear and imprecise terminology was particularly striking in a book by Eatwell and Goodwin (2018), in which the authors created an entirely new terminology 'national populism' in an attempt to dissociate contemporary movements from their 'evil' and less palatable forebears. This was also expressed by Kaufmann (2017; see also 2018a) in his report 'Racial self-interest is not racism' where he argued that Brexit was an expression of white, particularly working class, 'racial self-interest' (what Goodhart terms 'White Identity Politics'). For Kaufmann (2017: 4), it is crucial to 'avoid using charges of racism to side-line discussions of ethno-demographic interests' in relation to issues such as opposition to immigration. This is further emphasised on the Policy Exchange webpage for the report launch, where Goodhart comments that 'The liberal reflex to tar legitimate majority grievances with the brush of racism risks deepening western societies' cultural divides'.

## Racial and gender logics: anti-intersectionality intersectionality/ anti-identity politics identitarianism

There are several discursive and ideological functions of the white working class 'left behind' thesis. By racializing the working class as white and constructing whiteness and white interests in class terms, as well as being 'the demos', not only is the diversity of the working class denied (see Virdee 2014; Patel 2015), but anti-immigrant and racist positions, as well as Brexit and its implications, are granted legitimacy while also cast as the responsibility of the disenfranchised. According to Luke Gittos (2016) of *Spiked!*, in a context of a rise in hate crime and far right activism during the Brexit campaign: 'the onset of panic has revealed how the very publications and commentators who once claimed to stand up for the working class in fact view working-class people as a violent, racist horde'. This is also something we see in the work of Goodhart and Kaufmann. For Kaufmann (2018b), white majorities and culture are allegedly under threat and this causes and justifies racism and xenophobia:

> When whites can't express their sense of ethnic loss, they turn to the seemingly more 'respectable' alternatives of demonising Muslims, criticising immigrants who live in minority neighbourhoods, or voting for Brexit (a result of diverting concerns over ethnic change into hatred of the acceptably 'white' EU).

It is not only where 'blame' is apportioned, but that this construction also treats white 'indigenous' Britons as the most disenfranchised and victimised by their elected leaders and other racial and ethnic groups who are allegedly unfairly privileged over them. The source of this is attributed to everything from decolonization and deindustrialization, where white working-class men can no longer be providers and protectors, to political correctness, identity politics, intersectionality and 'wokeness' (usually anti-racism and feminism). As privileged white people are often left out of the race vs. class politics of the 'left behind' thesis, except where they are driving and benefitting from the analysis, and can be seen to be affected by anti-racism and feminism, it ceases to be about class and becomes about white, and often male, victimisation. The intersection of race and gender in right-wing and wider racist discourses is by no means new. Historically, racist discourses have been based around the construction of white men as protectors of women under threat by racialized men. While we still see this, particularly with liberal Islamophobia targeting Islam and Muslims in the name of women's rights (Mondon and Winter 2017), there has been a discursive change with white men increasingly represented as victims of social change and social forces in post-civil rights and post-industrial America and post-industrial Britain (see Daniels 1997; Faludi 1999; Ferber 1998; Gabriel 1998). In addition to the material conditions that may inform this construction, it is also predicated on the post-racial culture of equivalence. This is where real or perceived equality is not only equated with the loss of white privilege, but vulnerability and victimisation at the hands of others in a supposed reversal of the established racial and gender order that places white men at the bottom of the social hierarchy. White men come out as intersectional losers as a result of the intersection of their whiteness and masculinity, and women, people of colour and migrants are cast as winners. When pushed to its conclusion, this narrative argues that this leaves white men subject to so-called reverse racism and sexism.

In the current context, the articulation of loss and victimisation goes well beyond the 'left behind' constituency and discourse. It is a discursive strategy that also involves the appropriation of the very discourses through which racialized people and women, and those with intersecting identities, articulate their marginalisation and inequality historically (Crenshaw 1989; see also Olufemi 2020). It is an anti-intersectional intersectionality and an anti-identity politics identity politics. While seemingly opposing identity politics and intersectional theory, and so-called 'Grievance Studies', it is co-opted by them to represent white male interests and perceived reversal of the racial and gender order, using tools they may believe worked for other groups at their expense. Ironically, it often emanates from privileged actors, institutional positions, and platforms. Examples of this include the so-called Intellectual Dark Web (IDW) and 'Grievance Studies' hoax that sought to expose feminist and left wing scholarship for allegedly having a 'cynically biased perspective on men, masculinity, heterosexuality, and whiteness' (Lindsay et al. 2019). We also see this in its most extreme on the far right Identitarian movement and wider alt-right, and the misogynist Men's Rights Activists and Incels or 'involuntary celibates' (Winter 2019).

For University Professor and IDW associate Jordan Peterson, the concept of 'white privilege' is an attack on white people:

> [B]eing called out on their white privilege, identified with a particular racial group and then made to suffer the consequences of the existence of that racial group and its hypothetical crimes, and that sort of thing has to come to a stop…. [It's] racist in its extreme.
> *(Bandler 2016)*

What is typical is that white people deny expressions of racism, as can be seen in the case of Kaufmann's distinction between racism and racial self-interest, but criticism of racism is seen as anti-white racism.

In the United Kingdom, opposition to identity and intersectional politics and the representation of white men as a marginalised and victimised group are frequent talking points. According to *Spiked!* editor Brendan O'Neill (2020a), defending Terry Gilliam, another white man, following his criticism of #MeToo, transgender rights and self-identification as a 'black lesbian' for status in the context of identity and intersectional politics:

> The casual manner in which 'white man' has become a term of abuse is deeply worrying. It treats whiteness almost as an original sin. It turns the accident of white skin into a marker for evil, a sign that you're a morally questionable creature. It's time to bring this white-man-bashing to an end.

Perhaps, the most infamous and well-publicised example of this in recent times was the appearance of actor and recording artist Laurence Fox on BBC Question Time in January 2020. Fox, part of an acting dynasty and graduate of The Harrow School and RADA, is neither 'left behind', working class, nor an obvious candidate for the show. He is though part of a pattern in which reactionary identitarians are given a platform in the interests of so-called 'balance' and the appearance of 'free speech'. On the show, Fox clashed with audience member, academic Rachel Boyle, after she argued that Meghan Markle was the victim of racism. In response, Fox asserted that '[i]t's not racism' and, playing the post-race card, 'We're the most tolerant lovely country in Europe'. When, in response to his claim and lack of understanding, Boyle called Fox 'a white privileged male', he quickly abandoned post-racial colourblindness, co-opted the language of anti-racism for himself and claimed reverse racism: 'I can't help what I am, I was born like this, it's an immutable characteristic … So to call me a white privileged male is to be racist. You're being racist' (Jarvis 2020). Of course, in response to the exchange and criticism of Fox, a series of articles appeared in *Spiked!*. These included 'Laurence Fox and the woke McCarthyists' which used culture war framing to represent Boyle, a woman of colour, and other critics as 'elites' and Fox, a privileged white man, as a victim: 'Disagree with the cultural elites and they will try to destroy you' (O'Neill 2020b).

## Conclusion

It is not just that the representation of the white working class as the 'left behind' and white men as victims is ideological, it is also false and dangerous. The danger is that it legitimises racism and negates the experiences and needs of the most disenfranchised and at risk of both racism, sexism and inequality, who are purported to have power and status in this construct. For the Runnymede Trust (Khan and Shaheen 2017), the racialization of the working class and focus on white interests ignores the wider diversity of the working class and inequality faced by Black and minority ethnic communities, migrants, and refugees. This divide-and-rule politics constructed a zero-sum competition for representation and reduced resources between the 'indigenous' white working class and 'others', even though socio-economic inequality and related problems (poverty, lack of social mobility, low wages, housing, and institutional representation), predominantly represented as white working class problems, 'cut across racial groups', with ethnic minorities, particularly women of colour, suffering the brunt of austerity politics (Khan 2017; see also Runnymede Trust 2015, and Bassel and Emejulu 2017a, 2017b).

The white working class construct pits this elusive and narrowly defined group against racialized minorities and migrants, who are denied working class status, in a competition for scarce, deregulated and casualised employment and ever dwindling resources in neo-liberal Britain, and elsewhere. In addition to not addressing the inequality faced by 'white' working class people, it exacerbates the inequality and vulnerability faced by racialized and migrant working-class peoples, and particularly women of colour, and actually serves establishment political and economic interests. Nowhere has this been more evident than in the context of COVID-19 and the lockdown where working class people, and Black, Asian and Minority Ethnic (BAME) people and migrants have disproportionately been on the front line and affected, with death rates from COVID-19 in England being higher among people of Black and Asian origin than the white majority. Yet, all they received were rounds of applause and, in the case of migrants, a surcharge to use the National Health Service (NHS) and greater restrictions on what are termed 'unskilled' jobs until it was lifted in response to public pressure. Meanwhile, the reactionary advocates of the 'left behind' pushed for an end to the lockdown, a move which would predominantly serve their elitist interests, while putting more pressure on poorer communities and placing them in direct danger.

## Notes

1 The Leave.EU campaign was one of the two main organisations supporting the 'Leave' campaign, with Vote Leave. Leave.EU had close ties with UKIP, while Vote Leave was closer to the Conservative Party.
2 The Nouvelle Droite (New Right) was a political and intellectual movement which originated in France in the 1960s to revive the far right, building partly on Antonio Gramsci's theory of hegemony. Their work paved the way for the reconstruction of many far right parties and their shift to more cultural articulations of racism in particular.
3 For more on race, class and the deserving and underserving poor in the context of neoliberalism, see: S. Lawler 2005. 'Disgusted Subjects: The Making of Middle-Class Identities'. *Sociological Review*, 53 (3): 429–446; S. Lawler 2012. 'White like them: whiteness and anachronistic space in representations of the English white working class'. *Ethnicities*, 12 (4): 409–426; A. Kokoli and Winter, 2015. 'What a girl's gotta do: the labor of the biopolitical celebrity in austerity Britain'. *Women & Performance: a journal of feminist theory*, 25 (2): 157–174; R. Shilliam 2018. *Race and the Undeserving Poor: From Abolition to Brexit*. Newcastle: Agenda; I. Tyler 2013. *Revolting Subjects: Social Abjection and Resistance in Neoliberal Britain*. London: Zed Books.

# References

Bandler, A. 2016. 'EXCLUSIVE: Q&A with Prof. Jordan Peterson on Genderless Pronouns and the Left's "PC Game"', *The Daily Wire*, 4 November, viewed 19 June 2020, https://www.dailywire.com/news/exclusive-qa-prof-jordan-peterson-genderless-aaron-bandler.

Bar-On, T. 2013. *Rethinking the French New Right: Alternatives to Modernity*. London: Routledge.

Bassel, L. and Emejulu, A. 2017a. *Minority Women and Austerity: Survival and Resistance in France and Britain*. Bristol: Policy Press.

Bassel, L. and Emejulu, A. 2017b. Whose Crisis Counts? Minority Women, Austerity and Activism in France and Britain. In *Gender and the Economic Crisis in Europe*, ed. J. Kantola and E. Lombardo, pp. 185–208. London: Palgrave.

Begum, N. 2020. 'Race and the Referendum: An Intersectional Analysis of Ethnic Minority and White Voting Behaviour in the 2016 EU Referendum', PhD thesis, University of Bristol.

Bhambra, G. 2017. Brexit, Trump, and 'Methodological Whiteness': On the Misrecognition of Race and Class. *British Journal of Sociology: Special Issue on the Trump/Brexit Moment: Causes and Consequences*, 68 (S1): S214–S232. DOI: 10.1111/1468-4446.12317.

Crampton, C. 2016. 'Voting for Trump and Brexit: What the Working Class Revolt Is Really About', *The New Statesman*, 9 November, viewed 19 June 2020, http://www.newstatesman.com/world/north-america/2016/11/voting-trump-and-brexit-what-working-class-revoltreally-about.

Crenshaw, K. 1989. Demarginalizing the Intersection of Race and Sex: A Black Feminist Critique of Antidiscrimination Doctrine, Feminist Theory and Antiracist Politics. *University of Chicago Legal Forum*, 1989 (8), https://chicagounbound.uchicago.edu/uclf/vol1989/iss1/8.

Daniels, J. 1997. *White Lies: Race, Class, Gender, and Sexuality in White Supremacist Discourse*. New York: Routledge.

Dorling, D. 2016. Brexit: The Decision of a Divided Country. *BMJ*, 354. DOI: 10.1136/bmj.i3697.

Dorling, D. 2020. So, how did we end up with this government? *Public Sector Focus*, January/February, 14–17.

Eatwell, R. and Goodwin, M. 2018. *National Populism: The Revolt Against Liberal Democracy*. London: Pelican.

Faludi, S. 1999. *Stiffed: The Betrayal of the American Man*. New York: Perennial.

Farage, N. 2016. 'The Little People Have Had Enough', *The Telegraph*, 9 October, viewed 7 May 2020, https://www.telegraph.co.uk/opinion/2016/10/09/the-little-people-have-had-enough---not-just-here-but-in-america/.

Ferber, A. 1998. *White Man Falling: Race, Gender, and White Supremacy*. London: Rowman & Littlefield.

Ford, R. and Goodwin, M. 2017. Britain After Brexit: A Nation Divided. *Journal of Democracy*, 28: 17–30.

Gabriel, J. 1998. *Whitewash: Racialized Politics and the Media*. London: Routledge.

Garner, S. 2007. *Whiteness: An Introduction*. London: Routledge.

Gittos, L. 2016. 'Britain has not become Racist Overnight', *Spiked!*, 28 June, viewed 8 June, https://www.spiked-online.com/2016/06/28/britain-has-not-become-racist-overnight/.

Glynos, J. and Mondon, A. 2016. The Political Logic of Populist Hype: The Case of Right Wing Populism's 'Meteoric Rise' and Its Relation to the Status Quo. *Populismus* working paper series no. 4.

Goodhart, D. 2017. *The Road to Somewhere: The Populist Revolt and the Future of Politics*. London: C. Hurst.

Gutteridge, N. 2016. 'Working class revolution? Reports of huge EU referendum turnout which "would favour leave"', *The Express*, 24 June, viewed 20 January 2017, https://www.express.co.uk/news/politics/682890/EU-referendum-Reports-huge-EU-referendum-turnout-favour-Leave-Brexit.

Hall, M. and Maddox, D. 2016. 'FARAGE speech: Controlling mass immigration while Britain remains part of EU is IMPOSSIBLE', *The Express*, 29 April, viewed 10 May 2020, http://www.express.co.uk/news/politics/665446/Nigel-Farage-Ukipcontrol-immigration-leave-EU-referendum-June.

Harris, J. 2016. 'Britain is in the midst of a working-class revolt', *The Guardian*, 17 June, viewed 20 January 2017, https://www.theguardian.com/commentisfree/2016/jun/17/britain-working-class-revolt-eu-referendum.

Hobolt, S. B. 2016. The Brexit vote: a divided nation, a divided continent. *Journal of European Public Policy*, 23 (9): 1259–1277. DOI: 10.1080/13501763.2016.1225785.

Jarvis, J. 2020. 'Laurence Fox clashes with Question Time audience member over Meghan Markle racism row', *Evening Standard*, 17 January, viewed 10 May 2020, https://www.standard.co.uk/news/uk/laurence-fox-question-time-meghan-racism-a4336741.html.

Kaufmann, E. 2017. 'Racial Self-Interest' is not Racism. *Policy Exchange*, 3 March, viewed 10 January 2018, https://policyexchange.org.uk/publication/racial-self-interest-is-not-racism/.

Kaufmann, E. 2018a. *White Shift: Populism, Immigration and the Future of White Majorities*. London: Allen Lane.

Kaufmann, E. 2018b. 'White majorities feel threatened in an age of mass migration – and calling them racist won't help', *The New Statesman*, 17 October, viewed 18 June 2020, https://www.newstatesman.com/politics/uk/2018/10/white-majorities-feel-threatened-age-mass-migration-and-calling-them-racist-won.

Kennedy, J. 2018. *Authentocrats*. London: Penguin Random House.

Khan, O. 2017. 'Who Cares About The White Working Class?', *HUFFPOST*, 21 March, viewed 18 June 2020, https://www.huffingtonpost.co.uk/dr-omar-khan/white-working-class-disadvantages_b_15494046.html.

Khan, O. and Shaheen, F. 2017. 'Minority Report: Race and Class in post-Brexit Britain, Runnymede Trust and Class', *Runnymede Trust and CLASS*, March, http://www.runnymedetrust.org/uploads/publications/pdfs/Race%20and%20Class%20Post-Brexit%20Perspectives%20report%20v5.pdf.

Kokoli, A. and Winter, A. 2015. What a Girl's Gotta Do: The Labor of the Biopolitical Celebrity in Austerity Britain. *Women & Performance: A Journal of Feminist Theory*, 25 (2): 157–174.

Lawler, S. 2005. Disgusted Subjects: The Making of Middle-Class Identities. *Sociological Review*, 53 (3): 429–446.

Lawler, S. 2012. White Like Them: Whiteness and Anachronistic Space in Representations of the English White Working Class. *Ethnicities*, 12 (4): 409–426.

Lentin, A. 2020. *Why Race Still Matters*. Cambridge: Polity.

Lindsay, J., Boghossian, P. and Pluckrose, H. 2019. 'From dog rape to white men in chains: We fooled the biased academic left with fake studies', *USA Today*, 15 December, viewed 10 June 2020, https://www.usatoday.com/story/opinion/voices/2018/10/10/grievance-studies-academia-fake-feminist-hypatia-mein-kampf-racism-column/1575219002/.

Lyons, J. 2016. 'Farage campaign courted far right', *The Sunday Times*, 22 May, viewed 10 June 2020, http://www.thetimes.co.uk/article/farage-campaign-courted-far-right-njrqxhkqb.

Mondon, A. 2013. *The Mainstreaming of the Extreme Right in France and Australia: A Populist Hegemony?* Farnham: Ashgate.

Mondon, A. and Winter, A. 2017. Articulations of Islamophobia: From the Extreme to the Mainstream? *Ethnic and Racial Studies*, 13 (40): 2151–2179. DOI:10.1080/01419870.2017.1312008.

Mondon, A. and Winter, A. 2018. Whiteness, Populism and the Racialization of the Working Class in the United Kingdom and the United States. *Identities: Global Studies in Culture and Power*, 5 (26): 510–528. DOI:10.1080/1070289X.2018.1552440.

Mondon, A. and Winter, A. 2020. *Reactionary Democracy: How Racism and the Populist Far Right Became Mainstream*. London: Verso.

Norris, P. and Inglehart, R. 2019. *Cultural Backlash: Trump, Brexit, and Authoritarian Populism*. Cambridge: Cambridge University Press. DOI:10.1017/9781108595841.

Olufemi, L. 2020. *Feminism, Interrupted*. London: Pluto.

O'Neill, B. 2020a. 'It's time to stop bashing white men', *Spiked!*, 8 January, viewed 8 June 2020, https://www.spiked-online.com/2020/01/08/its-time-to-stop-bashing-white-men/.

O'Neill, B. 2020b. 'Laurence Fox and the woke McCarthyists', *Spiked!*, 20 January, viewed 10 May 2020, https://www.spiked-online.com/2020/01/20/laurence-fox-and-the-woke-mccarthyists/.

Patel, J. 2015. 'Both racism and anti-racism were present in the making of the English working class': An Interview with Satnam Virdee. *Media Diversified*, 18 November, viewed 20 May 2018, https://mediadiversified.org/2015/11/18/both-racism-and-anti-racism-were-present-in-the-making-of-the-english-working-class/.

Peck, T. 2016. 'Nigel Farage's triumphalist Brexit speech crossed the borders of decency', *The Independent*, 24 June, viewed 10 May 2020, http://www.independent.co.uk/news/uk/politics/brexit-recession-economy-what-happens-nigel-farage-speech-a7099301.html.

Runnymede Trust. 2015. 'The 2015 Budget Effects on Black and Minority Ethnic People', *Runnymede Trust*. http://www.runnymedetrust.org/projects-and-publications/employment-3/budget-2015-impact-on-bme-families.html.

Sayer, D. 2017. White riot—Brexit, Trump, and Post-Factual Politics. *Journal of Historical Sociology* 30 (1): 92–106. DOI:10.1111/johs.v30.1.

Shilliam, R. 2018. *Race and the Undeserving Poor: From Abolition to Brexit*. Newcastle: Agenda.

Song, M. 2014. Challenging a Culture of Racial Equivalence. *British Journal of Sociology*, 65: 107–129. DOI:10.1111/1468-4446.12054.

Spiked! 2016. 'The Brexit Vote Was a Revolt against the Establishment', *Spiked!/WorldBytes*, 24 August, viewed 20 January 2017, http://www.spiked-online.com/newsite/article/the-brexit-votewas-a-revolt-against-the-establishment/18693#.WWZEVYjytPY.

Stewart, H. and Mason, R. 2016. 'Nigel Farage's anti-migrant poster reported to police', *The Guardian*, 16 June, viewed 10 May 2020, https://www.theguardian.com/politics/2016/jun/16/nigel-farage-defends-ukip-breaking-point-poster-queue-of-migrants.

Tyler, I. 2013. *Revolting Subjects: Social Abjection and Resistance in Neoliberal Britain*. London: Zed Books.

Virdee, S. 2014. *Racism, Class and the Racialized Outsider*. Basingstoke: Palgrave.

Virdee, S. and McGeever, B. 2018. Racism, Crisis, Brexit. *Ethnic and Racial Studies*, 41 (10): 1802–1819. DOI: 10.1080/01419870.2017.1361544.

Winter, A. 2019. Online Hate: From the Far-Right to the 'Alt-Right', and from the Margins to the Mainstream. In *Online Othering: Exploring Digital Violence and Discrimination on the Web*, ed. K. Lumsden and E. Harmer, pp. 39–63. London: Palgrave.

# Part V

# Governmentalities: Formations, reproductions, and refusals of whiteness

This section engages with the ways in which whiteness frames and forms everyday practices of inclusion and exclusion across spheres of social life. It looks at the formal practices and processes of human governance and the state to explore how whiteness becomes institutionalised through contact with the state and its agents, and how ideals of whiteness define behaviour, either for sanction or punishment. These processes and practices operate as a systemically ordered, interconnected and shifting complex. They include criminalisation, school exclusion, development of curriculum materials and ethos, definitions of citizenship and rights, racialisation of mental health and unhealthiness, and reproduction, birthing and reproductive practices and aspirations, as in the case of transnational parental matching practices, as well as more everyday consumption practices.

The section contributions build on the significant body of empirical work focusing on institutional processes, professional practices in single sites, country or discipline-specific practices, to consider the extensive, multi-layered and interconnected nature of white governmentalities. Amrita Pande's chapter presents an ethnography of transnational 'repro-flows' of commercial fertility practices. Jamie Kherbaoui and Brittany Aronson's chapter unpicks the network of practices, policies, organisations and institutions making up the 'White Saviour Industrial Complex'. Javeria Shah presents a 'whiteness ecology' of Britishness established through interconnected catalysts for the percolation of racist ideologies in structures, systems, and interactions. Sarah Heinz follows Foucault to consider whiteness as a 'dispositif', 'a network of socially dispersed practices, discourses, systems of artefacts and modes of subjectification'. As part of the governmental practice of creating white people, states reach beyond their borders, redrawing them globally in more or less obvious ways. For Georgie Wemyss, this responsibility for the drawing of global borders is distributed to citizens through 'everyday bordering' practices which are a process of officially and unofficially racialising citizens inside and outside of whiteness through immigration legislation. Her focus is the creation of the racially subordinated category of 'lascar' by historical and geographical processes to contain a mobile Indian labour force. Together the contributions show a global system of interconnected governmentalities which sustain and reproduce global whiteness. Governmentalities also encompass the relationship with neoliberalism, with the instantiation of global neoliberal whiteness as a means to govern the social through the economic at the interpersonal and intimate levels. Choices about life,

DOI: 10.4324/9780429355769-105

bodies and births, idealisations of home, and practices of bodily and familial comfort are enacted through whiteness as a form of governmentality. Sarah Heinz considers the globality of home and the idealisation of home ownership to connect cultural practices of aspirational home making to settler colonial practices of possession and dispossession and contemporary welfare state institutional exclusions from housing across South Africa, Australia, Britain, Singapore, and Malaysia. For Wemyss, the establishment of an economic commonsense through work for her British Indian seafarers becomes a form of lived bodily common sense, a way of keeping friends and making enemies. Kherbaoui and Aronson develop a devastating analysis of the US context where philanthropic deceit works to produce the disastrous effects of the COVID-19 pandemic internal to the United States. Global colonial neoliberal economic commonsense orders the rules of supposedly universal human deservedness and worth by rewarding people who conform to certain governing norms and practices as 'inside', while positioning non-conforming outsiders as dispensable. Governmental abstractions are actually lived realities of whiteness that work to accord life and death.

# 19

# Assisted reproduction and assisted whiteness

*Amrita Pande*

## Introduction

In her review of what she labels 'anthropology of reproductive tourism', medical anthropologist Michal Nahman (2016) asks: 'What do the increasingly intensified and standardised practices of cross-border purchase of gametes tell us about what "IVF reproduces" other than babies?' In this chapter, based on a multi-sited global ethnography, I follow a chain of intended parents (IP), egg providers and gametes across borders and continents, to demonstrate that as IP search for the perfect egg provider and clinics collude to provide this service to them, in essence, the desirability of whiteness is reproduced. Assisted reproductive technologies assist the search for and desirability of whiteness.

## Reproductive travel and repro flows

Medical Travel, clients traveling for medical treatment, has been going on for centuries (Roberts and Scheper-Hughes 2011). Reproductive travel, or repro-travel, clients traveling for various forms of infertility treatment, is also a practice going on for decades. Historically, wealthy elites from the global south travelled to the global north in search of the best technologies and treatment, not available or not reliable at home. Now, we witness a reverse traffic – clients from all over the world are heading to the global south to get treatment at bargain prices, and get access to reproductive resources in ways that they cannot at home. My interest in this intriguing world of repro-travel started in 2006 and culminated into a monograph on gestational surrogacy in India (Pande 2014). In that I argued that despite warnings by radical feminists that this service is akin to baby farms where poor black women are breeding white babies, there is much more to debate. In their narratives, the women made it clear that surrogacy was exceptionally hard labour but it was also work where they produced something of value, and instead of glass bangles or shirts in a factory, they were now (re)'producing' a priceless baby. Yet, I highlighted the paradox of this temporary valuation of their bodies and celebration of their contribution – their fertile bodies were being taken care of, fed and pampered for the first time in an anti-natal state like India. For decades these women had been told that their excessive fertility was what was making their families and, in fact, the entire nation poor. Through long-term injectables and sterilisation, they

DOI: 10.4324/9780429355769-19

had been coerced into 'choosing' not to reproduce. Even when they needed to, they could not afford proper medical care for their own pregnancy and birth. Suddenly, this same class of women was being treated to the most sophisticated biomedical technologies because they were birthing children for other, richer, and often whiter parents to keep. This is what I called 'neo-eugenics', the new, subtle form of eugenics whereby the neo-liberal notion of consumer choice justifies promotion of assisted reproductive services for the rich and, at the same time, by portraying poor people (often in the global south) as strains on the world's economy and environment, justifies aggressive anti-natal policies.

Since 2016, commercial surrogacy has been banned in most parts of the global south, including India. But instead of closing the industry and my field, so to speak, the ban became the reason to expand the industry and the ethnography into a global one, connecting repro-flows across the world, especially the global south. As I connect my current research on 'repro-flows' with my previous works on gestational surrogacy, I realise that although race and whiteness were underlying my previous argument of neo-eugenics in cross-border gestational surrogacy, it was mostly invisible in the analysis itself. In this chapter, in some sense, I pick up where I had concluded by placing the two concepts at the centre of the analysis of cross border repro-flows.

In the next section, I outline the existing literature on transnational reproductions and liberal eugenics to argue that this scholarship is inadequate in addressing the reproduction of stratifications and reaffirmation of neo-eugenics by cross-border repro-flows. Instead, I engage with feminist research on race and reproduction, critical whiteness and critical race studies to address the complexities of the fertility industry.

## Transnational reproduction: Race and liberal eugenics

In the past decade, the growing scholarship on transnational reproduction has queried the multiple forms of power embedded in cross border *repro-flows*, the movement of reproductive bodies and substances across borders (Deomampo 2016; Nahman 2016; Pande 2014; Roberts, 2011; Rudrappa 2015; Speier 2016; Whittaker and Speier 2010). Scholars, within and outside of this cohort of transnational reproduction have been debating on the paradoxical and, often, contentious role of race in biomedicine genetic technologies and assisted reproduction in the twenty-first century (Kahn 2004; Kaufman and Hall 2003; Roberts 2011; Russell 2015). In these discussions around race and ART in the twenty-first century, there are emerging debates around the nature of 'reprogenetics', the merger of reproductive and genetic technologies 'to ensure or prevent the inheritance of particular genes in a child'. In my previous discussions of gestational surrogacy, my concept of neo-eugenics was in part a critical response to a strand of scholarship around such reprogenetics, or what some science and technology in society (STS) scholars have labelled 'liberal' eugenics (Agar 2004; Rose 2007) – a new era of biopolitics led by individual consumer choice, where the only role that the state plays is to 'foster the development of a range of technologies of enhancement' (Agar 2004: 5). The shift from a focus on the state to the individual and individual responsibility is fundamental to the argument being made. For instance, in *Politics of Life Itself*, sociologist Nikolas Rose, who since then has become foundational in all works on reproductive ethics and biotechnology, asserts that there is a concise break in the eugenic tendencies of the first four decades of the twentieth century and what we are witnessing in contemporary biopolitics. While genetic makeup of the population still remains a political concern, political obsession with race-based enhancements, and negative eugenics, Rose believes, is one of the past, or of countries with 'different rationalities' (p. 69). This 'transformed bio politics' of the twenty-first century is one that is about 'fostering individual life, not of eliminating those that threaten the quality of populations, it is a biopolitics that does not seek to legitimate inequality but to intervene on its consequences' (p. 167). The way forward, for the scholars of liberal eugenics, is to envision reproductive selection as an individual, voluntary, state neutral and, often, empowering, practice. Other scholars of 'liberal eugenics' have been as optimistic about this difference between state-sponsored eugenics of the past, and the private choices around technological enhancements prevalent today (Agar 2004; Blencowe 2011; Rose 2007). But are these practices merely a reflection of individual autonomy and choice, or are they also shaped by, and embedded within, power relations? In this chapter, through a systematic study of the transnational fertility industry, I challenge this assumed binary and the inadvertent depoliticising of racialised desires and choices. The focus on intimacy and privacy of choices around kinship, familial, and racial identity depoliticises questions of in-equalities, and of whiteness as an (embodied) privilege. To understand the complex interplay of consumer desires for their offspring, the political-economy of the fertility industry and its in-terlinkages with the history of eugenics, I move now to critical race and whiteness studies.

## Transnational reproduction: Critical race and critical whiteness theory

A body of research on critical whiteness studies, mostly emanating from the United States, has defined whiteness by its 'power to be invisible', wherein the attached privileges also tend to appear as natural, expected and universal (Dyer 1997). The critical agenda for these scholars is to subject whiteness to the same scrutiny that black bodies and blackness have been historically and analytically subjected to, to challenge this invisibility. Yet, another line of more recent studies on whiteness, South African critical whiteness studies, amongst others challenge this emphasis on 'invisible privilege alone' and instead focus on the stark embodiment and strategic manip-ulations of whiteness in particular times and spaces (De Klerk 2010; Steyn 2001; Willoughby-Herard 2007). One of the 'fundamental errors' of the first line of critical whiteness studies is to assume that the spectacular, pervasive and bio-logic basis of race and whiteness has disappeared from the current historical moment (Willoughby-Herard 2007: 487). In this chapter, I draw from this strain of critical whiteness scholarship emanating from the South to focus on the embodied and hypervisible manifestations of racialised desires embedded in the fertility industry.

One of the most vocal critics of the raced nature and impacts of ARTs is legal scholar Dorothy Roberts, who has systematically laid out the inherent 'whiteness' of ARTs, which normalises the invisibility of black women from the entire discussion of ARTs. Black women are deemed guilty of hyperfertility and hence their reproductive needs are denigrated and ig-nored. The only time blackness makes its media appearance is in stories of lawsuits and couples suing clinics and gamete banks for 'malpractice', very often involving a white woman being mistakenly inseminated with a 'black sperm' (see Cramblett vs. Midwest Sperm bank 2016 and Andrews vs. MYUMC case 2007).[1] Sensationalist media reports might equate the case of a white woman mistakenly inseminated by a black sperm to that of an African-American woman inseminated by a white sperm, yet, for those familiar with the history of racial purity, notions of contamination and white degeneracy, the two become substantially different 'fertility screw ups' (Quiroga 2007). While Roberts comments on the invisibility of blackness as a raced product of new ART, others observe the link between race and reproduction as an incessant desire to racially match one's offspring (Almeling 2007; Ikemoto 1995; Krolokke 2014; Quiroga 2007; Russell 2015). These scholars have demonstrated a fundamental irony of race in assisted reproduction – while social scientists continue to argue that race is a social construct, these technologies reinforce the concept of race as a biological category, and shared race as shared kinship. In the United States, for instance, Ikemoto (1995) highlights the naturalisation of the desire for a racial match within the egg provision industry. Although, in artificial in-semination, recipients routinely emphasised a racial match, this never becomes a topic of dis-cussion presumably because racial-matching is seen as an obvious and natural desire. It is only when black women choose 'white eggs' and colour lines are crossed that the topic is deemed newsworthy (Ikemoto 1995: 1016). Clinics and gamete banks become 'matchers' in actively shaping individual decision-making about reproduction and the need to form racially homo-genous families (Lenhardt 2017; Moll 2019). When one juxtaposes this normalisation of racial matching with the invisibility of blackness from the fertility industry, ART ultimately privilege genetic relatedness in ways that reaffirm and reproduce hegemonic notions of white hetero-patriarchal families (Quiroga 2007; Roberts 2011).

While phenotype matching has been observed in the fertility industry across the world, with IP, gametes and gamete providers crossing borders, 'whiteness' becomes a purchasable trait with multiple, and often conflicting, meanings. Scholars of assisted reproduction in Asia, for instance have focused on the 'match' as more than just racial matching, this hypervisible basis of ra-cialisation and race matching intersects with of religion, caste, skin colour in post-colonial locals. Charis Thompson, for instance, talks of a complex intertwining of post-colonial history with race, wherein desirability is embedded in colour and skin tone and yet is not limited to it. In her work with gamete donors, she brings up the example of a Japanese recipient who chose an Asian donor profile based on the desired skin tone but then rejected it when she learnt that it was from a Korean donor – Korea a former colony of Japan fell too low in the matrix of desirability to be pulled up solely on the basis of skin tone match. In another study of white desirability in Korea, media studies scholar Ji-Hyun Ahn deepens this criticism of the black and white binary assumed in scholarships on racialised desires and instead brings up ideas of white desirability that are embedded in celebration of 'hybridity'. The desirability of whiteness, Ahn demonstrates, is intricately woven together with a certain class of multiracialism, 'racial hy-bridity', and the neoliberal commodification of cosmopolitan whiteness 'as a marker of cool-ness' and of desirable beauty. Here, mixed whiteness becomes a marker of desirable otherness in terms of aesthetics – mixed race *white* individuals are celebrated as embodying beauty, cos-mopolitanisms, metrosexuality and the best of both worlds. In her work on 'Eurasian Mixed Race-ness', Matthews (2007) expands on this notion of cosmopolitan whiteness by debating the appeal of Eurasian/mixed race as 'cosmo chic', one who is 'familiar, knowable, sophisticated and worldly' (Matthews 2007: 51).

Recent scholarship on skin-whitening observes a similar shift towards the 'aesthetics' or 'affect' of cosmopolitan whiteness, wherein the demand for lighter skin in Asia and amongst people of Black African descent is theorised as something beyond the desire for 'Caucasian whiteness' (Ayu Saraswati 2010; Tate 2016). The embodiment of cosmopolitan whiteness, Saraswati argues, is not restricted to one race but requires embodying the *feelings* of cosmo-politanness and is embedded with many other 'positive affective qualities such as sophistication, beauty, or, as one of the whitening ads' slogans puts it, "skin of innocence"' (Ayu Saraswati 2010: 28). For Tate, skin lightening is akin to 'shade shifting', a 'post-race self-affirming aes-thetic enhancement and choice' (Tate 2016: 7). While I find the analytical frame of cosmo-politan whiteness compelling and critical in understanding the performativity of beauty and the 'fluidity of whiteness' (Pande 2021), I demonstrate that the language of 'individual choice' make invisible structures of inequality and power. I argue instead, that in choices made within the transnational fertility industry, such 'enhancements' do not challenge or subvert racialisation and racialised hierarchies. In the next sections, I highlight two such choices: *Desire for racial matching* (by some IP who identify as white) and desire *for cosmopolitan and mixed whiteness* (by some IP who do not identify as white). Both sets of desires are made purchasable by new technologies, and in effect, reaffirm the desirability of whiteness.

## Global ethnography

In 2010, when I started the fieldwork for this project, there were several countries, for instance Czech Republic, India, Mexico, Thailand, Ukraine, and the United States, that served as transnational reproductive hubs for third-party reproduction, especially gestational commercial surrogacy and egg provision. Since 2014, the industry has been scuttling around the globe, pushed out from one country to another, due to national laws banning either egg provision or cross border commercial surrogacy or both. IP now need to cross multiple borders to access services related to the various aspects of assisted fertility – from gamete provision, embryology to gestation. To fully understand the transnationality of this process as well as to map the global trajectory from egg retrieval to embryo implantation, I conducted research in three related sites – the 'preparation' of (white) egg providers by global egg agencies in South Africa before their travels to various global fertility clinics across the world, the egg retrieval and making of an embryo in a global fertility clinic in India, and finally the transfer of embryo into the womb of a gestational mother in a clinic in Cambodia.

For the first segment of my research, egg retrieval, I interacted with 'traveling egg providers' (Pande 2020; Pande and Moll 2018), women who regularly travel across the world to provide their eggs to various partner global fertility clinics, before and during their travels. Between 2012 and 2018, I travelled with three groups of egg providers from South Africa to India and Cambodia.[2] Additionally, I conducted detailed open-ended, semi-structured interviews with 15 medical professionals and fertility professionals. The agency managers and fertility professionals connected me to 21 egg providers and 28 IP who are using the services of these transnational fertility clinics. I conducted unstructured interviews with IP via Skype and/or had face–face interactions with them at hotels in India and Cambodia. The clients in these global fertility clinics are predominantly international. Although married heterosexual couples comprise a majority of users of ARTs within national fertility markets, LGBTQ clients, popularly labelled 'gay IP' are conspicuous at the transnational level as they are more likely to be barred from accessing ART services at home. Gay IPs are more likely to be implicated in the ethical and justice scandals around the industry, another reason for their disproportionate visibility (Mamo and Alston-Stepnitz 2014).

## Desiring whiteness for a racial match

There is a deep irony that the demand for whiteness within the transnational fertility industry is filled by women from South Africa, a country that is majority Black and where, more than two decades after apartheid has ended, racial classifications remain the foundation of society. Elsewhere (Pande 2018, 2020), I describe, in detail, the history and political-economy of the gamete industry emerging from within this racially bifurcated health-care industry. Here, I focus on the cross-border demand for white South African egg providers, and to understand the dynamics of this demand, I talk to Dr. Peter, a European fertility expert who consults for clinics in South Africa. Dr. Peter gives a quick explanation as to why the market for white South African traveling egg providers exists,

> See … An egg donation cycle in the United States can cost anywhere between 25 000 to 30 000 dollars. But, now think, if you were smart and instead recruited egg donors in

South Africa? You have to pay them only USD 2000 and they are happy to fly anywhere and donate! These girls are also white, have blue eyes and are blonde like the Americans … A white face is a white face and often that's what a person wants.

According to Dr. Peter, a simple substitution of North American 'whiteness' with South African whiteness reduces the costs substantially. IP narratives reveal a far more complicated motivation for desiring white (South African) gametes than sheer cost. In many cases, the clients choose a white egg provider because they identify as white and desire that the child born through assisted technologies to 'pass' as their own. Becker et al. (2005) relate this to the ubiquitous nature of 'resemblance talk', constant public observations about a child's physical similarity to parents. Other scholars have commented on racial matching and resemblance based on phenotypical similarities as kin-making tactics (Deomampo 2016: 96) and a way to avoid the stigma of using donor eggs. All respondents who identified as white gave some version of 'resemblance talk' to legitimise their hunt for white egg cells.

Cynthia, a 44-year-old white IP from Canada, confessed that after eight unsuccessful IVF attempts at home, she had decided to end her fertility treatment journey. One of her Indian friends informed her about a fertility clinic in India that provided surrogacy and egg provision services. The clinic, however, did not offer the services of their own egg bank, which has a database of over 300 Indian and Nepalese egg provider profiles. When I interviewed Cynthia, one of South Africa's biggest egg banks facilitated the movement of white South African egg providers to India. Cynthia was sent the details of this company and their 'girls'. She describes her determination to choose an appropriate egg provider as an 'obsession',

> Elizabeth (Liz), the manager of the South African egg bank became like a friend, I asked so many questions and wanted so many details! I felt possessed, it was like an obsession. I literally put all the qualities of the donors on an xl sheet and weighted them to choose the ultimate donor … All the girls that Liz offered were white, except one or two mixed race ones. I guess she knew what I wanted. I mean, I have no issues about race but honestly, I felt like I needed to have a whole spiritual connection with my donor, if this had to work. If not my own genes, then the closest imitation … I wanted the hair, the freckles, the eye colour, the works.

While Cynthia believes she has 'no issues with race', she simultaneously highlights the need for racial match to establish a spiritual connection with the child. All white couples I interviewed refrained from using the word 'race' when talking about the choice of gamete, and instead talked of skin tones, eye colour, and hair colour, yet the hunt for the closest imitation was 'a key part of maintaining a narrative of whiteness' (Ryan and Moras 2017: 590). Other scholars have noticed a similar 'coding' of racial desires in non-racial terms by white IP. In their study of white lesbian gamete recipients in the United States, Ryan and Moras talk of the 'the explicit mobilisation of "optional ethnicities" and a simultaneous silence around race', to highlight the white privilege of opting for a situationally specific ethnic identity – a privilege that is not available to many other racially marginalised groups (2017: 588).

Claudia, a white intended mother from Germany, was keen to avoid discussions of race and instead emphasised her Dutch ancestry as a reason for choosing an Afrikaans speaking white South African egg provider. I interviewed Claudia over Skype in 2015, while she was in the process of getting her egg provider from Liz's egg bank in South Africa and was to be treated in yet another clinic in India. Claudia describes her desire for a white South African egg provider as ancestry and ethnicity, and not a race-based choice.

I know I could have gone for the Indian ones (egg providers). It would have been simpler, I suppose … But I was looking for a deeper connection and when they (the clinic) offered me a South African girl, I read up all about the Afrikaans-speaking girls in South Africa … Did you know Afrikaans has both Dutch and German connections? That sealed it for me … For me it's not about race here, it's about my ancestors, our connected heritage.

Although Claudia mentions the importance of 'heritage', this can only be symbolic as the Afrikaans-speaking egg provider will have no real connection with the child borne out of these technologies, and hence little chance of transmitting any culture or linguistic ability to the child. Claudia's attempt at establishing deep connections, resonates with Laura Mamo's (2005) 'affinity ties', wherein IPs (intended mothers in case of sperm donation) imagine their sperm donors' characteristics, for instance a hobby, as rematerialised full personalities (Mamo 2005: 246). As discussed in an earlier section, this desire for racial matching has been observed in many parts of the world. Within the transnational fertility industry, this desire is not merely fulfilled but naturalised, for all white IP. Unexpectedly, the transnational fertility industry reveals another set of racialised desires – the desire for cosmopolitan whiteness by IP who do not identify as white.

## Desiring cosmopolitan 'mixed' whiteness

Orchid Fertility Clinic in Cambodia was founded as a clinic specialising in transnational surrogacy after India, Thailand, and Nepal prohibited the practice in their countries. In 2015 and 2016, Orchid's business flourished with clients coming from all parts of the globe – mostly same sex partners and single men searching for egg providers and gestational surrogates. All fertility professionals and matchers I interviewed commented on the stark differences in the needs and expectations of their 'gay' and heterosexual clients in the gamete selection process. Liz, the South African owner and manager of a global egg agency, makes a clear distinction between her 'straight' and 'gay' clients, and the egg provider traits they emphasise.

For straight couples, they want to choose a donor that matches the mom, the closest match the better. If she is a tall blonde, of course, she will choose a tall blonde donor … Because she is giving up her DNA and there is a whole lot of grief that goes with that. It's different for gay couples, you know! Gay couples just want an attractive donor, that's it. I would want to say that there is a deeper meaning in that, but I cannot! I maybe generalizing, but I often even tease this gay client of mine about his hunt for 'pretty donors'.

Liz does not comment on her white, heterosexual clients' desire for a racial match and, instead, naturalises it as the intended mothers' intense desire to have the highest possible degree of resemblance. Her 'gay' clients, however, are teased because of their, allegedly, shallow quest for a pretty donor. Although Liz's observation is stark in its crude generalisation, it is useful to ask: What do IP emphasise when they are not looking for a resemblance match with a partner?

David, 37, is a gay intended father from Israel, and his partner, Daniel, an Argentine Jew settled in the United States. David and Daniel's journey involved a white South African egg provider and Orchid fertility clinic. David relates, in detail, the complex mix of race, religion, and cultures in his family and in Israel. His grandparents trace their roots to places as varied as Turkey and Algeria, and the only time he automatically checked a 'white' box of racial classification was in a financial form in the United States. David, however, is candid about his choice of a white egg provider:

> In our country, everyone, gay or straight, is obsessed with kids! It has been in my sub conscious since I turned 16 and came out ... So when I chose to become a dad, and paid so much for it, I wanted the best option possible. Her health was important, height, overall her looks – I wanted a white donor with blue or green eyes. (He repeats) I wanted the best option possible, in a way, you can say ... for genetic improvement (he laughs). Why not? See for us (he means as a gay parents) genes are everything. Because one of us is already being left out of the gene pool of the family, we aren't getting pregnant, so we are not going to make a moral issue about choosing the best gene if we can.

Despite his knowledge of race politics in Israel and the United States, and his multiracial family, David makes a definite choice about the race of the gamete provider. He talks about her 'attractiveness' and emphasises whiteness as genetic improvement and the best gene money can buy. David's desires need to be unpacked within the rather complicated terrain of same-sex couples managing their bio-genetic parenting within the technological process of conception and birth. In her work with same sex users of ART in the United States, Dempsey (2013) finds a preoccupation with choosing a donor that is most likely to create a child who could pass as a 'genetic hybrid' of the same sex parents. For David, however, the desire is for a genetic hybrid of another kind – a concerted effort to technologically attain a mix of traits that is deemed universally appealing. I observed a similar desire for strategic hybridisation amongst some (single and same sex) intended fathers from Asia. The manager of Orchid clinic, Dr. Mia, explains that when there are no intending mother present, as in the case of her same sex male clients, the desire is often not about a resemblance match,

> Many of our Asian married patients (intended parents) choose from our Asian database ... *But yes, every third patient asks for white eggs.* Everyone wants a beautiful face for the next generation ... We let the patients make the choice, we don't question. And many don't ask for our advice ... They (the IP) hear from word of mouth that that is a possibility here— that you can get white egg donor. And they see these pictures of couples with lovely mixed-race babies and they say 'why not'? And we say 'why not'?

Dr. Mia's narrative above reveals a far more complex categorisation of racialised desires than the narratives in the previous section, which were about the desire for racial (white) purity and racial matching. What is striking is Dr. Mia's claim that *one out of three* of her Asian clients desire a white egg provider, and the clinic fulfills this desire by matching them with a global egg bank and a white provider. This desire for racial hybridity needs to be understood as a transnational moment interacting with particular local histories. Historically, in much of East Asia, racially mixed children were a reminder of colonial or Euro-American military presence and the related 'immoral' liaisons. This post-colonial desire for white-mixed race babies is thus distinct from both the desire for 'Caucasian' whiteness and from the historical and local discourse of race with clearly defined racial boundaries and an unquestioned desire for racial purity.

Unarguably, meanings and perceptions of race and whiteness are entrenched in a layer of histories and hierarchies, which cannot be reduced to skin colour. Yet, as much as these local co-creations of whiteness (by clinics and clients) is analytically revealing, it does have a common global denominator – of reaffirming white desirability. The popularity of a white mixed-race offspring, for instance is starkly distinct from the treatment received by black mixed-race individuals, who do not embody this desirable mix of white exoticism and familial familiarity. Scholars working with black mixed-race children in Asia notice a similar pattern of marginalising those who are seen to be 'undesirably' mixed. Mixed African-Chinese children, or the black *hunxueer* 'hybrid child', face intense marginalisation and even racial slurs as a cultural Other, or a *yizu* alien race (Wing-Fai 2015).[3] A desire for mixed-race whiteness does not erase miscegenation, or challenge racial hierarchies.

## Conclusion

In her book *Desiring Whiteness*, Seshadri–Crooks (2000) argues that although race can never be reduced to 'the look', it is fundamentally a 'regime of looking' and 'a practice of visibility' (2000). The peculiar resiliency of race, Seshadri-Crooks argues, has much to do with this the 'hyper-valorisation of appearance'. The world of assisted reproduction is indeed built on this hyper valorisation of appearance, and highlights the irony that although the scientific validity of race has been disproved, this does not undermine its biologism. Much like the 'fertility screw ups' have demonstrated, when a white woman is mistakenly inseminated with a black sperm, this 'mistake' determines the life of the baby. As critical whiteness scholars from the south have indicated, there is 'something' that is inherited as 'race', making whiteness both hypervisible and a blatant privilege. For some, for instance Claudia and Cynthia, this choice translates into a desire for visible resemblance, racial purity and whiteness. South African egg providers and eggs are racialised in particular ways to legitimise this cross-border hunt for gametes. For others, like David, and other Asian clients at Orchid fertility clinic, racial match becomes secondary as science, technology, and travel intersect to offer the opportunity for strategic hybridity and a cosmopolitan whiteness.

Within the transnational fertility industry, race becomes a manipulable resource available to IP and clinics, at large. On the one hand, the transnational fertility industry facilitates the co-production of multiple and varied desires, some of which challenge assumptions of the normative family ideal as both 'monoracial and heterosexual' (Ahmed 2018, p. 2080). While some heterosexual white IP, in their search for a resemblance match, emphasise monoraciality, other IP, often single and same sex intended fathers, desire other traits that subvert the assumed universal desire for racial matching. This diluting of the desire to 'match a partner' resonates with Diane Tober's observation of single women and lesbian couples in their choice of sperm donor. Tober finds her respondents emphasising traits that are not all about a resemblance match. This elaborate and diverse preference of desired traits, ranging from intelligence to race, which are assumed to be inheritable, is labelled 'grassroot eugenics' (Tober 2019). For Tober, this form of eugenics is individual, innocuous and starkly different from the race-based eugenics of the past. As ART becomes a mean to 'invest' in a child, IP, medical professionals, transnational agency managers, and gamete 'matchers' become co-producers in designing desires that reaffirm the hegemony of whiteness. Although we might want to believe that the days of state biopolitics and eugenics is over, and consumers are making rational and responsible choices about their desired child, individual desires are, in effect, deeply shaped by (post-)colonial ideas of racial hierarchies, race-based aesthetics and the desire for freedom and privilege that comes with a 'proximity to whiteness' (Ahmed 2007: 130).

## Acknowledgement

This research is funded by two National Research Foundation Grants (Grant number 118573 and 103712) of South Africa. Ethics approval was obtained from the Department of Sociology, Faculty of Humanities, University of Cape Town, South Africa (SOC20/04/2012). A version of this chapter was originally published as a journal article in the journal Medical Anthropology.

## Notes

1 These stark and crude race-based labels for reproductive matter reflect the norm in the fertility industry wherein gametes are often stored in colour-coded vials, white for white eggs, black for African-American eggs, and so on (Russell 2015).
2 Elsewhere (Pande 2020) I analyse, in greater detail, the desires of these traveling egg provider and their management by global fertility professionals.
3 The notion of racial purity continues in much of the conversations around mixed race individuals. In fact, even the Chinese term 'hunxueer' assumes that mixed race individuals are polluting the bloodline (Wing-Fai 2015).

## References

Agar, N. 2004. *Liberal Eugenics: In Defense of Human Enhancement*. Malden: Blackwell Publishing.

Ahmed, S. 2007. Multiculturalism and the Promise of Happiness. *New Formations*, 63: 121–137.

Ahmed, A. 2018. Race and Assisted Reproduction: Implications for Population Health. *Fordham Law Review*, 86 (6): 2801–2810.

Ahn, J.-H. 2015. Desiring Biracial Whites: Cultural Consumption of White Mixed-race Celebrities in South Korean Popular Media. *Media, Culture & Society*, 37 (6): 937–947.

Almeling, R. 2007. Selling Genes, Selling Gender: Egg Agencies, Sperm Banks, and the Medical Market in Genetic Material. *American Sociological Review*, 72: 319–340.

Ayu Saraswati, L. 2010. Cosmopolitan Whiteness: The Effects and Affects of Skin-Whitening Advertisements in a Transnational Women's Magazine in Indonesia. *Meridians*, 10 (2): 15–41.

Becker, G., Butler, A. and Nachtigall, R. 2005. Resemblance Talk: A Challenge for Parents Whose Children Were Conceived with Donor Gametes in the US. *Social Science and Medicine*, 61 (6): 1300–1309.

Daniels, C. R. and Heidt-Forsythe, E. 2012. Gendered Eugenics and the Problematic of Free Market Reproductive Technologies: Sperm and Egg Donation in the United States. *Signs*, 37 (3): 719–747.

De Klerk, E. 2010. White Curtains, Dark Thoughts. *English in Africa*, 37 (1): 41–62.

Dempsey, D. 2013. Surrogacy, Gay Male Couples and the Significance of Biogenetic Paternity. *New Genetics and Society*, 32 (1): 37–53.

Deomampo, D. 2016. *Transnational Reproduction: Race, Kinship, and Commercial Surrogacy in India*. New York: New York University Press.

Dyer, R. 1997. *White*. London: Routledge.

Frankenburg, R. 2002. *White Women, Race Matters: The Social Construction of Whiteness*. London: Routledge.

Gilbert, D. 2005. Interrogating Mixed-Race: A Crisis of Ambiguity? *Social Identities*, 11 (1): 55–74.

Ikemoto, L. C. 1995. The Infertile, the too Fertile, and the Dysfertile. *Hastings Law Journal*, 47 (4): 1007–1061.

Kahn, J. 2004. How a Drug Becomes "Ethnic": Law, Commerce, and the Production of Racial Categories in Medicine. *Yale Journal of Health Policy, Law, and Ethics*, 4 (1): 1–46.

Kaufman, J. S. and Hall, S. A. 2003. The Slavery Hypertension Hypothesis: Dissemination and Appeal of a Modern Race Theory. *Epidemiology 30*, 14 (1): 111–118.

Kr{\o}l{\o}kke, C. 2014. West is Best: Affective Assemblages and Spanish Oocytes. *European Journal of Women's Studies*, 21 (1): 57–71.

Lenhardt, R. 2017. The Color of Kinship, 102 IOWA. *Law Review*, 2071.

Mamo, L. 2005. Biomedicalizing Kinship: Sperm Banks and the Creation of Affinity-ties. *Science as Culture*, 14 (3): 237–264. DOI: 10.1080/09505430500216833.

Mamo, L. and Alston-Stepnitz, E. 2014. Queer Intimacies and Structural Inequalities: New Directions in Stratified Reproduction. *Journal of Family Issues*, 36: 519–540.

Matthews, J. 2007. Eurasian Persuasions: Mixed Race, Performativity and Cosmopolitanism. *Journal of Intercultural Studies*, 28 (1): 41–54.

Moll, T. 2019. Making a Match: Curating Race in South African Gamete Donation. *Medical Anthropology*, 38 (7): 588–602.

Nahman, M. 2016. Reproductive Tourism, Through the Anthropological 'Reproscope'. *Annual Review of Anthropology*, 45: 417–432.

Pande A. 2014. *Wombs in Labor: Transnational Commercial Surrogacy in India*. New York: Columbia University Press.

Pande, A. 2020. Visa Stamps for Injections: Traveling Biolabor and South African Egg Provision. *Gender & Society*, 34 (4): 573–596. DOI:10.1177/0891243220932147.

Pande A. 2021. Mix or Match?": Transnational fertility industry and White Desirability. *Medical Anthropology*. https://www.tandfonline.com/doi/full/10.1080/01459740.2021.1877289.

Pande, A. and Moll, T. 2018. Gendered Bio-responsibilities and Travelling Egg Providers from South Africa. *Reproductive Biomedicine & Society Online*, 6: 23–33.

Quiroga, S. S. 2007. Blood Is Thicker than Water: Policing Donor Insemination and the Reproduction of Whiteness. *Hypatia*, 22 (2): 143–161.

Roberts, D. 2011. *Fatal Invention: How Science, Politics, and Big Business Re-create Race in the Twenty-first Century*. New York: New Press.

Roberts, E. F. S. and Scheper-Hughes, N. 2011. Introduction: Medical Migrations. *Body & Society*, 17: 1–30.

Rose, N. 2007. *The Politics of Life Itself: Biomedicine, Power, and Subjectivity in the Twenty-First Century*. Princeton: Princeton University Press.

Rose, N. and Novas, C. 2005. Biological Citizenship. In *Global Assemblages: Technology, Politics, and Ethics as Anthropological Problems*, ed. A. Ong and S. Collier, pp. 439–463. Malden, USA: Blackwell Publishing.

Rudrappa S. 2015. *Discounted Life: The Price of Global Surrogacy in India*. New York: New York University Press.

Russell, C. 2015. The Race Idea in Reproductive Technologies: Beyond Epistemic Scientism and Technological Mastery. *Bioethical Inquiry*, 12: 601–612.

Ryan, M. and Moras, A. 2017. Race Matters in Lesbian Donor Insemination: Whiteness and Heteronormativity as Co-constituted Narratives. *Ethnic and Racial Studies*, 40 (4): 579–596.

Seshadri-Crooks, K. 2000. *Desiring Whiteness: A Lacanian Analysis of Race*. London: Routledge.

Speier, A. 2016. *Fertility Holidays. IVF Tourism and the Reproduction of Whiteness*. New York: New York University Press.

Steyn, M. 2001. '*Whiteness Just Isn't What It Used To Be': White Identity in a Changing South Africa*. Albany, NY: State University of New York Press.

Tate, S. 2016. *Skin Bleaching in Black Atlantic Zones. Shade Shifters*. Basingstoke, Hampshire: Palgrave Macmillan.

Taussig, K. S., Rapp, R. and Heath, D. 2008. Flexible Eugenics: Technologies of the Self in the Age of Genetics. In *Anthropologies of Modernity: Foucault, Governmentality, and Life Politics*, ed. J. X. Inda, pp. 194–212. Malden, MA: Blackwell Publishing Ltd.

Thompson, C. 2009. Skin Tone and the Persistence of Biological Race in Egg Donation for Assisted Reproduction. In *Shades of Difference: Why Skin Color Matters*, ed. E. Nakano Glenn, pp. 131–147. Palo Alto, California: Stanford University Press.

Thompson, C. 2011. Medical Migrations Afterword: Science as a Vacation? *Body & Society*, 17 (2–3): 205–213.

Tober, D. 2019. *Romancing the Sperm: Shifting Biopolitics and the Making of Modern Families*. New Brunswick, NJ: Rutgers University Press.

Whittaker, A. and Speier, A. 2010. 'Cycling Overseas': Care, Commodification, and Stratification in Cross-Border Reproductive Travel. *Medical Anthropology*, 29 (4): 363–383.

Willoughby-Herard, T. 2007. South Africa's Poor Whites and Whiteness Studies: Afrikaner Ethnicity, Scientific Racism, and White Misery. *New Political Science*, 29 (4): 479–500.

Wing-Fai, Leung (2015) Who Could Be an Oriental Angel? Lou Jing, Mixed Heritage and the Discourses of Chinese Ethnicity. *Asian Ethnicity*, 16 (3): 294–313.

# 20

# British Indian seafarers, bordering and belonging

*Georgie Wemyss*

## Introduction

> It is creating divisions in the society. Not only between the white indigenous people and the immigrant people. It could just be one of my friends who has fallen out with me... just to harass me ... so the Home Office are trying their best not to make a cohesive society although they preach for this ... they are trying to employ people as police against each other they are creating a situation of chaos in this society.
>
> *(Ahmed, British-Bangladeshi small business employer, London)*[1]

Ahmed is talking about increased immigration enforcement raids on British-Bangladeshi owned businesses happening as ordinary citizens were encouraged to report their suspicions of people living or working 'illegally' in the United Kingdom as part of creating a 'hostile environment' for UK immigration. He warned against the divisive impacts of this on British society whereby individuals acting as citizen border-guards are able to use their insider status to exclude and disrupt the lives of others. Through everyday bordering processes (Yuval-Davis et al. 2018), all citizens, including those who feel othered in their daily interactions, are encouraged to bolster their insider status by sustaining national borders through policing the lives of neighbours. This happens as part of the broader state induced compulsions to monitor the immigration status of their neighbours, tenants, or employees. Old scores with no obvious connection to immigration, 'race' or religion can be reignited when those confident in their legal status as citizens are enabled to use state immigration laws to harass those whom they perceive as less secure.

This chapter draws on theoretical approaches developed within critical race studies that understand whiteness as a social and cultural construction that is differentially and conditionally associated with skin colour. Whilst whiteness shifts over time and in different spaces, it has evolved as an organising principle of late modernity. It is linked to hierarchies of privilege and belonging and enacted through ideas of nation and formal and informal immigration status upheld in social policies (Hage 1998; Hunter et al. 2010; Nayak 2007; Wemyss 2006). Through the everyday actions of citizens encouraged or compelled to monitor immigration status of their neighbours, tenants or employees the twenty-first century hostile environment immigration policies that Ahmed is talking about codify whiteness, enacting racialised power, grown out of

DOI: 10.4324/9780429355769-20

British colonial expansion and destruction. All citizens are legally obliged to carry out everyday bordering duties (Yuval-Davis et al. 2019) via job application processes, health and other public and private service access monitoring. However, their targets are those thought of, using Nayak's expression (2007) as 'not white enough' to be included in the cultural construct of white Britishness. Successful business owners such as Ahmed may abide by the rules of the neoliberal cultures of whiteness in their daily lives by checking the immigration status of their employees. However, they are 'not white enough' to avoid rumour-triggered Border Force raids of their businesses or for their immigration status to not be questioned by bureaucrats who cannot imagine them as British citizens. For them whiteness and hence their status as British nationals is provisional.

Like many other British-Bangladeshis, Ahmed had been born in the district of Sylhet[2] and settled in London with his wife whose extended family members had migrated to the United Kingdom over different decades and generations. Their ancestors had included men employed on British merchant navy ships in the nineteenth and twentieth centuries – some of whom had settled in Britain whilst others built lives in port cities or inland across the British Empire and the United States or had returned to live in Sylhet (Adams 1987; Bald 2013; Goodall et al. 2008).

Ahmed's comment, identifying the apparently contradictory rhetoric and practice of the UK government, illustrates the perspectives of British citizens whose ancestors were born in the ex-Empire and for whom the borders of Britain have rarely appeared 'natural', one-dimensional or 'fair'. Neither did they experience borders as the impermeable linear constructions along the edges of state territories of nationalist discourses. In particular, the globally mobile, racialised colonial seafaring labour force were a motivation for the codification of white privilege into maritime and immigration laws that created and re-created state borders and ideologies of white nationhood across the British Empire. Seafarers also experienced the permeability and shifting characteristics of racialised legal employment categories and the conditionality of whiteness in maritime and imperial contexts. During wartime crises, a minority of British Indian seafarers managed to be recruited into white labour categories at sea whilst continuing to be targets of racist violence and discrimination on and offshore (Visram 2002).

In the following discussion, I use an analytical approach drawn from theories of global coloniality and critical whiteness studies (Hunter et al. 2010) to focus on selected histories of the colonial British Indian maritime labour force to expand understandings of different ways that white supremacy has framed and continues to form present-day state bordering practices that are part of hostile environment immigration policies that force citizens racialised as 'not white enough' to prove their right to live and work in the United Kingdom. Maritime labour histories evidence how colonial employment categories and other bordering discourses and immigration practices worked together over four centuries to produce enduring ideas of 'who is white' and who is 'not white enough' strengthening the relationship between whiteness and Britishness. Tlostanova and Mignolo explain global coloniality as the 'model of power relations that came into existence as a consequence of the Western imperial expansion but did not end with the official end of colonialism and colonial administrations' (2012: 7). Whilst historical European colonialism is (mostly) past, the relations of coloniality endure. The power relations of global coloniality include historical cultural and labour relations together with knowledge production that both enables and restricts the ways differently situated people imagine their position in the world and their relationships with others. In the following sections, I begin by briefly outlining how processes of bordering work to include and exclude differently situated people in the context of global coloniality. I then focus on how racialised hierarchies of Britishness and belonging have produced and been reproduced through historical maritime and immigration bordering legislation that created mobile labour categories that aimed to prevent British Indian subjects from settling in the United Kingdom and white settler colonies.

## Bordering, global coloniality, and exclusionary categories

Far from the natural barriers or solid constructions of nationalist imaginations, state borders have always been created, re-constructed and experienced in diverse ways, by differently situated people, at multiple levels and sites across time and space (Yuval-Davis et al. 2019). Borders act as filters – permeable for those permitted to or who manage to cross them – whilst they are intended to be impermeable to others. Bordering processes constitute a principal organising mechanism in constructing, maintaining, and controlling social and political order from local to global scales. Van Houtum et al. (2005) notion of 'b/ordering' – the interaction between the ordering of chaos and processes of border-making – succinctly encapsulates the relationship between bordering and governance whereby b/ordering discourses and practices create and recreate categories of those who are included and those who are excluded from national collectivities. Processes of bordering always differentiate between 'us' and 'them', those who are in and those who are out, those who are allowed to cross the borders and those who are not. Different political projects of belonging construct the borders as differentially permeable, view those who want to cross the border as more or less of a security or cultural threat and construct the borders around different criteria for participation and entitlement for those who do cross them (Yuval-Davis et al. 2019). 'Everyday bordering', which in this section I use to discuss contemporary hostile environment immigration policies, refers to the everyday construction of *state* borders through ideology, cultural mediation, discourses, political institutions, attitudes and everyday forms of transnationalism (Yuval-Davis et al. 2018). In the United Kingdom, discourses and practices of everyday bordering materially and culturally reproduce the relationship between whiteness and imagined Britishness and as such are enduring components of global coloniality.

Throughout the twentieth and twenty-first century, governments in the Global South and North have been visibly strengthening state borders that were commonly created through European wars and colonial treaties. External walls or fences are constructed in parallel with increasing border checks at internal sites. Whilst neoliberal globalisation has been associated with de-bordering for goods, financial service and global elites, it has also been accompanied by re-bordering inside and outside of state territories in the name of securitisation. For example, in Israel the concrete wall built in 2000, aimed at preventing terrorist attacks, also cut off Palestinians from fields and work in Palestinian West Bank territory. The steel wall along the Egyptian border and Sinai desert that was built a decade later to stop African migrants fleeing war and poverty was later used to stop ISIS attacks (Yuval-Davis 2019: 60).

As borders have moved into the centre of political and social life, processes of everyday bordering are redefining contemporary notions of citizenship and belonging for racialised minorities and for hegemonic majorities. In India, as well as the construction of fences to keep out Muslim Pakistani and Bangladeshi citizens, the world's most extensive biometric ID system extends the reach of the internal border. It monitors all Indian citizens whilst excluding from welfare services and pensions those, predominantly Muslims, labelled as Pakistanis, Bangladeshis, or from Myanmar, who cannot prove to bureaucrats that they are legal residents (Manhotra 2016). The internal bordering thus intensified the socio-economic inequalities and rigid hierarchies of belonging which were legacies of the partition of British-ruled India.

Immigration and nationality legislation have worked in bordering and racially ordering European nations over centuries of colonial expansion. Successive laws have created and policed borders that maintain a global racialised order established by colonisation. In the case of the United Kingdom, Nadine El-Enany (2020) has mapped out how past and present legislation relating to Britain and its colonies have resulted in wealth accumulated globally being located within the borders of the United Kingdom. Immigration legislation has ensured that assets in the form of infrastructure, welfare provision and future opportunities for citizens are inaccessible to most descendants of Britain's colonial subjects. In different times and colonial spaces, intentionally discriminatory legislation has been made to appear 'race-neutral' (El-Enany 2020). Post-independence, bordering technologies such as those that constitute the hostile environment, maintain a permeability in state borders for the citizens of Britain's white settler colonies whilst blocking citizens of Britain's African, Asian, and Caribbean colonies.

For post-imperial Britain, the relationship between whiteness and Britishness ensures that the spectacular bordering of immigration raids (De Genova 2012), the bordering of the 'culture of disbelief' – a starting point of extreme scepticism – that imbues Home Office bureaucrats in their interactions with those with family connections in the Global South, and the everyday bordering of hostile environment policies work together to construct racialised hierarchies of belonging, producing and re-producing ideas of who belongs or does not belong; who is white or not white enough to belong. In the United Kingdom, the 'Windrush scandal', created through the structural racialised violence of colonial bordering and postcolonial re-bordering processes, exemplifies the historical relationships between whiteness, governance, bordering, and belonging. The scandal is the most widely publicised consequence of UK hostile environment immigration policies embedded in the 2014 and 2016 Immigration Acts whereby regulations require employers, landlords and healthcare workers to carry out unpaid, untrained border-guarding roles on behalf of the British state (Yuval-Davis et al. 2019). As everyday border-guards, private citizens and public sector administrators denied employment, homes and healthcare to working class Black British citizens, most usually the children of British subjects who had moved from Caribbean colonies to the British mainland to work. Many of the 'Windrush generation' had arrived in the United Kingdom with their right to residence recorded on their parents' passports whilst others born in the United Kingdom had no documentary evidence to prove their citizenship. Individuals who could not prove their UK citizenship to citizen border-guards lost their livelihoods, many were detained, deported, and died before they received any state compensation (Gentleman 2019). The everyday bordering of the hostile environment legislation impacted beyond those of the Windrush generation. It led to discrimination in letting property to, or in employing British citizens and other legal residents deemed 'not white enough'. In addition, British employers in the so-called 'ethnic enclave economy', including Ahmed, faced targeted Border Force raids based on suspicions that they employed compatriots illegally or because their neighbours bore a grudge (Bloch and McKay 2015; Grant and Peel 2015: Wemyss 2015; Yuval-Davis et al. 2018).

The Windrush scandal exposed, momentarily, the exclusionary relationship between whiteness and Britishness. As the scandal progressed, the centrality of the enslavement of Africans and plantation economies to white Briton's wealth and British power and the related experiences of detention and deportation of Black British citizens were voiced in Parliament (Lammy 2018) and the Home Office commissioned a report that raised the need for staff to be educated in British Empire histories[3] (Williams 2020). The scandal demonstrated that to understand how contemporary immigration regimes and bordering practices reproduce notions of white Britishness and belonging it is essential to understand their colonial genealogies. In the following section, I focus on these relations of global coloniality as they inscribe the lives of descendants of British Indian seafarers. Four hundred years of colonialism rarely frames dominant media or political narratives about Britain's past and the specific histories of working class south Asian seafarers are typically absent. Present, though, are the impacts of colonial-era maritime legislation that racialised Indian British seafarers as not white and hence their British descendants as not white or not white enough. Like nineteenth century seafarers, they have come to embody the border becoming identified as suspected illegal border crossers and the targets of hostile environment policies. I show how selected historical material practices of state bordering have worked together over centuries to reproduce notions of white Britishness that sought to prevent British Indian seafarers from settling in the United Kingdom and continues to exclude their descendants from British citizenship and belonging.

## British Indian seafarers: Bordering at sea and onshore

Since the seventeenth century, immigration control through maritime legislation, immigration law and partnerships between state and private actors has, in specific times and spaces, been constructed to exclude Indian colonial subjects from settling in the United Kingdom, South Africa, Canada, Australia, and elsewhere. In this section, I consider selected examples of bordering that has impacted on the lives, including feelings of belonging and experiences of citizenship, of present-day racialised citizens of Britain and white settler colonies of its ex-Empire.

The historian Ravi Ahuja (2006) has demonstrated, the tension between the 'mobility' and 'containment' of British Indian subjects during a period of expanding mobility in the later decades of the British Empire. Following the abolition of slavery, Indian indentured labourers were transported to work in plantations in Fiji, Mauritius, South Africa, and the Caribbean and later labourers travelled to work on the railways in East Africa where many settled. In the First and Second World Wars, Indian soldiers were transported to fight, and many died in the Middle East, Europe, and South East Asia. Most mobile of all were the Indian seafarers who worked on the ships delivering the labourers, military and goods throughout the period of empire and global conflict. Gopalan Balachandran characterises the metropolitan response to the increased mobility from Asia as reinforcing 'tiered arrangements of racialized biopolitical borders' reaching into ships and foreign ports' (2016: 188). Bordering technologies constructed to 'contain' the Indian mobile labour force and prevent desertions and the settlement of working-class Indian men in the metropolis and white settler colonies mean that there is little material or discursive evidence of their time on land. However, as I show below, whilst dominant empire discourses represented white Europeans as imposing racialised order on migrations to their colonies, the borders were permeable and 'containment' never complete.

During the nineteenth and twentieth centuries a complex array of bordering techniques grew out of the economic priorities of shipping companies that strove to keep costs down through maintaining a segmented, racialised labour market with Indian seafarers kept at the bottom of a rigid hierarchy (Ahuja 2006; Tabili 1994; Visram 2002). These combined with bordering processes associated with racially exclusive immigration laws in Britain, North America, and Australia so that at different times and in different spaces, multiple state and privately administered bordering techniques were put in place attempting to 'contain' the itinerant seafarers at ports of departure in India, at sea and at ports of entry. Below, I explore these sites of bordering to show how they worked together to ensure that working class Indian seafarers faced considerable barriers in settling in Britain or the white settler colonies thereby producing their invisibility in national narratives and maintaining the dominant idea of the British nation as historically white.

## Maritime bordering legislation

Successive British maritime legislation created a mobile racialised category of people that was excluded from permanent settlement in the United Kingdom and white settler colonies through requiring private ship owners and others to manage their exclusion via a range of bordering practices. From the early days of the East India Company, maritime legislation codified whiteness materially and culturally, enshrining interconnected racial and class discrimination in law, so that south Asian seafarers from rural colonial peripheries were recruited under Indian Articles which, at different times, stipulated lower rates of pay, less cabin space, and lower quality food than their European counterparts (Balachandran 2012; Visram 2002). The 1823 Merchant Shipping Act, not repealed until 1963, extended earlier restrictions on Indian seafarers by confirming that Indian Articled Seafarers could only be paid off and discharged in India. The 1823 Act made official the racialised category of 'lascar', that had been commonly used to label men from south Asia or parts of Africa employed on European commanded ships. Seafarers from very diverse parts of the Indian subcontinent and some from parts of Africa were grouped into a single racialised category, employed on what became known as 'lascar' articles, compelling them to work in inferior conditions for less pay. 'Laskar' or 'lascar', became a term of racist abuse in the English language, described as the mobile equivalent of 'coolie'[4] (Balachandran 2012). Because Indian Articled seafarers were prohibited from terminating their contracts anywhere outside of British India, between voyages the East India Company was obliged to house them in barracks near the ports or in privately run boarding houses. In the days of sail seafarers would spend several months in the port areas before obtaining a return voyage and many became destitute and 'illegal' on the streets of London (Visram 2002).

From the 1870s, following the introduction of steamships and the opening of the Suez Canal, greater numbers of Indian seafarers were employed working as firemen, stoking coal in the ships' engines. Steamships spent less time in dock than sailing vessels and British Indian crew were not always allowed to land. For those who did, the 1894 Merchant Shipping Act bound them to return to India by giving ship owners powers to place them on vessels heading back to India even without work. Indian seafarers who deserted faced criminal prosecution (Balachandran 2012; Fisher 2004; Visram 2002). Balachandran has likened ships to 'camps' – spaces of confinement and exception where states and private employers exercise 'extraordinary power' (2016: 188). Up to the mid-twentieth century employers could insert a clause in 'lascar' contracts that prohibited men from taking any shore leave in European-ruled African and North American ports. The financial interests of the shipping companies were protected through the maritime laws which supported them in retaining a cheap labour force with seafarers employed on Indian Articles preferred to those employed on British contracts, because of the low costs of employment via the 'lascar' Articles and the stereotypes of the formers supposed 'docility' and compliance as opposed to the latter's 'drunkenness and absence without leave' (Ahuja 2006; Visram 2002). Constructions of the 'docility' of 'lascars' were produced through the racialised political and economic relations of domination on ship and on land where the ships officers wielded control over every aspect of their lives.

What was referred to in shipping company and government discourses as 'desertion' or 'jumping ship' was, apart from suicide, the only escape from the all-encompassing control of the shipping companies.[5] It involved Indian seafarers outwitting officers as they sought to cross the border illegally from ship to land. During war and post-war decades, they were actively recruited and employed illegally by onshore businesses. From the mid-1920s, despite the extension of maritime laws that required shipping companies to track down and prosecute British Indian 'deserters', only P&O did so because their trade, predominantly with Asia, depended to a greater extent on the low-waged 'lascar' Articled labour force. Other companies with more North Atlantic trade ignored desertions if it suited them economically (Balachandran 2012: 181–184). By the 1930s, desertion was spoken of by UK officials as a recognised means by which British Indian subjects could reach and settle in Britain (Visram 2002: 259–263).

Many men successfully escaped the ships and 'lascar' Articles, using growing Indian networks in port cities to find work on land and ways to get employed back onto ships on British contracts giving them the better conditions of the European crew (Ahuja 2006; Balachandran 2012; Visram 2002). The many names of Muslim seafarers on British Articles who died in the First and Second World Wars listed alongside European names on the Merchant Seafarers' Memorial next to the Tower of London evidence that British Indian men had been able to be re-employed on British Articles in wartime. The names of thousands of men who died when employed on inferior 'lascar' Articles are not moulded into the bronze plaques. Deceased men from both categories are mostly invisible in post-war narratives, consolidating the idea of the whiteness of the British nation. Sona Miah, from Sylhet, survived the 1939–1945 war. Like others, he was able to escape following multiple voyages on Indian Articles and after working informally in London was recruited on British Articles as the Second World War began:

> Coming to Glasgow 1937, I ran away from *Arcade* ship, to London. Other people telling, London very good … I came to a house near New Road … 1939 – I got English Articles… good money … I sent it to my brother [in Sylhet]…Wartime … five different ships … after the war I worked on 22 different ships … 1954 to 1967.
>
> *(Adams 1987: 137–138)*

Another Sylheti seafarer, Nawab Ali, recounted how after jumping ship illegally in Cardiff at the beginning of the same war, he was hidden by a friend before he was also 'brought' to London where he was later able to obtain documents that enabled him to work legally and later helped many other men to leave ships then to find jobs onshore or take them to the Shipping Office to be recruited on British Articles. He also took that route, working under British Articles until the end of the war after which he lived in the United Kingdom (Adams 1987: 70–89). Miah and Ali's experiences illustrate that the codification of whiteness into maritime legislation did not ensure the impermeability of the UK border to British Indian working-class men who left ships and shifted employment categories. However, through making it illegal to leave their ships, compelling them to hide and initially to live and work without documentation, the bordering legislation forced them to make themselves invisible to officials, further consolidating the idea of Britain as white.

## Immigration legislation in the United Kingdom and white settler colonies

Similar processes enacted through immigration legislation produced and maintained the material and cultural whiteness of the metropole and settler colonies. Immigration policies targeted at preventing Indian seafarers from settling and subsequently acquiring citizenship in the United Kingdom and white settler colonies combined with the maritime legislation to make it harder for working class British Indians to cross borders into the metropole or elsewhere. By 1855, all British merchant shipping companies were employing 12,000 men on 'lascar' Articles. By the end of the nineteenth century, most employees of the P&O Company were British Indian (Goodall et al. 2008). In 1897, the Immigration Restriction Act was imposed in the port of Durban in the British settler colony of Natal. As well as limiting the entrance of the categories of 'paupers' and 'criminals', it introduced a literacy test aimed at preserving the whiteness of the colony by keeping out Indians, including seafarers, intending to land. The Act required potential migrants to write a letter to the Colonial Secretary in any European Language chosen by the official – who could therefore ensure that English was not selected if the potential unwanted border-crosser spoke English. Seafarers circumvented the barriers constructed by this contrived 'race-neutral' legal route, by deserting and disappearing into the Durban Indian community. They sometimes entered official records if they were caught, imprisoned and/or put on board departing ships (Hyslop 2015) all contributing to the construction of the colony as a space of white cultural and material domination. In 1902, the colonial Australian Ministry introduced a policy aimed at 'preserving the purity of their race and to encourage the recruitment of British seamen' that would only contract P&O Company mail steamers if they did not employ 'lascar' crew. To assuage Australian fears, officials in British India offered to confine the Indian crews to the ships when they docked in Australia (Balachandran 2016: 197). However, the combination of maritime legislation combined with immigration policies may not have kept the rate of desertions of Indians from British Merchant ships at Australian ports as low as archival records suggest. As in Natal, Imperial records were themselves part of the 'mechanisms of control rather than proof that the controls worked' (Goodall et al. 2008: 47). Empire-authored records were part of an ideology of containment that sought to convey that imperial control was effective in imposing racialised order onto a chaotic and transient situation. Goodall et al. (2008) document seafarers who jumped ship or were abandoned at ports when ship owners went bankrupt, living in port cities, seeking work across the continent or settling in Aboriginal communities where they were not faced with daily racism by white settlers. The knowledge of Indian seafarer lives is absent from dominant Australian national narratives as in addition to the 'illegality' of those who had jumped ship and integrated into different communities, white settler political pressures led to mixed-heritage descendants of Indian and Aboriginal partnerships rejecting their Indian heritage to prove their Aboriginality and right to represent their communities in struggles against white cultural and economic domination (Goodall et al. 2008).

In Britain, racist campaigns built up against Indian, African, Chinese, and Caribbean seafarers throughout the nineteenth and early years of the twentieth centuries. The port riots in 1919 were started by local white men and women who attacked people and property in mixed neighbourhoods, blaming African and Asian labourers for the lack of employment during the economic downturn following the First World (Tabili 1994). One legislative response was the 1919 Aliens Restriction (Amendment) Act that ordered preference be given to British crews, assumed to be white, and the deportation of 'destitute coloured seamen'. Despite being officially categorised as British subjects and not 'Aliens' Indian seafarers were 'not quite white enough' to be thought of as British and often, without documentary proof of their status, many were deported alongside seafarers from different areas of Africa and the Caribbean. The 1925 Coloured Alien Seamen Order that consolidated the 1919 amendment required 'coloured seamen' to register with the police and be deported if 'destitute'. As well as African and Caribbean men, Goan Christian seafarers who were not categorised as 'British Indian' and British Indian crew without papers were deported (Ahuja 2006). Being intentionally or mistakenly deported as an 'Alien' or being forced to return to sea to escape the racist violence and discriminatory legislation further contributed to the strengthening of the dominant idea of the British nation as white in terms of population and culture.

## Bordering partnerships

Complex, multilayered partnerships between employers, unions and compatriots made up the everyday practice of bordering legislation in different colonial contexts. At different periods shipping companies made decisions about who they employed based on contemporary racialised stereotypes and links with diverse local networks they had built up in specific localities across Asia. In the early twentieth century P&O recruiting in Mumbai preferred Muslims from Punjab to work in the engines, deckhands from Gujarat and Christian stewards from Goa whilst the Clan Steamship Company chose crew from Sylhet recruited in Kolkata (Ahuja 2006: 130). Access to the ships and ensuing mobility reached inland to villages and households as influential crew members – such as *serangs* (boatswain) – recruited via their own networks. *Serangs* also controlled the lives of seafarers on board through bonds of debt that reached back to villages. Their own dependence on the white officers and financial obligations meant that it was in their interests to ensure that Indian seafarers were kept under surveillance when anchored in docks and caught and punished if they attempted to jump ship (Adams, 1987; Ahuja 2006: 136; Balachandran 2016: 198).

Shipping Companies also sought to control the onshore movements of Indian crews between voyages. In 1922, the P&O company requisitioned an old hulk in the Royal Albert Docks in London. Indian crews were forced to live in a camp-like exceptional state outside the jurisdiction of Britain's health, sanitation or labour laws and away from the local population (Balachandran 2016: 198; Tabili 1994: 60–61). Shipping companies also wanted to avoid aggravating white seamen's unions which had been opposing what they referred to as cheap Indian labour since the nineteenth century. Unions in the United Kingdom and Australia took P&O to court over employing 'coloured' seamen and supported their respective governments' efforts to stop Indians coming ashore and settling in the growing cosmopolitan dockside communities (Goodall et al. 2008: 57). In the United Kingdom, during the Second World War, British Indians were subjects of surveillance as both state and non-state actors took on bordering roles in port areas and inland. The National Union and Seamen and port authorities 'sought closer watch on Asian boarding-house keepers to check desertions' and 'any constable or military officer' was empowered to 'arrest an Indian on mere suspicion of desertion' (Balachandran 2012: 186–187). The border was potentially wherever an Indian seafarer was onshore. Working class men from south Asia were forced into legal categories that obliged them to embody the border. In the context of global coloniality, their descendants continue to be the subjects of continuing embodied bordering discourses and practices.

Whilst there is a genealogy in the onshore and onboard bordering practices and the subjects of bordering over time, the categories to which the border was applied in official discourse and practice has changed. Before 1947, Indian seafarers were British colonial subjects and borders experienced related not only to nationality but to their classification in the racialised and class-defined category of 'lascar'. Those borders were managed at ports by ship owners, *serangs* and unions and inland by police and the military. At independence, Bengal, including the district of Sylhet, was divided between India and East Pakistan. Sylheti seafarers had mostly been recruited after travelling to Kolkata which became part of India in 1947. Many went missing during the violence of Partition and later, as Pakistani citizens, faced extortion at the new border controls and found it progressively harder to be recruited in Kolkata as local interests dominated (Balachandran 2012: 277–280). Partition and Independence disrupted geographies of mobility whilst, in response to post-war labour shortages, British borders were open to citizens of the ex-Empire making it more straightforward for seafarers to work legally in manual industries in the United Kingdom (Thandi 2007). In the 1960s, ex-seafarer Aftab Ali from Sylhet, later a politician in East Pakistan, influenced the 'voucher system' that briefly gave thousands of former seafarers and other Sylhetis and Punjabis from East and West Pakistan respectively, legal access to the UK labour market and eventual settlement, establishing today's British-Bangladeshi and British-Pakistani populations (Adams 1987; Choudhury 1993, 1995; Visram 2002). However, voucher holders as well as British ex-seafarers, including those who owned successful businesses, experienced being thought of as 'not white enough' to be British as they faced further legislative barriers when they wanted to bring their families to live with them. Until DNA testing was used to prove paternity, immigration officials, operating under the Home Office's culture of disbelief, consistently denied family reunification to seafarer and voucher-holder families whose long-term settlement and future migration challenged the notion of the white British nation. In 1986, Sona Miah, quoted earlier, who had worked on over 30 British-owned ships over a 30-year period and was living in London recounted an experience he shared with many others:

> I married in 1943, went home again three times when my ship went to Calcutta [Kolkata] – got 6 children but the immigration don't believe they are mine …
>
> *(Adams 1987: 138)*

## Conclusion

Thousands of men sought to escape poverty, famine, and oppressive land-based racialised power relations of British-ruled India by working on British-owned merchant ships. Imperial governments constructed maritime legislation that created the inferior racialised outside, or 'not quite' white labour category 'lascar' forcing British Indian seafarers to embody the racialising border at sea and onshore. Metropolitan and colonial immigration legislation created further racialised bordering practices so that shipping companies, *serangs,* boarding house keepers and others were enabled to report and arrest men living in the United Kingdom or white settler colonies based on their perceived identity as 'lascar'. However, racialising borders are never impermeable and seafarers escaped 'lascar' articles at ports across the globe, going on to establish creative communities that in the twenty-first century link mixed-heritage families in the United Kingdom and ex-colonies on different continents (Bald 2013; Goodall et al. 2008). The mobile, global labour force of British Indian seafarers was central to the economies of the British Empire and to Britain's survival in two world wars. However, due to the invisibility of their bodies and experiences, produced and enforced by imperial, racialised, border legislation and everyday bordering practices, their lives have been ignored in dominant white narratives of British history and settler colonies. The partial accounts of south Asian populations as 'recent arrivals', low down a British hierarchy of belonging, continue to construct them as 'not quite white enough' British citizens as outsiders and thus as the 'common sense' targets of toxic everyday state bordering practices. This chapter presents a different story addressing this partiality and challenging this whitening of seafaring and its important role in establishing and resisting imperial national narratives of whiteness.

## Notes

1  I interviewed Ahmed (not their real name) as part of EUBORDERSCAPES research project funded by the European Community's Seventh Framework Programme 2012–16. This quote was used in our resulting publication, *Bordering* (Yuval-Davis et al. 2019: 108) anonymized as 'BJ'.

2  Sylhet district in the North-East of Bangladesh. The majority of British-Bangladeshis are descended from people who migrated from this district.

3  Recommendation 6 of the Windrush Lessons Learned Review was that 'The Home Office should: (a) devise, implement and review a comprehensive learning and development programme which makes sure all its existing and new staff learn about the history of the United Kingdom and its relationship with the rest of the world, including Britain's colonial history, the history of inward and outward migration and the history of black Britons' (Williams 2020).

4  'Lascar' originally a Persian word, became a racialised term used to categorise men from Africa or Asia employed on European commanded ships made official in the British 1823 Merchant Shipping Act. As 'Laskar or 'Lascar', it became a term of abuse in English language (Balachandran 2012). I therefore use the term 'Indian seafarer'.

5  Suicides from jumping overboard were also recorded as means by which seafarers escaped ships (Balachandran 2016).

## References

Adams, C. 1987. *Across Seven Seas and Thirteen Rivers: Life Stories of Pioneer Sylheti Settlers in Britain*. London: THAP Books.

Ahuja, R. 2006. Mobility and Containment: The Voyages of South Asian Seamen, c. 1900–1960. International Review of Social History Vol. 51, SUPPLEMENT 14: Coolies, Capital, and Colonialism: Studies in Indian Labour History, pp. 111–141.

Balachandran, G. 2012. *Globalizing Labour? Indian Seafarers and World Shipping, c 1870–1945*. New Delhi: Oxford University Press.

Balachandran, G. 2016. Indefinite Transits: Mobility and Confinement in the Age of Steam. *Journal of Global History*, 11 (2): 187–208.

Bald, V. 2013. *Bengali Harlem and the Lost Histories of South Asian America*. Harvard University Press.

Bloch, A. and McKay, S. 2015. Employment, Social Networks and Undocumented Migrants: The Employer Perspective. *Sociology*, 49 (1): 38–55.

Choudhury, Y. 1993. *The Roots and Tales of Bangladeshi Settlers*. Birmingham: Sylheti Social History Group.

Choudhury, Y. 1995. *Sons of the Empire: Oral History from the Bangladeshi Seamen Who Served on British Ships During the 1939–45 War*. Birmingham: Sylheti Social History Group.

De Genova, N. 2012. Border, Scene and Obscene. In *A Companion to Border Studies*, ed. T. M. Wilson and H. Donnan, ch. 28. Chichester: Wiley-Blackwell.

El-Enany, N. 2020. *(B)ordering Britain: Law, Race and Empire*. Manchester: Manchester University Press.

Fisher, M. 2004. *Counterflows to Colonialism: Indian Travellers and Settlers in Britain, 1600–1857*. Delhi: Permanent Black.

Gentleman, A. 2019. *The Windrush Betrayal: Exposing the Hostile Environment*. London: Faber & Faber.

Goodall, H., Ghosh, D. and Todd, L. R. 2008. Jumping Ship: Indians, Aborigines and Australians Across the Indian Ocean. *Transforming Cultures*, 3 (1): 44–74.

Goodfellow, M. 2019. *Hostile Environment: How Immigrants Became Scapegoats*. London: Verso Books.

Grant, S. and Peel, C. 2015. *'No Passport Equals No Home': An independent evaluation of the 'Right to Rent' scheme*. Joint Council for the Welfare of Immigrants, https://jcwi.org.uk/sites/default/files/documets/No%20Passport%20Equals%20No%20Home%20Right%20to%20Rent%20Independent%20Evaluation_0.pdf

Hage, G. 1998. *White Nation: Fantasies of White Supremacy in a Multicultural Society*. Annandale: Pluto Press.

Houtum, van H., Kramsch, O. and Zierhofen, W. 2005. Prologue: Bordering Space. In *Bordering Space*, ed. H. van Houtum, O. Kramsch and W. Zierhofen, pp. 1–13. Aldershot: Ashgate.

Hunter, S., Grimes, D. and Swan, E. 2010. Introduction: Reproducing and Resisting Whiteness in Organizations, Policies, and Places. *Social Politics*, 17 (4): 407–422.

Hyslop, J. 2015. Oceanic Mobility and Settler-Colonial Power: Policing the Global Maritime Labour Force in Durban Harbour c. 1890–1910. *Journal of Transport History*, 36 (2): 248–267.

Lammy, D. 2018. 'National day of shame: David Lammy criticises treatment of the Windrush Generation', *The Guardian*, 16 April, viewed 6 March 2021, https://www.theguardian.com/uk-news/video/2018/apr/16/national-day-of-shame-david-lammy-criticises-treatment-of-windrush-generation-video.

Manhotra, D. 2016. 'State takes steps to prevent illegal immigrants from getting Aadhaar', *The Tribune*, 17 March, viewed 30 September 2018, http://www.tribuneindia.com/news/jammu-kashmir/community/state-takes-steps-to-prevent-illegal-immigrants-from-getting-aadhaar/209709.html.

Mezzadra, S. and Neilson, B. 2013. *Border as Method, or, the Multiplication of Labour*. Durham, NC: Duke University Press.

Nayak, A. 2007. Critical Whiteness Studies. *Sociology Compass*, 1 (2): 737–755.

Tabili, L. 1994. *'We Ask for British Justice': Workers and Racial Difference in Late Imperial Britain*. New York: Cornell University Press.

Thandi, S. S. 2007. Migrating to the 'Mother Country', 1947–1980. In *A South-Asian History of Britain: Four Centuries of Peoples from the Indian Sub-Continent*, ed. M. H. Fisher, S. Lahiri and S. S. Thandi, ch. 7. Oxford and Westport, CT: Greenwood World Publishing.

Tlostanova, M. V. and Mignolo, W. 2012. *Learning to Unlearn: Decolonial Reflections from Eurasia and the Americas*. Columbus: The Ohio State University Press.

Visram, R. 2002. *Asians in Britain: 400 Years of History*. London: Pluto Press.

Wemyss, G. 2006. The Power to Tolerate: Contests Over Britishness and Belonging in East London. *Patterns of Prejudice*, 40 (3): 215–236.

Wemyss, G. 2009. *The Invisible Empire: White Discourse, Tolerance and Belonging*. Farnham: Ashgate.

Wemyss, G. 2012. Littoral Struggles, Liminal Lives: Indian Merchant Seafarers' Resistances. In *South Asian Resistances in Britain, 1858–1947*, ed. R. Ahmed and S. Mukherjee, ch. 3. London: Continuum.

Wemyss, G. 2015. Everyday Bordering and Raids Every Day: The Invisible Empire and Metropolitan Borderscapes. In *Borderscaping: Imaginations and Practices of Border Making,* ed. C. Brambilla et al., pp. 187. Farnham: Ashgate.

Williams, W. 2020. *Windrush lessons learned review: Independent review by Wendy Williams*. The Home Office, 19 March, https://assets.publishing.service.gov.uk/government/uploads/system/uploads/attachment_data/file/874022/6.5577_HO_Windrush_Lessons_Learned_Review_WEB_v2.pdf.

Yuval-Davis, N., Wemyss, G. and Cassidy, K. 2018. Everyday Bordering, Belonging and the Reorientation of British Immigration Legislation. *Sociology*, 52 (2): 228–244. DOI:10.1177/0038038517702599.

Yuval-Davis, N., Wemyss, G., and Cassidy, K. 2019. *Bordering*. Cambridge: Polity.

# 21

# Making yourself at home: Performances of whiteness in cultural production about home and homemaking practices

*Sarah Heinz*

In May 2017, UK conveyancing provider *My Home Move* conducted a survey in which they asked 700 people in Britain about their favourite property television show, their favourite presenter, and, finally, which 'iconic property would be their ideal home' (MyHomeMove 2017). The results to the last question are telling when it comes to the connection between whiteness, property, and ideas of home. The survey's participants most frequently named the fictional estate of Downton Abbey as their ideal of home (with 16%), with *Dallas'* Southfork Ranch coming second (14%), and Hogwarts School of Witchcraft and Wizardry from the *Harry Potter* franchise coming third (with 13%).[1] Doug Crawford, CEO of *My Home Move*, commented: 'Home ownership and the type of property we own in the United Kingdom has typically been an indicator of social status; the bigger the property is, the more successful we are, so it's no surprise that the Nation's dream home is that of the Earl of Grantham' (MyHomeMove 2017).

However, what Crawford seems to forget in his comment is that these three properties share more than size. Downton is tied to a class system associated with a land-owning, patrilineal aristocracy connected to empire, Hogwarts is modelled on a class-conscious public school system, and Southfork Ranch is connected to a masculinist settler colonial notion of property that wilfully 'forgets' the dispossession of Native peoples and the effects of slavery. These buildings are thus materialisations of white privilege, classism, sexism, and racism, all of which are problematically obscured by notions of home as a sense of organic belonging, destiny, or even as a birthright. Harry Potter's 'homecoming' to Hogwarts and the Earl of Grantham's frequent eulogies that 'Downton is in [his] bones' (Walderzak 2016: 14) vividly express a sense of home as a source of identity. Yet, this sense of identity is not only essentialist but also nostalgic for an imperialist past embodied in grand, historical buildings – a nostalgia that the participants of the survey seem to share.

It is this connection between imaginaries of home, the materialities of home, specifically property, and notions of whiteness that I am interested in. Despite its alleged stability and naturalness, whiteness is not a fixed identity but rather something we do and perform. This doing is not simply the choice of each individual. A dispositif of whiteness disposes us towards some rather than other practices, norms, and ideals, and we therefore 'do whiteness' within

DOI: 10.4324/9780429355769-21

institutionalised frameworks that are part of larger structures like the state as well as part of smaller institutions like the family. Exactly because whiteness is in constant need of affirmation through repetition, everyday practices and material contexts like buildings form the basis of people's performances of whiteness. The family home is a prime setting for such performances of whiteness. Although mostly thought of as a private space, home is intensely political and shaped by normative conventions, economic frameworks, and social expectations. It thus becomes a focal point for whitely practices and is configured by the normative position that whiteness has taken up in Western discourses. The chapter analyses cultural production surrounding home, specifically property-themed television shows and media about home improvement, to track how practices of doing home and doing whiteness intersect. Asking how a 'good' home is presented and who is or is not eligible for such a 'good' home makes it possible to uncover normative notions of the white subject and its agency that underlie Western ideals and practices of home and homemaking. To show this nexus of whiteness, home, property, and the self, I will begin my analysis with a focus on whiteness as a doing.

## Doing whiteness and its consequences

Most scholars in the field have described whiteness as an effect of social relations that are structured by inequality and hierarchies of power. Whiteness is neither an essential, biological identity nor the objective description of a homogeneous group of people with stable social relations. It rather is a location of structural advantage, a 'standpoint', as well as a 'set of cultural practices that are usually unmarked and unnamed' (Frankenberg 1993: 1). To debunk essentialist notions of race and whiteness, the focus on the relational and procedural nature of racialised (and, in turn, also gendered and classed) identifications is central: '[…] it is perhaps more profitable to [… engage with] what race *does* as well as what/whether it is' (St Louis 2005: 30, my emphasis; see also Miles and Brown 2003: 102). Such a focus on how people *do* whiteness zooms in on whiteness as 'an ascription' (Dyer 1997: 50) and a 'symbolic formation' (Bonnett 2000: 129) bound up with ideas about modernity and civilisation, property and capital, and, ultimately, notions of the human subject. If whiteness is more often than not constructed as a 'racialised norm' (Byrne 2006: 26), then Western ideas of the subject and its agency are an effect of normative notions of who is and who is not a (white) subject in the first place.

This definition of whiteness as a social and cultural construction with real and profound effects enables an analysis of both its material and discursive dimensions and of how they overlap in our daily practices and cultural representations. If we *do* whiteness in the most mundane activities of our daily lives, then whiteness is an (often unmarked) experience as well as the knowledge that a hierarchical and racialised system produces about 'us', 'them', and the world. This production of knowledge affects how we can relate to whom and with what consequences, how we deal with the spaces and institutions in which we live, how we engage with others, and how we imagine our ideal selves and environments, one of which is our home. Although the white subject is presented as stable and pre-existent, it is tied to constant performances in all areas of daily life, making it a 'situational accomplishment' (Messerschmidt 2004: 55) similar to gender or other processes of identification (see Butler 1990). Whiteness is performed incessantly and according to the rules and conventions of 'whiteliness' or 'whitely scripts' that govern people's behaviour if they want to be recognised as white (for whiteliness see Frye 1992; for whitely scripts see Bailey 1998; for a combination of both Frye's and Bailey's arguments see Gray 2002).

Using Foucault's notion of the dispositif, it is therefore helpful to understand whiteness as a whole network of socially dispersed practices, discourses, systems of artefacts, and modes of subjectification that are not homogeneous, but that establish seemingly necessary relations between its differing elements (Foucault 1980: 194). This construction of necessity within the dispositif makes individuals want to conform to its norms and values, because conformity results in being recognised as a subject, and it excludes those who perform 'un-white' behaviour, norms, values, or subjectivities (Butler 1997: 7). The white subject is thus not only brought into being through modes of subjectification, it also becomes governable via internalised regulatory regimes that Foucault has described as biopolitics (2010: 317). In this production, organisation, and management of governable bodies and their relations, our home spaces play a central role that I now turn to.

## The imaginaries and materialities of home

Power and politics literally find a home in our houses, apartments, and other dwellings, and they do so in the places and practices that are part of our homemaking routines. Thus, home is not a neutral or private space. Rather, it is 'intensely political both in its internal relationships and through its interfaces with the wider world over domestic, national, and imperial scales' (Blunt and Dowling 2006: 142). These politics of home are all the more important to scrutinise when we consider imaginaries of home in many Western cultures. Home is an auratic term that conjures up a host of associations such as family, comfort, or safety. In such imaginaries, home becomes the equivalent of the ideal home as a 'locale of human warmth and material suste-nance, moral probity and spiritual comfort' (Tuan 2012: 227). Of course, meanings of home are dependent on concrete social, cultural, and historical contexts and can differ widely in in-dividual experiences. In addition, home can be a site of negative feelings, exclusion, a loss of self, or even violence, especially for women (Madigan et al. 1990; Morley 2000: 56–85). Nevertheless, across many Western cultures since the eighteenth century, home has remained an often idealised, even romanticised setting for the self and communal ties, for nostalgia, *Heimat*, and *Heimweh* (Morley 2000: 31–33; Tuan 2012).

These imaginaries of home take on material form, creating spaces in which we 'do' home every day. Contemporary Western cultures have surprisingly similar and enduring conceptions of what a home looks like: mostly, a large, detached residential building made for one nuclear family, and, ideally, a garden or at least a yard. In addition, owner occupation is 'the social as well as political and economic norm; it remains the preferred housing outcome of the re-sponsible, risk-averse citizen' (Smith 2015: 62). Consequently, such a house is not just some architectural form but a 'dominant or ideal version of house-as-home' (Blunt and Dowling 2006: 100). It already implies who typically lives (or can afford to live) in such buildings, and it creates problematic hierarchies, for example of 'good' homeowners vs. their 'marginalised "Other", renting', often associated with 'passive welfare recipience' (Smith 2015: 62, 67).

How such idealised houses are lived in plays a crucial role in a culture's sense of what a good home and homeowner is. Houses are seen to turn into 'real' homes when they are used as settings for self-actualisation and social relations, primarily those of family. Thus, practices of homemaking are vital for houses to turn into homes in the first place, and these practices start with the choice of 'design, spatial organisation, and furnishings of domestic dwellings [that] influence and inflect concepts and/or ideologies of the home' (Mallett 2004: 66). However, what is seen as 'good' design, 'proper' ways of living, and 'properly' relating to other people within a home is intensely regulated and based on the normalisation of some forms of behaviour and community rather than others. For a biopolitics that requires ideal citizens to regulate themselves, the house-as-home becomes the central arena for practicing normative modes of identity and community, and it is specifically salient that many (if not most) homemaking practices seen as good, normal, and proper in contemporary Western society are connected to middle-class whiteness. As a normalised and invisible regime of self-regulation and empowerment, whiteness shapes the mundane daily expressions of a biopolitics of home and its connection to the body (Dyer 1997: 23f). From the way I am expected to park my car, arrange my flower beds, prepare and consume food, to the more complex matters of caring for my child, personal hygiene and sexual relations, or more communal matters like entertaining guests in my home, whitely scripts configure the practices that turn a house into a 'good' or 'ideal' home. Thus, homemaking practices are intimately tied to 'an imaginary of home that casts the social relations of middle-class, white, heterosexual, nuclear families, and its material manifestation in the form of the detached suburban house, as an ideal, or homely, home' (Blunt and Dowling 2006: 131f). Home is something that we do, and like whiteness, our ideas of home are culturally contingent and created through concrete daily practices. Nevertheless, within our cultural discourses, these contingent performances tend to take on a self-explanatory and natural quality that also finds expression in our way of approaching the economic dimension of home as property.

## Whiteness, home, and/as property

Property and material relations are tightly connected to the formations and effects of racialisation. Ever since critical whiteness studies came into being, property and structures of labour have been a central concern for researchers in the field, specifically in the context of American labour history (see Allen 1994; Ignatiev 1995; Jacobson 1998). What these early approaches share is the contention that whiteness is an invention to secure the economic privileges of those in power. For poor and immigrant workers in the United States, to be included in whiteness opened access to goods, jobs, health protection, or housing, and even when these material benefits were small, whiteness still functioned as a 'psychological wage' that prevented worker solidarity across racialised boundaries (Roediger 1991: 64, see also Leonard 2010: 21). This structure continues to have consequences for housing and homeownership, creating hurdles for some groups rather than others when it comes to acquiring property that can turn into 'good' homes. George Lipsitz has talked about a 'possessive investment in whiteness', arguing that 'patterns of lending for house purchases are a significant factor in the development of segregated housing in urban America' (Clarke and Garner 2010: 20, see also Lipsitz 1995).

In the context of the legislation of property in America, Cheryl Harris has similarly shown how specific ways of defining property as individual rather than communal made white, Western notions of the subject the foundation of what was assessed as property in the first place. Thus, white settlers could lay claim to the ownership of farms and land, while Indigenous peoples could not achieve legal ownership of their land, because their collective stewardship was not recognised as a relation of 'property' at all (Harris 1993: 1727). This normalisation of white subjectivity and Western notions of law was also a central issue in the practice of slavery that was only possible by reducing black people to bodies (rather than subjects) that could be owned, a commodification 'which granted relative privilege to all white Americans. [...] white dominated black without this being discriminatory, just normal' (Clarke and Garner 2010: 21). These powerful effects of defining all types of property along the lines of a white logic is the case in all settler colonies, for example in Australia where Native peoples and their claims to land or religious sites were ignored or denied for a long time under the doctrine of 'terra nullius' (Macintyre 1999: 34). White settlers could thus take *legal* possession of both the land and the 'indigenous population who appear[ed] to be part of the landscape' (Meinig 2004: 13).

Such legal and political structures not only enable access to Indigenous territories, but influence how white settlers 'do' home through whiteness, because these structures 'come to be lived as given, as simply the unmarked, generic conditions of possibility for occupancy, association, history, and personhood', an affective experience that Rifkin calls 'settler common sense' (2013: 323). It is no surprise, then, that up to the present day, property is a contentious issue in many former settler colonies like Australia. This becomes obvious in white Australians' fear of 'losing' home, a fear that underlies the sometimes angry reactions to Aboriginal claims to sovereignty and land like the Native Title Act of 1993 (Slater 2019: 133f). Settler colonies are thus based on a precarious sense of home that Moreton-Robinson has called 'white possessive logic': 'It is a learned and received way of being in the world, a privilege, a taken-for-grantedness that nonetheless has to be defended, reaffirmed and reproduced over and over' (Slater 2019: 32; see also Moreton-Robinson 2005: 22). Being at home as a white settler subject is founded on the disturbance of somebody else's homeland and a denial of 'Indigenous ontological relations to land' (Moreton-Robinson 2015: 21). And yet, white settlers' sense of home remains insecure and in need of constant reaffirmation through acts of doing home as whiteness.

## Improve yourself: The home and the (white) self

Property, home, and whiteness are not only linked economically, politically, and legally, but also ontologically in producing and maintaining a sense of self for the inhabitants of a home. If, as outlined earlier, houses are seen to only turn into 'real' homes when they are settings for self-actualisation, and if whiteness is produced in multiple and minute practices, then home is a source, a setting, as well as an extension of white subjectivity. This mapping of house, home, and the inhabitant's self becomes particularly tangible in cultural production on home improvement, DIY, and interior design, because these genres set out to perfect and enhance someone's home and, in extension, someone's self. People spend a sizeable portion of their income on home decor (an estimated $65.2 billion per year in the US alone), and they invest their time to both work on and consume media about home spaces (see Graham et al. 2015: 346). In discourses on home improvement, home does not only give shelter to a person but is an extension of a person's mood, personality, and, implicitly, their self-regulation and their relations with the outside world. Thus, 'interior design [can be seen] as a paradigm for subjectivity and homemaking' (Butter 2016: 266).

Television shows about renovation and home organisation often exhibit a similar therapeutic tone already apparent in their titles. On the Emmy-nominated Netflix show *Tidying Up with Marie Kondo* (aired 2019), Japanese host Marie Kondo helps Americans who live in messy, overcrowded homes to de-clutter and organise; on the British *DIY SOS,* later rebranded as *The Big Build* (airing since 1999), Nick Knowles and his team first helped homeowners 'rescue' DIY projects gone wrong and later on helped 'deserving families' develop their properties; and on the German show *Einsatz in vier Wänden* (*Mission within four walls*, my translation, 2003–2013), host Tine Wittler renovated 'nightmare' homes to a state 'fit for human beings' (RTL.DE. n.d). Despite their different approaches to home improvement, all these shows take on the character of an intervention, rescuing the houses as much as their inhabitants from both crumbling building fabric and their less-than-ideal homemaking practices. Episodes typically use editing techniques of 'before and after' to effectively contrast the 'shocking' initial conditions of houses and interiors with the bright and orderly spaces after the experts are done. Tearful homeowners are repeatedly shown thanking the show hosts for their 'new lives' and a 'happy end' that they had been unable to achieve themselves (see Raisborough 2011: 122). Here, home improvement becomes a route towards a better life along the lines of the dispositif of whiteness connected to control, enterprise, and responsibility (Dyer 1997: 23f).

In this 'whitely' improvement of home and self, the intersection of racialisation and class, education, and cultural capital plays a central role. Shows like the above give the homeowners a specific function for television audiences. Viewers are invited to evaluate the previous homemaking practices of the homeowners as in need of reform because they are set against a universalised white middle-classness (Wood and Skeggs 2008: 188). The German show *Einsatz in vier Wänden* is a good example for this. Show host Tine Wittler was presented as a 'Wohnexpertin' (RTL.DE. n.d), an untranslatable term that stresses both her expertise in interior design and her superior sense of good living or even a good life. The 'nightmarish' condition of the often messy, dark, or even rat-infested houses picked for the show was implicitly mapped onto their inhabitants who were predominantly lower class, overweight, unemployed, and presented as uneducated, specifically in contrast to 'expert' Tine Wittler, who would sometimes 'translate' the homeowners' comments about their new homes into standard German. While episodes began with the inhabitants of the home being consulted about their wishes, they were not allowed back into their houses or apartments until the experts were done. The final product of the expert intervention was then dramatically unveiled, and the show's editing, music, and voice-over focused on the overwhelmed gratefulness of the homeowners. Overall, this is a strategy that gives people on the show a child-like, dependent, and passive position typical of colonialist images of non-white populations in need of regulation and control (see McClintock 1995). At the same time, shows like *Einsatz in vier Wänden* connect this dependent position with a class-based take on the deficient lifestyles of an 'underclass' that is unfit for a neoliberal society of self-governing citizens, embodied by a tidy, functional, and tasteful home (see Heinz 2016).

Even on programmes that set out to help the 'deserving poor' by renovating or enlarging their often cramped quarters, for example the US-based *Extreme Makeover: Home Edition* (aired 2003–2012 and revived in 2020), the focus is on the family's self-reliance and hard work, stressing that despite their poverty, they are 'model citizens and deserving families whose problems are no fault of their own' (McMurria 2008: 320). Private sector solutions to issues like a lack of health care are foregrounded, while larger structural inequalities tied to race and class are ignored. Analyses of such docutainment formats have accordingly described these shows as 'Charity TV' (Ouellette and Hay, 2008: 33), 'goodwill reality TV' (McMurria 2008: 307), or even as 'poverty porn' (McKenzie 2015: 12). Tellingly, these formats as well as their white, neoliberal narrative have translated well in transnational broadcasting contexts, with a show like *Extreme Makeover: Home Edition* being licensed or copied in countries as varied as Albania, Argentina, Brazil, Israel, the Philippines, Romania, Serbia, or Spain.

If one also links the ideal home to owner occupation, then the connection between home, property, and white subjectivity comes full circle. The white possessive logic that Moreton-Robinson outlines as the basis for appropriating land also forms the foundation for a white sense of self-possession, agency, and self-worth that valorises a subject that 'owns', that is that maintains and regulates *itself*, its bodily urges, and its environments in the sense of the biopolitics outlined earlier. Smith accordingly talks about homeownership as an 'ideological imperative that is passed between generations' and an 'unquestioned [...] cultural norm' that continues to be central throughout the Western world (2015: 64). A *'home of one's own'* is *'a home that one owns'* (Smith 2015: 67), and whoever is unable or unwilling to invest in such a home (and, implicitly, in a self-possessed identity) is assessed as a deviant, non-agentive self in need of reform. Cultural production about the home as property and those who try to buy it is therefore a highly interesting source of how whiteness is supposed to be 'done'. I will thus conclude my discussion with a short analysis of property-themed television.

## Property TV and the 'good' citizen

Property-themed shows have been a staple of most Western television programming for decades. Even after the 2007/2008 crash in most Western housing markets, genres dealing with buying or improving property proved 'remarkably adaptable to new economic and ideological circumstances' (McElroy 2017: 525). Homeownership therefore is a highly relevant factor in the cultural, economic, and political landscape. England's housing system, for example, 'shifted from majority (90%) rent to majority (70%) own in less than a century' (Smith 2015: 65). By the end of 2003, 'about half of the personal wealth of the UK was […] invested in owned homes' (Smith 2015: 67). Even following the financial crisis and the implosion of the mortgage industry, owned homes continue to be assessed (paradoxically) as a responsible investment that provides security for the owners and their children (Doling and Ronald 2010; Smith 2015). Accordingly, the notion of the homeowner combines the possession of capital with the capability of 'creating a place that is secure, comfortable and welcoming' as well as a setting for self-actualisation and self-regulation (Blunt and Dowling 2006: 93).

I want to address the global dynamics of such ideals of home by shortly focusing on two final examples, *House Hunters Asia*, airing on HGTV Asia since 2016, and the South-African programme *All About Property*, airing since 2018. Both programmes are produced in contexts where white people are not numerically dominant and in which access to land and property ownership is unavailable for large parts of the general population. Yet, both shows vividly underline that the possessive investment in whiteness identified earlier still shapes homeowners' aspirations as well as their media representation on the small screen. This becomes obvious in *House Hunters Asia*, a show that uses the formula of the US-based programme of the same name, and follows prospective real estate buyers from across Asia on their search for a home. There is no presenter, but the show features an English voice-over whose received pronunciation often contrasts with the accented speech of the house hunters themselves. While on British property shows, most people look for historical buildings with 'character', the prospective homeowners in Singapore or Malaysia are shown to prefer modern, mostly high-rise apartments with open-plan spaces and modern amenities that both the agents and the voice-over present as highly desirable. For the locations, the show stresses an area's potential and its rising real estate value and illustrates this value by shots of glitzy shopping malls, art galleries, and Western-style residential buildings. In effect, *House Hunters Asia* presents homeownership as a badge of success given to already affluent middle-class people in Asia's urban centres who emulate a Westernized lifestyle connected to modernity and progress, while ignoring (both visually and narratively) the large social inequalities in terms of access to affordable housing, land, and basic homemaking necessities.

The concept of the South African programme *All About Property* is different in not following actual house hunters but providing the audience with everything they need to know about buying or selling a home in South Africa. The show therefore does not primarily address viewers as homemakers but as entrepreneurs who need to be aware of the financial, legal, and social contexts in which they act to maximise their return of investment. Nevertheless, the focus on property as wealth and success shares other property-themed programmes' enactment of ideals of a self-regulating subject whose hard work materialises in the shape of real estate. This combination of real estate know-how and property as the 'good' citizen's way towards prosperity is emblematic of the new post-apartheid South Africa that has positioned itself within a neoliberal capitalist order that sees social inequality less as a systemic issue and more as in-dividual failure. Here, the programme ties in with the home improvement shows discussed earlier and their emphasis on deserving 'model' citizens and their self-regulation and self-help.

In each episode of *All About Property*, presenter Cornelius Koopman, who was joined by Koketso Sylvia Milosevic in season 4, meets with real estate professionals, for example a home inspector pointing out how to spot damage, or they visit new, often luxurious developments such as the New Braamfontein Lofts in downtown Johannesburg. These lofts and other luxury developments, specifically in urban areas such as Johannesburg, are material manifestations of what has been termed post-apartheid South Africa's 'spatial inequality', enacted in evictions and the eradication of informal settlements and showing in the lack of housing for poor urban communities (Strauss and Liebenberg 2014: 428). These inequalities implicitly shape *All About Property* on many levels. The experts who give advice on the programme are predominantly white, urban professionals, for example lawyers, architects, or investors, who are interviewed in their own sprawling homes or their spacious offices. Koopman and Milosevic, who are mixed and Black South African, respectively, ask very short questions and are then shown attentively listening to the long and detailed answers given by the experts. In its spatialisation and narrative relations, the show thus suggests that the experts have already achieved the success and wealth that the viewers should aspire to and it implicitly codes this success as white, urban, and middle class. Consequently, property is again turned into a badge of success for the self-regulating, hard-working citizen while poverty, eviction, or depending on renting is turned into an in-dividual problem of those who lack perseverance and self-control.

## Conclusion: Whiteness, the eternal DIY project

Whiteness is an aspiration configured by the norms, ideals, and scripts of whiteness. This makes whiteness a performative and situational accomplishment that has to be repeated and enforced in a multiplicity of social situations over time. As I have shown, home shares this performative character with whiteness and is a point of intersection for multiple imaginaries, materialities, and politics of subjectivity. Far from being a private space or respite from the outside world, home spaces are settings, sources, and externalisations of the norms and conventions of a dis-positif of whiteness that sets up ideals of self-governed subjects and their homemaking practices. The homeowner as the standard of a responsible middle-class citizen thus turns out to be a focal point of Western practices of whiteness and is accordingly a figure represented in cultural production around home such as the property-themed media that I have analysed. This ima-ginary has translated successfully to multiple settings across the globe, holding them together in a global coloniality of whiteness and presenting similar ideals of tidy homes, responsible citizens, and the successful creation of wealth on small screens in South Africa, Germany, or Malaysia. Just as the homes presented on television or in glossy lifestyle magazines, whiteness becomes a lifelong DIY project for the enterprising, self-improving subject. And even though no one actually lives in Downton Abbey, the fact that many aspire to it is worthwhile investigating in a continued attempt to tackle the enduring effects of white privilege and racialisation.

## Note

1   *Downton Abbey* is a British television series, produced by ITV, that ran from 2010 to 2015, with a film being made in 2019. It focuses on the fate of the aristocratic Crawley family and their fictional estate that gives the series its title. *Dallas* is an American television soap opera, produced by CBS between 1978 and 1991, focusing on the affluent Ewing family from Texas who live on the iconic Southfork

Ranch. The *Harry Potter* franchise is based on J.K. Rowling's series of young adult novels about young wizard Harry Potter, first published between 1997 and 2007. Both the novels and their numerous spin-offs, for example the film adaptations, a play, or video game versions, feature the fictional boarding school Hogwarts, a castle-like structure set in Scotland that is central for the overall plot.

# References

Allen, T. 1994. *The Invention of the White Race. Vol. I: Racial Oppression and Social Control*. London: Verso.

Bailey, A. 1998. Locating Traitorous Identities: Toward a View of Privilege-Cognizant White Character. *Hypatia*, 13 (3): 27–42. DOI: 10.1111/j.1527-2001.1998.tb01368.x.

Blunt, A. and Dowling, R. 2006. *Home*. London: Routledge. DOI: 10.4324/9780203401354.

Bonnett, A. 2000. *White Identities: Historical and International Perspectives*. Harlow: Pearson Education Limited.

Butler, J. 1990. *Gender Trouble: Feminism and the Subversion of Identity*. New York: Routledge. DOI: 10.4324/9780203824979.

Butler, J. 1997. *The Psychic Life of Power*. Stanford, CA: University Press.

Butter, S. 2016. Representations of Ideal Homes in English Culture: Gracious Living and the Creative Self in Matthew Reynolds' Designs for a Happy Home. In *Subject Cultures: The English Novel from the 18th to the 21st Century*, ed. N. Kuster, S. Butter and S. Heinz, pp. 251–268. Tübingen: Narr.

Byrne, B. 2006. *White Lives: The Interplay of 'Race', Class and Gender in Everyday Life*. London: Routledge. DOI: 10.4324/9780203640043.

Clarke, S. and Garner, S. 2010. *White Identities: A Critical Sociological Approach*. London: Pluto Press. DOI: 10.2307/j.ctt183p383.

Doling, J. and Ronald, R. 2010. Home Ownership and Asset-Based Welfare. *Journal of Housing and the Built Environment*, 25 (2): 165–173. DOI: 10.1007/s10901-009-9177-6.

Dyer, R. 1997. *White*. London: Routledge. DOI: 10.4324/9781315003603.

Foucault, M. 1980. The Confession of the Flesh. In *Power/Knowledge: Selected Interviews and Other Writings 1972–1977*, ed. C. Gordon, pp. 194–228. New York: Harvester Wheatsheaf.

Foucault, M. 2010. *The Birth of Biopolitics: Lectures at the Collège de France, 1978-1979*. Basingstoke: Palgrave Macmillan. DOI: 10.1057/9780230594180.

Frankenberg, R. 1993. *The Social Construction of Whiteness: White Women, Race Matters*. Minneapolis, MN: University of Minnesota Press.

Frye, M. 1992. White Woman Feminist. In *Wilful Virgin: Essays in Feminist Theory*, ed. M. Frye, pp. 147–169. Freedom, CA: Crossing Press.

Graham, L. T., Gosling, S. D. and Travis, C. K. 2015. The Psychology of Home Environments: A Call for Research on Residential Space. *Perspectives on Psychological Science*, 10 (3): 346–356. DOI: 10.1177/1745 691615576761.

Gray, B. 2002. 'Whitely Scripts' and Irish Women's Racialized Belonging(s) in England. *European Journal of Cultural Studies*, 5 (3): 257–274. DOI: 10.1177/1364942002005003064.

Harris, C. I. 1993. Whiteness as Property. *Harvard Law Review*, 106 (8): 1707–1791. DOI: 10. 2307/1341787.

Heinz, S. 2016. Unhomely Spaces and Improper Houses: Representations of Whiteness and Class on British Television. In *Anglistentag 2015 Paderborn: Proceedings*, ed. C. Ehland, I. Mindt and M. Tönnies, pp. 77–88. Trier: WVT.

Ignatiev, N. 1995. *How the Irish Became White*. London: Routledge.

Jacobson, M. F. 1998. *Whiteness of a Different Color: European Immigrants and the Alchemy of Race*. Cambridge, MA: Harvard University Press. DOI: 10.2307/j.ctvjk2w15.

Leonard, P. 2010. *Expatriate Identities in Postcolonial Organizations: Working Whiteness*. Farnham: Ashgate. DOI: 10.1177/0957926511022030607.

Lipsitz, G. 1995. The Possessive Investment in Whiteness: Racialized Social Democracy and the 'White' Problem in American Studies. *American Quarterly*, 473: 369–387. DOI: 10.2307/2713291.

Macintyre, S. 1999. *A Concise History of Australia*. Cambridge: University Press. DOI: 10.1017/CBO9780511809996.

Madigan, R., Munro, M. and Smith, S. J. 1990. Gender and the Meaning of the Home. *International Journal of Urban and Regional Research*, 14 (4): 625–647. DOI:10.1111/j.1468-2427.1990.tb00160.x.

Mallett, S. 2004. Understanding Home: A Critical Review of the Literature. *The Sociological Review*, 52 (1): 62–89. DOI:10.1111/j.1467-954X.2004.00442.x.

McClintock, A. 1995. *Imperial Leather: Race, Gender and Sexuality in the Colonial Context*. New York: Routledge.

McElroy, R. 2017. Mediating Home in an Age of Austerity: The Values of British Property Television. *European Journal of Cultural Studies*, 20 (5): 525–542. DOI:10.1177/1367549417701758.

McKenzie, L. 2015. *Getting By: Estates, Class and Culture in Austerity Britain*. Bristol: Policy Press.

McMurria, J. 2008. Desperate Citizens and Good Samaritans: Neoliberalism and Makeover Reality TV. *Television & New Media*, 9 (4): 305–332.

Meinig, S. 2004. *Witnessing the Past: History and Post-Colonialism in Australian Historical Novels*. Tübingen: Narr.

Messerschmidt, J. W. 2004. *Flesh and Blood: Adolescent Gender Diversity and Violence*. Lanham: Rowman and Littlefield.

Miles, R. and Brown, M. 2003. *Racism*, 2nd edn. London: Routledge.

Moreton-Robinson, A. 2005. The House that Jack Built: Britishness and White Possession. *Australian Critical Race and Whiteness Studies Association Journal*, 1: 21–29.

Moreton-Robinson, A. 2015. *The White Possessive: Property, Power, and Indigenous Sovereignty*. Minneapolis, MN: University of Minnesota Press. DOI:10.5749/minnesota/9780816692149.001.0001.

Morley, D. 2000. *Home Territories: Media, Mobility and Identity*. London: Routledge. DOI:10.4324/97802 03444177.

Ouellette, L. and Hay, J. 2008. *Better Living Through Reality TV: Television and Postwelfare Citizenship*. Malden, MA: Blackwell Publications.

Raisborough, J. 2011. *Lifestyle Media and the Formation of the Self*. Houndmills and New York: Palgrave Macmillan.

Rifkin, M. 2013. Settler Common Sense. *Settler Colonial Studies*, 3 (3–4): 322–340. DOI:10.1080/22014 73X.2013.810702.

Roediger, D. R. 1991. *The Wages of Whiteness: Race and the Making of the American Working Class*. London, New York: Verso.

Slater, L. 2019. *Anxieties of Belonging in Settler Colonialism: Australia, Race and Place*. London: Routledge. DOI:10.4324/9780429433733.

Smith, S. J. 2015. Owner Occupation: At Home in a Spatial, Financial Paradox. *International Journal of Housing Policy*, 15 (1): 61–83. DOI:10.1080/14616718.2014.997432.

St Louis, B. 2005. Racialization in the 'Zone of Ambiguity'. In *Racialization: Studies in Theory and Practice*, ed. K. Murji and J. Solomos, pp. 29–50. Oxford: University Press. DOI:10.1177/0268580906067811.

Strauss, M. and Liebenberg, S. 2014. Contested spaces: Housing rights and evictions law in post-apartheid South Africa. *Planning Theory*, 13 (4): 428–448. DOI:10.1177/1473095214525150.

Tuan, Y.-F. 2012. Epilogue: Home as Elsewhere. In *Heimat: At the Intersection of Memory and Space*, ed. F. Eigler and J. Kugele, pp. 226–239. Berlin: De Gruyter. DOI:10.1515/9783110292060.226.

Walderzak, J. 2016. I May Be a Socialist, But I'm Not a Lunatic. In *Downton Abbey and Philosophy*, ed. A. Barkman and R. Arp, pp. 13–23. Chicago: Open Court.

Wood, H. and Skeggs, B. 2008. Spectacular Morality: 'Reality' Television, Individualisation and the Remaking of the Working Class. In *The Media and Social Theory*, ed. D. Hesmondhalgh and J. Toynbee, pp. 177–193. London and New York: Routledge.

## Audiovisual Sources

*All About Property*. 2018–present. TV, The Home Channel-DStv Channel 176.

*DIY SOS*, rebranded as *The Big Build*, 1999–present. TV, BBC1.

*Einsatz in 4 Wänden*, 2003–2013. TV, RTL.

*Extreme Makeover: Home Edition*, 2003–2012, 2020–present. TV, ABC and HGTV.

*House Hunters Asia*, 2016–present. TV, HGTV Asia.

*Tidying Up with Marie Kondo*, 2019. Streaming, Netflix.

Sarah Heinz

## *Online Sources*

MyHomeMove. 2017. 'Nick Knowles and DIY SOS nail top position in UK's favourite property TV survey', 22 May, viewed 3 July 2020, https://www.myhomemove.com/the-people-have-spoken-nick-knowles-and-diy-sos-nail-top-position-in-uks-favourite-property-tv-survey/.

RTL.DE. n.d. 'Einsatz in 4 Wänden', viewed 11 July 2020, https://www.rtl.de/themen/thema/einsatz-in-4-w-nden-t8474.html.

# 22

# Bleeding through the band-aid: The white saviour industrial complex

*Jamie Kherbaoui and Brittany Aronson*

## Introduction

The White Saviour Industrial Complex (WSIC) is a network of practices, policies, organisations, and institutions responsible for reifying historical inequities by continuing to maintain white control over Black, Indigenous, and People of Colour (BIPOC) through a complex system of predominantly white-led initiatives rooted in the preservation of dependence and powerlessness. The WSIC, an essential component to the construction and maintenance of whiteness, has shifted in form over time to adapt to the changing socio-political landscape. In doing so, the global white elite seek to maintain a narrative of white innocence and benevolence, while masking the role of the WSIC in acts of racial violence across the globe. While often critiqued on a global scale, we position the WSIC in our domestic United States context to illustrate how it harms BIPOC both domestically and globally. We situate our examination within the broader sociohistorical context of the globalization of white supremacy. We also frame the current COVID-19 global pandemic and the structural racism pandemic within the relationship between the non-profit industrial complex (NPIC) and the WSIC. Ultimately, we argue the WSIC, and thus white supremacy, are the cause of the mass devastation facing communities across the world, and without antiracist structural level change, the current aid paradigm and white-led band-aid solutions will only result in further harm to BIPOC communities.

## Our positionalities: Kherbaoui

Writing from my position of lived experiences as a white, temporarily able-bodied, cis-hetero woman and United States citizen raised in a middle-class, Catholic Minnesotan household, I am on a lifelong journey of unlearning my own internalised white saviour mentality. My white saviour mentality is part of a deeper internalization of white supremacy. This internalization is shaped by a series of racial projects, including the postcards I often found in my mailbox while I was growing up of images of Native American children being utilised by white Christian missionaries to solicit donations. What I did not learn during my childhood was the traumatic history of Native American boarding schools that white settler Christians in Minnesota created

DOI: 10.4324/9780429355769-22

to remove Native American children from their communities and strip them of their culture, language, and spiritual practices through US government policies of forced assimilation and cultural genocide. The WSIC thrives on centering the emotional desires of white individuals over the physical, material, and psychological harm being done to BIPOC (Aronson 2017; Cole 2012; Flaherty 2016; Willer 2019). As a white academic, it is easy for me to centre my own emotional desires for comfort by focusing on a structural analysis of the WSIC while detaching from the daily realities of how the WSIC has resulted in my ability to have the privilege to write this piece and work for a predominantly white institution that involves community engagement work with and in BIPOC communities. I cannot claim to examine the role of white United States citizens in creating and maintaining the WSIC without examining myself as one of those white United States citizens. Thus, as I approach writing this chapter, I must also grapple with the interconnectedness between the comfort and safety I am able to experience to write this publication during the global coronavirus pandemic and the disproportionate harm simultaneously being inflicted on BIPOC communities domestically and globally.

## Our positionalities: Aronson

In conceptualising this work, it is important that I situate my positionality to recognise who I am in connection to broader society and my interest in examining the WSIC. I identify as a white Latina cis-hetero women, able-bodied, middle-class, and born with American citizenship. Much of my earlier writings in the academy, I monolithically situated myself as 'white' with a goal to continuously reflect on and confront my privilege (Aronson 2016; Aronson 2017). As I continued upon my journey learning about race, racism, in whiteness, particularly in the United States, I realised by erasing a part of my identity, being one-half Colombian, I was actually reinforcing whiteness further by not interrogating why I did that. Later in my work, I began to grapple with this and have shifted my positionality statements to include this important tension. I have learned I can simultaneously recognise my privilege while also understanding the ways I have succumbed to whiteness by erasing myself. Whiteness as an ideology is dangerous and dehumanising.

Urrieta (2010) explains, 'whitestreaming' begins in schools through the curriculum that is founded on the 'practices, principles, morals, and values of white supremacy' and highlights white Anglo-American culture. He asserts that this is not exclusively the work of white people anymore: 'any person, including people of colour, actively promoting or upholding white models as the goal of standard is also involved in whitestreaming' (p. 181). I grew up in a home socialized into whiteness and thus became an active 'whitestreamer' that I brought with me into my teaching. In my earlier work (Aronson 2017), I unpacked my own complicity in the WSIC and the importance of disrupting this work in teacher education. Unlike what Jamie describes in her positionality statement of focusing on a structural level analysis of the WSIC, I previously centered a personal analysis of self-reflection (and honestly self-persecution) of my role embodying 'white privilege' and how I continued to reinforce oppression. I now know I need a critical interrogation of the systems that exist to sustain white supremacy and support a WSIC. I believe BOTH of these analyses are necessary as we work to be co-conspirators against oppression and the WSIC (Love 2019).

## Historical context

White saviourism can be traced back to white supremacist theology that has resulted in centuries of colonialism, imperialism, and the continued oppression of BIPOC, which was politically and religiously sanctioned through the Doctrine of Discovery in the papal bull Dum Diversas in 1452 and the bull Romanus Pontifex issued in 1455 by Pope Nicholas V., followed by the Inter Caetera in 1493 issued by Alexandar VI. These documents served as the foundation to justify the global slave trade in the fifteenth and sixteenth centuries, and the Age of Imperialism (*White Saviour: Racism in the American Church* 2019). The Doctrine of Discovery was utilised to justify land seizure through the 1823 United States Supreme Court Case, Johnson vs. McIntosh. In this case, Chief Justice John Marshall utilised this Doctrine to ignore aboriginal land possession and justify the United States federal government's seizure of land, arguing it belonged to the colonial powers who 'discovered' it (Native Voices n.d.; Indigenous Values 2018). These racial doctrines were crafted by white supremacist theologists who justified the denial of land possession to Native people and any non-Native people who were deemed not white through manifest destiny ideology.

Manifest destiny ideology was created to claim it was white peoples' God-given right and Christian duty to take whatever they wanted and do whatever they wanted to anyone who was not considered to be white. Manifest destiny ideology was also invoked to justify U.S. imperialism in the 1890s and early twentieth century, which led to the US control and possession of the Philippine Islands and Hawaii. The white man's burden narrative, a central component to manifest destiny ideology, was utilised in Rudyard Kipling's 'The White Man's Burden' poem published in 1899 as an appeal to the United States to assume control of the Philippines. At the historical moment this poem was published, US imperialism was beginning to take hold through the Philippine-American War and the Spanish-American War, which led to the US Senate ratification of the treaty that placed Puerto Rico, Guam, Cuba, and the Philippines under American control (History Matters n.d.).

Institutionalisation of white supremacy originating from the European colonizer's church is still alive today in our United States government's practices of imperialism, neoliberalism and the behaviours of white-led institutions. The present-day white American church has maintained its power through the WSIC, which disguises the continued white paternalistic control over BIPOC domestically and globally as charitable acts in the name of God. Contextualizing current aid and missionary work within the broader historical context of white supremacy illustrates why individual white people's work within the WSIC, even if guided by good intentions, will continue to perpetuate white supremacy.

In an interview for her Good Ancestor podcast with No White Saviours advocacy campaign leaders Olivia Alaso and Kelsey Nielsen, Layla F. Saad (2019) reflects,

> When you're coming into any situation, we're talking about aid workers right now or missionary workers coming to the African continent to volunteer, to help, to do whatever the stuff they're there to do. You have to remember; you're not just coming in as the single individual person. You're coming with the whole entire weight of the history of what it means to be white, to have a colonial history and in the present day you still have that power dynamic that's at play.

Whether it be through Christian missionaries bringing a white supremacist theological understanding of God to BIPOC around the world or international development and the aid industry, the WSIC maintains the legacy of the Doctrine of Discovery and its white supremacist theology. In doing so, it seeks to maintain the lie of American Exceptionalism by denying responsibility for any wrongdoing that has resulted in global inequality, while also claiming to save BIPOC from themselves in the name of God and democracy. Hickel (2018) argues the 'aid paradigm allows rich countries and individuals to pretend to fix with one hand what they destroy with the other, dispensing small bandages at the same time as they inflict deep injuries, and claiming the moral high ground for doing so' (p. 30). This has allowed white settler colonialists to talk about sins without naming their role as the sinner (Cole 2012). By reframing white saviourism within a historical context, the myth of the white saviour crumbles and the root causes of global racial inequality are exposed.

## Domestic issues of saviourism

The WSIC has gained international attention through critique of white saviour films (Hughey 2014), white missionaries and the voluntourism industry (Saad 2019), and an overrepresentation of white educators in BIPOC majority schools (Aronson 2017). This chapter focuses on the domestic manifestations of the WSIC in the United States to examine how it has been utilised to oppress BIPOC not only globally but also domestically. The existence of the WSIC already has manifested itself in the United States through a prison–industrial complex (Davis 1999), NPIC (Smith and INCITE! Women of Color Against Violence, 2007), and education–industrial complex (Aronson and Boveda 2017). With each of these complexes, white-led institutions and organisations are able to maintain control over BIPOC while also presenting white supremacist structures and systems as the solution to saving BIPOC from themselves.

The idea of American exceptionalism is nothing new in US ideology and it is directly connected to the globalization of white supremacy (Allen 2005; Leonardo 2002; Ortiz 2018). Sensoy and DiAngelo (2017) explain that ideology is 'the big, shared ideas of a society that are reinforced through all of the institutions and thus are very hard to avoid believing' (p. 224). US white American culture breeds ideologies of individualism and meritocracy starting at a young age through history lessons which romanticize the United States' past. White Americans are taught to believe that we are the best in the world because of our hard-earned merits and natural superiority, while the reality of how this country was built by looting from and pillaging BIPOC remains intentionally hidden (Flaherty 2016). Ortiz (2018) argues, '… the idea that the United States is the freest nation on the earth, the champion of the oppressed, and can do no wrong – or at least never intends to do wrong – is a myth' (p. 185). This way of thinking results in direct and indirect harm to BIPOC domestically and globally while dominant white society refuses to acknowledge any form of wrongdoing.

For this chapter, we further elaborate on the domestic manifestations of the WSIC by examining the relationship between the WSIC and the NPIC. As we are writing this chapter, we are living through the global COVID-19 pandemic. The COVID-19 pandemic and the pandemic of structural racism occurring simultaneously present a ripe example of the shortcomings and deceit of the WSIC. Thus, we have shifted our focus to position our conversation of the WSIC and NPIC in the context of the United States' response to both pandemics. In doing so, we seek to support the global call from BIPOC for white people to move away from the 'helping' mentality that is rooted in the WSIC towards long-term commitment to being actively antiracist and supporting Black-led organising.

## WSIC and the NPIC

Nonprofits, despite being portrayed as the bedrock of American generosity and exceptionalism, are a state-sanctioned mechanism designed by the wealthy, white elite to control BIPOC and destabilize social movements that pose a threat to white supremacy and our current capitalist system (Rodríguez and INCITE! Women of Color Against Violence, 2007). INCITE![1] contributors illustrate the harmful impacts the NPIC has on BIPOC. Foundations, established by white, corporate elitists have played an instrumental role in suppressing grassroots organizing efforts led by BIPOC. Rodríquez writes, '... the "ruling class" of philanthropic organisations and foundations may, at times, almost unilaterally determine whether certain activist commitments and practices are appropriate to their consensus vision of American democracy' (2007: 27). By maintaining control through the NPIC, those in power are able to reduce the possibility of effective efforts to dismantle white supremacy.

The NPIC is a present-day mechanism maintaining the ever-evolving WSIC. According to the Race to Lead: Confronting the Non-profit Racial Leadership Gap report, survey results consistently indicate less than 20% of executive directors/CEOs of non-profits are people of colour (Thomas-Breifeld and Kunreuther, 2019: 2). The NPIC's racial leadership gap cannot be disentangled from the role nonprofits play in upholding white supremacy through the WSIC. Nonprofits not only lack leadership of BIPOC, they enable white organisations and institutions to maintain power over BIPOC while denying access to funds to BIPOC leadership.

Even when BIPOC-led nonprofits are able to secure funds, research confirms 'unrestricted assets of groups with leaders of colour were 76% smaller than those led by whites' (Dorsey et al. 2020: 11). In 'The Case for Funding Black-Led Social Change', the authors refer to this as 'Philanthropic Redlining or the Philanthropic Black Codes' (Emergent Pathways LLC, 2020: 10). As a result, 'institutional philanthropy, acting in alignment with systems of anti-Black oppression, has thus contributed to the volatility of thousands of BLOs (Black Lead Organisations) and the porous organisational infrastructure for Black-led social change' (Emergent Pathways LLC, 2020: 4). Research on racism in philanthropy indicates the NPIC, despite being portrayed as the solution for addressing the harm caused by structural racism, is also complicit in maintaining white supremacy.

For white leadership and funders, the NPIC allows those in power to channel white guilt resulting from what Teju Cole (2012) describes as the 'unbearable pressures that build in a system built on pillage' into charity-oriented solutions that neglect to address structural racism. Foundations dictate who is deserving and undeserving. Andrea Smith connects Rockefeller's foundation strategy to the present-day approach that maintains 'people of colour deserve individual relief but people of colour organised to end white supremacy become a menace to society' (2007: 8). Regardless of the individual intentions of white non-profit staff members and missionary volunteers, the WSIC and thus the NPIC are actively maintaining white supremacy.

To ensure their control over who has access to resources and who does not, foundations direct money away from taxes towards private decision-making tables. This privatisation of public goods is a neoliberal control mechanism that is employed both domestically and globally through institutions like the IMF, World Bank, NGOs, and private foundations. Through privatisation, these institutions are able to maintain a system of dependency to justify external white-led entities maintaining control over BIPOC. The NPIC evolved out of a shift toward privatisation of public goods and services as part of the global neoliberal agenda. In the latter part of the twentieth century, the United States government shifted its responsibilities as the primary provider of social services to other levels of government, private companies, and non-profit organisations (Kettl 2000). By denying public goods are basic social rights, neoliberalist ideology treats certain groups of people as expendable.

Neoliberal paternalism allows white, wealthy individuals to dictate who is deserving and undeserving of basic human rights, like healthcare, food, water, and safe housing. When institutions oppress and exploit those who are deemed expendable, community leaders are forced to focus on providing human services to just survive. As a result, they have less capacity to address root causes of inequities so that all can thrive (Samimi 2010: 21). Kivel and INCITE! Women of Color Against Violence (2007) utilises the term 'buffer zone' to discuss how the ruling class 'prevent people at the bottom of the pyramid from organising to maintain the power, the control, and, most important, the wealth that they have accumulated' (p. 134). He argues the functions of the buffer zone include: *'taking care of* people at the bottom of the pyramid', *'keeping hope alive'*, and 'to maintain the system by *controlling* those who want to make changes' (p. 135). The buffer zone provides a way for the global elite to maintain white supremacy.

White-led foundations have played a critical role in attempting to co-opt the Black Power Movement and other BIPOC-led social movements by advancing a programme of domestic neocolonialism through philanthropic efforts while denying their responsibility for the harm that has caused the need for services in the first place. King Osayande and INCITE! Women of Color Against Violence (2007) argue,

> In reality, the wealth of most family foundations, not just the obvious culprits of op-
> pression, like Rockefeller, Ford, Getty, and other corporate foundations, has come from
> centuries of oppression and exploitation of African Americans, Native Americans,
> Mexicans, Chinese migrants and other people of colour and the poor in this country. Yet
> the idea that family foundations should be required as a community to pay reparations has
> never been a part of the analysis of the white Left.
>
> *(p. 87)*

Instead of reparations and structural change, the WSIC continues to exert control through an endless cycle of band-aid solutions, which neglect to reckon with not only historical wrong-doing, but also present-day neocolonialism. Globally, the aid paradigm justifying band-aid solutions over addressing root causes relies on the myth that rich countries are developing poor countries. In actuality, 'poor countries are effectively developing rich countries- and they have been since the late fifteenth century' (Hickel 2018: 30). The aid narrative is deployed as a form of propaganda to 'make the takers seem like the givers and conceals how the global economy actually works' (p. 30). The aid paradigm embedded in the WSIC serves as a racial project to uphold white supremacy. Critical interrogation of the underlying myth of the aid paradigm and how it falsely portrays the Global South as inferior can also be applied domestically to the United States context. When white-led non-profits and foundations share data in their annual reports to demonstrate how they are responsible for what they define as 'success' in BIPOC communities domestically, they do not put those stories in conversation with how BIPOC are responsible for their own accumulation of wealth.

## COVID-19

The deceitfulness of the aid paradigm is crucial to keep in mind when we look at how white US institutions frame narratives about who is responsible for getting communities through COVID-19. The United States is experiencing the worst COVID-19 outbreak in the world. Some argue it is because of American exceptionalism ideology and how the virus has ex-acerbated existing structural inequities (Friedman 2020). On 20 January 2020, the United States reported its first case of the newly recognised virus among the novel coronaviruses now known as COVID-19. This was the same day the first case was also reported in South Korea. However, there were drastically different responses in both how South Korea handled this epidemic as well as the rate of recovery the country initially experienced. The country's leadership acted fast with a motto of 'test, trace and treat' (Kim 2020). South Korea's healthcare system is well-funded and efficient at distributing public services, unlike the United States' healthcare system. Despite evidence demonstrating the United States was failing to contain the COVID-19 outbreak while South Korea was succeeding, during the White House briefing on 15 April 2020, Donald Trump stated, '[N]obody is able to do things like we can do. And we're going to be able to help other countries that are having tremendous problems, to put it mildly' (remarks by President Trump 2020). Yet, in March 2020, the Trump administration was requesting critical supplies from South Korea and other countries due to severe shortages in the United States. How is the nation (the United States) that is continuously lauded the 'best country' in the world by President Donald Trump going to help other countries, when healthcare workers in the United States are without proper protective gear and people are dying at alarming rates, disproportionately within the African-American (Black) community (Hlavinka 2020)? Why is there this desire to announce how the United States is going to be able to help those that the United States has exploited abroad, but not provide basic human rights to adequate healthcare to the BIPOC continuously exploited right here in the United States? American exceptionalism has always been a myth, long before the COVID-19 pandemic. The WSIC enables the maintenance of this deceitful ideology embedded in the global aid paradigm.

Despite the mantra 'We're all in this together', BIPOC have been impacted by this pandemic at disproportionately high rates. According to the PBS NewsHour series 'Race Matters' (2020), 'Health officials have stressed that novel coronavirus doesn't discriminate based on race or ethnicity. But disparities long present in the U.S. medical system are now driving what some call a crisis within a crisis: black and brown communities across the country are being hit harder, and with fewer resources to save them.' A guest on the show, Dr. Blackstock, a NYC physician working in an Urgent Care Center, emphasized the reality of how these racial health disparities are linked to structural racism. Dr. Ruha Benjamin, a Professor of African-American Studies at Princeton University, has argued while the media might be presenting statistics of the higher percentage of Black people dying from COVID-19 is connected to pre-existing health conditions such as asthma or diabetes, what rarely is acknowledged by the dominant white media are the pre-existing social conditions in housing, employment, education, mass incarceration, and healthcare that impacted communities well before COVID-19 showed up. The structures in US society have been built with racism embedded into our systems. The ideology of whiteness and American exceptionalism keep racism functioning, while enabling white individuals to believe 'we are all in this together' and to remain shocked at how this could happen to a country like the United States.

Early when the virus was first reported, some white Americans demonstrated behaviours suggesting the virus would not have any real impact on them, or that perhaps this was all a hoax created by the 'liberal media' (Hoskin 2020). As Hoskin (2020) reported in *Vox*,

> While it might seem ludicrous that whiteness and income level would somehow make people immune to infection, there is some truth to such beliefs. In the event that these rich white folks find themselves with a cough and fever, they are more likely to have the reassurance and privilege of access to local testing centers and quality, unbiased health care…Being white is the default identity in America. Whiteness is our cultural tapestry. It's America's norm, against which all others are measured, and there is a special kind of security that comes along with being the norm…That feeling of 'oppression' these white protesters have voiced is the residual effect of living in a country that has been shaped to cater to their racial majority status, and consequently, their perceived loss of power and privilege.
>
> (n.p.)

We have witnessed visual displays of such resistance as white protesters began showing up at courthouses, some armed and not wearing masks, demanding their liberties and rights be restored. These claims of 'oppression' many white protestors have deployed in relation to the lockdown protocols are directly connected to this idea of American exceptionalism of invincibility. Believing COVID-19 may not directly impact them, it is easy to not acknowledge or care how the Black community is most impacted by this pandemic. Building from Charles Mills' (1997) assertion that a *racial contract* exists as a set of rules that distinguishes how white people are allowed to move in society as compared to people of colour, Serwer (2020) explains,

> But the pandemic has introduced a new clause to the racial contract. The lives of disproportionately black and brown workers are being sacrificed to fuel the engine of a faltering economy, by a president who disdains them. This is the COVID contract.
>
> *(n.p.)*

It is under these circumstances – consequences from larger systemic inequalities rooted in our country's history of white supremacy – that exacerbate and maintain the WSIC. Thus, when we see the expansion of food banks and other white-led charities, this allows white non-profit leadership and white-led foundations to feel good about themselves, with no need to dismantle the structural racism that maintains their control over BIPOC. After the COVID-19 pandemic passes, how will white Americans operate in the future in light of this pandemic in response to the other existing pandemics, including structural racism, domestically, and globally? These are the questions we must raise to acknowledge the power of ideology impacting the WSIC which operates on US soil. The COVID-19 pandemic illustrates very clearly band-aid solutions being utilised by the NPIC continue to fall short in enabling all members of our society to not only survive but also thrive. Structural change is needed, as the Black Lives Matter movement has continued to demand. Brittany Packnett Cunningham, a lifelong activist and member of the Ferguson Uprising, tweeted, 'Charity only matters where solidarity is present. So systemic change thru voting is absolutely necessary' (Packnett 2019). White individuals have a responsibility to move beyond 'helping' mentalities to truly thinking about the impact their voting decisions, in addition to many other behaviours, have on a broader society and who we elect into offices at local, state, and federal levels.

Acknowledging how the WSIC has operated throughout history and the deceitfulness of the aid paradigm discussed earlier in this chapter, it is likely white-led institutions and organisations will attempt to utilise white saviour narratives to justify disaster capitalism practices and paternalistic neoliberal programmes. Yet, many will deny the disturbing reality of how those exploited and on the frontlines of keeping our communities alive were treated as expendable in the name of our capitalist system, and movements for structural change will continue to be co-opted. Naomi Klein (2007) argues capitalists utilise disasters, such as hurricanes, wars, and epidemics, to advance neoliberal policies and practices during times of chaos and shock. Klein has characterised the Trump Administration's current response to COVID-19 as a pandemic shock doctrine that is seeking to utilise the present chaos to further the privatization of public goods and services and erode our democracy, despite the widespread call from community activists for universal healthcare, universal housing, universal childcare, paid sick leave, decarceration, and other programmes that treat all human beings as deserving of basic social rights (Klein 2020).

Community organiser and artist Bree Newsome Bass and several other BIPOC activists argue it is disaster white supremacy that has built the foundation for the COVID-19 pandemic in the United States to be so much worse than in other countries. In the podcast,

'Intersectionality Matters' hosted by Kimberlé Crenshaw (2020), Newsome Bass describes how our current systems are organised around white supremacy and our essential workforce is treated as disposable, which is a status quo of racial violence that is built into the foundation of this country. She traces the current treatment of the essential labour force to the dehumanization of enslaved people who were an essential part of how the economy is maintained. Yet, when the dominant news stories cover how white-led institutions are on the frontlines to treating patients, who are disproportionately BIPOC, they do not grapple with how these essential workers have been treated as disposable because of whiteness (Crenshaw 2020).

## Conclusion

By acknowledging the reality that white American Exceptionalism is a myth and white supremacy is the reason the United States has a remarkably high COVID-19 death rate, the centuries-old white saviour narrative that has been the backbone of stories of white American 'generosity' is exposed as harmful and deceitful. White saviour narratives feed white egos with every call for donations while intentionally denying the role white individuals must take responsibility in addressing the structural racism being exacerbated by COVID-19. The donations are not the problem, as in kind and monetary donations are critical to supporting Black-led organising efforts. The problem is rooted in how white supremacy has resulted in structural racism that necessitates white donations to BIPOC in the first place and the lack of commitment to antiracist action from these same white donors.

## Note

1   INCITE! is a network of radical feminists of colour organising to end state violence and violence in [their] homes and communities, who held 'The Revolution Will Not Be Funded: Beyond the Nonprofit Industrial Complex' conference in 2004 (INCITE! n.d.).

## References

Allen, R. L. 2005. The Globalization of White Supremacy: Toward a Critical Discourse on the Racialization of the World. *Educational Theory*, 51 (4): 467–485.

Aronson, B. A. 2017. The White Savior Industrial Complex: A Cultural Studies Analysis of a Teacher Educator, Savior Film, and Future Teachers. *Journal of Critical Thought and Praxis*, 6 (3): 36–54.

Aronson, B. A. 2020. From Teacher Education to Practicing Teacher: What Does Culturally Relevant Praxis Look Like? *Urban Education*, 55 (8–9): 1115–1141.

Aronson, B. A. and Boveda, M. 2017. The Intersection of White Supremacy and the Education Industrial Complex: An Analysis of #BlackLivesMatter and the Criminalization of People with Disabilities. *Journal of Educational Controversy*, 12 (1): 1–20.

Cole, T. 2012. 'The White-Savior Industrial Complex', *The Atlantic*, 21 March, viewed 4 April 2019, https://www.theatlantic.com/international/archive/2012/03/the-white-savior-industrial-complex/254843/.

Crenshaw, K. 2020. 'Pt 4- Under the Blacklight: COVID & Disaster White Supremacy', podcast, 21 April, viewed 6 May 2020, https://soundcloud.com/intersectionality-matters/13pt-4-under-the-blacklight.

Davis, A. Y. 1999. *The Prison Industrial Complex*. Chico, CA: AK Press.

Dorsey, C., Bradach, J. and Kim, P. 2020. *Racial Equity and Philanthropy: Disparities in Funding for Leaders of Color Leave Impact on the Table*', The Bridgespan Group & Echoing Green, viewed 15 June 2020, https://www.bridgespan.org/bridgespan/Images/articles/racial-equity-and-philanthropy/racial-equity-and-philanthropy.pdf?ext=.pdf.

Emergent Pathways LLC. 2020. *The Case for Funding Black-Led Social Change*, Emergent Pathways LLC, viewed 15 June 2020, http://www.blacksocialchange.org/wp-content/uploads/2020/05/BSCFN_BLSCO_Report.pdf.

Flaherty, J. 2016. *No More Heroes: Grassroots Challenges to the Savior Mentality*. Chico, CA: AK Press.

Friedman, U. 2020. 'Why America Resists Learning From Other Countries', *The Atlantic*, 14 May, viewed 25 May 2020, https://www.theatlantic.com/politics/archive/2020/05/coronavirus-could-end-american-exceptionalism/611605/.

Hickel, J. 2018. *The Divide: Global Inequality from Conquest to Free Markets*. New York: W. W. Norton & Company.

History Matters. n.d. 'The White Man's Burden: Kipling's Hymn to U.S. Imperialism', viewed 6 April 2020, http://historymatters.gmu.edu/d/5478/.

Hlavinka, E. 2020. 'COVID-19 Killing African Americans at Shocking Rates', *MedPage Today*, 1 May, viewed 5 May 2020, https://www.medpagetoday.com/infectiousdisease/covid19/86266.

Hoskin, M. N. 2020. 'The whiteness of anti-lockdown protests: How ignorance, privilege, and anti-black racism is driving white protesters to risk their lives', *Vox*, 25 April, viewed 2 May 2020, https://www.vox.com/first-person/2020/4/25/21234774/coronavirus-covid-19-protest-anti-lockdown.

Hughey, M. 2014. *The White Savior Film: Content, Critics, and Consumption*. Philadelphia: Temple University Press.

INCITE! n.d. 'Beyond the non-profit industrial complex', *INCITE!*, viewed 21 May 2020, https://incite-national.org/beyond-the-non-profit-industrial-complex/.

Indigenous Values. 2018. 'Dum Diversas', *Doctrine of Discovery*, viewed 6 April 2020, https://doctrineofdiscovery.org/dum-diversas.

Kettl, D. F. 2000. The Transformation of Governance: Globalization, Devolution, and the Role of Government. *Public Administration Review*, 60 (6): 488–497.

Kim, T. 2020. 'Why is South Korea beating coronavirus? Its citizens hold the state to account', *The Guardian*, 11 April, viewed 15 April 2020, https://www.theguardian.com/commentisfree/2020/apr/11/south-korea-beating-coronavirus-citizens-state-testing.

King, T. L. and Osayande, E. 2007. The filth on philanthropy: Progressive philanthropy's agenda to misdirect social justice movements. In *The Revolution Will Not Be Funded: Beyond the Non-Profit Industrial Complex*, ed. INCITE! Women of Color Against Violence, pp. 79–89. Cambridge, MA: South End Press.

Kivel, P. 2007. Social Service or Social Change? In *The Revolution Will Not Be Funded: Beyond the Non-Profit Industrial Complex*, ed. INCITE! Women of Color Against Violence, pp. 129–149. Cambridge, MA: South End Press.

Klein, N. 2007. *The Shock Doctrine: The Rise of Disaster Capitalism*. New York: MacMillan.

Klein, N. 2020. '"Coronavirus Capitalism": Naomi Klein's Case for Transformative Change Amid Coronavirus Pandemic', *Democracy Now*, 19 March, viewed 20 April 2020, https://www.democracynow.org/2020/3/19/naomi_klein_coronavirus_capitalism.

Leonardo, Z. 2002. The Souls of White Folk: Critical Pedagogy, Whiteness Studies, and Globalization Discourse. *Race Ethnicity and Education*, 5 (1): 29–50.

Love, B. L. 2019. *We Want to Do More Than Survive: Abolitionist Teaching and The Pursuit of Educational Freedom*. Boston: Beacon Press.

Mills, C. W. 1997. *The Racial Contract*. Ithaca, NY: Cornell University Press.

Native Voices. n.d. 'Supreme Court rules American Indians do not own land', *National Library of Medicine*, viewed 6 April 2020, https://www.nlm.nih.gov/nativevoices/timeline/271.html.

Ortiz, P. 2018. *An African American and Latinx History of the United States*, vol. 4. Boston: Beacon Press.

Packnett Cunningham, B. 2019. 'It's important to remember…/', Twitter, 22 November, viewed 19 May 2020, https://twitter.com/mspackyetti/status/1198011858374004741.

PBS. 2020. 'COVID-19 may not discriminate based on race—but U.S. health care does', *PBS News Hour*, 2 April, viewed 5 April 2020, https://www.pbs.org/newshour/show/covid-19-may-not-discriminate-based-on-race-but-u-s-health-care-does?fbclid=IwAR3XS1qfBL3YfWDglC4v91IEQoIGcgGkBUonBmn1FbnpbpmGzLqW4mprv5Q.

*Remarks by President Trump, Vice President Pence, and Members of the Coronavirus Task Force in Press Briefing* 2020, television programme, The White House, Washington D.C., 15 April.

Rodríguez, D. 2007. The political logic of the non-profit industrial complex. In *The revolution will not be funded: Beyond the non-profit industrial complex*, ed. INCITE! Women of Color Against Violence, pp. 21–40. Cambridge, MA: South End Press.

Saad, L. 2019. 'No white saviors on saying "no" to white saviorism', podcast, 19 December, viewed 3 March 2020, http://laylafsaad.com/good-ancestor-podcast/ep012-no-white-saviors.

Samimi, J. C. 2010. Funding America's nonprofits: The nonprofit industrial complex's hold on social justice. *Columbia Social Work Review*, pp. 17–25. DOI: 10.7916/D8QC0DC7.

Sensoy, O. and DiAngelo, R. 2017. *Is Everyone Really Equal?: An Introduction to Key Concepts in Social Justice Education*. New York: Teachers College Press.

Serwer, A. 2020. 'The Coronavirus Was an Emergency Until Trump Found Out Who Was Dying', *The Atlantic*, 8 May, viewed 25 May 2020, https://www.theatlantic.com/ideas/archive/2020/05/americas-racial-contract-showing/611389/?fbclid=IwAR1U9MCac43OPcn2hY-FLLg1KMlajnpgA0zH898kR3vOyzcdZuntli-xDY4.

Smith, A. 2007. 'Introduction'. In *The Revolution Will Not Be Funded: Beyond the Non-Profit Industrial Complex*, ed. INCITE! Women of Color Against Violence, pp. 1–18. Cambridge, MA: South End Press.

Thomas-Breifeld, S. and Kunreuther, F. 2019. *Race to Lead: Confronting the Racial Leadership Gap*, Building Movement Project, viewed 15 June 2020, https://buildingmovement.org/wp-content/uploads/2019/08/Race-to-Lead-Confronting-the-Nonprofit-Racial-Leadership-Gap.pdf.

Urrieta, L. 2010. *Working from Within: Chicana and Chicano Activist Educators in Whitestream Schools*. Tucson: University of Arizona Press.

*White Savior: Racism in The American Church*, 2019, film, 1517 Media. Directed by A. J. Christopher.

Willer, J. 2019. *Working through the Smog: How White Individuals Develop Critical Consciousness of White Saviorism*, Master's Thesis, Merrimack College, North Andover, viewed 25 May 2019, https://scholarworks.merrimack.edu/soe_student_ce/29/.

# 23

# An ecological exploration of whiteness: Using imperial hegemony and racial socialisation to examine lived experiences and social performativity of melanated communities

*Javeria Khadija Shah*

## Introduction

Inspired by Bronfenbrenner's (1975) bio-ecological theory this chapter's treatment of whiteness as an ecology is elaborated using concepts of imperial hegemony and racial socialisation, that centralise whiteness. The chapter connects Anoop Nayak's (2007) definition of whiteness to ecological framings of whiteness in the context of physical and ideological colonisation and its manifestation as racial socialisation, which is rooted in white supremacy. Nayak (2007) contends that whiteness

1.  is a modern invention; it has changed over time and place.
2.  is a social norm and has become chained to an index of unspoken privileges.
3.  the bonds of whiteness can yet be broken/deconstructed for the betterment of humanity.

*(2007: 738)*

The discussion shifts to a challenging of 'Whiteness as social norm ...' (2007: 738) through de-socialisation *as* decolonisation and treats this as an *ecological disruption*. This strand of the discussion aligns with the 'third wave' (Garner 2017: 1583) of critical whiteness which aims to extend focus on whiteness in the context of power dynamics. The chapter draws on examples from within UK policy, education, and news, to demonstrate the percolation of whiteness across social systems and interactions. Communities that are racialised as other to white are referenced as 'melanated' except for specific references to granular data or discourse, where the terms 'Black' or 'Brown' or 'BAME'[1] are used as reflective of the originating context.

DOI: 10.4324/9780429355769-23

## Bronfenbrenner's bio-ecological theory

In the past century, there has been a steady growth in ecological approaches within the social and natural sciences (Greenfield 2012: 2) and recent trends in the rejection of linear approaches that have been criticised for overlooking 'social complexity' (Johnson 2008: 2) in favour of theorists such as Urie Bronfenbrenner and his ecological systems theory (Härkönen 2007). The theory is considered to enable understandings of the individual in the context of their social influences and cultural and environmental interactions (Bronfenbrenner 1975) and in the recent years, there has been a steady growth in the use of Bronfenbrenner's (1975) ideas in social research (compare Halliday et al. 2018; Hodgson and Spours 2009, 2017; Hong 2011; Hong and Garbarino 2012; Ivankova and Plano Clark 2018; Johnson 1994; Waters et al. 2009; Marks and Grzywacz 2017; Nitsch 2009 Hong 2011; Quin 2016 Hodgson 2017; Renn 2003).

As Figure 23.1 represents, Bronfenbrenner presents a nuanced ecological system, which considers social interaction in a multitude of shapes and possibilities. Weisner suggests that the core of Bronfenbrenner's theory is represented in a dynamic and enmeshed social-ecological system of process, person, context, and time (PPCT) (Weisner 2008: 258). Bronfenbrenner defines a social ecology that surrounds the individual and represents the broader environmental influences and interactions that affect the individual (Santrock 2007).

A bio-social ecology is modelled using interconnecting layers constituting of a chronosystem,[2] macrosystem,[3] exsosytem,[4] mesosystem,[5] and microsystem.[6] Each ecological interaction or influence is defined as a system within itself to build a broader ecology.

While some have stayed true to Bronfenbrenner's (1975) original ideas, others such as Neville and Mobley (2001) and Weaver-Hightower (2008) have adopted aspects of his theory to develop hybrid approaches to the ecological analysis of social processes and interplay. These recent developments have demonstrated the potential of ecological approaches in assisting holistic understandings of systems, processes, and society as a whole through the lens of actor participants (Weaver-Hightower 2008).

## Applying this theoretic to whiteness

In using Bronfenbrenner's approach to develop an understanding of whiteness as an ecology, this section of the chapter is premised in two main assumptions. First, that conceptual whiteness is a social construction which has emerged from western colonisation (Guess 2006). Second, that the experience of melanated individuals and communities will differ within a whiteness socio-ecological system to those that are racialised as white. Connecting these two points to develop a holistic understanding of ideological whiteness as a socio-ecological articulation, it can be argued that a whiteness ecology is rooted in white supremacy which by design positions whiteness as the norm. Moreover, that individuals racialised as white benefit from this normalisation by default which 'plays in sustaining social privilege beyond that which is accorded marginalised others' (Guess 2006: 650). Extending this point further, it can be argued that in the positioning of whiteness as normative, knowledge tropes such as ideological beliefs, political positionings, and historical narratives are ecologically reinforced to sustain structural inequality, which prevents the incorporation of different world views, histories, and ideological beliefs on equal footingGarner 2017.

Working from these two assumptions, I present a whiteness ecosystem though a framing of each ecological layer using a social phenomenon or interaction that represents the percolation of white supremacy and its impact on melanated communities.

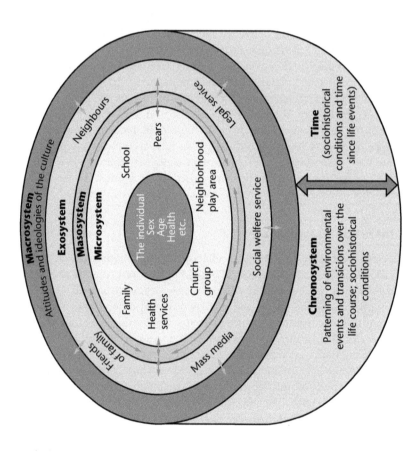

*Figure 23.1* Bio-Ecological Theory. Source: Santrock (2007). *Child Development*, 11th edn. NY: McGraw-Hill Companies Inc.

## Chronosystem through the lens of time

The chronosystem speaks to the time dynamics of an ecological system which Bronfenbrenner (1975) frames as environmental timings. In a whiteness ecology, this layer of the ecosystem can also be aligned with Nayak's (2007) premise that '*Whiteness is a modern invention (that) has changed over time and place*' (2007: 738) in its enactment through the colonial legacies of racism and contemporary coloniality.

I argue that whiteness as an environ has been upheld through a range of social systems, communications, and interactions, which reinforce a white supremacist model that inevitably impacts on the quality of lived experience and the trajectories of melanated individuals who are navigating this ecology. Extending this point by drawing on the work of Stuart Hall, I also argue that this dynamic is a hegemonic articulation which connects colonial racial constructions and dominant ideological formations and their reinforcement through the use of popular culture and the media over time (Hall 1997a). These points are amplified when considered through the lens of UK citizenship and national identity and the way Englishness is synonymised with whiteness, while a British identity is conditional for melanated communities. In the recent years, this has been captured in the Windrush scandal[7] and the Shamima Begum[8] story. Both examples of situations where melanated British citizens were effectively stripped of their citizenship because of the disproportionate burden of 'proof' placed on them to justify their rights to their Britishness, rather than the according of their citizenship as a right through birth or naturalisation.

The chronosystemic shape of whiteness represents across all facets of society and is upheld through a re-telling of history, which centralises whiteness, and through media representations which compound the otherness of melanated communities and positions national identity and citizenship as conditional to race. An English identity is synonymous with a white identity, even if that identity may historically belong to non-English geographical contexts or origins, this hegemonic dynamic is represented in social systems such as education and state systems such as legal infrastructures, which by design disadvantages melanated communities (Garner 2017; Hughes 2007). Furthermore, that historical and representational omission of melanated British communities from the national narrative compounds disadvantage in a racism through omission.

Approaching this point through the lens of socialisation, it can be argued that racial socialisations that were once constructed and upheld within the British Empire are now ecologically reproduced in our social experiences and interactions. That this dynamic is upheld through racial socialisation and attached hierarchies of human importance based on race. The continuation of racial socialisation and connected hierarchies can be drawn on using a socio-historic lens to conclude that colonial violence continues in its legacy form and that this now manifests in an ideological reinforcement. Moreover, that white supremacist ideology has strengthened through continuous social enactment over time and now percolates across all layers of a whiteness social ecology. Social enactments which articulate across all facets of society, as individuals navigate educational, legal, policy enactments that are underpinned by a 'social performativity' of their socialised identities. In the context of a whiteness ecology, this manifests in racial inequality and articulates as performance of race. This manifestation is framed through the other aspects of the bio-ecology suggested by Bronfenbrenner.

## Macrosystem through the lens of policy

Taking her cue from a long line in feminist postcolonial analysis of the state Critical Whiteness Studies scholar Shona Hunter has shown the relational and dynamic enactment of whiteness producing the contemporary British (neo)liberal state enactment (see Hunter 2015). The notion of a whiteness ecology can be used to compliment this sort of analysis to consider how this relational dynamic percolates as a whiteness ecology.

Weaver-Hightower's (2008) reimagining of Bronfenbrenner's (1975) bio-ecological systems theory develops a policy ecology model which is constituted by five main factors of actors, relationships, environments, structures, and processes (2008: 155–156). He also considers notions of agency and power and the positioning of policy resistant groups that can influence and alter ecologies (2008, p. 156). Using this ecological interpretation, we can begin to see an interaction forming between melanated individuals' policy enactment and broader macro, meso, and microsystemic white supremacy – in which their interests, trajectories, socialisation, and equality are all impacted upon negatively. In this context, policy resistance from melanated communities is represented through varying forms of activism.

In a post-millennial UK context, the described policy dynamic is captured in recent criminal justice policy, which continues to pathologize melanated communities particularly men. Whether this is through new terror laws that enable the state with more powers over the individual based on suspicion only, or in the disproportionate volume of stop and searching of melanated men by the police. The following section draws on some specific examples of such policy and uses existing research to examine the impacts of this on the lived experience of melanated communities – to situate the policy praxis as a key hegemonic device which sustains a whiteness macrosystem.

To conclude on policy as a macrosystemic constituent, if the state itself is generating racist policy, and the policing of that policy is also entrenched in institutional and societal racism – then we may be prompted to ask, what is the social purpose of the melanated individual? Is the melanated other simply performing a binary, othered role … a counter narrative, as a way of sustaining a whiteness ecology? After all, can whiteness really exist without melanated communities to set up its binary?

## Prevent duty

Introduced in 2011 and drawing on the UK Home Office's 2003 Prevent strategy, the Prevent Duty was the UK government's principal response to the threat of terrorism and radicalisation (Dudenhoefer 2018). The strategy is multiagency in its approach which is implemented 'with police working alongside statutory partners and communities to support those at risk from all forms of extremism' (National Police Chiefs' Council 2020). This multiagency nature has drawn much criticism. The UK prevent duty is perhaps the most prevalent example of state led Islamophobic ideological implementation and an example of state violence at its most obvious.

In their paper, *The banality of counterterrorism 'after, after 9/11'? Perspectives on the Prevent duty from the UK health care sector*, Heath-Kelly and Strausz (2019) problematize the 'anticipatory counterterrorism under the rubric of welfare and care' (2019: 89). Busher et al. (2017) have acknowledged the uneasy tension between the state and the multi-agencies that it has relied on to deliver this strategy. The most notable difference in this particular state intervention from other policies in the criminal justice area has been its reliance on the education system and teachers for implementation (Dudenhoefer 2018). Home Office statistics from 2019 show that 'the Education sector made the most referrals (33%; 1,887), followed by the police (29%; 1,650)' (2019: 5).

Teachers and school/college leaders, as well as prominent academics, the National Union of Teachers and civil society organisations, such as the human rights groups Liberty and Rights Watch UK, and Muslim organisations such as the Muslim Council of Britain have expressed a number of concerns about the duty. These concerns include that shifting previously existing counter-terrorism responsibilities onto a statutory footing would put undue pressure on educational institutions and teachers; that many educators may not have the skills or confidence to facilitate discussion of such issues; that the pressure to report terrorism-related concerns might contribute to the 'securitising' of education and could have a 'chilling effect' on free speech in the classroom; that the Prevent duty may deepen stigmatisation and suspicion of British Muslims; and that the new measures might even intensify feelings of suspicion towards the state, thereby playing into the hands of those seeking to recruit young people into terroristic activities.

In March 2019, the Court of Appeal ruled that a guidance paragraph contained within the Prevent Duty for higher and further education institutions was 'unlawful' (Home Office 2020). The strategy has since been subject to controversy and criticism because of its 'predominant targeting of British Muslims' (2018: 1).

The multiagency approach adopted for Prevent provides an interesting insight into the interplay between different ecological layers towards a shared agenda, even where this agenda is contested from within by the professionals tasked with administering it and an example of how such ecological inter-play can negatively impact melanated communities and individuals. Another example of such impact is the British police's rights to stop and search.

## Stop and search

In the recent years, there has been an ongoing debate on the disproportionate stop and search policing of Black and Brown men (Parmar 2011; Yesufu 2013). Statistics for 2007 to 2008 for England and Wales presented that there were '150,000 stop and searches' of Black men in England, '28,000 in Wales', and '104,000 in London'. In parallel, to these statistics, there were '52,000 excessive stop and searches of Asian men in England', '17,000 in Wales', and '19,000 in London' (Yesufu 2013: 289).

Framing this macrosystemic occurrence from a chronosystemic perspective, the context to such policy levered policing in connection to Black men is not new and can be dated as far back as the 'Vagrancy Act of 1894', and then later, the 'Suspect Laws' of the 1970s (Yesufu 2013: 284) – representing the colonial underpinnings to whiteness construction which pathologizes Black and Brown men as criminal, dangerous, and suspicious reflects and anticipates the other as a threat to society. Moreover, the evolution of such beliefs and their percolation in different facets of state and society represent the clear binary between White and Black that exists. This binary is perhaps most aptly captured in the difference in policing towards those racialised as white. This point links to research findings from a 2011 study, which presented that

> There was a strong feeling amongst Asian youth that they felt labelled, and as though they were not treated fairly by the ways in which the police made their decisions about who to stop and search. Such protests about questioning why they had been stopped were generally absent from the interviews with White citizens.
>
> *(Parmar 2011: 375–376)*

It has been argued by some such as Yesufu (2013) that policing itself is a racist enterprise which upholds societal and instititional racism. Yesufu (2013) moves on to share a response from the Black Police Association to racism in the police which challenges issues of whiteness, mono culture, and outright racism within the police

> We still have a monocultural police service. I find that if you want to survive in the police service you have to adopt the culture or the white culture if you want to be specific. Now

the disproportional factor that we are talking about here is about racism full stop. From the last time I checked the statute books, there is no offence Driving Whilst Black or Walking Whilst Black. That has to stop.

*(2013: 289)*

This discussion on the anticipatory pathologising and criminalisation of Black and then Brown men, reinforces earlier discussions on hegemony as a state tool and its use as a device to oppress melanated communities. In the case of the two policies discussed thus far, the state oppression manifest specifically for Black (Glynn 2016) and then Brown men. Linking to the earlier point on racial inequality and associated social performance, this dynamic can be seen to articulate in Black and Brown men deliberately avoiding policed public spaces. Long (2018) discusses this dynamic in connection to the experiences of Black men in her exploration of the racialisation and criminalisation of Blackness and concludes that 'in a racially ordered society, Blackness is a symbol of inferior race and inferior class in the police imagination' (Long 2018: 204).

## Exosystem though the lens of the legality and media representation

There is a broad range of literature which discusses structural and institutional racism in the United Kingdom in different contexts. For example, Glynn (2016) draws on Critical Race Theory to explore the lived experience of Black male offenders. He connects historical racial trauma and contemporary racism to develop holistic understandings into how these aspects percolate to shape individual trajectories and outcomes for offenders racialised as Black – and concludes that a singular race classification of 'Black' to define offenders fails to consider the intersectional, socio-historic, and socio-economic contexts that constitute the black criminological experience.

Others such as Williams (1987) and Cole (2009) have taken a macro approach to assessing racism in British society. Cole (2009) argues old and new forms of racism, connecting the older forms to Britain's imperial past and labels Islamaphobic and anti-asylum seeking attitudes as a form of a new 'hybridist racism' (Cole 2009). There is also an interesting body of work from Kyriakides and Virdee (2003), Vautier (2009), Webster (2018), and Wigger (2019), which examines racism through the lens of hegemonic violence. Framing such discourse using an exosystemic lens, it is possible to situate racism as the rippling ecological effects on the individual suggested by Hong and Garbarino (2012).

These framings connect to an ongoing socio-cultural discourse relating to negative racial representations in the media as an articulation of cultural hegemony. As Hall (1997b) has argued, the stratified positioning of various melanated communities and individuals is upheld though negative media representations and stereotypes. Extending this analysis, I argue that negative media representations play a part in reinforcing racial socialisation though which members of white and melanated groups either enact their perceived positions in society or resist as the 'London Riots' demonstrated. The London 'riots' erupted in 2011 in response to the shooting of Mark Duggan by the police. Civil unrest soon spread to several UK cities including Liverpool, Bristol, and Birmingham. 'Rioters' mainly consisted of the 'poor/Black/unemployed' people (Till 2013: 72). Media coverage of the 'riots' was carefully constructed to reinforce damaging racial tropes (Shah 2019). Moreover, the state took a decision for tougher sentencing for over a 1,000 participants in the riots, hence leading to the subsequent criminalisation of poor Black individuals involved (Pina-Sánchez et al. 2017). This factor stood in stark contrast to the state's handling of the white collar criminals responsible for the financial crisis where just 47 were sentenced (Noonan et al. 2018). The media plays a significant role in steering public political and social opinion. In the United Kingdom, the state also holds powers over the British Broadcasting Cooperation (BBC) which is funded by the public through the form of a licence fee.

The media we consume forms part of our macrosystem and can determine our world view of people, individuals, society, politics, and social situations – and media representation itself is a crucial component in furthering the state's dominant ideologies (Hall 1997a). However, representation is not limited to the media only. As Hall (1997a) asserts, representations are a process whereby individuals' worldviews are informed by the representations that they encounter and that these, in turn, are led to our constructions of personal meanings, which we reconstruct and represent to the world through language (1997a: 18). According to Hall (1997a), this process manifests in a combination of conceptual and linguistic systems defined by 'cultural codes' that underpin our social interplay (1997a: 22–23). For the melanated individual within a whiteness ecology, representation can either play out through absence as a form of racism through omission, or through negative stereotyping. By not seeing themselves mirrored in the workplace or seeing those like them disproportionately represented in the criminal and mental health systems, or to see negative stereotyping and representation of communities that they originate from or belong to … the violence of representation in its lack or in its inaccuracy is a form of white violence.

Extending this point, it is important to recognise that whiteness is upheld through state's use of media to sustain its normalisation. Through not seeing positive representations of melanated communities or individuals (if at all), you are constantly reminded that white is the good binary, the normative, and the universal standard.

## Mesosystem through the lens of education

This layer represents the interaction between the exo and microsystem. In a whiteness ecology context, this layer is premised in that the quality of individual experience is shaped by one's racialisation and influenced by factors such as familial background, access to particular neighbourhoods and thus neighbours. The intersectional angle to this dynamic brings an additional complexity to the experiences of melanated individuals navigating more than one othering identity, see Modood (1988), Rattansi (2000), Reay (2001), and Harris (2009) on intersectional Black and Asian identity in reference to class, religion, and structural inequality.

In 2018, I completed a socio-ecological qualitative longitudinal study into the policy enactment and lived educational experiences of post 14 low level vocational learners classified as of 'low ability'. My study revealed that learners were being classified with labels such as 'underachieving', 'non-academic', 'special needs', or 'with behavioural issues' by their secondary schools. Moreover, that the labelling being used in schools was echoed in the language of policy and following individuals into their further education and determining their access to educational choices and opportunities. The study indicated that young peoples socialised identities were being predetermined at school level based on a categorisation system that influenced learners perceived academic abilities, and future life chances, educational trajectories, and professional destinations.

Findings from the study also revealed that melanated learners faced more barriers to academic opportunities than their white peers and in some cases were classified as of 'low ability' irrespective of previous grades and qualifications. An example of this arose in the case of a Black learner who was steered by a college admissions team to enrol on to a low-level vocational qualification even though they held higher qualifications. This incident resulted in unnecessarily elongating the student's time at the college and negatively impacted their higher education options.

My study revealed the significance of the maesosystemic layer to the individual, through its exploration of the relationship between educational policy, institutional enactment, pedagogic spaces, and policy actors. Institutional enactment demonstrated a socialised dynamic, which is heavily dependent on categorising. Using a whiteness ecology framing, the study indicated that melanated learners were more likely to come under scrutiny and be negatively labelled based on behaviour or perceived ability from the onset.

Education can be a crucial tool for democracy and equalising society – but it can also uphold state ideological agendas as some, such as Foucault (2005) have argued. Some examples of stratification from within the British education system include the Higher Education BAME attainment gap (Universities UK and National Union of Students 2019), the lack of Black and Brown representation in classrooms (Farinde et al. 2016) and educational leadership (Miller 2019) – and the volume of school expulsion of Black boys – for instance, government statistics report that in the 2017/2018 school year, 'Mixed White and Black Caribbean, and Black Caribbean pupils had high exclusion rates, and were both nearly three times as likely to be permanently excluded as White British pupils' (Race Disparity Unit 2020).

## Microsystem through the lens of situating the individual

The microsystemic layer is the closest to the individual in terms of influence and interaction (Swick and Williams 2006). The layer is constituted by factors such as family, education, social groups, peers, and healthcare access. In a UK context, this may manifest in the postcodes where you live, your access to state education, and the national health service.

As I write this chapter I am drawn to a number of 'recent' national stories that amplify this point, particularly the disproportionate COVID-19 related BAME (Black, Asian, Minority, Ethnic)[9] deaths (Aldridge et al. 2020) – and the way in which the very presentation of this social narrative has represented entrenched white supremacy. Whether this has been through the use of pseudo race science, socio-economic, or cardiometabolic justifications, or through a delay in the UK government's release of the BAME COVID-19 review finding no significant racialised dynamic to the Pandemic. A review that was consequently contradicted by the Labour Lawrence Review (2020). On a microsystemic level, this health narrative would play out in affecting health and access and causing medical vulnerabilities for individuals racialised as other to white. The policy ecology model recognises the individual that Bronfenbrenner (1975) locates at the centre of his model as policy actors. Weaver-Hightower (2008) presents the mobility of these actors across ecological levels based on two key factors. First, the level of individual enactment, and second the simultaneous roles that individuals fulfil as they enact policy.

Examining this point through the lens of race and socialisation, it can be argued that individuals not racialised as white are tied to their racialisation through a state induced socialisation, in ways that white people are not. A 'hegemonic enactment' ensues in which, those racialised as white are socialised into dominant hierarchies that exist by default. In contrast, melanated individuals unwillingly enact their own oppression by remaining in a whiteness ecology as they continue to occupy a dynamic that is designed to disadvantage them.

A whiteness ecology consists of social performativity which socialises individuals based on factors such as class and race to uphold legacy categorisations from Britain's colonial past. The current socialisation and ecological dynamics in British society are a living record left of its colonial past. Using this framing I argue that holding on to this dynamic is vital to the national identity narrative which is synonymous with whiteness. However, it is important to acknowledge some of the present-day dichotomies in these presentations of the individual. For examples Holmes' (2017) assertion that the individual is a passive recipient of dominant ideologies, defined by social hierarchical systems, is perhaps over simplistic? As it can be argued that contemporary contexts such as the rise of the digital age (Shah 2017) have given way to an increase in individual reflexivity that was perhaps previously lacking? (Holmes 2017: 4). It can also be argued that it is becoming possible to challenge ideological power (Alvesson and Sköldberg 2009) in an increasingly interactive and globalised digital culture (Shah 2017). The chapter concludes in its framing of decolonisation as an act of 'de-socialisation' and a function of 'ecological disruption' to dismantle colonial legacies of racism.

## Conclusion

A whiteness ecology cannot be dismantled unless we become conscious of our social performativity. What role are we playing in this praxis? How do our racialised identities play out in society and how much of this playing out should we take for granted or challenge? Part of this reflexivity calls on us to interrogate the power dynamics that uphold whiteness (Hunter 2015) and to question the extent of our racial performance and our role in sustaining a whiteness ecology through our hegemonic enactment. To challenge our hegemonic enactments through a dismantling and reassessment of language and interaction. For me, the challenging articulates in the right to self-define myself racially. I resist homogenised identities such as BAME, Brown, Political Black, or Person of Colour. If I must be defined by not being white in a whiteness ecology, then I prefer melanated over of colour, and global majority over ethnic minority. The first step for me is centring myself on my own terms within a whiteness ecology that aims to omit and erase me.

The challenging continues through activism. I draw on my work as this articulates via the Social Performance Network project to argue 'de-socialisation' *as* decolonisation, with the first stage of self-educating on the past.

> We cannot decolonize until we acknowledge and understand our colonial pasts and the whitewashing of British history. In recent years, contemporary British identity appears to have become synonymous with whiteness and the histories of Empire have become slowly omitted from national consciousness. The nuanced and often difficult narratives of Empire that live as legacy in many facets of British society, are now replaced with binary narratives of white and black and immigration leading to white English poverty. Complexed identities and contexts reduced to simplified and bigoted narratives of difference and colourism.

> The challenge that confronts movements like ours, are such barriers, that present in our societal structures and systems and that represent colonial legacies of erasure and omission. Without an acknowledgement of the invisible othered, a decolonization process cannot occur. So, I call on to all colleagues, practitioners, students, and peers to begin engaging with histories and stories of Empire to understand why decolonization is so important. Without an existing knowledge of these contexts, we cannot dismantle the dangerous messages that have become indoctrinated into every layer of our knowledge systems and structures.

> *(Shah 2018)*

Next, we must work on ensuring that all perspectives, world views, histories, experiences, sciences, and approaches, are incorporated into all facets of our society, whether that is through a more balanced curriculum, a fairer approach to the law and order, or a restorative approach to reforming criminals. Fundamentally, we must deconstruct ideas of white as normative and as synonymous with privilege – and begin working together at reimagining a society in which we are all creators and collaborators.

Finally, to engage with a de-socialising process, which involves individual, community, and social engagement in which we take ownership of our narratives and identities and break the cycle of defaulting to social performativity. For those racialised as white, this process involves giving up privilege and reconciling with new truths. De-socialising *as* Decolonising activism requires us to collectively reimagine each other. We cannot do this until we all begin doing the work on ourselves in our relationship to white supremacy. This chapter closes on an invitation to join the work being carried out in this area to reimagine an equitable society to which we all belong.

## Notes

1   Black, Asian, Minority, Ethnic.
2   The chronosystem is represented in the environmental timings and events that affect the development of the individual. In a practical sense, this can be understood through the lens of factors such as the socio-historical (Leonard 2011). This layer can also be framed as constituting the longitudinal element to an overarching social ecology.
3   Bronfenbrenner (1975) classifies the top and outer tier of the ecological system as the macrosystem. The macrosystem consists of broader ideological attitudes and values that form the culture of the society to which the individual belongs (Neville and Mobley 2001: 473).
4   The exsosytem (Bronfenbrenner 1975) includes influencing factors such as the individual's broader family networks, friends, neighbours and the mass media that represent interaction and interrelations between two or more environments. This level does not directly connect to the individual but re-presents as an indirect influence that can be farmed as a ripple style effect (Hong and Garbarino 2012: 276).
5   The mesosystem represents the relationship between the microsystem and the broader environment that include the individual and therefore directly affect the individual (Hong and Garbarino 2012: 276).
6   Bronfenbrenner (1975) presents the microsystem level that represents the individual's immediate environments and closest influences and interactions (Swick and Williams 2006). This level consists of factors such as immediate family, education, social groups, peers, and the individual's healthcare access.
7   In the Windrush example, the Home Office approach to developing a 'hostile environment' for immigration resulted in the loss of the right to employment, housing, health, and social care of approximately 5,000 citizens (Lammy 2020) and lead to the deportation of approximately 160 of post-war Caribbean migrants (Lawford and Rose 2020) many of whom had migrated as children in the context of post war rebuilding.
8   In the Shamina Begum example, the situation is of a person stripped of citizenship as an adult because of her recruitment into ISIS (Islamic State group) at 15.
9   The minority ethnic in this classification includes 'white other' such as first generation EU migrants or the gypsy traveller communities. The term homogenises 'the other' to a single category and the specific contexts, experiences, and racialised dynamics are convoluted and lost within this broad category.

## References

Aldridge, R. W. et al. 2020. Black, Asian and Minority Ethnic Groups in England are at Increased Risk of Death from COVID-19: Indirect Standardisation of NHS Mortality Data. *Wellcome Open Research*, 5: 1–19.

Alvesson, M. and Sköldberg, K. 2009. *Reflexive Methodology: New Vistas for Qualitative Research*, 2nd edn. Los Angeles, London: SAGE.

Bronfenbrenner, U. 1975. Reality and Research in the Ecology of Human Development. *Proceedings of the American Philosophical Society*, 119 (6): 439–469.

Busher, J. et al. 2017. What the Prevent Duty Means for Schools and Colleges in England: An Analysis of Educationalists' Experiences. *Aziz Foundation*, July: 1–68.

Cole, M. 2009. A Plethora of 'Suitable Enemies': British Racism at the Dawn of the Twenty-first Century. *Ethnic and Racial Studies*, 32: 1671–1685.

Dudenhoefer, A. 2018. Resisting Radicalisation: A Critical Analysis of the UK Prevent Duty. *Journal for Deradicalization*, 14 (Spring): 153–191.

Farinde, A. A., Allen, A. and Lewis, C. W. 2016. Retaining Black Teachers: An Examination of Black Female Teachers' Intentions to Remain in K-12 Classrooms. *Equity and Excellence in Education*, 49 (1): 115–127.

Foucault, M. 2005. The Subject and Power. *Critical Inquiry*, 8 (4): 777–795.

Garner, S. 2017. Surfing the Third Wave of Whiteness Studies: Reflections on Twine and Gallagher. *Ethnic and Racial Studies*, 40 (9): 1582–1597.

Glynn, M. 2016. Towards an Intersectional Model of Desistance for Black Offenders. *Safer Communities*, 15 (1): 24-32.

Greenfield, E. A. 2012. Using Ecological Frameworks to Advance a Field of Research, Practice, and Policy on Aging-in-Place Initiatives. *Gerontologist*, 52 (1): 1–12.

Guess, T. J. 2006. The Social Construction of Whiteness: Racism by Intent, Racism by Consequence. *Critical Sociology*, 32 (4): 649–673.

Hall, S. 1997a. *Representation: Cultural Representations and Signifying Practices.* SAGE Publications & Open University.

Hall, S. 1997b. The Spectacle of the 'Other'. In *Representation: Cultural Representations and Signifying Practices.* London: Open University.

Halliday, A. J., Kern, M. L., Garrett, D. K. and Turnbull, D. A. 2018. The Student Voice in Well-being: A Case Study of Participatory Action Research in Positive Education. *Educational Action Research*, 0792: 1–24.

Härkönen, U. 2007. 'The Bronfenbrenner ecological systems theory of human development'. Scientific Articles of V International Conference, pp. 1–17.

Harris, R. 2009. Black British, Brown British and British Cultural Studies. *Cultural Studies*, 23 (4): 483–512.

Heath-Kelly, C. and Strausz, E. 2019. The Banality of Counterterrorism 'After, After 9/11'? Perspectives on the Prevent Duty from the UK Health Care Sector. *Critical Studies on Terrorism*, 12 (1), 89–109.

HM Home Office. 2019. 'Individuals Referred to and Supported Through the Prevent Programme', April 2018 to March 2019 (December).

Hodgson, A. and Spours, K. 2009. *Collaborative Local Learning Ecologies: Reflections on the Governance of Lifelong Learning in England.* Inquiry into the Future for Lifelong Learning (IFLL), National Institute of Adult Continuing Education, Sector Paper 6, 1–27.

Hodgson, A. and Spours, K. 2017. *Education, Skills and Employment in East London: An Ecosystem Analysis.* London: UCL Insititute of Education.

Holmes, M. 2017. Sociology for Optimists. *Discover Society*, 43: 1–10.

Home Office. 2020. 'Prevent duty guidance' [online], viewed 7 June 2020, https://www.gov.uk/government/publications/prevent-duty-guidance.

Hong, J. S. 2011. An Ecological Understanding of Kinship Foster Care in the United States. *Journal of Child and Family Studies*, 20 (6): 863–872.

Hong, J. S. and Garbarino, J. 2012. Risk and Protective Factors for Homophobic Bullying in Schools: An Application of the Social-Ecological Framework. *Educational Psychology Review*, 24 (2): 271–285.

Hughes, R. L. 2007. A Hint of Whiteness: History Textbooks and Social Construction of Race in the Wake of the Sixties. *The Social Studies*, 98 (5), 201–208.

Hunter, S. 2015. *Power, Politics and the Emotions: Impossible Governance?* 1st edn. (21 April). London: Routledge.

Ivankova, N. V. and Plano Clark, V. L. 2018. Teaching Mixed Methods Research: Using a Socio-ecological Framework as a Pedagogical Approach for Addressing the Complexity of the Field. *International Journal of Social Research Methodology*, 5579: 1–16.

Johnson, E. S. 2008. Toward an Alternative Model of Accountability in Education. *Complicity: An International Journal of Complexity and Education*, 5 (1): 1–10.

Johnson, G. M. 1994. An Ecological Framework For Conceptualizing Educational Risk. *Urban Education*, 29 (1): 34–49. DOI:10.1177/0042085994029001004.

Kyriakides, C. and Virdee, S. 2003. Migrant Labour, Racism and the British National Health Service. *Ethnicity and Health*, 8 (4): 283–305.

Lammy, D. 2020. 'Two years after Windrush, we're deporting people who've only known Britain as home', *The Guardian*, 10 February, viewed 10 December 2020, https://www.theguardian.com/commentisfree/2020/feb/10/windrush-deporting-people.

Lawford, E. and Rose, E. 2020. 'Windrush scandal explained: Who was involved in the deportation crisis?', *The Evening Standard*, 8 June, viewed 1 February 2021, https://www.standard.co.uk/news/world/windrush-scandal-generation-explained-a4463106.html.

Lawrence, D. 2020. 'An avoidable crisis', viewed 3 March 2021, https://www.lawrencereview.co.uk/.

Leonard, J. 2011. Using Bronfenbrenner's Ecological Theory to Understand Community Partnerships: A Historical Case Study of One Urban High School. *Urban Education*, 46 (5): 987–1010.

Lindsay, S. et al. 2018. Applying an Ecological Framework to Understand Transition Pathways to Post-secondary Education for Youth with Physical Disabilities. *Disability and Rehabilitation*, 40 (3): 277–286.

Long, L. 2018. *Perpetual Suspects: A Critical Race Theory of Black and Mixed-Race Experiences of Policing*, 1st edn. 20. London: Palgrave Macmillan.

Marks, N. F. and Grzywacz, J. G. 2017. Social Inequalities and Exercise during Adulthood: Toward an Ecological Perspective. *Journal of Health and Social Behavior*, 42 (2): 202–220.

Martin, G. 2016. Towards an Intersectional Model of Desistance for Black Offenders. *Safer Communities*, 15 (1): 24–32.

Miller, P. W. 2019. 'Tackling' Race Inequality in School Leadership: Positive Actions in BAME Teacher Progression – Evidence from Three English Schools. *Educational Management Administration & Leadership*. 48 (6): 986–1006. DOI:10.1177/1741143219873098.

Modood, T. 1988. 'Black', Racial Equality and Asian Identity. *Journal of Ethnic and Migration Studies*, 14 (3): 397–404.

National Police Chiefs' Council. 2020. 'Delivering prevent' [online], viewed 7 May, https://www.npcc.police.uk/CounterTerrorism/Prevent.aspx.

Nayak, A. 2007. Critical Whiteness Studies. *Sociology Compass*, 1 (2): 737–755.

Neville, H. and Mobley, M. 2001. Social Identities in Contexts: An Ecological Model of Multicultural Counseling Psychology Processes. *The Counseling Psychologist*, 29 (4): 471–486.

Nitsch, J. R. 2009. Ecological Approaches to Sport Activity: A Commentary from an Action-Theoretical Point of View. *International Journal of Sport Psychology*, 40 (1): 152–176.

Noonan, L. et al. 2018. 'Who went to jail for their role in the financial crisis?', *Financial Times*, 20 September, viewed 1 February 2021, https://ig.ft.com/jailed-bankers/.

Parmar, A. 2011. Stop and Search in London: Counter-Terrorist or Counter-Productive? *Policing and Society*, 21 (4): 369–382.

Pina-Sánchez, J. Lightowlers, C. and Roberts, J. 2017. Exploring the Punitive Surge: Crown Court Sentencing Practices Before and After the 2011 English Riots. *Criminology and Criminal Justice*, 17 (3): 319–339.

Quin, D. 2016. Longitudinal and Contextual Associations Between Teacher-Student Relationships and Student Engagement: A Systematic Review. *Review of Educational Research*, 87 (2): 345–387.

Race Disparity Unit. 2020. Pupil Exclusions. London: Cabinet Office.

Rattansi, A. 2000. On Being And Not Being Brown/Black-British: Racism, Class, Sexuality and Ethnicity in Post-imperial Britain. *Interventions*, 2 (1): 118–134.

Reay, D. 2001. Finding or Losing Yourself?: Working-Class Relationships to Education. *Journal of Education Policy*, 16 (4): 333–346.

Renn, K. A. 2003. Understanding the Identities of Mixed-Race College Students Through a Developmental Ecology Lens. *Journal of College Student Development*, 44 (3): 383–403.

Santrock, J. W. 2007. *Child Development*, 11th edn. NY: McGraw-Hill Companies, Inc.

Shah, J. 2017. Informal Learning in a Digital Landscape: A Higher Education Drama Conservatoire Case Study. In *Informal Learning: Perspectives, Challenges, and Opportunities*, ed. S. Rutherford, p. 314. Nova.

Shah, J. 2018. 'Decolonising Statement', *Social Performance Network*, viewed 11 December 2020, https://socialperformanceacademy.wpcomstaging.com/decolonising-statement/.

Shah, J. 2019. 'London Spring, Arab Riots', *State Violence*. University of Manchester, 4 April 2018. London: Social Performance Network.

Swick, K. J. and Williams, R. D. 2006. An Analysis of Bronfenbrenner's Bio-ecological Perspective for Early Childhood Educators: Implications for Working with Families Experiencing Stress. *Early Childhood Education Journal*, 33 (5): 371–378.

Till, J. 2013. The Broken Middle: The Space of the London Riots. *Cities*, 34: 71–74.

Universities UK and National Union of Students, 2019. Black, Asian and minority UK universities: Attainment at ethnic student #Closingthegap, May, 83, viewed 11 December 2020, https://www.universitiesuk.ac.uk/policy-and-analysis/reports/Documents/2019/bame-student-attainment-uk-universities-closing-the-gap.pdf.

Vautier, E. 2009. Playing the 'Race Card': White Anxieties and the Expression and Repression of Popular Racisms in the 1997 UK Election. *Patterns of Prejudice*, 43 (2): 122–141.

Waters, S. K., Cross, D.S. and Runions, K. 2009. Social and Ecological Structures Supporting Adolescent Connectedness to School: A Theoretical Model. *Journal of School Health*, 79 (11): 516–524.

Weaver-Hightower, M. B. 2008. An Ecology Metaphor for Educational Policy Analysis: A Call to Complexity. *Educational Researcher*, 37 (3): 153–167.

Webster, C. S. 2018. Turning the Tables: Media Constructions of British Asians from Victims to Criminals, 1962 to 2011. In *Media, Crime, Racism*, ed. M. Bhatia, S. Poynting and W. Tufail, pp. 11–32. Basingstoke: Palgrave Macmillan.

Weisner, T. S. 2008. The Urie Bronfenbrenner Top 19: Looking Back at His Bioecological Perspective. *Mind, Culture, and Activity*, 15 (3): 258–262.

Wigger, I. 2019. Anti-Muslim Racism and the Racialization of Sexual Violence: 'Intersectional Stereotyping' in Mass Media Representations of Male Muslim Migrants in Germany. *Culture and Religion*, 20 (3): 248–271.

Williams, F. 1987. Racism and the Discipline of Social Policy: A Critique of Welfare Theory. *Critical Social Policy*, 7 (20): 4–29.

Yesufu, S. 2013. Discriminatory Use of Police Stop-and-Search Powers in London, UK. *International Journal of Police Science & Management*, 15 (4): 281–293.

# Part VI

# Provocations:
# Debates and dilemmas

Whiteness as a concept has proven its relevance in making sense of racial power relations, exemplified by the burgeoning volume of academic work and research, and how the concept is taken up in popular and political discourses. As a relatively recent inter- and transdisciplinary field, critical studies in whiteness serves as a lively intellectual space for theoretical and political contestation and rethinking, including challenges to the very existence of the field. Controversies have ranged from whether race should be abolished, or can be abolished, to whiteness studies being deployed as a ruse for white people to re-centre themselves. The contributions in this section confront essentialising and fetishising understandings of whiteness; the socio-political and ethical complexities of racialised existence; problematics of white antiracism; and the rejuvenation of white supremacism in expected and unexpected ways. Bernard Matolino opens this section with a confrontation of the elevation of Western epistemology at the expense of the West's others through the foundational discipline of philosophy. He proposes that whiteness be suspended to address the paradox that contemporary African philosophy is labouring under, defined as it is by a founding text written by a European but caught in a cycle of protest thought against whiteness. What would be the shape of African philosophy without whiteness, if this is even thinkable? Amanpreet Ahluwalia then takes the discussion to normative Critical Whiteness Studies, challenging the field to engage with the complexities and sometimes contradictory lived experiences of people racialised as other to whiteness. Can Critical Whiteness Studies interrogate the ways in which *antiracist* white subjects are implicated in the violences of whiteness? As one answer to the previous chapter, Samantha Vice confronts the clashing demands when a white subject pursues an ethics of integrity in conditions of systemic and structural injustice. Addressing white privilege may have repercussions difficult to balance out with subjective attachments. In the next chapter, Phillip W. Gray shows how the Alt-Right as a political identification and movement has given whiteness a new lease on life by explicitly claiming whiteness as an identity, in contrast to (neo)liberal racelessness. The Alt-Right position updates white supremacism with a tone and tenor pilfered from twenty-first century leftist politics, while effecting reversals of the Black Feminist theory of intersectionality to declare white subjects as 'marginalised'. The section concludes with Colleen E. Boucher and Cheryl E. Matias, who draw the argument in this volume together with their analysis of how colour-blind (neo)liberalism has been supplanted by a new aggressive form of whiteness that still evades race but deploys violence akin to the pre-Civil Rights era in the United States. It is an emboldened whiteness that works as an 'evolutionary terror'.

DOI: 10.4324/9780429355769-106

# 24

# Curtailing imagination: Modern African philosophy's struggle against whiteness

*Bernard Matolino*

## Introduction

My aim in this chapter is threefold. I start by pointing out the pervasiveness of whiteness in a field I am most familiar with – African philosophy – followed by evidence of how whiteness has shaped that field. Second, I argue against the raising of whiteness to such prominence. I seek to demonstrate that the very act of thinking in reaction to whiteness, has retarded possibilities that African philosophy could have turned itself into. Third, I seek to propose what African philosophy could begin to become, once freed from whiteness. This freedom involves suspension of whiteness as a category that matters in both life and systems of thought. While whiteness's powers, both socially and academically, are real and have serious consequences for African people, I shall argue that overcoming those pervasive powers does not lie in direct confrontations with them by insisting on the African difference or credibility of African thought. Such moves in my view will only lead to the imprisonment of African thought. Rather, I am interested in pursuing a thought system that would operate as if whiteness either never mattered or never existed. Such a move disempowers whiteness while freeing African thought to be authentic and organic to its own purpose. For such a move to succeed, I will have to argue for why whiteness should no longer matter for African philosophy.

## Whiteness and thought systems

Whiteness is foremost a thought system. It is an attitude and belief that is grounded in well-coordinated ideas of what it means to be white and what it takes for one who bears the mark of whiteness to carry such an identity successfully. It is also an expression of values that whites have, prefer, advocate or live by. These values become markers of difference between whites and people racialized as non-whites. These values easily legitimate whiteness. They justify the very possibility of whiteness not only as a viable approach to life but also as a different approach that is rooted in a shared and viable understanding of the world and life. At times whiteness just makes itself visible thus creating discomfort for people of colour. At other times, it is aggressive in attempting to impose its own ways on other systems. One of the fascinating developments of white thought systems is their association with Christian civilization (Jun et al. 2018). Historically,

DOI: 10.4324/9780429355769-24

whites were not always Christians. But through the grace of Rome, when they eventually Christianized, they conflated whiteness with Christianity to form a hybridized civilization. It was this civilization, packed with elaborate beliefs and arguments for its superior truths, which made its way to the shores and eventually to the most interior capillaries of African existence. As this civilization made its way into Africa, it did not encounter a space that was bereft of ideas about the nature of the world and its fundamental truths. However, the ideas permeating Africa were deemed pagan and far from Christian truths and European civilization. This immediately necessitated the mission to save the wretched Africans from both their erroneous ways and backward station. They were to be introduced to civilization and the best way to do that was to colonize them into the future of civility. This, of course was a terrible contradiction, as Taiwo (2010) argues. But ahead did the colonial mission steam and it produced colonies that were Christianized and Europeanized to varying degrees. This process had a lasting and detrimental effect on the trajectory that African life could have taken.

I shall be interested in how the colonial mission, as a process steeped in whiteness, affected philosophy on the continent (see Serequeberhan 1994: 62–67). My interest in philosophy is twofold; first I identify as a professional philosopher with interest and expertise in African philosophy. Hence, I am invested in understanding its history and why it went through the stages it did. Second, philosophy is an important aspect of any people's interaction with reality. It is the provider of reason and justification of why people have the sort of ideas they have about themselves and the world. In addition, philosophy has been used as a measure of a people's civilization. If it turns out to be the case that philosophy has always been a part of people, then it will be said that those people were civilized. If, however, their philosophy was imported or imposed from somewhere then their project of civilization did not originate from within.

The history of modern African philosophy starts with the preacher Rev Fr Placide Tempels (1959), a Belgian Franciscan missionary working among the Baluba of modern Democratic Republic of Congo as a missionary. His little book, first published in Flemish and later translated into English, *Bantu Philosophy*, has attracted both scorn and admiration in equal measure. As D.A. Masolo (1994) correctly points out, the most inhospitable reaction to the book has emerged from French speaking Africans while English speaking Africans do not seem to mind the contents of the book. I am not going to discuss the claims of the book or recycle the arguments contained therein. What I am interested in pursuing is how this book, written by a missionary, represents as a founding text for modern African philosophy how a field is forced to define itself under the gaze of whiteness. Whether one agrees with Tempels's thesis or not, one cannot ignore the role that he plays as the foremost thinker in both colonial and post-colonial African philosophy. The degree to which Tempels shapes African philosophy is of the same magnitude as the role colonialism played in shaping the fate of African citizens. Every time the foundations of African philosophy are sought, the name that is invoked is that of a Belgian missionary. A missionary who openly confessed in his book that his aim of writing that book was for the benefit of all colonial administrators and officials in their quest to civilize the Bantu. The truths, half-truths, and oblique mischaracterizations contained in Tempels's book have to be affirmed, corrected, and dismissed by African thinkers long after Tempels has left the scene.

But what does it do to a field for its foundational text not only to originate from the mind of a missionary but also one who openly declares that he is writing for the benefit of the colonial mission? What sort of damage or prospect does such a text present to the inheritors of the field after the missionary has accomplished his task? One of the consequences is the sort of doubt that Tempels created for African thinkers about their relationship to their chosen pursuit – philosophy. Tempels was able to plant seeds of self-doubt deep in the minds of the first generation of professional philosophers of African descent so much that they dedicated a lot of their energy and intellectual talent to the question of whether African philosophy exists or not. While we cannot quantify how Tempels in direct ways contributed to this knee jerk reaction, the signs are there of his colonial ghost casting its shadow for a long time, being present on philosophical tables and gatherings, more than it should have been allowed.

Hence, we see the founding texts (after Tempels's book) written by Africans primarily devoting themselves to the nature and possibility of the existence of African philosophy. The debates pursued by these texts ranged from the difference that existed between African philosophy and its Western counterpart to naming the trends of African philosophy. They also extended themselves to cover what were considered to be necessary discussions of the topics seen as appropriate to African philosophy as well as how these topics differed from their Western counterparts. If one looks at the texts between 1960 and 1990, there is overarching concern with addressing the African difference. Whether the authors were in support or opposition to that difference, this theme became very visible as an aid to establishing what the project of African philosophy would look like.

I suppose what must be addressed is what this obsession with the existence of African philosophy represented in relation to whiteness (see Eze 1999). Is there a way that we could create a direct link between African philosophy's questions about its own existence and the effects of whiteness on African people? I think we could succeed in establishing such a link. The prospects for establishing such a link do not lie in the project of African philosophy or what African philosophers had conceived that project to be. Rather, the link lies in the project to decolonize and reactions to this project. We must not make light of the fact that modern African philosophy emerges in the same period of the arrival of independence. This is not a coincidence or lucky chance. On the contrary, it is part of the struggle for freedom and the need for the black person to assert her dignity in the face of the desecration caused by conquest. The best way to go about the assertion of dignity, for African philosophers, is to prove that they have an equivalent thought system (though dissimilar in method and content) to the Westerner. The primary reason for that need arises from the role that Western philosophy played in both furthering the thesis of difference between races and asserting the superiority of the white race. The reality for African philosophy, then, did not just become a fight for the superiority or even origins of ideas. It became a fight against other political forces of race and racial discrimination with the accompanying realities of colonial conquest and oppression.

It could then be that the development of African philosophy was, in very large part, an exercise in fighting whiteness or was counter-hegemonic to the pervasive effects of whiteness on black Africa. The theoretical and practical consequences of colonialism, as whiteness, were dealt with at various levels of African consciousness including philosophical theoretical formulations.

## Retarding effects of whiteness

While it is easy to trace how whiteness has affected the development of African philosophy as a counter-hegemonic voice, what is not always easy to establish is the damage that has been caused to African systems of thought in the process of the development of this counter-hegemonic voice. The most prominent discussion of this damage is to be found in the assessments of theories advocating the existence of the African personality/consciencism advanced by Kwame Nkrumah, Negritude advanced by Léopold Sédar Senghor, and Julius Nyerere's Ujamaa. I will not be outlining the details of these theories and the specific points they advance save to point out their similarities and associated effects.

A shared feature of these theories is that their foundation is African exceptionalism. They advance the thesis that there is something fundamentally different about Africans that deserves special attention or special categories of thought to fully capture what Africanness is. A significant part of this difference is said to lie in how the African is to be seen as a communal entity who avoids individualist inclinations as well as liberal politics. However, what has arisen from the pursuit of this system of thought and subsequent commitment has been the construction of the African as a person who is averse to forms of reason that are not communitarian or that do not endorse lines of thought that prioritize a certain form of reason. Take, for example, Senghor's insistence that Africans are not analytical by nature but emotional. What does such a commitment do besides casting the African as essentially inept in analytical forms of reason? Or take the insistence on the foundations of African communities and politics as anything but communitarian, as Nyerere and Nkrumah argue, what does that insistence do except denying Africans the possibility of exposure to other systems that could prove more efficient than traditional communitarianism?

What these theories have done is to support and continue with views central to whiteness regarding the difference that exists between whites and Africans. These differences never promote or succeed in casting the African as superior. If anything they always succeed in showing the African as fundamentally distinct, misunderstood, or as someone who is committed to some system of thought that require special understanding. This mirrors the very thesis that Tempels was advancing when he insisted that the African was different from the Westerner and had to be understood on her own terms. The implicit denigration in this thinking must worry those interested in genuine liberation of Africans as well as those interested in the advancement of African thought as non-essentialist.

Yet, there is another danger lurking nearby. This has to do with how the field is constrained to unfold in very specific ways as a result of pressures to first justify its existence and then promulgate topics considered proper to its parameters of justification. The problem is that the discussants are not the agenda setters but they are confined to reacting to an agenda that is set elsewhere by other people. Let us take the much recognised idea that the emergence of African philosophy is counter-hegemonic to the dominant Western paradigm. On the face of it, this move not only looks legitimate but also admirable. It appears to be the sort of move that is necessary to ensure that the African's voice is heard. It appears to be the sort of move that will ensure that the African's views are eventually allowed a fair chance amongst other voices. However, there is a serious danger hidden within this move. The voice that is being allowed to emerge, or more precisely, the voice that is being forced to emerge is one that is conditioned by its experiences of whiteness. It seeks to articulate that experience, first, then moves on to attempt overcoming it.

If we look at the emergence of modern African philosophy as a distinct field concerned with so-called African issues, these issues are a reflection of the problems arising from encounters with whiteness. While the issues appear to be about African concerns, they actually are about engagement with whiteness. This engagement creates boundaries of thought and how that thought is exercised. By so doing, they limit the very possibility of thought or direct thought to be obsessed about only one object. As we have discussed earlier, this may create a fundamentalist attitude towards finding African essences or insisting on differences between white and black people. But this limitation also serves the purpose of diverting attention from other considerations that may be in need of intellectual attention. Such considerations could be about Africans as a people without any regard to judgements from whiteness.

What this does, in my view, is to create a prison of thought. Africans become imprisoned in categories that are pre-determined by the effects of whiteness. The idea of freethinking intellectuals as responsible for the formulation and pursuit of their own thoughts is never realized under these conditions. While I am advocating the idea of freethinking, it is important to keep in mind that this process is executed within historical and social settings. These settings provide the thinker with a context to work in, to think from and to refer to. What this context has said about the thinker's social and historical standing matters in giving the thinker horizons of possibilities of thought. A slave, for example, can only think about her wretched conditions and possibilities of freedom and escape – in a way that only a slave can. The same notions – possibilities of freedom and escape – do not appear to the nobleman in the same way they appear to the slave. The very idea of freedom does not even mean the same thing to both the slave and the nobleman. They may both, in their very quiet moment, ponder on the meaning and reality of freedom; but if you ask them to explicate what the contents of their thoughts are, you would soon be confronted with stark differences.

Notwithstanding the facts of history and social context from which the thinker emerges, it is necessary to ask whether the thinker has freedom to choose a different set of problems from ones that her history presents. For example, what sort of concern could be legitimately uppermost in the mind of a political philosopher in Africa in the 1980s? The answer that we will yield depends on whether we choose to take an obvious and easy route or a not so obvious and not so easy route. The obvious and easy route is to go with the descriptions I have provided of the social and historical background that appear inescapable in conditioning the thinker. The not so obvious and not so easy route is to deny the restrictions imposed by these historical and social facts. I do not suggest that in the latter case what is being done is to deny the effects of historical or social facts. Rather there is a need to see what the history and social facts one inherits may offer and may be unable to offer. While the African political philosopher of the 1980s may feel constrained by the immediacy of the colonial experience and may need to deal with it extensively, as a thinker she is also called on to go beyond the limits of such facts. She is not in the strictest of senses at par with the actual slave who is dreaming (thinking) of her freedom. The African thinker is an examiner of what has been, what could possibly have been, and what could possibly be. In weighing all these positions and possibilities, the thinker must come up with a clear plan of where her responsibilities are most required and where her energies are supposed to be invested for maximal effect.

My argument may sound misdirected or not serious at all until we consider something fundamentally dubious about whiteness. Whiteness, like its companion racism, is false. Racism is based on the belief that there exists distinct races that are deserving of different treatment. A racist not only believes in the existence of races but also in that it is morally acceptable to afford different races different treatment (in accordance with whatever criteria the racist is working with). Of course, this is all false. There are, strictly, no races. There is just the human race with different phenotypical presentation of its subsets/members. These different phenotypical presentations are not radically different to warrant constitution of the belief in different races. A racist, therefore, believes erroneously that there are races. If we turn our attention to whiteness the same sort of problems arise. As human beings, we have fallen into the convention of talking of differences amongst us in terms of colour. We all know that strictly speaking there is no person whose skin colour matches the colour white just as much as there is no person whose skin colour matches the colour black (Chimakonam 2019). Whatever we are trying to do in talking about white and black people, at the very least it achieves the purpose of capturing and communicating the phenotypical differences between people we are talking about. This type of talk, in and of itself, has no further use other than to describe differences in appearance. However, some people have fallen into the trap of assigning to whiteness and blackness, more than descriptions of differences in appearance. Such people have assigned positive attributes to whiteness while reserving negative attributes for blackness (see Mills 2007; Tsri 2016). This is racism, which is false, since whiteness and blackness have no known essences as they are categories that (strictly) do not exist. Blackness does not exist, in the same way as whiteness does not exist. Talking about them as if they really existed beyond simple descriptions of phenotypical difference is false talk.

However, these falsehoods have become an integral part of how most of us think about the world and frame reality. They may also have become an indispensable part of how we choose to make judgements on important things. These falsehoods have not only become a part of stories we tell but also stories we believe. Therein lies the challenge of false accounts. They are not only easily believable; they are also stubbornly enduring as they refuse to be shaken off by contrary evidence. Falsehoods relating to racism and whiteness must be treated as special categories because they have a long history of justification in all sorts of fields that one can think of. Some of this evidence is not invoked to support straight bigotry but is drawn to aid descriptions such as Africans' failure and whites' progress. These facts are turned to suggest that there is something fundamentally wrong with Africans.

Whatever the history of whiteness or debates on the origins or motives of such history, what cannot be denied is that whiteness is a false doctrine. This doctrine has been used by discredited colonial, apartheid, oppressive, and reactionary regimes to justify their politics of exclusion and oppression. The fact that such regimes have collapsed under the scorn and resistance they occasioned shows too well the falsity of whiteness. The fact that whiteness has succeeded in detaining thinkers in Africa for so long under different schools and orientations is a regrettable waste of energy if not the greatest diversion in the history of Africans. Above, I referred to work that has come for sharp criticism for its attempt at developing accounts of blackness that are deemed problematic. However, I propose that it is not only Senghor or Nyerere's essentialism that is problematic. Approaches steeped in attempts at overcoming the effects of colonialism such as decolonial theories or postcolonial theories or respectable albeit exclusivist versions of Africanism all fall prey to adding to the already oversubscribed confrontation with whiteness. This confrontation may prove least beneficial to the African condition.

My problem with these theories is that they are unable to provide frameworks of empowering Africans in any way beyond blueprints of understanding the operations of whiteness as part of the racism of colonialism and subsequent neo-colonialisms. While these analyses may prove to be useful for their intended purposes, we must venture to inquire what the actual benefit of those intended purposes are beyond their findings. If the postcolony or post-colony or post colony, for example, was to understand how it was damaged by racisms that supported whiteness and spread falsehoods about black people, then what? If the intellectual effort we see in the brilliant articulation of various points of relations coming together to form a basis of black exclusion was to be directed towards other intellectual needs, what would both the intellectual and developmental landscape of Africa look like?

There is something that we as Africans must be very careful about when we engage in theorization that seeks to contest whiteness (not that the falsehood of whiteness should not be contested). There is a danger that accompanies such projects. These dangers have to do with how we end up choosing to understand our situation or reasons why Africa as a continent is in its current condition. We cannot engage with the fictions of whiteness without eventually coming to exculpating ourselves from any blame for the way we have turned out. The effect of this insincerity is, as Jean Paul Sartre would name it, false consciousness. If our gaze is permanently fixed on whiteness, not only do we deny ourselves the possibility of thinking through other things that affect our existence, we also begin to be obsessed about whiteness to a point where everything has to be traced to what whiteness did. This view lessens our agency and it reduces us to pawns that have been moved around for so long and are only interested in understanding why they were moved in the way they were. Yet, there are so many things that we have done to each other and with each other that demand a more robust engagement with who we are without always referencing our experiences to whiteness. We need to be brutally honest about the role we have played in at least contributing to impoverishing ourselves, killing each other in senseless bush wars, the political intolerance we have shown each other and the collapse of institutions and societies that we have presided over since independence.

In assessing why Africa is the way it is, we have ended at a place where internalists and externalists differ on who is pulling the trigger on Africa. This debate appears to have merit but one would think that the case is a bit of both. Yet what is required for Africa to improve its station is not to concentrate on what some discredited people did but what credible people can do with their insightful minds in advancing African agency.

## Possibilities of African thought systems

In this concluding section, I seek to advocate discarding of whiteness. This process of discarding whiteness, viewed from the prism of African philosophy, will present the most viable possibility of African philosophy freeing itself first from the hold of whiteness, and becoming free to pursue what it must.

A significant part of what I propose here involves treating whiteness as if it did not matter. This may immediately raise the difficulty of contradiction if not downright nonsense. Whiteness does matter, the retort may protest. The damage it has caused through slavery, colonialism and other continued practices of domination are real, and their consequences re-main intact long after formal discontinuation of such practices. Social structures created by racist and oppressive regimes remain intact in their continued favouring of whites at the expense of racial others. Institutions continue with their favourable dispositions towards white people long after official proclamations of white superiority have been banned. Through whiteness, the white race continues to benefit from long established economic privileges, institutional dom-inance and access to connections not possible for the majority of Africans. Because of whiteness, generational wealth is a possibility for the white race while inter-generational poverty is the lived reality for the majority of Africans. My response to this position is that I do not even seek to contest or query the legitimacy of all the grievances against whiteness. I accept such grie-vances and their effects as accurately presented.

Yet despite this correct description, I only see one way out of whiteness; ditching it completely. Before outlining what this process involves, I think it is important to separate issues of practicality from the development of ideas. While it is true, in some cases, that these two are inter-related, it is also quite possible to separate them. For example, reversing long lasting practical effects of whiteness requires different strategies from reversing effects that whiteness has had on thought systems that seek to undo it. My conviction arises from the tenuous re-lationship that exists between thoughts and practical social systems. While there are thoughts behind systems, it does not follow that there is a perfect match between the two. As a result, systems may take a life of their own depending on a number of other factors that seek to influence how the system eventually looks like. With systems of thought, it is entirely up to the individual thinkers to shape the final outlook.

What I advocate, then, is a system of thought that treats whiteness for what it is: a false doctrine. Whiteness has been unmasked as false. What then is left is for the logical consequence of that unmasking to follow: ditch whiteness. This process of ditching whiteness is not a re-actionary antithesis to whiteness comparable to the development of what are considered as counterhegemonic voices to the overarching determinism of whiteness. Rather, this process of ditching whiteness is first a process of claiming true intellectual freedom, and second a process of empowering the African through admitting multiple sources of thought.

My idea of a claim to true freedom is through decentering the ubiquity of the effects of Africa's historical encounter with white Europe that aimed to expand the power of whiteness. The idea I have in mind is one that does not reject facts of history or consequences of processes of history. It is one that takes a stance against that history and its consequences. Such a stance is one that is committed to the view that African agency is not to be determined by facts of colonialism. It sees African agency as a continuous process aimed at not only making sense of the past but of making sense of possibilities that are available to Africans now and how these can shape their future for the better. Such thinking prioritizes responsibility taking, inventiveness, and a willingness to overcome any obstacle as primary to its approach to the world. A significant part of this thinking is the rejection of thinking of Africanness in relation to what whiteness has done. To reject the effects of whiteness on thought systems means rescuing those thought systems from imprisoned references to essences of blackness or limited and narrow comparisons of differences between whiteness and blackness. It means thinking afresh in relation to the present. It is to be bound to only what is possible as both original and future looking. It is not ahistorical thought, but thought that understands the pitfalls of historical determinism. It is a rejection of the viability of blackness as a category of thought but an embrace of the viability of thought that proceeds from blackness. It is a rejection of viewing blackness as a summation of what its experiences were but an embrace of possibilities of how blackness can forge its own way in response to its context and how it assesses that context.

In as far as that thought system is African and philosophical, it is committed primarily to improving what the conditions of the immediate environment are in relation to how they construct our visions of reality. While the immediate environment has a long history, including effects of whiteness, the possibilities that the environment presents without consideration of whiteness are great. The suspension of whiteness is a reclaiming of power, power to reform thought so that other categories that are deserving of attention may also begin to show up and be attended to. In rejecting whiteness, there is an opening of a possibility of a re-imagination of a world of equals, a world that is not pained by its unjust past. A key element of thought is imagination. Imagination has the capacity to free. Without imagination, one is restricted to the drudgery of the usual. To think and imagine whiteness as having never occurred leads to new constructions that are both black and earnest for whatever purpose the thinker might have.

Thus, the intellectual freedom I envisage is one that goes beyond limits of identities created by historical facts and reactions to them. Philosophically, this form of thinking takes seriously the situationality of the thinker in relation to how she understands her immediate environment to be an impediment or an aid to her own ideas and what she wants those ideas to do. This is particularly so for present generations of African thinkers who are born after the attainment of independence. If they find Africa to be a frustrating place, can they honestly without a grain of deceit think in terms of how whiteness has caused them the particular frustration they feel? When the youths of Africa go to public institutions with expectations of getting decent services from state officials, but get nothing except inefficiency and recklessness, can they sincerely blame London or Paris for their unprocessed passport or shortage of drugs at the local hospital? If they were to do so, that would be a tragic and unproductive way of thinking.

The second process, which seeks to admit multiple sources of thought, is nothing short of an affirmation of the diversity of African thought and how that diversity is representative of the multiple identities that constitute the reality of this continent. The creation of African philosophy with a view to developing a counterhegemonic voice might have meant that, for a while, it was necessary to punt a single Africanist view. Or that it was necessary to develop an authentic African voice or system of thought. The need for such a move would easily have been rooted in an attempt to counter both the false claims of superiority by whiteness as well as the damaging consequences of those claims. Hence it could have been both necessary and desirable to formulate a coherent body of work that would identify as African by virtue of its methodology and content. Such a commitment would, inevitably, have led to the creation of similar views on fundamental topics such as the nature of persons and the importance of community in African ontologies. Even if this were the case, there were voices that claimed that African philosophy is not a monolith. However, those voices had to compete against views that favoured a less diverse account of African thought.

I will not rehash the path that these differing views eventually took and how they contributed to the prospects and at times stagnation of African philosophy. Rather, I wish to comment on the idea of African, as experience, in relation to philosophy. Whether in its traditional set up or in its modern appearance, the fact of being Africa has to be necessarily diverse. Diversity is only human and if Africans are humans, they will not be exempted from it. This diversity spreads itself from experiences of life to thoughts on that life. Hence to be African is to live and think in accordance with one's particular experiences. While it could be true that to a great degree, life in traditional society was not highly distinguishable, that is not necessarily true in modern Africa. While the source of value and interpretation of life was narrow, in traditional Africa, it has become much more varied in modern Africa. What this points to is the divergence of sources of identity that are now characteristic of the people of this continent. Even in a single individual, it is not unusual to find a multiplicity of sources informing the identity of that individual. This is even truer for African communities that are wont to draw on a number of sources for either the shared or the contested identity of their members. Nothing is as illustrative of this point as political membership. There are as many political parties on the continent and each of these parties is sharply opposed to the other. Yet, all members of these parties are enjoined to live together amicably despite their intolerance of each other's political commitments. What this shows is not only the need to be embrace a commitment to recognizing pluralism; it also shows the need to embrace pluralism in thought and possibility of ideas that are said to be responsible for what an African is.

Thinking of the formation of the identity of Africans or what identity they bear as a result of historical factors, may include considerations of the historical impact of whiteness. But that consideration must be proper to the effects of whiteness. It is now but only a small part of reality for many an African. Let us return to the political experience of many Africans, to make the point I have in mind. The majority of African citizens are young people below the age of 40. They would have been born after the end of colonialism and would not have memories and experiences of white men swathed in corrupted views of their natural superiority. The majority of African citizens have no memory of white colonial administrators or of visuals of segregation. Instead, they have very distinct memories and immediate experiences of dysfunctionality, poverty, and wretchedness caused by their black presidents. If they were to reflect on their situation, and they were displeased with it, they would lay blame on their black governments for rampant corruption and general decay.

## Conclusion

Problems besetting Africa today need to be faced with an openness to framing their origins as well as their solutions beyond the limitations of whiteness. Both conceptually and methodologically, African philosophy has an obligation to open itself to as diverse sources of problems and imaginations of their solutions, as possible. If thought is freed up from restrictions of whiteness, then it can begin to develop a multifaceted comprehension of its environment as well as responses that are needed to re-order the deficiencies emerging from such an environment. Thoughts systems that are not restrained by essentialisms of whiteness and reactions to them, hold better promise for engaging with Africa's future prospects or limitations.

## References

Chimakonam, J. O. 2019. Why the Racial Politic of Colour-branding should be Discontinued. *Phronimon*, 20 (1): 1–24. DOI:10.25159/2413-3086/6600.

Eze, E. C. 1999. Philosophy and the 'Man' in the Humanities. *Topoi*, 18: 49–58.

Jun, A. *et al.* 2018. *White Jesus: The Architecture of Racism in Religion and Education*. New York: Peter Lang.

Masolo, D. A. 1994. *African Philosophy in Search of Identity*. Nairobi: East African Educational Publishers.

Mills, C. W. 2007. White Ignorance. In *Race and Epistemologies of Ignorance*, ed. S. Sullivan and N. Tuana, pp. 13–38. Albany: State University of New York Press.

Serequeberhan, T. 1994. *The Hermeneutics of African Philosophy: Horizon and Discourse*. New York: Routledge.

Taiwo, O. 2010. *How Colonialism Preempted Modernity in Africa*. Bloomington: Indiana University Press.

Tempels, P. 1959. *Bantu Philosophy*. Paris: Présence Africaine.

Tsri, K. 2016. Africans are not Black: Why the Use of the Term 'Black' for Africans should be Abandoned. *African Identities*, 14 (2): 147–160. DOI:10.1080/14725843.2015.1113120.

# 'The Feeling in my Chest': Unblocking space for people of colour in critical whiteness studies

*Amanpreet Ahluwalia*

## The improbability of *us*

I am a Sikh woman of Punjabi descent; the love of my life is a white German man. We often marvel at the improbability of *us* – that one evening, the first time we met, changed the whole course of our lives and yet, it almost never was. My epic Punjabi–British–German tale of love starts not with our chance encounter, but begins with the histories that made *us* possible. *We*, our stories, begin to intersect through the Spice Trade, with the European colonial project, in the throes and aftermath of the Second World War, with the rebuilding of Europe using labour from the colonies, with the European Union and the modern project of Globalisation. For any of us to sincerely honour our origin story, we must employ the concept of *presencing* as a tool. Gail Lewis writes:

> … presencing is an epistemological and ontological praxis of emergence based on felt connection among human and non-human; ancestral and contemporary life. It contests and has the potential to detoxify the effects of colonial discourse (historical and contemporary) in which indigenous people are rendered invisible and/or insensible.
>
> *(Lewis 2017: 4)*

*Presencing* refers to a bringing forth of that which has become buried or rendered invisible. *Presencing*, similarly to *wonder* (Ahmed 2004), allows us to see the world '*as made* and as such … opens up … historicity' (2004: 179).

When I refer to these events, I refer not only to the spatial possibilities that, when layered together through history culminate in our physical presence that night but also how these histories produced the social and psychic overlaps that shaped our compatible subjectivities and ontologies. The fact that Germany lost the war and spent many years reconciling with the reality of their modern imperialist project and the devastation it caused, acted as an interruption in the flow of the social relations of power that we understand as white privilege in Germany. My partner grew up as a young man in the 1990s with interests in history, politics and sociogeny which meant that interrogating, reckoning with and identifying the dangers and mechanisms of imperialism, racism, ethno-nationalistic supremacy and political projects of 'othering' eventually *became possible* for him.

DOI: 10.4324/9780429355769-25

It is our shared understanding of the 'produced' nature of social relations and of our social world more widely which form the foundation that our relationship is built on. This alone, however, is not enough to make us *both* legible to one another. *We* are also made possible because of the privileges that flow into me as a colonial subject from India, one of the most historically significant British colonies. I currently reside at the heart of empire, in London, England, and benefit from all of the advantages this comes with. I have internalised and benefitted from *whiteness* enough to be legible to my partner, he has developed a sense of criticality that makes him legible to me. I find it important to say here that I love him, not because I hate my people or my culture or myself, as has sometimes been suggested, but because my lived experience is evidence that subjectivity *is* multiple.

My intention here was to draw attention to how strangely complex the existence of our compatibilities are, some of which are personal (a love of Death Metal being one of them) but many shaped by our respective, but familiar to one another, socio-historical contexts. It is important to say too, that *we* are also not *inevitable*, my partner has a twin brother, whose politics are the polar opposite to his own – the way in which our world shapes us, is often un-predictable. For me then, any discipline called 'Critical Whiteness Studies' must be able to hold space open for complicated interpersonal analyses of the lived experience of people like me whose relationship to whiteness is not linear, unidirectional, or singular.

Throughout this chapter, I use my own lived experience as a woman of colour, an antiracist activist and someone who has intimately built her life with white people, to dream new po-tentialities for the discipline; to explore what happens when we make space for thinking people of colour into the work of CWS. I ask what happens when we centre antiracism, decoloniality and intimacy in this frame? I also employ the tool of wonder to explore what it might look like to *really* honour the word 'critical' in 'Critical Whiteness Studies'? I argue that for CWS to be a relevant contribution to the project of racial justice, contributors to the discipline must grapple with the way in which the discipline engenders an anti-relational, substantialist, essentialising way of theorising that we see from normative social science. I conclude that if, as a critical discipline, CWS is to be relevant to the project of social progress, racial equality or social justice, contributions to the discipline must grapple with the lived complexities, ambiguities, and contradictions in living *and* labouring towards social justice (Gunaratnam 2003).

## (Un)critical whiteness studies?

At the time of writing, engagement, both public and academic, with CWS is burgeoning. More and more people in Western contexts are trying to make sense of the myriad ways in which white supremacy has been normalised in places such as Brexit Britain and Post-Trump United States. The renewed interest in CWS suggests that it is here to stay, problematic and contested as it might be. As a social justice practitioner, my investment in academia and in critical dis-ciplines is in their application; for me, theory is the place I come to help me unpick or un-derstand the relational messes that I sometimes find myself in, and to use what I learn to labour towards change. To do my work well, I am consistently untangling. Considering that CWS is a site that people rely on to untangle their racialized messes, I am interested in exploring new possibilities for the subject. I myself had high hopes for my first encounter with CWS ten years ago; I had hoped the discipline would be a place of richness for me. At the time, I had been a community development practitioner for some years, a young woman of colour and somebody who had been active in anti-oppressionist struggle; I was desperate to find ways to understand the confusing dynamics that I found myself in whilst engaged with antiracist work with my white colleagues. I was trying to understand how they could have perpetuated such violence in our shared spaces while being so aware of structural racism, white privilege and while being so committed to realising an antiracist future.

Our love for one another was real and deep, we lived so intimately in the work of challenging racism together, but still, so many aspects of our relationships remained complicatedly entangled in racialized power; so many forms of abuse were replicated in our shared spaces. The confusing thing was that the gaslighting, the abusive behaviour, the refusal to imagine that we (as people of colour) could have the same levels of agency and potential for liberation (as white people), *were not consistent*, and were also accompanied by a deep caring. It took years to identify the behavioural patterns attached to their racism, and to recognise that many of the ways that the racism manifested was truly related to people's individual traumas and subjectivities as well as their whiteness. Gail Lewis (2009) talks beautifully and achingly about the 'proximity of love and racism' in her relationship with her white mother; about the pains and joys of moving 'in and out of the economies of whiteness, and the habits of thinking that it sometimes generates' (2009: 14).

I can wholeheartedly say that the inability to understand or identify the multiplicity and complicatedness of the relational dynamics that I was stuck in, was just as damaging as the behaviours themselves. Given these experiences and the answers that I was searching for, my engagement with CWS was incredibly fraught. I have often felt frustrated at the ways in which CWS scholars simplify the way that we *live* racialized power in the everyday. The replication of normalised academic method in CWS – of theorising 'whiteness' as a '*thing*', an 'organising principle' (Nayak 2007); 'unmarked ideal' or 'universal norm' (Dyer 1997; Fine et al. 2004; Garner 2007; Nayak 2007; Steyn and Conway 2010) is a simplification of the complex processes, paradoxes, and ambivalences that labouring to develop our ontologies in service of social justice births. Before continuing, I would like to make a distinction here between theorists who belong to different disciplines, but write about whiteness, and theorists who align themselves with CWS as an academic discipline. CWS scholars tend to write about whiteness from a 'substantialist' perspective; from the point of view that social life and social relations are made up of 'things ... acting under their own powers, independently of all other substances' (Dewey and Bentley 1949, in Emirbayer 1997).

It is here that I would like to pick up on the dangers of CWS existing as a substantialist canon can pose. The tendency of CWS theorists to write about whiteness *only,* as if it possesses an Aristotelian 'Being', has many damaging implications; 'each time critics focus on the object and not the human labour of production, [social forces] assume a life and logic, an autonomy and agency of their own, independent of the actors who produced them' (Lea 2008: 19). As a critical discipline, I argue that if CWS is to be relevant to the project of social progress, racial equality or social justice, theorists must not replicate the same anti-relational, substantialist, essentialising theorising that we see from normative social science. This form of theory erases the centuries of intentional, industrial-scale practices that went into producing racial inequality (see Said 2003) and also simplifies the ambivalence that we all experience in how we live racialized power in the everyday. Even Adolf Hitler issued his Jewish family physician, Eduard Bloch, protection to allow for him to flee Austria to the United States and saved his life. In the rest of this chapter, I draw on Black Feminist theory and method to explore some of the ways in which CWS can centre relationality and subjectivity. I use ideas of feeling work and emotional labour to discover how closely our selfhoods, hurts, traumas, and joys are a central part of being able to think decolonial possibilities into existence.

Learning to *truly see* power and resist perpetuating inequality or participating in the subjection of others and ourselves is deeply internal. Patrisse Cullors, one of the co-founders of Black Lives Matter (BLM), talks about the work of BLM as spiritual, as healing, as a project of 'rehumanising' (Cullors 2019). For me, in my writing, thinking and in my work, this starts with understanding the effects of, and uncovering and identifying the different textures and residues that the trauma of racism has left behind in my life.

When I first started the work of conceiving this article, I was in the middle of an intense period of self-reflection, the fourth of my life. It was six years since the storms within had called me to live in their crosscurrents, so that I might understand more about those forces that are invisible to me in my everyday but that direct my life, nonetheless. Many years ago, I came to understand just how much being forged in the throes of structural, cultural, and personal trauma affected how I experience the world. Relational theory exists as the antithesis to substantialist theorising (Emirbayer 1997); it is the study of how two or more things are connected, and more importantly, what those connections *produce in relationship with one another*. I explore the relational connections between racialized trauma, writing, and imagining decolonial possibilities later.

I argue that any theorist that wants to say something important about race or whiteness, must do so in a way that helps us to come to terms with the ways we may have been hurt, broken, or traumatised by the violence of racialization and project of colonisation – all of us, no matter where we sit on this spectrum at any one time. Developing a shared language that helps us name how these traumas live in our bodies, what they enable and constrain, is imperative for this work. I also argue that any work that has anything of interest to say about liberation must also be *healing*. Black Feminism is such an incredible roadmap for how an academic discipline can create a shared language for this work; a cannon that heals. Van Der Kolk (2015) tells us, 'the challenge of recovery [from trauma] is to establish ownership of your own body and your mind – of your self. This means feeling free to know what you know, and feel what you feel without becoming overwhelmed, enraged, ashamed, or collapsed' (p. 204). I argue that developing a shared language for describing and therefore enabling comprehension of the significance of bodily knowledge, feelings, and ways of thinking and knowing that relate to racialized and racial trauma, is essential for the work of CWS.

As anyone who has tried to overcome their demons will know, this ability to 'show up', to feel still or to think freely, is not easily accessible to me all the time. It comes to me in the line of a book, in a thought in the shower, in the beauty of friendship; in fits, bursts, starts and paragraphs. When I started writing this chapter, I was in a wonderful place emotionally, this allowed me to *really notice* the 'stuckness' that I felt in trying to start writing. I sat in-front of a blank page for days; writing and rewriting the first paragraph for more than two weeks. Not because I did not know what to say, but because *something is not fitting*. My heart skips a beat, is this my way in? What am I trying to fit, and where? Why does it not fit? I often write on race and racism without issue, but somehow having to directly centre CWS in this frame was *doing* something, blocking something within me. In the past, I would have blamed myself for being 'stupid' when experiencing such mad-making obstructions in my ability to think. I have since learned, just like all the historicity that has made me legible to my partner, much of this has also made me illegible to myself, the psychic block making it impossible to know where to go from here. It is being caught in this dynamic that I call *unthinkability*.

So where do we go when we are caught in a place which feels so alien, that the language in which it writes itself, does not allow space for us to speak ourselves into existence? I find Gail Lewis' (2017) work on 'presence' and 'presencing' offers us a great conceptual starting point. I have to be honest; the article is so rich I cannot be sure that I grasp it fully, but she says thatpresence is about 'here-ness' and 'alive-ness' and 'presencing' is 'a decolonial move through which counter-histories, counter-spatialities, subaltern epistemologies and modes of being' generate meaning. She argues that 'for meaning to be generated and the possibility of a third space to emerge a capacity for symbolic thought is required and this in its turn is both an effect of, and occurs in, the dynamic space between presence and absence' (Lewis 2017: 3). For me, if CWS is ever truly to fulfil its mission, the 'third space' between the myriad presences and absences needs to be interrogated. Especially important is making space for people of colour to interrogate our own relationship to whiteness. My experience has been that as a person of colour, I struggled to do this, and I explore this in more detail in the next section.

## Opening up the 'third space'

By now, my trauma work and the healing that followed, has taught me one thing above all else: The body knows. So, how can I understand what is being stirred up in me as I try to do this work? What is the 'presence' and 'absence' in this situation, and what does the relationship between them tell me? I search for a presence to help me unpick myself out of this mess, and I come to Audre Lorde. With two chapters of her work 'Poetry is not a Luxury' and 'The Transformation of Silence into Language and Action', Audre Lorde (2007) taught me more about the importance of tending to my spirit, my soul, my flesh and down to the very marrow of my bones, in recovering my own agency, my best thinking, my most creative, still and loving self than years of therapy. Each time I deeply convene with Audre, her work gifts me with new freedoms that allow me to 'show up' in my life in ways that I never knew I could. So I live in the lines of those chapters again as she tells me:

> This is poetry as illumination, for it is through poetry that we give name to those ideas – which are – until the poem – nameless and formless, about to be birthed, but already felt … as we come into touch with our own ancient, non-European consciousness of living as a situation to be experienced and interacted with, we learn more and more to cherish our feelings, and to respect those hidden sources of power from where true knowledge and, therefore, lasting action comes … we can train ourselves to respect our feelings, and to transpose them into a language so they can be shared.
>
> *(Lorde 2007: 36)*

I heed her advice, her wisdom, it grounds me. She too talks about presence, absence and *process of producing* language. I pay disciplined attention to speaking myself into existence, bringing the feelings that I must work through, forward in my consciousness. I sit in my chair, stuck, and begin to do the work of listening to my body; I track the sensation, it is a pressure in the middle of my diaphragm. Still leaning on Audre Lorde, I pay attention to transposing my feelings into words and naming this psychic blockage which manifests in my body, slowly comprehending the weight of the work that I am beginning to undertake. The blockage was a bodily feeling of frustration, when I dig deeper it is not only an epistemic stuck-ness, but feels like an ontological repression in my very *being;* I am cornered, and I am caught, bodily, in the very dynamic that I wanted to explore; how the anti-relational approach of CWS limits my ability to speak easily to the ideas that I want to speak to. I am directly caught in the trap that I am writing to challenge.

But my body takes me back to this weight, and I trust where I am stuck is an important place to stay, I am *presencing*. I realise clearly for the first time how *sentient* this work somehow is; the work of decolonial thinking. It is structured by the very forms of language that we use. This is exactly why the canon of 'Critical Whiteness Studies' is so important, the very form of thinking instituted by the discipline structures our ability to imagine otherwise. *Is this my third space?* Of course, discourse analysis makes this clear, but what I had not understood *bodily*, or experienced in a way that I could put words to, was that the way that language is structured carries its own *ontology*. The feeling in my chest is made up of my present struggle, but also the ways in which the violence of the past materialises in my present. Hortense Spillers speaks to this so masterfully when she describes the sorts of work we have to do as women of colour. She says:

> Let's face it. I am a marked woman, but not everybody knows my name ... I describe a locus of confounded identities, a meeting ground of investments and privations ... In order for me to speak a truer word concerning myself, I must strip down through layers of attenuated meanings, made in excess of time, over time, assigned by a particular historical order, and there await the marvels of my own inventiveness.
>
> *(Spillers 2003: 65)*

What I think Spillers is talking about here, is the materialisation of the historic processes of colonization onto/into her own being, and specifically important for this chapter, in the ways that affects the way that she is able to think about, or know herself. I feel I also experienced this in real-time: the emotional and intellectual labour required to do this work. It became an active site of intense struggle – not in the struggle to access myself per se, but to bring those internal thoughts and feelings into being through modes of production incompatible with their expression, for the comprehension of an audience which may also not understand why what I am saying is important. My internal struggle was also compounded by a sense of the violent history that produced it; the weight of colonialism and the way it constrains my ability to express and know myself materialised in these moments; I felt a genuine sense of *oppression* – I mean that with the full weight that this word carries. *The absence has been presenced.* I had to do the work of re-joining and recreating myself, undoing the ways that I compartmentalise to survive, rather than hiding in myself and disengaging entirely. I had to *presence* the atemporal oppressions that I was experiencing internally to really get to the core of what I wanted to say. For me, the most important question to ask here is, what might have happened if I had not known how to resolve my *unthinkability*?

Returning to that weight in my diaphragm: I think about racialized trauma, the ongoing struggle to 'be'. The code switching, the self-censorship, the total terror as I walk to school as a 6-year-old girl and crowds of grown men shout racial slurs at me. I start to think of the 'tremendous energy to keep functioning while carrying the memory of terror, and the shame of utter weakness and vulnerability' (Van Der Kolk 2014: 89). *I also think about how hard the work of birthing these thoughts, feelings and ideas are in the wake of the terror and trauma that we carry.* I think of Toni Morrison's Beloved (1987): she talks about how 'out there they don't love our children'. What does it mean to strip through the layers that Spillers talks about, and speak yourself into existence, and what happens is that *you speak yourself out of the mouth of a white man, maybe even for the white man, for people who do not love you*? What damage does it do, to live so many years without even realising that the weight in your diaphragm is both the psychic presence and absence of these things? For many years, I carried all of these unspoken traumas around with me. I held them bodily; and they accumulated, they formed a heavier weight over the years in different classrooms, lecture theatres and writing practices, and so the familiar weight 'presenced' itself when writing the first sentence of this chapter, that weight has a *history*. As the CWS project continues, I genuinely want to ask contributors, teachers, activists, academics and students to think deeply about what it means to improve the 'quality of light' that CWS provides, in a way that has an impact on the ways in which 'we live, and upon the changes which we hope to bring about through those lives' (Lorde 2007: 36). What presences and absences can you feel? How might the space between them contribute to a more profound method of meaning making in CWS?

## Complicatedness as an analytic

Being a person of colour, belonging to a racialized community and living in the West is complicated. I would describe the way that I grew up as living between *many* extremes; relative privilege and relative subjection, the intense love and joy of belonging to a huge family and the repression of belonging to a traditional Sikh family, the violence of racism in the 1980s and 1990s, truly loyal and life-giving friendships, feeling alien, total withdrawal, intensely anxious presence, violence and shame from many places, loving and hating being British, loving and hating being Indian, loving and hating my family, *loving and hating my life*. Those periods of intense self-reflection that I mentioned earlier were often about trying to make sense of these extremes, of trying to understand what holding them all together meant for who I am. I am reminded here of how Avery Gordon starts her book 'Ghostly Matters'. Inspired by Patricia Williams, she offers us the following; 'that life is complicated may seem a banal expression of the obvious, but it is nonetheless ... perhaps the most important theoretical statement of our time' (Gordon 2008: 3). When I first read this sentence, I felt so validated; like she'd described something that was so fundamental to the way that I live, but that I had never quite been able to articulate.

Those periods of self-reflection were also about survival. When I talk about survival, I mean much more than physical survival, I mean to have survived as a *whole* person. I love how Christina Sharpe talks about this process. She calls it making liveable relationships, places and moments in all that feels unliveable; working at joy, bringing beauty, of recognising that while I have lived, and continue to experience subjection, I can do the work of 'not living *as* the subjected' (Sharpe 2016: 4). Learning to live not '*as* the subjected' is not only about unlearning the ways that we learn to think of ourselves as less than human but also, in refusing to see myself as a victim, I must face my clear privilege and the ways in which I am complicit with whiteness. So, what does it mean to understand ourselves as complicated? The decolonial frame calls for us to embrace both our privileges and subjections. To be aware of the social, political, cultural, and economic forces through history up until this day which shape my present, including my privilege and the way that I perpetuate an unfair system. As Sharpe and other Black Feminists such as Audre Lorde, Saidiya Hartman, Tina Campt, Hortense Spillers, bell hooks and especially Sylvia Wynter have shown, knowing differently reaches its deepest and most meaningful level when we are able to use this knowledge in service of *living* differently.

What does it really mean to engage with complicatedness as an analytic for understanding how power works through us? What does this mean again, for us as writers, or people who are labouring towards social justice? My own subjectivity is so interlaced with the privilege and oppression that there have been times when, from one frame, one part of myself, I am a complete stranger to myself in the other. And so, what does it mean to do the work of *presencing* (Lewis 2017) myself as a *whole* person not only as a personal practice, but also in service of social justice? I am a woman of colour who lives in a racist society. I am a first-generation British Indian woman who grew up with the privileges of the global North. I have an education that is valued globally. I did not have access to the same opportunities as many connected middle- to upper-class students at my university. I grew up in a loving family. I co-own a gorgeous (to me) flat in London. I grew up relatively poor. My roots are firmly working-class but I have royal ancestry and firmly established middle-class family in India. I only recently realised how much both my royal ancestry, and my familial experience of the trauma of partition has affected my family. My privileges and my subjection are wildly bound up with the project of colonization; I see the intense damage this has caused my family, myself. My family live the privileges of whiteness every day.

The truth is, creating liveability within all of this, *psychically*, is not simple work; to claim myself slowly back from the entrapment of colonial violence, racism, sexism, intergenerational trauma and every other force that was designed to make me feel wrong in my body while simultaneously claiming my privilege is sometimes mad-making. I found an intense power in deciding that I deserved better than to live half a life, always denying or hiding one or more parts of myself. While I continue to find personal power in healing the fault lines, fractures and compartmentalisation by challenging the assumption of the incompatibility of 'whiteness' and 'otherness', this work is politically relevant because healing those fractures taught me a lot about how I *live* power. I learned that I had the power to weaken the links in the chains that whiteness places around us, making it possible to *think* a different future. When I started this work at 14 years of age, my only expectation was to cheat my own living death, to somehow find a stable middle ground between numbness and heightened terror – both in many ways linked to the pain in living in the afterlife of colonization.

Over time, I found that in working to actively heal myself, in taking the fractured, bruised and bloody bits that were hastily stitched together out of necessity to survive at the time, to live in them that I give the shame less power over me, to radically accept these experiences as part of myself and to rebuild around them, I have learned more than anything that this healing work is a *radical act of service*. In learning how to connect and locate my struggles in events across time and space, to labour to release the violences that I had internalised, to unwaveringly nurse the strength and beauty of the lessons learned in those places in service of teaching myself how to *live* differently 'Healing the fractures' has become an analytic; learning how to craft stories and analysis that bring together those things that we have been taught to be incompatible; for me this means finding power in creating a fluidity in my subjectivity between those parts of my identity that were never meant to live together; my whiteness, my blackness, my queerness, my privilege, my subjection, they were never meant to exist in harmony. I think this radical fluidity, is the place from which my ability to think of being human anew comes. Sylvia Wynter taught me this, in referring to her work, McKittrick tells us:

> … think carefully about the ways in which those currently inhabiting the underside of the category Man-as-human – under our current epistemological regime, those cast out as impoverished and colonized and undesirable and lacking reason – can, and do, provide a way to think about being human anew.
>
> *(Wynter and McKittrick 2015: 3)*

Over time, I learned that labouring in service of living better for myself, was also a deeply spiritual practice of social justice, a practice in service of my loved ones and others like me – in doing the work, in refusing to be a carrier of hurts and horrors that have wracked the lives of my family, my friends and community, in reimagining a different life for myself, I refuse my own undoing (see Hartman 2020). But, more importantly, I can use this time to practise refusing to contribute to the undoing of other people *like me*. This work is also a strong recognition of how power *lives in me*. In working to insulate myself from the fundamental anti-relational currents of whiteness, I was actively working towards not perpetuating its power and violence on others through me. My hope for this work is to call CWS contributors to develop analyses, or analytic methods complex enough to hold all of the complicated ways in which we *live* racialised power, and for us all to use the work of healing the fractures between those parts of us that we have been taught are incompatible, to come to a more complex understanding of human life.

So I ask, one last time, what must you do?

## Conclusion

If we are to understand Critical Whiteness Studies as an antiracist discipline, we must challenge the normative reproductions of substantialist, anti-relational and essentialising academic method and that has tended to form the canon. Racism and whiteness are complicated and simplified theorising endangers our ability to fully comprehend and interrupt the byzantine technologies of racism and white supremacy that we live. That CWS scholars replicate methodologies used to produce colonial 'worlding' (Said 1984) absolutely limits the potential of CWS to be the radical, useful and complicated discipline that it needs to be to support people to identify racism and practice racial justice.

Furthermore, CWS as a discipline holds an ethical responsibility to be a site of critical engagement with whiteness as power. The global shift to a more outwardly imperial politics, especially in the West but further afield too, means that people are both relying on, and using CWS to interrogate, and untangle the web of racialized violences that we all live. In this work, I have explored what opening up a 'third space' for more complicated, relational analyses of power can do. If, as a critical discipline, CWS is to be relevant to the project of social progress, racial equality, or social justice, contributions to the discipline must grapple with the lived complexities, ambiguities, and contradictions in living *and* labouring towards racial justice (Gunaratnam 2003).

One aspect in particular that I have explored in this work is that opening up a 'third space' for people of colour to explore the complicated ways in which we are both caught in, and perpetuate the violences of whiteness. Interestingly, I would conceptualise this work as a Black Feminist critique of Critical Whiteness Studies, but would also argue that bringing Black Feminism into the work of CWS is imperative. If CWS is ever to achieve its full potential, it must make space for the experiences complicated relationships with racialized power, but especially those of people of colour/racialized people.

## References

Ahmed, S. 2004. *The Cultural Politics of Emotion*. Edinburgh: Edinburgh University Press.

Cullos, P. in Tippett, K. (Host) 2019, May 15. The Spiritual Work of Black Lives Matter. [Audio podcast Episode] in On Being. Krista Tippett Public Productions.

Dyer, R. 1997. *White*. London: Routledge.

Emirbayer, M. 1997. Manifesto for a Relational Sociology. *American Journal of Sociology*, 103 (2): 281–317.

Fine, M. et al. 2004. *Off White. Readings on Power, Privilege, and Resistance*. London: Routledge.

Garner, S. 2007. *Whiteness. An Introduction*. London: Routledge.

Gopal, P. 2019. *Insurgent Empire: Anticolonial Resistance and British Dissent*. London: Verso.

Gordon, A. F. 2008. *Ghostly Matters: Haunting and the Sociological Imagination*. Minneapolis: University of Minnesota Press.

Gunaratnam, Y. 2003. *Researching 'Race' and Ethnicity: Methods, Knowledge and Power*. London: SAGE Publications.

Hartman, S. 2020. *Notes on Feminisms: The Plot of Her Undoing*. Feminist Art Coalition, available at https://static1.squarespace.com/static/5c805bf0d86cc90a02b81cdc/t/5db8b219a910fa05af05dbf4/157238530 5368/NotesOnFeminism-2_SaidiyaHartman.pdf.

Lea, T. 2008. *Bureaucrats & Bleeding Hearts: Indigenous Health in Northern Australia*. Sydney: UNSW Press.

Lewis, G. 2009. Birthing Racial Difference: Conversations with my Mother and Others. *Studies in the Maternal*, 1 (1): 1–21.

Lewis, G. 2017. Questions of Presence. *Feminist Review*, 117 (1): 1–19.

Lorde, A. 2007. *Sister Outsider: Essays and Speeches*. New York: Ten Speed Press.

Morrison, T. 1987. *Beloved*. New York: Knopf.

Nayak, A. 2007. Critical Whiteness Studies. *Sociology Compass*, 1 (2): 737–755.

Nayak, S. 2015. *Race, Gender and the Activism of Black Feminist Theory. Working with Audre Lorde.* East Sussex: Routledge.

Said, E. 1984. *The World, The Text and The Critic.* Cambridge: Harvard University Press.

Said, E. 2003. *Orientalism.* London: Penguin Books.

Sharpe, C. 2016. *In the Wake. On Blackness and Being.* Durham, NC: Duke University Press.

Spillers, H. J. 2003. Mama's Baby, Papa's Maybe: An African American Grammar Book. In *Black, White and in Color: Essays on American Literature and Culture,* ed. H. Spillers, pp. 203–229. Chicago and London: University of Chicago Press.

Steyn, M. and Conway, D. 2010. Introduction: Intersecting whiteness, interdisciplinary debates. *Ethnicities,* 10 (3): 283–291.

Van Der Kolk, B. 2015. *The Body Keeps the Score: Mind, Brain and Body in the Transformation of Trauma.* UK: Penguin Books.

Wynter, S. 1990. Afterword: Beyond Miranda's Meanings: Un/silencing the 'Demonic Ground' of Caliban's Woman. In *Out of the KUMBLA: Caribbean Women and Literature,* ed. C. Boyce Davies and E. Savory Fido, pp. 355–372. Trenton, NJ: Africa World Press.

Wynter, S. 1995. But what does 'wonder' do? Meanings, canons too. *Stanford Humanities Review, 4* (1): 124–129.

Wynter, S. and McKittrick, K. 2015. Unparalleled Catastrophe for our Species? Or, to give Humanness a Different Future: Conversations. In *On Being Human as Praxis,* ed. K. McKittrick, pp. 9–89. Durham, NC: Duke University Press.

# 26

# Integrity, self-respect, and white privilege

*Samantha Vice*

## Introduction

How are we to live a morally decent life in a world that is systematically and recalcitrantly unjust? However noble one's intentions, such circumstances often make it very difficult to do the right thing, or to do it without personal sacrifice. In this chapter, I explore how one is to retain integrity and self-respect when one is on the wrong side of justice, not because (or not only because) of personal wrongdoing, but because of one's group identity. In particular, I am interested in white racial identity in the democratic South Africa, where apartheid has left an enduring legacy of racial injustice and inequality from which whites have benefitted.[1]

Whatever one's personal virtues and self-conception, under such conditions – which are overwhelmingly but not uniquely present in South Africa – one's group membership is significant to how others see one, and how one comes to see oneself. Race is not a merely incidental feature, like eye colour or being right- or left-handed; rather, it is morally relevant and identity-constituting, whether one likes it or not. As a white South African, I have been forced by circumstances to see myself as others see me, as not only an individual, but a person who is also a symbol of a painful history and ongoing hardship for many, and in whose name these injustices were systematically carried out. Whether my conclusions and explorations here are relevant for other kinds of privilege I cannot address sufficiently here, but I would argue that racial privilege is only one example of a deeper phenomenon that assails most of us in some guise or other – that of our being morally in the wrong partly because of social features over which we have little unmediated control.

My question, then, is: How is a racially privileged person to retain self-respect and integrity in conditions of systematic injustice? Can they be retained? I will assume that self-respect and integrity are praiseworthy character traits and constituents of a morally good character, and shall refer to them as 'personal' or 'self-related' virtues or values for short.[2] If they are undermined or are difficult to achieve in certain conditions, this is an ethically significant conclusion. Before I begin, however, I need briefly to state the other assumptions and foci that guide my exploration.

First, I assume that there is structural injustice in our social, economic, and political institutions, apart from whether we can identify and hold particular people responsible. That is, patterns of privilege and deprivation are not arbitrary or neutral; we can predict people's life

DOI: 10.4324/9780429355769-26

chances if we know their relative position in the social structures. Current conditions are often a legacy of past injustice, and even well-meaning people can find themselves invidiously positioned in ways that prejudice the life chances of others, and which influence their character and relations.

Second, however, I assume that the privileged are not simply innocent and exempt from responsibility. They are implicated in the injustices, even if their particular causal influence cannot be identified and even if structural injustices exist independently from their individual actions (Young 2003). People can be implicated in something in different ways – by being causally involved in its creation or continuation; by being symbolically identified with it; by benefitting from it; by supporting it or not fighting against it. Different kinds of implication will carry different kinds of responsibility and censure, and I am also assuming that we should sometimes still take responsibility for what we might not directly be responsible for bringing about (Card 1996; Walker 1991). I will therefore use 'implication' generally, though as a pejorative term: to be 'implicated in X' is to be in a morally problematic position.

Third, I shall use the ambiguous notion of 'privilege' in the following ways (Vice 2019): 'Privilege' first names problematic habits of being in the world – complacency, entitlement, arrogance, assumptions about what is 'normal', valuable and right. Privilege of this kind is habitual, often working beneath the level of consciousness (Sullivan 2006; Vice 2010); we can be quite unwitting about it until someone points it out, usually to our shock. Second, 'privileges' can be material or status goods, and the benefits that go with them – being deferred to and treated as an authority; higher salaries; wealth and property ownership; and the socioeconomic power this brings. In both these senses, privilege is a group-based, relational and pejorative notion; members of one group are privileged relative to another, their goods (their 'privileges') are ill-gotten or unjustly retained, and privilege is a mark of being somehow in the wrong.

These features of a privileged life are especially prevalent for white people in South Africa. While they are a minority, they are still economically and culturally powerful and so have not entirely shed the benefits that went with being white in apartheid South Africa. The discourse and efforts of reconciliation and forgiveness that so strikingly marked the early years of the new democracy in the 1990s have now been overtaken by those of 'radical economic transformation'. Some within the ruling ANC are openly suspicious of the much-praised constitution, declaring it to be a liberal instrument to entrench white supremacy and prevent the redistribution of land and wealth that might make good post-apartheid promises. In light of the evidence of staggering government corruption during Jacob Zuma's presidency (2009–2018), this can sound expedient, but it is also not surprising given the continuing inequalities in South Africa. For instance, Statistics South Africa reports in 2019 that while inequality is slowly improving, the average real earnings of whites is more than three times that of black Africans,[3] and their asset scores remain the highest of all population groups.[4] Whites are in an uncomfortable position if they condemn the ills of apartheid, strive to live by values of equality and justice, and yet continue to benefit from its legacy; their self-respect and integrity is very much at stake. 'Being white' in South Africa, therefore, both marks a racial category and identity, as well as a position of economic and social privilege.

Finally, I focus on those white people who are both morally conscientious and concerned to lead a more than bearable life. That is, they are reflective and care about the injustices of their society, but also want a fulfilling life for themselves in which they can concentrate on personal commitments and special relationships. And I assume that they are at least reasonable in these desires.

So, recognising the ills of her society and the way she benefits from ongoing inequality, recognising her implication in injustice, but also wanting a personally good life, how can a white South African retain self-respect and integrity? I begin by offering rough working accounts of those virtues, drawing from many sources.

## Integrity and self-respect

Integrity and self-respect are clearly related notions and central to our conception of a morally admirable person. While I shall try to keep them distinct, it is somewhat artificial to do so.

## Integrity

Central to the notion of integrity is that of 'standing for something', as Cheshire Calhoun (1995) writes – instantiating our deeply held values in our behaviour, demeanour and, ideally, our inner life, and responding as they direct even in the face of temptation to do otherwise. We could add that it also requires standing up for something – defending our values and their expression in one's own behaviour and responses. Raimond Gaita (1981: 163) writes that the person of integrity 'stands fast in seriousness'; we can 'find him behind his words'. He will put his name to a position and is prepared to be identified with it, not subordinating his own judgment to others, nor to expediency, comfort, or gain (Calhoun 1995:238). In this way, integrity can confirm and protect identity.

Descriptions of integrity suggest *activity* and *response* (or their refusal) – the person of integrity does or says or thinks certain things (or refrains from them), and her integrity is tested and revealed in those activities (or refusals). It therefore includes sincerity, coherence between values, beliefs, and behaviour. However, given that nobody is perfect, it must be possible to show or partly regain integrity in the acknowledgement of faults and the effort to improve oneself. And given that we reasonably change our minds and develop our values, it must be compatible with moments of doubt, inner turmoil and conflict. Our notion of integrity must therefore be flexible, allowing for 'a kind of continual remaking of the self as well as a capacity to balance competing commitments and values and to take responsibility for one's work and thought' (Cox et al. 2003:41).

So far, I have described integrity formally: Someone has integrity if she stands by and for her commitments and principles, regardless of their content. This has three related ramifications: First, someone with integrity could 'stand for' non-moral values, like artistic or professional values. Second, as long as the relevant principles are significantly a person's own, they need not also be right; she could get things wrong, morally, and still have integrity (Calhoun 1995: 248). And third, a dedicated, strongly principled but morally odious person could also conceivably have integrity. There is no conclusive argument in favour of a substantial rather than a formal account, but we can point to integrity's role in our moral practices. It is usually a term of praise, and so some substantial conditions on the content of principles seems called for – we do not want to praise a fanatic Nazi (Cox et al. 2003: 69; McFall 1987: 9). It will also be difficult to stand for a commitment publicly if it is morally despicable, so as a matter of fact integrity regarding obnoxious commitments will probably not be common, even if it is possible. Here I will be concerned with morally acceptable values and principles, even if they are not themselves moral, and will remain neutral about whether integrity is essentially substantial.

## Self-respect

I characterised integrity in terms of activities or omissions. Respect is in the first instance a recognition of the nature and value of the object. In Kant's influential account, respect is the appropriate response to the special value of rational humanity; we all possess a '*dignity* (an absolute inner worth)' which demands respect for others and oneself: A person can therefore 'measure himself with every other being of this kind and value himself on a footing of equality with them' (Kant 1996 [1797], 6: 434–435). To lack *self*-respect is not to recognise one's actual worth, to act in ways contrary to that worth, or to subordinate one's worth to another person; the servile person, says Kant (1996 [1797], 6: 435), 'disavows' his dignity, and pursues his ends 'as if he were seeking a favour'.[5] Self-respect is thus the sense of oneself as entitled to represent and claim rights for oneself, to be an equal participant and interlocutor in a community of equals. It is therefore an essentially substantial notion.

Robin Dillon (1992) calls this Kantian conception *recognition* self-respect, and distinguishes it from two other kinds – *evaluative* and *basal* self-respect.[6] Evaluative self-respect 'involves an appreciation of one's earned worth, a positive appraisal of one's quality as a person in light of the standards given in one's self-ideal' (Dillon 1992: 134). It is still moral appraisal, and in that way contrasts with self-esteem, which need not involve moral evaluation, nor evaluation of a morally significant feature (see Dillon 2016). I could esteem myself for carrying off impossibly high heels, keeping to the tune, or achieving my personal best time. Although Dillon does not put it in this way, evaluative self-respect seems to involve and require integrity, for integrity is living up to those standards on which one's self-conception is grounded. Evaluative self-respect could then be the response to the recognition that one has shown integrity. Unlike recognition self-respect, it can be lost – if one really does fall below one's reasonable standards, one will justifiably lose the sense that one has earned further respect, even if one retains recognition self-respect of oneself as, simply, a person. Basal self-respect then underlies both recognition and evaluative self-respect; it 'involves an implicit confidence in the rightness of one's being', a fundamental security about one's worth that 'reverberates throughout one's self-experiences and life' (Dillon 2001: 68).

I will focus on recognition and evaluative self-respect in this chapter. Of these, recognition self-respect is the most fundamental, a deep sense of being decent, fundamentally valuable and an equal with others. Without it, as John Rawls (1973: 440) writes, 'nothing may seem worth doing'.[7] You may lose or damage your integrity and so want to hide from others, and yet you can continue acting in the world. Without self-respect, in contrast, there can be no overriding reason to continue at all.

## Private and social virtues

I take self-respect and integrity to be fundamentally personal, self-directed notions, but they do have a social dimension as well. That is, they involve your having a proper relation to yourself (recognition of your worth, commitment to your principles) and to others (being an equal among others, standing for something before others and thus being vulnerable to their opinion). Calhoun (1995: 252), however, does not think that integrity is a personal virtue at all, because it is threatened by 'our own vulnerability to other people'. Without the social dimension, it 'ultimately reduces to "standing *by*" the line that demarcates self from not-self' (1995: 253–254), so that '[a]cting without integrity undermines the boundaries of the self' and one's standing in relations to others drops out (1995: 254). I agree that integrity is a matter of standing for something as an equal before and within a moral community, yet I also think we should retain its personal dimension. If our core principles and commitments are partly constitutive of the self, then betraying them to the judgments of others is a way of dissolving the contours of the self; of losing what constitutes you as unique and gives your life its substance. As I argue later, maintaining a boundary is also a way of protecting self-respect, and demanding some basic respect from others. That said, it is important to remember that how we feel about ourselves – our self-relation – is also crucially dependent on how we believe others feel about us.

I now explore the effect that acknowledging racial privilege can have on these virtues. I will often speak in the first person, as this is a personally resonant exploration and pursued from my own (hopefully not too idiosyncratic) point of view.

## Privilege and the sense of self

Integrity requires that I act on my convictions, and self-respect will not countenance remaining in a morally compromised position. My recognition that I am implicated in racial injustice and that I am arbitrarily privileged puts pressure on self-respect, integrity, and the sincerity of my moral convictions. It seems clear that I am in many respects not the person I aspire to be, or perhaps thought I was. Once I take to heart these realisations, I will want to try to change what I can while retaining a positive enough self-conception to enable such work at all. So integrity and self-respect for a white South African like me seems to require 'taking to heart' uncomfortable truths. But what does it mean to 'take something to heart' and are there ethical limits to the process?

## Taking to heart

Generally, we say we 'take something to heart' only if it has personal significance for us and if it promises to change our beliefs, values or self-conception. Taking to heart is personal; it requires taking responsibility for the beliefs and values that are criticised or questioned, and for their implications. As I mentioned earlier, I can take ethical responsibility for something even if its metaphysical status is unclear – for my naturally gloomy temperament or the behaviour of my child or fellow citizens, or for the harm done in my name. In doing so, says Margaret Urban Walker, we can be expected 'to muster certain resources of character to meet the synergy of choice and fortune' (1991: 19), and in the process, temptations to 'self-deception, self-indulgence, and wishful thinking' will need to be overcome (1991: 20). This work is necessary, but it will not be easy to begin or sustain.

Jennifer Church (2002) argues that 'taking to heart' is a matter of how we use our beliefs. What she calls 'deep beliefs' 'operate unreflectively, automatically generating a wide range of thoughts, feelings, and behaviour (much of which I may be quite unaware)' (2002: 366). We need to add to this, however. While there will be cases where over time some belief has sunk deep and is altering or guiding our other mental states, we also speak of a *moment* or *experience* of taking something to heart in a more general sense, and we know how painful and disorienting this can be. Here, to take to heart is to appreciate the full significance of new information or criticism about ourselves – it 'strikes us', we say; our self-conception feels unstable or shifts abruptly; we are motivated to change ourselves as a result. Over time, the realisation may become deep, but in order for our acknowledgment and the changes it motivates to be possible, we must be aware of it, and it is unlikely that such awareness could easily dissipate, especially if it is taken up and used against what is unreflective and habitual.[8] This work will require vigilance and effort; it will probably be a long time before the changes and the original criticism that guide them could operate automatically. There is therefore a difference, I am suggesting, between 'taking to heart' in a practically relevant way, and the unreflective operations of Church's sense of 'taking to heart'. I will now look in more detail at how taking privilege to heart would affect our sense of self.

## Taking privilege to heart

Taking privilege to heart is a complex process, with aspects that do not always cohere, and with diverging implications for integrity and self-respect. It is important to bear in mind my assumption that we all have a reasonable desire to lead more than minimally bearable lives, to care for our loved ones, to pursue those interests that give our lives meaning. We cannot in good faith deny the importance of this partial dimension of our lives, and we are rational in wanting to protect it. This leads, however, to one dimension of the conflict that interests me: We must protect and stand for this part of our lives or risk our integrity and self-respect. And this means that we must focus a significant amount of attention *here*. Squandering our own talents and abilities or selling them cheaply; neglecting those we are responsible for or love; not pursuing a personally flourishing life – such neglect would undermine those virtues (Hill 1991; Kant 1996 [1797], 6 and 1998 [1785], 4: 430: 444–446; Williams 1973, 1981).

On the other hand, another dimension of the conflict cannot be ignored either: The fact that others' lives are as important to them as ours are to us (Nagel 1991) and that taking up an impartial perspective requires justice and opportunities for all the millions of others with whom we share our world. Many of those lives are already relatively deprived, especially in South Africa and other countries of the global south. Recognising that we – as white people – still hold a privileged position in South Africa calls on our sense of justice, and if we take our position to heart, integrity and self-respect are at stake here too, though in a different way.

Taking racial privilege to heart requires fully appreciating the meanings of whiteness, how it is embedded in social structures in ways that are often invisible to those of us who are white. It requires taking responsibility for that privilege and one's membership of a morally and politically problematic group. This is to accept that the negative meanings of white privilege apply to us, not only those who are crudely and obviously racist, and that privilege might make us into people we cannot approve of. In taking all of this to heart, we learn to see ourselves as those on the receiving end of the racial injustice associated with whiteness often see us, to see ourselves from the outside, as inescapably and most significantly members of groups with violent histories and symbolism. This external view might not cohere with how we think of ourselves, and so there are plenty of opportunities for self-deception and moral shirking. There might be a more-or-less plausible story to be told which would exempt us from straightforward causal responsibility, for example, and there will be a great temptation to accept it. Taking responsibility might then itself be a moral choice, which reveals or chooses a certain view of our place in a community, the significance of group membership, and our relation to others.

Recognition of whiteness now places us in the kind of moral space previously (and often still) occupied by those who are not white – that is, being in the wrong, not just doing wrong. We are *nothing but*, or *significantly nothing but* our skin colour in the eyes of many (Vice 2016). We know that we are perceived as a certain kind of person ('entitled', 'complacent', 'privileged', and 'wealthy') and might in fact *be* such a person – that is why it would be appropriate to feel shame (Vice 2010). It can feel like there is no 'gap' between our whiteness and our self. We *are* white, and that is all that matters. When we take up the external view, our being collapses into our whiteness, and this collapse, I suggest, leads to a more profound diminishment of integrity and self-respect. This is a collapse into moral inequality; we cannot act and converse as moral equals. Appraisal self-respect diminishes, because we have failed to display integrity, to be in the ways required by our avowed moral standards; recognition self-respect diminishes as we feel diminished amongst others. The basic sense of being a moral equal with others, in a moral community in which we are equal participants and interlocutors, is difficult to retain when we see ourselves as many others do. There is a sense in which we cannot meet others as equals if we take up their view completely, and we are lowered not only in our own eyes, but also in the eyes of those we must face.[9] While we might retain a theoretical belief in our equal Kantian worth to all others, it might be difficult for this belief to be practically operative.[10]

However, we are not in the position by choice and cannot change it by an act of will. Because racialised injustice is not only a result of individual actions, but embedded in the nature of our institutions and social structures, our moral position is unstable. On the one hand, we find ourselves positioned in structures we do not fully approve, even as we undeniably benefit from them. This seems to take some responsibility out of our hands and thus enables the maintenance of some self-respect and integrity. As long as society remains structured in the way it is now, we can only with immense and collective effort rid ourselves of privilege. We may repudiate the security or financial comfort of being middle-class or white, or give up some worldly goods, but we will still fit into certain settings, be accepted as 'one of us', or have authority in certain situations. But at the same time, privilege inclines us to be a certain sort of person, which we also cannot condone and to which we cannot be indifferent. We must take responsibility for who we are; repudiating responsibility for what we have no control over, or what did not originate from a choice, will remove most of ourselves from our responsibility. That would amount to seeing ourselves not as agents but as passive recipients of influences – not, that is, as persons at all (Nagel 1979). Within this complicated and seemingly endless dialectic between personal responsibility and structural constraints, it is difficult to settle on any view of ourselves.[11]

So integrity in one mode – the maintenance of our moral principles – will demand that we take the criticisms of the deprived and denigrated to heart and recognise the deep, constitutive failings in our relations with others. It will reveal just how far we are from the standards we set for ourselves (appraisal self-respect) and the principles we thought we avowed (integrity). However, taking privilege to heart might require us to give less weight to our personal commitments and projects, diminishing integrity within that realm of life. It will also diminish recognition self-respect as our sense of moral equality is diminished. Typically, self-respect and integrity work together, and typically in one direction: A person will lose self-respect if she acts in ways that damage her integrity; she will gain self-respect if she responds with integrity. Integrity can therefore affect self-respect, and self-respect can help us to act with integrity. Here, however, they can come apart, a problem when in the most literal sense I have to *live with myself*, a phrase associated both with integrity and self-respect. If these values can pull in different directions in this context, then I may not be able to 'live with myself' in either case.

Taking privilege to heart will therefore certainly be uncomfortable, and can lead to potentially corrosive moral emotions like self-contempt, shame, or hopelessness (Hook 2011). Even if one thinks these are a fair price for the privileged to pay, or that they can be morally helpful (Vice 2010), there are further moral dangers which are worth taking seriously. One is the general moral problem of being reduced practically to one trait, which does damage to the particularity of persons and which is precisely one of the mechanisms and costs of prejudice. Whether this reduction is intentionally imposed by others or by oneself in light of their judgement, it involves a 'masking of individuality', as Lawrence Blum (2005: 271) writes. Stereotyping, he says, 'involves seeing individual members through a narrow and rigid lens of group-based image, rather than being alive to the range of characteristics constituting each member as a distinct individual' (p. 271). The reduction of a white South African to privilege, even if she does it to herself, is a reduction to group identity and denial of ethically significant individuality. While this reduction is in no way equivalent to the harm done to black South Africans by racial stereotypes, and while it is a reaction to an already unjust situation, we may still admit that it is an ethically problematic phenomenon.

Another danger is suggested by Kant's (1996 [1797], 6: 449) remark that the principle of respect for each other 'admonishes' us to keep ourselves 'at a distance from one another'. Taking many liberties with this idea, I suggest that the collapse of the self into its worst aspect can be experienced as a too intimate and presumptuous closeness: First, of other people to yourself; second, of yourself to those personal aspects you have with difficulty learnt to see as vicious. You may acknowledge the justice in being identified with your racial group, while finding it objectionable to be exhausted by the label. Again, it is the structural aspect of the injustice in which white South Africans are implicated that renders our position more complex – we are not only, or not simply, morally compromised in a way that makes ascriptions of responsibility obvious. A healthy relation to the self seems, therefore, to require that we maintain a boundary between our personal conception of ourselves, and the identity that characterises us in our public relations with others.[12]

Besides these difficult personal consequences, there are troubling social and political con-sequences. First, constructive conversation is only possible when interlocutors consider themselves to be equals, and this is impossible for those without self-respect. Not being able with integrity and self-respect to trust one's judgment and stand up for one's beliefs before others, makes respectful conversation and effort difficult. Without faith in the other's charitable spirit, the hard work of building something together is impossible. If we know that our fellows ignore all our qualities besides privilege, and if we see those others only as critics, a shared and good-willed effort to improve our overlapping world becomes more difficult. (Again, the parallel with apartheid attitudes is instructive.)

A second consequence is suggested by Rawls (1973). Self-respect, he says, has two aspects: First, 'a person's sense of his own value, his secure conviction that his conception of his good, his plan of life, is worth carrying out' (1973: 440). Second, it implies a confidence that one will be able to carry out one's intentions and plan of life:

> When we feel that our plans are of little value, we cannot pursue them with pleasure or take delight in their execution. Nor plagued by failure and self-doubt can we continue in our endeavours. ... Without [self-respect] ... nothing may seem worth doing, or if some things have value for us, we lack the will to strive for them. All desire and activity becomes empty and vain, and we sink into apathy and cynicism.
>
> (Rawls 1973: 440)

Taking privilege deeply to heart can equally lead to corrosive apathy, cynicism or self-contempt, making it difficult to lead a fulfilling life and to contribute to efforts to rebuild society.

If we value integrity and self-respect, and consider them to be constituents of an admirable character, we are left with a problem. When we are privileged in conditions of structural injustice, integrity and self-respect seem to require that we take to heart our morally dubious situation; however, we are in certain respects morally damaged by just that process. The de-mands on integrity and self-respect are demands issuing both from the situation and ourselves. That is, taking to heart is required and justified by the facts of injustice and the perverse influence of privilege on our characters. Morality demands that we act to change this, and for the morally conscientious, the demands of morality are also the demands of their integrity and self-respect. If this is correct, then being in the right is hardly possible in this situation.

Some might say that this is how it should be, and the privileged must learn to live with an unliveable self and, as a minority in South Africa, an often precarious and violently resented presence. But if privilege is structural and remains even after our best efforts to change ourselves, and if our desires to sustain and develop the personal dimension of our lives is reasonable, this strikes me as too glib. The problems are not all of our own making, the responsibility is also political and dispersed; we are positioned in privilege and do not only position ourselves. The morally conscientious person should be able to live with herself, even if uncomfortably and critically.

## Conclusion

What should we conclude about taking privilege to heart, given these personal and social moral dangers? If we think that integrity and self-respect are essential for healthy moral agency and personality, and that ongoing work to improve ourselves requires them, then doing what we should do – taking privilege to heart – must, it seems, meet a limit. Whether this means that we should not take it to heart at all, or weaken the process in some way, or stop its progress at some point, I do not yet know. What seems clear, and yet perverse, is that doing what we think we ought to do – taking our privilege and everything it means to heart – potentially leaves us where we ought not, for other reasons, to be either.

In conclusion, what is the status of these reflections? There is nothing inevitable about the broadly Kantian moral framework I depend on, and I cannot defend it here, except indirectly by showing its value in explaining the phenomenon that interests me. I have argued that while self-respect and integrity are conceptually and normatively concerned with our relation to ourselves, that relation is crucially dependent on how we perceive ourselves to be perceived. Others, however, would offer a more strongly relational framework that might emphasise the positive relations on which a society depends (communality and solidarity, relations of care and emotional inter-dependence – Metz 2013), or the negative relations which might undermine them (power, potential violence, and oppression – Young 1990). My approach is perhaps more pessimistic than the former and more optimistic than the latter.

Finally, I have spoken in the first person, singular and plural, and to many that will be an unbearable imposition – how can I speak for all white South Africans and say what will, or ought to, happen in the mind of each person? This is a real question, to which I can respond only by saying that I am interested in exploring 'taking to heart' as I have experienced it, that is, exploring what seems to me to occur quite properly when we take white privilege to heart and when we follow through the logic of self-respect and integrity. I assume that I am not unlike many South Africans who think about their roles in racial injustice, although we may use different terms and frameworks. But the tentative conclusions I reach have much broader implications for our understanding of those self-directed values in times of systematic injustice, and the risks of taking that injustice seriously to heart. These risks might be justified, but they should concern us because they put at risk the very virtues of character that allow us to undertake the journey towards this knowledge.[13]

## Notes

1 Racial terminology is a controversial matter. Unless indicated, I use 'white' and 'black' in the inclusive sense familiar in South Africa, to pick out those groups that were benefitted and oppressed by the apartheid regime. Both groups therefore include identities that in other contexts would be importantly distinct.

2 I put aside the debate about whether both strictly count as virtues; for a survey of the issues, see Cox et al. (2003: Ch. 2).

3 Statistics South Africa (2019: 146). Here, 'black African' does not include coloureds, Indians and Asians, groups that Stats SA continues to recognise.

4 Statistics South Africa Stats SA (2019: 51). Here, 'black African' does not include coloureds, Indians and Asians, groups that Stats SA continues to recognise.

5 And see the essays in Hill (1991) for a Kantian account of self-respect and servility.

6 She draws on Darwall (1977).

7 Rawls (1973) calls self-respect the most important of the primary social goods, and a value which a just society will foster.

8 Church allows that we may take something to heart gradually or suddenly; something may take time to sink in, or 'hit home' with a sudden force (2002: 367). But these descriptions sit uncomfortably with the unreflective and automatic work that such beliefs then play.

9 Basal self-respect may remain relatively unscathed through the process of taking to heart if it developed sturdily enough in childhood.

10 I set aside the tricky question of whether those whose critical views positions the privileged in these morally problematic ways are blameworthy in doing so. Perhaps there are more or less virtuous ways of behaving *qua* oppressed, or *qua* disadvantaged. See Hay (2011).

11 See Bailey (1999) and Blum (2011) for alternative explorations of how to respond to one's racial privilege.

12 Although this thought takes us to tricky territory, there may be something disrespectful in relating to people in such a way that they cannot but lose self-respect – again, a familiar point after centuries of oppressing others.

13 My thanks to the editors for their helpful comments, and to Vida Yao, who insightfully commented on an earlier version of this chapter.

## References

Bailey, A. 1999. Despising an Identity They Taught Me to Claim. In *Whiteness: Feminist Philosophical Reflections*, ed. C. J. Cuomo and K. Q. Hall, pp. 85–107. Rowman and Littlefield.

Blum, L. 2005. Stereotypes and Stereotyping: A Moral Analysis. *Philosophical Papers*, 33 (3): 251–289.

Blum, L. 2011. Anti-Racist Moral Identities, or Iris Murdoch in South Africa. *South African Journal of Philosophy*, 30 (4): 440–451.

Calhoun, C. 1995. Standing for Something. *The Journal of Philosophy*, 92 (5): 235–260.

Card, C. 1996. *The Unnatural Lottery: Character and Moral Luck*. Philadelphia: Temple University Press.

Church, J. 2002. Taking it to Heart: What Choice Do We Have? *The Monist*, 85 (3): 361–380.

Cox, D. et al. 2003. *Integrity and the Fragile Self*. Aldershot: Ashgate.

Darwall, S. 1977. Two Kinds of Respect. *Ethics*, 88: 36–49.

Dillon, R. S. 1992. How to Lose Your Self-Respect. *American Philosophical Quarterly*, 29 (2): 125–139.

Dillon, R. S. 2001. Self-Forgiveness and Self-Respect. *Ethics*, 112 (1), 53–83.

Dillon, R. S. 2016. Respect. In The Stanford Encyclopedia of Philosophy, ed. E. N. Zalta [online], viewed 10 March 2020, https://plato.stanford.edu/archives/win2016/entries/respect/.

Gaita, R. 1981. Integrity. *Proceedings of the Aristotelian Society*, 55: 161–176.

Hay, C. 2011. The Obligation to Resist Oppression. *Journal of Social Philosophy*, 42 (1): 21–45.

Hill Jr., T. E. 1991. *Autonomy and Self-Respect*. Cambridge: Cambridge University Press.

Hook, D. 2011. White Privilege, Psychoanalytic Ethics, and the Limitations of Political Silence. *South African Journal of Philosophy*, 30 (4): 494–501.

Kant, I. 1996 [1797]. *The Metaphysics of Morals*, tr. and ed. M. Gregor. Cambridge: Cambridge University Press.

Kant, I. 1998 [1785]. *Groundwork of the Metaphysics of Morals*, tr. and ed. M. Gregor. Cambridge: Cambridge University Press.

McFall, L. 1987. Integrity. *Ethics*, 98 (1): 5–20.

Metz, T. 2013. The Western Ethic of Care, or an Afro-Communitarian Ethic? Specifying the Right Relational Morality. *Journal of Global Ethics*, 9 (1): 77–92.

Nagel, T. 1979. *Mortal Questions*. Cambridge University Press.

Nagel, T. 1991. *Equality and Partiality*. Oxford University Press.

Rawls, J. 1973. *A Theory of Justice*. Oxford University Press.

Statistics South Africa (Stats SA). 2019. *Inequality Trends in South Africa*. Pretoria: Statistics South Africa, available at https://www.afd.fr/en/ressources/inequality-trends-south-africa-multidimensional-diagnostic-inequality.

Sullivan, S. 2006. *Revealing Whiteness: The Unconscious Habits of Racial Privilege*. Bloomington and Indianapolis: Indiana University Press.

Vice, S. 2010. How Do I Live in this Strange Place? *Journal of Social Philosophy*, 41 (3): 323–342.

Vice, S. 2016. Essentialising Rhetoric and Work on the Self. *Philosophical Papers*, 45 (1–2): 103–131.

Vice, S. 2019. Impartiality, Partiality and Privilege. The View from South Africa. In *Debating African Philosophy*, ed. G. Hull, pp. 130–145. London and New York: Routledge.

Walker, M. U. 1991. Moral Luck and the Virtues of Impure Agency. *Metaphilosophy* 22 (1–2): 14–27.

Williams, B. 1973. A Critique of Utilitarianism. In *Utilitarianism: For and Against,* ed. B. Williams and J. J. C. Smart, pp. 77–155. Cambridge University Press.

Young, I. M. 1990. *Justice and the Politics of Difference*. Princeton University Press.

Young, I. M. 2003. 'Political Responsibility and Structural Injustice,' Lindley Lecture, 5 May, [online], viewed 10 April 2020, http://www.bc.edu/content/dam/files/schools/cas_sites/sociology/pdf/PoliticalResponsibility.pdf.

# 27

# Whiteness as resistance: The intersectionality of the 'Alt-Right'

*Phillip W. Gray*

Is it okay to be white? At first, this seems an odd question, but the responses to this question, and the uses of it, provide insight into how whiteness operates for the 'Alt-Right'. This chapter begins with the constructed nature of the 'Alt-Right': in effect, the 'Alt-Right' is a useful catch-all term for a new tendency within Rightist political thought, but one that contains a substantial level of contestation on meaning and boundaries. This chapter then turns to the self-definition of 'whiteness' within the 'Alt-Right:' 'whiteness' is contested while also acting as a form of 'Ur' oppression, on which the other potential coalition members in the 'Alt-Right' frame their own views and movements. The next section illustrates the central importance of resistance in defining 'White'[1] for the 'Alt-Right'. In particular, the 'Alt-Right' views itself as resisting against neoliberal and progressive narratives that define 'White' as simultaneously a null category as well as inherently negative/evil. This chapter concludes with some thoughts on the possibility of white identitarianism becoming more mainstream.

## The ambiguous nature of the 'Alt-Right'

The 'Alt-Right' is a term of convenience, as defining it is a challenge (Gray and Jordan 2018). The origin of the term is usually attributed to Richard Spencer (Hawley 2017: 51–58; and see Johnson 2018a: 4–5), while other writers/groups labelled as 'Alt-Right' have preferred terms such as 'New Right', or 'Dissident Right'. Although these different labels may reflect a desire for separate 'branding' or to distinguish themselves from Spencer, these different terms also indicate variations in ideology and prioritisation. As a clear ideological tendency/movement with a major organisational 'spine' connecting disparate groups, the 'Alt-Right' does not exist, and the term within popular language is an artificial construct. Many of those called 'Alt-Right' have discarded the label (such as Greg Johnson of Counter-Current Publications) or never accepted it at all (for instance, many of the writers at VDARE): in practice, the moniker 'Alt-Right' exists now more as a weaponised label used by opponents to accuse others of extremism.[2] However, this term is useful for identifying a form of Rightist political thought/action that does not 'fit' within other areas associated with the contemporary political Right or with earlier forms of extremist Right politics, such as the Axis Powers or explicitly white supremacist writers/organisations like William L. Pierce and the National Alliance.[3]

DOI: 10.4324/9780429355769-27

As long as this new form is understood as developing within contested boundaries, we can use 'Alt-Right' as a descriptive term for understanding this constellation of ideas and organisations. For this chapter, the 'Alt-Right' will be construed broadly to include groups/ideas/thinkers who may overlap or be adjacent to the 'core' Alt-Right without necessarily being a part of it in an organisational or self-identified sense (comparable with the instrumental notion of coalitions in Collins 2000: 38). What types of ideologies/groups are included is best summarised by Greg Johnson, writing about his initial hopes for the 'Alt-Right', which would include '… race realism, White Nationalism, the European New Right, the Conservative Revolution, Traditionalism, neo-paganism, agrarianism, Third Positionism, anti-feminism, and Right-wing anti-capitalists, ecologists, bioregionalists, and small-is-beautiful types …' (quoted in Johnson 2018a: 8). This eclectic mix of worldviews/interests illustrates the developing nature of the 'Alt-Right', as well as its internal diversity on many points. The constructed use of 'Alt-Right' in this chapter will be broader: it will also include those individuals/organisations that evince particular concern about White identity, White populations, or White racial consciousness. Under this broader construal, groups such as VDARE and individuals such as Pat Buchanan, Peter Brimelow, and perhaps Steve Sailor[4] would be 'Alt-Right' (noting that most of these individuals/groups have explicitly rejected the 'Alt-Right' label, and many would adamantly and sincerely reject the idea that they are white identitarians).

Finally, this chapter focuses on the 'strong case' of the 'Alt-Right': specifically, the individuals/groups analysed present the most articulate views of this movement. As with most movements, no doubt there is a substantial difference in sophistication between the 'strong case' advocates and rank-and-file members. I focus on the 'strong case' for two reasons. First, investigations of the 'Alt-Right' – and of white identity politics in general – often exhibit a type of 'discount psychoanalysis' in their examinations of these movements. Rather than seeking to analyse these movements/ideas as their members themselves understand them, there is too frequently a tendency to dismiss these views merely as 'fear' of 'losing power', primitive thinking, or simple 'white fragility' (DiAngelo 2018). While this style of discourse may provide a sense of intellectual/emotional superiority among its speakers, it is less than enlightening in understanding what these movements actually believe. Rather than seeking to understand these ideological forms as a complex of ideas, motivations, and structures, these simplistic (and in some ways 'therapeutic') methods used by various 'antiracist' authors merely reaffirm their own assumptions and prejudices, leading to a problematic feedback loop that prevents critical analysis of both the 'Alt-Right' as well as one's own theories. Within the American context of the 'culture wars', this form of psychologising ideological differences is highly detrimental: one is less inclined to engage in forms of 'training' that *a priori* dictate that one's ideological views reflect an 'unconscious' will-to-dominate or are merely mental disturbances pretending to be ideas. Second, by investigating the strongest arguments presented by this ideological tendency, one is in a better position to combat it: as these ideas 'seep down' to the broader movement, understanding these ideas at their most sophisticated provides a better means to contest them.

## 'White', ethnonationalism, and bioculture

What does 'White' mean for the 'Alt-Right'? We start by noting what it is not. The 'Alt-Right' notion of whiteness diverges from earlier, explicitly supremacist forms in two ways. First, 'White' is less narrow among the 'Alt-Right' than for earlier racialists. For Nazi theorists, and even later racialist vanguardists such as Pierce, focused on 'pure' White populations, generally identified as Nordic and/or Aryan, contrasted with less 'pure' forms (such as 'Alpine' or 'Mediterranean' types). While the concentration on 'purity' can still exist, there is substantially less emphasis about White 'purity' than in the distinction between White and non-White. For much of the European 'Alt-Right', the specific 'ethnos' of a population (Flemish, English, Finnish, and so forth) holds a more fundamental position than 'White', but 'White' also serves as a general 'grouping' for Western ethnic groups. For the 'Alt-Right' in America, these ethnic connotations may exist, but often instead view White Americans as a specific 'ethnos' itself (or possibly multiple White 'peoples'). Second, the 'Alt-Right' tends to be white nationalist/separatist in its view of whiteness, rather than supremacist. For many analysts – and certainly in popular usage – 'nationalism' and 'supremacy' are distinctions without a difference, but this is erroneous. Most of the contemporary 'Alt-Right' is nationalist/separatist in nature, focusing on maintaining White populations/norms. In contrast to earlier forms of White identity (such as that of Nazi Germany), there is little desire for rule over other racialised populations: the main focus is on being *away* from other populations, not *dominating* them. Separation of races into their own racially homogenous enclaves, rather than a White imperialist control over People of Color (POC) populations, is generally a common aim. In this view, true diversity exists when 'peoples' (defined along racial, ethnic, and 'biocultural' lines) are free to organise their own societies, in contrast to multiethnic societies (viewed as inherently conflictual) or to a more 'globalised' and 'cosmopolitan' society (viewed as creating a stultifying standardisation, beneficial only to well-connected elites and large corporations).

One must distinguish between 'supremacy' and 'preference for one's own'. Put simply: the Alt-Right generally does not desire White hegemony over races; rather, it seeks separation of races into their own homogenous states, primarily as a means of protecting Whites. On the one hand, the 'Alt-Right' is, for the most part, not 'white supremacist', as it does not seek universal dominance by Whites and often advocates for forms of racial/ethnic self-determination for groups that are not White, such as Palestinians (for instance, see Johnson 2013: 108–115). In contrast to explicit white supremacists who advocated for the extermination of other racial groups, most 'Alt-Right' thinkers desire separation, with races living in their own homogenous communities rather than intermixed within one, multiracial state. Often, this translates as a type of 'ethnonationalism for everyone', with Japan offered as a positive example of such an ethnostate. Much of this non-supremacy arises from the broader movement's own theories. 'White' is not viewed as universal, but particular, just as with other races and ethnicities. In this perspective, all races should be able to arrange their societies as they see fit: but this applies for Whites in their own 'homelands' as well. Without such homogenous societies, this perspective believes Whites in particular are threatened with elimination, with the increased risks to Boer populations in post-apartheid South Africa seen as a cautionary example of the dangers for White minority populations in multiracial states (see Mercer 2011; Nowicki 2016). Operating under the belief that evolutionary adaptions in the 'biocultural' foundations of races/ethnicities shape the forms of social organisation that best 'fit' for any given racial/ethnic group, the 'Alt-Right' believes that a multiethnic society must necessarily lead to conflict, as the foundational bases for 'correct' organisation are fundamentally different between racial/ethnic groups. For Michael Levin, declaring a specific form of social organisation as universally 'better' is meaningless among races: evolutionary differences developing from millennia of separation between races means there is no racial 'Archimedean point' from which a universal standard can arise. Rather, forms of social organisation can only be judged as 'better' or 'worse' for specific racial populations (Levin 2005, p. 161–189): as such, social/political structures that operate effectively among Whites will be oppressive to other populations (and similarly, effective social/political structures among those of African ancestry would likewise be oppressive for White populations). One sees similar notions in the emphasis on 'genetic similarity theory' in Jared Taylor's writing (2011), with genetic similarity serving as a major foundation for 'ethnostates' by individuals such as Greg Johnson (2019: 27–30). This 'Alt-Right' view of ethnonationalism for all is a type of mirror reflection of collective, group-focused concerns for justice in some elements of intersectionality and critical theory, where 'What makes critical theory 'critical' is its commitment to justice, *for one's own group and for other groups*' (emphasis added) (Collins 2000: 31). However, it is clear that much of the 'Alt-Right' does believe in some type of superiority among Whites, at least on some measures, such as average group intelligence (although here, most also acknowledge the higher average group intelligence of North Asians and Ashkenazi Jews to White populations: see Lynn 2015: 150–152, 192–198; MacDonald 2002: 33–34). This is framed as a fundamental 'preference for one's own': that the behaviours, norms, and customs of one's own population are viewed as better for one's own population (similar to viewing one's neighbourhood traditions as better, because it is one's *own* neighbourhood): 'White Americans must once again believe in themselves and assert their own consciousness as a people, which is not the case now' (Auster 2019: 215). This is a preference, viewed as biologically (or bio-culturally) hard-wired within all populations, to prefer what is 'ours' to what is not. As Dutton explains, '...in-group preference and out-group negativity are useful because genes can be passed on not only from parents to offspring but also via kin. Accordingly, kin-preference will increase one's "inclusive fitness"' (Dutton 2019: 80–81).[5] In this perspective, the 'Alt-Right' is 'supremacist', but in a manner that all races/ethnicities are 'supremacist' about their own group.

What 'whiteness' means for the Alt-Right is contested. As a marker of identity, 'White' maintains priority over other identity traits; but the specific nature of 'whiteness' can vary. There is a general notion that 'White' entails a 'biocultural' (O'Meara 2013) connection within the specific population. 'Biocultural' denotes a connection between genetic/biological traits and cultural traits, with biology playing a significant role in cultural development (and similarly, that culture can have a 'feedback' function on what traits are 'selected' over generations within a population). The stringency of this biological/cultural connection varies within the 'Alt-Right'. For European schools of thought – such as the French 'New Right' of *Groupement de Recherches et d'Études pour la Civilisation Européene* as well as various identitarian movements, including *Génération Identitaire*[6] – there is a broad notion of a connection between biology and culture, but they focus more specifically upon ethnic divisions and cultural norms as part of a broader 'ethnos' (or 'people') rather than delving deeply into biology (see Willinger 2014). For these strands of the 'Alt-Right', 'White' is a general term for European populations and their homelands, which includes the various 'peoples' within Europe.

For American strands of the 'Alt-Right', biology plays a much larger role. This focus likely reflects the historical differences between Europe and North America.[7] While overlapping with the European strands' notion of 'bioculture', the American strands focus more on the under-lying genetics (and evolutionary psychology) of group racial differences and of White identity. Under this view, the millennia of separation between races, adapting to substantially different environments, created evolutionary differences in discrete populations, which include differ-ences in intelligence, time preference and impulse control (resulting in emotionality and hy-persexuality), rule-following, and child-rearing, susceptibility to certain types of illnesses, compatibility of blood plasma, and so forth (see Jensen 1998; Rushton 2000). Statements that racial differences are only 'skin deep' or social constructions are viewed as highly unscientific and a form of 'cognitive creationism'. Connected to this focus on genetics is the importance of evolutionary psychology. The works of Kevin MacDonald (2002) and others provide key examples, noting that White group survival strategies operate differently than methods of other races, with White populations being less ethnocentric and group-oriented than other groups. For the 'Alt-Right', this comparative *lack* of racial ethnocentrism and collectivism is the central problem facing Whites: as White populations tend to be more individualistic and less inclined towards racial collectivism (although some on the 'Alt-Right' argue these traits are the result of Christianity's negative influence rather than reflecting fundamental elements of White/European bioculture), Whites are at a substantial disadvantage for group survival against more racially-aware, collectivist groups.

For American strands of the 'Alt-Right', a major differentiating feature between Whites and other racial groups is that the former are less collectivist, less ethnocentric, and more focused on reciprocity than the latter: 'The common thread is an abiding sense of reciprocity, a conviction that others have rights that must be respected. This conviction, which can be described as a kind of public morality, is at the heart of the institutions that are common to most white societies and absent from most non-white ones: democracy, free speech, and the rule of law' (Taylor 2017: 15). While these traits might at first appear positive, this American strand emphasises that these very traits now undermine White survival, as a form of 'pathological altruism': the proclivity of Whites to distance themselves from their own racial group interests becomes self-destructive when other racial populations are fully willing to use these rules for their own collective, racial group interests. Reciprocity, rule-following, and free speech, in this view, depend on a population capable of elevating the interests of its individual members above its racial collective interests: from the 'Alt-Right' perspective, this proclivity is lacking in POC populations. While mainstream conservatives (sometimes called 'Conservativism Inc.': Kirkpatrick 2019) tend to view institutions like the free market, democracy, and free inquiry as universal human traits, the 'Alt-Right' views these traits as highly particular to specific ethnic populations. The failure of conservatism, in this view, is in universalising rules/principles that are instead racially/ethnically particular.

Along similar lines, globalised neoliberalism itself (a system sometimes referred to as 'GloboHomo') is viewed as inherently anti-White. For the 'Alt-Right', globalised neoliberalism homogenises, destroying the diversity of cultures generally (and White culture specifically) in a morass of lowest-common-denominator consumerism and libertinism. The Alt-Right views neoliberalism as benefiting a narrow range of 'globalists' while substantially harming grounded, concrete communities: to increase profits/control, elites encourage offshoring of work from Western countries to cheaper areas in the developing world, while simultaneously pushing for significant levels of immigration into White countries (both to depress labour prices while also undermining labour solidarity through ethnic division). This concurrent undermining of Whites (through the export of jobs) with substantial immigration (the importation of non-White populations) leads to the view of 'the Great Replacement' (see Camus 2018) within 'Alt-Right' circles. As such, a major defining element of 'White' for the 'Alt-Right' is resistance.

## Whiteness as resistance

Many White identitarians avoid giving a specific list of traits for Whites, beyond some broad categorisations. This avoidance may reflect differences between 'Alt-Right' thinkers (for instance, Taylor tends to be more individualist and more free market-oriented in comparison to Johnson), as well as seeking to avoid infighting typical of earlier white identitarians. Taylor emphasises the rule of law, individualism, and reciprocity, while Johnson focuses on more collectivist traits (see Johnson 2015). But currently, a major defining and unifying trait of 'White' is resistance: resistance to the decrease in White populations (especially through immigration), resistance to a perceived 'degrading' of White culture (against the view that White culture is non-existent or purely negative), and resistance to what is understood as the removal of White norms from predominantly White countries (including Europe, the United States,

Canada, Australia, and New Zealand) (see Willinger 2013: 17). For the 'Alt-Right', anti-White activities/patterns in predominantly White societies lead to inevitable 'white genocide' (see Johnson 2018b). While the language appears extreme, the 'Alt-Right' justifies this language by making comparisons: imagine these same demographic/cultural practices occurring in a non-White society, being committed by Whites (for instance extensive White immigration into Saudi Arabia or Guatemala, with demands that the dominant culture 'transform' to accept the newcomers, re-interpret its past based on White minority experience, change its norms for White minority populations, and permit extensive White immigration that would lead to the native population becoming a minority ethnicity: see Houck 2018: 285, 342). Were these practices occurring elsewhere, so the argument goes, the 'genocide' label would be used by the same people who dismiss its usage by White populations. That other countries are not committing 'ethnosuicide' (see Krebs 2012) – and that there is no demand for them to do so – reflects, to the 'Alt-Right', that the drive for multiethnic societies is not from a desire for 'diversity', but rather from an inherently anti-White animus.

In various ways, the contemporary 'Alt-Right' is similar to what perhaps could be called the 'preliminary' stage of intersectionality, where one can locate '"intersectionality-like" thinking' (Hancock 2016: 79) but without an overarching unified discourse yet formulated (see Gray 2018). While the intersectional 'social locations' of oppression play an increasing role in discussions, the current state of the 'Alt-Right' is closer to the period of various marginalised groups seeking coalitions while simultaneously encountering internal divisions. In the case of intersectionality, the 'Ur' example of oppression at this earlier juncture (within the United States) was that of the Black woman; for the contemporary 'Alt-Right', this exemplar role is filled by the White man. In both cases, many other populations are also engaged, but the underlying discourse/ideology is guided and shaped by these exemplar models. For intersectionality, Black feminist thought – informed by certain strands of critical theory – served as the paradigm discourse, while the 'Alt-Right' instead often relies upon elements of the German 'conservative revolution', evolutionary psychology, and/or genetics research as the paradigm discourse.

Psychology plays a particular role both for some intersectional as well as some 'Alt-Right' thinkers, but the similarity does not appear significant: while intersectional thinkers rely more on studies focused on implicit bias and stereotype threat, 'Alt-Right' writers primarily look to research on intelligence, evolutionary psychology, and the role of genetics on human cognition. In theoretical analysis, however, the overlap in influences between the 'Alt-Right' and some elements of intersectionality (or perhaps, in the genealogy of intersectionality's development) can be noticed. In terms of direct appropriation, various 'Alt-Right' authors (such as Johnson and De. Benoist) have explicitly made use of Antonio Gramsci's concepts, such as 'hegemony' and 'meta-politics'. For these authors, Gramsci's prioritisation of culture as a necessary means of raising consciousness and gaining power is tactically sound and a model to follow. In their view, the expansion of 'Cultural Marxism'[8] reveals Gramsci's insights, as the 'long march through the institutions' revolutionised the West gradually rather than through an explicit, militant use of power. Other influences on the 'Alt-Right' are not appropriations from the Left, *per se*: instead, both ideological tendencies gain insights from the same authors, but with significantly different interpretations. Friedrich Nietzsche provides a good example: an anti-foundationalist rebelling against the logocentric nature of modernity and emphasising the aesthetic, the non-rational, and the linguistic, Nietzsche plays a significant role in the development of both intersectional and 'Alt-Right' ideational systems. However, while intersectionality focuses on the agonistic elements of Nietzsche, the 'Alt-Right' makes use of his anti-egalitarian perspectives. These differences become clearer with the importance of the German 'conservative revolution' (see Mohler and Weissmann 2018) – referring to a collection of Rightist German thinkers and authors in the interwar period – on the 'Alt-Right'.

Among these 'revolutionaries' that influence the 'Alt-Right', some have little to no influence on intersectionality, such as Oswald Spengler and Ernst Jünger. Other authors in this 'revolution', however, have influenced both tendencies: Martin Heidegger and Carl Schmitt. As with Nietzsche, the implications drawn from these two thinkers vary substantially between intersectional and 'Alt-Right' authors, although both tend to emphasise the importance of going outside of *Logos*-centric paradigms, the dangers of neoliberalism and the technologicalisation of life, and the ongoing relevance of 'states of emergency' and 'exceptions' in the globalised world. These shared influences also result in some shared concerns (and shared enemies): much of the 'Alt-Right' stands in vehement opposition to neoliberalism. The 'Alt-Right' stance against globalism shares many similarities with intersectional criticisms: the main difference is that the 'Alt-Right' believes that the group most in danger of seeing its population eliminated (culturally and potentially physically) by neoliberalism is White populations.

A unifying element for most of the 'Alt-Right' is resistance against the dominant framing of 'White' in popular culture, academic research, and other powerful institutions of society. From their perspective, the elite hegemonic (in a Gramscian sense) culture presents 'White' in two uncomplimentary contradictory ways: in Nell Irvin Painter's words, 'Whiteness is on a toggle switch between bland nothingness and racist hatred' (quoted in Houck 2018: 183). First, 'White' is presented as a null set: there is no 'White' culture of any worth, but instead merely an insipid group of practices that mimics a culture. While the hegemonic, elite culture (including mass media, academia, major corporations, government, and others) can present positive instances of 'Black' or 'indigenous' cultures without difficulty, the descriptor 'White' is singular in being hollow and empty. 'White' entails 'bland' and 'dull'. Among the limited number of potential positive aspects of what could be called 'White' culture, these elements are usually accused of appropriation: that a 'White' cultural norm/custom was 'stolen' from another population, directly or indirectly.

This notion of appropriation leads to a second frame within the hegemonic culture: 'White' as evil. Where 'White' does provide meaning, it is solely negative: 'whiteness' means oppression, colonialism, imperialism, genocide, neoliberalism, and homogenisation. 'White' becomes the negative other – a singular encompassing entity on which all negative traits are assigned. In general, the 'Alt-Right' would take a similar perspective as Collins that '[m]aintaining images of US Black women as the other provides ideological justification for race, gender, and class oppression. Certain basic ideas crosscut these and other forms of oppression' (Collins 2000: 70), but would maintain that it is the US White man who is now configured as the Other, with the crosscutting forms of oppression arising in this combination. 'Critical Whiteness Studies' itself would be an example for the 'Alt-Right' of this second frame: the 'whiteness' examined has few to no positive traits, where '[w]hiteness is a sociohistorical form of consciousness, given birth at the nexus of capitalism, colonial rule, and the emergent relationships among dominant and subordinate groups' (McLaren 1998: 66), with this area of study primarily focused on purging those negative elements of 'whiteness' that pervade the culture, or dismantling whiteness *in toto*. Within intersectional-like (the stage at which the 'Alt-Right' appears to be now) thinking, there is a strong tendency to merge various 'Enemy' populations or movements together. Part of this tendency arises from historical developments in the second half of the twentieth century (see Gray 2020: 154–161), but it is also fundamentally entwined with the idea of cross-cutting social locations of oppression. At a theoretical level, neoliberalism *must* be connected with 'whiteness', 'patriarchy', 'heteronormativity', and other oppressive social locations: while the marginalised are many, the 'oppressor' must be singular. The 'Alt-Right' construction of 'whiteness' presents us with a notable contrast, as many of its adherents typically are strong and vocal opponents of neoliberalism and global homogenisation:

rather than 'whiteness' and neoliberalism working hand in hand, the 'Alt-Right' argues that neoliberal 'globalism' is one of the greatest enemies of Whites, working in tandem with the ideologies of 'diversity'.

For much of the 'Alt-Right', 'White' reflects a resistance to the dual forces of neoliberalism's homogenising consumerism and to the 'ethno-narcissism' of other ethnic groups in 'white homelands'. The 'Alt-Right' sees neoliberalism and various 'woke'[9] or 'progressive' movements/ideologies (such as intersectionality) working hand-in-hand (Crowley 2020; Joyce 2020). In this view, neoliberalism desires an atomised population of consumers defined by mere commercial preferences, with the identitarian elements of 'woke' ideologies often being an identity-based form of consumer preference. For other racial/ethnic groups (already inclined towards group collectivist strategies and strongly imbued with a group/racial consciousness), neoliberal activities that hollow out White racial consciousness/culture provide avenues to advance their own racial groups. In this view, both neoliberalism and non-White identity groups share a common enemy: White racial identity. For neoliberalism, White racial identity presents a threat insofar as White collective action would undermine the purely economic reasoning that wrecks White 'homelands' through employment exportation and foreign population importation. For progressive identitarianism, White racial identity is the central enemy for various reasons, including the general tendency towards group conflict between racial/ethnic groups, as well as racial resentment. Additionally, White racial identity is a needful enemy, as the coalition of the 'marginalised' in intersectional or other discourse can be highly unstable (reflected in, for instance, ethnic animus between Black and Latinx populations, or various PoC populations and LGBTQ+ populations): the common enemy of 'Whiteness' serves to keep these unstable coalitions together, if not in commonality of purpose, then in commonality of the hated 'Other'.

A significant activity for the 'Alt-Right' is raising White racial consciousness, which includes 'taking back' the term 'White', similar to how LGBT+ 'took back' the term 'queer'. The viral campaigns stating 'It is okay to be White' are instances of this 'taking back' attempt, aiming both to convey a political preference while simultaneously goading opponents into overreaction, such as in the outcry that this message is 'hate speech'. In this manner, the 'Alt-Right' seeks to show hypocrisy (only some identities can be 'okay'), as well as to provide critique (arguing that 'diversity, inclusion, and equity' is a dog-whistle for anti-White actions/opinions). However, the 'Alt-Right' is not simply reflected in ideological texts or organisational structures: its most popular aspects may be reflected in what could be called 'meme warfare'.[10] In practice, memes act as a form of meta-political resistance to hegemonic 'woke' narratives in Western societies. These memes will present tropes/images as a means of advancing ideological views, while also providing information deemed 'politically incorrect' that (if presented openly) may result in suspensions from social media platforms, social ostracism, and even possible ramifications for continued employment. In this view, the requirement for 'politically correct' speech restrictions comes under attack for two primary reasons. First, the restrictions are viewed as puritanical impositions by those with power, and thus memes act to puncture the sanctimony of the powerful, similar to anti-establishment humour from earlier generations (targeting, for instance, established religious sensibilities or societal demands for proper 'patriotism'). Second, 'politically correct' restrictions are perceived as creating barriers to spreading accurate information, if such information should undercut progressive or Leftist narratives: these language restrictions, in this view, act as a form of Orwellian 'Newspeak' that prevents the presentation of even true information if the 'hate facts' (as they are sometimes called) are accurate. One example is the '13/50' meme, indicating the Black percentage of the US population compared the Black percentage of murderers (as listed in US Department of Justice statistics): using an explicit statement – 'despite being 13% of the population, Blacks commit over 50% of murders' – can result in suspension or worse, but if the information is conveyed more ambiguously, or perhaps put in an image form, then it may fly 'under the radar' of censors. A substantial amount of this 'meme warfare' is simply for fun, not dissimilar to earlier cases of dissident views 'sticking it' to what are perceived as puritanical and/or irrational authorities and reigning *mores* (see also Hawley 2017: 107–108). But these memes also act a form of meta-politics: a humorous picture can reach substantially more (and different) audiences than a tract or pamphlet, while also encouraging the questioning of dominant paradigms (as a means of 'red-pilling'). Often explicitly referencing Gramsci's views of hegemony, some Alt-Right thinkers present 'meme warfare' as assisting in creating the cultural shifts necessary for political changes, and often point to the New Left's successes as an illustration of how these activities can be fruitful.

## Conclusion

For the 'Alt-Right', whiteness is the exemplar, foundational identity for resistance against a hegemonic culture dominated by neoliberalism, globalism, and cultural Marxism, where seeking profits and global standardisation buries White populations through migrations of other races to White states and by undermining institutions that could protect White populations. But this framework also presents avenues for coalitions among other resisting identities that operate within it. Although these disparate identities vary significantly, a common undercurrent that provides discursive unity is White identitarianism. At this point, White identitarianism and the 'Alt-Right' are marginal movements: no major political party or movement within the United States aligns with them, no major corporation or institution provides support, and those associating with these movements can anticipate potential social ostracism, 'doxxing',[11] as well as loss of employment for themselves and possibly for family members. And yet, there are reasons to believe that elements of this tendency may become more popular, if not mainstream, in the future. As critical race theory and intersectional discourse becomes more predominant in American (and Western) popular culture rather than primarily occupying academic spaces (and thus, away from the notably ideologically homogenous spaces of the academy to the more ideologically heterogenous spaces of the broader society), as mandated 'conversations' on 'white privilege' become more typical in corporate and other settings (and likely viewed less like 'conversations' and more like struggle sessions), and as these White populations discover that they can at best only hope to be 'anti-racist racists' (Katz 2003), one might hear many more voices saying, quite explicitly, 'it's okay to be White'.

## Notes

1 Throughout this chapter, 'White' will be capitalised to indicate the substantive identity element in whiteness among the 'Alt-Right'. For the 'Alt-Right', White populations share a fundamental unity in genetics, geographical origin, and culture: they view genetics and culture as intimately connected in the 'biocultural' structure of 'peoples'. In attempting to understand the 'Alt-Right' as it understands itself, the capitalisation underscores how 'White' is not only a social construct or descriptor in this movement, but rather a substantive, unified, foundational identity.

2 Counter-Currents Publications is a major 'Alt-Right', White Nationalist, and alternative publisher within the United States, managed by its editor-in-chief, Greg Johnson. In addition to publishing many books, it maintains an active webpage that serves both to spread its ideas as well as to provide a venue for discussion among like-minded individuals. As Johnson shows notable sympathies with parts of the French 'New Right', Counter-Currents maintains a combination of European and American far-right ideologies. VDARE, founded in 1999 by Peter Brimelow (a former writer in mainstream conservative journals such as *National Review*), focuses on the dangers of mass immigration to the

American system. Its main venue is VDARE.com. Although it will publish self-identified 'race realists', VDARE itself is more nationalist than explicitly racialist in orientation.

3  The National Alliance was an American white supremacist organisation formed in 1974 founded by its leader, William L. Pierce (1933–2002), an important figure in white supremacist movements during the latter part of the twentieth century. Pierce's best-known text was *The Turner Diaries*, a near-future novel about a secretive white supremacist terrorist organisation. The National Alliance also published various other works, and founded a record company. The National Alliance fell into infighting after Pierce's death.

4  Pat Buchanan is an American paleoconservative, and author of *The Death of the West*. He served in the three presidential administrations, and was a regular commentator on various political programmes. Buchanan also ran for the Republican Presidential nomination in the 1992 and 1996 and for the Reform Party nomination in 2000. Peter Brimelow is the founder of VDARE (see endnote 2 for details). Steve Sailer is a writer whose work regularly appears in alternative venues. Notable for his work on 'Human Biodiversity' and the role of evolution on population differences, Sailer's writings often focus on group-level variations between racial populations on education, crime, and other topics.

5  For the 'Alt-Right', 'fitness' typically is used in a Darwinian sense, and often derives from the discipline of evolutionary psychology. 'Fitness' indicates the ability/inability of a population to maintain its distinctive qualities, as well as to reproduce itself over time: for instance, MacDonald (2002) focused on Jewish group-survival strategies. In its use of 'fitness', much of the 'Alt-Right' is somewhat eugenicist, as it encourages pro-natalist policies by White populations/states, and emphasises behaviours (such as strength training) to increase 'fitness' for Whites overall. But this 'Alt-Right' view is not 'Social Darwinism': the term is usually associated with laissez-faire economic systems and the 'Robber Baron' style of big business. In contrast, many on the 'Alt-Right' consider that style of economic organisation as highly dysgenic (particularly for Whites), reflected in their strong rejection of neoliberalism.

6  GRECE (the 'Research and Study Group for European Civilization'), founded in 1968, primarily focuses on '*ethnos*' within Europe, and underlying foundations of, and perceived threats to, European cultures. It has included Alain de Benoist, Guillaume Faye, Pierre Vial, and Dominque Venner, among others. *Génération Identitaire* (GI), founded in 2012 in France, is a self-described 'patriotic youth movement' with branches in numerous European states. Involved in various protests and actions, GI focuses on maintaining of European identity and curbing mass (particularly Islamic) immigration from outside Europe.

7  Europe has extended historical roots to various 'homelands' (be they broadly understood as 'Germania', or more narrowly focused, such as Flanders or Wales) which can still point to linguistic, historical, and ethnic differences: at least theoretically, populations in these 'homelands' can trace their lineage in these areas back by hundreds of years, if not millennia. For the 'Alt-Right', these ethnicities are the indigenous populations of Europe, similar to the Inuit of Canada. In the American case, the connections to these 'homelands' among those of European descent are looser to non-existent: many European-descended Americans may have a vague knowledge that their ancestors originated in Scotland or Finland (for instance), but lack a rooted connection to the customs/traditions of these areas. Similarly, the American narrative of 'a nation of immigrants' and/or settlers loosens the felt connections with a specific European ethnicity, leading instead to a broader racial solidarity. Finally, the significant population heterogeneity within American society creates greater emphasis on broadly racial (over ethnic) identity formation: some note this change would reflect the expansion of 'whiteness' over time (see Jacobson 1998), but some on the 'Alt-Right' do not see this expansion as positive, rather viewing it as a means of 'cleansing' ethnic specificity from populations like the Irish and Polish while simultaneously undermining the ethnic specificity of American Anglo-Saxon Protestants (see Jones 2004).

8  'Cultural Marxism' is a term broadly used not only by the 'Alt-Right' but also by more mainstream Rightist and conservative authors. Generally, it refers to critical theory, inclusive of the Frankfurt School as well as its various permutations into the present. This term indicates the Marxian nature of critical theory, even if its adherents have abandoned the economic determinism and class-prioritisation in Marxism proper for cultural/sociological prioritisation instead. While at times used equivocally, it indicates that current critical theories are a 'rehashed' form of Marxism, replacing the 'world-historic' proletariat with new 'saviour classes', such as BIPOC, various genders, or other populations.

9  'Woke', within the American Left, indicates consciousness-raising: that a person has 'woken up' to systemic injustices and inequities within society against marginalised groups (BIPOC, certain gender

groups, and so forth). Within the American Right (including, but not limited to, the 'Alt-Right'), 'red-pilled' refers to a similar idea: 'woken up', but with different notions of who is suffering injustice (the working class, 'white trash', and the like). 'Red-pill' itself is a reference to the film *The Matrix* (1999).

10 Many of the memes discussed here will be dated by the time of this chapter's publication. Memes change quickly in the 'Alt-Right' for two reasons. First, the decentralised, online nature of the 'Alt-Right' emphasises the new, shocking, and interesting: a meme will go through various iterations/changes, where it may become more mainstreamed, or become 'stale'. The second reason reflects self-preservation: once a meme gains the attention of groups such as the Anti-Defamation League (ADL: a Jewish non-governmental organisation, primarily focused on combatting anti-Semitism) or the Southern Poverty Law Center (SPLC: an American non-governmental organisation initially formed to combat the Klu Klux Klan), and/or mainstream media, meme-users may be targeted for algorithmic bans on social media sites. Even memes that are not specifically 'Alt-Right' (such as the 'NPC' or 'Learn to Code' memes) have led to mass bans/suspensions on social media sites, so knowing when to drop a meme becomes important. To (cyber)survive, successful 'Alt-Right' users remain attentive not only to when a meme becomes 'stale', but also when a meme places a target upon them.

11 'Doxxing' refers to the practice of revealing identifying information about a person. Originally, 'doxxing' indicated the practice of revealing the true name of an anonymous writer on the Internet, but its meaning has expanded over time.

# References

Auster, L. 2019. *Our Borders, Ourselves: America in the Age of Multiculturalism.* Litchfield: VDARE.com Books.

Camus, R. 2018. *You Will Not Replace Us!* Plieux: Chez l'auteur.

Collins, P. H. 2000. *Black Feminist Thought: Knowledge, Consciousness, and the Politics of Empowerment*, 2nd edn. New York: Routledge. DOI:10.4324/9780203900055.

Crowley, C. 2020. 'Coronavirus and the crisis of neoliberalism', *Occidental Observer*, 26 April, viewed 22 June 2020, https://www.theoccidentalobserver.net/2020/04/26/coronavirus-and-the-crisis-of-neoliberalism/.

DiAngelo, R. 2018. *White Fragility: Why It's So Hard for White People to Talk About Racism.* Boston: Beacon Press.

Dutton, E. 2019. *Race Differences in Ethnocentrism.* London: Arktos.

Gray, P. W. 2018. 'The Fire Rises': Identity, the 'Alt-right', and Intersectionality. *Journal of Political Ideologies*, 23 (2): 141–156. DOI:10.1080/13569317.2018.1451228.

Gray, P. W. 2020. *Vanguardism: Ideology and Organization in Totalitarian Politics.* New York: Routledge. DOI:10.4324/9780429318252.

Gray, P. W. and Jordan, S. R. 2018. Revealing the Alt-right: Exploring Alt-right History, Thinkers and Ideas for Public Officials. *Public Voices*, 15 (2): 31–49.

Hancock, A. 2016. *Intersectionality: An Intellectual History.* Oxford: Oxford University Press. DOI:10.1093/acprof:oso/9780199370368.001.0001.

Hawley, G. 2017. *Making Sense of the Alt-Right.* New York: Columbia University Press. DOI:10.7312/hawl18512.

Houck, R. 2018. *Liberalism Unmasked.* London: Arktos.

Jacobson, M. F. 1998. *Whiteness of a Different Color: European Immigrants and the Alchemy of Race.* Cambridge: Harvard University Press.

Jensen, A. R. 1998. *The G Factor: The Science of Mental Ability.* Westport: Praeger.

Johnson, G. 2013. *New Right Versus Old Right: And Other Essays.* San Francisco: Counter-Current Publishing Ltd.

Johnson, G. 2015. *Truth, Justice, and a Nice White Country.* San Francisco: Counter-Current Publishing Ltd.

Johnson, G. 2018a. What is the Alternative Right? In *The Alternative Right*, ed. G. Johnson, pp. 1–28, San Francisco: Counter-Current Publishing Ltd.

Johnson, G. 2018b. *The White Nationalist Manifesto.* San Francisco: Counter-Current Publishing Ltd.

Johnson, G. 2019. *Toward a New Nationalism.* San Francisco: Counter-Current Publishing Ltd.

Jones, E. M. 2004. *The Slaughter of Cities: Urban Renewal as Ethnic Cleansing.* South Bend: Fidelity Press.

Joyce, A. 2020. 'Multiculturalism in the age of coronavirus', *Occidental Observer*, 14 April, viewed 22 June 2020, https://www.theoccidentalobserver.net/2020/04/14/multiculturalism-in-the-age-of-coronavirus/.

Katz, J. H. 2003. *White Awareness: Handbook for Anti-Racism Training*, 2nd edn. Norman: University of Oklahoma Press.

Kirkpatrick, J. 2019. *Conservatism Inc.: The Battle for the American Right*. London: Arktos.

Krebs, P. 2012. *Fighting for the Essence: Western Ethnosuicide or European Renaissance?* London: Arktos.

Levin, M. 2005. *Why Race Matters: Race Differences and What They Mean*. Oakton: New Century Foundation.

Lynn, R. 2015. *Race Differences in Intelligence: An Evolutionary Analysis*, 2nd edn. Arlington: Washington Summit Publishers.

MacDonald, K. 2002. *The Culture of Critique: An Evolutionary Analysis of Jewish Involvement in Twentieth-Century Intellectual and Political Movements*. 1st Books.

McLaren, P. 1998. Whiteness is …: The Struggle for Postcolonial Hybridity. In *White Reign: Deploying Whiteness in America*, ed. J. L. Kincheloe *et al.* New York: St. Martin's Griffin.

Mercer, I. 2011. *Into The Cannibal's Pot: Lessons for America from Post-Apartheid South Africa*. Seattle: Stairway Press.

Mohler, A. and Weissmann, K. 2018. *The Conservative Revolution in Germany 1918-1932: A Handbook*. Whitefish: Washington Summit Publishers.

Nowicki, A. 2016. The Niggers of the Earth. In *The Uprooting of European Identity*, ed. R. B. Spencer, pp. 31–70. Arlington: Washington Summit Publishers.

O'Meara, M. 2013. *New Culture, New Right: Anti-Liberalism in Postmodern Europe*. London: Arktos.

Robertson, W. 1993. *The Ethnostate: An Unblinkered Prospectus for an Advanced Statecraft*. Ostara Publications.

Rushton, J. P. 2000. *Race, Evolution, and Behavior: A Life History Perspective*. Port Huron: Charles Darwin Research Institute.

Taylor, J. 2011. *White Identity: Racial Consciousness in the 21st Century*. New Century Books.

Taylor, J. 2017. *If We Do Nothing: Essays and Reviews from 25 Years of White Advocacy*. No Location: New Century Books.

Willinger, M. 2013. *Generation Identity: A Declaration of War Against The '68ers*. David Schreiber, trans. London: Arktos.

Willinger, M. 2014. *A Europe of Nations: A Declaration of Independence*. London: Arktos.

# 28

# An evolutionary terror: A critical examination of emboldened whiteness and race evasion

*Colleen E. Boucher and Cheryl E. Matias*

Imagine an ignorance that resists

Imagine an ignorance that fights back

Imagine an ignorance militant, aggressive, not to be intimidated, an ignorance

that is active, dynamic, that refuses to go quietly – not at all confined to the

illiterate and uneducated but propagated at the highest levels of the land, indeed

presenting itself unblushingly as knowledge.

*(Mills 2007: 13)*

## Introduction

The evolution of whiteness and its racist byproducts can only be understood when situated historically and socially (Mills 2007), as the contexts of time and location reveal the identities of the oppressed, the oppressors, and the de jure and de facto systems of dominance that exist among them. The United States, with its long history of white dominance and oppression of People of Colour (POC)[1] has strong epistemological roots in white supremacist soil. Meaning, the ways that white people construct their knowledge around race are based in their dominance over POC groups, and thus their racial (racist) reality is created in the image of whiteness (Scheurich and Young 1997). Yet, as much as race is permanent (Bell 1992), when the historical and social contexts change with time, ways of understanding race and racism evolve, too. While this can lead to the interrogation and shedding of racist thinking (Kendi 2016) or the ability to overcome white ignorance (Mills 2007), this chapter argues that at this epistemological moment in US history, whiteness has also taken on an emboldened nature, an evolutionary terror by which the roots of whiteness reach deeper for supremacy and foster the growth of intimidation, violence, and abusive emotional tactics to maintain dominance. According to Matias and Newlove (2017), the use of these emboldened tactics comes from a perversion of knowledge, such that these white racists have rationalised and justified their epistemological

DOI: 10.4324/9780429355769-28

stance in a twisted reversal of false victimhood. To evaluate these tactics, the use of new terminology in the field of Critical Whiteness Studies (CWS) helps to elucidate the insidious nature of evolutionary whiteness.

It is worthwhile to acknowledge the American-centric nature of this chapter's examples of whiteness and the evolution of racism in recent years. Both authors live in the United States, which provides a close-up view of American politics and the prominent racial issues of the country. We recognise, though, that there are international examples of whiteness, racism, and scholarship that does not originate in the United States.

## Framing theory and terminology

CWS are used to explicate the ways 'whiteness as embodied racial power' (Bonilla-Silva 2003: 271) presents itself in society, at micro- and macro-levels. POC scholars have been researching and writing about whiteness for nearly a hundred years (Baldwin 1963; Du Bois 1935; Fanon 1967), elucidating the ways in which white supremacy is the basis for institutional and individual racism. Central to CWS and this chapter is Critical Race Theory and the reality that white people generally benefit from the very same societal elements that harm POC. As a recent example, the US policing controversy during the summer of 2020, after multiple Black[2] people were killed by police in separate events, has drawn increased attention to disparities in justice for whites versus POC. Black people are far more likely to be killed by police than whites in the United States; meanwhile, white people tend to view the police as a protective force (Berman et al. 2020). In this contemporary example, Black people in America are literally being killed by the same institution that white people find comforting. Similar examples repeat this story, and to best understand the multidimensionality embedded in such stories we operationally employ CWS. CWS provide a framework for understanding how the tactics, emotionalities, and epistemologies of whiteness impact both whites and POC within a white supremacist power structure. Drawing from Matias's (2016: 185) work, Figure 28.1 displays a conceptualisation of whiteness and racism as stemming from an overarching institutional white supremacy that impacts POC and white people differently.

In recent years, CWS became popularised with terminology such as 'white privilege' (McIntosh 1989) and 'white fragility' (DiAngelo 2018). White privilege, as popularised by McIntosh (1989) is a metaphorical knapsack of unearned privileges that whites carry and can be 'unpacked'. White fragility, per DiAngelo (2018), provides a concept to understand the discomfort whites feel when engaging in any racial dialogue. Both concepts have provided richer context in understanding whiteness. Yet, despite the heralding of the terms' innovativeness, those concepts are nothing new to POC. In fact, much like Leonardo and Porter's (2010) argument about inter-race race dialogues, whites always seem impressed with how much they have learned while having what they believe to be a 'real' inter-race dialogue, while POC feel they have not learned anything new.

Meanwhile, as CWS shines a spotlight onto mechanisms of whiteness, the campaign and resulting election of Donald Trump as president of the United States suggests an epistemological perversion. That is, Trump 'capitalised off whiteness rhetoric as a means to rally those individuals who already harboured deep-rooted prejudices' (Matias and Newlove 2017: 926). We are reminded that although whiteness and racism are not new, a campaign that promulgates whiteness publicly allows emboldened white racists to vocalise and act on their hatred more visibly. Such a phenomenon demonstrates the evolutionary patterns of whiteness from the overt racist of yesteryear to covert racist and now back again to proud and emboldened overt racism. Just as whiteness and responses to whiteness have changed and evolved over time, so must the

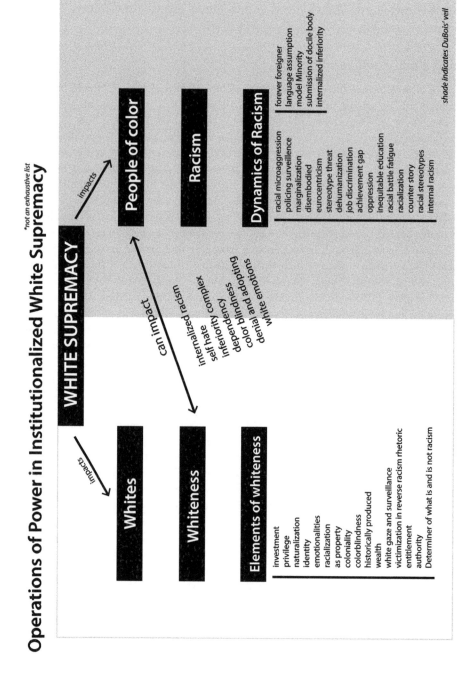

*Figure 28.1* Operations of Power in Institutionalised White Supremacy. Source: C.E. Matias 2016. *Feeling White*. Rotterdam: Sense Publishers. p. 185.

very terminology we use for racial justice. To analyse the current evolutionary terror of whiteness, two terms need evaluation: 1) the name (and thus theoretical focus of) CWS, and 2) the use of 'colour-blind' racism.

## Towards a use of critical studies of whiteness

While there are certainly benefits to whiteness studies that help to move white people towards awareness of their own privileges and fragility, some whiteness scholars have raised concerns about narrowly focusing more on the humanisation of whites than the harm it does to POC (Matias and Boucher, forthcoming). As such, whiteness scholars have reached an epistemological fulcrum whereby they must choose whether to assign innocence to the ignorance of whiteness (Mills 2007) which focuses on their privileges and fragility, or to critically examine the intentionality of whites refusing to face whiteness as a problem of their own making (Matias and Boucher, forthcoming). The use of CWS to frame the realities of whiteness can fall short of pivoting away from simple answers to white ignorance, which narcissistically works to re-centre whiteness, as a disease not of white people's doing (Matias 2016).

Since CWS is not itself a theory, but a transdisciplinary approach that draws on several critical theoretical perspectives, Matias and Boucher (forthcoming) offer a focal shift by turning toward several racial theories that place the 'critical studies' in front of 'whiteness' (thus, a critical study of whiteness approach). One such racial theory is Yancy's (2008) phenomenological approach to understanding the racial interpellation of white bodies surveilling Black bodies. Yancy's (2008) racial analysis centres on the epistemological perversion, where white minds pervert their entitled sense of power to displays of fear (justifying anti-Blackness) which then leads to literal and figurative policing of Black bodies. As Yancy (2008) describes, 'Whites "see" the Black body through the medium of historically structured forms of "knowledge" that regard it as an object of suspicion' (p. 3). He further explicates that his Blackness, as this 'suspicious' object, is inherently-so in the white mind, due to years of historical and social permission to believe whiteness is the norm while POC are perceived as abnormal. Yet, whites frequently refuse to consciously draw the racial contrasts between themselves and a POC (what many call colour-blindness), while subconsciously recognising colour and reacting in visceral, fearful ways (i.e. the purse clutching by the white woman near a Black man in Yancy's (2008) narrative). Outside of its juxtaposition to Blackness, whiteness does not exist in the white mind, because what is normal, or standard, needs no interrogation; it can remain invisible by the sort of intentional ignorance purported by Leonardo (2002) and Mills (2007). There is a great hypocrisy here: whites will refuse to admit that they recognise racial differences, while simultaneously behaving in ways that decry their stance because they react to POC as abnormal and fear-inducing as the 'other'. This intentional focus on Othering is a crucial element of a critical study of whiteness (Matias and Boucher, forthcoming) because it rightfully places valuable attention on the dehumanisation of POC through whiteness instead of only focusing on the rehumanising efforts of unpacking privilege and noticing fragility in white people.

Fanon (1967) corroborates this need to decentre whiteness using racial psychoanalytics to juxtapose Blackness with whiteness, arguing 'he [a Black man] must be black in relation to the white man … a real dialectic between my body and the world' (p. 110–111). Once again, the importance lies in critically analysing the harm generated by whiteness. In doing so, the study of whiteness is dethroned of its power because such an approach refuses to coddle or stoke the supposed woes of privilege loss. Many other scholars of colour provide theoretical perspectives on the inter-connectedness of whiteness and its harm to POC (as listed in Matias and Boucher, forthcoming): Black, Chicana, and AAPI[3] feminism (e.g. bell hooks, Alma Garcia, Sara Ahmed, and Allyson Tintinangco-Cubales), postcolonial theories (e.g. Albert Memmi, and Edward Said), and sociological theories of race (e.g. W.E.B. Dubois and Eduardo Bonilla-Silva). However, their insights are often left out in literature on CWS. This is of grave importance in that the voices of POC scholars who have deconstructed whiteness in relation to the racial oppression of POC are ignored and the recentering of white humanity is transfixed. How then does that narcissistic recentering (that dismisses the voices of the racially oppressed) mirror emboldening racists of today?

## Towards a use of race-evasion

Related to the narcissism ever-present in whiteness (Matias 2016), the term 'colour-blind' has been used to describe the 'raceless' reality of white people who claim to not 'see' race. One critical problem with this terminology is that it produces what Bonilla-Silva (2003) calls, 'racism without racists' when in reality, their colour-blind mentality is racism (Bonilla-Silva 2010). The term has a long history in the United States, reaching back to the Plessy vs. Ferguson (1895) case where Justice Harlan stated, 'our constitution is colour-blind... takes no account of his surroundings or of his colour' and then ruled in favour of separate but equal segregation that led to many years of Jim Crow laws in the country. From this early example, two important results of colour-blind rhetoric manifested. First, a person's colour is actually noticed, but simply not taken into account when considering legal matters, including the highest laws of the land. Second, a racist law (legal segregation in separate but equal policies) can be enacted within a supposedly colour-blind system. Thus, colour-blindness acknowledges colour but refuses to respect it; additionally, colour-blindness protects the legal, systemic racism of the United States even in the highest court of the land.

On the individual level, as Annamma et al. (2017) put it, in America 'to refuse to acknowledge race is to be morally superior' (p. 148). In fact, many white parents pride themselves on teaching their children to not see colour; and herein lies one of the problems with the term itself: colour-blind racism is taught, not inherited or acquired passively. Using the term colour-blind to describe a way of understanding race and racism is to treat it like an affliction that one did not choose, which is not in need of any treatment because to be colour-blind is the most non-racist way to be. Colour-blindness on the personal level allows someone to refuse to acknowledge race in any circumstance, simultaneously allowing for the purposeful act of ignoring white supremacy in any racist form it takes. Taking the lens of a critical study of whiteness, the harm to POC with this colour-blind terminology and mentality is significant. When white people choose to ignore race, it generates an epistemological point of view by which any discriminatory act they see can be explained another way; essentially, colour-blindness allows for whiteness to erase racism from existence. For POC, the effect is gaslighting (Matias 2020), told repeatedly that they misunderstood something as racist when an oft rationale of 'certainly it wasn't meant that way' is invoked.

Finally, Annamma et al. (2017) alert scholars that from a DisCrit point of view, 'disabilities are metaphors for weakness or limitations' (p. 153) and so the use of 'colour-blind' not only misunderstands and co-opts a disability term, but also assigns deficit language to that disability in the effort of explaining a form of racism. While it could be argued that colour-blindness as a form of racism is a weakness and a limitation in many ways, as mentioned already, appropriating the term from a disability to do so doubly insults a population living with the difficulties of blindness.

Thus, the legal/systemic use of colour-blind terminology that leads to protected racial analysis (Annamma et al. 2017), the trauma to POC from gaslighting and the re-centering of whiteness as innocent that a critical study of whiteness illuminates (Matias and Boucher, forthcoming), and misappropriation of a term that devalues different sight abilities (Annamma et al. 2017), colour-blind racism needs a new term. Based on the reasoning described here, and in light of the emboldened en-whitening moments analysed next in this chapter, the term 'race-evasion' (Annamma et al. 2017: 147) better describes the epistemological and behavioural reality of today.

Rather than being blind to race, the U.S. legal system evades race as a factor in determining justice and uses its purported blindness to claim innocence when its very laws and policies discriminate against POC. Clearly, the term 'colour-blind' is not enough to account for how whiteness evolves in ways that manipulate the terminology for its own benefit. As such a critical study of whiteness adopts an approach that confronts race-evasion by removing the innocence from whiteness that claims to not see colour, instead acknowledging that they are purposely avoiding the race they do see, and all of its discriminatory acts. For POC, the gaslighting and narcissistic power is squelched as the white gaze admits to seeing colour and discrimination based on that colour. For the deficit lens of disability, the use of race-evasion eliminates any dis/ability relationship. Importantly, the use of the term race-evasion as a replacement of colour-blindness does not end the phenomenon. Rather, it evokes truth and disarms the innocence of whiteness. It is here that an analysis of the current epistemological moment of emboldened en-whitening in the United States can begin.

## Critical studies of whiteness and race-evasion in the current evolutionary terror

The rise of white nationalism and racist xenophobia in the United States in recent years can be best understood through a critical study of whiteness and race-evasive tactics. Certainly, the increase in public acts of racism and support of racist policies from political institutions was born of hundreds of previous racist years in American history (see Anderson 2017; Kendi 2016). In other words, racism was deeply embedded in the policies and hearts of Americans long before the 2016 US presidential campaign, which was characterised in part by racially charged rhetoric among the candidates. The current evolutionary terror of emboldened en-whitening has been bolstered by this campaign rhetoric and then post-election policies as embodied white racial power. As Bobo (2017) so cogently puts it, 'There are deep, ongoing and highly adaptive conditions of racism at the institutional, cultural and individual levels that prefigure and play out in our national political discourse'. It is the notion that racism is highly adaptive, indeed, evolutionary, that explains how a politician can impact ideologies like white nationalism and lead to two forms of backlash.

## Rhetorical encouragement of white nationalism and xenophobia

The US presidential campaign in 2016 was characterised partly by rhetoric that ostracised and demeaned immigrants and POC. During and immediately after Trump's election in November 2016 a sharp increase in hate crimes and vocal, public racist acts rose across the country (Reilly 2016). These were not the subtle hate crimes so emblematic of the 1980 colour-blind era. Instead these were full-fledged overtly racist attacks that eerily resembled the racism pre-1960s Civil Rights Era. Examples of hate crimes flooded the nation in the weeks after the 2016 election, echoing Trump's nationalistic and xenophobic campaign rhetoric, with some white nationalists attributing their inspiration to the new president (Reilly 2016). Even his main campaign slogan, 'Make America Great Again' was a subtle call for a previous time 'to an America where the material well-being and privileged position of white citizens would be protected' (Bobo 2017: 100). The use of an authoritative platform helped to restore racism as an unofficial but acceptable policy in the country.

Through a critical study of whiteness in this situation, Trump has performed the narcissistic reversal of victimhood where a white person declares that white Americans are victims of POC. In one classic example, Trump spoke about immigrants during his official announcement that he was running for president. He said,

> When Mexico sends its people, they're not sending their best. They're not sending you. They're not sending you. They're sending people that have lots of problems, and they're bringing those problems with us. They're bringing drugs. They're bringing crime. They're rapists. And some, I assume, are good people. But I speak to border guards and they tell us what we're getting. And it only makes common sense. It only makes common sense. They're sending us not the right people.
>
> *(Trump 2015)*

Several elements of this speech display narcissistic reverse victimhood as viewed through a critical study of whiteness and the abusive gaslighting of race-evasion (Matias 2020). First, claiming that Mexico is sending bad people plays to the assumption that immigrants are criminals (Sharpless 2016). In doing so, this speech traumatises Latinx communities, already harmed by racism and normalising the perversion of truth.

By then saying, 'they are not sending you' to a mainly white audience, the speech symbolically reaffirms white morality at the expense of racially oppressed Mexican immigrants. In fact, these words come after claiming that Mexico is sending criminals and rapists to imply that all Mexican immigrants bear such labels. Oddly enough, by castigating Mexican immigrants as the racial Other the rhetoric also reaffirms white morality by positing that unlike those Mexican criminals and rapists, whites are not these things. This race-evasion quietly centres whiteness by not specifically mentioning it but implying the superior morality of the white audience. To attach these criminal behaviours to the entire body of immigrants from Mexico worked to drum up fear in white Americans that they are the victims of individual and collective immigration. Thus, xenophobic racism lead to white nationalism.

Further gaslighting immigrants, Trump used a false corroboration from border guards, the trusted protection between Mexicans and white Americans, to substantiate his point that immigrants are dangerous. The statement 'they're not sending us the right people' (Trump 2015) again draws a line of moral superiority between his white audience and Mexican immigrants entering the United States. The 'right' people are white Americans, and 'wrong' people are immigrants. Perhaps most insidiously harmful of all, saying 'It only makes common sense' twice in this section of the speech (Trump 2015), twists the narrative of victimhood further into narcissistic whiteness; it does not even require evidence, or thinking, or any other perspectives to understand the moral superiority of white Americans over immigrants – common sense is all you need. This racist epistemological stance originates in a perversion of reality such that Trump and his followers have 'the rationale and justification for their discriminatory behaviours' (Matias and Newlove 2017: 923).

As reported by Serwer (2019), 'the most devastating consequences of the Trump presidency have been policy decisions'. Much like the rest of US history (Supreme Court 1895; Anderson 2017; Kendi 2016) racist policies have driven racist thinking. This leads to a lack of protection for POC and the privileged position of whites in the system of (in)justice, a typical example of whiteness as embodied racial power. Some examples of discriminatory policies in the United States in the recent years include: the travel ban on many predominantly Muslim countries, bringing clear partisans into the Supreme Court, supporting police brutality policies, supporting child abuse as a deterrent to illegal immigration, and the caging of immigrant children in detention centres separate from their parents (Serwer 2019). While not an exhaustive list, the reality is that recent policies have supported discriminatory practices in the United States, and these policies join the rhetoric of unchecked whiteness. As Kendi (2016) argues, 'Time and again, powerful and brilliant men and women have produced racist ideas to justify the racist policies of their era' (p. 9). The same can be said of today's era, where the public display of the rhetoric of whiteness ultimately upholds racist policies.

Alongside several nationally recognised racialised incidents during and after the 2016 election, the popularised use of whiteness rhetoric coupled with race evasiveness serve to illustrate how whiteness has evolved in ways that are almost *en vogue*. Terms like colour-blindness just do not get at the ever-evolving state of race. This was exemplified during the 2017 social media and human rights campaign of #BlackLivesMatter. Initially, protesting police brutality and the disproportionality of how Black people are institutionally murdered by police, the movement became a global phenomenon in 2020 with regards to ending racism. In fact, according to their website the #BlackLivesMatter movement's mission is to 'eradicate white supremacy and build local power to intervene in violence inflicted on Black communities by the state and vigilantes' (BlackLivesMatter.com 2020). As frequent Black murders by police or vigilantes occurred in subsequent years, often filmed and made viral on the Internet, this attention to Black lives stirred up an 'all lives matter' whitelash – typically a backlash that harbours whiteness sentiment. As an attempt at returning to the colour-blind racism so beloved in America, the 'all lives matter' response is an act of race evasion intending to gaslight: for the Black community it attempts to manipulate them into thinking these increasingly commonplace murders are not racial, while also suggesting to non-Black POC and whites that it is not worthy of attention. By evading the inherent racism embedded in how police enact institutional murder of Blacks, whiteness proclaims itself innocent; simply if it is not about race, then those who claim that it is, must be the problem. Clearly, evading racism is just another manoeuvre to reify whiteness in ways that keep its racial power. As such, a critical study of whiteness allows for a deeper investigation of whiteness that operates in ways that narcissistically presumes itself as a victim at the lives of Black and other POC. Much like Yancy's (2008) juxtaposition of the white gaze on the Black body, where the white woman clutches her purse and slightly shifts her body away from the Black man, the innocence of the white person is emphasised while the Black body is profiled as guilty by mere existence. Or, stated another way, the rhetoric of whiteness in this case is to absolve the white woman of her racist behaviours towards the Black man, and thus she never owns up to such behaviours and how they impact the Black man. In much the same way, saying 'all lives' or 'blue lives' matter in response to #BlackLivesMatter, is just another evolved practice of whiteness where white innocence and race-evasion take centre stage from the ones actually being harmed: Black lives.

Though there are many more examples, we, the authors, share one more. The COVID-19 pandemic hit the globe in 2020. The death toll as of June 2020 continues to rise in ways that make COVID-19 the leading cause of death worldwide. Nations responded with mandatory self-quarantining, all non-mandatory businesses and public places closed, and people were instructed to wear masks and maintain social distances at least 6 feet apart. Though the Center for Disease Control stated that the virus originated in China there were no inherent racist practices beyond that fact. When the president of the United States in 2020 publicly labelled the Coronavirus as the Chinese Virus, spikes of anti-Asian American racist surfaced in epic proportions. Words hold power, especially when spoken by someone who symbolically represents the leadership in the United States. In fact, those words mattered so much that in March 2020 a Texas man, claiming inspiration from the presidency, stabbed a young family of four who were of Asian descent (Kim 2020). Outrageous hate crimes against AAPI continued to grow; many of these perpetrators later stated they placed blame of the virus on Asian people (Mangan 2020). But often these events are popularised in US media as raceless, again evading race, moreover white supremacy. In doing so, these events reify whiteness rhetoric while offering the misled idea that whites are the victim of Asian sabotage: a falsity that is being gaslighted as truth.

## Two forms of backlash

For some white Americans and non-Black POC, these racially tense times fuelled by and through the presidency sparked two kinds of responses. One response is to continue to reject the existence of whiteness (however, this time with greater vehemence and entitlement) and claim a perverted sense of victimhood. The other response is to call out racism and whiteness by name, condemning it and focusing on white privileges. In fact, in a day and age where racist acts are caught on camera and made viral the latter response is also becoming increasingly vehement in stopping racism. The reason for these responses is the same: whiteness, generally 'the great unsaid' (Thandeka 1999: 3) is thrust into the white consciousness and demands a response. Much like Matias's (2016) argument that whiteness, when backed into a corner, will have to acknowledge its presence to defend its honour, the reification of whiteness nationally is also acknowledging its presence and defending its honour.

When asked about their personal identity, whites tend to mention all manner of characteristics besides being white. This is a 'normal' phenomenon of whiteness because the dominant or advantaged group in a society considers itself normal, and often goes unmentioned, reinforcing its ubiquitous quality (Tatum 2013). An essential element of race-evasion is a deep denial of a white person's own whiteness and the privileges whiteness affords, the damages it invokes, and the innocence it automatically embeds. In fact, these easily connect to colour-blind racism so frequently taught to white children in the United States; whiteness is not real if colour-blindness exists (see Matias 2016). When whiteness was thrust onto the white American consciousness, colour-blindness became more difficult to maintain, illuminating its epistemological perversion; and race-evasion became the modus operandi for many whites in response to modern day race conscious race-based incidents.

For others who choose to square off with whiteness, they stand as human beings to bear true witness to the increasing hostility to Blacks and other POC, especially when viral video captures it all on social media. Simply, they cannot deny what they see. In response, these individuals became protesters for #BlackLivesMatter, flooding the streets of most major US American cities in May and June of 2020. While many white people became newly aware of police brutality on Black bodies, started researching systemic racism, and joined book clubs to read DiAngelo's (2018) *White Fragility* while posting memes on Facebook about their white privilege, some of the protests began to include violence and looting. While this situation is ongoing at the time of writing this chapter, the very fact that so many white people became suddenly 'woke'[4] to their whiteness and in many cases became less race-evasive, whiteness evolved yet again. The looting, in particular, led to many white people, who had previously been online voices for #BlackLivesMatter and acknowledging their privilege, to invoke specific (and partial) quotes from Martin Luther King, Jr., calling on protesters to be peaceful. The use of one famous Black Civil Rights activist, who often called for peaceful protests, was a clever way to remind Black people that if they want to be respected, they need to do it in a certain way. A critical study of whiteness illuminates that yet again whiteness seeks moral superiority even in the face of hypocrisy. Meaning, as whites police Black bodies, speech, and behaviour, they hypocritically do so under the guise of *saving* them by controlling and dictating the terms of what should constitute Black liberation.

## Conclusion

The US presidency and presidential campaign are emblematic of the evolution of whiteness. By adopting and publicly pronouncing a rhetoric of whiteness that then justify racist policies and by generating new ways to twist narratives that centre whiteness and its inherent innocence while policing and murdering BIPOC, race and white supremacy evolve into new dimensions. Through understanding the insidious ways whiteness operates as embodied racial power (Bonilla-Silva 2003), a critical study of whiteness can help to refocus the analysis on how white supremacy harms POC (Matias and Boucher, forthcoming). As a vital part of a critical study of whiteness, noticing and calling out ways that colour-blindness is evoked by white people and reframing that narrative as race-evasion further illuminates the way that whiteness continually re-centres itself. This re-centering gaslights people to believe that white race-evaders are the victims and that POC are the perpetrators. In this delusional reality, racism and white supremacy reign. Through an analysis of several racially charged events in the US presidency and presidential campaign a critical study of whiteness determines that whiteness has evolved in ways that wrongfully maintain its perceived innocence, masking its maintenance in racial power. In a world of uncertainty, this is a terrorising revelation. That a virus can infect us inasmuch as evolutionary whiteness can, is recognising the full terror of it all. But much like any other terror or threat, many of us will fight back and survive. That is *our* evolutionary path.

## Notes

1  In this chapter, POC refers to People of Colour that do not benefit from phenotypic societal elements of white skin. Recent scholarship uses the acronym BIPOC which stands for Black, Indigenous, and People of Colour. In this chapter, when Black, Indigenous, or other specific groups such as Asians specifically pertain to the narrative, the group will be specifically named.
2  In this chapter, we choose to capitalise the terms Black, Indigenous, and People of Colour, and leave the term white and whiteness in the lower case. While many respected scholars disagree on this choice, our reasoning is that groups in BIPOC refer to specific racial groups, whereas being white or performing whiteness is not necessarily based on a specific race.
3  AAPI refers to Asian Americans and Pacific Islanders.
4  The term 'woke' in this sense refers to people (usually white) who have become aware of racial realities such as whiteness and the oppression of POC. The term originates from Black people warning one another to 'stay woke' to oppressive practices.

## References

Anderson, C. 2017. *White Rage*. New York: Bloomsbury.

Annamma, S. A., Jackson, D. D. and Morrison, D. 2017. Conceptualizing Color-Evasiveness: Using Dis/ability Critical Race Theory to Expand a Color-blind Racial Ideology in Education and Society. *Race Ethnicity and Education*, 20 (2): 147–162.

Baldwin, J. 2008 [1963]. A Talk to Teachers. *Yearbook of the National Society for the Study of Education*, 107 (2): 15–20. View at http://richgibson.com/talktoteachers.htm.

Bell, D. 1992. *Faces at the Bottom of the Well: The Permanence of Racism*. New York, NY: Basic Books.

Berman, M. *et al.* 2020. 'Protests spread over police shootings. Police promised reforms. Every year, they still shoot and kill nearly 1,000 people', *Washington Post*, 8 June, viewed 13 June 2020, https://www.washingtonpost.com/investigations/protests-spread-over-police-shootings-police-promised-reforms-every-year-they-still-shoot-nearly-1000-people/2020/06/08/5c204f0c-a67c-11ea-b473-04905b1af82b_story.html.

Black Lives Matter. 2020. https://blacklivesmatter.com/about/.

Bobo, L. D. 2017. Racism in Trump's America: Reflections on Culture, Sociology, and the 2016 US Presidential Election. *The British Journal of Sociology*, 68 (S1): 85–104.

Bonilla-Silva, E. 2003. 'New Racism', Color-blind Racism, and the Future of Whiteness in America. In *White Out: The Continuing Significance of Racism*, ed. A. Doane and E. Bonilla-Silva, pp. 271–284. New York: Routledge.

Bonilla-Silva, E. 2010. *Racism Without Racists: Color-Blind Racism and The Persistence of Racial Inequality in The United States*, 3rd edn. Lanham, MD: Rowman & Littlefield.

DiAngelo, R. 2018. *White Fragility*. Boston, MA: Beacon Press.

Du Bois, W. E. B. 1935. Does the Negro need Separate Schools? *The Journal of Negro Education*, 4 (3): 328–335.

Fanon, F. 1967. *Black Skin, White Masks*. New York: Grove Press.

Johnson, A. 2006. *Privilege, Power, and Difference*, 2nd edn. New York, NY: McGraw Hill.

Kendi, I. X. 2016. *Stamped from the Beginning*. New York: Nation Books.

Kim, J. 2020. 'Report: Sam's Club stabbing suspect thought family was "Chinese infecting people with coronavirus"', *KTSM News*, 7 April, viewed 25 June 2020, https://www.ktsm.com/news/report-sams-club-stabbing-suspect-thought-family-was-chinese-infecting-people-with-coronavirus/.

Leonardo, Z. 2002. The Souls of White Folk: Critical Pedagogy, Whiteness Studies, and Globalization Discourse. *Race Ethnicity and Education*, 5 (1): 29–50.

Leonardo, Z. and Porter, R. K. 2010. Pedagogy of Fear: Toward a Fanonian Theory of 'Safety' in Race Dialogue. *Race Ethnicity and Education*, 13 (2): 139–157.

Mangan, D. 2020. 'Trump defends calling coronavirus "Chinese virus" – "it's not racist at all"', *CNBC*, 18 March, viewed 17 June 2020, https://www.cnbc.com/2020/03/18/coronavirus-criticism-trump-defends-saying-chinese-virus.html.

Matias, C. E. 2016. *Feeling White*. Rotterdam: Sense Publishers.

Matias, C. E., ed. 2020. *Surviving Becky(s): Pedagogies for Deconstructing Whiteness and Gender*. Lexington Books.

Matias, C. E. and Newlove, P. M. 2017. Better the Devil You See, Than the One You Don't: Bearing Witness to Emboldened En-whitening Epistemology in the Trump Era. *International Journal of Qualitative Studies in Education*, 30 (10): 920–928.

Matias, C. E. and Boucher, C. Forthcoming. Putting the Criticality Back in Critical Whiteness Studies. In *Critical Theories for School-Based Practice: A Foundation for Equity and Inclusion in Practice and Supervision*, ed. S. L. Proctor and D. Rivera. To be published by Routledge.

McIntosh, P. 1989. White Privilege: Unpacking the Invisible Knapsack. *Peace and Freedom Magazine*, July/August 10 unknown 12 unknown.

Mills, C. 2007. White Ignorance. In *Race and Epistemologies of Ignorance*, ed. S. Sullivan and N. Tuana, pp. 11–38. State University of New York Press.

Plessy vs. Ferguson 1895. Judgement, Decided May 18, 1896; Records of the Supreme Court of the United States; Record Group 267; Plessy v. Ferguson, 163, #15248, National Archives.

Reilly, K. 2016. 'Racist Incidents Are Up Since Donald Trump's Election. These Are Just a Few of Them', *TIME*, 13 November, viewed 12 June 2020, https://time.com/4569129/racist-anti-semitic-incidents-donald-trump/.

Scheurich, J. J. and Young, M. D. 1997. Coloring Epistemologies: Are Our Research Epistemologies Racially Biased? *Educational Researcher*, 26 (4): 4–16.

Serwer, A. 2019. 'The President's Pursuit of White Power', *The Atlantic*, 14 January, viewed 13 June 2020, https://www.theatlantic.com/politics/archive/2019/01/trump-embraces-white-supremacy/579745/.

Sharpless, R. 2016. 'Immigrants Are Not Criminals': Respectability, Immigration Reform, and Hyperincarceration. *Houston Law Review*, 53 (3): 691.

Supreme Court of The United States. 1896. *U.S. Reports: Plessy v. Ferguson, 163 U.S. 537*. [Periodical]. View at https://www.loc.gov/item/usrep163537/.

Tatum, B. 2013. The Complexity of Identity: 'Who am I?' In *Readings for Diversity and Social Justice*, 3rd edn., ed. Adams *et al.*, pp. 6–9. New York: Routledge.

Thandeka. 1999. *Learning to be White*. New York: Continuum.

Trump, D. J. 2015. 'Transcript: Donald Trump announces his presidential candidacy', *CBS News*, 16 June, viewed 15 June 2020, https://www.cbsnews.com/news/transcript-donald-trump-announces-his-presidential-candidacy/.

Yancy, G. 2008. *Black Bodies, White Gazes*. Maryland: Rowman & Litchfield Publishers.

# Epilogue: Reflections

*Michelle Fine and William E. Cross Jr.*

We are privileged to draft an epilogue, offering reflections on the volume and the project. We read with great interest the introduction and reviewed the chapters. There is a seductive brilliance to the volume. With vibrant language of 'space invaders', whiteness as a 'somatic norm' (Puwar 2004) and of course Charles Mills' notion of 'white unknowing', the editors Shona Hunter and Christi van der Westhuizen have curated a set of essays that promise to unpack the triage of white *invisibility, ignorance, and innocence*. We were impressed by the transnational sweep of the volume and topics. Deep interrogation across these seemingly disparate spaces and landscapes of coloniality forces us to think about imperial whiteness from afar, up close, in the past and haunting the present.

In this brief closing piece, we have organised our thoughts around what we learned from the volume, what has been provoked in us as critical psychologists and where we imagine this intellectual/political/epistemic project moves next. We cannot ignore that at this moment, in the post-Trump early Biden years, white nationalisms and state-sponsored violence by police and ICE, prison guards, and military flare; calls for 'homeland' and evidence of domestic terrorism, accumulate aggressively within global consciousness, right now particularly in Israel and in the United States. At the same time, we cannot ignore that corporations and the 1% have profited in abundance during pandemic times of gross poverty, housing insecurity and food insecurity, and 'deaths of despair' among poor whites have skyrocketed. And still, in the dizzying affective jazz of the moment, we find hope in global and local solidarity movements, mobilised with rage and passion, demanding justice, land, water, equitable education, economic restructuring, prison and policing abolition, transnational labour solidarities, campaigns for environmental justice, defunding the police and reparations. These are head spinning times.

In our country, and surely yours – wherever you are – the current 'crises' are indeed nested and multiple, unmasked by COVID-19 and sutured into stubborn, persistent and relentless grooves of racial capitalism, occupation, state inspired racial violence, voter suppression, misogyny, transphobia, and ableism. Public health crisis, of course, both racialised and classed, and at the same time women of all colours and classes continue to be beaten and killed, while trans and gender expansive people remain ever vulnerable, white nationalisms flare, police shoot, indigenous lands stolen, eviction rates rise, environmental assaults worsen, and migrants seek asylum.

DOI: 10.4324/9780429355769-107

We are indebted to the editors of the Handbook, provoked by the authors and greedily yearning for more. And so, we begin our multi-raced dialogue on whiteness analytics sketched into this multi-voiced volume. To situate our discussion of white supremacy and logics, we extract from the doubled writings of Franz Fanon and Jean Paul-Sartre as they open, separately and yet in synchrony, an edition of *Wretched of the Earth*, speaking respectively to Black Algerians and white citizens of France about the evils of white supremacy and colonialism.

## White logics, colonialism and the making of zombies

In the opening pages of his short-lived preface to the original volume of Frantz Fanon's *Wretched of the Earth*, Jean Paul Sartre writes to the French: *'It is you who are zombies'*. Confronting White Europeans with complicity in birthing scars, chains and trauma throughout the African continent, Sartre challenges white silence, denial and the systematic turning away from the bloody footprints of colonialism. The preface, of course, precedes Fanon's brilliant and highly circulated text and was removed soon after original publication. But while the twinned texts existed, linking arms, emboldened, between the same covers, they were directed to two distinct audiences. Sartre opens his preface with an attack on the colonial project in Algeria:

> The European elite undertook to manufacture a native elite. They picked out promising adolescents; they branded them, as with a red-hot iron, with the principles of western culture, they stuffed their mouths full with high sounding phrases, grand glutinous words that stuck to the teeth. These walking lies had nothing left to say to their brothers; they only echoed … it was a golden age.

He then implores his fellow Europeans, 'Europeans, you must open this book and enter into it. After a few steps in the darkness, you will see strangers gathered around a fire; come close and listen for they are talking of the destiny they will mete out to your trading centres and to the hired soldiers who defend them. They will see you perhaps but they will go on talking among themselves, without even lowering their voices. This indifference strikes home: their fathers, shadowy creatures, your creatures were but dead souls; you it was who allowed them glimpses of light, to you only did they dare speak and you did not bother to reply to such zombies. Their sons ignore you; a fire warms them and sheds light around them and you have not lit it. Now at a respectful distance, it is you who will feel furtive … and perished with cold. Turn and turn about; in these shows from whence a new dawn will break, it is you who are the zombies …'.

Sartre accuses his French readers of complicity: 'It is not right, my fellow countrymen, you who know very well all the crimes committed in our name. It is not at all right that you do not breathe a word about them to anyone not even to your own soul, for fear of having to stand in judgment on yourself. I am willing to believe that at the beginning you did not realise what was happening; later you doubted whether such things could be true; but now you know, and still hold your tongues. Eight years of silence; what degradation! And your silence is all of no avail; today the years of silence; what degradation!'

Fanon wrote for/to Algerians; Sartre to the French. For a short few years, they performed a tragic duet, as if both on stage, speaking to different audiences, hitting a few shared notes, a jazz of descriptive narrative, reversals, rage, comedy, dystopic imaginaries, and calls for action.

***

We appreciate the jazz of dialogue between Fanon and Sartre, speaking with twinned tongues to colonised and coloniser about the brutal consequences – uneven of course – of the white colonial project. We, too, engage a kind of intellectual/political/intimate jazz between ourselves, over two decades. Bill an aficionado of the genre, Michelle an admirer. We are long friends, allies, writers on/through critical race theory. For over two decades, we have relied on each other when we need to touch ground with someone who knows us each, intellectually, emotionally, through vulnerability. Bill, an internationally recognised scholar of Black history, racial identities and analyst of how Black people in the United States have historically made sense, joy, love, labour, humour, money in a nation dedicated to black death, black denial, and racial capitalism; Michelle, a scholar-activist who writes with and on critical participatory praxis, alongside struggles for justice – economic, racial, gendered, and carceral – drawing largely on decolonial feminist theory to design projects of use for justice movements. When Michelle was asked to sketch an epilogue, I knew I needed Bill to complete my thoughts/finish my sentences/interrupt my ignorance/gently nudge me to see what my biography has kept me from knowing.

Together we read the volume, emailed, and chatted on zoom. Our epilogue rises from each of our lives, and our shared understandings of how scholarship can provoke radical imagination, a re-membering and re-visioning, through critical race and now critical whiteness as a deeply troubling centre and anchor in racial formations.

## Appreciations

We begin with appreciations, loving the radical internationalism of the volume, attending at once to the stubborn particulars of place and animating, also, the relentless global flow of white dominance, logics, and violence. With essays drawn from theoretical, historic and global expansiveness, whiteness swells and complicates as if atmospheric. Both abstract and embodied; structural and dynamic. As the editors argue, 'This volume builds on newer, more explicitly integrated critiques that analyse whiteness as part of a broader racial formation, which is material, affective, and discursive'.

The everywhereness of whiteness creates a text that can overwhelm. Sometimes it is difficult to breathe; hard to see where the fugitive pathways to radical transformation might be carved; where solidarities have been hatched; where love can snuggle within; where structural fractures have been pried open by multiracial movements for justice; where freedom dreams have unleashed. The enclosure and suffocation of whiteness as an inescapable object of inquiry is perhaps intentional. We are reminded of and challenged by what critical South African psychological Puleng Segalo would argue is the *poison in the marrow* – even after apartheid, even in black bodies, even in movements for justice, the residue of the untroubled norm, in the very air we (can't) breathe – in every social indicator and piece of evidence – housing/health/education/incarceration statistics – we 'see' how whiteness flourishes/how 'others' pale. We are reminded to be always suspect of the predictability by which whiteness bubbles to the top and enraged by the endless droning on of Black death/deficit as banal.

The stunning and radical internationalism of the text invites readers to absorb the stubborn racialised particulars of place. At the same time, one cannot help but notice the deadly drum beat of racialised patterns and hierarchies that cut across. Herein lies a big idea, tucked into the volume, about a small rhythm that runs across the chapters. The writers span the globe, with roots in Zimbabwe, South Africa, India, Israel/Palestine, Sweden, Japan, New Zealand, as well as sites in the Global North including the United Kingdom, United States, Canada, and

Germany. Quite a number of the essays introduce what might be considered idiosyncratic 'sites of racial analysis' that could easily be minimised as 'outliers' but instead reveal the dynamics of racial formation that refract across. South Africa and Israel/Palestine are situated not as aberrations, but as racialised cauldrons where, at various points in history, uninhibited ejaculations of the racialised bile explode, reliably predicting Black/Palestinian death. The volume refuses 'unremembering' (Pumla Gqola 2010: 8) – 'a calculated act of exclusion and erasure.'

We were also impressed with the vast expanse of the topics covered. Across the sections on Epistemologies, Conspiracies, Colonialities, Intersectionalities, Governmentalities and Provocations, authors theorise and deploy critical, anti-racist and fugitive forms of knowledge production, both intellectual and activist. The landscapes for exploration stretch across sex/romance tourism, adoption, health, #Trad cultural narratives, Zionism, empire, anti-Muslim racism, lovemaking and necking as national past-times, Meghan Markle, war, genocide, immigration, assisted reproduction, Alt-Right, images of domesticity and home, 'global gays', seafarers, white saviours, the sprawling carceral state and the insidious bleeding of whiteness into hierarchies that constitute education.

This vast topical landscape is a gift, and also a challenge for this text. A gift because the writers craft exquisite individual pieces dissecting *how* whiteness rises to the top – most generous, most gifted, best seafarers, most innocent, across place, scale and topic. A challenge ... because there is a mischievous coyness attached to the variations of whiteness that dance across the pages of the volume. One can never quite be sure of the 'what' of whiteness. Goldberg references the problem: white logics are promiscuous, nimble, and mutating. Whiteness 'commits to anything at all, to remaking and replication as the locally same, as the particular instantiation of the unchanging Universal and therefore recognisable. Its trick is to be anywhere by going nowhere. A culture of pure replicability via a culture of cloning' (Goldberg 2009: 364). Even more exacting, Mbembe writes, 'Whiteness is... most corrosive and ... most lethal when it makes us believe that it is everywhere; that everything originates from it and it has no outside' (2015: 31).

While we found, across the chapters, a flurry of white-enactments, a few essays were particularly useful for framing whiteness as an assemblage of power. These essays, by Goldberg and Mbembe, as well as others, refuse to shrink whiteness to white subjects and argue instead that the experiences and analyses of racialised peoples should centre on analyses of racial formations. Like Fanon and Sartre, we find most useful frameworks that interrogate how white logics move across scale, and under the skin. By so doing we can see white logics within policing, the Immigration and Customs Enforcement (ICE) staff, the US tax code, public education and child protective services. Clearly these systems are designed and infused with the logics of white supremacy, framed as 'protection' and increasingly enforced by people of all racial/ethnic groups including people of colour.

As Michael Omi and Howard Winant suggest across their three editions of *Racial Formation in the United States* (2014), whether we consider neoliberalism, the body, intersectionality or the relationship between structural racism and racial identity, it is imperative for critical scholars to make visible how white supremacist logics and consolidations of power insinuate themselves, occupy and metastasize within ideologies, state policies, public and private institutions, social relations, movements and subjectivities.

## Longings and provocations: Entanglements of whiteness with racial capitalism, neoliberal accountability regimes, and solidarities

The book is a vast invitation, a bath into uncomfortable and jarring lines of analysis; making visible and troubling that which has been naturalised as white merit, deservingness, innocence and most recently fragility.

Together, however, Bill in Denver and Michelle outside New York City, we write from within a nation ravaged by class/race inequalities that paper the walls and historic soul of the United States. To read on white supremacy without deep attention to racial capitalism feels like a powerful but partial story. We both wish there were more attention in the Handbook paid to the weaving of whiteness and political economy, racial capitalism, as we live in a time of extraordinary and violent evidence of wealth gaps, deaths of despair, elites and corporations profiting from denial of power/money/resources to the 99% – especially to Black people. There is no shame in the Congressional Republicans and their audacious wealth and whiteness as they refuse to support any redistributive policies and mobilise aggressively to restrict voting rights to people of colour and people of poverty. The entanglements of white supremacist logics and capitalism deserve dedicated theoretical and empirical engagement. And so we offer some thoughts …

## Racial capitalism and whiteness

The chapters are consistently stunning in their insights, analysis, and cogency. While many chapters engage rich and lively intersectional analyses of whiteness and gender, sexuality, popular culture, and ideologies, an important limitation concerns the near total absence of chapters that address the political economy and the strategic appropriation of whiteness.

An important exception can be found in the chapter by Neema Begum, Aurelien Mondon, and Aaron Winter, 'Between the 'left behind' and 'the people': Racism, populism and the construction of the 'white working class' in the context of Brexit'. These authors grapple skilfully, and with complexity, over the wretched political consequences of pitting white working class against people of colour in the struggle over Brexit (and by extension in the United States). Figuring the Brexit problematic at centre, Begum, Mondon, and Winter unpack the dominant story of who voted for Brexit and dissect the strategic use of the 'aggrieved white working class' trope. They trouble the framing of pro-Brexit voters as working class and challenge the distorted representation of working class as (only) white. They offer a particularly compelling chapter for understanding how race and racism have been appropriated by elites and the far right in the United Kingdom to advance the interests of wealth and nationalism, to obscure and advance the political interests of the wealthy, to elide how wealth and whiteness propel far right ideology, and to attribute responsibility for conservative swings toward immigrants and racialised minority groups:

> Our argument is that the focus on the white working class has not only racialised and divided the most diverse section of our society, but displaced racism, white supremacy, and Brexit itself onto the working class. In the process, it not only served to exculpate the middle and upper classes and rendered their racism and white supremacy relatively in-visible, but allowed elites to serve and protect their own economic and political interests, while appearing to be looking out for the so-called 'legitimate' concerns of the 'left behind'.

These authors make clear that mainstream political and media articulations 'shift responsibility for inequalities and the rise of far right politics away from elites, institutes and structures and onto racialised immigrants'. This essay gets messy, in delicious ways, untangling how popular media could, at once, advance the interests and obscure the involvement, of elites. The authors expose two erasures are accomplished in this discursive portrait of the white working class left behind: First, the 'working class' in the United Kingdom (and United States) is racialised as white; literally whiting out people of colour, refugees and asylum seekers among the working class. Second, the interests/motives/money and influence of elites are obscured. Discursively pit against each other, tensions between working class whites and people of colour inflame. With analytic clarity and substantial evidence, this chapter dives into the knotty intersection of white logics and racial capitalism, by tracing systematically how elite white interests are masked, racialised minorities blamed for the glide to the Right, and inter-group tensions between working class whites and people of colour undermined, with solidarities stifled.

## The seductive intimacy of white logics, racial capitalism, and splitting

In the recent writings on racial (in)justice, Bill has wandered down a simple analytic path, trying to unpack how the white working class subjectivities are seduced, formed and deformed under capitalism. So in a revised edition of this *Handbook* published sometime in the future, Bill hopes to imagine a new chapter on political economy written by two scholars standing-in for the likes of Jane Mayer and the late Manning Marable. Part of the focus would be to interrogate the triumph of American capitalism in cannibalising and seducing white workers, while provoking the barest of resistance, as captured by the title of Steve Fraser's amazing work: *The Age of Acquiescence* (Fraser 2015). Fraser's work presents, at the more granular level, the story of how the conservative movement, which is to say, *unrepentant capitalists,* thoroughly and successfully miseducated members of the white working class to the point that they – white workers – blamed other workers, that is people of colour, women, and especially feminists, for the personal misery and social decay linked to loss of employment. In the logic of a *Mighty Python Script,* minoritised groups, who neither own nor control industry, are seen, not as working-class partners, but as progenitors of white working-class pain. In nursing angst over the loss of 'white' jobs, taken by the wrong type of Americans and immigrants, white workers failed to notice that *everyone's job* was eliminated by shutting down factories altogether and that all workers with a high school degree or less were now disposable, redundant, and expendable (Bluestone and Harrison 1982). Whiteness was manufactured, exploited and split under capitalism in ways structural, social, intra-psychic, religious, and stitched into family lore.

The miseducation of white workers in the United States began in slavery (Taylor 2018), when the propertied class – owners of land and slaves – worked to pass laws meant to place social constraints on the everyday life of poor white people, who, because of their numbers, posed a hypothetical threat to the designs of landed elites. People [poor whites] who did not own property [land or slaves] were arrested for vagrancy then hired out to perform work for the propertied class, at a salary guaranteed to result in abject poverty. The use of vagrancy laws to entrap white workers became the *modus operandi* for re-enslavement of blacks, at the end of Reconstruction, but it was first put to practice during slavery to control 'surplus' white labour (Brown 2013; Dickerson 1986). In addition, white elites manipulated the political systems such that the vote of white workers was suppressed because truth be told, the southern propertied class *did not believe in democracy*, reflecting the perspective of the most conservative and reactionary politician and political theorist from South Caroline – John C. Calhoun (circa 1782–1850) – who believed the nation's fate should be decided by persons of property, with nearly zero input from the poor. One hundred and fifty years later, Calhoun's sociopathic perspective would inspire Milton Freedman and the pseudo-economist, James McGill Buchanan, who with the lavish support provided by the Koch Brothers (MacLean 2017), mounted the counter narrative to Keynesian economics whereby the rich are freed from any obligation to support 'socialistic' adventures such as water purification and sewage treatment, public education, social security, and Medicare (MacLean 2017). Returning, to an earlier point, there is much irony that white workers in the present should wave the confederate flag, as the flag not only symbolised slavery, but subjugation of white wage earners and the suppression of their political voice (Brown 2013; Rothman 2018).

During the first 12 years of Reconstruction (1865–1877), Union solders occupied key locations throughout the South and this afforded psychological and legal space within which Blacks evidenced amazing progress to a degree that seriously threatened plans by white elites to constrain the choices and options of Black wage labour (Gates 2020). The 1877 Hayes/Tilden Compromise put an end to Black protection (Woodward 1991) and while making it possible to reduce black labour to a form of neoslavery, white labour was provided, not a wage increase, but the promise to never be placed on the same plain as Black labour. This privileging of white labour as 'you are better than black labour' was short lived. During the Coal Miner's War of 1891, working class whites were again treated with distain by capital. The Tennessee coal miner's union objected to the owner's use of leased prison labour to break the strike, a variation of vagrancy laws. The owners controlled important political voices so that the state militia was pitted against the strikers. In breaking the coal miner's strike, Gatling guns capable of firing 200 rounds per minute and bombs dropped from planes helped break the will of the workers (Derickson 1988; Lewis 1987).

If 'disdain' captures the use of vagrancy laws in the antebellum south as well as the deployment of machine guns and aerial bombing, then cannibalism may not be too strong a description of capitalism's attitudes toward white labour in the aftermath of deindustrialisation. A slightly less repugnant term is *disposability*. Clinging to and achieving very little warmth from the shredded strands of the now totally weathered whiteness comforter, poor whites drank the Kool-aide, aligned in solidarity with white grievance animated by elites. They rose to elect a president who, having proposed to reinvigorate their special status as white and working class, passed instead, a tax bill that 'promised' trickle down benefits to the poor, *after* it filled the oversized wine glasses of those already satiated and obscenely rich. The executives of industry quickly discovered that by buying back company stock, this made it possible to increase management salaries 10-fold and more, reversing the trickle-down thesis to produce a flood of money going into the pockets of top management. Enthralled by a cult of personality, the miseducation of white workers reached a new high, when they associated social safety net programs with the underserving poor that is people of colour, while in interviews with Jennifer Silva, they *blamed themselves* for the downturn in their lives (Silva 2019). The philosophy of individualism run amok.

In the meantime, spatial separation of Black and white communities made it easier for pejorative myths about Black people to take on new life, and in 1965 non-other than Patrick Moynihan, who first started out on the right track by identifying unemployment as the cause of the fall from grace of so many Black families, subsequently turned around and blamed Black people themselves for being unemployed (Moynihan 1965), Black single mothers in particular. For the same period in history, when deindustrialisation and globalisation were unleashing widespread unemployment, President Bill Clinton formulated a social safety net for which *proof of current employment* was required. In effect, working class people were coerced into seeking employment in low paying service positions, at a salary positioning them 'below' the poverty line. Even working two jobs or doing double-shifts at one, failed to bring earnings back to the level of the wages paid at their now defunct industrial jobs, and in the absence of health care, their families lived a life on the razors edge, until, inevitably, someone became sick. Many of their jobs were branded as essential, during the pandemic, resulting in constant risk exposure and as scientifically predicted, increased likelihood of infection and death.

In the absence of mainstream employment, and a social safety net depleted by legislative fiat, some Black and Brown men, and women made street life the site for their economic survival. Peering across the housing/spatial divide separating the races, whites quickly racialised black and brown gangsterism as proof that 'those' people were psychopathically inclined at birth. Thus, when a white woman was brutally raped in Central Park, the police rounded up five black male youth and charged them with the rape. Although physical evidence was collected at the scene, none of it matched or connected any of the five accused youth, but this did not delay their prosecution. The five were convicted based on assumptions and hypotheticals, not proof. The *Central Park Five* became the Central Park *savages*. The prosecuting attorney was convinced of their genetic predispositions and the five were found guilty (Byfield 2014). Donald Trump paid for a full-page ad in the New York Times calling for the death penalty. Eventually another person confessed to the crime and the forensic evidence collected at the crime scene matched and thus connected the person to the crime, plus he provided additional evidence only the rapist could possibly know. Nevertheless, the prosecuting attorney tried to argue the central park five did not deserve exoneration! In her mind, myth and stereotypes trumped actual evidence. This led Jeremi Duru to title his law review article about the case in these words: 'The Central Park Five, the Scottsboro Boys, and the myth of the bestial black man' (Duru 2003).

After the radicalism of 1968, white awareness about race goes back into hibernation, as housing and community *Apartheid* makes it possible for the two groups to *seldom* interact. It is the task of the police to keep the communities apart, and to surveil the borders such that few Blacks can cross over the imaginary divide, other than for purposes of employment. Even then, Blacks cross over with great trepidation. For years, cries of police brutality fell on death ears (Moore 2010); however, as the COVID-19 pandemic expanded the amount of time allotted to monitoring social media and televised news reportage, the televised recording of the murder of George Floyd and the graphic details about the 'accidental' shooting by police of Breonna Taylor, broke through centuries of white resistance to racial truths and the social organisation known as *Black Lives Matter* was transformed into a social movement of international proportions.

As this piece is written, the United States is on the cusp of a new direction in its treatment and support of the working class, and in particular, people of colour. Joe Biden, normally a centrist, has put forth a revitalisation plan in the tradition of the New Deal that if enacted will lift a large portion of Black people, and white working class, out of the grips of extreme poverty, and given its educational supports, may promote even higher levels of uplift. However, it is important to recall that the GI Bill did not contain the word 'race', yet its enactment was quickly racialised through various political machinations. One hopes that can be avoided this time around. Our point here is simple: there is a need for rigorous conceptual work at the intersection of white logics/supremacy and racial capitalism, within the United States and as importantly transnationally. We turn now to the seepage of white logics inside governmentality and neoliberal accountability regimes.

## White logics and seepage through governmentality and neoliberal accountability regimes

In this section, we animate yet another enactment of white logics, through the relentless, invasive, profit making empire of neoliberal accountability regimes. These logics/policies/big data surveillance systems, enacted in the name of efficiency, accountability and protection, have devastated universities, K-12 schooling, perpetrated 'predictive policing', and spawned PREVENT programs throughout the United Kingdom and the United States to identify young people who might turn to terrorism and radicalism (not white nationalism, mind you). Implemented with a vengeance on people of colour, and a profit largely for whites. The seepage of white logics as a metric/standard has infiltrated the very structures and processes of educational and carceral accountability regimes, increasingly enforced by people who work for 'the state', who find themselves entrapped, enforcing white logics against communities under siege. And so we want to problematise the seepage of white logics into governmentalities; the naturalising of 'disparities', and the sense of complicity coagulating in the veins of those who work for the state.

Seepage: Especially during COVID-19, but even before, any graphs/charts/statistics you read on educational disparities, health disparities, economic disparities, housing and food insecurity... predictably assemble along the melanin arc. Whites rise to the top, Blacks fall to the bottom, with varied racial/ethnic/immigrant groups in the mid. Some read these patterns as 'natural', others as tragic, and many view these patterns as evidence of cumulative and sustained racial violence in state policies. As the editors of this volume argue, 'Whiteness involves a mind track universalising itself as a pre-given norm to the extent that the foundational Western binarism of white/black is obscured'.

We should all be provoked to notice and disrupt how white logics and metric madness have occupied management systems of state institutions. We should all be encouraged to re-think, document, and decolonise the penetration of white logics into school assessments, psychiatric diagnoses, the definitions of criminality/innocence, and 'child protective services'. Testing has become a corporate intrusion into the public sphere, trans-nationally; a profit making re-instantiation of white merit/Black and Brown deficits. Care and protection systems, enacted by many well-intentioned individuals, are often viewed, in communities of colour, as white supremacy in drag. Governmental metrics and policies, demanding evidence and 'data-driven' decision-making, have been mobilised in ways that reproduce and scientise racial hierarchies and end up converting structural violence into 'evidence' of pathology or deficit that sticks to people of colour. Metric madness has become a profit-making industry for privatising public sector institutions, certainly in the United States and United Kingdom, and sprawling globally: pathologising people of colour (in the name of 'care' or 'protection') and laminating whites – particularly elite whites. And, at least in the United States, being used to delegitimate public sector unions.

And then there is the question of who is enforcing these systems, whose souls are saturated in affects of complicity. Again we take seriously the relentless power of these logics and assemblages beyond the 'who' of front line workers. We hear people who work in government projects – education, social welfare, charity, NGOs – and then find themselves as midwives of a punishing white logic dressed up as care. Especially people of colour working as educators, government officials, immigration professionals, social workers ... trying to penetrate/occupy/transform systems from within, find themselves, instead, offering 'Invitations to come into the human race [that] operate as invitations into neoliberal whiteness' (Hunter 2015: 12). Consider for a moment those who work in the state sponsored space between those who have been oppressed/marginalised and the state/volunteers/charity/NGOs. These are often young people who want to 'be of use', make 'good trouble' and 'help' communities they care about. And yet today, the beads of complicity coagulate in their veins. Almost every system they are working within is structured with banal carceral and white supremacist/nationalist 'logics' – to 'prevent' terrorists, to 'diagnose' learning needs, to 'remove children from homes for their own good', to 'predict' danger to self and others, to 'protect' national security. Intentions aside, in the aggregate, much of this work ends up in removal, separation, containment and deportation of largely people of colour.

The aches of complicity are growing louder, as turn-over rates accelerate, particularly for instance for teachers of colour in the United States. The rates of burn out and health problems among the 'helping professions' are amplifying, as progressives working 'within' find themselves reinforcing whiteness as 'somatic norm'. The bleeding of white logics into neoliberal assessment (of schools? Clinical practice? Universities? Teacher effectiveness? Evidence based practice? Psychological wellbeing?) deserves critical interrogation as a flow of scienticised disposability drenched in whiteness as punitive logics. Recall the writing of Jackie Wang; 'We need to consider the extent to which racial violence is the unspoken and necessary underside of security, particularly white security. Safety requires the removal and containment of people deemed to be threats' (Wang 2018: 287). Whose logics are dominant, and who is asked to do the dirty work?

## Social interactions and racialised white violence: the intimate praxis of #KARENS

We read through the volume in the heat of George Floyd protests and the verdict, after a summer of endless videos streaming white women calling the police on Black men (#KARENS). Earlier we have considered how white logics work in concert with racial capitalism and through government institutions and neoliberal accountability regimes. We now consider a third level of white logic penetration, asking how do white supremacist logics insert themselves, as if banal, in social relations? Michelle thought we should address the viral spread of #KARENS videos, as they emerged all summer and beyond, white women who demand comfort even from their/our own paranoid fantasies of black invasion, calling police on Black men who dis-order, who occupy bodies out of order. These embodiments of white *fearage* are experienced as fragility and vulnerability but expressed as a lethal extension of the state, calling on the carceral capillaries of 'protection' to contain Blackness as if white 'fear' were normal and the cause found in HIM. These women again are not outliers – they are bold/unapologetic/flamboyant displays of white violence, caught on video, spewing white entitlement to land/space/time/gaze/the resources of the carceral state.

Michelle was moved to write to #KAREN this summer, those white women who believe our comfort requires the forced removal of Black people/voices/bird watching/stoop sitting:

Dear #Karen:

You, the blonde, we have to talk. In my humiliating unknowing, I didn't know there were so many of you; I didn't know your heart stops, you grab a phone, like white men grab a gun. Self defense from the anxiety within, provoked by black bodies, as if the police, the carceral state were an extension of our skin. When did we join the force, the soft complicit outer rim? You tell me you're a liberal, not a racist, you were just scared. Stand your ground, anyone would do the same. I am embarrassed I didn't know that so many of you – us? – existed; I don't know if COVID made us madder, more paranoid, quicker to dial or maybe the cameras, the summer of George Floyd, Breonna Taylor, Elijah McClain have risen our collective blood pressure, and the videos can't be denied. We can't white this out of history – although we sure try.

*White men quick to trigger; white women quick to call*

In 1992, bell hooks wrote a powerful essay, 'whiteness in the Black imagination'. I thought it brilliant then and for me embarrassing that I didn't realise the terror whites caused Blacks in the everyday, fears of going to parks, quiet walks in forests, cutting through a neighbour's back yard, stealing an apple from a local tree. I read, through hooks' searing words the terror that lives in black bodies as they wander into a white neighbourhood, cross a lawn to get to school faster, bump into a white person in the supermarket, as a white woman on a train throws a glance at Black mother if her son drops a toy, or throws it, even as white children run up and down the corridor in Union Station Newark waiting for the Acela – the speed train. I never thought about it. (OK, Charles Mills, I hear you.)

I knew or thought I knew – I have written about whiteness, white stereotypes, white microaggressions onto Black bodies. I have spent decades reading/teaching/writing with Franz Fanon, Du Bois, Ida B. Wells about the ways in which colonialism and racism move under the skin, into the body. There is a book (1988, 2004) called *Nervous Conditions* by Tsitsi Dangarembga, about a Black African girl, plucked from community, sent to a white school, to learn; it's the story of how her neurons betray her and police her from within. I now see the hole in my understanding – I thought I understood white cognitive stereotypes and Black rage… but in my Venn diagram of race and thoughts/emotion was constrained by my own ignorance. I failed to appreciate the hole where white fearage festers – our deeply embodied fearage fed by generations of whispers and headlines about black danger, desire to kill us. And so we – white women – have, in the aggregate, sutured ourselves to the carceral state, to police, to prisons.

Susan on Marion Road [a woman in my own community who made national headlines as she threatened to call the police on her Black neighbours over whether or not they had a permit to build a patio] has haunted me – terrible of course; traumatising, yes; guilty obviously. And yet I remain curious about what moved through her body, whose racialised voices and repulsions and desires, crawled under her skin to threaten with police, knowing of course that she could accelerate the murder of a Black man on Marian Road, feuding about a patio, even as her white neighbours circled around and begged her to stop taunting him.

Transgenerational terrors: George Floyd spoke to his long dead mother as he was losing breath; Nora (pseudonym), the Black mother on Marian Road, could barely produce words through a tightened throat and impending tears, 'take the children into the house, I don't want them to see the police'.

Among my neighbours perhaps there is a closet Karen lurking – maybe we all are. For 30 years, my sons always have friends of colour, close friends who sleep and eat here. And yet, as they dribbled in basketball or threw a football on the street (admittedly at midnight), we would get a call, or a glance, or an email. And the football scene we heard nothing until police cars rode up. Two officers exited the car, said there was a complaint, and according to Caleb, my white son, the officer grabbed the football and joined the game.

Only learned of this recently, when Susan provoked conversations that sounded like 'did you know about all these Karens?' across our back porch, as Caleb and Chris his best friend, sat in our back yard. Chris admitted that as one of the few Black males at Cornell, yes, he met a few Karens and some white boys like Supreme Court Justice Kavanaugh, so he wasn't surprised.

Whiteness moves through power, enacts with rage, relies upon the carceral state, assumes we own the land/air/affect, and now mutating variants flourish in our midst. Even, softly, through the rage and fear embodied and enacted by white women.

We end with one more corner of social life somewhat under-represented in the Handbook; a corner where we believe whiteness needs to be interrogated, in intimacies and struggles for justice. We draw from the writings of decolonial feminist Maria Lugones, and lift up with appreciation one of the chapters in the volume, by Amanpreet Ahluwalia.

Michelle Fine and William E. Cross

## Rooting our work in intimacies and solidarities

'The starting point ... is coalitional because the fractured locus is in common, the histories of resistance at the colonial difference are where we need to dwell, learning about each other' (Lugones 2010: 753).

We are, at base, scholars and friends moved by solidarities – intellectually and intimately, in our work and in our lives. When we taught together, and since, we have come of age in the fractured locus, marinating in histories of resistance, exploring with curiosity and care, learning about each other and ourselves, and the worlds we have inhabited and dreamed of.

We found those essays that were rooted in sweet/troubled solidarities to be extraordinary: rich, generative, expansive and forward looking. Consider the beautifully crafted piece by Amanpreet Ahluwalia, '"The feeling in my chest": Unblocking Space for People of Colour in Critical Whiteness Studies'. Ahluwalia opens at a vulnerable and expansive hinge of *We* speaking as a South Asian woman in love with a white European man:

> *We*, our stories, begin to intersect through the Spice Trade, the European colonial project, in the throes and aftermath of World War Two, with the rebuilding of Europe using labour from the colonies and in the modern project of Globalisation and of the European Union. When I refer to these events, I refer not only to the spatial possibilities that, when layered together culminate in our physical presence on that night at the Town Crier, but also to the social and psychic overlaps that produced our compatible subjectivities and ontologies. My partner grew up as a young man in 90s Germany with interests in history and politics, this meant that understanding the dangers and mechanisms of imperialism, racism, ethno-nationalistic supremacy and shared political projects of 'othering' eventually became second nature to him. Our shared understanding of the 'produced' nature of social relations and our social world more widely is the foundation that our relationship is built on ...

> *We* are possible because of the privileges that flow to me as a colonial subject who belongs to one of the most historically significant British colonies and who benefits from all of the advantages that come from living in the heart of empire. I have internalised *whiteness* enough to be legible to my partner, and together, we have a shared discourse that allows us to communicate across our divides and become legible to the other. I find it important to say here that I love him, not because I hate my people or my culture or myself, as has sometimes been suggested, but because my lived experience is evidence that subjectivity *is* multiple, and for many reasons, our subjectivities connect and intersect in many ways – a love of Death Metal and good food being two of them... For me then, any discipline called 'Critical Whiteness Studies' must be able to hold space open for complicated interpersonal analyses of the lived experience of people like me whose relationship to whiteness is not linear, unidirectional or singular.

Embracing the affects voiced by Ahluwalia, we close out with a presencing of solidarities ground in the intimacies of friendship, intellectual and political comradeship. Our conversations, over 30 years, have been so rich, so provocative. We have taught together, written together, and stretched to embrace each other through the 'betweens' of our lives and work. At the Graduate Center, over students and texts, we chiselled a space both of and between; a Black man and a white woman, captured by the discipline of psychology, itchy to engage activism and scholarship, to write for/with/despite. We taught together a course called Beyond Damage.

When we reach out to each other – with drafts and vulnerabilities – emails and phone calls – we know we are about to be provoked and calmed. We carve a small space where we speak through who we are and have been, and what we make, together. When I (Michelle) was asked to write this epilogue, I knew it had to be with Bill; he would make my head explode a little, expand a lot. That we would laugh, argue about what we read and draft an essay rooted in critique and possibilities, respect and dignity.

The words of Amanpreet Ahluwalia call for relationality, not binaries; a recognition of wounds and complexities: 'I argue that any theorist that wants to say something important about race or whiteness, must do so in a way that helps us to come to terms with the ways we may have been hurt, broken or traumatised by the violence of racialisation and project of colonisation – all of us, no matter where we sit on this spectrum at any one time. Developing a shared language that helps us name how these traumas live in our bodies, what they enable and constrain, is imperative for this work'.

This epistemic mooring, within relationships and solidarities, recognising us all to be broken, obligated to attend to power inequities, enriched by our differences and yet sutured in struggle together, marks the kind of activist scholarship that we have engaged for 30 years.

At the Public Science Project at the Graduate Center, CUNY, where Michelle's scholarship/activism is situated, we craft solidarity projects with activists and movements for justice (www.publicscienceproject.org). Years ago, Bill joined us for a gathering with women at Bedford Hills Correctional Facility, a women's prison, as we took up a participatory analysis of college in prison, anchored in the perspective of those women most impacted by the carceral state. Another moment of stitching solidarities across barbed wire, race/ethnicity, biography, mistakes. Critical participatory action research (Fine 2017) marks an epistemic refusal of white logics in research, a contestation of where knowledge lives, a recognition of wisdom in the margins/shadows and a messy gesture towards epistemic justice. Walking into the prison together, to create research 'with' not 'on' marked a stretch toward solidarity. (see Fine et al. 2001; https://www.prisonpolicy.org/scans/changing_minds.pdf).

The lineage of critical participatory action research is long, rooted in the Global South, attached to Freire, Fals-Borda, Ignacio Martin-Baro, and also Ida B. Wells and W.E.B. Du Bois in the Global North. The commitments are simple – no research on us without us. Those of us who are marked as white people have a responsibility to engage boldly – not retreat – with humility and resources, to investigate 'with'/alongside, the very systems, institutions, ideologies, relationships, opportunities that privilege us, devastate others, reproduce racial hierarchies and racialised state violence, and still function as well-oiled machines of fairness and security, like schools and policing. In these projects we form participatory contact zones of very differently positioned people, studying, for instance, domestic violence and carceral state violence against women of colour; queer youth and activism; foster youth and college; the unfulfilled promise of racial desegregation in schooling; sustained discrimination against formerly incarcerated college students; police violence … Please check out the Public Science Project website to review some of our projects (www.publicscienceproject.com). Solidarity based inquiries are rooted in a radical commitment to document what is, privileging the perspective of those most impacted, and interrogating who is vulnerable to state violence, who is protected and how might things be otherwise. Whiteness is neither a reason to retreat, nor to take over. White logics and violence require interrogation from all of us.

Epistemic justice requires a bending toward the perspectives of those most impacted. But let us not forget that whiteness – as punitive logic and colonial assemblage – is at the heart of unjust schools and violent policing; whiteness embraces capitalism and struggles over land and housing security; whiteness impacts who police are protecting and assaulting; and so the sticky entanglements with capitalism, the carceral state, misogyny, need to be interrogated. The praxis of solidarity could not be more urgent, and for us, delicious in 'revolting' times.

****

We end where we began, with rhythms of pain, desire, and radical imagination swirling. When we write, we always have music playing in the background. Three songs held us through this collaboration; dominated our listening while completing this chapter. 'Juicy', by Biggy Smalls, as it best captures the resistance and resilience of victims of white racism. Joni Mitchell's 'Drink a case of you' as once we started reading the chapters it was hard to work on any of our other assignments. And finally, Marvin Gaye's 'What's Going on' as the Handbook covers so much material in speaking truth to power.

Thanks for the opportunity to move, together, across space and time, to the rhythms of rage and radical possibility.

# References

Berezow, A. 2018. 'White Overdose Deaths 50% Higher Than Blacks, 167% Higher Than Hispanics'. American Council on Science and Health blog, 5 April, viewed 22 February 2019, https://www.acsh.org/news/2018/04/05/white-overdose-deaths-50-higher-blacks-167-higher-hispanics-12804.

Bluestone, B. and Harrison, B. 1982. *The Deindustrialization of America*. New York, NY: Basic Books.

Brown, D. 2013. A Vagabond's Tale: Poor Whites, Herrenvolk Democracy, and the Value of Whiteness in the Late Antebellum South. *The Journal of Southern History*, 79 (4): 799–840.

Byfield, N. 2014. *Savage Portrayals: Race, Media and the Central Park Jogger Story*. Temple University Press.

Dangarembga, T. (1988, 2004) *Nervous Conditions*. London: Ayebia Clarke Publishers.

Derickson, A. 1988. *Workers' Health, Workers' Democracy: The Western Miners' Struggle, 1891–1925*. Cornell University Press.

Dickerson, D. C. 1986. *Out of the Crucible: Black Steel Workers in Western Pennsylvania, 1875-1980*. Albany, NY: SUNY Press.

Duru, N. J. 2003. The Central Park Five, the Scottsboro Boys, and the Myth of the Bestial Black Man. *Cardozo L. Rev.*, 25: 1315.

Fanon, F. 1961. *Wretched of the Earth*. Paris: Maspero.

Fine, M. 2017. *Just Research in Contentious Times*. New York: Teachers College Press.

Fine, M. *et al.* 2001. *Changing Minds: The Impact of College on Women in a Maximum Security Prison*. View at https://www.prisonpolicy.org/scans/changing_minds.pdf.

Fraser, S. 2015. *The Age of Acquiescence: The Life and Death of American Resistance to Organized Wealth and Power*. Boston, MA: Little, Brown and Company.

Gates Jr, H. L. 2020. *Stony the Road: Reconstruction, White Supremacy, and the Rise of Jim Crow*. New York: Penguin Books.

Goldberg, D. T. 2009. *The Threat of Race: Reflections on Racial Neoliberalism*. Hoboken, NJ: Wiley-Blackwell.

Gqola, P. 2010. *What is Slavery to Me? Postcolonial/Slave Memory in Post-apartheid South Africa*. Johannesburg: Wits University Press.

Hooks, B. (1992) Representing Whiteness in the Black Imagination. *Cultural Studies*, ed. L. Grossberg et al. London: Routledge, 1992, pp. 338–342.

Hunter, S. 2015. *Power, Politics and the Emotions: Impossible Governance?* London: Routledge.

Lewis, R. L. 1987. *Black Coal Miners in America: Race, Class, and Community Conflict, 1780–1980*. University Press of Kentucky.

Lugones, M. 2010. Toward a Decolonial Feminism. *Hypatia*, 25 (4): 742–759.

MacLean, N. 2017. *Democracy in Chains: The Deep History of the Radical Right's Stealth Plan for America*. New York: Penguin.

Mbembe, A. 2015. 'Decolonizing Knowledge and the Question of the Archive', UCT lecture [online], view at https://wiser.wits.ac.za/system/files/Achille%20Mbembe%20-%20Decolonizing%20Knowledge%20and %20the%20Question%20of%20the%20Archive.pdf

Moore, L. N. 2010. *Black Rage in New Orleans: Police Brutality and African American Activism from World War II to Hurricane Katrina*. LSU Press.

Moynihan, D. P. 1965. Employment, Income, and the Ordeal of the Negro Family. *Daedalus*, Fall (94): 745–770.

Omi, M. and Winant, H. 2014. *Racial formation in the United States*. New York: Routledge.

Puwar, N. 2004. *Space Invaders: Race, Gender and Bodies Out of Place*. Oxford: Berg.

Rothman, J. D. 2018. Masterless Men: Poor Whites and Slavery in the Antebellum South. *Labour/Le Travail*, 82: 266–269.

Sartre, J. P. 1961. Preface. In *Wretched of the Earth*, ed. F. Fanon. Paris: Maspero.

Segalo, P. 2020. Poison in the Marrow: Complexities of Liberating and Healing the Nation. *HTS Teologiese Studies/Theological Studies*, 76 (3): a6047.

Silva, J. M. 2019. *We're Still Here: Pain and Politics in the Heart of America*. Oxford University Press.

Taylor, A. M. 2018. *Embattled Freedom: Journeys through the Civil War's Slave Refugee Camps*. UNC Press Books.

Wang, J. 2018. *Carceral Capitalism. Semiotext(e)/Intervention Series, Vol. 21*. Cambridge, MA: The MIT Press.

Woodward, C. V. 1991. *Reunion and Reaction: The Compromise of 1877 and the End of Reconstruction*. Oxford University Press.

# Index

Milton Keynes UK
Ingram Content Group UK Ltd.
UKHW052108111223
434200UK00008B/65